KU-481-396

SOCIOLOGY OF EDUCATION

Withdrawn

T05,4957

370.19

SOCIOLOGY OF EDUCATION

A CRITICAL READER

Edited by Alan R. Sadovnik

Routledge
Taylor & Francis Group
New York   London

Routledge
Taylor & Francis Group
270 Madison Avenue
New York, NY 10016

Routledge
Taylor & Francis Group
2 Park Square
Milton Park, Abingdon
Oxon OX14 4RN

© 2007 by Taylor & Francis Group, LLC
Routledge is an imprint of Taylor & Francis Group, an Informa business

Printed in the United States of America on acid-free paper
10 9 8 7 6 5 4 3

International Standard Book Number-10: 0-415-95497-5 (Softcover) 0-415-95496-7 (Hardcover)
International Standard Book Number-13: 978-0-415-95497-6 (Softcover) 978-0-415-95496-9 (Hardcover)

No part of this book may be reprinted, reproduced, transmitted, or utilized in any form by any electronic, mechanical, or other means, now known or hereafter invented, including photocopying, microfilming, and recording, or in any information storage or retrieval system, without written permission from the publishers.

Trademark Notice: Product or corporate names may be trademarks or registered trademarks, and are used only for identification and explanation without intent to infringe.

Library of Congress Cataloging-in-Publication Data

Sociology of education : a critical reader / edited by Alan R. Sadovnik.
    p. cm.
   Includes bibliographical references and index.
   ISBN 978-0-415-95496-9 (alk. paper) -- ISBN 978-0-415-95497-6 (pbk : alk. paper)
   1. Educational sociology. 2. Educational sociology--United States. I. Sadovnik, Alan R.

LC191.2.S632 2006
306.43--dc22
                                                          2006100283

Visit the Taylor & Francis Web site at
http://www.taylorandfrancis.com

and the Routledge Web site at
http://www.routledge.com

For Mags

We're working on it!

Contents

Acknowledgments

This book would not have been possible without the help of a number of important individuals. At Rutgers, Lachone McKenzie and her work-study students provided essential secretarial support. My graduate assistants, Elizabeth Morrison and Tara Davidson, provided important administrative support; and Princeton University intern, Ralph Schaefer, provided excellent technical and administrative support.

At Routledge, my editor Catherine Bernard provided helpful support and advice at all stages of the project. Lynn Goeller and Judith Simon provided helpful assistance and advice during production.

My wife and collaborator on many other scholarly projects, Susan F. Semel, provided effective and cheerful assistance in proofreading the final page-proofs. Mags Semel provided helpful assistance in the final stages of production.

This book is dedicated to Mags Semel, my developmentally disabled stepdaughter, who has taught me what living up to one's potential really means.

BISHOP BURTON COLLEGE
LIBRARY

Introduction

The sociology of education has provided important insights to the ways in which schools affect individuals and groups. Through an examination of the relationships among societal factors such as political, economic, and cultural systems and schools, sociologists have uncovered how educational processes affect the way people think, live and work, their place in society and their chances for success or failure. From the famous Coleman Report, *Equality of Educational Opportunity* in 1966, research in the sociology of education has attempted to understand whether educational systems and their practices provide opportunities for all children to achieve based on their merits or whether they reproduce existing social inequalities. From the beginning of the twenty-first century, with educational policy in the United States emphasizing the concurrent themes of standards and equity and the reduction of the achievement gap among groups, based on social class, race, ethnicity, gender, and disability, sociologists of education continue to provide important empirical findings on the effects of education.

Theory and research in the sociology of education seek to understand, in Christopher Hurn's (1993) words, "the limits and possibilities of schooling." In a country that has placed enormous faith in the power of schools to ameliorate all types of social problems, including poverty, and has viewed schools as the central institutions for social mobility, the sociology of education provides evidence about the extent to which schools can solve social problems.

The discipline of sociology developed at the end of the nineteenth century amid the promise and problems of industrialization, urbanization, and a developing belief in education in Europe and the United States. During this period, more and more children were required to go to school and sociologists began to examine the relationship between school and society. As schooling became more available to increased numbers of children, many believed that schools would be critical to a modern era where merit, talent, and effort would replace privilege and inheritance as the most significant factor for social and occupational mobility (Sadovnik, Cookson, & Semel, 2006, p. 20).

Until the 1960s, sociologists, for the most part, shared this optimism about the role of education in a modern society. They examined important themes, including how children are socialized for adult roles, the school as a social organization, and the effects of schooling on students' life chances. Beginning in the 1960s, sociologists of education began to doubt that schools, by themselves, could solve social problems, especially problems of economic and social inequality. These sociologists questioned whether schools were or could be, in the words of U.S.-nineteenth-century educational reformer Horace Mann, "the great equalizer" (Sadovnik, Cookson, & Semel, 2006 p. 20).

Sociologists of education continued to believe that they could improve education through the application of scientific theory and research. Because of their scientific orientation, they are more likely to ask *what is* rather than *what ought to be*, although sociological research has been the basis for trying to improve and change schools. They want to discover what occurs inside of schools and what the effects of schooling are on individuals and groups. The distinctive feature of the sociology of education is empiricism, or the collection and analysis of empirical data within a theoretical context in order to construct a logical set of conclusions (Sadovnik, Cookson, & Semel, 2006, p. 20).

Thus, *The Sociology of Education* relies on empirical methods to understand how schools are related to society, how individuals and groups interact within schools, and what the effects of schooling are for individuals and groups of children. Its findings are based on an attempt to be objective and scientific. It examines individuals and groups in their social context and examines the social forces that affect them. The sociological approach to education is crucial because it provides conclusions based on focused and tested observations. Without such an analysis, one cannot know *what is*; and without knowing *what is*, one cannot *make what ought to be* a reality (Sadovnik, Cookson, & Semel, 2006, p. 20).

In his important book *The Sociological Imagination* (1959), C. Wright Mills argued that the sociological imagination was vital for understanding society. The sociological imagination, according to Mills, allows individuals to transcend the often-narrow boundaries of their lives and to see the world from the larger context of history and society. Using the sociological imagination allows individuals to relate their own lives with the social, cultural, and historical factors that have affected them, and ultimately enables individuals to understand how and why these forces are crucial in shaping our lives (Sadovnik, Cookson, & Semel, 2006, p. 5). Based on this, the relationship between school and society is at the heart of the sociology of education. Without an understanding of how the components of society fit together, it is impossible to understand how schools work and their effects within a particular society. In an increasingly multiethnic and multiracial society, the need for such a sociological perspective remains as important as ever.

In her book, *Education and Inequality* (1977), Caroline Persell provided a model for understanding the relationship between school and society through four interrelated levels of sociological analysis. These include the societal, institutional, interpersonal, and intrapsychic levels (for the complete model, see Sadovnik, Cookson, & Semel, 2006, p. 111). The *societal* level encompasses the most general structures of society, including its political and economic systems, its level of development, and its system of social stratification (or institutionalized levels of inequality). The *institutional* level includes a society's main institutions, including the family, the schools, churches, synagogues, and mosques, business and government agencies, and the media, all of which play an essential part in the socialization of children into adult roles and responsibilities. The *interpersonal* level includes the processes, symbols, and interactions that occur within institutional settings. These include language, dress, face-to-face interactions, gestures, and rituals, which comprise everyday life. The *intrapsychic* level includes individual thoughts, beliefs, values, and feelings, which are, to a large extent, shaped by a society's institutions and interactions. For sociologists of education, the degree to which external forces determine individual actions or whether they are capable of freely shaping the world is a crucial dialectic. A sociological perspective, although recognizing the human ability for free will, stresses the power of external forces in shaping individual choices and how these are often related to group differences within the stratification system. As you will see in Part I, functionalism is concerned with the societal, institutional, and interpersonal processes that create what Emile Durkheim termed the collective conscience (society internalized in the individual). Conflict theory is concerned with the ways in which social, political, cultural, and economic differences among groups at the societal level produce conflict that often results in change (Sadovnik, Cookson, & Semel, 2006, p. 111).

In order to understand these issues, *The Sociology of Education: A Critical Reader* provides some of the most important readings in the field. The reader is designed for advanced undergraduate and graduate students in the sociology of education and related courses. It is organized into six parts. Part I examines theory and method in the sociology of education. Through both classic and contemporary readings, you will explore the major theoretical and methodological issues in the field. Part II examines school organization and processes through an exploration of teaching, learning, and curriculum. Although the majority of the book focuses on education in the United States, Part III examines international education in order to analyze the similarities and differences in educational systems throughout the world, how schools reflect national character and culture, and the degree to which schooling as an institution has become a worldwide phenomena, with far more similarities than differences among national systems. Part IV examines higher education in the United States and focuses on issues related to access and opportunity. This section explores whether American higher education has become more democratic and meritocratic or whether it remains highly stratified according to race, social class, and gender. Within this context, it analyzes access and opportunity in different sectors of the higher educational system, two- and four-year colleges and universities, both public and private. Part V examines, arguably, the most important area in the field: the relationship between education and inequality. It examines the role of schools in reproducing existing inequalities or in providing opportunities for mobility for students from lower socioeconomic backgrounds. Further, it examines the effects of educational processes such as tracking and ability grouping. Finally, it analyzes the effects of education on different groups, including African Americans, Latinos, Asian Americans, Native-Americans, women and men, different social classes, and students with disabilities. Part VI examines educational policy and reform by examining the limits and possibilities of various policies, including district and school-based reforms, standards-based reforms, school choice, and the No Child Left Behind Act (2001). This section provides important insight into the extent to which school reform alone can ameliorate the effects of factors outside the schools, including poverty and families.

Selecting 27 articles for inclusion was no easy task, given the hundreds that are suitable for inclusion in this reader. They are in no way meant to be exhaustive or to cover all the important topics in the field. In addition, unlike many readers that include edited selections of articles and can include many more, this reader primarily includes articles in their entirety. The reason for this is to ensure that advanced undergraduate and graduate students have the opportunity to read sociological research as it is written and to engage in critical analyses of full texts. Obviously, what is gained in depth is lost in breadth. My criteria for selection included the following:

1. With a small number of exceptions, sociologists or researchers closely associated with the sociology of education have written all of the articles. Although there have been many important articles written by economists, political scientists, anthropologists, and historians of education, a reader in the sociology of education ought to include work done mostly by sociologists.

2. The articles apply a sociological perspective to the study of education. Such a sociological perspective views schools and schooling as part of the larger social order, examines the effects of schooling on individuals and groups, and analyzes the factors external to the individual that affect individual and group behavior.

3. The articles make an important theoretical and/or research contribution to our understanding of the main issues and problems in the sociology of education. Within this context, the selections include various theoretical perspectives and methodological approaches.

4. The articles represent either classical or contemporary approaches to the sociology of education.

5. The articles are written in a language that is understandable to advanced undergraduate and graduate students. Although this is the case for most of the articles, some are theoretically and/or methodologically difficult and are included because they represent an essential contribution to the field.

6. The articles following Part I provide empirical evidence on a problem in the sociology of education and illustrate the power of the sociology of education for understanding educational problems.

7. The articles as a whole are representative of the diversity of researchers and problems in the field, with respect to race, ethnicity, and gender. Although there was no quota used to ensure that a diversity of authors and topics was included (the volume does not include equal representation), I attempted to choose articles that represented such diversity.

The readings in *Sociology of Education: A Critical Reader* are meant to stimulate your thinking about the important roles that schools play in contemporary society and their ability to solve fundamental social, economic, and political problems.

References

Coleman, J., et al. (1966). *Equality of educational opportunity.* Washington D.C.: U.S. Government Printing Office.
Hurn, C. (1993). *The limits and possibilities of schooling.* Needham Heights, MA: Allyn and Bacon.
Mills, C. W. (1959). *The Sociological imagination.* New York: Oxford University Press.
Sadovnik, A. R., Cookson, P. W., & Semel, S. F. (2006). *Exploring education: An introduction to the foundations of education* (3rd ed.). Boston: Allyn and Bacon.

Suggested Readings

The following texts are excellent sources for all of the sections of the reader:

Ballantine, J. (2001). *The sociology of education: A systematic analysis (5th Edition)*. Saddle River, NJ: Prentice Hall.

Brint, S. (1998). *Schools and society*. Thousand Oaks, CA: Pine Forge.

Karabel, J. & Halsey, A.H. (1977) *Power and ideology in education*. New York: Oxford.

Hallinan, M. (2000). *Handbook of the sociology of education*. New York: Kluwer.

Halsey, A.H. et al. (1997). *Education: Culture, economy, society*. New York: Oxford.

Hurn, C. (1993) *The limits and possibilities of schooling*. Needham Heights, MA: Allyn and Bacon.

Levinson, D., Cookson, P.W. & Sadovnik, A.R. (2002). *Sociology and education: An encyclopedia*. New York: Routledge/Falmer.

Riordan, C. (2003). *Equality and achievement: An introduction to the sociology of education*. (Second edition). Boston: Allyn and Bacon.

Sadovnik, A.R., Cookson, P.W. & Semel. S.F. (2006). *Exploring education: An introduction to the foundations of education* (Third Edition). Boston: Allyn and Bacon.

Theory and Method in the Sociology of Education

Part I provides some of the most important theoretical readings in the sociology of education. They examine the development of theory and research in the sociology of education.

Chapter 1, "Theory and Research in the Sociology of Education" by Rutgers University sociologist Alan R. Sadovnik, provides an overview of classical and contemporary theories and quantitative, qualitative, and mixed-methods approaches in sociological and educational research.

Chapter 2, "On Education and Society" by classical nineteenth century sociologist Emile Durkheim, provides the foundation for the development of functionalist theories in the sociology of education, popularized in the mid-twentieth century by Talcott Parsons.

Chapter 3, "Functional and Conflict Theories of Educational Stratification" by University of Pennsylvania sociologist Randall Collins, provides a comparison of functionalist and conflict theories in the sociology of education and the foundation of his status-competition theory of educational expansion.

Chapter 4, "Broken Promises: School Reform in Retrospect," from their classic book *Schooling in Capitalist America* (1976), by University of Massachusetts political economists Samuel Bowles and Herbert Gintis, applies their neo-Marxist correspondence theory to the history of school reform in the United States.

Chapter 5, "On Understanding the Processes of Schooling: The Contributions of Labeling Theory" by sociologist Ray Rist, provides an overview of the contributions of interactionist theory in general and labeling theory in particular to understanding the processes of schooling.

Chapter 6, "The Forms of Capital" by the late French sociologist Pierre Bourdieu, provides a conflict analysis of the role of different types of capital (human, economic, cultural, and social) in reproducing social class advantages.

Chapter 7, "Social Class and Pedagogic Practice" by the late British sociologist Basil Bernstein, uses functionalist (Durkheimian), conflict (neo-Marxist and Weberian), and interactionist approaches to analyze the relationship between social class and educational practices and how power and economic relations help to reproduce social class inequalities.

Chapter 8, "The Effects of Education as an Institution" by Stanford University sociologist John Meyer, provides the foundation for institutional theory as developed by Meyer and his colleagues since the 1980s. Institutional theory argues that mass public education as an institution has been a worldwide phenomenon and examines comparative and international similarities and differences among educational institutions as they have developed in different countries since the nineteenth century.

Questions for Reflection and Discussion

1. How do functionalist and conflict theorists differ in their assessment of the role of schools in helping to change societies?

2. How does interactionist theory differ in its focus from functionalist and conflict theory? Can it complement one or both of the other theories?

3. Is research in the sociology of education scientific? Should it be? What do you think of trying to make educational research similar to medical or pharmaceutical research?

4. What did Emile Durkheim see as the major functions of schools? Can you give some contemporary examples of these functions in the present century?

5. How do Bowles and Gintis view the potential for educational reforms to reduce poverty and to provide economic mobility for low-income children?

6. How would Randall Collins view proposals to require a master's degree as the entry level credential to become a teacher or a nurse?

7. How would Ray Rist analyze the process under IDEA (Individuals with Disabilities and Education Act) by which children with disabilities are tested, identified, and then educated according to their disabilities?

8. In the 1970s, Basil Bernstein was criticized as a cultural deprivation theorist; that is one who argued that low-income children do less well in school because their culture is deficient when compared to middle- and upper-class children. Do you agree with this criticism and why? Do you think that Bourdieu's theories of cultural and social capital are examples of cultural deprivation theory? What are the similarities and differences between Bourdieu's and Bernstein's theories?

9. Many economists argue that mass public educational systems developed around the world to meet the increasing demands of technology and the high-level skills required by technological societies. How would John Meyer respond to this argument? How would Randall Collins? How would Bowles and Gintis?

1
Theory and Research in the Sociology of Education[1]

ALAN R. SADOVNIK

The sociology of education has mirrored the larger theoretical debates in the discipline of sociology. From its roots in the classical sociology of Karl Marx, Max Weber, and Emile Durkheim to the contemporary influences of symbolic interactionism, postmodernism, and critical theory, sociology of education research has been influenced by a number of different theoretical perspectives. This chapter provides an overview of the major theoretical perspectives in the sociology of education—functionalism, conflict theory, and symbolic interactionism—as well as contemporary theoretical approaches: the code theory of Basil Bernstein, the cultural capital theory of Pierre Bourdieu, the status-competition theory of Randall Collins, the institutional theory of John Meyer, and postmodern critical theory.

Functionalist Theory[2]

Functionalist sociologists begin with a picture of society that stresses the interdependence of the social system; these researchers often examine how well parts are integrated with each other. Functionalists view society as a kind of machine, where one part articulates with another to produce the dynamic energy required to make society work. Most important, functionalism stresses the processes that maintain social order by stressing consensus and agreement. Although functionalists understand that change is inevitable, they underscore the evolutionary nature of change. Further, although they acknowledge that conflict between groups exists, functionalists argue that without a common bond to unite groups, society will disintegrate. Thus, functionalists examine the social processes necessary to the establishment and maintenance of social order.

Functionalist theories of school and society trace their origins to the French sociologist Emile Durkheim's (1858–1917) general sociological theory. At its center, Durkheim's sociology (1893/1947; 1915/1954) was concerned with the effects of the decline of traditional rituals and community during the transition from traditional to modern societies. Durkheim's analysis of the differences between mechanical and organic solidarity in the *Division of Labor* (1893/1947) and his concept of anomie in *Suicide* (1897/1951) examined the need for societies to create rituals and institutions to provide for social cohesion and meaning. Like Ferninand Tönnies' (1887/1957) analysis of Gemeinschaft and Gesellschaft, Durkheim provided a sociological analysis of the effects of modernity on community.

For Durkheim, the processes of industrialization, urbanization, and modernization led to the breakdown of traditional rituals and methods of social control, which in turn led to the breakdown of social solidarity and cohesion. In *Suicide* (1897/1951), he demonstrated empirically how the breakdown in traditional community resulted in the decline of collective conscience and the rise of individualism. Such a breakdown lead to what Durkheim called anomie, the condition of norm-lessness in individuals and society.

As the bonds that connected individuals to each other and to society became unhinged, modern societies faced disintegration from within. Durkheim, however, was not a reactionary; he did not believe that the solution to social disintegration was a return to the past, with its strict forms of social control and regulation. Rather, he believed that modern societies had to develop new forms of social control and cohesion that would allow for the newly developed individualism of modernity to exist within a cohesive modern society. Such a society, what Durkheim called organic solidarity, would allow for a balance between individualism and community.

Durkheim was the first sociologist to apply sociological theory to education. His major works on education include *Moral Education* (1962), *The Evolution of Educational Thought* (1977), and *Education and Sociology* (1956). While Durkheim recognized that education had taken different forms at different times and places, he believed that in virtually all societies, education was of critical importance in creating the moral unity necessary for social cohesion and harmony. For Durkheim, moral values were the foundation of society.

Durkheim's emphasis on values and cohesion set the tone for how present-day functionalists approach the study of education. Functionalists tend to assume that consensus is the normal state in society and that conflict represents a breakdown of shared values. In a highly integrated, well functioning society, schools socialize students into the appropriate values and sort and select students according to their abilities. From a functional point of view, then, educational reform is supposed to create structures, programs, and curricula that are technically advanced and rational and that encourage social unity. It should be evident that most American educators and educational reformers implicitly base their reform suggestions on functional theories of schooling. When, for example, *A Nation at Risk*, a government report on U.S. schools, was released in 1983, its authors argued that our schools were responsible for a whole host of social and economic problems. There was no suggestion that perhaps education might not have the power to overcome deep social and economic problems without changing other aspects of American society.

Functionalism is concerned with the functions of schooling in the maintenance of social order. Whereas conflict theory (see the next section) argues that schools function in the interests of the dominant groups in a society, functionalism sees schools as functioning in the interests of the majority of citizens, at least within democratic societies. Therefore functionalists examine the specific purposes of schooling and their role in society. These purposes or functions are intellectual, political, social, and economic (Bennett & LeCompte, 1990, pp. 5–21) and refer to their role within any existing society. Functionalists, however, are most concerned with the role of schools in modern, democratic societies.

The intellectual purposes of schooling include the following: to teach basic cognitive skills such as reading, writing, and mathematics; to transmit specific knowledge, for example, in literature, history, and the sciences; and to help students acquire higher order thinking skills such as analysis, evaluation, and synthesis.

The political purposes of schooling are to inculcate allegiance to the existing political order (patriotism); to prepare citizens who will participate in this political order (for example, in political democracies); to help assimilate diverse cultural groups into a common political order; and to teach children the basic laws of the society.

The social purposes of schooling are to socialize children into the various roles, behaviors, and values of the society. This process, referred to by sociologists as socialization, is a key ingredient in the stability of any society; it enables members to help to solve social problems; and by participating in socialization, schools work, along with other institutions such as the family, and the church or synagogues, to ensure social cohesion. The economic purposes of education are to prepare students for their later occupational roles and to select, train, and allocate individuals into the division of labor. Whereas the degree to which schools directly prepare students for work varies from society to society, most schools have at least an indirect role in this process.

Sometimes these purposes contradict each other. For example, the following question underscores the clash between the intellectual and political purposes of the school. If it is the intellectual purpose of the school to teach higher order thinking skills such as critical thinking and evaluation, then can the school simultaneously engender patriotism and conformity to society's rules?

Modern functionalist theories of education have their origin in the work of Talcott Parsons (1959). Parsons (1902–1979) believed that education was a vital part of a modern society, a society that differed considerably from all previous societies. From this perspective, schooling performs important functions in the development and maintenance of a modern, democratic society, especially with regard to equality of opportunity for all citizens. Functionalists such as Kingsley Davis and Wilbert Moore (1945) argued that inequality was functional and necessary in all societies, as it ensured that the most talented individuals would fill the functionally most important positions. Nonetheless, modern democratic societies differ from previous, traditional agrarian societies because they are meritocratic; that is, talent and hard work should determine the allocation of individuals to positions, rather than accidents of birth. Thus, in modern societies education becomes the key institution in a meritocratic selection process.

This democratic-liberal functionalist perspective views education as a vital institution in a modern capitalist society defined by its technocratic, meritocratic, and democratic characteristics (Hurn, 1993, pp. 44–47). Although considerable inequality remains, society in this framework is characterized by the evolutionary movement from ascription to achievement, with equal educational opportunity the crucial component. According to this perspective, the historical pattern of academic failure by minority and working-class students was a blemish on the principles of justice and equality of opportunity expounded by a democracy. This educational pattern necessitated the formulation of reform programs to ensure equality of opportunity. While functionalist theorists disagreed on the causes of academic failure, they vigorously believed that the solutions to both educational and social problems were possible within the capitalist social structure. As Diane Ravitch argued:

> It is indisputable that full equality has not been achieved, but equally indisputable in the light of the evidence is the conclusion that a democratic society can bring about effective social change, if there is both the leadership and the political commitment to do so. To argue, against the evidence, that meaningful change is not possible is to sap the political will that is necessary to effect changes (1977, pp. 114–115).

The central distinction made by the functionalist perspective was between equality of opportunity and equality of results. A democratic society is a just society, according to this tradition, if it generates the former. Therefore, functionalist theory rested on a positive view of meritocracy as a laudable goal, with education viewed as the necessary institutional component in guaranteeing a fair competition for unequal rewards. The just society, then, is one where each member has an equal opportunity for social and economic advantages and where individual merit and talent replace ascriptive and class variables as the most essential determinants of status. Education is thus the vehicle in ensuring the continual movement toward this meritocratic system.

In addition to its role in a meritocratic society, education plays a significant function in the maintenance of the modern democratic and technocratic society. In a political democracy, schools provide citizens with the knowledge and dispositions to participate effectively in civic life. In an ever increasingly technical society, schools provide students with the skills and dispositions to work in such a society. Although schools do teach specific work skills, they also teach students how to learn so they may adapt to new work roles and requirements.

Functionalist theory was the dominant paradigm in sociology and the sociology of education until the 1960s. In the 1960s, conflict theory emerged as a significant critique and alternative to functionalism. Conflict theorists argued that schools functioned in the interests of dominant groups, rather than everyone, and that functionalists confused what is with what ought to be. According to this critique, whereas schools ought to be democratic and meritocratic, the empirical evidence did not support the functionalist contention that they were. Although the specific nature of conflict theory is developed in the next section, it is important to note some of the problems with functionalism. First, conflict theorists argue that the relationship between schooling, skills, and jobs is far less rational than functionalists suggest (Hurn, 1993, pp. 50–52). Second, conflict theorists point out that the role of schools in providing equality of opportunity is far more problematic than functionalists suggest (Hurn, 1993, pp. 52–54). Third, large-scale empirical research on the effects of schooling casts significant doubt on the functionalist assertion that the expansion of schooling brings about an increasingly just and meritocratic social order (Hurn, 1993, pp. 54–55).

Conflict Theory[3]

As suggested above, not all sociologists of education believe that society is held together by shared values and collective agreement alone, but on the ability of dominant groups to impose their will on subordinate groups through force, cooptation, and manipulation. In this view the glue of society is economic, political, cultural, and military power. Ideologies or intellectual justifications created by the powerful are designed to enhance their position by legitimizing inequality and the unequal distribution of material and cultural goods. One argument, for instance, is that differences are an inevitable outcome of biology or history. Clearly, conflict sociologists see the relation between school and society as problematic. Whereas functionalists emphasize cohesion in explaining social order, conflict sociologists emphasize struggle. From a conflict point of view, schools are similar to social battlefields, where students struggle against teachers, teachers against administrators, and so on. These antagonisms, however, are most often muted for two reasons: the authority and power of the school and the achievement ideology. In effect, the achievement ideology convinces students and teachers that schools promote learning and sort and select students according to their abilities, not according to their social status. In this view, the achievement ideology disguises the "real" power relations within the school, which, in turn, reflect and correspond to the power relations within the larger society (Bowles and Gintis, 1976).

Although Karl Marx (1818–1883) did not write a great deal about education specifically, he is the intellectual founder of the conflict school in the sociology of education. His analytic imagination and moral outrage were sparked by the social conditions found in Europe in the late 19th century. Industrialization and urbanization had produced a new class of workers—the proletariat—who lived in poverty, worked up to 18 hours a day, and had little, if any, hope of creating a better life for their children. Marx believed that the class system, which separated owners from workers and workers from the benefits of their own labor, made class struggle inevitable. He believed that, in the end, the proletariat would rise up and overthrow the capitalists, and in doing so, establish a new society where men and women would no longer be "alienated" from their labor. Marx's powerful and often compelling critique of early capitalism has provided the intellectual energy for subsequent generations of liberal and leftist thinkers who believe that the only way to a more just and productive society is the abolition or modification of capitalism and the introduction of socialism. Political economists Samuel Bowles and Herbert Gintis in their book, *Schooling in Capitalist America* (1976), use a Marxist perspective for examining the growth of the American public school. To their minds, there is a direct "correspondence" between the organization of schools and the organization of society; and until society is fundamentally changed, there is little hope of real school reform. Other conflict sociologists of education, however, argue that traditional Marxism is too deterministic and overlooks the power of culture and human agency in promoting change. That is, they suggest that Marxism places too much emphasis on the independent effects of the economy and not enough on the effects of cultural, social, and political factors.

An early conflict sociologist who took a slightly different theoretical orientation when viewing society was Max Weber (1864–1920). Like Marx, Weber was convinced that power relations between dominant and subordinate groups structured societies, but unlike Marx, Weber believed that class differences alone could not capture the complex ways human beings form hierarchies and belief systems that make these hierarchies seem just and inevitable. Thus, Weber examined status cultures as well as class position. Status is an important sociological concept because it alerts us to fact that people identify their group by what they consume and with whom they socialize. Weber also recognized that political and military power could be exercised by the State, without direct reference to the wishes of the dominant classes. Moreover, Weber had an acute and critical awareness of how bureaucracy was becoming the dominant type of authority in the modern state and how bureaucratic ways of thinking were bound to shape educational reforms. Weber made the distinction between the "specialist" and the "cultivated man." What should be the goal of education—training individuals for employment or for thinking? Or are these two goals compatible?

The Weberian approach to studying the relation between school and society has developed into a compelling and informative tradition of sociological research. Researchers in this tradition tend to analyze school organizations and processes from the point-of-view of status competition and organizational constraints. One of the first American sociologists of education to use these concepts was Willard Waller. In his book, *The Sociology of Teaching* (1965), Waller portrays schools as autocracies in a state of "perilous equilibrium." Without continuous vigilance, schools would erupt into anarchy because students are essentially forced to go to school against their will. To Waller's mind, rational models of school organization only disguise the inherent tension that pervades the schooling process. Waller's perspective is shared by many contemporary conflict theorists who see schools as oppressive and demeaning and portray student noncompliance with school rules as a form of resistance.

Contemporary conflict theory includes a number of important approaches. First, a major research tradition that has emerged from the Weberian school of thought is represented by Randall Collins (1978). He believes that educational expansion is best explained by status group struggle. He argues that educational credentials, such as college diplomas, are primarily status symbols, rather than indicators of actual achievement. The rise of "credentialism" does not indicate that society is becoming more expert but that education is increasingly used by dominant groups to secure more advantageous places in the occupational and social structure for themselves and their children.

A second school of conflict theory is based on the work of Stanford sociologist John Meyer and his collaborators. Called institutional theory, Meyer argues that the expansion of education worldwide has not been due to functional requirements or labor market demands but rather to the worldwide process of citizenship and the democratic belief that educational development is a requirement of a civil society. Like Collins, Meyer does not believe that such expansion is a proof of democracy, but rather the belief that educational expansion is necessary. Through comparative, historical, and institutional analysis Meyer and his colleagues (Meyer and Rowan, 1977, 1978; Meyer et al., 1992; Rubinson, 1986) demonstrate that educational expansion often preceded labor market demands and that educational expansion is legitimated by institutional ritual and ceremony rather than actual practices.

Third, a variation of conflict theory, referred to as the "new sociology of education" (Young, 1971) began in France and England during 1960s. Unlike most Marxists, who tend to emphasize the economic structure of society, social and cultural reproduction theorists argued that school processes reflect the interests of cultural and social elites. The "new sociologists of education" attempted to link micro and macro processes into a comprehensive theory of school and society. Pierre Bourdieu (1931–2002) examined how cultural capital (particular forms of culture, such as knowledge of music, art, and literature) is passed on by families and schools (1977). The concept of "cultural capital" is important because it suggests that, in understanding the transmission of inequalities, we ought to recognize that the cultural characteristics of individuals and groups are significant indicators of status and class position. There is a growing body of literature that suggests schools pass on to graduates specific social identities that either enhance or hinder their life chances. For example, a graduate from an elite prep school has educational and social advantages over many public school graduates in terms of acceptance to elite colleges and occupational mobility. This advantage has very little to do with what prep school students learn in school and a great deal to do with the power of their schools' reputations for educating members of the upper class. Bourdieu's theories extend the work of other sociologists who have argued persuasively that human culture cannot be understood as an isolated and self-contained object of study but must be examined as part of a larger social and cultural structure. To understand the impact of culture on the lives of individuals and groups we must understand the meanings that are attributed to cultural experiences by those who participate in them (Mannheim, 1936).

Another social reproduction theorist, Basil Bernstein (1924–2000) synthesized macro- and micro-sociological approaches, primarily using a conflict perspective (1990a, b, c, d). He argued that the structural aspects of the educational system and the interactional aspects of the system reflect each other and must be viewed holistically. He examined how speech patterns reflect students' social class backgrounds and how students from working class backgrounds are at a disadvantage in the school setting because schools are essentially middle class organizations. Bernstein combined a class analysis with an interactional analysis, which links language with educational processes and outcomes. Bernstein demonstrated empirically how school processes at the micro-level result in the reproduction of social stratification at the macro-level. Later in the chapter, the work of Bernstein, Bourdieu and Collins will be examined in more detail.

Interactionist Theory[4]

In general, interactionist theories about the relation of school and society are critiques and extensions of the functionalist and conflict perspectives. The critique arises from the observation that functionalist and conflict theories are very abstract and emphasize structure and process at a societal (macro-sociological) level of analysis. While this level of analysis helps us to understand education in the "big picture," macro-sociological theories hardly provide us with an interpretable snap-shot of what schools are like on an everyday level. What do students and teachers actually do in school? Interactionist theories attempt to make the "commonplace strange" by turning on their heads everyday taken-for-granted behaviors and interactions between students and students and between students and teachers. It is exactly what most people do not question that is most problematic to the interactionist. For example, the processes by which students are labeled "gifted" or "learning disabled" are, from an interactionist point of view, important to analyze because such processes carry with them many implicit assumptions about learning and children. By examining the micro-sociological or the interactional aspects of school life, we are less likely to create theories that are logical and eloquent, but without meaningful content.

Interactionist theory has its origins in the social psychology of early twentieth century sociologists George Herbert Mead (1863–1931) and Charles Horton Cooley (1864–1929). Mead and Cooley examined the ways in which the individual is related to society through ongoing social interactions. This school of thought, known as symbolic interactionism, viewed the self as socially constructed in relation to social forces and structures and the product of ongoing negotiation of meanings. Thus, the social self is an active product of human agency rather than a deterministic product of social structure. This more existential perspective, with its origins in the school of philosophy known as phenomenology (Giddens, 1975), stresses what sociologists Peter Berger and Thomas Luckmann (1963) called the social construction of reality.

Interactionist theory is usually combined with functionalism and/or conflict theory to produce a more comprehensive theory of society. One of the most influential interactionist theorists was Canadian-born sociologist Erving Goffman, whose work examined the microsociology of everyday life and the functions of interaction rituals in holding society together. Trained as an anthropologist in the functionalist tradition of Emile Durkheim and A. R. Radcliffe-Brown, Goffman was interested in how everyday taken-for-granted patterns of interactions serve to hold society together. Goffman's brand of interactionism was functionalist, as he viewed social interaction patterns as rituals that served to maintain society through an invisible micro-social order. Although Goffman did not directly study education, his writings on mental hospitals in *Asylums* (1961a), on the labeling of so-called deviant behavior in *Stigma* (1963a), and of patterns of interpersonal behavior in *The Presentation of Self in Everyday Life* (1959), *Encounters* (1961b), *Behavior in Public Places* (1963b), and *Interaction Ritual* (1967) have provided a rich tapestry of concepts for sociologists of education, particularly through the use of labeling theory, which has been applied to the study of teacher expectations (Persell, 1977), ability grouping and tracking (Oakes, 1985), and the study of schools as total institutions (Cookson and Persell, 1985).

Ray Rist has provided some of the most important insights on the ways in which school proesses affect educational achievement. Rist's (1970, 1973, 1977) research into the everyday processes of schooling in an inner city school provided an understanding of how school practices, such as labeling and ability grouping, contribute to the reproduction of educational and social inequalities. In his classic essay, "On understanding the processes of schooling: the contributions of labeling theory" (1977), Rist argued that interactionism has provided important understandings of the way in which the everyday workings of schools (including teacher and student interactions), labeling, and linguistic discourse are at the root of unequal educational outcomes. Drawing upon labeling theory, originally a key approach in the sociology of deviance, Rist demonstrated how teacher expectations of students based on categories such as race, class, ethnicity, and gender affect student perceptions of themselves and their achievment. In another classic essay, "Student social class and teacher expectations: the self fulfilling prophecy in ghetto education" (1970), Rist reported findings from his ethnographic study of a St. Louis elementary school, consisting of primarily African American students. Rist demonstrated how African American teacher labeling of students based on their different social class backgrounds resulted in low-income students being placed in lower ability reading groups and middle class students in higher ability groups, independent of ability. These labels became "life sentences" that had profoundly negative effects on the achievement of the low-income students, who remained in low ability groups throughout their careers. Rist concludes that the interactional processes of the school resulted in educational inequality mirroring the larger structures of society. He concluded that "the system of public education in reality perpetuates what it is ideologically committed to—eradicating class barriers which result in inequality in the social and economic life of the citizenry" (Rist, 1970, p. 449). Combined with the findings of conflict theory, Rist's interactionist approach provides an empirical documentation of how schools reproduce inequality.

Contemporary Approaches in the Sociology of Education

Code Theory: Basil Bernstein's Contribution to Understanding Education[5]

Code theory is the term used to describe the theoretical and empirical project of British sociologist Basil Bernstein. This approach is concerned with how the macro-level (social, political, and economic structures and institutions) is dialectically related to the way in which people understand systems of meaning (codes). For over three decades, Bernstein was one of the centrally important and controversial sociologists, whose work influenced a generation of sociologists of education and linguists. From his early works on language, communication codes, and schooling to his later works on curriculum and pedagogy (teaching methods), Bernstein attempted to produce a theory of social and educational codes (meaning systems) and their effect on social reproduction. Although structuralist in its approach, Bernstein's sociology drew on the essential theoretical orientations in the field—Durkheim, Weber, Marx, and interactionist—and provided the possibility of an important synthesis.

Bernstein's early work on code theory was highly controversial because it discussed social class differences in language that some labeled a deficit theory. Nonetheless, the work raised crucial questions about the relationships among the social division of labor, the family, and the school and explored how these relationships affected differences in learning among social classes. His later work (1977a) began the difficult project of connecting macropower and class relations to the microeducational processes of the school. Whereas class reproduction theorists such as Bowles and Gintis (1976) offered an overtly deterministic view of schools, viewing education as exclusively influenced by the economy without describing or explaining what goes on in schools, Bernstein's work promised to connect the societal, institutional, interactional, and intrapsychic levels of sociological analysis. In doing so, it presented an opportunity to synthesize the classical theoretical traditions of the discipline: Marxist, Weberian, and Durkheimian.

The concept of code is central to Bernstein's structural sociology. From the outset of its use in his work on language (restricted and elaborated codes), the term refers to a "regulative principle which underlies various message systems, especially curriculum and pedagogy" (Atkinson, 1985, p. 136). Bernstein's early work on language (1958, 1960, 1961) examined the relationship between public language, authority, and shared meanings (Danzig, 1995, pp. 146–147). By 1962, Bernstein began to develop code theory through the introduction of the concepts of restricted and elaborated codes (1962a, 1962b). In *Class, Codes, and Control*, Volume 1 (1973a), Bernstein's sociolinguistic code theory was developed into a social theory examining the relationships between social class, family, and the reproduction of meaning systems.

For Bernstein, there were social class differences in the communication codes of working class and middle class children, differences that reflect the class and power relations in the social division of labor, family, and schools. Based upon empirical research, Bernstein distinguished between the restricted code of the working class and the elaborated code of the middle class. Restricted codes are context dependent and particularistic, whereas elaborated codes are context independent and universalistic. For example, when asked to tell a story describing a series of pictures, working-class boys used many pronouns, and their stories could only be understood by looking at the pictures. Middle-class boys, on the other hand, generated descriptions rich in nouns, and their stories could be understood without the benefit of the pictures (Bernstein, 1970). Although Bernstein's critics (see Danzig, 1995) argued that his sociolinguistic theory represented an example of deficit theory (alleging that he was arguing that working-class language was deficient) Bernstein consistently rejected this interpretation (see Bernstein, 1996, pp. 147–156). Bernstein argued that restricted codes are not deficient, but rather are functionally related to the social division of labor, where context-dependent language is necessary in the context of production. Likewise, the elaborated code of the middle classes represents functional changes necessitated by changes in the division of labor and, as a result, by the middle class's new position in reproduction rather than production. That schools require an elaborated code for success means that working class children are disadvantaged by the dominant code of schooling, not deficient. For Bernstein, difference becomes deficit in the context of macro-power relations.

In the third, fourth, and fifth volumes of *Class, Codes, and Control* (1977a, 1990, 1996), Bernstein developed code theory from its sociolinguistic roots to examine the connection between communication codes and curriculum and teaching methods. In this respect, code theory became concerned with the processes of schooling and how they related to social class reproduction. Bernstein analyzed the significant differences between different forms of educational transmission and suggested that social class differences in curriculum and pedagogy are related to inequalities of educational achievement between working-class and middle-class students. Schools that serve middle-class students have different curricula and teaching methods than schools that serve working-class students, and these differences result in educational inequality. Through a careful and logical consideration of the inner workings of the dominant forms of educational practice, Bernstein contributed to a greater understanding of how the schools (especially in the United Kingdom and United States) reproduce what they are ideologically committed to eradicating—social-class advantages in schooling and society. Bernstein's analysis of the social-class assumptions of pedagogic practice is the foundation for linking microeducational processes to the macrosociological levels of social structure and class and power relations.

Despite the criticisms that Bernstein's work is sometimes complex and difficult, it is undeniable that it represented one of the most sustained and powerful attempts to investigate significant issues in the sociology of education. Over 35 years ago, Bernstein began with a simple but overwhelming issue: how to find ways to "prevent the wastage of working-class educational potential" (1961, p. 308). Taken as a whole, Bernstein's work provided a systematic analysis of the relationship between society, schools, and the individual and of how schooling systematically reproduces social inequality.

Cultural Capital and Symbolic Violence: The Contributions of Pierre Bourdieu

Like Bernstein, Pierre Bourdieu (Bourdieu and Passeron, 1977; Bourdieu, 1973, 1977, 1984) attempted to test empirically a theory of society, culture, and education that synthesizes Durkheim and Marx (Swarz, 1997). As the director of the Centre de Sociologie Europeenne in Paris, Bourdieu and his research colleagues provided a theoretical and empirical understanding of culture and stratification. As Collins (Collins and Makowsky, 1993, p. 259) notes, for Bourdieu "culture itself, is an economy.... Stratification in the cultural economy and in the material economy are reciprocally related. For Bourdieu, culture is a realm of power struggle, related to the struggle over the means of violence that characterizes the realm of politics."

Thus, Bourdieu's central concepts of cultural capital and symbolic violence, which were developed in Bourdieu and Passeron's *Education, Society, and Culture* (1977), are used to understand how schooling is part of a symbolic process of cultural and social reproduction. Symbolic violence is "power which manages to impose meanings and to impose them as legitimate by concealing the power relations which are the basis of its force" (Collins and Makowsky, p. 259). This type of power is found not only in schooling but also in other educational realms, including such arenas as child-rearing, museums, musical and artistic institutions. Although schools appear to be neutral, they actually advantage the upper and middle-classes through their symbolic representations. These classes possess cultural capital, or symbolic representations of cultural domination, such as language, ideas, and knowledge of music, art, and literature, all of which have important exchange value in the educational and cultural marketplace.

Drawing upon the functionalism in the sociology of Durkheim and the anthropology of Lévi-Strauss, Bourdieu, like Bernstein, provided more of a conflict, neo-Marxist dimension that demonstrates that cultural capital reproduces social classes and that schooling reproduces cultural capital unevenly among social classes. Schooling corresponds to the dominant interests of society; as a result, upper and middle-class forms of cultural capital become codified in the school's curriculum. Unlike functionalists, Bourdieu and Bernstein did not view these patterns as leading to social cohesion and agreement but rather to class domination.

Bourdieu was not without his critics. According to Collins (Collins and Makowsky, 1993, p. 264), "Bourdieu's theory is completely closed. It is totally cynical, totally pessimistic. We are eternally doomed to stratification.... We cannot get outside our skins; we can only change places inside an iron circle." This view, as Collins suggests, fails to point out the intense organizational and societal conflicts that often result in some reshaping of social stratification (p. 265). Nevertheless, Collins (1993) includes Bourdieu as among the most influential European sociologists of the late twentieth century.

Status Competition and Interaction Ritual: The Contributions of Randall Collins

Like Bourdieu and Bernstein in Europe, U.S. sociologist Randall Collins has attempted to synthesize Marx, Weber, and Durkheim, as well as the microsociologist Erving Goffman, into an overall conflict theory of society. The role of education is central to his theory.

In *Conflict Sociology* (1975), Collins outlined a theory of sociology as an explanatory science, and tested a series of propositions about the nature of social order and change. In it, Collins, although rooted in a Weberian conflict perspective, attempted to synthesize the sociologies of Marx, Weber, Durkheim, and Goffman. Beginning in this ambitious volume, Collins argues that the role of sociology is to understand scientifically the relationship between macro power relations and micro social processes. From Durkheim and Freud, Collins argues that the world is held together by nonrational as well as rational factors and, from Weber, that conflict between social groups over wealth, power, and status are the fuel of social life. Collins (1978) distinguishes between productive and political labor within organizations: Productive labor represents the rational and functional processes that are related to goals and objectives; political labor represents the often nonrational processes related to status competition and group domination and advantage. Although most groups argue that their work in organizations is functional and productive, it is often nonrational and used as a means to legitimate control and domination by dominant groups. Unlike Marxists, who see dominant groups as defined largely by economic forces, Collins provides a Weberian analysis that sees group formation as defined by cultural and political forces as well.

Collins's work on education began with his important article, "Functionalist and conflict theories of educational stratification" (1971), which provided a critique of functionalist theories of social stratification. Unlike functionalists, who viewed the expansion of education as a result of an ongoing expansion of democracy, meritocracy, and technology, Collins argued that educational expansion was far less rational. Rather than seeing the expansion of educational systems in democratic-liberal societies as a rational response to democratic processes of equality of opportunity and meritocratic ideology, and as a result of the rise in requirements for expert knowledge in a highly technological society, Collins (1978) argues that the rise in credentials cannot be explained by the demands of political process or the needs of the labor market.

In *The Credential Society* (1978), Collins suggests that the expansion in educational credentials has been a result of status-competition among groups who engage in symbolic conflict over scarce cultural, political, and economic rewards. For example, elevation of the college degree over the high school degree as an entry-level requirement is not, as functionalists argue, the result of the higher skills and knowledge required in an increasingly technological society. Rather, Collins argues, the competition for good positions, combined with the expansion of opportunities in higher education in response to democratic claims for equality of opportunity made by historically marginalized groups, has raised the stakes for all groups. As groups who historically had not attended college gained access, advantaged groups did not sit by idly, waiting for them to catch up. Rather, through professional organizations they raised the entry-level requirements for professions by using a rational-functional argument that such credentials were necessitated by increased skills of the professions.

Based on a historical and empirical analysis of the requirements of different professions, Collins demonstrated that educational credentials have increased far in excess of an increase in occupational skills and requirements. For example, whereas pharmacists now need a five-year college program rather than the apprenticeship program of the 1930s, the actual knowledge and skills of the profession have not increased dramatically. In fact, in the 1930s pharmacists were called chemists because they made medication from scratch. Today, most pharmacists distribute manufactured medications from bottles and use computer programs to prevent harmful drug interactions. Certainly medical knowledge has increased; however, the requirements of the profession have not increased to a level that justifies the increase in educational requirements.

A second example is the rising educational requirements for nurses. Although it is still possible to become a registered nurse through a two-year community college associate degree program, the movement to require a four-year bachelor's degree is becoming the norm. Proponents of the Bachelor of Science in Nursing argue that the explosion of medical knowledge, combined with the need for a liberally educated nurse who can think on her feet, necessitates elevating the requirement. Collins, however, suggests that there is little empirical evidence to support these claims or that nurses with baccalaureate degrees are more effective than those with degrees in Associate Arts and Sciences. Rather, the movement for increased credentials is an attempt by nurses to raise their own status, especially in relation to doctors, through increased educational levels. Likewise, the increased educational credentials required by pharmacists is viewed as their attempt to raise their own status and income. Similar movements are now occurring for teachers, where teacher-educators and policymakers are arguing that a master's degree should be the minimum entry-level requirement rather than the baccalaureate because of the increased knowledge required to teach children. Although this argument is presented as a rational and functional requirement, there is little evidence to suggest that teachers who enter teaching with master's degrees are more effective.

The rise of credentials, according to Collins, is a result of middle-class professional attempts to raise their status—and to raise the stakes. As historically marginalized groups struggle to catch up, advantaged groups use professional organizations not only to raise their own status but also to increase their advantage in the competition for professional positions. Since they already possess higher credentials, they can continue to distance themselves from competitors who do not have them.

Critics of Collins suggest that his view is too cynical and nonrational and often denies the important functional aspects of educational expertise and the need for increased education. Although these critics are correct in suggesting that, given rising technological demands, increased education is sometimes important, it is also the case that the dramatic increase in credentials cannot be explained by functional demands alone.

Institutional Theory: The Contributions of John Meyer

The work of John Meyer and his colleagues on the development of mass systems of public education worldwide has been an important theoretical approach in the sociology of education since the 1970s. Called institutional theory, Meyer argued that schools are global institutions and have developed similarly throughout the world since the 19th century. Although schools do reflect national cultures and there are differences among national school systems, Meyer and his colleagues have argued that mass educational systems have developed as part of international patterns of democratization and globalization. Meyer argues that all over the world mass systems of public education have developed giving access to more and more people. Meyer, however, does not necessarily agree with the functionalist argument that such expansion is automatically democratic, but rather like conflict theorists, he argues that education as an institution is often controlled by dominant groups and that like Collins, he does not believe that educational expansion is predominantly caused by the needs of the labor market. Rather, it is the belief in education in a democratic civil society that fuels demands for mass schooling. Finally, Meyer and his colleagues have applied institutional theory internationally and comparatively to provide a global analysis of educational systems.

David Baker and Gerald LeTendre (2005) have applied institutional theory to a comparative analysis of international educational systems and processes. Based on Meyer's theory, they argue that there are a number of related themes in the development of worldwide educational systems. These include "the worldwide success of mass schooling," that "schooling is an institution," and that "educational change is institutional change" (Baker and LeTendre, 2005, pp. 6–12). They argue that there are a fundamental set of beliefs that have influenced the development of mass schooling, including that all children should be educated, that nations should invest in schooling; that education functions for the collective good of society; that children should receive early and ongoing schooling; that the types of cognitive skills learned in schools are good for individuals and society; and that one's social, economic, or racial status should not limit access to schooling (Baker and LeTendre, 2005, pp. 7–8). Although these are similar to the democratic-liberal functions of schooling outlined by functionalists, institutional theorists also see how conflict between groups over access and opportunity to mass schooling has affected educational institutions. According to Baker and Letendre, "Over a thirty-year research program with colleagues, institutional theorist and comparative sociologist John Meyer has convincingly established a strong case for thinking about schooling as a product of a world culture that renders education as a resilient and powerful institution in modern society (see, as examples, Baker, 1999; Meyer, 1977; Ramirez and Boli, 1987; Meyer, Ramirez and Soysal, 1992; Fuller and Rubinson, 1992). They have shown that mass schooling takes similar forms throughout the world, and that there are common beliefs in what schooling can and should do for society. This process, they argue, has to a large degree been driven by a dynamic world culture" (Baker and LeTendre, 2005, p. 10). Although Meyer and colleagues believe that national differences are important, they stress the commonalities among educational institutions and the worldwide belief than mass schooling is important.

Postmodern critical theory [6]

Postmodernism developed out of a profound dissatisfaction with the modernist project of enlightenment and reason. Beginning with the poststructural writings of Jacques Derrida (1973, 1981, 1982) and Jean Baudrillard (1981, 1984), social theorists, particularly in France, questioned the appropriateness of modernist categories for understanding what they saw as a postmodern world, a world that transcended the economic and social relations of the industrial world that modernist thought had sought to understand. In particular, the work of Jean Francois Lyotard (1984) rejected the Marxist perspective and the Enlightenment and modernist assumptions underlying Marxist theory and sought to create a different theory for the late twentieth century.

Postmodernist thought consists of many interrelated themes. First, postmodernism insists on what Lyotard (1984) has labeled the rejection of all metanarratives. By this, Lyotard meant that modernist preoccupation with grand, total, or all-encompassing explanations of the world need to be replaced by localized and particular theories. Second, postmodernism stresses the necessary connection between theory and practice as a corrective to the separation of them in much modernist thought. Third, postmodernism stresses the democratic response to authoritarianism and totalitarianism. In particular, Stanley Aronowitz and Henry Giroux (1991), Giroux (1991), and Peter McLaren and R. Hammer (1989) call for a democratic, emancipatory, and antitotalitarian theory and practice, with schools seen as sites for democratic transformation. Fourth, postmodernism sees modernist thought as Eurocentric and patriarchal. Giroux (1991), Patricia Lather (1991), Elizabeth Ellsworth (1989), and others provide an important critique of the racism and sexism in some modernist writings and of the failure of modernism to address the interests of women and people of color. Fifth, postmodernist theorists believe that all social and political discourses are related to structures of power and domination. Sixth, postmodernism stresses what Nicholas Burbules and Susan Rice (1991) term "dialogue across differences." Recognizing the particular and local nature of knowledge, postmodern theorists call for the attempt to work through differences rather than to see them as hopelessly irreconcilable. Thus, postmodern theories of education call for teachers and students to explore the differences between what may seem like inherently contradictory positions in an effort to achieve understanding, respect, and change.

Although much of postmodern theory developed as a critical theory of society and a critique of modernism, it quickly became incorporated into radical writings on education that are often called critical theory. Critical educational theory, which over the past two decades has involved an interdisciplinary mixture of social theory, sociology, and philosophy, has been profoundly affected by postmodernist thought. In particular, by the 1980s critical theories of education, which from the late 1970s attempted to provide an antidote to the over-determinism of Bowles and Gintis (1976), regularly incorporated postmodern language and concerns. There have been numerous postmodern theories of education or applications of postmodernism to education, which will be referred to a postmodern-critical theory. Postmodern-critical theories of education often draw heavily on the work of the Brazilian educator Paolo Freire (1972, 1985, 1987), whose influential work *Pedagogy of the Oppressed* (1972) became the foundation for critical educational theory in the United States (Macedo, 1990, 1994; Kincheloe and Steinberg, 1998). Postmodern-critical theories of education are similar to neo-Marxist theory with respect to curriculum and pedagogy. A school of thought called critical pedagogy (Kincheloe and Steinberg, 1998, ch. 1) stresses the classroom as a site for political action and teachers as agents of change. Finally, postmodern theories of education eschewed what it saw as the overly quantitative approach of traditional sociology of education research and instead argued for more qualitative, narrative, autobiographical approaches to research (Denzin and Lincoln, 2006).

Sadovnik (1995) points out a number of problems with postmodern-critical theories of education. First, postmodern theories of education often are written in a language that is difficult to understand. While this is problematic for all academic work, it is more so for a theory that purports to provide an agenda for critique and change in the school. Second, they usually eschew empirical methods to study schools. As a result, they are sometimes long on assertion and short on evidence. Finally, and most importantly, postmodernist theories of education often fail to connect theory to practice in a way that practitioners find meaningful and useful. Although this does not suggest that postmodernists write exclusively for practitioners, if one of the stated aims of theorists such as Giroux is to develop teachers as transformative intellectuals and to provide a critical pedagogy for school transformation, then the problem of language is of central importance. How can we have dialogues across difference if teachers are excluded from the dialogue?

What separates postmodern critical theory from the rest of the sociology of education is the absence of empirical evidence. Although many of the sociological approaches discussed in this chapter are conceptual and theoretical, theory is the foundation for empirical research. For example, functionalist theory resulted in a rich empirical research project on the relationship between education, achievement, and mobility. Conflict theory resulted in a rich array of comparative, historical, and empirical research on the relationship between education and social reproduction, between educational expansion and labor market requirements, and on the beliefs in citizenship. Interactionist theory resulted in a rich variety of qualitative, ethnographic studies of schools and classroom practices, describing how school processes related to social stratification.

Postmodern-critical theory does not provide sufficient empirical research to test its often tautological propositions. Therefore, although it represents an important social theory, it fails to live up to the promise of sociology: to develop a scientific, empirically tested set of propositions about how the social world works. The following section examines the different types of social scientific research employed in by sociologists of education.

The Rise of Empirical Sociology of Education: Methodological Approaches to Studying Educational Effects

Beginning in the 1960s, quantitative methods dominated research in the sociology of education. Large scale data sets, such as High School Beyond, the National Educational Longitudinal Study, and the

School and Staffing Surveys collected by organizations such as the National Opinion Research Center at the University of Chicago and the National Center for Educational Statistics were mined using sophisticated statistical techniques, including multivariate analysis, hierarchical linear modeling, path analysis, and others. The purpose of this type of research was to examine the independent effects of schooling on educational and economic outcomes, while controlling for a series of independent variables, both inside and outside of schools. Beginning with the Coleman Report in the 1960s (Coleman et al., 1966) and Jenck's analyses of family and school (1972 et al., 1979), these quantitative analyses examined the explained and unexplained variation in academic achievement among different groups, based on race, social class, ethnicity, gender, age, disability and others. This type of research also examined school effects on these groups by comparing different types of schools, including public, private, and charter schools, as well as the effects of school organization and processes, including ability grouping, tracking, and school and class size (Hallinan, 2000; Levinson, Cookson and Sadovnik, 2002).

Although this type of research provided important evidence on the effects of school organization and processes and the independent effects of factors outside of schools, such as poverty, family, neighborhood, community, and peer groups, interactionist sociologists of education argued that research based on large scale data sets often missed the reasons for these effects, as they did not examine school processes. As an antidote to large data set quantitative research, qualitative researchers provided complementary approaches to understanding schooling using ethnographic methods. Based on the methods of the Chicago School of Sociology in the 1930s (Vidich and Lyman, 1994) researchers such as Annette Lareau (1989, 2004), Lois Weis (1990, 2005), and Michelle Fine (1992) provided important analyses of how school processes affect students from various backgrounds.

Some qualitative researchers have remained squarely in the scientific tradition of positivism insisting on objectivity, rigorous research design, and examining causality (Maxwell, 2004). Others are more rooted within interpretive traditions, including symbolic interactionism, ethnomethodology, hermeneutics, postmodernism, feminism, critical theory, and cultural studies (Riehl, 2001: 116) and in varying degrees reject post-positivist notions of scientific rigor. As noted above, many of the postmodern critical studies prefer narrative and autobiographical approaches. Despite critiques of qualitative research as unscientific (see Denzin and Lincoln, 2006), qualitative research continues to be an important part of research in the sociology of education.

By the beginning of the 21st century, as a response to this critique of the unscientific nature of some qualitative educational research, policy makers and governmental officials at the U.S. Department of Education called for educational research to mirror the scientific methods of the natural sciences. Arguing that experimental research design with randomized trials, "the gold standard" of medical and pharmaceutical research should be the preferred method in educational research, the U.S. Department of Education issued guidelines for funded educational research privileging experimental design in particular and quantitative methods in general. In addition, the Department of Education's policies, including the federal No Child Left Behind Act (2001) required scientific evidence for programs and curricula to appear on its What Works Clearinghouse list, or to be eligible for federal funds in Title I (high poverty) districts or for comprehensive school reform model grants. Although social science and educational research organizations such as the American Educational Research Association issued statements opposing this strict definition of scientific research and called for the inclusion of qualitative studies on an equal footing, federal policy and funding continues to privilege quantitative methods.

A number of researchers have argued that there are weaknesses in both quantitative and qualitative research methods and that mixed-methods approaches make more sense (Chatterji, 2005; Johnson and Onwuegbuzie, 2004; Maxwell, 2004). Based upon these strengths and weaknesses, it is clear that both quantitative and qualitative methods should be an important part of sociology of education research. Riehl (2001) argues that qualitative research in the sociology of education has made valuable contributions to our understanding of educational problems and has offered policy makers useful data for school improvement. Large scale data set analyses have provided essential evidence on the effects of schooling and have been invaluable to policy makers. In an age where educational research is dominated by the Institute of Education Sciences at the U.S. Department of Education labeling of experimental research design and randomized field trials modeled after the pharmaceutical and medical research communities as the "gold standard" for evaluating what works and recommending policy and programmatic interventions, it is imperative that both quantitative and qualitative research are recognized as important tools for policy makers. Whether studies are totally quantitative or totally qualitative or part of a mixed-method approach that uses both quantitative and qualitative methods, sociology of education research provides important data for public policy. Chatterji (2005) argues convincingly that a mixed-method approach rich in qualitative methods must be part of extended-term mixed-method (ETMM) evaluation designs to ensure researchers provide policy makers with the best evidence of what works in education, although this approach is difficult and costly.

Conclusion

The sociology of education originated in the concerns of classical sociology in the 19th and early 20th centuries. It came of age in from the 1960s onward and concentrated on the significant questions regarding meritocracy and equality. Contemporary theories in the sociology of education have attempted to synthesize the major theories in the field, functionalism, conflict theory, and interactionism and have provided a rich theoretical foundation for empirical work. At the same time, the concern with educational inequalities has resulted in a preoccupation with empirical, mostly quantitative investigations of school effects. Using large data sets such as High School and Beyond and the National Education Longitudinal Study, these investigations have focused on school processes such as tracking and their effects. Although these studies have provided important findings on educational outcomes and the independent effects of schooling, family, and other student background characteristics, they have often lacked theoretical sophistication.

Today, the sociology of education is at a crossroads. The 20th century represented the attempt to refine and empirically test the theoretical insights of the classical sociology of the 19th century. Through sophisticated methodological approaches, sociologists of education provided important empirical evidence on the effects of education on different groups and have been an important source of data for discussions of the achievement gap. However, postmodern theorists and researchers, usually using qualitative methods, provided an alternative to what they perceived as the overly scientific, quantitative focus of much of the sociology of education research. For many sociologists of education, this response has weakened the scientific base of educational research. For others (Cookson, 1987; Hallinan, 1996), sociology of education of all types has been too removed from policy and practice. In the coming years, sociologists of education need to combine varied research methodologies, quantitative and qualitative, to examine the most important question common to functionalist and conflict theory: to understand why students from lower socioeconomic backgrounds do less well in school and to provide pragmatic policy recommendations for successful school reform and to reduce the achievement gap. Although sociological theory in the sociology of education will continue to be an important part of this project, the separation of theory, research, and practice needs to be diminished.

Notes

1. Earlier versions of this chapter appeared in A.R. Sadovnik, "Theories in the Sociology of Education." Pp. 7–26 in *Schools and Society: A Sociological Approach to Education, Second Edition.* edited by J. Ballantine and J. Spade, Wadsworth, 2004 and A.R Sadovnik, "Theories in the Sociology of Education." Pp. 15–34 in *Schools and Society: A Sociological Approach to Education*, edited by J. Ballantine and J. Spade, Wadsworth, 2001.

2. Adapted from A. R. Sadovnik and P. W. Cookson, Jr. "Functionalism," in *Education and Sociology: An Encyclopedia*. New York and London: Routledge, 2002.
3. This section is adapted from A. R. Sadovnik, P. W. Cookson, Jr., & S. F. Semel, *Exploring Education: An Introduction to the Foundations of Education,* chapter 4. Boston: Allyn and Bacon, 1994; 2001, 2006.
4. This section is adapted from A. R. Sadovnik, P. W. Cookson, Jr., & S. F. Semel, *Exploring Education: An Introduction to the Foundations of Education,* chapter 4. Boston: Allyn and Bacon, 1994; 2001, 2006.
5. This section is adapted from A. R. Sadovnik, "Basil Bernstein's theory of pedagogic practice: A structuralist approach," *Sociology of Education* 64(1), January 1991: 48–63. Reprinted by permission of the American Sociological Association.
6. This section is adapted from A. R. Sadovnik, "Postmodernism and the sociology of education: Closing the rift among scholarship, research, and practice." In George Noblit and William Pink (Eds.), *Continuity and contradiction: The futures of the sociology of education* (Hampton Press, 1995).

References

Aronowitz, S., & Giroux, H. (1991). *Postmodern education: Politics, culture and social criticism.* Minneapolis: University of Minnesota Press.

Atkinson, P. (1985). Language, structure and reproduction: An introduction to the sociology of Basil Bernstein. London: Methuen.

Baker, D. P. (1999). Schooling all the masses: Reconsidering the origins of American schooling in the post-bellum era. *Sociology of Education*, 72(4), 197-215.

Baker, D. P., & LeTendre, G. K. (2005). *National differences, global similarities: World culture and the future of schooling.* Palo Alto, CA: Stanford University Press.

Baudrillard, J. (1981). *For a critique of the political economy of the sign* (Charles Leaven, Trans.). St. Louis: Tellos Press.

Baudrillard, J. (1984). The precession of simulacra. In B. Wallis, (Ed.), *Art after modernism: Rethinking representation* (pp. 213–281). Boston: David Godine.

Bennett, K. P., & LeCompte, M. D. (1990). *How schools work.* New York: Longmann.

Berger, P., & Luckmann, T. (1963). *The social construction of reality.* Garden City, NY: Doubleday.

Bernstein, B. (1958). Some sociological determinants of perception: An enquiry into sub-cultural differences. *British Journal of Sociology*, 9, 159–174.

Bernstein, B. (1960). Language and social class: A research note. *British Journal of Sociology*, 11, 271–276.

Bernstein, B. (1961). Social class and linguistic development: A theory of social learning. In A. H. Halsey, J. Floud, & C. A. Anderson (Eds.), *Education, economy and society*, pp. 288–314. New York: Free Press.

Bernstein, B. (1962a). Linguistic codes, hesitation phenomena and intelligence. *Language and Speech*, 5, 31–46.

Bernstein, B. (1962b). Social class, linguistic codes and grammatical elements. *Language and Speech*, 5, 221–240.

Bernstein, B. (1970). Education cannot compensate for society. *New Society*, 387, 344–347.

Bernstein, B. (1973a). *Class, codes, and control* (Vol. 1). London: Routledge & Kegan Paul. (Original published 1971)

Bernstein, B. (1973b). *Class, codes, and control* (Vol. 2). London: Routledge & Kegan Paul. (Original published 1971)

Bernstein, B. (1973c) On the classification and framing of educational knowledge. In B. Bernstein, *Class, codes, and control* (Vol. 1, pp. 202–230; Vol. 2, 85–115). London: Routledge & Kegan Paul. (Originally published in *Knowledge and control: New directions for the sociology of education*, M. F. D. Young, Ed., 1971, London: Collier-Macmillan.)

Bernstein, B. (1977a). *Class, codes, and control.* (Vol. 3). London: Routledge & Kegan Paul. (Original published 1971)

Bernstein, B. (1977b). Class and pedagogies: Visible and invisible (Rev. ed.). In B. Bernstein, *Class, codes, and control* (Vol. 3, pp. 116–156). London: Routledge & Kegan Paul.

Bernstein, B. (1986). On pedagogic discourse. In J. G. Richardson (Ed.), *Handbook for theory and research in the sociology of education*, (pp. 205–240). New York: Greenwood. (Revised and reprinted in B. Bernstein, pp. 165–218, 1990.)

Bernstein, B. (1990a). *Class, codes and control: Vol. 4: The structuring of pedagogic discourse.* London: Routledge.

Bernstein, B. (1990b). Social class and pedagogic practice. In B. Bernstein, *Class, codes, and control: Vol. 4: The structuring of pedagogic discourse* (pp. 63–93). London: Routledge.

Bernstein, B. (1990c). Elaborated and restricted codes: Overview and criticisms. In B. Bernstein, *Class, codes and control: Vol. 4: The structuring of pedagogic discourse* (pp. 94–130). London: Routledge.

Bernstein, B. (1990d). The social construction of pedagogic discourse. In B. Bernstein, *Class, codes, and control: Vol. 4: The structuring of pedagogic discourse* (pp. 165–218). London: Routledge.

Bernstein, B. (1995). A response. In A. R. Sadovnik (Ed.), *Knowledge and pedagogy: The sociology of Basil Bernstein* (pp. 385–424). Norwood, NJ: Ablex Publishing Corporation.

Bernstein, B. (1996). *Pedagogy, symbolic control and identity: Theory, research, critique.* London: Taylor & Francis.

Bourdieu, P. (1973). Cultural reproduction and social reproduction. In R. Brown (Ed.), *Knowledge, education, and cultural change* (pp. 71–112). London: Tavistock.

Bourdieu, P. (1977). *Outline of a theory of practice.* Cambridge, UK: Cambridge University Press.

Bourdieu, P. (1984). *Distinction: A social critique of the judgment of taste.* Cambridge, MA: Harvard University Press.

Bourdieu, P., & Passeron, J. C. (1977). *Reproduction in education, society and culture.* London: Sage.

Bowles, S., & Gintis, H. (1976). *Schooling in capitalist America.* New York: Basic Books.

Burbules, N., & Rice, S. (1991). Dialogue across differences: Continuing the conversation. *Harvard Educational Review*, 61 (4), 393–416.

Burbules, N., & Rice, S. (1992). Can we be heard? A reply to Leach. *Harvard Educational Review*, 62 (2), 264–271.

Chatterji, M. (2005), Evidence on "What Works": An Argument for Extended-Term Mixed-Method (ETMM) Evaluation Designs. *Educational Researcher*, 34(5), 14–24.

Coleman, J. et al. (1966). *Equality of educational opportunity*. Washington D.C.: U.S. Government Printing Office.

Collins, R. (1971). Functional and conflict theories of educational stratification. *American Sociological Review*, 36 (6), 1002–1019.

Collins, R. (1975). *Conflict sociology*. New York: Academic Press.

Collins, R. (1978). *The credential society*. New York: Academic Press.

Collins, R., & Makowsky, M. (1993). *The discovery of society*. New York: McGraw Hill.

Cookson, P. W. (1987). Closing the rift between scholarship and practice: The need to revitalize educational research. *Educational Policy*, 1, 321–331.

Cookson, P. W., Jr., & Persell, C. H. (1985). *Preparing for power: America's elite boarding schools*. New York: Basic.

Danzig, A. (1995). Applications and distortions of Basil Bernstein's code theory. In A. R. Sadovnik (Ed.), *Knowledge and pedagogy: The sociology of Basil Bernstein* (pp. 145–170). Norwood, NJ: Ablex Publishing Corporation.

Davis, K., & Moore, W. (1945). Some principles of stratification. *American Sociological Review*, 10, 242–249.

Denzin, N. K., & Lincoln, Y.S. (2006). *Handbook of qualitative research* (Third ed.). Thousand Oaks, CA: Sage.

Derrida, J. (1973). *Speech and phenomenon*. Evanston, IL: Northwestern University Press.

Derrida, J. (1981). *Positions*. Chicago: University of Chicago Press.

Derrida, J. (1982). *Of grammatology*. Baltimore: Johns Hopkins University Press.

Durkheim, E. (1947). *The division of labor in society*. Glencoe, IL: Free Press. (Original work published 1893)

Durkheim, E. (1951). *Suicide*. Glencoe, IL: Free Press. (Original work published 1897)

Durkheim, E. (1954). *The elementary forms of religious life*. Glencoe, IL: Free Press. (Original work published 1915)

Durkheim, E. (1956). *Education and sociology*. New York: Free Press.

Durkheim, E. (1962). *Moral education*. New York: Free Press.

Durkheim, E. (1977). *The evolution of educational thought* (P. Collins, Trans.). London: Routledge & Kegan Paul.

Ellsworth, E. (1989). Why doesn't this feel empowering? Working through the repressive myths of critical pedagogy. *Harvard Educational Review*, 59 (3), 297–324.

Fine, M. (1992). *Framing Dropouts*. Albany, New York: SUNY Press.

Freire, P. (1972). *Pedagogy of the oppressed*. New York: Herder & Herder.

Freire, P. (1985). *The politics of education*. South Hadley, MA: Bergin & Garvey.

Freire, P. (1987). *A pedagogy for liberation*. South Hadley, MA: Bergin & Garvey.

Fuller, B., & Rubinson, R. (eds.) (1992). The political construction of education. New York: Praeger.

Giddens, A. (1975). *The new rules of sociological method*. London: Cambridge University Press.

Giroux, H. (1991). *Postmodernism, feminism, and cultural politics: Redrawing educational boundaries*. Albany, NY: SUNY Press.

Goffman, E. (1959). *The presentation of self in everyday life*. Garden City, NY: Doubleday.

Goffman, E. (1961a). *Asylums*. Garden City, NY: Doubleday.

Goffman, E. (1961b). *Encounters*. Indianapolis, IN: Bobbs-Merrill.

Goffman, E. (1963a). *Stigma*. Englewood Cliffs, NJ: Prentice-Hall.

Goffman, E. (1963b). *Behavior in public places*. Garden City, NY: Doubleday.

Goffman, E. (1967). *Interaction ritual*. Garden City, NY: Doubleday.

Hallinan, M.T. (1996). Bridging the gap between scholarship and practice. *Sociology of Education* 69 (Extra Issue), 131-134.

Hallinan, M.T. (Ed) (2000). *Handbook of sociology of education* New York: Kluwer.

Hurn, C. (1993). *The limits and possibilities of schooling*. Needham Heights, MA: Allyn & Bacon.

Johnson, R., & Onwuegbuzie, A. (2004). Mixed methods: a research paradigm whose time has come. *Educational Researcher*, 33(7), 14-26.

Kincheloe, J. L., & Steinberg, S. R. (Eds.). (1998). *Unauthorized methods: Strategies for critical teaching*. New York: Routledge.

Lareau, A. (1989). *Home Advantage*. New York: Routledge.

Lareau, A. (2004). *Unequal Childhood: Class, Race and Family Life*. Berkeley: University of California Press.

Lather, P. (1991). *Getting smart: Feminist research and pedagogy with/in the postmodern*. New York: Routledge.

Levinson, D.L., Cookson, P.W., & Sadovnik, A.R. (2002). *Encyclopedia of education and sociology*. New York: Routledge.

Lyotard, J. F. (1984). *The postmodern condition* (G. Bennington & B. Massumi, Trans.). Minneapolis: University of Minnesota Press.

Mannheim, K. (1936). *Ideology and utopia*. New York: Harcourt & Brace.

Maxwell, J. Causal explanation, qualitative research and scientific inquiry in education. *Educational Researcher*, 33(2), 3-11.

McLaren, P., & Hammer, R. (1989). Critical pedagogy and the postmodern challenge: Toward a critical postmodernist pedagogy of liberation. *Educational Foundations*, 3(3), 29–62.

Meyer, J. (1977). The effects of education as an institution. *American Journal of Sociology*, 83(1), 55–77.

Meyer, J., Kamens, D., Benavot, A., Cha, Y. K., & Wong, S. Y. (1992). *School knowledge for the masses: World models and national primary curriculum categories in the twentieth century*. London: Falmer.

Meyer, J., & Rowan, B. (1977). The structure of educational organizations. In M. Meyer & Associates (Eds.), *Environments and organizations* (pp. 78–109). San Francisco: Jossey-Bass.

Meyer, J., Ramirez, F. O., Rubinson, R., & Boli, J. (1977). The world of educational revolution, 1950–1970. *Sociology of Education*, 50, 242–258.

Meyer, J., & Rowan, B. (1978). Institutionalized organizations: Formal structure as myth and ceremony. *American Journal of Sociology*, 83, 340–363.

Meyer, J., Ramirez, F., & Soysal, Y. (1992). World expansion of mass education, 1870–1980. *Sociology of Education*, 65, 128–149.

Oakes, J. (1985, 2005). *Keeping track: How schools structure inequality*. New Haven: Yale.

Parsons, T. (1959). The school as a social system. *Harvard Educational Review*, 29, 297–318.

Persell, C. H. (1977). *Education and inequality*. New York: Free Press.

Ramirez, F., & Boli, J. (1987). The political construction of mass schooling: European origins and worldwide institutionalization. *Sociology of Education*, 60, 2–17.

Ravitch, D. (1977). *The revisionists revisited*. New York: Basic Books.

Riehl, C. (2001). Bridging to the future: The contributions of qualitative research to the sociology of education. *Sociology of Education*, 74 (Extra Issue): 115–134.

Rist, R. (1970). Student social class and teacher expectations: The self fulfilling prophecy in ghetto education. *Harvard Educational Review*, 40, 411–451.

Rist, R. (1973). *The urban school: Factory for failure*. Cambridge, MA: MIT Press.

Rist, R. (1977). On understanding the processes of schooling: The contributions of labeling theory. In J. Karabel & A. H. Halsey, *Power and ideology in education* (pp. 292–305). New York: Oxford University Press.

Rubinson, R. (1986). Class formation, politics and institutions: Schooling in the United States. *American Journal of Sociology*, 92, 519–548.

Sadovnik, A. R. (1991). Basil Bernstein's theory of pedagogic practice: A structuralist approach. *Sociology of Education*, 64(1), 48–63.

Sadovnik, A. R. (Ed.). (1995). *Knowledge and pedagogy: The sociology of Basil Bernstein*. Norwood, NJ: Ablex Publishing Corporation.

Sadovnik, A. R. (1995). Postmodernism and the sociology of education: Closing the rift among scholarship, research, and practice. In George Noblit & William Pink (Eds.), *Continuity and contradiction: The futures of the sociology of education*. Cresskill, NJ: Hampton Press.

Swartz, D. (1997). *Culture and power: The sociology of Pierre Bourdieu*. Chicago: University of Chicago Press.

Tönnies, F. (1957). *Community and society*. New York: Harper. (Original work published 1887)

U.S. Department of Education. (1983). *A nation at risk*. Washington, DC: U.S. Government Printing Office.

Vidich, A. J., & Lyman, S.M. (1994). Qualitative methods: Their history in sociology and anthropology. In N. K. Denzin& Y. S. Lincoln (Eds.), *Handbook of qualitative research* (First ed., pp. 23–59). Thousand Oaks, CA: Sage Publications, Inc.

Weis, L. (1990). *Working class without work*. New York: Routledge.

Weis, L. (2004). *Class reunion*. New York: Routledge.

Young, M. F. D. (Ed.). (1971). *Knowledge and control: New directions of the sociology of education*. London: Collier-Macmillan.

Suggested Reading

Atkinson, P. (1981). Bernstein's structuralism. *Education Analysis*, 3, 85–96.

Atkinson, P., Davies, B., & Delamont, S. (1995). *Discourse and reproduction: Essays in honor of Basil Bernstein*. Cresskill, NJ: Hampton Press.

Bernstein, B. (1961). Social structure, language, and learning. *Educational Research*, 3, 163–176.

Bernstein, B. (1971). A sociolinguistic approach to socialisation with reference to educability. In D. Hymes & J. Gumperz (Eds.), *Directions in sociolinguistics*. New York: Holt, Rinehart & Winston. (Reprinted in B. Bernstein, *Class, codes and control (Vol. 1)*. London: Routledge & Kegan Paul, 1973.)

Bernstein, B. (1973). *Class, codes, and control* (Vol. 3). London: Routledge & Kegan Paul. (Original published 1975)

Bernstein, B., & Cook-Gumperz, J. (1976). The coding grid, theory and operations. In J. Cook-Gumperz (Ed.), *Social control and socialization: A study of social class differences in the language of maternal control* (pp. 48–72). London: Routledge & Kegan Paul.

Cherryholmes, C. (1988). *Power and criticism: Poststructural investigations in education*. New York: Teachers College Press.

Dewey, J. (1916). *Democracy and education*. New York: Free Press.

Dewey, J. (1984). *The public and its problems*. In John Dewey: The later works, Vol. 2: 1925–1927. Carbondale & Edwardsville, IL: Southern Illinois University Press. (Original work published 1927)

Giroux, H. (1981). *Ideology, culture and the process of schooling*. Philadelphia: Temple University Press.

Giroux, H. (1983). *Theory and resistance in education*. South Hadley, MA: Bergin & Garvey.

Giroux, H. (1988). *Teachers as intellectuals*. South Hadley, MA: Bergin & Garvey.

Habermas, J. (1979). *Communication and the evolution of society*. Boston: Beacon Press.

Habermas, J. (1981). Modernity versus postmodernity. *New German Critique*, 8(1), 3–18.

Habermas, J. (1982). The entwinement of myth and enlightenment. *New German Critique*, 9(3), 13–30.

Habermas, J. (1983). Modernity: An incomplete project. In H. Foster (Ed.), *The anti-aesthetic: Essays on postmodern culture* (pp. 3–16). Seattle, WA: Bay Press.

Habermas, J. (1987). *The philosophical discourse of modernity* (F. Lawrence, Trans.). Cambridge, MA: MIT Press.

Harvey, D. (1989). *The condition of postmodernity: An inquiry into the origins of cultural change*. Cambridge, MA: Basil Blackwell.

Holland, J. (1986). Social class differences in adolescents' conception of the domestic and industrial division of labor. *C.O.R.E.*, 10(1). University of London, Institute of Education.

Jameson, F. Postmodernism and consumer society. In H. Foster (Ed.), *The antiaesthetic: Essays on postmodern culture* (pp. 11–125). Seattle: Bay Press.

Jencks, C. (1979). *Who Get's Ahead.* New York: Basic Books.

Jencks, C. (1987). *What is post-modernism?* New York: St. Martin's.

Jencks, C. et al. (1972). *Inequality.* New York: Basic Books.

Jenkins, C. (1990). The professional middle class and the origins of progressivism: A case study of the new educational fellowship, 1920–1950. *C.O.R.E.*, 14(1). University of London, Institute of Education.

Karabel, J., & Halsey, A. H. (1977). *Power and ideology in education.* New York: Oxford University Press.

Lather, P. (1989). Critical theory, curriculum transformation, and feminist mainstreaming. *Journal of Education*, 1966 (March), 49–62.

Lather, P. (1989). Postmodernism and the politics of enlightenment. *Educational Foundations*, 3(3), 8–9.

Marx, K. (1971). *The poverty of philosophy.* New York: International Publishers.

Marx, K., & Engles, F. (1947). *The German ideology.* New York: International Publishers. (Original work published 1846)

McLaren, P. (1991). Schooling and the postmodern body: Critical pedagogy and the politics of enfleshment, In H. Giroux, *Postmodernism, feminism, and cultural politics: Redrawing educational boundaries.*(pp. 144–173). Albany, NY: SUNY Press, 1991.

Semel, S. F. (1995). Basil Bernstein's theory of pedagogic practice and the history of American progressive education: Three case studies. In A. R. Sadovnik (Ed.), *Knowledge and pedagogy: The sociology of Basil Bernstein* (pp. 337–358). Norwood, NJ: Ablex Publishing Corporation.

Weber, M. (1978). *Economy and society* (Vols. 1 & 2). (G. Roth & C. Wittich, Eds.) Berkeley: University of California Press.

Wexler, P. (1987). *Social analysis: After the new sociology.* London: Routledge & Kegan Paul.

2

On Education and Society

ÉMILE DURKHEIM

Educational transformations are always the result and the symptom of the social transformations in terms of which they are to be explained. For a people to feel at any given moment the need to change its educational system, it is necessary that new ideas and needs have emerged for which the old system is no longer adequate. But these needs and ideas do not arise spontaneously; if they suddenly come to the forefront of human consciousness after having been ignored for centuries, it is necessarily the case that in the intervening period there has been a change and that it is this change of which they are an expression. Thus, in order to understand the educational achievement of the sixteenth century, we need as a preliminary to know in a general way what constituted the great social movement that historians call the Renaissance and of which a new educational theory was but one manifestation.

The essence of the Renaissance has often been identified with a return to the spirit of classical times; and indeed this is precisely the meaning of the word normally used to designate this period of European history. The sixteenth century is supposed to have been a period when man, abandoning the gloomy ideals of the Middle Ages, reverted to the gayer and more self-confident view of life which prevailed in the ancient pagan world. As to the cause of this change of direction, it allegedly consisted in the rediscovery of classical literature, the principal masterpieces of which were rescued during this period from the oblivion in which they had languished for centuries. On this view it was the discovery of the great works of classical literature that brought about this new change of outlook in the western European mind. But to speak of the Renaisssance in this way is only to point in the most superficial way to its façade. If it were indeed true that the sixteenth century simply took up the classical tradition at the point it had reached when the Dark Ages arrived and temporarily blotted it out, the Renaissance would emerge as a movement of moral and intellectual reaction that would be hard to account for. We would have to assume that humanity had strayed from its natural path for fifteen centuries, since it had to retrace its steps back over a period of such length in order to embark upon a whole new stage in its career. Certainly progress does not proceed in a straight line; it makes turnings and detours; advances are followed by recessions but that such an aberration should be prolonged over a period of fifteen hundred years is historically incredible. It is true that this view of the Renaissance accords with the way in which the eighteenth-century-writers spoke of it. But just because they felt a kind of admiration for the simple life of primitive societies, are we to say that then social philosophy was an attempt to restore prehistoric civilization? Because the men of the Revolution thought that they were imitating the actions of the ancient Romans, are we to view the society that resulted from the Revolution as an imitation of the ancient city? People involved in action are the least well placed to see the causes that underlie their actions, and the way in which they represent to themselves the social movement of which they are a part should always be regarded as suspect and should by no means be thought of as having any special claim to credibility.

Besides, it is simply not true that classical literature was unknown during the centuries we have just been considering, that it was only discovered towards the beginning of the sixteenth century, and that it was this revelation that suddenly expanded the intellectual horizons of Europe. The fact is that there was not a single period during the whole of the Middle Ages when these literary masterpieces were not known; in every generation we find a few people sufficiently intelligent and sensitive to be able to appreciate their worth. Abélard, the hero of dialectic, was at the same time a literary scholar; Virgil, Seneca, Cicero, and Ovid were just as familiar to him as were Boethius and Augustine. During the twelfth century there was a famous school at Chartres which, inspired by its founder, Bernard de Chartres, offered a classical education similar to what would later be offered by the Jesuits. One could multiply examples of this type. It is true that these attempts to introduce classical literature into education remained isolated cases; they never succeeded in capturing the imagination of the Scholastics, who cast them back into obscurity. But they are nonetheless real, and they are sufficient to prove that if classical literature was not appreciated in the Middle Ages, if it played no part in education, this was not because people did not know of its existence. In short, the Middle Ages knew about all the main aspects of classical civilization, but it only retained what it regarded as important, what answered to its own needs. Its entire attention was caught by logic, and this eclipsed everything else. Thus, if everything changed in the sixteenth century, if suddenly Greek and Roman art and literature were recognized as being of incomparable educational value, this clearly must have been because at that moment in history, as a consequence of a change that had taken place in the public mind, logic lost its former prestige—while by contrast an urgent need was felt for the first time for a kind of culture that would be more refined, more elegant or literary. People did not acquire this taste because they had just discovered classical antiquity; rather, they demanded from the antiquity they already knew the means of satisfying the new taste they had just acquired. What we must seek, therefore, is an account of this change of direction in the intellectual and moral outlook of the European peoples, if we wish to understand the nature of the Renaissance insofar as it affected educational thought no less than scientific and literary thought. A people only modifies its mental outlook to such an enormous extent when very fundamental features of social life have themselves been modified. We can therefore be certain in advance that the Renaissance derives, not, I repeat, from the fortuitous fact that certain classical works were exhumed at this time, but rather from profound changes in the organization of European societies. I cannot, of course, attempt here to paint a complete and detailed picture of these transformations, but I should like at least to point out the most important of them so as to be able to relate the educational movement we shall be exploring to its social roots.

In the first place, there was a group of interrelated changes in the economic sphere. People had finally got away from the paltry life-style of the Middle Ages, when the general insecurity of relations paralyzed the spirit of enterprise, when the limited number of markets stifled great ambition, when only the extreme simplicity of their tastes and needs enabled men to live in harmony with their environment. Gradually order had been established; better government and more efficient administration had rallied people's confidence. Towns had proliferated and become more populous. Most important of all, the discovery of America and the trade route via the Indies had galvanized economic activity by opening up new worlds in which it could operate. Consequently, the general welfare had been increased; vast fortunes had been amassed; and the acquisition of wealth stimulated and developed a taste for the easy, elegant life of luxury....

However, if this transformation had been limited to the world of the aristocracy, it probably would not have had such extensive social consequences. But one of the effects of accrued wealth was to produce at the same time a narrowing of the gaps between social classes. Up till then the bourgeoisie had not even dared raise its eyes to look at the aristocracy across what it felt to be a great fixed gulf. And it found it natural to lead quite a different existence. But now that the bourgeoisie had become richer and consequently more powerful, it also became more ambitious and sought to narrow the gap. Its expectations had increased with its resources, making the life it had led up till then appear intolerable. It was no longer afraid to cast its gaze upwards and it wanted as well to live the life of the nobles, to imitate their style, their manners, their luxury. As one writer puts it: "Pride was reaching ever higher peaks in every section of the community. The bourgeoisie in the towns have started wanting to dress in the same way as the aristocracy…and the people from the villages in the same way as the bourgeoisie in the towns." According to another author, the bourgeois ladies grew bored with their life of obscurity; they now wanted to copy the great ladies. "One can scarcely distinguish any longer between a noble lady and a plebeian…one sees women who are worse than plebeian dressing in flowing robes embroidered in gold and silver…their fingers are loaded with emeralds and other precious stones … in the old days the practice of kissing a lady's hand in greeting was restricted to aristocrats, and noble ladies did not offer their hand to the first comer, let alone to anyone at all. Today men smelling of leather rush to kiss the hand of a woman whose escutcheon is exclusively aristocratic. Patrician ladies marry plebeian men, plebeian women marry patrician men; thus we are breeding hybrid creatures." It is easy to guess that so considerable a change in the way life was understood would inevitably be accompanied by a change in the way education was understood, and that instruction designed to produce a good bachelor of arts, versed in all the secrets of syllogism and argument, would be quite unsuited to the enterprise of producing an elegant and fluent nobleman able to hold his own in a salon and possessing all the social graces.

However, in addition to this transformation, there was another one, no less important, which took place in the world of ideas.

By the sixteenth century, the great nation states of Europe had been in large measure established. Whereas in the Middle Ages there had been but one Europe, one Christendom, which was united and homogeneous, there now existed great individual collectivities with their own intellectual and moral characters. England found its identity and its unity with the Tudors, Spain with Ferdinand of Castile and his successors. Germany with the Hapsburgs (albeit more vaguely), and France did so before any of the others under the Capetians. The old unity of Christendom had thus been definitively shattered. However much people continued to profess respect for the fundamental doctrines, which still appeared highly abstract, each of the groups which had thus been formed had its own special mode of thought and feeling, its own national temperament whose particular emphasis tended to affect the systems of belief that had been accepted until that time by the vast majority of the faithful. And since the great moral figures that had arisen could only develop their individual natures, since they could not organize their thoughts and beliefs according to their own lights unless they were granted the right to deviate from accepted beliefs, they claimed this right and in claiming it they proclaimed it; that is to say they claimed the rights of schism and of free inquiry—albeit only to a limited extent, and not as absolute rights, since such a thing would have been inconceivable at the time. It is here that we find the root cause of the Reformation, that other aspect of the Renaissance that was the natural result of the movement towards individualization and differentiation taking place at that time within the homogeneous mass of Europe. In one sense, of course, Scholasticism had paved the way for it. Scholasticism had taught reason to be more self-confident by confronting it with monumental questions and equipping it with a rigorous logical training so that it might make fresh conquests. However, between the audacities of Scholasticism, especially at the end of the fifteenth century, which were always relatively moderate—between the more or less bold claims made by a few thinkers whose voices were scarcely heard outside the schools, and the sudden explosion that was the Reformation and that shook the whole of Europe, there is clearly a radical break, which bears witness to the fact that new forces had come into play.

Here we have a new causal factor, which was to bring about a change in the theory and practice of education. The Christian faith had played too large a part in medieval education for the educational system not to be affected by the upheavals that faith was undergoing. Moreover, there were other ways in which the economic factor exercised a parallel influence. It is clear, in fact, that the aesthetic ideal of the Middle Ages was quite unsuited for pupils who had acquired a taste for luxury and the life of leisure. And since this aesthetic ideal was the ideal of Christianity, Christianity itself was affected by the same phenomenon. For it was not possible that the aversion felt henceforth for the old view of life should not be extended to the whole system of beliefs upon which that view of life was grounded. If, as we have argued, Christianity was accepted so readily by the barbarians, this was precisely because of its starkness, its indifference towards the products of civilization, its disdain for the joys of existence. But the same reasons that accounted for its triumph then were now to diminish its authority over people's minds. Societies that had learned to savor the joy of living could no longer put up with a doctrine that rendered sacrifice, self-denial, abstinence, and suffering in general the supreme objects of desire.

Individuals, sensing that this system ran counter to their deepest feelings and opposed the satisfaction of needs they regarded as quite natural, could only be disposed to cast doubt upon it, or at least to cast doubt upon the way it had been interpreted up to that time; for it is impossible to accept uncritically, unreservedly, and without sufficient reason a doctrine that in certain respects seems to go against nature. Without renouncing it completely, people came to feel the need to revise it, to interpret it afresh, in such a way that it would harmonize with the aspirations of the age. Now, any such revision and reinterpretation presuppose the right to revise, to inspect, and to interpret, in some sense the right to examine, which, however one looks at it, implies a diminution of faith....

Now, it is clear that there is nothing in Scholasticism that could have satisfied these new tastes: on the contrary, it was bound to be hostile to them. Since it attached no importance to form, it did not hesitate to twist language savagely in order to satisfy all the needs of thought, without regard to considerations of purity or harmony. As a result of the very great place it accorded to debate, it developed a taste not for ideas that were delicate, subtle, measured, but rather for opinions that were dogmatic and clear-cut and whose features stood out in such a way that conflicting opinions could be clearly contrasted. Moreover, the violent arguments that were born of these contrasts could only encourage a coarseness in manners comparable to what had been upheld for so long by the noble knights in their tourneys and similar practices. The student of the Middle Ages was primarily concerned with crushing his opponent beneath the weight of his arguments and did not care in the least whether his presentation was attractive. His unkempt appearance and his rustic deportment and manners were expressions of this same state of mind.

Here we have the explanation of why the men of the new generation were quite literally horrified by Scholasticism and its methods. The extreme virulence of their polemics seems at first sight to be out of place in a purely educational quarrel. But the fact is that the issue was really more wide-ranging. The sixteenth century did not accuse Scholasticism simply of having engaged in certain debatable or regrettable academic practices but rather of having constituted a school of barbarousness and coarseness. Hence the frequency with which the words *barbarus, stoliditas, rusticitas* recur in the writings of Erasmus. To these refined minds a Scholastic is quite literally a barbarian (remember the title of Erasmus's book *Antibarbaros),* who speaks a language scarcely human, crude-sounding, formally inelegant; who delights only in arguments, in deafening yells, in verbal and other battles; who is ignorant, in sum, of all the benefits of civilization, of everything that contributes to the charm of life. We can readily conceive of the feeling such an educational system would be capable of arousing in men whose aim was to render humanity more tender, more elegant, more cultivated.

The only way to succeed in ridding the human intellect of its coarseness, to polish and refine it, was to introduce it to and make it intimate with an elegant and refined civilization, so that it might become imbued with its spirit. Now, the only civilization that could satisfy this condition at that time was that of the classical peoples as it had been expressed and preserved in the works of their great writers, poets, and orators. It was thus quite natural that these should be seen as providing the schoolteachers needed by the young. "What then," says Erasmus, "what then could have guided these coarse men of the Stone Age towards a more human life, towards being more gentle of character and more civilized in morals? Was it not literature? It is literature that molds the mind, that mollifies passions, that checks the untamed outbursts of natural temperament." For this purpose there existed no other established and developed literatures apart from those of Rome and Greece.

With this in view, the moral milieu in which the child was to be molded had to be made up of all the extant elements of these literatures. Hence the enormous attention accorded by the public at this time to the masterpieces of Greco-Roman civilization. If people esteemed and admired them, if they sought to imitate them, this is not because they were exhumed at this moment in history and, by being discovered, suddenly inculcated in people a taste for literature. Quite the reverse: it was because a taste for literature, a taste for a new kind of civilization, had just been acquired that they suddenly became objects of enthusiastic veneration; for they appeared, and quite rightly so, as the only means available of satisfying this new need. If this vast body of literature had hitherto been neglected, this was not because nothing was known of it (we have already seen that the major works were known); rather, its virtues were not appreciated because they did not meet any contemporary need. If, by contrast, they were then regarded in the eyes of public opinion, or at least of a certain section of it, as being of incomparable value, this was because a new attitude of mind was in the process of developing and could only be fully realized in the school of the classics. And one may even wonder whether the greater frequency of the finds and exhumations that occurred at this period was not a result of the fact that since, henceforth, the value of these discoveries was fully appreciated people devoted more of their ingenuity to making them. To find, one must seek, and one only seeks in earnest when one attaches importance to what one hopes to find.

Thus the educational ideas of the humanists were not the result of simple accidents. They derived, rather, from a fact whose influence on the moral history of our country it is difficult to exaggerate; I refer to the establishment of polite society. If France did indeed become from the sixteenth century onwards a center of literary life and intellectual activity, this was because, at this same period, there had developed among us a select society, a society of intellectually cultivated people to whom our writers addressed themselves. It was the ideas and the tastes of this society that they communicated; it was for this society that they wrote and for it that they thought. It was here in this particular environment that the driving force of our civilization from the sixteenth century to the middle of the eighteenth century arose. And the object of education as Erasmus conceived of it was to prepare man for this special and restricted society.

Here too we can see the essential character and at the same time the radical flaw of this educational theory. It is the fact that it is essentially aristocratic in nature. The kind of society that it seeks to fashion is always centered around a court, and its members are always drawn from the ranks of the aristocracy or at least from the leisured classes. And it was indeed here and here alone that that fine flowering of elegance and culture could take place, the nurturing and development of which were regarded as more important than anything else. Neither Erasmus nor Vivès had any awareness that beyond this small world, which for all its brilliance was very limited, there were vast masses who should not have been neglected and for whom education could have brought about higher intellectual and moral standards and an improved material condition.

When such a thought did occur to them it disappeared again very quickly without their thinking it necessary to examine it at length. Since he realizes that this expensive education is not suitable for everyone, Erasmus wonders what the poor will do; his answer to this objection is utterly simple. "You ask," he says, "what the poor will be able to do. How will those who can scarcely feed their children be able to give them over a sustained period of time the right kind of education? To this I can only reply by quoting the words of the comic writer: 'You can't ask that what we are capable of achieving should be as great as what we would like to achieve.' We are expounding the best way of bringing up a child, we cannot produce the means of realizing this ideal." He restricts himself to expressing the wish that the rich will come to the help of those who are well-endowed intellectually but who would be prevented by poverty from developing their aptitudes. But he seems not to realize that even if this education were made available to everybody the difficulty would not be resolved, for this generalized education would not meet the needs of the majority. Indeed, for the majority the supreme need is survival, and what is needed in order to survive is not the art of subtle speech, it is the art of sound thinking, so that one knows how to act. In order to struggle effectively in the world of persons and the world of things more substantial weapons are needed than those glittering decorations with which the humanist educationalists were concerned to adorn the mind to the exclusion of anything else.

Think now how much Scholasticism, for all its abstractness, was imbued with a more practical, more realistic, and more social spirit. The fact is that dialectic answered real needs. Intellectual conflict, competition between ideas, constitutes a genuinely important part of life. Moreover, the strength and virility of thought which were acquired as a result of such arduous mental gymnastics could be used in the service of socially useful ends. Thus we must beware of thinking that the medieval schools served only to produce dreamers, seekers after quintessences, and useless pettifogging quibblers. The truth is quite the opposite. It was there that the statesmen, the ecclesiastical dignitaries, and the administrators of the day were brought up. This training, which has been so denigrated, created men of action. It was the education recommended by Erasmus that forms a totally inadequate preparation for life. In it, rhetoric supplants dialectic. Now, if rhetoric had good reason for featuring in the education of the classical world, where the practice of eloquence constituted not only a career but the most important career, this was by no means the case in the sixteenth century, when it played only a very small part in the serious business of life. A theory of education that made rhetoric the principal academic discipline could thus only develop qualities related to the luxuries of existence and not at all to its necessities.…

In order to know what became of the educational theories of the Renaissance when they were translated into practice, it would thus seem that we have only to investigate how the University understood them and applied them. But what makes such a procedure impossible, what makes the whole question more complicated, is the great change that took place at this very moment in our academic organization. Up till that time the University had a complete monopoly on and sole responsibility for education, and consequently the future of any educational reforms was dependent upon the University and upon the University alone. However, towards the middle of the sixteenth century, over and against the University corporation there was established a new teaching corporation, which was to break the University's monopoly and which was even to achieve with quite remarkable rapidity a kind of hegemony in academic life. This was the corporation of the Jesuits.

The Jesuit order arose from the need felt by the Catholic Church to check the increasingly threatening progress of Protestantism. With extraordinary speed the doctrines of Luther and Calvin had won over England, almost the whole of Germany, Switzerland, the Low Countries, Sweden, and a considerable part of France. In spite of all the rigorous measures taken, the Church felt itself impotent and began to fear that its dominion in the world would collapse completely. It was then that Ignatius Loyola had the idea of raising a wholly new kind of religious militia the better to combat and, if possible to crush, heresy. He realized that the days were over when people's souls could be governed from the depths of a cloister. Now that people, carried by their own momentum, were tending to elude the Church, it was essential that the Church move closer to them so as to be able to influence them. Now that particular personalities were beginning to stand out from the homogeneous moral and intellectual mass that had been the rule in preceding centuries, it was essential for the Church to be close to individuals, to accommodate its influence over them to intellectual and temperamental diversities. In short, the vast monastic masses familiar to the Middle Ages, which, stationary at their post, had restricted themselves to repulsing such attacks as occurred, without, however, knowing how to take the offensive themselves, had to be replaced. An army of light troops would be established that would be in constant contact with the enemy and consequently well-informed about all his movements, but at the same time sufficiently alert and mobile to be able to go at the slightest signal wherever there was danger, and yet sufficiently flexible to be able to vary its tactics in accordance with the diversity of people and circumstances; its troops would do all this while always and everywhere pursuing the same goal and cooperating in the same grand design. This army was the Company of Jesus.

What was distinctive about it was that it was able to contain within itself two characteristics, which the Middle Ages had adjudged irreconcilable and contradictory. On the one hand, the Jesuits belong to a religious order in the same way as the Dominicans or the Franciscans; they have a head, they are all subject to one and the same rule, to a communal discipline; indeed passive obedience and unity of thought and action have never been carried to such an extreme degree in any militia whether secular or religious. The Jesuit is thus a regular priest. But, on the other hand, he simultaneously possesses all the characteristics of the secular priest; he wears his habit; he fulfills his functions, he preaches, he hears confessions, he catechizes; he does not live in the shadow of a monastery, he rather mingles in the life of the world. For him duty consists not in the mortification of the flesh, in fasting, in abstinence, but in action, in the realization of the goal of the Society. "Let us leave the religious orders," Ignatius Loyola used to say, "to outdo us in fasts, in watches, in the austerity of the regime and habit that, out of piety, they impose upon themselves." "I believe that it is more valuable, for the glory of Our Lord, to preserve and to fortify the stomach and other natural faculties rather than enfeebling them . . . you should not assault your own physical nature, because if you exhaust it your intellectual nature will no longer be able to act with the same energy."

Not only must the Jesuit mingle with the world, he must also open himself up to the ideas that are dominant within it. The better to guide his age he must speak its language, he must assimilate its sports. Ignatius Loyola sensed that a profound change had taken place in manners and that there was no going back on this: that a taste for well-being, for a less harsh, easier sunnier existence had been acquired that could not conceivably be stifled or fobbed off; that man had developed a greater degree of pity for his own sufferings and for those of his fellowmen, that there was more sparing of pain, and consequently that the old ideal of absolute renunciation was finished. To prevent the faithful from drifting away from religion, the Jesuits devoted their ingenuity to divesting religion of its former austerity: they made it pleasant and devised all kinds of accommodating arrangements to make it easy to observe. It is true that in order to remain faithful to the mission they had assigned themselves, to avoid seeming to encourage the innovators against whom they were struggling by their own example, they had at the same time to stick to the letter of immutable dogma. It is well known how they extricated themselves from this difficulty and were able to reconcile these conflicting demands thanks to their casuistry, whose excessive flexibility and over ingenious refinements have frequently been pointed out. While maintaining in their sacred form the traditional prescriptions of Roman Catholicism, they were still able to place these within the scope not only of human weakness in general—there is no religion that has ever managed to escape this necessity—but of the elegant frivolousness of the leisured classes of the sixteenth century in particular; it was these leisured classes that it was so important to keep free from heresy and to preserve in the faith. And this is how, while they became essentially men of the past, defenders of the Catholic tradition, the Jesuits were able to exhibit towards the idea, the tastes, and even the defects of the time an attitude of indulgence for which they have often, and not without reason, been reproached. They thus had a dual identity as conservatives, even as reactionaries, on the one hand, and as liberals on the other: a complex policy the nature of which we needed to show here, for we shall encounter it again in the foundations of their educational theory.

But they very quickly came to realize that in order to achieve their end it was not enough to preach, to hear confession, to catechize: the really important instrument in the struggle for mastery of the human soul was the education of the young. Thus they resolved to seize hold of it. One fact in particular made them acutely aware of the urgent need for this; one would have had to be blind to all the evidence not to see that the new methods taking root in the schools could only have the effect of opening up the road to heresy. Indeed, the greatest minds of the time, the most illustrious of the humanists, had openly been converted to the new religion; this was the case with Dolet, with Ramus, with Mathurin Cordier, with the majority of teachers in the College de France, recently founded by Francois I. Thus humanism by its very nature constituted a threat to the fait. And indeed it is clear that an inordinate taste for paganism was bound to cause people's minds to dwell in a moral environment with absolutely nothing Christian about it. Accordingly, if the evil was to be attacked at it sources it would be necessary instead of abandoning the humanist movement to its own devices, to gain control of it and to direct it.

The aim of the Jesuits thus had nothing to do with getting the pupil acquainted with and able to understand classical civilizations; it was exclusively concerned with teaching them to speak and write in Greek and Latin. This explains the importance attributed to written assignments and the nature of these assignments. This is why in the grammar classes prose composition prevailed and was far more important than translation from Latin, which was scarcely practiced at all. This is why stylistic exercises were so numerous and so varied. This attitude even influenced the way the expositions were carried out. Father Jouvency has left us model expositions of Latin authors; one has only to read them to see that their main aim is to get the pupils to appreciate the author's Latin and his literary style, and to encourage them to imitate these same qualities.

Far from seeking to get their pupils to think again the thoughts of antiquity, far from wishing to steep them in the spirit of classical times, the Jesuits had precisely the opposite aim. Indeed, this was because they could see no other way of extricating themselves from the contradictory situation in which they had quite deliberately placed themselves. Because the fashion was for humanism, because classical letters were the object of a veritable cult, the Jesuits, always sensitive to the spirit of their age, professed, as we have just seen, a form of humanism–even quite an uncompromising one, since Greek and Latin alone were permitted entry into their colleges. But from another point of view, as we have said, they realized full well that humanism constituted a threat, that there was a real danger in wishing to fashion Christian souls in the school of paganism. How could these two contradictory needs be reconciled? How could the faith be defended and safeguarded as was required by the self-imposed mission of the Jesuits, while they simultaneously made themselves the apologists and exegetes of pagan literature?

There was only one way of resolving this antinomy: this was, in the very words used by Father Jouvency, to expound the classical authors in such a way "that they became, although pagan and profane, the eulogists of the faith." To make paganism serve the glorification and the propagation of the Christian ethic was a daring undertaking and, it would appear, remarkably difficult; and yet, the Jesuits had enough confidence in their ability to attempt it and to succeed in it. But in order to do this they had deliberately to denature the ancient world; they had to show the authors of antiquity, the men they were and the men they portray for us, in such a way as to leave in the shadows everything that was genuinely pagan about them, everything that makes them men of a particular city at a particular time, in order to highlight only those respects in which they are simply men, men as they are at all times and in all places. All the legends, all the traditions, all the religious ideas of Rome and Greece were interpreted in this spirit so as to give them a meaning any good Christian could accept.

Thus the Greco-Roman environment in which they made their pupils live was emptied of everything specifically Greek or Roman, so that it became a kind of unreal, idealized environment peopled by personalities who had no doubt historically existed but who were presented in such a way that they had, so to speak, nothing historical about them. They were now simply figures betokening certain virtues and vices and all the great passions of humanity. Achilles is courage; Ulysses is wily prudence; Numa is the archetype of the pious king; Caesar, the man of ambition; Augustus, the powerful monarch and lover of learning; etc. Such general and unspecific types could easily be used to exemplify the precepts of Christian morality.

Such disinheriting of antiquity was made easier for the Jesuits by the fact that, at least for a long time, all teaching of history was almost completely absent from their colleges. Even literary history was unknown. A writer's works were expounded without anyone's bothering to notice the physiognomy of the author, his manner, the way he related it to his age, to his environment, to his predecessors. His historical personality mattered so little that it was normal to study not an author, not even a work, but selected passages and extracts. How was it possible to form a picture of a specific man out of such sparse and disjointed fragments, among which his individuality was dispersed and dissolved? Each of these pieces could scarcely appear to be anything other than an isolated model of literary style, a sort of fair copy of exceptional authoritativeness.

We can now understand better how it came about that the Jesuits, and perhaps to a lesser extent so many other educators, tended to attribute to the past and especially to the distant past an educational value greater than that which they attributed to the present. This was because the past, at least at a time when the historical sciences have not advanced sufficiently to render it almost as precise and specific as the present—the past, because we see it from afar, naturally appears to us in vague, fluid, unstable forms, which are consequently all the easier to mold according to our will. It constitutes a more malleable and plastic substance that we can transform and present according to our fancy. It is thus easier to bend it for educational purposes. These people, these things from former times, we embellish without realizing we are deceiving ourselves in order to turn them into models for youth to imitate. The present, because it is before our very eyes, forces itself upon our attention and does not lend itself to this kind of reworking; it is virtually impossible for us to see it other than as it is with its ugliness, its mediocrity, its vices, and its failings; and this is why it seems to us ill-adapted to serve our educational ends. It was in this way that antiquity in the hands of the Jesuits could become an instrument for Christian education, whereas they would not have been able to utilize literature of their own age in the same way, imbued as it was with the spirit of rebellion against the church. In their desire to attain their goal, they had a powerful vested interest in fleeing from the moderns and taking refuge in antiquity....

But so far we have only studied the Jesuits' teaching. We must now consider their disciplinary structures. It is perhaps in this area that they showed the most art and originality and it is their superiority in this respect that best explains their success.

Their entire discipline was founded upon two principles.

The first was that there can be no good education without contact at once continuous and personal between the pupil and the educator—and this principle served a dual purpose. First, it ensured that the pupil was never left to his own devices. To be properly molded he had to be subjected to pressure that never let up or flagged; for the spirit of evil is constantly watchful. This is why the Jesuits' pupil was never alone. "A supervisor would follow him everywhere, to church, to class, to the refectory, to his recreation; in the living quarters and sleeping quarters he was always there examining everything." But this supervision was not intended only to prevent misconduct. It was also to enable the Jesuit to study at his ease "character and habits so that he might manage to discover the most suitable method of directing each individual child." In other words, this direct and constant intercourse was supposed not only to render the educational process more sustained in its effect but also to make it more personal and better suited to the personality of each pupil. Father Jouvency never stops recommending that a teacher not limit himself to exerting a general and impersonal influence on the anonymous crowd of pupils but rather graduate his influence and vary it according to age, intelligence, and situation. If he is conversing with a child in private, "let him examine the child's character so that he can mold what he says in accordance with it and, as they say, 'hook' his interlocutor with the appropriate bait." And the better to get the pupils to open their minds to him, he will need to make them open their hearts by endearing himself. Indeed there can be no doubt that in the course of the relationships thus cemented between teachers and pupils, bonds of friendship were frequently formed that survived school life. Thus Descartes remained very sincerely attached to his former teachers at La Flèche.

One can readily imagine how effective this system of continuous immersion must have been. The child's moral environment followed him wherever he went; all around him he heard the same ideas and the same sentiments being expressed with the same authority. He could never lose sight of them. He knew of no others. And in addition to the fact that this influence never ceased to make itself felt, it was also all the more powerful because it knew how best to adapt to the diversity of individual personalities, because it was most familiar with the openings through which it could slip and insinuate itself in the pupil's heart. By comparison with the style of discipline that had been practiced in the Middle Ages this represented a major revolution. The medieval teacher addressed himself to large and impersonal audiences, among which each individual, that is to say each student, was lost, drowned, and consequently abandoned to his own devices. Now, education is essentially an individual matter, and as long as the medieval teacher was dealing with vast masses he could obtain only very crude results. Hence the rowdy indiscipline of the students of the Middle Ages, which the establishment of the fully residential colleges was an attempt—never fully successful—to counter. For the colleges did not have at their disposal a staff of teachers and supervisors sufficiently numerous or perhaps sufficiently committed to the task of supervision to be able to exercise the necessary control and influence over each individual.

But in order to train pupils in intensive formal work, which was moreover pretty lacking in substance, it was not enough to surround them, to envelop them at close quarters with solicitude and vigilance; it was not enough to be constantly concerned to contain and sustain them; it was also necessary to stimulate them. The goad which the Jesuits employed consisted exclusively of competition. Not only were they the first to organize the competitive system in the colleges, they also developed it to a greater intensity than it has ever subsequently known.

Although today in our classrooms this system still has considerable importance, nevertheless it no longer functions without interruption. It is fair to say that with the Jesuits it was never suspended for a single moment. The entire class was organized to promote this end. The pupils were divided into two camps, the Romans on the one hand and the Carthaginians on the other, who lived, so to speak, on the brink of war, each striving to outstrip the other. Each camp had its own dignitaries. At the head of the camp there was an imperator, also known as dictator or consul, then came a praetor, a tribune, and some senators. These honors, which were naturally coveted and contested, were distributed as the outcome of a competition, which was held monthly. From another point of view, each camp was divided into groups consisting of ten pupils each ("decuries"), commanded by a captain (called the "decurion") who was selected from among the worthies we have just mentioned. These groups were not recruited at random. There was a hierarchy among them: the first groups were composed of the best pupils, the last groups of the weakest and least industrious of the scholars. Thus just as the camp as a whole was in competition with the opposite camp, so in each camp each group had its own immediate rival in the other camp at the equivalent level. Finally, individuals themselves were matched and each soldier in a group had his opposite number in the opposing group. Thus academic work involved a kind of perpetual hand-to-hand combat. Camp challenged camp; group struggled with group; pupils supervised one another, corrected one another, and took one another to task. On some occasions the teacher was not supposed to be afraid of pitting together two pupils of unequal ability. For example, an able pupil would have his work corrected by a less able pupil, says Father Jouvency, "so that those who have made mistakes may be the more ashamed and the more mortified by them." It was even possible for any pupil to do battle with a pupil from a higher group and, if victorious, to take his place.

It is interesting to note that these various ennoblements carried with them not only honorific titles but also active functions; and indeed it was these that constituted the prize. The captain enjoyed extensive powers. Seated opposite his group he was responsible for maintaining silence and attentiveness among his ten scholars, noting down absences, making the scholars recite their lessons, ensuring that assignments had been done with care and completed. The consuls exercised the same authority over the captains in their camp that these did over their own group members. Everyone was thus kept constantly in suspense. Never has the idea that the classroom is a small organized society been realized so systematically. It was a city-state where every pupil was a functionary. Moreover, it was thanks to this division of labor between the teacher and the pupils that one teacher was able without too much difficulty to run classes that sometimes numbered as many as two or three hundred pupils.

In addition to such regularly recurring competitions there were intermittent competitions too numerous to list. From time to time the best pieces of work were affixed to the classroom doors; the most noteworthy were read publicly in either the refectory or the Hall of Acts. Aside from the annual prize-giving, which took place solemnly to the sound of trumpets, prizes were given out spasmodically in the course of the year for a good piece of declamation, for a meritorious literary work, for a well executed dance, etc. From the second form onwards there was in each grade an Academy to which only the best pupils belonged. Then there were all kinds of public meetings in which the most brilliant pupils appeared and to which the families came to hear and applaud them. Thus an infinite wealth of devices maintained the self-esteem of the pupils in a constant state of extreme excitation.

Here again the Jesuits were effecting a revolution compared with what had gone before. We have seen that in the University and the colleges of the Middle Ages the system of competition was completely unknown; there were no rewards to recompense merit and induce effort, and exams were organized in such a way that for conscientious pupils they were little more than a formality. And here we have, quite suddenly, a totally different system, which not only establishes itself but which instantaneously develops to the point of superabundance. It is easier to understand now how the training given by the Jesuits managed to acquire the intensive character which we were recently remarking upon. Their entire system of discipline was organized towards this goal. The state of constant competition in which the pupils lived incited them to strain all the resources of their intelligence and will-power and indeed rendered this essential. At the same time the careful supervision to which they were subjected diminished the possibility of lapses. They felt themselves guided, sustained, encouraged. Thus everything induced them to exert themselves. As a result, within the colleges there was genuinely intense activity, no doubt flawed by being expended on the superficial rather than on the profound, but whose existence was incontestable.

However, now that we have noted the transformations that the Jesuits initiated in the realm of school discipline, we must seek their causes. Where did these two new principles come from? Did they derive exclusively from the particular aim the Jesuits were pursuing, from the very nature of their institution, from the mission they had assigned themselves, or were they not, by contrast, rather the effect of more general causes, were they not a response to some change that had occurred in public thought and ethics?

What must immediately rule out the first hypothesis is the fact that if the Jesuits were the first to realize these principles in academic practice, they had nevertheless been recognized and proclaimed already by the educational thinkers of the Renaissance. We remember Montaigne's protests against teachers unintelligent enough to wish to regiment the minds of all individuals in identical fashion. He too wants teachers to study the temperament of the pupil, to test him in order to understand him better, to make him, as he says, "run in front of himself" in order to be able to guide him in an enlightened way. And from another point of view, we have seen that the love of glory, the thirst for praise, and the sentiment of honor were for Rabelais and for Erasmus, as for the major thinkers of the sixteenth century, the essential motives for all intellectual activity and consequently for all academic activity. The Jesuits were thus on these two points, at least in principle, in agreement with their time. It is interesting to note that we know of at least one college where, before the time of the Jesuits, the competitive system was organized and practiced, moreover, in a form that in more than one respect resembled the one we have just described. This is the college at Guyenne, where Montaigne spent several years. The pupils in any one class were divided according to ability into sections that bore considerable resemblance to the Jesuits' groups of ten. Examinations took place frequently in which the pupils of one class were questioned by the pupils from a higher class or section. And here again we encounter competitions in public speaking, which took place before the assembly of all the classes.

It was the fact that a great change had taken place in the moral constitution of society that made this double change in the system of academic discipline necessary. In the seventeenth century the individual played a much greater part in social life than that which had hitherto been accorded to him. If, in the Middle Ages, teaching was impersonal, if it could be addressed diffusely to the indistinct crowd of pupils without any disadvantage, this was because at that time the notion of individual personality was still relatively undeveloped. The movements that occurred in the Middle Ages were mass movements carrying along large groups of human beings in the same direction, in the midst of which individuals became lost. It was Europe in its entirety that rose up at the time of the Crusades; it was the whole of cultivated European society that soon afterwards, under the influence of a veritable collective urge, flooded towards Paris to receive instruction. The didactic style of the time was thus in accord with the moral condition of society.

With the Renaissance, by contrast, the individual began to acquire self-consciousness; he was no longer, at least in enlightened circles, merely an undifferentiated fraction of the whole; in a sense, he was himself already a whole, he was a person with his own physiognomy who had and who experienced at least the need to fashion for himself his own way of thinking and feeling. We know that at this period there occurred, as it were, a sudden blossoming of great personalities. Now, it is quite clear that in proportion as people's consciousness becomes individualized, education itself must become individualized. From the moment it is required to exert its influence on distinct and heterogeneous individuals it cannot continue to develop in blanket fashion, homogeneously and uniformly. Thus education had to be diversified, and this was only possible if the educator, instead of remaining distant from the pupil, came close to him to get to know him better and to be able to vary his actions according to his individual nature.

But from another point of view, it is equally clear that an individual possessed of self-awareness, with his own set of beliefs and interests, cannot be motivated or trained to act by the methods applicable to an amorphous crowd. For the latter methods mighty shakings of the foundations are needed, powerful collective impressions of a rather vague and general kind, like those that sent tremors through the multitudes gathered around Abélard on the Montagne Sainte-Geneviève. By contrast, in proportion as each individual has his own particular moral life he must be moved by considerations specifically appropriate to him. Thus one must indeed appeal to self-esteem, to the sense of personal dignity, to what the Germans call *Selbstgefühl*. It is no accident that competition becomes more lively and plays a more substantial role in society as the movement towards individualization becomes more advanced. And so, since the moral organization of the school must reflect that of civil society, since the methods that are applied to the child cannot differ in essence from those that later on will be applied to the man, it is clear that the processes of the medieval disciplinary system could not survive; it is clear that discipline had to become more personal, to take greater account of individual feelings, and consequently to allow for a degree of competitiveness.

There was thus nothing intrinsically arbitrary about the two innovations the Jesuits introduced into the disciplinary system: the principle underlying them, at least, was well-grounded in the nature of things, that is to say in the condition of society in the sixteenth century. But if the principle was right, if it was to be retained, if it deserved to survive, the Jesuits applied it in the spirit of extremism that is one feature of their academic policy and, simply by doing this, they denatured it. It was good to keep close to the child in order to be able to guide him confidently; the Jesuits came so close to him that they inhibited all his freedom of movement. And in this way the method worked against the end it was meant to serve. It was wise to get to know the child well in order to be able to help in the development of his nascent personality. The Jesuits, however, studied him in order to stifle more effectively his sense of self—and this was a potential source of schism. At least, once they had recognized the value of rivalry and competitiveness, they made such immoderate use of them that the pupils were virtually at war with one another. How can we fail to consider immoral an academic organization that appealed only to egotistical sentiments? Was there then no means of keeping the pupils active other than by tempting them with such paltry bait?

3

Functional and Conflict Theories of Educational Stratification

RANDALL COLLINS

Education has become highly important in occupational attainment in modern America, and thus occupies a central place in the analysis of stratification and of social mobility. This paper attempts to assess the adequacy of two theories in accounting for available evidence on the link between education and stratification: a functional theory concerning trends in technical skill requirements in industrial societies; and a conflict theory derived from the approach of Max Weber, stating the determinants of various outcomes in the struggles among status groups. It will be argued that the evidence best supports the conflict theory, although technical requirements have important effects in particular contexts. It will be further argued that the construction of a general theory of the determinants of stratification in its varying forms is best advanced by incorporating elements of the functional analysis of technical requirements of specific jobs at appropriate points within the conflict model. The conclusion offers an interpretation of historical change in education and stratification in industrial America, and suggests where further evidence is required for more precise tests and for further development of a comprehensive explanatory theory.

The Importance of Education

A number of studies have shown that the number of years of education is a strong determinant of occupational achievement in America with social origins constant. They also show that social origins affect educational attainment, and also occupational attainment after the completion of education (Blau and Duncan, 1967:163–205; Eckland, 1965; Sewell et al., 1969; Duncan and Hodge, 1963; Lipset and Bendix, 1959:189–192). There are differences in occupational attainment independent of social origins between the graduates of more prominent and less prominent secondary schools, colleges, graduate schools, and law schools (Smigel, 1964:39, 73–74, 117; Havemann and West, 1952:179–181; Ladinsky, 1967; Hargens and Hagstrom, 1967).

Educational requirements for employment have become increasingly widespread, not only in elite occupations but also at the bottom of the occupational hierarchy (see Table 3.1). In a 1967 survey of the San Francisco, Oakland, and San Jose areas (Collins, 1969), 17% of the employers surveyed required at least a high school diploma for employment in even unskilled positions;[1] a national survey (Bell, 1940) in 1937–1938 found a comparable figure of 1%. At the same time, educational requirements appear to have become more specialized, with 38% of the organizations in the 1967 survey which required college degrees of managers preferring business administration training, and an additional 15% preferring engineering training; such requirements appear to have been virtually unknown in the 1920s (Pierson, 1959:34–54). At the same time, the proportions of the American population attending

Table 3.1 Percent of Employers Requiring Various Minimum Levels of Employees, by Occupational Level

	Unskilled	Semiskilled	Skilled	Clerical	Managerial	Professional
National Survey, 1937–38						
Less than high school	99%	97%	89%	33%	32%	9%
High school diploma	1	3	11	63	54	16
Some college				1	2	23
College degree				3	12	52
	100%	100%	100%	100%	100%	100%
San Francisco Bay Area, 1967						
Less than high school	83%	76%	62%	29%	27%	10%
High School diploma	16	24	28	68	14	4
Vocational training beyond high school	1	1	10	2	2	4
Some college				2	12	7
College degree					41	70
Graduate degree					3	5
	100%	100%	100%	101%	99%	100%
	(244)	(237)	(245)	(306)	(288)	(240)

schools through the completion of high school and advanced levels have risen sharply during the last century (Table 3.2). Careers are thus increasingly shaped within the educational system.

The Technical-Function Theory of Education

A common explanation of the importance of education in modern society may be termed the technical-function theory. Its basic propositions, found in a number of sources (see, for example, B. Clark, 1962;

Table 3.2 Percentage Educational Attainment in the United States, 1869–1965

Period	High School graduates/ pop. 17 yrs. old	Resident college students/ pop. 18–21	B.A.s or 1st prof. degrees/ 1/10 of pop. 15–24	M.A.s or 2nd prof. degrees/ 1/10 of pop. 25–34	Ph.D.s 1/10 of pop. 25–34
1869–1870	2.0	1.7			
1879–1880	2.5	2.7			
1889–1890	3.5	3.0			
1899–1900	6.4	4.0	1.66	0.12	0.03
1909–1910	8.8	5.1	1.85	0.13	0.02
1919–1920	16.8	8.9	2.33	0.24	0.03
1929–1930	29.0	12.4	4.90	0.78	0.12
1939–1940	50.8	15.6	7.05	1.24	0.15
1949–1950	59.0	29.6	17.66	2.43	0.27
1959–1960	65.1	34.9	17.72	3.25	0.42
1963	76.3	38.0			
1965			19.71	5.02	0.73

Kerr et al., 1960), may be stated as follows: (1) the skill requirements of jobs in industrial society constantly increase because of technological change. Two processes are involved: (a) the proportion of jobs requiring low skill decreases and the proportion requiring high skill increases; and (b) the same jobs are upgraded in skill requirements. (2) Formal education provides the training, either in specific skills or in general capacities, necessary for the more highly skilled jobs. (3) Therefore, educational requirements for employment constantly rise, and increasingly larger proportions of the population are required to spend longer and longer periods in school.

The technical-function theory of education may be seen as a particular application of a more general functional approach. The functional theory of stratification (Davis and Moore, 1945) rests on the premises (A) that occupational positions require particular kinds of skilled performance; and (B) that positions must be filled with persons who have either the native ability, or who have acquired the training, necessary for the performance of the given occupational role.[2]

The technical-function theory of education may be viewed as a subtype of this form of analysis, since it shares the premises that the occupational structure creates demands for particular kinds of performance, and that training is one way of filling these demands. In addition, it includes the more restrictive premises (1 and 2 above) concerning the way in which skill requirements of jobs change with industrialization, and concerning the content of school experiences.

The technical-function theory of education may be tested by reviewing the evidence for each of its propositions (1a, 1b, and 2).[3] As will be seen, these propositions do not adequately account for the evidence. In order to generate a more complete explanation, it will be necessary to examine the evidence for the underlying functional propositions, (A) and (B). This analysis leads to a focus on the processes of stratification—notably group conflict—not expressed in the functional theory, and to the formalization of a conflict theory to account for the evidence.

Proposition (1a): *Educational requirements of jobs in industrial society increase because the proportion of jobs requiring low skill decreases and the proportion requiring high skill increases.* Available evidence suggests that this process accounts for only a minor part of educational upgrading, at least in a society that has passed the point of initial industrialization. Fifteen percent of the increase in education of the U. S. labor force during the twentieth century may be attributed to shifts in the occupational structure—a decrease in the proportion of jobs with low skill requirements and an increase in proportion of jobs with high skill requirements (Folger and Nam, 1964). The bulk of educational upgrading (85%) has occurred *within* job categories.

Proposition (1b): *Educational requirements of jobs in industrial society rise because the same jobs are upgraded in skill requirements.* The only available evidence on this point consists of data collected by the U. S. Department of Labor in 1950 and 1960, which indicate the amount of change in skill requirements of specific jobs. Under the most plausible assumptions as to the skills provided by various levels of education, it appears that the educational level of the U. S. labor force has changed in excess of that which is necessary to keep up with skill requirements of jobs (Berg, 1970:38–60). Over-education for available jobs is found particularly among males who have graduated from college and females with high school degrees or some college, and appears to have increased between 1950 and 1960.

Proposition (2): *Formal education provides required job skills.* This proposition may be tested in two ways: (a) Are better educated employees more productive than less educated employees? (b) Are vocational skills learned in schools, or elsewhere?

(a) *Are better educated employees more productive?* The evidence most often cited for the productive effects of education is indirect, consisting of relationships between *aggregate* levels of education in a society and its overall economic productivity. These are of three types:

(i) The national growth approach involves calculating the proportion of growth in the U. S. Gross National Product attributable to conventional inputs of capital and labor; these leave a large residual, which is attributed to improvements in skill of the labor force based on increased education (Schultz,

1961; Denison, 1965). This approach suffers from difficulty in clearly distinguishing among technological change affecting productive arrangements, changes in the abilities of workers acquired by experience at work with new technologies, and changes in skills due to formal education and motivational factors associated with a competitive or achievement-oriented society. The assignment of a large proportion of the residual category to education is arbitrary. Denison (1965) makes this attribution on the basis of the increased income to persons with higher levels of education interpreted as rewards for their contributions to productivity. Although it is a common assumption in economic argument that wage returns reflect output value, wage returns cannot be used to prove the productive contribution of education without circular reasoning.

(ii) Correlations of education and level of economic development for nations show that the higher the level of economic development of a country, the higher the proportion of its population in elementary, secondary, and higher education (Harbison and Myers, 1964). Such correlations beg the question of causality. There are considerable variations in school enrollments among countries at the same economic level, and many of these variations are explicable in terms of political demands for access to education (Ben-David, 1963–64). Also, the overproduction of educated personnel in countries whose level of economic development cannot absorb them suggests the demand for education need not come directly from the economy, and may run counter to economic needs (Hoselitz, 1965).

(iii) Time-lag correlations of education and economic development show that increases in the proportion of population in elementary school precede increases in economic development after a takeoff point at approximately 30–50% of the 7–14 years old age-group in school. Similar anticipations of economic development are suggested for increases in secondary and higher education enrollment, although the data do not clearly support this conclusion (Peaslee, 1969). A pattern of advances in secondary school enrollments preceding advances in economic development is found only in a small number of cases (12 of 37 examined in Peaslee, 1969). A pattern of growth of university enrollments and subsequent economic development is found in 21 of 37 cases, but the exceptions (including the United States, France, Sweden, Russia, and Japan) are of such importance as to throw serious doubt on any *necessary* contribution of higher education to economic development. The main contribution of education to economic productivity, then, appears to occur at the level of the transition to mass literacy, and not significantly beyond this level.

Direct evidence of the contribution of education to *individual* productivity is summarized by Berg (1970:85–104, 143–176). It indicates that the better educated employees are not generally more productive, and in some cases are less productive, among samples of factory workers, maintenance men, department store clerks, technicians, secretaries, bank tellers, engineers, industrial research scientists, military personnel, and federal civil service employers.

(b) *Are vocational skills learned in school, or elsewhere?* Specifically vocational education in the schools for manual positions is virtually independent of job fate, as graduates of vocational programs are not more likely to be employed than high school dropouts (Plunkett, 1960; Duncan, 1964). Most skilled manual workers acquire their skills on the job or casually (Clark and Sloan, 1966:73). Retraining for important technological changes in industry has been carried out largely informally on-the-job; in only a very small proportion of jobs affected by technological change is formal retraining in educational institutions used (Collins, 1969: 147–158; Bright, 1958).

The relevance of education for nonmanual occupational skills is more difficult to evaluate. Training in specific professions, such as medicine, engineering, scientific or scholarly research, teaching, and law can plausibly be considered vocationally relevant, and possibly essential. Evidences comparing particular degrees of educational success with particular kinds of occupational performance or success are not available, except for a few occupations. For engineers, high college grades and degree levels generally predict high levels of technical responsibility and high participation in professional activities, but not necessarily high salary or supervisory responsibility (Perrucci and Perrucci, 1970).

At the same time, a number of practicing engineers lack college degrees (about 40% of engineers in the early 1950s; see Soderberg, 1963:213), suggesting that even such highly technical skills may be acquired on the job. For academic research scientists, educational quality has little effect on subsequent productivity (Hagstrom and Hargens, 1968). For other professions, evidence is not available on the degree to which actual skills are learned in school rather than in practice. In professions such as medicine and law, where education is a legal requirement for admission to practice, a comparison group of noneducated practitioners is not available, at least in the modern era.

Outside of the traditional learned professions, the plausibility of the vocational importance of education is more questionable. Comparisons of the efforts of different occupations to achieve "professionalization" suggest that setting educational requirements and bolstering them through licensing laws is a common tactic in raising an occupation's prestige and autonomy (Wilensky, 1964). The result has been the proliferation of numerous pseudo-professions in modern society; nevertheless these fail to achieve strong professional organization through lack of a monpolizable (and hence teachable) skill base. Business administration schools represent such an effort. (See Pierson, 1959: 9, 55–95, 140; Gordon and Howell, 1959:1–18, 40, 324–337). Descriptions of general, nonvocational education do not support the image of schools as places where skills are widely learned. Scattered studies suggest that the knowledge imparted in particular courses is retained only in small part through the next few years (Learned and Wood, 1938:28), and indicate a dominant student culture concerned with nonacademic interests or with achieving grades with a minimum of learning (Coleman, 1961; Becker et al., 1968).

The technical-function theory of education, then, does not give an adequate account of the evidence. Economic evidence indicates no clear contributions of education to economic development, beyond the provisions of mass literacy. Shifts in the proportions of more skilled and less skilled jobs do not account for the observed increase in education of the American labor force. Education is often irrelevant to on-the-job productivity and is sometimes counter-productive; specifically, vocational training seems to be derived more from work experience than from formal school training. The quality of schools themselves, and the nature of dominant student cultures suggest that schooling is very inefficient as a means of training for work skills.

Functional and Conflict Perspectives

It may be suggested that the inadequacies of the technical-function theory of education derive from a more basic source: the functional approach to stratification. A fundamental assumption is that there is a generally fixed set of positions, whose various requirements the labor force must satisfy. The fixed demand for skills of various types, at any given time, is the basic determinant of who will be selected for what positions. Social change may then be explained by specifying how these functional demands change with the process of modernization. In keeping with the functional perspective in general, the needs of society are seen as determining the behavior and the rewards of the individuals within it.

However, this premise may be questioned as an adequate picture of the fundamental processes of social organization. It may be suggested that the "demands" of any occupational position are not fixed, but represent whatever behavior is settled upon in bargaining between the persons who fill the positions and those who attempt to control them. Individuals want jobs primarily for the rewards to themselves in material goods, power, and prestige. The amount of productive skill they must demonstrate to hold their positions depends on how much clients, customers, or employers can successfully demand of them, and this in turn depends on the balance of power between workers and their employers.

Employers tend to have quite imprecise conceptions of the skill requirements of most jobs, and operate on a strategy of "satisficing" rather than optimizing—that is, setting average levels of performance as satisfactory, and making changes in procedures or personnel only when performance falls noticeably below minimum standards (Dill et al., 1962; March and Simon, 1958:140–141). Efforts to predict work performance by objective tests have foundered due to difficulties in measuring performance (except on specific mechanical tasks) and the lack of control groups to validate the tests (Anastasi, 1967). Organizations do not force their employees to work at maximum efficiency; there is considerable insulation of workers at all levels from demands for full use of their skills and efforts. Informal controls over output are found not only among production workers in manufacturing but also among sales and clerical personnel (Roy, 1952; Blau, 1955; Lombard, 1955). The existence of informal organization at the managerial level, the widespread existence of bureaucratic pathologies such as evasion of responsibility, empire-building, and displacement of means by ends ("red tape"), and the fact that administrative work is only indirectly related to the output of the organization, suggest that managers, too, are insulated from strong technological pressures for use of technical skills. On all levels, wherever informal organization exists, it appears that standards of performance reflect the power of the groups involved.

In this light, it is possible to reinterpret the body of evidence that ascriptive factors continue to be important in occupational success even in advanced industrial society. The social mobility data summarized at the onset of this paper show that social origins have a direct effect on occupational success, even after the completion of education. Both case studies and cross-sectional samples amply document widespread discrimination against Negroes. Case studies show that the operation of ethnic and class standards in employment based not merely on skin color but on name, accent, style of dress, manners, and conversational abilities (Noland and Bakke, 1949; Turner, 1952; Taeuber et al., 1966; Nosow, 1956). Cross-sectional studies, based on both biographical and survey data, show that approximately 60 to 70% of the American business elite come from upper-class and upper-middle-class families, and fewer than 15% from working-class families (Taussig and Joselyn, 1932:97; Warner and Abegglen, 1955:37–68; Newcomer, 1955:53; Bendix, 1956:198–253; Mills, 1963:110–139). These proportions are fairly constant from the early 1800s through the 1950s. The business elite is overwhelmingly Protestant, male, and completely white, although there are some indications of a mild trend toward declining social origins and an increase of Catholics and Jews. Ethnic and class background have been found crucial for career advancement in the professions as well (Ladinsky, 1963; Hall, 1946). Sexual stereotyping of jobs is extremely widespread (Collins, 1969:234–238).

In the traditional functionalist approach, these forms of ascription are treated as residual categories: carry-overs from a less advanced period, or marks of the imperfections of the functional mechanism of placement. Yet available trend data suggest that the link between social class origins and occupational attainment has remained constant during the twentieth century in America (Blau and Duncan, 1967:81–113); the proportion of women in higher occupational levels has changed little since the late nineteenth century (Epstein, 1970:7); and the few available comparisons between elite groups in traditional and modern societies suggest comparable levels of mobility (Marsh, 1963). Declines in racial and ethnic discrimination that appear to have occurred at periods in twentieth-century America may be plausibly explained as results of political mobilization of particular minority groups rather than by an increased economic need to select by achievement criteria.

Goode (1967) has offered a modified functional model to account for these disparities: that work groups always organize to protect their inept members from being judged by outsiders' standards of productivity, and that this self-protection is functional to the organizations, preventing a Hobbesian competitiveness and distrust of all against all. This argument re-establishes a functional explanation, but only at the cost of undermining the technological view of functional requirements. Further, Goode's conclusions can be put in other terms: it is to the advantage of groups of employees to organize so that they will not be judged by strict performance standards; and it is at least minimally to the advantage of the employer to let them do so, for if he presses them harder he creates dissension and alienation. Just how hard an employer *can* press his employees is not given in Goode's functional model. That is, his model has the disadvantage, common to functional analysis in its most general form, of covering too many alternative possibilities to provide testable explanations of specific outcomes. Functional analysis too easily operates as a justification for whatever particular pattern exists, asserting in effect that there is a proper reason for it to be so, but failing to state the conditions under which a particular pattern will hold rather than another. The technical version of job requirements has the advantage of specifying patterns, but it is this specific form of functional explanation that is jettisoned by a return to a more abstract functional analysis.

A second hypothesis may be suggested: the power of "ascribed" groups may be the *prime* basis of selection in all organizations, and technical skills are secondary considerations depending on the balance of power. Education may thus be regarded as a mark of membership in a particular group (possibly at times its defining characteristic), not a mark of technical skills or achievement. Educational requirements may thus reflect the interests of whichever groups have power to set them. Weber (1968:1000) interpreted educational requirements in bureaucracies, drawing especially on the history of public administration in Prussia, as the result of efforts by university graduates to monopolize positions, raise their corporate status, and thereby increase their own security and power vis-à-vis both higher authorities and clients. Gusfield (1958) has shown that educational requirements in the British Civil Service were set as the result of a power struggle between a victorious educated upper-middle-class and the traditional aristocracy.

To summarize the argument to this point: available evidence suggests that the technical-functional view of educational requirements for jobs leaves a large number of facts unexplained. Functional analysis on the more abstract level does not provide a testable explanation of which ascribed groups will be able to dominate which positions. To answer this question, one must leave the functional frame of reference and examine the conditions of relative power of each group.

A Conflict Theory of Stratification

The conditions under which educational requirements will be set and changed may be stated more generally, on the basis of a conflict theory of stratification derived from Weber (1968:926–939; see also Collins, 1968), and from advances in modern organization theory fitting the spirit of this approach.

A. *Status groups*. The basic units of society are associational groups sharing common cultures (or "subcultures"). The core of such groups is families and friends, but they may be etxended to religious, educational, or ethnic communities. In general, they comprise all persons who share a sense of status equality based on participation in a common culture: styles of language, tastes in clothing and decor, manners and other ritual observances, conversational topics and styles, opinions and values, and preferences in sports, arts, and media. Participation in such cultural groups gives individuals their fundamental sense of identity, especially in contrast with members of other associational groups in whose everyday culture they cannot participate comfortably. Subjectively, status groups distinguish themselves from others in terms of categories of *moral evaluation* such as "honor," "taste," "breeding," "respectability," "propriety," "cultivation," "good fellows," "plain folks," etc. Thus the exclusion of persons who lack the ingroup culture is felt to be normatively legitimated.

There is no *a priori* determination of the number of status groups in a particular society, nor can the degree to which there is consensus on a rank order among them be stated in advance. These are not matters of definition, but empirical variations, the causes of which are subjects of other developments of the conflict theory of stratification. Status groups should be regarded as ideal types, without implication of *necessarily distinct* boundaries; the concepts remain useful even in the case where associational groupings and their status cultures are fluid and overlapping, as hypotheses about the conflicts among status groups may remain fruitful even under these circumstances.

Status groups may be derived from a number of sources. Weber outlines three: (a) differences in life style based on economic situation (i.e., class); (b) differences in life situation based on power position; (c) differences in life situation deriving directly from cultural conditions or institutions, such as geographical origin, ethnicity, religion, education, or intellectual or aesthetic cultures.

B. *Struggle for Advantage.* There is a continual struggle in society for various "goods"—wealth, power, or prestige. We need make no assumption that every individual is motivated to maximize his rewards; however, since power and prestige are inherently scarce commodities, and wealth is often contingent upon them, the ambition of even a small proportion of persons for more than equal shares of these goods sets up an implicit counter-struggle on the part of others to avoid subjection and disesteem. Individuals may struggle with each other, but since individual identity is derived primarily from membership in a status group, and because the cohesion of status groups is a key resource in the struggle against others, the primary focus of struggle is between status groups rather than within them.

The struggle for wealth, power, and prestige is carried out primarily through organizations. There have been struggles throughout history among organizations controlled by different status groups, for military conquest, business advantage, or cultural (e.g., religious) hegemony, and intricate sorts of interorganizational alliances are possible. In the more complex societies, struggle between status groups is carried on in large part *within* organizations, as the status groups controlling an organization coerce, hire, or culturally manipulate others to carry out their wishes (as in, respectively, a conscript army, a business, or a church). Organizational research shows that the success of organizational elites in controlling their subordinates is quite variable. Under particular conditions, lower or middle members have considerable *de facto* power to avoid compliance, and even to change the course of the organizations (see Etzioni, 1961).

This opposing power from below is strengthened when subordinate members constitute a cohesive status group of their own; it is weakened when subordinates acquiesce in the values of the organization elite. Coincidence of ethnic and class boundaries produces the sharpest cultural distinctions. Thus, Catholics of immigrant origins have been the bulwarks of informal norms restricting work output in American firms run by WASPs, whereas Protestants of native rural backgrounds are the main "ratebusters" (O. Coffins *et al.,* 1946). Selection and manipulation of members in terms of status groups is thus a key weapon in intraorganizational struggles. In general, the organization elite selects its new members and key assistants from its own status group and makes an effort to secure lower-level employees who are at least indoctrinated to respect the cultural superiority of their status culture.[4]

Once groups of employees of different status groups are formed at various positions (middle, lower, or laterally differentiated) in the organization, each of these groups may be expected to launch efforts to recruit more members of their own status group. This process is illustrated by conflicts among whites and blacks, Protestants and Catholics and Jews, Yankee, Irish and Italian, etc. found in American occupational life (Hughes, 1949; Dalton, 1951). These conflicts are based on ethnically or religiously founded status cultures; their intensity rises and falls with processes increasing or decreasing the cultural distinctiveness of these groups, and with the succession of advantages and disadvantages set by previous outcomes of these struggles which determine the organizational resources available for further struggle. Parallel processes of cultural conflict may be based on distinctive class as well as ethnic cultures.

C. *Education As Status Culture.* The main activity of schools is to teach particular status cultures, both in and outside the classroom. In this light, any failure of schools to impart technical knowledge (although it may also be successful in this) is not important; schools primarily teach vocabulary and inflection, styles of dress, aesthetic tastes, values and manners. The emphasis on sociability and athletics found in many schools is not extraneous but may be at the core of the status culture propagated by the schools. Where schools have a more academic or vocational emphasis, this emphasis may itself be the content of a particular status culture, providing sets of values, materials for conversation, and shared activities for an associational group making claims to a particular basis for status.

Insofar as a particular status group controls education, it may use it to foster control within work organizations. Educational requirements for employment can serve both to select new members for elite positions who share the elite culture and, at a lower level of education, to hire lower and middle employees who have acquired a general respect for these elite values and styles.

Tests of the Conflict Theory of Educational Stratification

The conflict theory in its general form is supported by evidence (1) that there are distinctions among status group cultures—based both on class and on ethnicity—in modern societies (Kahl, 1957:127–156, 184–220); (2) that status groups tend to occupy different occupational positions within organizations (see data on ascription cited above); and (3) that occupants of different organizational positions struggle over power (Dalton, 1959; Crozier, 1964). The more specific tests called for here, however, are of the adequacy of conflict theory to explain the link between education and occupational stratification. Such tests may focus either on the proposed mechanism of occupational placement, or on the conditions for strong or weak links between education and occupation.

Education as a Mechanism of Occupational Placement. The mechanism proposed is that employers use education to select persons who have been socialized into the dominant status culture: for entrants to their own managerial ranks, into elite culture; for lower-level employees, into an attitude of respect for the dominant culture and the elite which carries it. This requires evidence that: (a) schools provide either training for the elite culture, or respect for it; and (b) employers use education as a means of selection for cultural attributes.

(a) Historical and descriptive studies of schools support the generalization that they are places where particular status cultures are acquired, either from the teachers, from other students, or both. Schools are usually founded by powerful or autonomous status groups, either to provide an exclusive education for their own children, or to propagate respect for their cultural values. Until recently most schools were founded by religions, often in opposition to those founded by rival religions; throughout the 19th century, this rivalry was an important basis for the founding of large numbers of colleges in the U. S., and of the Catholic and Lutheran school systems. The public school system in the U. S. was founded mainly under the impetus of WASP elites with the purpose of teaching respect for Protestant and middle-class standards of cultural and religious propriety, especially in the face of Catholic, working-class immigration from Europe (Cremin, 1961; Curti, 1935). The content of public school education has consisted especially of middle-class, WASP culture (Waller, 1932:15–131; Becker, 1961; Hess and Torney, 1967).

At the elite level, private secondary schools for children of the WASP upper class were founded from the 1880s, when the mass indoctrination function of the growing public schools made them unsuitable as means of maintaining cohesion of the elite culture itself (Baltzell, 1958:327–372). These elite schools produce a distinctive personality type, characterized by adherence to a distinctive set of upper-class values and manners (McArthur, 1955). The cultural role of schools has been more closely studied in Britain (Bernstein, 1961; Weinberg, 1967), and in France (Bourdieu and Passeron, 1964), although Riesman and his colleagues (Riesman, 1958; Jencks and Riesman, 1968) have shown some of the cultural differences among prestige levels of colleges and universities in the United States.

(b) Evidence that education has been used as a means of cultural selection may be found in several sources. Hollingshead's (1949:360–388) study of Elmtown school children, school dropouts, and community attitudes toward them suggests that employers use education as a means of selecting employees with middle-class attributes. A 1945–1946 survey of 240 employers in New Haven and Charlotte, N. C. indicated that they regarded education as a screening device for employees with desirable (middle-class) character and demeanor; white-collar positions particularly emphasized

BISHOP BURTON COLLEGE
LIBRARY

educational selection because these employees were considered most visible to outsiders (Noland and Bakke, 1949:20–63).

A survey of employers in nationally prominent corporations indicated that they regarded college degrees as important in hiring potential managers, not because they were thought to ensure technical skills, but rather to indicate "motivation" and "social experience" (Gordon and Howell, 1959:121). Business school training is similarly regarded, less as evidence of necessary training (as employers have been widely skeptical of the utility of this curriculum for most positions) than as an indication that the college graduate is committed to business attitudes. Thus, employers are more likely to refuse to hire liberal arts graduates if they come from a college which has a business school than if their college is without a business school (Gordon and Howell, 1959:84–87; see also Pierson, 1959:90–99). In the latter case, the students could be said not to have had a choice; but when both business and liberal arts courses are offered and the student chooses liberal arts, employers appear to take this as a rejection of business values.

Finally, a 1967 survey of 309 California organizations (Collins, 1971) found that educational requirements for white-collar workers were highest in organizations which placed the strongest emphasis on normative control over their employees.[5] Normative control emphasis was indicated by (i) relative emphasis on the absence of police record for job applicants; (ii) relative emphasis on a record of job loyalty; (iii) Etzioni's (1961) classification of organizations into those with high normative control emphasis (financial, professional services, government, and other public services organizations) and those with remunerative control emphasis (manufacturing, construction, and trade). These three indicators are highly interrelated, thus mutually validating their conceptualization as indicators of normative control emphasis. The relationship between normative control emphasis and educational requirements holds for managerial requirements and white-collar requirements generally, both including and excluding professional and technical positions. Normative control emphasis does not affect blue-collar education requirements.

Variations in Linkage between Education and Occupation

The conflict model may also be tested by examining the cases in which it predicts education will be relatively important or unimportant in occupational attainment. Education should be most important where two conditions hold simultaneously: (1) the type of education most closely reflects membership in a particular status group, and (2) that group controls employment in particular organizational contexts. Thus, education will be most important where the fit is greatest between the culture of the status groups emerging from schools, and the status group doing the hiring; it will be least important where there is the greatest disparity between the culture of the school and of the employers.

This fit between school-group culture and employer culture may be conceptualized as a continuum. The importance of elite education is highest where it is involved in selection of new members of organizational elites, and should fade off where jobs are less elite (either lower level jobs in these organizations, or jobs in other organizations not controlled by the cultural elite). Similarly, schools which produce the most elite graduates will be most closely linked to elite occupations; schools whose products are less well socialized into elite culture are selected for jobs correspondingly less close to elite organizational levels.

In the United States, the schools which produce culturally elite groups, either by virtue of explicit training or by selection of students from elite backgrounds, or both, are the private prep schools at the secondary level; at the higher level, the elite colleges (the Ivy league, and to a lesser degree the major state universities); at the professional training level, those professional schools attached to the elite colleges and universities. At the secondary level, schools which produce respectably socialized, nonelite persons are the public high schools (especially those in middle-class residential areas); from the point of view of the culture of WASP employers, Catholic schools (and all-black schools) are less acceptable. At the level of higher education, Catholic and black colleges and professional schools are less elite, and commercial training schools are the least elite form of education.

In the United States, the organizations most clearly dominated by the WASP upper class are large, nationally organized business corporations, and the largest law firms (Domhoff, 1967:38–62). Those organizations more likely to be dominated by members of minority ethnic cultures are the smaller and local businesses in manufacturing, construction, and retail trade; in legal practice, solo rather than firm employment. In government employment, local governments appear to be more heavily dominated by ethnic groups, whereas particular branches of the national government (notably the State Department and the Treasury) are dominated by WASP elites (Domhoff, 1967: 84–114, 132–137).

Evidence on the fit between education and employment is available for only some of these organizations. In a broad sample of organizational types (Collins, 1971), educational requirements were higher in the bigger organizations, which also tended to be organized on a national scale, than in smaller and more localistic organizations.[6] The finding of Penned and Perrucci (1970) that upper-class social origins were important in career success precisely within the group of engineers who graduated from the most prestigious engineering schools with the highest grades may also bear on this question; since the big national corporations are most likely to hire this academically elite group, the importance of social origins within this group tends to corroborate the interpretation of education as part of a process of elite cultural selection in those organizations.

Among lawyers, the predicted differences are clear: graduates of the law schools attached to elite colleges and universities are more likely to be employed in firms, whereas graduates of Catholic or commercial law schools are more likely to be found in solo practice (Ladinsky, 1967). The elite Wall Street law firms are most educationally selective in this regard, choosing not only from Ivy League law schools but from a group whose background includes attendance at elite prep schools and colleges (Smigel, 1964: 39, 73–74, 117). There are also indications that graduates of ethnically-dominated professional schools are most likely to practice within the ethnic community; this is clearly the case among black professionals. In general, the evidence that graduates of black colleges (Sharp, 1970:64–67) and of Catholic colleges (Jencks and Riesman, 1968:357–366) have attained lower occupational positions in business than graduates of white Protestant schools (at least until recent years) also bolsters this interpretation.[7]

It is possible to interpret this evidence according to the technical-function theory of education, arguing that the elite schools provide the best technical training, and that the major national organizations require the greatest degree of technical talent. What is necessary is to test simultaneously for technical and status-conflict conditions. The most direct evidence on this point is the California employer study (Collins, 1971), which examined the effects of normative control emphasis and of organizational prominence, while holding constant the organization's technological modernity, as measured by the number of technological and organizational changes in the previous six years. Technological change was found to affect educational requirements at managerial and white-collar (but not blue-collar) levels, thus giving some support to the technical-function theory of education. The three variables—normative control emphasis, organizational prominence, and technological change—each independently affected educational requirements, in particular contexts. Technological change produced significantly higher educational requirements only in smaller, localistic organizations, and in organizational sectors not emphasizing normative control. Organizational prominence produced significantly higher educational requirements in organizations with low technological change, and in sectors de-emphasizing normative control. Normative control emphasis produced significantly higher educational requirements in organizations with low technological change and in less prominent organizations. Thus, technical and normative status conditions all affect educational requirements; measures of association indicated that the latter conditions were stronger in this sample.

Other evidence bearing on this point concerns business executives only. A study of the top executives in nationally prominent businesses indicated that the most highly educated managers were not found in the most rapidly developing companies, but rather in the least economically vigorous ones, with highest education found in the traditionalistic financial and utility firms (Warner and Abegglen, 1955:141–143, 148). The business elite has always been highly educated in relation to the American populace, but education seems to be a correlate of their social origins rather than the determinant of their success (Mills, 1963:128; Taussig and Joslyn, 1932:200; Newcomer, 1955:76). Those members of the business elite who entered its ranks from lower social origins had less education than the businessmen of upper and upper-middle-class origins, and those businessmen who inherited their companies were much more likely to be college educated than those who achieved their positions by entrepreneurship (Bendix, 1956:230; Newcomer, 1955:80).

In general, the evidence indicates that educational requirements for employment reflect employers' concerns for acquiring respectable and well-socialized employees; their concern for the provision of technical skills through education enters to a lesser degree. The higher the normative control concerns of the employer, and the more elite the organization's status, the higher his educational requirements.

Historical Change

The rise in educational requirements for employment throughout the last century may be explained using the conflict theory, and incorporating elements of the technical-functional theory into it at appropriate points. The principal dynamic has centered on changes in the supply of educated persons caused by the expansion of the school system, which was in turn shaped by three conditions:

(1) Education has been associated with high economic and status position from the colonial period on through the twentieth century. The result was a popular demand for education as mobility opportunity. This demand has not been for vocational education at a terminal or commercial level, short of full university certification; the demand has rather focused on education giving entry into the elite status culture, and usually only those technically-oriented schools have prospered which have most closely associated themselves with the sequence of education leading to (or from) the classical Bachelor's degree (Collins, 1969:68–70, 86–87, 89, 96–101).

(2) Political decentralization, separation of church and state, and competition among religious denominations have made founding schools and colleges in America relatively easy, and provided initial motivations of competition among communities and religious groups that moved them to do so. As a result, education at all levels expanded faster in America than anywhere else in the world. At the time of the Revolution, there were nine colleges in the colonies; in all of Europe, with a population forty times that of America, there were approximately sixty colleges. By 1880 there were 811 American colleges and universities; by 1966, there were 2,337. The United States not only began with the highest ratio of institutions of higher education to population in the world, but increased this lead steadily, for the number of European universities was not much greater by the twentieth century than in the eighteenth (Ben-David and Zloczower, 1962).

(3) Technical changes also entered into the expansion of American education. As the evidence summarized above indicates: (a) mass literacy is crucial for beginnings of full-scale industrialization, although demand for literacy could not have been important in the expansion of education beyond elementary levels. More importantly, (b) there is a mild trend toward the reduction in the proportion of unskilled jobs and an increase in the promotion of highly skilled (professional and technical) jobs as industrialism proceeds, accounting for 15% of the shift in educational levels in the twentieth century (Folger and Nam, 1964). (c) Technological change also brings about some upgrading in skill requirements of some continuing job positions, although the available evidence (Berg, 1970:38–60) refers only to the decade 1950–1960. Nevertheless, as Wilensky (1964) points out, there is no "profes-

sionalization of everyone," as most jobs do not require considerable technical knowledge on the order of that required of the engineer or the research scientist.

The existence of a relatively small group of experts in high-status positions, however, can have important effects on the structure of competition for mobility chances. In the United States, where democratic decentralization favors the use of schools (as well as government employment) as a kind of patronage for voter interests, the existence of even a small number of elite jobs fosters a demand for *large-scale* opportunities to acquire these positions. We thus have a "contest mobility" school system (Turner, 1960); it produced a widely educated populace because of the many dropouts who never achieve the elite level of schooling at which expert skills and/or high cultural status are acquired. In the process, the status value of American education has become diluted. Standards of respectability are always relative to the existing range of cultural differences. Once higher levels of education become recognized as an objective mark of elite status, and a moderate level of education as a mark of respectable middle-level status, increases in the supply of educated persons at given levels result in yet higher levels, becoming recognized as superior, and previously superior levels become only average.

Thus, before the end of the nineteenth century, an elementary school or home education was no longer satisfactory for a middle-class gentleman; by the 1930s, a college degree was displacing the high school degree as the minimal standard of respectability; in the late 1960s, graduate school or specialized professional degrees were becoming necessary for initial entry to many middle-class positions, and high school graduation was becoming a standard for entry to manual laboring positions. Education has thus gradually become part of the status culture of classes far below the level of the original business and professional elites.

The increasing supply of educated persons (Table 3.2) has made education a rising requirement of jobs (Table 3.1). Led by the biggest and most prestigious organizations, employers have raised their educational requirements to maintain both the relative prestige of their own managerial ranks and the relative respectability of middle ranks.[8] Education has become a legitimate standard in terms of which employers select employees, and employees compete with each other for promotion opportunities or for raised prestige in their continuing positions. With the attainment of a mass (now approaching universal) higher education system in modern America, the ideal or image of technical skill becomes the legitimating culture in terms of which the struggle for position goes on.

Higher educational requirements, and the higher level of educational credentials offered by individuals competing for position in organizations, have in turn increased the demand for education by the populace. The interaction between formal job requirements and informal status cultures has resulted in a spiral in which educational requirements and educational attainments become ever higher. As the struggle for mass educational opportunities enters new phases in the universities of today and perhaps in the graduate schools of the future, we may expect a further upgrading of educational requirements for employment. The mobilization of demands by minority groups for mobility opportunities through schooling can only contribute an extension of the prevailing pattern.

Conclusion

It has been argued that conflict theory provides an explanation of the principal dynamics of rising educational requirements for employment in America. Changes in the technical requirements of jobs have caused more limited changes in particular jobs. The conditions of the interaction of these two determinants may be more closely studied.

Precise measures of changes in the actual technical skill requirements of jobs are as yet available only in rudimentary form. Few systematic studies show how much of particular job skills may be learned in practice, and how much must be acquired through school background. Close studies of what is actually learned in school, and how long it is retained, are rare. Organizational studies of how employers rate performance and decide upon promotions give a picture of relatively loose controls over the technical quality of employee performance, but this no doubt varies in particular types of jobs.

The most central line of analysis for assessing the joint effects of status group conflict and technical requirements are those which compare the relative importance of education in different contexts. One such approach may take organization as the unit of analysis, comparing the educational requirements of organizations both to organizational technologies and to the status (including educational) background of organizational elites. Such analysis may also be applied to surveys of individual mobility, comparing the effects of education on mobility in different employment contexts, where the status group (and educational) background of employers varies in its fit with the educational culture of prospective employees. Such analysis of "old school tie" networks may also simultaneously test for the independent effect of the technical requirements of different sorts of jobs on the importance of education. Inter-nation comparisons provide variations here in the fit between types of education and particular kinds of jobs which may not be available within any particular country.

The full elaboration of such analysis would give a more precise answer to the historical question of assigning weight to various factors in the changing place of education in the stratification of modern societies. At the same time, to state the conditions under which status groups vary in organizational power, including the power to emphasize or limit the importance of technical skills, would be to state the basic elements of a comprehensive explanatory theory of the forms of stratification.

Notes

1. This survey covered 309 establishments with 100 or more employees, representing all major industry groups.
2. The concern here is with these basic premises rather than with the theory elaborated by Davis and Moore to account for the universality of stratification. This theory involves a few further propositions: (C) in any particular form of society certain occupational positions are functionally most central to the operation of the social system; (D) the ability to fill these positions, and/ or the motivation to acquire the necessary training, is unequally distributed in the population; (E) inequalities of rewards in wealth and prestige evolve to ensure that the supply of persons with the necessary ability or training meshes with the structure of demands for skilled performance. The problems of stating functional centrality in empirical terms have been subjects of much debate.
3. Proposition 3 is supported by Tables 3.1 and 3.2. The issue here is whether this can be explained by the previous propositions and premises.
4. It might be argued that the ethnic cultures may differ in their functionality: that middle-class Protestant culture provides the self-discipline and other attributes necessary for higher organizational positions in modern society. This version of functional theory is specific enough to be subject to empirical test: are middle-class WASPs in fact better businessmen or government administrators than Italians, Irishmen, or Jews of patrimonial or working class cultural backgrounds? Weber suggested that they were in the initial construction of the capitalist economy within the confines of traditional society; he also argued that once the new economic system was established, the original ethic was no longer necessary to run it (Weber, 1930:180–183). Moreover, the functional explanation also requires some feedback mechanism whereby organizations with more efficient managers are selected for survival. The oligopolistic situation in large-scale American business since the late 19th century does not seem to provide such a mechanism; nor does government employment. Schumpeter (1951), the leading expositor of the importance of. managerial talent in business, confined his emphasis to the formative period of business expansion, and regarded the large, oligopolistic corporation as an arena where advancement came to be based on skills in organizational politics (1951:122–124); these personalistic skills are arguably more characteristic of the patrimonial cultures than of WASP culture.
5. Sample consisted of approximately one-third of all organizations with 100 or more employees in the San Francisco, Oakland, and San Jose metropolitan areas. See Gordon and Thal-Larsen (1969) for a description of procedures and other findings.
6. Again, these relationships hold for managerial requirements and white-collar requirements generally, both including and excluding professional and technical positions, but not for blue-collar requirements. Noland and Bakke (1949:78) also report that larger organizations have higher educational requirements for administrative positions than smaller organizations.
7. Similar processes may be found in other societies, where the kinds of organizations linked to particular types of schools may differ. In England, the elite "public schools" are linked especially to the higher levels of the national civil service (Weinberg, 1967:139–143). In France, the elite Ecole Polytechnique is linked to both government and industrial administrative positions (Crozier, 1964: 238–244). In Germany, universities have been linked principally with government administration, and business executives are drawn from elsewhere (Ben-David and Zloczower, 1962). Comparative analysis of the kinds of education of government officials, business executives, and other groups in contexts where the status group links of schools differ is a promising area for further tests of conflict and technical-functional explanations.

8. It appears that employers may have raised their wage costs in the process. Their behavior is nevertheless plausible, in view of these considerations: (a) the thrust of organizational research since Mayo and Barnard has indicated that questions of internal organizational power and control, of which cultural dominance is a main feature, take precedence over purely economic considerations; (b) the large American corporations, which have led in educational requirements, have held positions of oligopolistic advantage since the late 19th century, and thus could afford a large internal "welfare" cost of maintaining a well-socialized work force; (c) there are inter-organizational wage differentials in local labor markets, corresponding to relative organizational prestige, and a "wage-escalator" process by which the wages of the leading organizations are gradually emulated by others according to their rank (Reynolds, 1951); a parallel structure of "educational status escalators" could plausibly be expected to operate.

References

Anastasi, Anne, 1967 "Psychology, psychologists, and psychological testing." *American Psychologist* 22 (April): 297–306.

Baltzell, E. Digby, 1958 *An American Business Aristocracy*. New York: Macmillan.

Becker, Howard S., 1961 "Schools and systems of stratification." Pp. 93–104 in A. H. Halsey, Jean Floud, and C. Arnold Anderson (eds), *Education, Economy, and Society*. New York: Free Press.

Becker, Howard S., Blanche Geer, and Everett C. Hughes, 1968 *Making the Grade: The Academic Side of College Life*. New York: Wiley.

Bell, H. M., 1940 *Matching Youth and Jobs*. Washington: American Council on Education.

Ben-David, Joseph, 1963– "Professions in the class systems of present-64 day Societies." *Current Sociology* 12:247–330.

Ben-David, Joseph and Awraham Floczower, 1962 "Universities and academic systems in modern societies." *European Journal of Sociology* 31:45–85.

Bendix, Reinhard, 1956 *Work and Authority in Industry*. New York: Wiley.

Berg, Ivar, 1970 *Education and Jobs*. New York: Praeger.

Bernstein, Basil, 1961 "Social class and linguistic development." Pp. 288–314 in A. H. Halsey, Jean Floud, and C. Arnold Anderson (eds), *Education, Economy, and Society*. New York: Free Press.

Blau, Peter M., 1955 *The Dynamics of Bureaucracy*. Chicago: University of Chicago Press.

Blau, Peter M. and Otis Dudley Duncan, 1967 *The American Occupational Structure*. New York: Wiley.

Bourdieu, Pierre and Jean-Claude Passeron, 1964 *Les Heritiers: Les Etudiants et la Culture*. Paris: Les Editions de Minuit.

Bright, James R., 1958 "Does automation raise skin requirements?" *Harvard Business Review* 36 (July–August):85–97.

Clark, Burton R., 1962 *Educating the Expert Society*. San Francisco: Chandler.

Clark, Harold F. and Harold S. Sloan, 1966 *Classrooms on Main Street*. New York: Teachers College Press.

Coleman, James S., 1961 *The Adolescent Society*. New York: Free Press.

Collins, Orvis, Melville Dalton, and Donald Roy 1946 "Restriction of output and social cleavage in industry." *Applied Anthropology* 5 (Summer): 1–14.

Collins, Randall, 1968 "A comparative approach to political sociology." Pp. 42–67 in Reinhard Bendix et at. (eds.), *State and Society*. Boston: Little, Brown.

———— 1969 Education and Employment. Unpublished Ph.D. dissertation, University of California at Berkeley.

———— 1971 "Educational requirements for employment: A comparative organizational study." Unpublished manuscript.

Cremin, Lawrence A., 1961 *The Transformation of the School*. New York: Knopf.

Crozier, Michel, 1964 *The Bureaucratic Phenomenon*. Chicago: University of Chicago Press.

Curti, Merle, 1935 *The Social Ideas of American Educators*. New York: Scribners.

Dalton, Melville, 1951 "Informal factors in career achievement." *American Journal of Sociology* 56 (March): 407–415.

———— 1959 *Men Who Manage*. New York: Wiley.

Davis, Kingsley and Wilbert Moore, 1945 "Some principles of stratification." *American Sociological Review* 10:242–249.

Denison, Edward F., 1965 "Education and economic productivity." Pp. 328–340 in Seymour Harris (ed.), *Education and Public Policy*. Berkeley: McCutchen.

Dill, William R., Thomas L. Hilton, and Walter R. Reitman, 1962 *The New Managers*. Englewood Cliffs: Prentice-Hall.

Domhoff, G. William, 1967 *Who Rules America?* Englewood Cliffs, New Jersey: Prentice-Hall.

Duncan, Beverly, 1964 "Dropouts and the unemployed." *Journal of Political Economy* 73 (April):121–134.

Duncan, Otis Dudley and Robert W. Hodge, 1963 "Education and occupational mobility: A regression analysis." *American Journal of Sociology* 68:629–644.

Eckland, Bruce K., 1965 "Academic ability, higher education, and occupational mobility." *American Sociological Review* 30:735–746.

Epstein, Cynthia Fuchs, 1970 *Woman's Place: Options and Limits in Professional Careers*. Berkeley: University of California Press.

Etzioni, Amitai, 1961 *A Comparative Analysis of Complex Organizations*. New York: Free Press.

Folger, John K. and Charles B. Nam, 1964 "Trends in education in relation to the occupational structure." *Sociology of Education* 38:19–33.

Goode, William J., 1967 "The protection of the inept." *American Sociological Review* 32:5–19.

Gordon, Margaret S. and Margaret Thal-Larsen, 1969 *Employer Policies in a Changing Labor Market*. Berkeley: Institute of Industrial Relations, University of California.

Gordon, Robert A. and James E. Howell, 1959 *Higher Education for Business*. New York: Columbia University Press.

Gusfield, Joseph R., 1958 "Equalitarianism and bureaucratic recruitment." *Administrative Science Quarterly* 2 (March):521–541.

Hagstrom, Warren O. and Lowell L. Hargens, 1968 "Mobility theory in the sociology of science." Paper delivered at Cornell Conference on Human Mobility, Ithaca, N.Y. (October 31).

Hall, Oswald, 1946 "The informal organization of the medical profession." *Canadian Journal of Economic and Political Science* 12 (February): 30–44.

Harbison, Frederick and Charles A. Myers, 1964 *Education, Manpower, and Economic Growth*. New York: McGraw-Hill.

Hargens, Lowell and Warren O. Hagstrom, 1967 "Sponsored and contest mobility of American academic scientists." *Sociology of Education* 40:24–38.

Havemann, Ernest and Patricia Salter West, 1952 *They Went to College*. New York: Harcourt, Brace.

Hess, Robert D. and Judith V. Torney, 1967 *The Development of Political Attitudes in Children*. Chicago: Aldine.

Hollingshead, August B., 1949 *Elmtown's Youth*. New York: Wiley.

Hoselitz, Bert F., 1965 "Investment in education and its political impact" Pp. 541–565 in James S. Coleman (ed.), *Education and Political Development*. Princeton: Princeton University Press.

Hughes, Everett C., 1949 "Queries concerning industry and society growing out of the study of ethnic relations in Industry." *American Sociological Review* 14:211–220.

Jencks, Christopher and David Riesman, 1968 *The Academic Revolution*. New York: Doubleday.

Kahl, Joseph A., 1957 *The American Class Structure*. New York: Rinehart.

Kerr, Clark, John T. Dunlop, Frederick H. Harbison, and Charles A. Myers, 1960 *Industrialism and Industrial Man*. Cambridge: Harvard University Press.

Ladinsky, Jack, 1963 "Careers of lawyers, law practice, and legal institutions." *American Sociological Review* 28 (February):47–54.

——— 1967 "Higher education and work achievement among lawyers." *Sociological Quarterly* 8 (Spring):222–232.

Learned, W. S. and B. D. Wood, 1938 *The Student and His Knowledge*. New York: Carnegie Foundation for the Advancement of Teaching.

Lipset, Seymour Martin and Reinhard Bendix, 1959 *Social Mobility in Industrial Society*. Berkeley: University of California Press.

Lombard, George F., 1955 *Behavior in a Selling Group*. Cambridge: Harvard University Press.

March, James G. and Herbert A. Simon, 1958 *Organizations*. New York: Wiley.

Marsh, Robert M., 1963 "Values, demand, and social mobility." *American Sociological Review* 28 (August): 567–575.

McArthur, C., 1955 "Personality differences between middle and upper classes." *Journal of Abnormal and Social Psychology* 50:247–254.

Mills, C. Wright, 1963 *Power, Politics, and People*. New York: Oxford University Press.

Newcomer, Mabel, 1955 *The Big Business Executive*. New York: Columbia University Press.

Noland, E. William and E. Wight Bakke, 1949 *Workers Wanted*. New York: Harper.

Nosow, Sigmund, 1956 "Labor distribution and the normative system." *Social Forces* 30:25–33.

Peaslee, Alexander L., 1969 "Education's role in development." *Economic Development and Cultural Change* 17 (April): 293–318.

Perrucci, Carolyn Cummings and Robert Perrucci, 1970 "Social origins, educational contexts, and career mobility." *American Sociological Review* 35 (June):45l–463.

Pierson, Frank C., 1959 *The Education of American Businessmen*. New York: McGraw-Hill.

Plunkett, M., 1960 "School and early work experience of youth." *Occupational Outlook Quarterly* 4:22–27.

Reynolds, Lloyd, 1951 *The Structure of Labor Markets*. New York: Harper.

Riesman, David, 1958 *Constraint and Variety in American Education*. New York: Doubleday.

Roy, Donald, 1952 "Quota restriction and goldbricking in a machine shop." *American Journal of Sociology* 57 (March):427–442.

Schultz, Theodore W., 1961 "Investment in human capital." *American Economic Review* 51 (March):1–16.

Schumpeter, Joseph, 1951 *Imperialism and Social Classes*. New York: Augustus M. Kelley.

Sewell, William H., Archibald O. Halter, and Alejandro Portes, 1969 "The educational and early occupational attainment process." *American Sociological Review* 34 (February):82–92.

Sharp, Laure M., 1970 *Education and Employment: The Early Careers of College Graduates*. Baltimore: Johns Hopkins Press.

Smigel, Erwin O., 1964 *The Wall Street Lawyer*. New York: Free Press.

Soderberg, C. Richard, 1963 "The American engineer." Pp. 203–230 in Kenneth S. Lynn, *The Professions in America*. Boston: Beacon Press.

Taeuber, Alma F., Karl E. Taeuber, and Glen G. Cain, 1966 "Occupational assimilation and the competitive process: A reanalysis." *American Journal of Sociology* 72:278–285.

Taussig, Frank W. and C. S. Joslyn, 1932 *American Business Leaders*. New York: Macmillan.

Turner, Ralph H., 1952 "Foci of discrimination in the employment of nonwhites." *American Journal of Sociology* 58:247–256.

——— 1960 "Sponsored and contest mobility and the school system." *American Sociological Review* 25 (October):855–867.

Waller, Willard, 1932 *The Sociology of Teaching*. New York: Russell and Russell.

Warner, W. Lloyd and James C. Abegglen, 1955 *Occupational Mobility in American Business and Industry, 1928–1952*. Minneapolis: University of Minnesota Press.

Weber, Max, 1930 *The Protestant Ethic and the Spirit of Capitalism*. New York: Scribner's.

——— 1968 *Economy and Society*. New York: Bedminster Press.

4

Broken Promises

School Reform in Retrospect

SAMUEL BOWLES AND HERBERT GINTIS

We shall one day learn to supercede politics by education.—Ralph Waldo Emerson

. . .

Democracy and Technology in Educational Theory

The minds... of the great body of the people are in danger of really degenerating, while the other dements of civilization are advancing, unless care is taken, by means of the other instruments of education, to counteract those effects which the simplifications of the manual processes has a tendency to produce.—James Mill, 1824

Scholars abhor the obvious. Perhaps for this reason it is often difficult to find a complete written statement of a viewpoint which is widely accepted. Such is the case with modern liberal educational theory. Discovering its conceptual underpinnings thus requires more than a little careful searching. What exactly is the theory underlying the notion of education as "panacea"? In reviewing the vast literature on this subject, we have isolated two intellectually coherent strands, one represented by John Dewey and his followers—the "democratic school"—and the other represented by functional sociology and neoclassical economics—the "technocratic-meritocratic school." These approaches are best understood by analyzing the way they deal with two major questions concerning the limits of educational policy. The first concerns the compatibility of various functions schools are supposed to perform. The second concerns the power of schooling to perform these functions. We shall treat each in turn.

In the eyes of most liberal reformers, the educational system must fulfill at least three functions. First and foremost, schools must help integrate youth into the various occupational, political, familial, and other adult roles required by an expanding economy and a stable polity. "Education," says John Dewey in *Democracy and Education,* probably the most important presentation of the liberal theory of education, "is the means of [the] social continuity of life." We refer to this process as the "integrative" function of education.

Second, while substantial inequality in economic privilege and social status are believed by most liberals to be inevitable, giving each individual a chance to compete openly for these privileges is both efficient and desirable. Dewey is representative in asserting the role of the school in this process:

It is the office of the school environment... to see to it that each individual sets an opportunity to escape from the limitations of the social group in which he was born, and to come into living contact with a broader environment.[1]

Many liberal educational theorists—including Dewey—have gone beyond this rather limited objective to posit a role for schools in equalizing the vast extremes of wealth and poverty. Schooling, some have proposed, cannot only assure fair competition, but can also reduce the economic gap between the winners and the losers. We shall refer to this role of schooling in the pursuit of equality of opportunity, or of equality itself, as the "egalitarian" function of education.

Lastly, education is seen as a major instrument in promoting the psychic and moral development of the individual. Personal fulfillment depends, in large part, on the extent, direction, and vigor of development of our physical, cognitive, emotional, aesthetic, and other potentials. If the educational system has not spoken to these potentialities by taking individual development as an end in itself, it has failed utterly. Again quoting Dewey:

> The criterion of the value of school education is the extent in which it creates a desire for continued growth and supplies the means for making the desire effective in fact.... The educational process has no end beyond itself it is its own end.[2]

We refer to this as the "developmental" function of education.

For Dewey, the compatibility of these three functions—the integrative, the egalitarian, and the developmental—derives from basic assumptions concerning the nature of social life. First, he assumed that occupational roles in capitalist society are best filled by individuals who have achieved the highest possible levels of personal development. For Dewey, personal development is economically productive. Second, Dewey assumed that a free and universal school system can render the opportunities for self-development independent of race, ethnic origins, class background, and sex. Hence the integrative, egalitarian, and developmental functions of schooling are not only compatible, they are mutually supportive....

Dewey argues the necessary association of the integrative, egalitarian, and developmental functions of education in a democracy. A more recent liberal perspective argues only their mutual compatibility. This alternative view is based on a conception of the economy as a technical system, where work performance is based on technical competence. Inequality of income, power, and status, according to this technocratic-meritocratic view, is basically a reflection of an unequal distribution of mental, physical, and other skills. The more successful individuals, according to this view, are the more skillful and the more intelligent. Since cognitive and psychomotor development are vital and healthy components of individual psychic development and can be provided equally according to the "abilities" of the students upon their entering schools, the compatibility of these three functions of the educational system in capitalism is assured.

The popularity of the technocratic-meritocratic perspective can be gleaned from the policy-maker's reaction to the "rediscovery" of poverty and inequality in America during the decade of the 1960s. Unequal opportunity in acquiring skills was quickly isolated as the source of the problems.[3] Moreover, in assessing the efficacy of the educational system, both of preschool enrichment and of other school programs, measures of cognitive outcomes—scholastic achievement, for example—have provided the unique criteria of success.[4] Finally, the recent failure of educational policies significantly to improve the position of the poor and minority groups has, among a host of possible reappraisals of liberal theory, raised but one to preeminence: the nature-nurture controversy as to the determination of "intelligence."[5]

This technocratic-meritocratic view of schooling, economic success, and the requisites of job functioning supplies an elegant and logically coherent (if not empirically compelling) explanation of the rise of mass education in the course of industrial development. Because modern industry, according to this view, consists in the application of increasingly complex and intellectually demanding production technologies, the development of the economy requires increasing mental skills on the part of the labor force as a whole. Formal education, by extending to the masses what has been throughout human history the privilege of the few, opens the upper levels in the job hierarchy to all with the ability and willingness to attain such skills. Hence, the increasing economic importance of mental skills enhances the power of a fundamentally egalitarian school system to equalize economic opportunity....

The modern technocratic-meritocratic perspective avoids Mann's [Horace Mann was the father of the Common School movement in the 19th century who viewed schools as a great equalizer] class analysis but retains his basic assertions. According to the modern view, the egalitarianism of schooling is complemented by the meritocratic orientation of industrial society. Since in this view ability is fairly equally distributed across social class, and since actual achievement is the criterion for access to occupational roles, differences of birth tend toward economic irrelevance. Since whatever social-class based differences exist in an individual's "natural" aspirations to social status are minimized by the competitive orientation of schooling, expanding education represents a potent instrument toward the efficient and equitable distribution of jobs, income, and status. If inequalities remain at the end of this process, they must simply be attributed to inevitable human differences in intellectual capacities or patterns of free choice.

Thus as long as schooling is free and universal, the process of economic expansion will not only be consistent with the use of educational as an instrument for personal development and social equality; economic expansion, by requiring educational expansion, will necessarily enhance the power of education to achieve these ends. So the argument goes.[6]

If we accept for the moment the compatibility of various functions of education, we are confronted with a second group of questions concerning the power of education to counteract opposing tendencies in the larger society. If the educational system is to be a central social corrective, the issue of its potential efficacy is crucial to the establishment of the liberal outlook. Dewey does not withdraw from this issue:

...The school environment...establishes a purified medium of action.... As society becomes more enlightened, it realizes that it is responsible not to transmit and conserve the whole of its existing achievements but only such which make for a better future society. The school is its chief agency for the accomplishment of this end.[7]

But such generalizations cannot substitute for direct confrontation with the thorny and somewhat disreputable facts of economic life. In the reality of industrial society, can the school environment promote either human development or social equality? Self-development may be compatible with ideal work roles, but can education change the seamy realities of the workaday world? Equality may be compatible with the other functions of education, but can the significant and pervasive system of racial, class, and sexual stratification be significantly modified by "equal schooling"?

...

This approach became a fundamental tenet of educational reformers in the Progressive Era. Education, thought Dewey, could promote the natural movement of industrial society toward more fulfilling work, hence bringing its integrative and developmental functions increasingly into a harmonious union.

To complete our exposition of liberal theory, we must discuss the power of the educational system to promote social equality. For Dewey, of course, this power derives from the necessary association of personal growth and democracy—whose extension to all parts of the citizenry is a requisite of social development itself. In the technocratic version of liberal theory, however, the egalitarian power of the educational system is not automatically fulfilled. Were economic success dependent on race or sex, or upon deeply rooted differences in human character, the ability of schooling to increase social mobility would of course be minimal. But according to the modern liberal view, this is not the case. And where equal access is not sufficient, then enlightened policy may devise special programs for the education of the poor: job training, compensatory education, and the like.

Poverty and inequality, in this view, are the consequences of individual choice or personal inadequacies, not the normal outgrowths of our economic institutions. The problem, clearly, is to fix up the
people, not to change the economic structures which regulate their lives. This, indeed, is the meaning
of the "social power" of schools to promote equality.

Despite persistent setbacks in practice, the liberal faith in the equalizing power of schooling has
dominated both intellectual and policy circles. Education has been considered not only a powerful
tool for self-development and social integration; it has been seen, at least since Horace Mann coined
the phrase well over a century ago, as the "great equalizer."

Education and Inequality

Universal education is the power, which is destined to overthrow every species of hierarchy.
It is destined to remove all artificial inequality and leave the natural inequalities to find their
true level. With the artificial inequalities of caste, rank, title, blood, birth, race, color, sex, etc.,
will fall nearly all the oppression, abuse, prejudice, enmity, and injustice, that humanity is now
subject to. Lester Frank Ward, *Education* c. 1872

Much of the content of education over the past century and a half can only be construed as an unvar-
nished attempt to persuade the "many" to make the best of the inevitable. The unequal contest between
social control and social justice is evident in the total functioning of U.S. education. The system as it
stands today provides eloquent testimony to the ability of the well-to-do to perpetuate in the name
of equality of opportunity an arrangement which consistently yields to themselves disproportional
advantages, while thwarting the aspirations and needs of the working people of the United States.
However grating this judgment may sound to the ears of the undaunted optimist, it is by no means
excessive in light of the massive statistical data on inequality in the United States. Let us look at the
contemporary evidence.

We may begin with the basic issue of inequalities in years of schooling. As can be seen in Figure
4.1, the number of years of schooling attained by an individual is strongly associated with parental
socioeconomic status. This figure presents the estimated distribution of years of schooling attained
by individuals of varying socioeconomic backgrounds, If we define socioeconomic background by
a weighted sum of income, occupations, and educational level of the parents, a child from the ninetieth percentile may expect, on the average, five more years of schooling than a child in the tenth
percentile.[8]

A word about our use of statistics is in order. Most of the statistical calculations which we will
present have been published with full documentation in academic journals.... Those interested in
gaining a more detailed understanding of our data and methods are urged to consult our more technical articles.

The data, most of which was collected by the U.S. Census Current Populations Survey in 1962,
refers to "non-Negro" males, aged 25–64 years, from "non-farm" background in the experienced labor
force.[9] We have chosen a sample of white males because the most complete statistics are available for
this group. Moreover, if inequality for white males can be documented, the proposition is merely
strengthened when sexual and racial differences are taken into account.

Additional census data dramatize one aspect of educational inequalities: the relationship between
family income and college attendance. Even among those who had graduated from high school in
the early 1960s, children of families earning less than $3,000 per year were over six times as likely
not to attend college as were the children of families earning over $15,000.[10] Moreover, children from
less well-off families are *both* less likely to have graduated from high school and more likely to attend

inexpensive, two-year community colleges rather than a four-year B.A. program if they do make it to college.[11]

Not surprisingly, the results of schooling differ greatly for children of different social backgrounds. Most easily measured, but of limited importance, are differences in scholastic achievement. If we measure the output of schooling by scores on nationally standardized achievement tests, children whose parents were themselves highly educated outperform the children of parents with less education by a wide margin. Data collected for the U.S. Office of Education Survey of Educational Opportunity reveal, for example, that among white high school seniors, those whose parents were in the top education decile were, on the average, well over three grade levels in measured scholastic achievement ahead of those whose parents were in the bottom decile.[12]

Given these differences in scholastic achievement, inequalities in years of schooling among individuals of different social backgrounds are to be expected. Thus one might be tempted to argue that the close dependence of years of schooling attained on background displayed in the left-hand bars of Figure 4.1 is simply a reflection of unequal intellectual abilities, or that inequalities in college attendance are the consequences of differing levels of scholastic achievement in high school and do not reflect any additional social class inequalities peculiar to the process of college admission.

This view, so comforting to the admissions personnel in our elite universities, is unsupported by the data, some of which is presented in Figure 4.1. The right-hand bars of Figure 4.1 indicate that even among children with identical IQ test scores at ages six and eight, those with rich, well-educated, high status parents could expect a much higher level of schooling than those with less-favored origins. Indeed, the closeness of the left-hand and right-hand bars in Figure 4.1 shows that only a small portion of the observed social class differences in educational attainment is related to IQ differences across social classes.[13,14] The dependence of education attained on background is almost as strong for

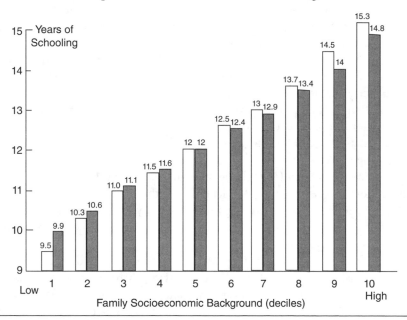

Figure 4.1 Educational attainments are strongly dependent on social background even for people of similar childhood IQs.

Notes: For each socioeconomic group, the left-hand bar indicates the estimated average number of years of schooling attained by all men from that group. The right-hand bar indicates the estimated average number of years of schooling attained by men with IQ scores equal to the average for the entire sample. The sample refers to "non-Negro" men of "nonfarm" backgrounds, aged 35–44 years in 1962.[14]

Source: Samuel Bowles and Valerie Nelson, "'The Inheritance of IQ,' and the Intergenerational Transmission of Economic Inequality," *The Review of Economics and Statistics,* Vol. LVI, No. 1. February 1974. Reprinted by persmission.

individuals with the same IQ as for all individuals. Thus, while Figure 4.1 indicates that an individual in the ninetieth percentile in social class background is likely to receive five more years of education than an individual in the tenth percentile, it also indicated that he is likely to receive 4.25 more years schooling than an individual from the tenth percentile with the same IQ. Similar results are obtained when we look specifically at access to college education for students with the same measured IQ. Project Talent data indicates that for "high ability" students (top 25 percent as measured by a composite of tests of "general aptitude"), those of high socioeconomic background (top 25 percent as measured by a composite of family income, parents' education, and occupation) are nearly twice as likely to attend college than students of low socioeconomic background (bottom 25 percent). For "low ability" students (bottom 25 percent), those of high social background are more than four times as likely to attend college as are their low social background counterparts.[15]

Inequality in years of schooling is, of course, only symptomatic of broader inequalities in the educational system. Not only do less well-off children go to school for fewer years, they are treated with less attention (or more precisely, less benevolent attention) when they are there. These broader inequalities are not easily measured. Some show up in statistics on the different levels of expenditure for the education of children of different socioeconomic backgrounds. Taking account of the inequality in financial resources for each year in school and the inequality in years of schooling obtained, Jencks estimated that a child whose parents were in the top fifth of the income distribution receives roughly twice the educational resources in dollar terms as does a child whose parents are in the bottom fifth.[16]

The social class inequalities in our school system, then, are too evident to be denied. Defenders of the educational system are forced back on the assertion that things are getting better; the inequalities of the past were far worse. And, indeed, there can be no doubt that some of the inequalities of the past have been mitigated. Yet new inequalities have apparently developed to take their place, for the available historical evidence lends little support to the idea that our schools are on the road to equality of educational opportunity. For example, data from a recent U.S. Census survey reported in Spady indicate that graduation from college has become no less dependent on one's social background. This is true despite the fact that high-school graduation is becoming increasingly equal across social classes.[17] Additional data confirm this impression. The statistical association (coefficient of correlation) between parents' social status and years of education attained by individuals who completed their schooling three or four decades ago is virtually identical to the same correlation for individuals who terminated their schooling in recent years.[18] On balance, the available data suggest that the number of years of school attained by a child depends upon family background as much in the recent period as it did fifty years ago.

Thus, we have empirical reasons for doubting the egalitarian impact of schooling. But what of those cases when education has been equalized? What has been the effect. We will investigate three cases: the historical decline in the inequality among individuals in years of school attained, the explicitly compensatory educational programs of the War on Poverty, and the narrowing of the black/white gap in average years of schooling attained.

Although family background has lost none of its influence on how far one gets up the educational ladder, the historical rise in the minimum legal school-leaving age has narrowed the distance between the top and bottom rungs. Inequality of educational attainments has fallen steadily and substantially over the past three decades.[19] And has this led to a parallel equalization of the distribution of income? Look at Figure 4.2. The reduction in the inequality of years of schooling has not been matched by an equalization of the U.S. income distribution,[20] In fact, a recent U.S. Labor Department study indicates that as far as labor earnings (wages and salaries) are concerned, the trend since World War II has been unmistakably away from equality. And it is precisely inequality in labor earnings which is the target of the proponents of egalitarian school reforms.[21] But does the absence of an overall trend toward income

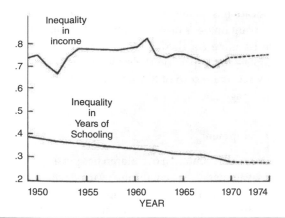

Figure 4.2 Equalization of education has not been associated with equalization of income.

Notes: The upper line shows the trend over time in the degree of inequality of income, as measured by the standard deviation of the natural logarithm of annual income of males aged twenty-five or older. The lower line shows the trend over time in the degree of inequality of years of schooling, as measured by the coefficient of variation (the standard deviation divided by the mean) of the years of schooling attained by males aged twenty-five and older. Data for 1970 to 1974 are estimates based on U.S. Census data.

Source: Barry Chiswick and Jacob Mincer, "Time Series Changes in Personal Income Inequality in the U.S.," *Journal of Political Economy*, Vol. 80, No. 3, Part II (May–June 1972).

equality mask an equalizing thrust of schooling that was offset by other disequalizing tendencies? Perhaps, but Jacob Mincer and Barry Chiswick of the National Bureau of Economic Research, in a study of the determinants of inequality in the United States, concluded that the significant reduction in schooling differences among white male adults would have had the effect—even if operating in isolation—of reducing income inequality by a negligible amount.[22]

Next, consider that group of explicitly egalitarian educational programs brought together in the War on Poverty. In a systematic economic survey of these programs, Thomas Ribich concludes that with very few exceptions, the economic payoff to compensatory education is low.[23] So low, in fact, that in a majority of cases studied, direct transfers of income to the poor would have accomplished considerably more equalization than the education programs in questions. The major RAND Corporation study by Averch came to the same conclusion.

Lastly, consider racial inequalities. In 1940, most black male workers (but a minority of whites) earned their livelihoods in the South, by far the poorest region; the education gap between nonwhites and whites was 3.3 years (38 percent of median white education).[24] By 1972, blacks had moved to more affluent parts of the country, and the education gap was reduced to 18 percent (4 percent for young men aged 25–34 years).[25] Richard Freeman has shown that this narrowing of the education gap would have virtually achieved black/white income equality had blacks received the same benefits from education as whites.[26] Yet the income gap has not closed substantially: The income gap for young men is 30 percent, despite an education gap of only 4 percent.[27] Clearly as blacks have moved toward educational (and regional) parity with whites, other mechanisms—such as entrapment in center-city ghettos and suburbanization of jobs, and perhaps increasing segmentation of labor markets—have intensified to maintain a more or less constant degree of racial income inequality. Blacks certainly suffer from educational inequality, but the root of the their exploitations lies outside of education, in a system of economic power and privilege in which racial distinctions play an important role.

The same must be concluded of inequality of economic opportunity between men and women. Sexual inequality persists despite the fact that women achieve a level of schooling (measured in years) equivalent to men.

We conclude that U.S. education is highly unequal, the chances of attaining much or little schooling being substantially dependant on one's race and parents' economic level. Moreover, where there is a discernible trend toward a more equal educational system—as in the narrowing of the black educational deficit for example—the impact on the structure of economic opportunity is minimal at best. As we shall presently see, the record of the U.S. school system as a promoter of full human development is no more encouraging.

Education and Personal Development

While the educational practice of regimentation of children has persisted, the fundamentalist conception of a child as immoral or savage has given way, through various stages, to a more appreciative view. To modern educators, the child appears as the primitive embodiment of the good and the natural—the noble savage, if you will. Children are spontaneous and joyful, unpredictable and trusting—traits to be cherished but sadly evanescent in the path toward maturity.[28]

At the same time, the educator's view of the family has changed. Once the trusted engine of moral training for youth, to which the school was considered a complement and ballast, the family increasingly appears in the writings of educators as the source of the child's inadequacy. Thus in the thought of the culture of poverty and cultural deprivation advocates, the school has been elevated to the status of family surrogate in the well engineered Society.[29] The social roots of this transformed concept of the family-school relationship have little to do with any alteration in family structure, and less to do with any heightening of the public morality. The impetus stems rather from the professional educator's profound mistrust of, and even fear of, the families of black and poor children, and in an earlier period, of Irish and other immigrant families.[30] Nor is this mistrust alien to the logic of social control. For all its nobility, the noble savage remains savage, and integration into the world of adults requires regimentation.

The most striking testimonial to the hegemony of the social-control ideology is perhaps its clear primacy even among those who opposed such obvious manifestations of the authoritarian classroom as corporal punishment and teacher-centered discussion. The most progressive of progressive educators have shared the commitment to maintaining ultimate top-down control over the child's activities. Indeed, much of the educational experimentation of the past century can be viewed as attempting to broaden the discretion and deepen the involvement of the child while maintaining hierarchical control over the ultimate processes and outcomes of the educational encounter. The goal has been to enhance student motivation while withholding effective participation in the setting of priorities.

Hence, like the view of the child, the concept of discipline has itself changed. Two aspects of this change are particularly important. First, the once highly personalized authority of the teacher has become a part of the bureaucratic structure of the modern school. Unlike the teachers in the chaotic early nineteenth-century district schools, modern teachers exercise less personal power and rely more heavily on regulations promulgated by higher authorities. Although frequently prey to arbitrary intervention by parents and other community members, the nineteenth-century teacher was the boss of the classroom. The modern teacher is in a more ambiguous position. The very rules and regulations which add a patina of social authority to his or her commands at the same time rigidly circumscribe the teacher's freedom of action.

Second, the aim of discipline is no longer mere compliance: The aim is now "behavior modification." Prompt and obedient response to bureaucratically sanctioned authority is, of course, a must, But sheer coercion is out of keeping with both the modern educator's view of the child and the larger social needs for a self-controlled not just controlled-citizenry and work force. Discipline is still the theme, but the variations more often center on the "internalization of behavioral norms," on equipping the child with a built-in supervisor than on mere obedience to external authority and material sanctions.[31]

The repressive nature of the schooling process is nowhere more clearly revealed than in the system of grading, the most basic process of allocating rewards within the school. We will have gone some distance toward comprehending the school as it is—in going behind the educational rhetoric—if we can answer the question: Who gets what and why?

Teachers are likely to reward those who conform to and strengthen the social order of the school with higher grades and approval, and punish violators with lower grades and other forms of disapproval, independent of their respective academic and cognitive accomplishments. This fact allows us to investigate exactly what personality traits, attitudes, and behavioral attributes are facilitated by the educational encounter.

Outside of gross disobedience, one would suspect the student's exhibition of creativity and divergence of thought to be most inimical to the smooth functioning of the hierarchical classroom. For the essence of the modern educational encounter is, to use Paolo Freire's words, that teaching:

> …becomes an act of depositing, in which the students are the depositories and the teacher is the depositor. Instead of communicating, the teacher issues communiques and makes deposits which the student patiently receive, memorize, and repeat. This is the "banking" concept of education.… The teacher teaches and the students are taught.… The teacher chooses and enforces his choice and the students comply. The teacher acts and the students have the illusion of acting through the action of the teacher.[32]

Others refer to this conception as the "jug and mug" approach to teaching whereby the jug fills up the mugs.

Thus the hostility of the school system to student behavior even approaching critical consciousness should be evident in the daily lives of students. Getzels and Jackson[33] have shown that high school students perceive this to be the case. They subjected a group of 449 high school students to an IQ test and a battery of exams which purport to measure creativity.[34] They found no appreciable correlation between measured IQ and measured "creativity." The top 20 percent in IQ on the one hand, and in creativity on the other, were singled out and asked to rank certain personality traits (a) on the degree to which they would like to have these traits, and (b) on the degree to which they believed teachers would like the student to have. There was virtually complete agreement by the high IQ and the high creatives on which traits are preferred by teachers; in other words, these students view the demands made upon them in a similar way. However, the two groups disagreed on what traits they themselves would like to have: The correlation between the two groups' ratings of the personality traits "preferred for oneself" was quite low.[35] Most striking of all, however, was the finding that, while the high IQs' "preferred traits" correspond closely to their perception of the teachers' values, the high creatives ranking of preferred traits was actually inversely related to the perceived teachers' ranking.[36] The high creatives do not fail to conform; rather they do not wish to conform.[37]

Getzel and Jackson's is but one of the many studies which link personality traits to school grades. We have undertaken a review of this literature, the results of which support the following interpretation.[38] Students are rewarded for exhibiting discipline, subordinancy, intellectually as opposed to emotionally oriented behavior, and hard work independent from intrinsic task motivation. Moreover, these traits are rewarded independently of any effect of "proper demeanor" on scholastic achievement.

Rather than plowing through this mass of data, we shall present the results of the most extensive of our sources. In the early 1960s, John L. Holland undertook a study of the determinants of high school success among a group of 639 National Merit Scholarship finalists—males for the most part in the top 10 percent of students in IQ and the top 15 percent in class rank.[39] Holland collected four objective measures of cognitive development from his subjects' College Entrance Examination Board tests.[40] In addition, he collected some sixty-five measures of personality, attitude, self-concept, creativity, and home life through testing the students, their parents, and obtaining various ratings from their teachers.[41]

We have extensively analyzed this massive body of data.[42] Our first conclusion is that, while the group's high academic rank is doubtless related to their above-average IQs, differences in scholastic achievement among them were not significantly related to their grades, despite a good deal of variation in both achievement and grades within the group. More telling, however, is the fact that many of the personality variables were significantly and positively related to grades. Most important were the teachers' ratings of the students' *Citizenship* and the students' self evaluation of *Drive to Achieve*.[43] Neither of these variables had any significant impact on actual achievement measures!

These results are not in themselves surprising. It is to be expected that students will be rewarded for their conformity to the social order of the school *(Citizenship)* as well as their personal motivation to succeed within the nexus of this social order *(Drive to Achieve)*. Only the most naive would expect school grades to depend on scholastic achievement alone.

But what do *Citizenship* and *Drive to Achieve* really reflect? In a liberated educational encounter, we would expect these traits to embody some combination of diligence, social popularity, creativity, and mental flexibility. Yet statistical analysis *of* the Holland data reveals a strikingly different pattern. Students who are ranked by their teachers as high on *Citizenship* and *Drive to Achieve* are indeed more likely to be diligent (e.g., they are high on such measures as *Deferred Gratification, Perseverance,* and *Control*) and socially popular (e.g., they are high on *Social Leadership* and *Popularity*). But they are, in fact, significantly below average on measures of creativity and mental flexibility (e.g., they are low on such measures as *Cognitive Flexibility, Complexity of Thought, Originality, Creativity,* and *Independence of Judgment*).[44] Moreover, further statistical analysis shows that these same traits of creativity and mental flexibility are directly penalized in terms of school grades, holding constant test scores, *Citizenship,* and *Drive to Achieve.*

The conclusions from this body of data seem inescapable. Conformity to the social order of the school involves submission to a set of authority relationships which are inimical to personal growth. Instead of promoting a healthy balance among the capacity for creative autonomy, diligence, and susceptibility to social regulation, the reward system of the school inhibits those manifestations of personal capacity which threaten hierarchical authority.

We have emphasized elements on the "hidden curriculum" faced in varying degrees by all students. But schools do different things to different children. Boys and girls, blacks and whites, rich and poor are treated differently. Affluent suburban schools, working-class schools, and ghetto schools all exhibit a distinctive pattern of sanctions and rewards. Moreover, most of the discussion here has focused on high-school students. In important ways, colleges are different; and community colleges exhibit social relations of education which differ sharply from those of elite four-year institutions. In short, U.S. education is not monolithic; our analysis will be expanded accordingly in future chapters.

Why do schools reward docility, passivity, and obedience? Why do they penalize creativity and spontaneity? Why the historical constancy of suppression and domination in an institution so central to the elevation of youth? Surely this is a glaring anomaly in terms of traditional liberal educational theory. The naive enthusiasm of the contemporary free-school movement suggests the implicit assumption that no one bad ever tried to correct this situation—that the ideal of liberated education is simply a new conception which has never been tried. Even sophisticated critics, such as Charles Silberman, tend to attribute the oppressiveness of schooling to simple oversight and irrationality:

> What is mostly wrong with public schools is not due to venality or indifference or stupidity but to mindlessness...It simply never occurs to more than a handful, to ask why they are doing

what they are doing to think seriously or deeply about the purposes or consequences of education.[45]

Yet, the history of the progressive-education movement attests to the intransigence of the educational system to "enlightened change" within the context of corporate capitalism.

Progressivism has been the keynote of modern educational theory embracing such pillars of intellect and influence as John Dewey, Charles W. Elliot, Alfred North Whitehead, William James, and G. Stanley Hall. The birth of the Association for the Advancement of Progressive Education in 1918 was merely the political codification of an already active social movement whose aim, in the words of its founder Stanwood Cobb, "...had little of modesty.... We aimed at nothing short of changing the entire school system of America."[46] Subscribing to Dewey's dictum that "... education is the fundamental method of social reform,...." the statement of principles of the Association for the Advancement of Progressive Education had its aim to be "...the truest and fullest development of the individual, based upon the scientific study of his mental, physical, spiritual, and social characteristics and needs."[47] However avant-garde today's liberal educationists feel themselves to be, they envision little more than did the Progressives in the dawning years of the century. Schooling was to provide the child with the freedom to develop "naturally" with a teacher as guide, not taskmaster. Intrinsic interest not external authority was to motivate all work. The leitmotif of the day was "taking the lid off kids," and the aim was to sublimate natural creative drives in fruitful directions rather than to repress them. Emotional and intellectual development were to hold equal importance, and activity was to be "real life" and "student directed."

The mass media dramatically attest to the ideological victory of the Progressives: Professional journals, education textbooks, and even the various publications of the U.S. Office of Education mouthed the rhetoric of Progressivism. As Lawrence A. Cremin, a foremost historian of the Progressive Movement in education, notes:

> There is a "conventional wisdom"... in education... and by the end of World War II progressivism had come to be that conventional wisdom. Discussions of educational policy were liberally spiced with phrases like "recognized individual differences," "personality development," "the whole child," "the needs of learners," "intrinsic motivation," "persistent life situations," "bridging the gap between home and school," "teaching children, not subjects," "adjusting the school to the child," "real-life experiences," "teacher pupil relationships," and "staff planning." Such phrases... signified that Dewey's forecast of the day when progressive education would eventually be accepted as good education had now finally come to pass.[48]

Yet the schools have changed little in substance.

Thus we must reject mindlessness along with venality, indifference, and stupidity as the source for oppressive education. A more compelling explanation of the failure to combat repression in U.S. schooling is simply that progressive education, though triumphant in educational theory, was never given a chance in practice. Indeed, this argument is often used by those adhering to the liberal perspective. Thus Raymond E. Callahan traces the failure of Progressivism to the growing preoccupation with order and efficiency in educational practice at the same time that progressive education was capturing hearts and minds in educational theory. Callahan argues that:

> ... Very much of what has happened in American education since 1900 can be explained on the basis of the extreme vulnerability of our schoolmen to public criticism and pressure and that this vulnerability is built into our pattern of local support and control.[49]

The direction the formal educational system took in this situation was dictated by the power of business interests and the triumphant ideology of "efficient management." Again Callahan:

> What was unexpected (in my investigation) was the extent not only of the power of the business-industrial groups, but of the strength of the business ideology. I had expected more professional autonomy and I was completely unprepared for that extent and degree of capitulation by administrators to whatever demands were made upon them.[50]

This vulnerability had great implications for student, teacher, and administrator alike. "Business methods" in schools meant that administrators were to be recruited from the ranks of politicians and especially businessmen, rather than professional educators, and their orientation was toward cost-saving and control rather than quality of education. Business methods also meant that the teacher was to be reduced to the status of a simple worker, with little control over curriculum, activities, or discipline, and whose accountability to the administrator again involved classroom authority rather than the quality of classroom experience. Lastly, the student was reduced to an "object" of administration, "busy-work," and standardized tests coming to prevail over play and self-development.

In short, the history of twentieth-century education is the history not of Progressivism but of the imposition upon the schools of "business values" and social relationships reflecting the pyramid of authority and privilege in the burgeoning capitalist system. The evolution of U.S. education during this period was not guided by the sanguine statements of John Dewey and Jane Addams, who saw a reformed educational system eliminating the more brutal and alienating aspects of industrial labor. Rather, the time motion orientation of Frederick Taylor and "Scientific Management," with its attendant fragmentation of tasks, and imposition of bureaucratic forms and top-down control held sway.

Thus there are some grounds for the opinion that the modern liberal view of the self-development capacities of schooling has not been falsified by recent U.S. experience; rather it has never been tried. A historian of Progressivism in U.S. education might well echo Gandhi's assessment of Western civilization: "It would be a good idea."

A Preface to the Critique of Liberal Educational Reform

> Ignorance is the mother of industry as well as of superstition. Reflection and fancy are subject to err; but a habit of moving the hand or the foot is independent of either. Manufacture, accordingly, prospers most where the mind is least consulted, and where the workshop may . . . be considered an engine, the parts of which are men.—Adam Ferguson, *An Essay on the History of Civil Society,* 1767

Decades of broken promises cast strong doubt on modern liberal educational theory. But the anomalies which arise when theory and practice are juxtaposed cannot lay it finally to rest. As Thomas Kuhn has noted, even in the physical sciences, only a recognizably superior alternative seals the fate of faulty but generally accepted dogma.[51]

All the more true is this observation in the social sciences. In the case of liberal educational theory, the failures of educational reform we have presented are by no means decisive. The "necessary connection" among the integrative, egalitarian, and developmental functions of education may appear only in the long run. Capitalism may still be young, and does seem to promote a rhetoric of tolerance and egalitarianism, as well as a supreme emphasis on individualism and human development. That this rhetoric is consistently thwarted in practice may simply represent a perverse institutional inertia. While educational policy has failed in the past, maturity and increased expertise may render it vastly more potent in the future. No one ever claimed reform to be easy—only ultimately possible with proper dedication. Finally, there may be tangible limits—technologically determined—to the degree of social mobility, due to inherent differences in mental ability. The possibility has been asserted forcefully by such writers as Arthur Jensen and Richard Herrnstein.[52]

In short, decent respect for liberal theory demands it be critiqued on theoretical grounds as well as in terms of the social outcomes it predicts, and, preferably with an alternative in mind. This will be our goal. While detailed presentation of our alternative will await future chapters, our argument may be summarized simply enough here: the failure of progressive educational reforms stems from the contradictory nature of the objectives of its integrative, egalitarian and developmental functions in a society whose economic life is governed by the institutions of corporate capitalism.

Both the democratic and technocratic versions of liberal education theory focus on the relationships into which individuals enter upon adulthood. In Dewey's democratic version, political life is singled out as central, while for the technocratic version, the technical aspects of production hold the honored position. Both have been blind to—or at least treated in quite unrealistic manner—the social relationships of capitalist production. Dewey's overall framework seems eminently correct. His error lies in characterizing the social system as democratic, whereas, in fact, the hierarchical division of labor in the capitalist enterprise is politically autocratic. Moreover, his central thesis as to the economic value of an educational system devoted to fostering personal growth is untrue in capitalist society. Dewey's view requires that work be a natural extension of intrinsically motivated activity. The alienated work of corporate life is inimical to intrinsic motivation.

In corporate capitalist society, the social relations of production conform, by and large, to the "hierarchical division of labor," characterized by power and control emanating from the top downward through a finely gradated bureaucratic order.[53] The social relationships of the typically bureaucratic corporate enterprise require special attention because they are neither democratic nor technical.

For Dewey, democracy is, in essence, "…a mode of conjoint communicative experience…" which "…repudiates the principle of external authority…in favor of voluntary disposition and interest." In this sense, the dominant forms of work for which the educational system prepares youth are profoundly antidemocratic. Under capitalism, work is characterized not by conjoint, but by hierarchical "communicative experience," and rigid patterns of dominance and subordinacy, where personal interaction is dictated primarily by rules of procedure set by employers: Dewey's "voluntary disposition" of the worker extends only over the decision to work or starve.

Dewey is of course aware of the undemocratic control of production in capitalist society; indeed, he refers explicitly to "…those in control of industry—those who supply its aims." But he avoids the fatal consequence of this admission for his theory by de-emphasizing democratic process and focusing on outcomes: the quality of the decision made by industrial aristocrats. The dehumanized nature of work in Dewey's time, exemplified by Taylorism and time-motion studies, and today, by the "human relations" school of organizational theory—is attributed to their "one-sided stimulations of thought," and hence responsive to liberal educational exposure. Here Dewey exhibits in raw form the liberal proclivity to locate the source of systemic failures in the shortcomings of individuals aim to propose "expert" solutions which respect—even reinforce—the top-down control of social life under corporate capitalism.[54] Surely he could not have been unaware of the forces in a market-oriented economy forcing managerial decision continually toward profit maximization to which end secure hierarchical authority and flexible control of the enterprise from the top are prime requisites.[55]

Similarly, the technocratic version of liberal educational theory suffers from an extremely partial characterization of the capitalist system. The major error in the technocratic school is its overemphasis on cognitive skills as the basic requirement of job adequacy. We shall show that cognitive requirements are by no means determinant, and indeed, can account for little of the association of education and economic success, Had the technocratic school looked at the social rather than the technical relations of production, it might have been more circumspect in asserting the compatibility of the integrative, egalitarian, and developmental functions of schooling. Indeed, it might have found that the way in which the school system performs its integrative function—through its production of stratified labor force for the capitalist enterprise—is inconsistent with its performance of either developmental or egalitarian functions. Focusing on cognitive variables, it cannot even entertain the idea that the correspondence between the social relations of production and the social relations of education—the essential mechanism of the integrative function of schooling—might preclude an egalitarian or truly humanistic education.

Thus the modern economy is a product of a social as well as a technical revolution. In the development of productive organization from precapitalist forms, through the relativity simple entrepreneur-worker relationship of the early factory system based on piecework, immediate supervision, and direct worker assessment to the modern complex, stratified, and bureaucratically ordered corporation or governmental organ, not simply the technical demands of work, but its social organization have changed drastically. Seen from the present, the Industrial Revolution may appear as a simple upgearing of the pace of technological change. From the point of view of those experiencing it, however, it constituted a thorough-going social upheaval involving not only radically new institutions in the governance of economic activity, but a radically different pattern of social interactions with demanding and pervasive requirements on the level of individual psychic functioning. Values, beliefs, modes of personal behavior, and patterns of social and economic loyalties were formed, transformed, and reproduced in the process of bringing the individual into line with the needs of capital accumulation and the extension of the wage labor system.

Conclusion

Of manufactures, of commerce, of both individual and national prosperity, nay even of science itself, the extended and abundant increase tends to complete the fatal circle: and, by decay, convulsion, anarchy, and misery, to produce a new and renovated order of things. In an advanced state of society, where the meridian is attained or passes, nothing can prevent or even protract the evil day, except the revivifying influence of education.—Thomas Bernard, "Extract from an account of the Mendip Schools," *Report of the Society for the Better Condition of the Poor,* 1799

The record of actual successes and failures of education as reform is not sufficient either to accept or to reject the liberal outlook. But it must be a point of departure in any serious inquiry into its potential contribution to social improvement. The record, as we have shown, is not encouraging. First, despite the concerted efforts of progressive educators of three generations, and despite the widespread assimilation of their vocabulary in the United States, schools, by and large, remain hostile to the individual's needs for personal development. Second, the history of U.S. education provides little support for the view that schools have been vehicles for the equalization of economic status or opportunity. Nor are they today. The proliferation of special programs for the equalization of educational opportunity had precious little impact on the structure of the U.S. education, and even less on the structure of income and opportunity in the U.S. economy. It is clear that education in the United States is simply too weak an influence on the distribution of economic status and opportunity to fulfill its promised mission as the Great Equalizer. Schooling remains a meager instrument in promoting full participation of racial minorities in the United States—indeed, even the expensive pilot projects in this direction seem to have failed rather spectacularly.

The educational system serves—through the correspondence of its social relations with those of economic life—to reproduce economic inequality and to distort personal development. Thus under corporate capitalism, the objectives of liberal educational reform are contradictory: It is precisely because of its role as producer of an alienated and stratified labor force that the educational system has developed its repressive and unequal structure. In the history of U.S. education, it is the integrative function which has dominated the purpose of schooling, to the detriment of the other liberal objectives.

More fundamentally, the contradictory nature of liberal educational reform objectives may be directly traced to the dual role imposed on education in the interests of profitability and stability; namely, enhancing workers' productive capacities and perpetuating the social, political, and economic conditions for the transformation of the fruits of labor into capitalist profits. It is these overriding objectives of the capitalist class—not the ideals of liberal reformers—which have shaped the actuality of U.S. education, had left little room for the school to facilitate the pursuit of equality or full human development. When education is viewed as an aspect of the reproduction of the capitalist division of labor, the history of school reforms in the United States appears less as a story of an enlightened but sadly unsuccessful corrective and more as an integral part of the process of capitalist growth itself.

We cannot rule out the possibility that a future dramatic and unprecedented shift toward equality of educational opportunity might act as a force for equality. Nor do we exclude the possibility that open classrooms and free schools might make a substantial contribution to a more liberating process of human development. Indeed, we strongly support reforms of this type is part of a general strategy of social and economic transformation. But to consider educational change in isolation from other social forces is altogether too hypothetical. The structure of U.S. education did not evolve in a vacuum; nor will it be changed, holding other things constant. Education has been historically a device for allocating individuals to economic positions, where inequality among the positions themselves is inherent in the hierarchal division of labor, differences in the degree of monopoly power of various sectors of the economy, and the power of different occupational groups to limit the supply or increase the monetary returns to their services. Thus equalization of educational outcomes, rather than reducing inequality, would more likely simply shift the job of allocating individuals to economic positions to some other "institution." Similarly, a less repressive educational system will produce little more than the "job blues" unless it can make an impact upon the nature of work and the control over production.

This much, at least, we can say with some certainty: Repression, individual powerlessness, inequality of incomes, and inequality of opportunity did not originate historically in the educational system, nor do they derive from unequal and repressive schools today. The roots of repression and inequality lie in the structure and functioning of the capitalist economy. Indeed, we shall suggest in the next chapter that they characterize any modern economic system—including the socialist state—which denies people participatory control of economic life.

Notes

1. John Dewey, *Democracy and Education* (New York: The Free Press, 1966), p. 20.
2. *Ibid.*, pp. 50–53.
3. Theodore W. Schultz, "Investment in Poor People," Seminar on Manpower Policy and Programs, Office of Manpower Policy Evaluation Research, Washington: Department of Labor, 1966.
4. Harvey Averch *et al.*, "How Effective Is Schooling: A Critical Review and Synthesis of Research Findings" (Santa Monica: The Rand Corporation, 1972).
5. Samuel Bowles and Herbert Gintis, "IQ in the U.S. Class Structure," in *Social Policy*, November–December 1972 and January–February 1973.
6. Arthur A. Jensen, "How Much Can We Boost IQ and Scholastic Achievement?" *Havard Educational Review*, Vol. 39, No. 1, 1969; Richard Herrnstein, "IQ," *Atlantic Monthly*, Vol. 228, No, 3, September 1971; Edward C. Banfield, *The Unheavenly City* (Boston: Little, Brown and Company, 1968); Daniel P. Moynihan and Nathan Glazer, *Beyond the Melting Pot* (Cambridge, Mass.: MIT Press, 1970).
7. Dewey (1966), *op. cit.*, p. 20.
8. This calculation is based on data reported in full in Samuel Bowles and Valerie Nelson, "The 'Inheritance of IQ' and the Intergenerational Transmission of Economic Inequality," *The Review of Economics and Statistics*, Vol. LVI, No.1, February 1974. It refers to non-Negro males from non-farm backgrounds, aged 35–44 years. The zero-order correlation coefficient between socioeconomic background and years of schooling was estimated at 0.646. The estimated standard deviation of years of schooling was 3.02. The results tor other age groups are similar.
9. See Appendix A, footnote 14, in Chapter 4 and the following sources: Bowles and Nelson (1974), *op. cit.* Peter Blau and Otis D. Duncan, *The American Occupational Structure* (New York: John Wiley, 1967); Otis D. Duncan, D. C. Featherman, and Beverly Duncan, *Socioeconomic Background and Occupational Achievement, Final Report,* Project No, S-0074 (EO-191) (Washington, D.C.: Department of Health, Education and Welfare, Office of Education, 1968); Samuel Bowles, "Schooling and Inequality from Generation to Generation," *The Journal of Political Economy,* Vol. 80, No.3, Part II, May-

June 1972.

10. These figures refer to individuals who were high-schoo! seniors in October, 1965, and who subsequently graduated from high school. College attendance refers to both two- and four-year institutions, Family income is for the twelve months preceding October 1965. Data is drawn from U.S. Bureau of the Census, *Current Population Reports,* Series P-60, No. 183, May 1969.

11. For further evidence, see U.S. Bureau of the Census (1969), *op. cit.,* and Jerome Karabel, "Community Colleges and Social Stratification," *Harvard Educational Review,* Vol. 424, No. 42, November 1972.

12. Calculation based on data in James S. Coleman *et al., Equality of Educational Opportunity* (Washington, D.C.: U.S. Government Printing Office, 1966), and Bowles and Gintis (1972), *op. cit.*

13. The data relating to IQ are from a 1966 survey of veterans by the National Opinion Research Center; and from N. Bayley and E. S. Schaefer, "Correlations of Material and Child Behaviors with the Development of Mental Ability: Data from the Berkeley Growth Study," *Monographs of Social Research in Child Development,* 29, 6 (1964).

14. This figure is based on data reported in full in our Appendix A and in Bowles and Nelson (1974), *op. cit.* The left-hand bars of each pair were calculated using the estimated corrdation coefficient between socioeconomic background and education of 0.65. The results for other age groups were similar: 0.64 for ages 25–34 and 44–54, and 0.60 for ages 55–64 years. The right-hand bars were calculated from thc normalized regression coefticient on socioeconomic background from an equation using background and early childhood IQ to predict years of schooling, which was estimated at 0.54. The results for other age groups were similar: 0.54 for ages 25–34 and 45–54, and 0.48 for ages 55–64. Socioeconomic background is defined as normalized sum of father's education, father's occupational status, and parents' income. The mean and standard deviation of years of schooling were estimated at 11.95 and 3.02, respectively.

15. Based on a large sample of U.S. high-school students as reported in: John C. Flannagan and William. W. Cooley, *Project Talent, One Year Follow-up Study,* Cooperative Research Project, No. 2333, University of Pittsburgh: School of Education, 1966.

16. Christopher Jencks *et al., Inequality: A Reassessment of the Effects of Family* and *Schooling in America* (New York: Basic Books, 1972), p.48.

17. William L. Spady, "Educational Mobility and Access: Growth and Paradoxes," in *American Journal of Sociology,* Vol. 73, No. 3, November 1967; and Blau and Duncan, *op. cit.* (1967).

18. Blau and Duncan (1967), *op. cit.* See the reported correlations in Appendix A.

19. We estimate the coefficient of variation of years of schooling at about 4.3 in 1940 (relying on Barry Chiswick and Jacob Mincer, "Time Series Changes in Personal Income Inequality in the U.S." *Journal of Political Economy,* Vol. 80, No. 3, Part II [May–June 1972], Table 4 tor the standard deviation of schooling and the Decennial Census for the mean), and at 2.95 in 1969 (relying on Chiswick and Mincer [1972] Table B10).

20. Calculated from Table B1 and Table B10 in Chiswick and Mincer (1972), *op. cit.*

21. Peter Henle, "Exploring the Distribution of Earned Income," *Monthly Labor Review,* Vol. 95, No. 12, December 1972. Inequalities in income (profit, rent interest, and transfer payments plus labor earnings) may also have increased if the unmeasured income from capital gain and other tax shelters for the rich are taken into acount. See Jerry Cromwell, "Income Inequalities, Discrimination and Uneven Development," unpublished Ph.D. dissertation, Harvard University, May 1974.

22. Chiswick and Mincer (1972), op. *cit.*

23. Thomas I. Ribich, *Education and Poverty* (Washington, D.C.: Brookings Institution, 1968).

24. United States Bureau of the Census, *Current Population Reports,* Series P-60, October 1970, Table 75, p. 368.

25. United States Bureau of the Census, *Curren. Population Reports,* series P-60, November, 1972, Table 1, p. 14.

26. Michael Reich, *Racial Discrimination and the Distribution of Income,* Ph.D. dissertation, Harvard University, May 1973.

27. United States Bureau of the Census, *op. cit.* (Dccember 1973), Table 47, p. 114.

28. Whence e. e. cummings' sharp lines: "...the children knew, but only a few/ and down they forgot as up they grew." e. e. cummings, *Poems, 1923–1954* (New York: Harcourt, Brace and World, 1954), p. 370.

29. cf. Charles Valentine, *Culture and Poverty* (Chicago: University of Chicago Press, 1968). Early in the nineteenth century, Robert Dale Owen, the renowned utopian, had proposed that the interests of social equality dictated that the children of the poor be raised in public institutions.

30. Tyack (1967), *op. cit.;* Katz (1971), *op. cit.*

31. In Chapter 5 we will argue that both changes in the approach to discipline reflect the changing social relationships of production in the corporate capitalist economy.

32. Paulo Freire, *Pedagogy of the Oppressed* (New York: Herder and Herder, 1972), pp. 58–59.

33. J. W. Getzels and P. W. Jackson, "Occupational Choice and Cognitive Functioning," in *Journal of Abnormal and Social Psychology,* February 1960.

34. For a general discussion of the content and meaning of creativity tests, see Michael W. Wallach, *The Intelligence of Creativity Distinction* (New York: General Learning Corporation, 1971),

35. The exact correlation was r = 0.41.

36. The correlations between own and teacher's desired personality traits were r = 0.67 for the high IQs and r = 0.25 for the high creatives.

37. Both groups had similar scores on tests of achievement motivation—McClelland n-ach and Strodtbeck V-score,

38. Herbert Gintis, "Education, Technology, and the Characteristics of Worker Productivity," *American Economic Review,* May 1971.

39. John L. Holland, "Creative and Academic Performance Among Talented Adolescents," *Journal of Educational Psychology,* No. 52, 1961.

40. Verbal and Mathematical sections of the Scholastic Achievement Test, Humanities and Scientific Comprehension.
41. The interested reader should consult Holland (1961), *op. cit.* and Herbert Gintis, *Alienation and Power,* Ph.D. dissertation for Harvard University, May 1969.
42. Gintis (1969), *op. cit.* and (1971), *op. cit.*
43. Holland's personality measures will be presented in italics. Unless otherwise indicated, all are statistically significant at the 1 percent level.
44. In addition to the good citizenship—externally motivated student, a small portion of the high *Drive to Achieve* students exhibit a set of personality traits quite similar to those of the *Deviant Creatives* described in Getzel and Jackson's study, already presented. These students, high on *Artistic Performance and Creative Activities,* evidently reject the pressure to define their personal goals in terms compatible with high grades and teacher approbation, and their positive personality traits are uniformly penalized in terms of grades and teacher ratings for *Citizenship.*
45. Charles Silberman (1971), *op. cit.*
46. As quoted in Lawrence Cremin (1964), *op. cit.,* p. 241.
47. *Ibid.,* pp. 240–241.
48. *Ibid.,* p. 328.
49. Raymond Callahan, *Education and the Cult of Efficiency* (Chicago; University of Chicago Press, 1962), preface.
50. *Ibid.*
51. Thomas S. Kuhn, *The Structure of Scientific Revolutions (Chicago:* The University of Chicago Press, 1962), p. 53.
52. Arthur A. Jensen, *Educability and Group Differences* (New York: Harper & Row, 1973); and Richard Herrnstein, *IQ in the Meritocracy* (Boston: Little, Brown and Company, 1973).
53. For a more complete discussion, see Richard C. Edwards, Michael Reich, and Thomas Weisskopf, *The Capitalist System* (Englewood Cliffs, NJ: Prentice-Hall, 1972); André Gorz, "Technical Intelligence and the Capitalist Division of Labor," *Telos,* Summer 1972; and Chapter 3.
54. Clarence Karier, *Shaping the American Educational State: 1900 to the Present* (New York: The Free Press, 1975); and Clarence Karier, Joel Spring, and Paul C. Violas (1973), *op. cit.*
55. Indeed, it has been pointed out to us by Dr. F. Bohnsack in a personal communication that Dewey did begin to revise his views, especially after World War I:

For this later time, at least, I would doubt whether we could say he characterized the social system as democratic. He saw and criticized the totalitarian features of existing society and the missing "... intrinsic growth orientation of education." As self development and equality of opportunity, to him, were inconsistent with preparing workers for existing [alienated] jobs, he criticized such a preparation and wanted to change existing industrial education as well as industrial work.

See A. G. Wirth, *The Vocational-Liberal Studies Controversy between John Dewey and Others (1900–1917)* (Washington, D.C., 1970), and John Dewey, "Education vs. Trade-training," *The New Republic,* Vol. 3, No. 15, May 1915.

As Virginia Held has pointed out to us, Dewey, in his mature work, *Art as Experience* (New York: Minton, Balch and Company, 1934), went further to claim:

The labor and employment problem of which we are so acutely aware cannot be solved by mere changes in wage, hours of work, and sanitary conditions. No permanent solution is possible save in a radical alteration, which affects the degree and kind of participation the worker has in the production and social disposition of the wares he produces. (p. 343)

5

On Understanding the Processes of Schooling

The Contributions of Labeling Theory

RAY C. RIST

There have been few debates within American education which have been argued with such passion and intensity as that of positing causal explanations of success or failure in schools.[1] One explanation which has had considerable support in the past few years, particularly since the publication of *Pygmalion in the Classroom* by Rosenthal and Jacobson (1968), has been that of the "self-fulfilling prophecy." Numerous studies have appeared seeking to explicate the mechanisms by which the teacher comes to hold certain expectations of the students and how these are then operationalized within the classroom so as to produce what the teacher had initially assumed. The origins of teacher expectations have been attributed to such diverse variables as social class, physical appearance, contrived test scores, sex, race language patterns, and school records. But from the flurry of recent research endeavors, there has emerged a hiatus between this growing body of data and any larger theoretic framework. The concept of the self-fulfilling prophecy has remained simply that—a concept. The lack of a broader conceptual scheme has meant that research in this area has become theoretically stymied. Consequently, there has evolved instead a growing concern over the refinement of minute methodological nuances.

The thrust of this [article] is to argue that there is a theoretical perspective developing in the social sciences which can break the conceptual and methodological logjam building up on the self-fulfilling prophecy. Specifically, the emergence of *labeling theory* as an explanatory framework for the study of social deviance appears to be applicable to the study of education as well. Among the major contributions to the development of labeling theory are Becker, 1963, 1964; Broadhead, 1974; Lemert, 1951, 1972, 1974; Douglas, 1971, 1972; Kitsuse, 1964; Loffland, 1969; Matza, 1964, 1969; Scheff, 1966; Schur, 1971; Scott and Douglas, 1972; and Rubington and Weinberg, 1973.

If the labeling perspective can be shown to be a legitimate framework from which to analyze social processes influencing the educational experience and the contributions of such processes to success or failure in school, there would then be a viable *interactionist* perspective to counter both biological and cultural determinists' theories of educational outcomes. While the latter two positions both place ultimate causality for success or failure *outside* the school, the labeling approach allows for an examination of what, in fact, is happening *within* schools. Thus, labeling theory would call our attention for example, to the various evaluative mechanisms (both formal and informal) operant in schools, the ways in which schools nurture and support such mechanisms, how students react, what the outcomes are for interpersonal interaction based on how these mechanisms have evaluated individual students, and how, *over time,* the consequences of having a certain evaluative tag influence the options available to a student within a school. What follows first is a summary of a number of the key aspects of labeling theory as it has been most fully developed in the sociological literature; second is an attempt to integrate the research on the self-fulfilling prophecy with the conceptual framework of labeling theory. Finally, the implications of this synthesis are explored for both future research and theoretical development.

Becoming Deviant: The Labeling Perspective

Those who have used labeling theory have been concerned with the study of *why* people are labeled, and *who* it is that labels them as someone who has committed one form or another of deviant behavior. In sharp contrast to the predominant approaches for the study of deviance, there is little concern in labeling theory with the motivational and characterological nature of the person who committed the act.

Deviance is understood, not as a quality of the person or as created by his actions, but instead as created by group definitions and reactions. It is a social judgment imposed by a social audience. As Becker (1963:9) has argued:

> The central fact of deviance is that it is created by society. I do not mean this in the way it is ordinarily understood, in which the causes of deviance are located in the social situation of the deviant, or the social factors, which prompted his action. I mean, rather, that social groups create deviants by making the rules whose infraction constitute deviance, and by applying those rules to particular people and labeling them as outsiders. From this point of view, *deviance is not the quality of the act the person commits, but rather a consequence of the application by others of rules and sanctions to an "offender." This deviant is one to whom the label has been successfully applied. Deviant behavior is behavior that people so label.* (emphasis added)

The labeling approach is insistent on the need for a shift in attention from an exclusive concern with the deviant individual to a major concern with the *process* by which the deviant label is applied. Again citing Becker (1964:2):

> The labeling approach sees deviance always and everywhere as a process and interaction between at least two kinds of people: those who commit (or who are said to have committed) a deviant act, and the rest of the society, perhaps divided into several groups itself.... One consequence is that we become much more interested in the process by which deviants are defined by the rest of the society, than in the nature of the deviant act itself.

The important questions, then, for Becker and others, are not of the genre to include, for example: Why do some individuals come to act out norm-violating behavior? Rather, the questions are of the following sort: Who applied the deviant label to whom? Whose rules shall prevail and be enforced? Under what circumstances is the deviant label successfully and unsuccessfully applied? How does a community decide what forms of conduct should be singled out for this kind of attention? What forms of behavior do persons in the social system consider deviant, how do they interpret such behavior, and what are the consequences of these interpretations for their reactions to individuals who are seen as manifesting such behavior? (See Akers, 1973.)

The labeling perspective rejects any assumption that a clear consensus exists as to what constitutes a norm violation—or for that matter, what constitutes a norm—within a complex and highly heterogeneous society. What comes to be determined as deviance and who comes to be determined as a deviant is the result of a variety of social contingencies influenced by who has the power to enforce such determinations. Deviance is thus problematic and subjectively given. The case for making the societal reaction to rulebreaking a major independent variable in studies of deviant behavior has been succinctly stated by Kitsuse (1964:101):

A sociological theory of deviance must focus specifically upon the interactions which not only define behaviors as deviant, but also organize and activate the application of sanctions by individuals, groups, or agencies. For in modern society, the socially significant differentiation of deviants from the nondeviant population is increasingly contingent upon circumstances of situation, place social, and personal biography, and the bureaucratically organized activities of agencies of social control.

Traditional notions of who is a deviant and what are the causes for such deviance are necessarily reworked. By emphasizing the processual nature of deviance, any particular deviant is seen to be a product of being caught, defined, segregated, labeled, and stigmatized. *This is one of the major thrusts of the labeling perspective—that forces of social control often produce the unintended consequence of making some persons defined as deviant even more confirmed as deviant because of the stigmatization of labeling. Thus, social reactions to deviance further deviant careers.* Erikson (1966) has even gone so far as to argue that a society will strive to maintain a certain level of deviance within itself as deviance is functional to clarifying group boundaries, providing scapegoats, creating out-groups who can be the source of furthering in-group solidarity, and the like.

The idea that social control may have the paradoxical effect of generating more of the very behavior it is designed to eradicate was first elaborated upon by Tannenbaum. He noted (1938:21):

> The first dramatization of the "evil" which separates the child out of his group . . . plays a greater role in making the criminal than perhaps any other experience. . . . He now lives in a different world. He has been tagged. . . . The person becomes the thing he is described as being.

Likewise, Schur (1965:4) writes:

> The societal reaction to the deviant, then, is vital to an understanding of the deviance itself and a major element in—if not the cause of—the deviant behavior.

The focus on outcomes of social control mechanisms has led labeling theorists to devote considerable attention to the workings of organizations and agencies which function ostensibly to rehabilitate the violator or in other ways draw him back into conformity. Their critiques of prisons, mental hospitals, training schools, and other people-changing institutions suggest that the results of such institutions are frequently nearly the opposite of what they were theoretically designed to produce. These institutions are seen as mechanisms by which opportunities to withdraw from deviance are sealed off from the deviant, stigmatization occurs, and a new identity as a social "outsider" is generated. There thus emerges on the part of the person so labeled a new view of himself which is one of being irrevocably deviant.

This movement from one who has violated a norm to one who sees himself as a habitual norm violator is what Lemert (1972:62) terms the transition from a primary to a secondary deviant. A primary deviant is one who holds to socially accepted roles, views himself as a nondeviant, and believes himself to be an insider. A primary deviant does not deny that he has violated some norm, and claims only that it is not characteristic of him as a person. A secondary deviant, on the other hand, is one who has reorganized his social-psychological characteristics around the deviant role. Lemert (1972:62) writes:

> Secondary deviation refers to a special class of socially defined responses which people make to problems created by the societal reaction to their deviance. These problems . . . become central facts of existence for those experiencing them. . . . Actions, which have these roles and self-attitudes as their referents make up secondary deviance. The secondary deviant . . . is a person whose life and identity are organized around the facts of deviance.

A person can commit repeated acts of primary deviation and never come to view himself or have others come to view him as a secondary deviant. Secondary deviation arises from the feedback whereby misconduct or deviation initiates social reaction to the behavior which then triggers further misconduct. Lemert (1951:77) first described this process as follows:

> The sequence of interaction leading to secondary deviation is roughly as follows: 1) primary deviation; 2) societal penalties; 3) further primary deviation; 4) stronger penalties and rejections; 5) further deviations, perhaps with hostilities and resentments beginning to focus upon those doing the penalizing; 6) crisis reached in the tolerance quotient, expressed in formal action by the community stigmatizing of the deviant; 7) strengthening of the deviant conduct as a reaction to the stigmatizing and penalties; and 8) ultimate acceptance of deviant social status and efforts at adjustment on the basis of the associated role.

Thus, when persons engage in deviant behavior they would not otherwise participate in and when they develop social roles they would not have developed save for the application of social control measures, the outcome is the emergence of secondary deviance. The fact of having been apprehended and labeled is the critical element in the subsequent construction of a deviant identity and pursuit of a deviant career.

The Origins of Labeling: Teacher Expectations

Labeling theory has significantly enhanced our understanding of the process of becoming deviant by shifting our attention from the deviant to the judges of deviance and the forces that affect their judgment. Such judgments are critical, for a recurrent decision made in all societies, and particularly frequent in advanced industrial societies, is that an individual has or has not mastered some body of information, or perhaps more basically, has or has not the capacity to master that information. These evaluations are made periodically as one moves through the institution of school and the consequences directly affect the opportunities to remain for an additional period. To be able to remain provides an option for mastering yet another body of information, and to be certified as having done so. As Ivan Illich (1971) has noted, it is in industrial societies that being perceived as a legitimate judge of such mastery has become restricted to those who carry the occupational role of "teacher." A major consequence of the professionalization of the role of teacher has been the ability to claim as a near exclusive decision whether mastery of material has occurred. Such exclusionary decision-making enhances those in the role of "teacher" as they alone come to possess the authority to provide certification for credentials (Edgar, 1974).

Labeling theorists report that in making judgments of deviance, persons may employ information drawn from a variety of sources. Further, even persons within the same profession (therapists, for example) may make divergent use of the same material in arriving at an evaluative decision on the behavior of an individual. Among the sources of information available to labelers, two appear primary: first-hand information obtained from face-to-face interaction with the person they may ultimately label, and second-hand information obtained from other than direct interaction.

The corollary here to the activities of teachers should be apparent. Oftentimes, the evaluation by teachers (which may lead to the label of "bright," "slow," etc.) is based on first-hand information gained through face-to-face interaction during the course of the time the teacher and student spent together in the classroom. But a goodly amount of information about the student which informs the teacher's evaluation is second-hand information. For instance, comments from other teachers, test scores, prior report cards, permanent records, meetings with the parents, or evaluations from welfare agencies and psychological clinics are all potential informational sources. In a variation of the division between first-hand and second-hand sources of information, Johnson (1973) has suggested that there are three key determinants of teacher evaluations: student's prior performance, social status characteristics, and present performance. Prior performance would include information from cumulative records (grades, test scores, notes from past teachers or counselors, and outside evaluators) while social status and performance would be inferred and observed in the ongoing context of the classroom.

What has been particularly captivating about the work of Rosenthal and Jacobson (1968) in this regard is their attempt to provide empirical justification for a truism considered self-evident by many in education: School achievement is not simply a matter of a child's native ability, but involves directly and inextricably the teacher as well. Described succinctly, their research involved a situation where, at the end of a school year, more than 500 students in a single elementary school were administered the "Harvard Test of Inflected Acquisition." In actuality this test was a standardized, relatively nonverbal test of intelligence, Flanagan's (1960) Test of General Ability (TOGA). The teachers were told that such a test would, with high predictive reliability, sort out those students who gave strong indication of being intellectual "spurters" or "bloomers" during the following academic year. Just before the beginning of school the following fall, the teachers were given lists with the names of between one and nine of their students. They were told that these students scored in the top twenty percent of the school on the test, though, of course, no factual basis for such determinations existed. A twenty percent subsample of the "special" students was selected for intensive analysis. Testing of the students at the end of the school year offered some evidence that these selected children did perform better than the nonselected. The ensuing debate as to the validity and implications of the findings from the study will be discussed in the next section.

The findings of Deutsch, Fishman, Kogan, North, and Whiteman (1964); Gibson (1965): Goslin and Glass (1967); McPherson (1966); and Pequignot (1966) all demonstrate the influence of standardized tests of intelligence and achievement on teacher's expectations. Goaldman (1971), in a review of the literature on the use of tests as a second-hand source of information for teachers, noted: "Although some of the research has been challenged, there is a basis for the belief that teachers at all levels are prejudiced by information they receive about a student's ability or character." Mehan (1971, 1974) has been concerned with the interaction between children who take tests and the teachers who administer them. He posits that testing is not the objective use of a measurement instrument, but the outcome of a set of interactional activities which are influenced by a variety of contingencies which ultimately manifest themselves in a reified "test score." Mehan suggests (1971):

> Standardized test performances are taken as an unquestioned, non-problematic reflection of the child's underlying ability. The authority of the test to measure the child's real ability is accepted by both teachers and other school officials. Test results are accepted without doubt as the correct and valid document of the child's ability.

Characteristics of children such as sex and race are immediately apparent to teachers. Likewise, indications of status can be quickly inferred from grooming, style of dress, need for free lunches, information on enrollment cards, discussion of family activities by children, and visits to the school by parents. One intriguing study recently reported in this area is that by two sociologists, Clifford and Walster (1973:249). The substance of their study was described as follows:

> Our experiment was designed to determine what effect a student's physical attractiveness has on a teacher's expectations of the child's intellectual and social behavior. Our hypothesis was that a child's attractiveness strongly influences his teachers' judgments; the more attractive the child, the more biased in his favor we expect the teachers to be. The design required to test this hypothesis is a simple one: Teachers are given a standardized report card and an attached photograph. The report card includes an assessment of the child's academic performance as

well as of his general social behavior. The attractiveness of the photos is experimentally varied. On the basis of this information, teachers are asked to state their expectations of the child's educational and social potential.

Based on the responses of 404 fifth grade teachers within the state of Missouri, Clifford and Walster concluded (1973:255):

> There is little question but that the physical appearance of a student affected the expectations of the teachers we studied. Regardless of whether the pupil is a boy or girl, the child's physical attractiveness has an equally strong association with his teacher's reactions to him.

The variables of race and ethnicity have been documented, by Brown (1968), Davidson and Lang (1960), Jackson and Cosca (1974), and Rubovits and Maehr (1973), among others, as powerful factors in generating the expectations teachers hold of children. It has also been documented that teachers expect less of lower-class children than they do of middle-class children (cf. Becker, 1952; Deutsch, 1963; Leacock, 1969; Rist, 1970, 1973; Stein, 1971; Warner, Havighurst, and Loeb, 1944; and Wilson, 1963). Douglas (1964), in a large-scale study of the tracking system used in British schools, found that children who were clean and neatly dressed in nice clothing, and who came from what the teachers perceived as "better" homes, tended to be placed in higher tracks than their measured ability would predict. Further, when placed there they tended to stay and perform acceptably. Mackler (1969) studied schools in Harlem and found that children tended to stay in the tracks in which they were initially placed and that such placement was based on a variety of social considerations independent of measured ability. Doyle, Hancock, and Kifer (1971) and Palardy (1969) have shown teacher expectations for high performance in elementary grades to be stronger for girls than boys.

The on-going academic and interpersonal performance of the children may also serve as a potent source of expectations for teachers. Rowe (1969) found that teachers would wait longer for an answer from a student they believed to be a high achiever than for one from a student they believed to be a low achiever. Brophy and Good (1970) found that teachers were more likely to give perceived high achieving students a second chance to respond to an initial incorrect answer, and further, that high achievers were praised more frequently for success and criticized less for failure.

There is evidence that the expectations teachers hold for their students can be generated as early as the first few days of the school year and then remain stable over the months to follow (Rist, 1970, 1972, 1973; Willis, 1972). For example, I found during my three-year longitudinal and ethnographic study of a single, *de facto* segregated elementary school in the black community of St. Louis, that after only eight days of kindergarten, the teacher made permanent seating arrangements based on what she assumed were variations in academic capability. But no formal evaluation of the children had taken place. Instead, the assignments to the three tables were based on a number of socio-economic criteria as well as on early interaction patterns in the classroom. Thus, the placement of the children came to reflect the social class distinctions in the room—the poor children from public welfare families all sat at one table, the working class children sat at another and the middle class at the third. I demonstrated how the teacher operationalized her expectations of these different groups of children in terms of her differentials of teaching time, her use of praise and control, and the extent of autonomy within the classroom. By following the same children through first and second grade as well, I was able to show that the initial patterns established by the kindergarten teacher came to be perpetuated year after year. By second grade, labels given by another teacher clearly reflected the reality each of the three groups experienced in the school. The top group was called the "Tigers," the middle group the "Cardinals," and the lowest group, the "Clowns." What had begun as a subjective evaluation and labeling by the teacher took on objective dimensions as the school proceeded to process the children on the basis of the distinctions made when they first began.

Taken together, these studies strongly imply that the notion of "teacher expectations" is multi-faceted and multi-dimensional. It appears that when teachers generate expectations about their students, they do so not only for reasons of academic or cognitive performance, but for their classroom interactional patterns as well. Furthermore, not only ascribed characteristics such as race, sex, class, or ethnicity are highly salient, interpersonal traits are also. Thus, the interrelatedness of the various attributes which ultimately blend together to generate the evaluation a teacher makes as to what can be expected from a particular student suggests the strength and tenacity of such subsequent labels as "bright" or "slow" or "trouble-maker" or "teacher's little helper." It is to the outcomes of the student's having one or another of these labels that we now turn.

An Outcome of Labeling: The Self-Fulfilling Prophecy

W. I. Thomas, many years ago, set forth what has become a basic dictum of the social sciences when he observed, "If men define situations as real, they are real in their consequences." This is at the core of the self-fulfilling prophecy. An expectation which defines a situation comes to influence the actual behavior within the situation so as to produce what was initially assumed to be there. Merton (1968:477) has elaborated on this concept and noted: "The self-fulfilling phase is, in the beginning, a *false* definition of the situation evoking a new behavior which makes the originally false conception come true" (emphasis in the original).

Here it is important to recall a basic tenet of labeling theory—that an individual does not become deviant simply by the commission of some act. As Becker (1963) stressed, deviance is not inherent in behavior *per se,* but in the application by others of rules and sanctions against one perceived as being an "offender." Thus, the only time one can accurately be termed a "deviant" is after the successful application of a label by a social audience. Thus, though many persons may commit norm violations, only select ones are subsequently labeled. The contingencies of race, class, sex, visibility of behavior, age, occupation, and who one's friends are all influence the outcome as to whether one is or is not labeled. Scheff (1966), for example, demonstrated the impact of these contingencies upon the diagnosis as to the severity of a patient's mental illness. The higher one's social status, the less the willingness to diagnose the same behavioral traits as indicative of serious illness in comparison to the diagnosis given to low status persons.

The crux of the labeling perspective lies not in whether one's norm violating behavior is known, but in whether others decide to do something about it. Further, if a label is applied to the individual, it is posited that this in fact causes the individual to become that which he is labeled as being. Due to the reaction of society, the change in the individual involves the development of a new socialized self-concept and social career centered around the deviant behavior. As Rubington and Weinberg (1973:7) have written:

> The person who has been typed, in turn, becomes aware of the new definition that has been placed upon him by members of his groups. He, too, takes this new understanding of himself into account when dealing with them....When this happens, a social type has been ratified, and a person has been socially reconstructed.

Rosenthal and Jacobson's *Pygmalion in the Classroom* (1968) created wide interest in the notion of the self-fulfilling prophecy as a concept to explain differential performance by children in classrooms. Their findings suggested that the expectations teachers created about the children randomly selected as "intellectual bloomers" somehow caused the teachers to treat them differently, with the result that the children really did perform better by the end of the year. Though the critics of this particular research (Snow, 1969; Taylor, 1970; Thorndike, 1968, 1969) and those who have been unsuccessful in

BISHOP BURTON COLLEGE LIBRARY

replicating the findings (Claiborn, 1969) have leveled strong challenges to Rosenthal and Jacobson, the disagreements are typically related to methodology, procedure, and analysis rather than to the proposition that relations exist between expectations and behavior.

The current status of the debate and the evidence accumulated in relation to it imply that teacher expectations are *sometimes* self-fulfilling. The early and, I think, overenthusiastic accounts of Rosenthal and Jacobson have obscured the issue. The gist of such accounts have left the impression, as Good and Brophy (1973:73) have noted, that the mere existence of an expectation will automatically guarantee its fulfillment. Rather, as they suggest:

> The fact that teachers' expectations can be self-fulfilling is simply a special case of the principle that any expectations can be self-fulfilling. This process is not confined to classrooms. Although it is not true that "wishing can make it so," our expectations do affect the way we behave in situations, and the way we behave affects how other people respond. In some instances, our expectations about people cause us to treat them in a way that makes them respond just as we expect they would.

Such a position would be borne out by social psychologists who have demonstrated that an individual's first impressions of another person do influence subsequent interactions (Dailey, 1952; Newcomb, 1947) and that one's self-expectations influence one's subsequent behavior (Aronson and Carlsmith, 1962; Brock and Edelman, 1965; Zajonc and Brinkman, 1969).

The conditionality of expectations related to their fulfillment is strongly emphasized by labeling theorists as well. Their emphasis upon the influence of social contingencies on whether one is labeled, how strong the label, and if it can be made to stick at all, points to a recognition that there is a social process involved where individuals are negotiating, rejecting, accepting, modifying, and reinterpreting the attempts at labeling. Such interaction is apparent in the eight stages of the development of secondary deviance outlined above by Lemert. Likewise, Erikson (1964:17), in his comments on the act of labeling as a rite of passage from one side of the group boundary to the other, has noted:

> The common assumption that deviants are not often cured or reformed, then, may be based on a faulty premise, but this assumption is stated so frequently and with such conviction that it often creates the facts which later "prove" it to be correct. If the returning deviant has to face the community's apprehensions often enough, it is understandable that he, too, may begin to wonder whether he has graduated from the deviant role—and *so respond to the uncertainty by resuming deviant activity.* In some respects, this may be the only way for the individual and his community to agree as to what kind of person he really is, for it often happens that the community is only able to perceive his "true colors" when he lapses, momentarily into some form of deviant performance. (emphasis added)

Explicit in Erikson's quote is the fact of the individual's being in interaction with the "community" to achieve some sort of agreement on what the person is "really" like. Though Erikson did not, in this instance, elaborate upon what he meant by "community," it can be inferred from elsewhere in his work that he sees "community" as manifesting itself in the institutions persons create in order to help organize and structure their lives. Such a perspective is clearly within the framework of labeling theory, where a major emphasis has been placed upon the role of institutions in sorting, labeling, tracking, and channeling persons along various routes depending upon the assessment the institution has made of the individual.

One pertinent example of the manner in which labeling theory has been applied to the study of social institutions and their impact upon participants has been in an analysis of the relation of schooling to juvenile delinquency. There have been several works which suggest as a major line of argument that schools, through and because of the manner in which they label students, serve as a chief instrument in the creation of delinquency (Hirschi, 1969; Noblit and Polk, 1975; Polk 1969; Polk and Schafer, 1972; Schafer and Olexa, 1971). For example, Noblit and Polk (1975:3) have noted:

> In as much as the school is the primary institution in the adolescent experience—one that promises not only the future status available to the adolescent, but also that gives or denies status in adolescence itself—it can be expected that its definitions are of particular significance for the actions of youth. That is, the student who has been reported from success via the school has little reason to conform to the often arbitrary and paternalistic regulations and rules of the school. In a very real sense, this student has no "rational constraints" against deviance. It is through the sorting mechanisms of the school, which are demanded by institutions of higher education and the world of work, that youth are labeled and thus sorted into the situation where deviant behavior threatens little while providing some alternative forms of status.

It is well to reiterate the point—interaction implies behavior and choices being made by both parties. The person facing the prospect of receiving a new label imputing a systemic change in the definition of his selfhood may respond in any of a myriad number of ways to this situation. Likewise, the institutional definition of the person is neither finalized nor solidified until the end of the negotiation as to what precisely that label should be. But, in the context of a single student facing the authority and vested interests of a school administration and staff, the most likely outcome is that over time, the student will increasingly move towards conformity with the label the institution seeks to establish. Good and Brophy (1973:75) have elaborated upon this process within the classroom as follows:

1. The teacher expects specific behavior and achievement from particular students.
2. Because of these different expectations, the teacher behaves differently toward the different students.
3. This teacher treatment tells each student what behavior and achievement the teacher expects from him and affects his self-concept, achievement motivation, and level of aspiration.
4. If this teacher treatment is consistent over time, and if the student does not actively resist or change it in some way, it will tend to shape his achievement and behavior. High-expectation students will be led to achieve at high levels, while the achievement of low-expectations students will decline.
5. With time, the student's achievement and behavior will conform more and more closely to that originally expected of him.

The fourth point in this sequence makes the crucial observation that teacher expectations are not automatically self-fulfilling. For the expectations of the teacher to become realized, both the teacher and the student must move towards a pattern of interaction where expectations are clearly communicated and the behavioral response is consonant with the expected patterns. But as Good and Brophy (1973:75) also note:

> This does not always happen. The teacher may not have clear-cut expectations about a particular student, or his expectations may continually change. Even when he has consistent expectations, he may not necessarily communicate them to the student through consistent behavior. In this case, the expectation would not be self-fulfilling even if it turned out to be correct. Finally, the student himself might prevent expectations from becoming self-fulfilling by overcoming them or by resisting them in a way that makes the teacher change them.

Yet, the critique of American education offered by such scholars as Henry (1963), Katz (1971), Goodman (1964), or Reimer (1971) suggests the struggle is unequal between the teacher (and the institution a teacher represents) and the student. The vulnerability of children to the dictates of adults in positions of power over them leaves the negotiations as to what evaluative definition will be tagged on the children more often than not in the hands of the powerful. As Max Weber himself stated, to have power is to be able to achieve one's ends, even in the face of resistance from others. When that resistance is manifested in school by children and is defined by teachers and administrators as truancy, recalcitrance, unruliness, and hostility, or conversely defined as a lack of motivation, intellectual apathy, sullenness, passivity, or withdrawal, the process is ready to be repeated and the options to escape further teacher definitions are increasingly removed.

Postscript: Beyond the Logjam

This paper has argued that a fruitful convergence can be effected between the research being conducted on the self-fulfilling prophecy as a consequence of teacher expectations and the conceptual framework of labeling theory. The analysis of the outcomes of teacher expectations produces results highly similar to those found in the study of social deviance. Labels are applied to individuals which fundamentally shift their definitions of self and which further reinforce the behavior which had initially prompted the social reaction. The impact of the self-fulfilling prophecy in educational research is comparable to that found in the analysis of mental health clinics, asylums, prisons, juvenile homes, and other people-changing organizations. What the labeling perspective can provide to the study of educational outcomes as a result of the operationalization of teacher expectations is a model for the study of the *processes* by which the outcomes are produced. The detailing over time of the interactional patterns which lead to changes in self-definition and behavior within classrooms is sadly lacking in almost all of the expectation research to date. A most glaring example of this omission is the study by Rosenthal and Jacobson themselves. Their conclusions are based only on the analysis of a pre- and post-test. To posit that teacher expectations were the causal variable that produced changes in student performances was a leap from the data to speculation. They could offer only suggestions as to how the measured changes in the children's performance came about, since they were not in the classrooms to observe how assumed teacher attitudes were translated into subsequent actual student behavior.

To extend the research on the educational experiences of those students who are differentially labeled by teachers, what is needed is a theoretical framework which can clearly isolate the influences and effects of certain kinds of teacher reactions on certain types of students, producing, certain typical outcomes. The labeling perspective appears particularly well-suited for this expansion of both research and theoretical development on teacher expectations by offering the basis for analysis at either a specific or a more general level. With the former, for example, there are areas of investigation related to 1) types of students perceived by teachers as prone to success or failure; 2) the kinds of reactions, based on their expectations, teachers have to different students; and 3) the effects of specific teacher reactions on specific student outcomes. At a more general level, fruitful lines of inquiry might include 1) the outcomes in the post-school world of having received a negative vs. a positive label within the school; 2) the influences of factors such as social class and race on the categories of expectations teachers hold; 3) how and why labels do emerge in schools as well as the phenomenological and structural meanings that are attached to them; and 4) whether there are means by which to modify or minimize the effects of school labeling processes on students.

Labeling theory provides a conceptual framework by which to understand the processes of transforming attitudes into behavior and the outcomes of having done so. To be able to detail the dynamics and influences within schools by which some children come to see themselves as successful and act as though they were, and to detail how others come to see themselves as failures and act accordingly, provides in the final analysis an opportunity to intervene so as to expand the numbers of winners and diminish the numbers of losers. For that reason above all others, labeling theory merits our attention.

Note

1. The preparation of this paper has been aided by a grant (GS-41522) from the National Science Foundation—Sociology Program. The views expressed here are solely those of the author and no official endorsement by either the National Science Foundation or the National Institute of Education is to be inferred.

References

Akers, R. L. *Deviant Behavior: A Social Learning Approach.* Belmont, Cal.: Wadsworth, 1973.

Aronson, E., and Carlsmith, J. M. "Performance Expectancy as a Determinant of Actual Performance." *Journal of Abnormal and Social Psychology* 65 (1962):179–182.

Becker, H. S. "Social Class Variations in the Teacher–Pupil Relationship." *Journal of Educational Sociology* 25 (1952):451–465.

Becker, H. S. *Outsiders.* New York: The Free Press, 1963.

Becker, H. S. *The Other Side.* New York: The Free Press, 1964.

Broadhead, R. S. "A Theoretical Critique of the Societal Reaction Approach to Deviance." *Pacific Sociological Review* 17 (1974):287–312.

Brock, T. C., and Edelman, H. "Seven Studies of Performance Expectancy as a Determinant of Actual Performance." *Journal of Experimental Social Psychology* 1 (1965):295–310.

Brophy, J., and Good, T. "Teachers' Communications of Differential Expectations for Children's Classroom Performance: Some Behavioral Data." *Journal of Educational Psychology* 61 (1970):365–374.

Brown, B. *The Assessment of Self-Concept among Four Year Old Negro and White Children: A Comparative Study Using the Brown IDS Self-Concept Reference Test.* New York: Institute for Developmental Studies, 1968.

Claiborn, W. L. "Expectancy Effects in the Classroom: A Failure to Replicate." *Journal of Educational Psychology* 60 (1969):377–383.

Clifford, M. M., and Walster, E. "The Effect of Physical Attractiveness on Teacher Expectations." *Sociology of Education* 46 (1973):248–258.

Dailey C. A. "The Effects of Premature Conclusion upon the Acquisition of Understanding of a Person." *Journal of Psychology* 33 (1952):133–152.

Davidson, H. H., and Lang. G. "Children's Perceptions of Teachers' Feelings toward Them." *Journal of Experimental Education* 29 (1960): 107–118.

Deutsch, M. "The Disadvantaged Child and the Learning Process." in *Education in Depressed Areas,* edited by H. Passow. New York: Teachers College Press, 1963.

Deutsch, M., Fishman, J. A., Kogan, L., North, R., and Whiteman, M. "Guidelines for Testing Minority Group Children." *Journal of Social Issues* 20 (1964): 129–145.

Douglas. J. *The Home and the School.* London: MacGibbon and Kee, 1964.

Douglas, J. *The American Social Order.* New York: The Free Press, 1971.

Douglas, J. (ed.). *Deviance and Respectability.* New York: Basic Books, 1972.

Doyle, W., Hancock, G., and Kifer, E. "Teachers' Perceptions: Do They Make a Difference?" Paper presented at the meeting of the American Educational Research Association, 1971.

Edgar, D. E. *The Competent Teacher.* Sydney, Australia: Angus & Robertson, 1974.

Erikson, K. T. "Note on the Sociology of Deviance," in *The Other Side,* edited by H. S. Becker. New York: The Free Press, 1964.

Erikson, K. T, *Wayward Puritans.* New York: Wiley, 1966.

Flanagan, J. C. *Test of General Ability: Technical Report.* Chicago: Science Research Associates, 1960.

Gibson, G. "Aptitude Tests." *Science* 149 (1965):583.

Goaldman, L. "Counseling Methods and Techniques: The Use of Tests," in *The Encyclopedia of Education,* edited by L. C. Deighton. New York: Macmillan, 1971.

Good, T., and Brophy, J. *Looking in Classrooms.* New York: Harper and Row, 1973.

Goodmam, P. *Compulsory Mis-Education* New York: Random House, 1964.

Goslin, D. A., and Glass, D. C. "The Social Effects of Standardized Testing on American Elementary Schools." *Sociology of Education* 40 (1967): 115–131.

Henry, J. *Culture Against Man.* New York: Random House, 1963.

Hirschi, T. *Causes of Delinquency.* Berkeley: University of California Press, 1969.

Illich, I. *Deschooling Society.* New York: Harper and Row, 1971.

Jackson, G., and Cosca, C. "The Inequality of Educational Opportunity in the Southwest: An Observational Study of Ethnically Mixed Classrooms." *American Educational Research Journal* 11 (1974):219–229.

Johnson, J. *On the Interface between Low income Urban Black Children and Their Teachers during the Early School Years: A Position Paper.* San Francisco: Far West Laboratory for Educational Research and Development. 1973.

Katz, M. Class, *Bureaucracy and Schools.* New York: Praeger, 1971.

Kitsuse, J. "Societal Reaction to Deviant Behavior: Problems of Theory and Method," in *The Other Side,* edited by H. S. Becker. New York: The Free Press, 1964.

Leacock, E. *Teaching and Learning in City Schools.* New York: Basic Books, 1969.

Lemert, E. *Social Pathology.* New York: McGraw-Hill, 1951.

Lemert, E. *Human Deviance, Social Problems and Social Control.* Englewood Cliffs, N.J.: Prentice-Hall, 1972.

Lemert, E. "Beyond Mead: The Societal Reaction to Deviance." *Social Problems* 21 (1974):457–468.

Lofland, J. *Deviance and Identity.* Englewood Cliffs, N.J.: Prentice-Hall, 1969.

Mackler, B. "Grouping in the Ghetto." *Education and Urban Society* 2 (1969):80–95.

Matza, D. *Delinquency and Drift.* New York: Wiley, 1964.

Matza, D. *Becoming Deviant.* Englewood Cliffs, N.J.: Prentice-Hall, 1969.

McPherson, G. H. *The Role-set of the Elementary School Teacher: A case study.* Unpublished Ph.D. dissertation, Columbia University, New York, 1966.

Mehan, H. B. *Accomplishing Understanding in Educational Settings.* Unpublished Ph.D. dissertation, University of California, Santa Barbara, 1971.

Mehan, H. B. *Ethnomethodology and Education.* Paper presented to the Sociology of Education Association conference, Pacific Grove, California, 1974.

Merton, R. K. "Social Problems and Social Theory," in *Contemporary Social Problems,* edited by R. Merton and R. Nisbet. New York: Harcourt, Brace and World, 1968.

Newcomb, T. M. "Autistic Hostility and Social Reality." *Human Relations* 1 (1947):69–86.

Noblit, G. W., and Polk, K. *Institutional Constraints and Labeling.* Paper presented to the Southern Sociological Association meetings, Washington, D.C., 1975.

Palardy, J. M. "What Teachers Believe—What Children Achieve." *Elementary School Journal,* 1969, pp. 168–169 and 370–374.

Pequignot, H. "L'équation Personnelle du Juge." In *Semaine des Hopitaux* (Paris), 1966.

Polk, K. "Class, Strain, and Rebellion and Adolescents." *Social Problems* 17 (1969):214–224.

Polk, K., and Schafer, W. E. *Schools and Delinquency.* Englewood Cliffs, N.J.: Prentice-Hall, 1972.

Reimer, E. *School Is Dead.* New York: Doubleday, 1971.

Rist, R. C. "Student Social Class and Teachers' Expectations: The Self-fulfilling Prophecy in Ghetto Education." *Harvard Educational Review* 40 (1970):411–450.

Rist, R. C. "Social Distance and Social Inequality in a Kindergarten Classroom: An Examination of the 'Cultural Gap' Hypothesis." *Urban Education* 7 (1972):241–260.

Rist, R. C. *The Urban School: A Factory for Failure.* Cambridge, Mass.: The M.I.T. Press, 1973.

Rosenthal, R., and Jacobson, L. "Teachers' Expectancies: Determinants of Pupils' IQ Gains." *Psychology Reports* 19 (1966):115–118.

Rosenthal, R., and Jacobson, L. *Pygmalion in the Classroom.* New York: Holt, Rinehart and Winston, 1968.

Rowe, M. "Science, Silence and Sanctions." *Science and Children* 6 (1969):11–13.

Rubington, E., and Weinberg, M. S. *Deviance: The Interactionist Perspective.* New York: Macmillan, 1973.

Rubovits, P., and Maehr, M. L. "Pygmalion Black and White." *Journal of Personality and Social Psychology* 2 (1973):210–218.

Schafer, W. E., and Olexa, C. *Tracking and Opportunity.* Scranton, Pa.: Chandler, 1971.

Scheff, T. *Being Mentally Ill.* Chicago; Aldine, 1966.

Schur, E. *Crimes without Victims.* Englewood Cliffs, N.J.: Prentice-Hall, 1965.

Schur, E. *Labeling Deviant Behavior.* New York: Harper and Row, 1971.

Scott, R. A., and Douglas, J. C. (eds.). *Theoretical Perspectives on Deviance.* New York: Basic Books, 1972.

Snow, R. E. "Unfinished Pygmalion." *Contemporary Psychology* 14 (1969):197–199.

Stein, A. "Strategies for Failure." *Harvard Educational Review* 41 (1971):158–204.

Tannenbaum, F. *Crime and the Community.* New York: Columbia University Press, 1938.

Taylor, C. "The Expectations of Pygmalion's Creators." *Educational Leadership* 28 (1970):161–164.

Thorndike, R. L. "Review of Pygmalion in the Classroom." *Educational Research Journal* 5 (1968): 708–711.

Thorndike, R. L. "But Do You Have to Know How to Tell Time?" *Educational Research Journal* 6 (1969):692.

Warner, W. L.; Havighurst, R.; and Loeb, M.B. *Who Shall be Educated?* New York: Harper and Row, 1944.

Willis, S. *Formation of Teachers' Expectations of Student Academic Performance.* Unpublished Ph.D. dissertation, University of Texas, Austin, Texas, 1972.

Wilson, A. B. "Social Stratification and Academic Achievement," in *Education in Depressed Areas,* edited by H. Passow. New York: Teachers College Press, 1963.

Zajonc, R. B., and Brinkman, P. "Expectancy and Feedback as Independent Factors in Task Performance." *Journal of Personality and Social Psychology* 11 (1969):148–150.

6

The Forms of Capital

PIERRE BOURDIEU

The social world is accumulated history, and if it is not to be reduced to a discontinuous series of instantaneous mechanical equilibria between agents who are treated as interchangeable particles, one must reintroduce into it the notion of capital and with it, accumulation and all its effects. Capital is accumulated labor (in its materialized form or its 'incorporated,' embodied form) which, when appropriated on a private, i.e., exclusive, basis by agents or groups of agents, enables them to appropriate social energy in the form of reified or living labor. It is a *vis insita*, a force inscribed in objective or subjective structures, but it is also a *lex insita*, the principle underlying the immanent regularities of the social world. It is what makes the games of society—not least, the economic game—something other than simple games of chance offering at every moment the possibility of a miracle. Roulette, which holds out the opportunity of winning a lot of money in a short space of time, and therefore of changing one's social status quasi-instantaneously, and in which the winning of the previous spin of the wheel can be staked and lost at every new spin, gives a fairly accurate image of this imaginary universe of perfect competition or perfect equality of opportunity, a world without inertia, without accumulation, without heredity or acquired properties, in which every moment is perfectly independent of the previous one, every soldier has a marshal's baton in his knapsack, and every prize can be attained, instantaneously, by everyone, so that at each moment anyone can become anything. Capital, which, in its objectified or embodied forms, takes time to accumulate and which, as a potential capacity to produce profits and to reproduce itself in identical or expanded form, contains a tendency to persist in its being, is a force inscribed in the objectivity of things so that everything is not equally possible or impossible.[1] And the structure of the distribution of the different types and subtypes of capital at a given moment in time represents the immanent structure of the social world, i.e., the set of constraints, inscribed in the very reality of that world, which govern its functioning in a durable way, determining the chances of success for practices.

It is in fact impossible to account for the structure and functioning of the social world unless one reintroduces capital in all its forms and not solely in the one form recognized by economic theory. Economic theory has allowed to be foisted upon it a definition of the economy of practices which is the historical invention of capitalism; and by reducing the universe of exchanges to mercantile exchange, which is objectively and subjectively oriented toward the maximization of profit, i.e., (economically) *self-interested*, it has implicitly defined the other forms of exchange as noneconomic, and therefore *disinterested*. In particular, it defines as disinterested those forms of exchange which ensure the *transubstantiation* whereby the most material types of capital—those which are economic in the restricted sense—can present themselves in the immaterial form of cultural capital or social capital and vice versa. Interest, in the restricted sense it is given in economic theory cannot be produced without producing its negative counterpart, disinterestedness. The class of practices whose explicit purpose is to maximize monetary profit cannot be defined as such without producing the purposeless finality of cultural or artistic practices and their products; the world of bourgeois man, with his double-entry accounting, cannot be invented without producing the pure, perfect universe of the artist and the intellectual and the gratuitous activities of art-for-art's sake and pure theory. In other words, the constitution of a science of mercantile relationships which, inasmuch as it takes for granted the very foundations of the order it claims to analyze—private property, profit, wage labor, etc.—is not even a science of the field of economic production, has prevented the constitution of a general science of the economy of practices, which would treat mercantile exchange as a particular case of exchange in all its forms.

It is remarkable that the practices and assets thus salvaged from the 'icy water of egotistical calculation' (and from science) are the virtual monopoly of the dominant class—as if economism had been able to reduce everything to economics only because the reduction on which that discipline is based protects from sacrilegious reduction everything which needs to be protected. If economics deals only with practices that have narrowly economic interest as their principle and only with goods that are directly and immediately convertible into money (which makes them quantifiable), then the universe of bourgeois production and exchange becomes an exception and can see itself and present itself as a realm of disinterestedness. As everyone knows, priceless things have their price, and the extreme difficulty of converting certain practices and certain objects into money is only due to the fact that this conversion is refused in the very intention that produces them, which is nothing other than the denial (*Verneinung*) of the economy. A general science of the economy of practices, capable of reappropriating the totality of the practices which, although objectively economic, are not and cannot be socially recognized as economic, and which can be performed only at the cost of a whole labor of dissimulation or, more precisely, *euphemization*, must endeavor to grasp capital and profit in all their forms and to establish the laws whereby the different types of capital (or power, which amounts to the same thing) change into one another.[2]

Depending on the field in which it functions, and at the cost of the more or less expensive transformations which are the precondition for its efficacy in the field in question, capital can present itself in three fundamental guises: as *economic capital*, which is immediately and directly convertible into money and may be institutionalized in the form of property rights; as *cultural capital*, which is convertible, on certain conditions, into economic capital and may be institutionalized in the form of educational qualifications; and as *social capital*, made up of social obligations ('connections'), which is convertible, in certain conditions, into economic capital and may be institutionalized in the form of a title of nobility.[3]

Cultural Capital

Cultural capital can exist in three forms: in the *embodied state*, i.e., in the form of long-lasting dispositions of the mind and body; in the *objectified* state, in the form of cultural goods (pictures, books, dictionaries, instruments, machines, etc.), which are the trace or realization of theories or critiques of these theories, problematics, etc.; and in the *institutionalized* state, a form of objectification which must be set apart because, as will be seen in the case of educational qualifications, it confers entirely original properties on the cultural capital which it is presumed to guarantee.

The reader should not be misled by the somewhat peremptory air which the effort at axiomization may give to my argument.[4] The notion of cultural capital initially presented itself to me, in the course of research, as a theoretical hypothesis which made it possible to explain the unequal scholastic achievement of children originating from the different social classes by relating academic success, i.e., the specific profits which children from the different classes and class fractions can obtain in the academic market, to the distribution of cultural capital between the classes and class fractions. This starting point implies a break with the presuppositions inherent both in the commonsense view, which sees academic success or failure as an effect of natural aptitudes, and in human capital theories.

Economists might seem to deserve credit for explicitly raising the question of the relationship between the rates of profit on educational investment and on economic investment (and its evolution). But their measurement of the yield from scholastic investment takes account only of *monetary* investments and profits, or those directly convertible into money, such as the costs of schooling and the cash equivalent of time devoted to study; they are unable to explain the different proportions of their resources which different agents or different social classes allocate to economic investment and cultural investment because they fail to take systematic account of the structure of the differential chances of profit which the various markets offer these agents or classes as a function of the volume and the composition of their assets (see esp. Becker 1964b). Furthermore, because they neglect to relate scholastic investment strategies to the whole set of educational strategies and to the system of reproduction strategies, they inevitably, by a necessary paradox, let slip the best hidden and socially most determinant educational investment, namely, the domestic transmission of cultural capital. Their studies of the relationship between academic ability and academic investment show that they are unaware that ability or talent is itself the product of an investment of time and cultural capital (Becker 1964a: 63–6). Not surprisingly, when endeavoring to evaluate the profits of scholastic investment, they can only consider the profitability of educational expenditure for society as a whole, the 'social rate of return,' or the 'social gain of education as measured by its effects on national productivity' (Becker 1964b: 121, 155). This typically functionalist definition of the functions of education ignores the contribution which the educational system makes to the reproduction of the social structure by sanctioning the hereditary transmission of cultural capital. From the very beginning, a definition of human capital, despite its humanistic connotations, does not move beyond economism and ignores, *inter alia*, the fact that the scholastic yield from educational action depends on the cultural capital previously invested by the family. Moreover, the economic and social yield of the educational qualification depends on the social capital, again inherited, which can be used to back it up.

The Embodied State

Most of the properties of cultural capital can be deduced from the fact that, in its fundamental state, it is linked to the body and presupposes embodiment. The accumulation of cultural capital in the embodied state, i.e., in the form of what is called culture, cultivation, *Bildung*, presupposes a process of embodiment, incorporation, which, insofar as it implies a labor of inculcation and assimilation, costs time, time which must be invested personally by the investor. Like the acquisition of a muscular physique or a suntan, it cannot be done at second hand (so that all effects of delegation are ruled out).

The work of acquisition is work on oneself (self-improvement), an effort that presupposes a personal cost (*on paie de sa personne*, as we say in French), an investment, above all of time, but also of that socially constituted form of libido, *libido sciendi*, with all the privation, renunciation, and sacrifice that it may entail. It follows that the least inexact of all the measurements of cultural capital are those which take as their standard the length of acquisition—so long, of course, as this is not reduced to length of schooling and allowance is made for early domestic education by giving it a positive value (a gain in time, a head start) or a negative value (wasted time, and doubly so because more time must be spent correcting its effects), according to its distance from the demands of the scholastic market.[5]

This embodied capital, external wealth converted into an integral part of the person, into a habitus, cannot be transmitted instantaneously (unlike money, property rights, or even titles of nobility) by gift or bequest, purchase or exchange. It follows that the use or exploitation of cultural capital presents particular problems for the holders of economic or political capital, whether they be private patrons or, at the other extreme, entrepreneurs employing executives endowed with a specific cultural competence (not to mention the new state patrons). How can this capital, so closely linked to the person, be bought without buying the person and so losing the very effect of legitimation which presupposes the dissimulation of dependence? How can this capital be concentrated—as some undertakings demand—without concentrating the possessors of the capital, which can have all sorts of unwanted consequences?

Cultural capital can be acquired, to a varying extent, depending on the period, the society, and the social class, in the absence of any deliberate inculcation, and therefore quite unconsciously. It always remains marked by its earliest conditions of acquisition which, through the more or less visible marks they leave (such as the pronunciations characteristic of a class or region), help to determine its distinctive value. It cannot be accumulated beyond the appropriating capacities of an individual agent; it declines and dies with its bearer (with his biological capacity, his memory, etc.). Because it is thus linked in numerous ways to the person in his biological singularity and is subject to a hereditary transmission which is always heavily disguised, or even invisible, it defies the old, deep-rooted distinction the Greek jurists made between inherited properties (*ta patroa*) and acquired properties (*epikteta*), i.e., those which an individual adds to his heritage. It thus manages to combine the prestige of innate property with the merits of acquisition. Because the social conditions of its transmission and acquisition are more disguised than those of economic capital, it is predisposed to function as symbolic capital, i.e., to be unrecognized as capital and recognized as legitimate competence, as authority exerting an effect of (mis)recognition, e.g., in the matrimonial market and in all the markets in which economic capital is not fully recognized, whether in matters of culture, with the great art collections or great cultural foundations, or in social welfare, with the economy of generosity and the gift. Furthermore, the specifically symbolic logic of distinction additionally secures material and symbolic profits for the possessors of a large cultural capital: any given cultural competence (e.g., being able to read in a world of illiterates) derives a scarcity value from its position in the distribution of cultural capital and yields profits of distinction for its owner. In other words, the share in profits which scarce cultural capital secures in class-divided societies is based, in the last analysis, on the fact that all agents do not have the economic and cultural means for prolonging their children's education beyond the minimum necessary for the reproduction of the labor-power least valorized at a given moment.[6]

Thus the capital, in the sense of the means of appropriating the product of accumulated labor in the objectified state which is held by a given agent, depends for its real efficacy on the form of the distribution of the means of appropriating the accumulated and objectively available resources: and the relationship of appropriation between an agent and the resources objectively available, and hence the profits they produce, is mediated by the relationship of (objective and/or subjective) competition between himself and the other possessors of capital competing for the same goods, in which scarcity—and through it, social value—is generated. The structure of the field, i.e., the unequal distribution of capital, is the source of the specific effects of capital, i.e., the appropriation of profits and the power to impose the laws of functioning of the field most favourable to capital and its reproduction.

But the most powerful principle of the symbolic efficacy of cultural capital no doubt lies in the logic of its transmission. On the one hand, the process of appropriating objectified cultural capital and the time necessary for it to take place mainly depend on the cultural capital embodied in the whole family—through (among other things) the generalized Arrow effect and all forms of implicit transmission.[7] On the other hand, the initial accumulation of cultural capital, the precondition for the fast, easy accumulation of every kind of useful cultural capital, starts at the outset, without delay, without wasted time, only for the offspring of families endowed with strong cultural capital; in this case, the accumulation period covers the whole period of socialization. It follows that the transmission of cultural capital is no doubt the best hidden form of hereditary transmission of capital, and it therefore receives proportionately greater weight in the system of reproduction strategies, as the direct, visible forms of transmission tend to be more strongly censored and controlled.

It can immediately be seen that the link between economic and cultural capital is established through the mediation of the time needed for acquisition. Differences in the cultural capital possessed by the family imply differences first in the age at which the work of transmission and accumulation begins—the limiting case being full use of the time biologically available, with the maximum free time being harnessed to maximum cultural capital—and then in the capacity, thus defined, to satisfy the specifically cultural demands of a prolonged process of acquisition. Furthermore, and in correlation with this, the length of time for which a given individual can prolong his acquisition process depends on the length of time for which his family can provide him with the free time, i.e., time free from economic necessity, which is the precondition for the initial accumulation (time which can be evaluated as a handicap to be made up).

The Objectified State

Cultural capital, in the objectified state, has a number of properties which are defined only in the relationship with cultural capital in its embodied form. The cultural capital objectified in material objects and media, such as writings, paintings, monuments, instruments, etc., is transmissible in its materiality. A collection of paintings, for example, can be transmitted as well as economic capital (if not better, because the capital transfer is more disguised). But what is transmissible is legal ownership and not (or not necessarily) what constitutes the precondition for specific appropriation, namely, the possession of the means of 'consuming' a painting or using a machine, which, being nothing other than embodied capital, are subject to the same laws of transmission.[8]

Thus cultural goods can be appropriated both materially—which presupposes economic capital—and symbolically—which presupposes cultural capital. It follows that the owner of the means of production must find a way of appropriating either the embodied capital which is the precondition of specific appropriation or the services of the holders of this capital. To possess the machines, he only needs economic capital; to appropriate them and use them in accordance with their specific purpose (defined by the cultural capital, of scientific or technical type, incorporated in them), he must have access to embodied cultural capital, either in person or by proxy. This is no doubt the basis of the ambiguous status of cadres (executives and engineers). If it is emphasized that they are not the possessors (in the strictly economic sense) of the means of production which they use, and that they derive profit from their own cultural capital only by selling the services and products which it makes possible, then they will be classified among the dominated groups; if it is emphasized that they draw their profits from the use of a particular form of capital, then they will be classified among the dominant groups. Everything suggests that as the cultural capital incorporated in the means of production increases (and with it the period of embodiment needed to acquire the means of appropriating it), so the collective strength of the holders of cultural capital would tend to increase—if the holders of the dominant type of capital (economic capital) were not able to set the holders of cultural capital in competition with one another. (They are, moreover, inclined to competition by the very conditions in which they are selected and trained, in particular by the logic of scholastic and recruitment competitions.)

Cultural capital in its objectified state presents itself with all the appearances of an autonomous, coherent universe which, although the product of historical action, has its own laws, transcending individual wills, and which, as the example of language well illustrates, therefore remains irreducible to that which each agent, or even the aggregate of the agents, can appropriate (i.e., to the cultural capital embodied in each agent or even in the aggregate of the agents). However, it should not be forgotten that it exists as symbolically and materially active, effective capital only insofar as it is appropriated by agents and implemented and invested as a weapon and a stake in the struggles which go on in the fields of cultural production (the artistic field, the scientific field, etc.) and, beyond them, in the field of the social classes—struggles in which the agents wield strengths and obtain profits proportionate to their mastery of this objectified capital, and therefore to the extent of their embodied capital.[9]

The Institutionalized State

The objectification of cultural capital in the form of academic qualifications is one way of neutralizing some of the properties it derives from the fact that, being embodied, it has the same biological limits as its bearer. This objectification is what makes the difference between the capital of the autodidact, which may be called into question at any time, or even the cultural capital of the courtier, which can yield only ill-defined profits, of fluctuating value, in the market of high-society exchanges, and the cultural capital academically sanctioned by legally guaranteed qualifications, formally independent of the person of their bearer. With the academic qualification, a certificate of cultural competence which confers on its holder a conventional, constant, legally guaranteed value with respect to culture, social alchemy produces a form of cultural capital which has a relative autonomy vis-à-vis its bearer and even vis-à-vis the cultural capital he effectively possesses at a given moment in time. It institutes cultural capital by collective magic, just as, according to Merleau-Ponty, the living institute their dead through the ritual of mourning. One has only to think of the *concours* (competitive recruitment examination) which, out of the continuum of infinitesimal differences between performances, produces sharp, absolute, lasting differences, such as that which separates the last successful candidate from the first unsuccessful one, and institutes an essential difference between the officially recognized, guaranteed competence and simple cultural capital, which is constantly required to prove itself. In this case, one sees clearly the performative magic of the power of instituting, the power to show forth and secure belief or, in a word, to impose recognition.

By conferring institutional recognition on the cultural capital possessed by any given gent, the academic qualification also makes it possible to compare qualification holders and even to exchange them (by substituting one for another in succession). Furthermore, it makes it possible to establish conversion rates between cultural capital and economic capital by guaranteeing the monetary value of a given academic capital.[10] This product of the conversion of economic capital into cultural capital establishes the value, in terms of cultural capital, of the holder of a given qualification relative to other qualification holders and, by the same token, the monetary value for which it can be exchanged on the labor market (academic investment has no meaning unless a minimum degree of reversibility of the conversion it implies is objectively guaranteed). Because the material and symbolic profits which the academic qualification guarantees also depend on its scarcity, the investments made (in time and effort) may turn out to be less profitable than was anticipated when they were made (there having been a *de facto* change in the conversion rate between academic capital and economic capital). The strategies for converting economic capital into cultural capital, which are among the short-term factors of the schooling explosion and the inflation of qualifications, are governed by changes in the structure of the chances of profit offered by the different types of capital.

Social Capital

Social capital is the aggregate of the actual or potential resources which are linked to possession of a durable network of more or less institutionalized relationships of mutual acquaintance and recognition—or in other words, to membership in a group[11]—which provides each of its members with the backing of the collectivity-owned capital, a 'credential' which entitles them to credit, in the various senses of the word. These relationships may exist only in the practical state, in material and/or symbolic exchanges which help to maintain them. They may also be socially instituted and guaranteed by the application of a common name (the name of a family, a class, or a tribe or of a school, a party, etc.) and by a whole set of instituting acts designed simultaneously to form and inform those who undergo them; in this case, they are more or less really enacted and so maintained and reinforced, in exchanges. Being based on indissolubly material and symbolic exchanges, the establishment and maintenance of which presuppose reacknowledgment of proximity, they are also partially irreducible to objective relations of proximity in physical (geographical) space or even in economic and social space.[12]

The volume of the social capital possessed by a given agent thus depends on the size of the network of connections he can effectively mobilize and on the volume of the capital (economic, cultural, or symbolic) possessed in his own right by each of those to whom he is connected.[13] This means that, although it is relatively irreducible to the economic and cultural capital possessed by a given agent, or even by the whole set of agents to whom he is connected, social capital is never completely independent of it because the exchanges instituting mutual acknowledgment presuppose the reacknowledgment of a minimum of objective homogeneity, and because it exerts a multiplier effect on the capital he possesses in his own right.

The profits which accrue from membership in a group are the basis of the solidarity which makes them possible.[14] This does not mean that they are consciously pursued as such, even in the case of groups like select clubs, which are deliberately organized in order to concentrate social capital and so to derive full benefit from the multiplier effect implied in concentration and to secure the profits of membership—material profits, such as all the types of services accruing from useful relationships, and symbolic profits, such as those derived from association with a rare, prestigious group.

The existence of a network of connections is not a natural given, or even a social given, constituted once and for all by an initial act of institution, represented, in the case of the family group, by the genealogical definition of kinship relations, which is the characteristic of a social formation. It is the product of an endless effort at institution, of which institution rites—often wrongly described as rites of passage—mark the essential moments and which is necessary in order to produce and reproduce lasting, useful relationships that can secure material or symbolic profits (see Bourdieu 1982). In other words, the network of relationships is the product of investment strategies, individual or collective, consciously or unconsciously aimed at establishing or reproducing social relationships that are directly usable in the short or long term, i.e., at transforming contingent relations, such as those of neighborhood, the workplace, or even kinship, into relationships that are at once necessary and elective, implying durable obligations subjectively felt (feelings of gratitude, respect, friendship, etc.) or institutionally guaranteed (rights). This is done through the alchemy *of consecration,* the symbolic constitution produced by social institution (institution as a relative—brother, sister, cousin, etc.—or as a knight, an heir, an elder, etc.) and endlessly reproduced in and through the exchange (of gifts, words, women, etc.) which it encourages and which presupposes and produces mutual knowledge and recognition. Exchange transforms the things exchanged into signs of recognition and, through the mutual recognition and the recognition of group membership which it implies, reproduces the group. By the same token, it reaffirms the limits of the group, i.e., the limits beyond which the constitutive exchange—trade, commensality, or marriage—cannot take place. Each member of the group is thus instituted as a custodian of the limits of the group: because the definition of the criteria of entry is at stake in each new entry, he can modify the group by modifying the limits of legitimate exchange through some form of misalliance. It is quite logical that, in most societies, the preparation and conclusion of marriages should be the business of the whole group, and not of the agents directly concerned. Through the introduction of new members into a family, a clan, or a club, the whole definition of the group, i.e., its fines, its boundaries, and its identity, is put at stake, exposed to redefinition, alteration, adulteration. When, as in modern societies, families lose the monopoly of the establishment of exchanges which can lead to lasting relationships, whether socially sanctioned (like marriage) or not, they may continue to control these exchanges, while remaining within the logic of laissez-faire, through all the institutions which are designed to favor legitimate exchanges and exclude illegitimate ones by producing occasions (rallies, cruises, hunts, parties, receptions, etc.), places (smart neighborhoods, select schools, clubs, etc.), or practices (smart sports, parlor games, cultural ceremonies, etc.)

which bring together, in a seemingly fortuitous way, individuals as homogeneous as possible in all the pertinent respects in terms of the existence and persistence of the group.

The reproduction of social capital presupposes an unceasing effort of sociability, a continuous series of exchanges in which recognition is endlessly affirmed and reaffirmed. This work, which implies expenditure of time and energy and so, directly or indirectly, of economic capital, is not profitable or even conceivable unless one invests in it a specific competence (knowledge of genealogical relationships and of real connections and skill at using them, etc.) and an acquired disposition to acquire and maintain this competence, which are themselves integral parts of this capital.[15] This is one of the factors which explain why the profitability of this labor of accumulating and maintaining social capital rises in proportion to the size of the capital. Because the social capital accruing from a relationship is that much greater to the extent that the person who is the object of it is richly endowed with capital (mainly social, but also cultural and even economic capital), the possessors of an inherited social capital, symbolized by a great name, are able to transform all circumstantial relationships into lasting connections. They are sought after for their social capital and, because they are well known, are worthy of being known ('I know him well'); they do not need to 'make the acquaintance' of all their 'acquaintances'; they are known to more people than they know, and their work of sociability, when it is exerted, is highly productive.

Every group has its more or less institutionalized forms of delegation which enable it to concentrate the totality of the social capital, which is the basis of the existence of the group (family or a nation, of course, but also an association or a party), in the hands of a single agent or a small group of agents and to mandate this plenipotentiary, charged with *plena potestas agendi et loquendi*,[16] to represent the group, to speak and act in its name and so, with the aid of this collectively owned capital, to exercise a power incommensurate with the agent's personal contribution. Thus, at the most elementary degree of institutionalization, the head of the family, the *pater familias*, the eldest, most senior member, is tacitly recognized as the only person entitled to speak on behalf of the family group in all official circumstances. But whereas in this case, diffuse delegation requires the great to step forward and defend the collective honor when the honor of the weakest members is threatened, the institutionalized delegation, which ensures the concentration of social capital, also has the effect of limiting the consequences of individual lapses by explicitly delimiting responsibilities and authorizing the recognized spokesmen to shield the group as a whole from discredit by expelling or excommunicating the embarrassing individuals.

If the internal competition for the monopoly of legitimate representation of the group is not to threaten the conservation and accumulation of the capital which is the basis of the group, the members of the group must regulate the conditions of access to the right to declare oneself a member of the group and, above all, to set oneself up as a representative (delegate, plenipotentiary, spokesman, etc.) of the whole group, thereby committing the social capital of the whole group. The title of nobility is the form *par excellence* of the institutionalized social capital which guarantees a particular form of social relationship in a lasting way. One of the paradoxes of delegation is that the mandated agent can exert on (and, up to a point, against) the group the power which the group enables him to concentrate. (This is perhaps especially true in the limiting cases in which the mandated agent creates the group which creates him but which only exists through him.) The mechanisms of delegation and representation (in both the theatrical and the legal senses) which fall into place—that much more strongly, no doubt, when the group is large and its members weak—as one of the conditions for the concentration of social capital (among other reasons, because it enables numerous, varied, scattered agents to act as one man and to overcome the limitations of space and time) also contain the seeds of an embezzlement or misappropriation of the capital which they assemble.

This embezzlement is latent in the fact that a group as a whole can be represented, in the various meanings of the word, by a subgroup, clearly delimited and perfectly visible to all, known to all, and recognized by all, that of the *nobiles*, the 'people who are known', the paradigm of whom is the nobility, and who may speak on behalf of the whole group, represent the whole group, and exercise authority in the name of the whole group. The noble is the group personified. He bears the name of the group to which he gives his name (the metonymy which links the noble to his group is clearly seen when Shakespeare calls Cleopatra 'Egypt' or the King of France 'France', just as Racine calls Pyrrhus 'Epirus'). It is by him, his name, the difference it proclaims, that the members of his group, the liegemen, and also the land and castles, are known and recognized. Similarly, phenomena such as the 'personality cult' or the identification of parties, trade unions, or movements with their leader are latent in the very logic of representation. Everything combines to cause the signifier to take the place of the signified, the spokesmen that of the group he is supposed to express, not least because his distinction, his 'outstandingness', his visibility constitute the essential part, if not the essence, of this power, which, being entirely set within the logic of knowledge and acknowledgment, is fundamentally a symbolic power; but also because the representative, the sign, the emblem, may be, and create, the whole reality of groups which receive effective social existence only in and through representation.[17]

Conversions

The different types of capital can be derived from *economic capital*, but only at the cost of a more or less great effort of transformation, which is needed to produce the type of power effective in the field in question. For example, there are some goods and services to which economic capital gives immediate access, without secondary costs; others can be obtained only by virtue of a social capital of relationships (or social obligations) which cannot act instantaneously, at the appropriate moment, unless they have been established and maintained for a long time, as if for their own sake, and therefore outside their period of use, i.e., at the cost of an investment in sociability which is necessarily long-term because the time lag is one of the factors of the transmutation of a pure and simple debt into that recognition of nonspecific indebtedness which is called gratitude.[18] In contrast to the cynical but also economical transparency of economic exchange, in which equivalents change hands in the same instant, the essential ambiguity of social exchange, which presupposes misrecognition, in other words, a form of faith and of bad faith (in the sense of self-deception), presupposes a much more subtle economy of time.

So it has to be posited simultaneously that economic capital is at the root of all the other types of capital and that these transformed, disguised forms of economic capital, never entirely reducible to that definition, produce their most specific effects only to the extent that they conceal (not least from their possessors) the fact that economic capital is at their root, in other words—but only in the last analysis—at the root of their effects. The real logic of the functioning of capital, the conversions from one type to another, and the law of conservation which governs them cannot be understood unless two opposing but equally partial views are superseded: on the one hand, economism, which, on the grounds that every type of capital is reducible in the last analysis to economic capital, ignores what makes the specific efficacy of the other types of capital, and on the other hand, semiologism (nowadays represented by structuralism, symbolic interactionism, or ethnomethodology), which reduces social exchanges to phenomena of communication and ignores the brutal fact of universal reducibility to economics.[19]

In accordance with a principle which is the equivalent of the principle of the conservation of energy, profits in one area are necessarily paid for by costs in another (so that a concept like wastage has no meaning in a general science of the economy of practices). The universal equivalent, the measure of all equivalences, is nothing other than labor-time (in the widest sense); and the conservation of social energy through all its conversions is verified if, in each case, one takes into account both the labor-time accumulated in the form of capital and the labor-time needed to transform it from one type into another.

It has been seen, for example, that the transformation of economic capital into social capital presupposes a specific labor, i.e., an apparently gratuitous expenditure of time, attention, care, concern, which, as is seen in the endeavor to personalize a gift, has the effect of transfiguring the purely monetary import of the exchange and, by the same token, the very meaning of the exchange. From a narrowly economic standpoint, this effort is bound to be seen as pure wastage, but in the terms of the logic of social exchanges, it is a solid investment, the profits of which will appear, in the long run, in monetary or other form. Similarly, if the best measure of cultural capital is undoubtedly the amount of time devoted to acquiring it, this is because the transformation of economic capital into cultural capital presupposes an expenditure of time that is made possible by possession of economic capital. More precisely, it is because the cultural capital that is effectively transmitted within the family itself depends not only on the quantity of cultural capital, itself accumulated by spending time, that the domestic group possess, but also on the usable time (particularly in the form of the mother's free time) available to it (by virtue of its economic capital, which enables it to purchase the time of others) to ensure the transmission of this capital and to delay entry into the labor market through prolonged schooling, a credit which pays off, if at all, only in the very long term.[20]

The convertibility of the different types of capital is the basis of the strategies aimed at ensuring the reproduction of capital (and the position occupied in social space) by means of the conversions least costly in terms of conversion work and of the losses inherent in the conversion itself (in a given state of the social power relations). The different types of capital can be distinguished according to their reproducibility or, more precisely, according to how easily they are transmitted, i.e., with more or less loss and with more or less concealment; the rate of loss and the degree of concealment tend to vary in inverse ratio. Everything which helps to disguise the economic aspect also tends to increase the risk of loss (particularly the intergenerational transfers), Thus the (apparent) incommensurability of the different types of capital introduces a high degree of uncertainty into all transactions between holders of different types. Similarly, the declared refusal of calculation and of guarantees which characterizes exchanges tending to produce a social capital in the form of a capital of obligations that are usable in the more or less long term (exchanges of gifts, services, visits, etc.) necessarily entails the risk of ingratitude, the refusal of that recognition of nonguaranteed debts which such exchanges aim to produce. Similarly, too, the high degree of concealment of the transmission of cultural capital has the disadvantage (in addition to its inherent risks of loss) that the academic qualification which is its institutionalized form is neither transmissible (like a title of nobility) nor negotiable (like stocks and shares). More precisely, cultural capital, whose diffuse, continuous transmission within the family escapes observation and control (so that the educational system seems to award its honors solely to natural qualities) and which is increasingly tending to attain full efficacy, at least on the labor market, only when validated by the educational system, i.e., converted into a capital of qualifications, in subject to a more disguised but more risky transmission than economic capital. As the educational qualification, invested with the specific force of the official, becomes the condition for legitimate access to a growing number of positions, particularly the dominant ones, the educational system tends increasingly to dispossess the domestic group of the monopoly of the transmission of power and privileges—and, among other things, of the choice of its legitimate heirs from among children of different sex and birth rank.[21] And economic capital itself poses quite different problems of transmission, depending on the particular form it takes. Thus, according to Grassby (1970), the liquidity of commercial capital, which gives immediate economic power and favors transmission, also makes it more vulnerable than landed property (or even real estate) and does not favor the establishment of long-lasting dynasties.

Because the question of the arbitrariness of appropriation arises most sharply in the process of transmission—particularly at the time of succession, a critical moment for all power—every reproduction strategy is at the same time a legitimation strategy aimed at consecrating both an exclusive appropriation and its reproduction. When the subversive critique which aims to weaken the dominant class through the principle of its perpetuation by bringing to light the arbitrariness of the entitlements transmitted and of their transmission (such as the critique which the Enlightenment *philosophes* directed, in the name of nature, against the arbitrariness of birth) is incorporated in institutionalized mechanisms (for example, laws of inheritance) aimed at controlling the official, direct transmission of power and privileges, the holders of capital have an ever greater interest in resorting to reproduction strategies capable of ensuring better-disguised transmission, but at the cost of greater loss of capital, by exploiting the convertibility of the types of capital. Thus the more the official transmission of capital is prevented or hindered, the more the effects of the clandestine circulation of capital in the form of cultural capital become determinant in the reproduction of the social structure. As an instrument of reproduction capable of disguising its own function, the scope of the educational system tends to increase, and together with this increase is the unification of the market in social qualifications which gives rights to occupy rare positions.

Notes

1. This inertia, entailed by the tendency of the structures of capital to reproduce themselves in institutions or in dispositions adapted to the structures of which they are the product, is, of course, reinforced by a specifically political action of concerted conservation, i.e., of demobilization and depoliticization. The latter tends to keep the dominated agents in the state of a practical group, united only by the orchestration of their dispositions and condemned to function as an aggregate repeatedly performing discrete, individual acts (such as consumer or electoral choices).

2. This is true of all exchanges between members of different fractions of the dominant class, possessing different types of capital. These range from sales of expertise, treatment, or other services which take the form of gift exchange and dignify themselves with the most decorous names that can be found (honoraria, emoluments, etc.) to matrimonial exchanges, the prime example of a transaction that can only take place insofar as it is not perceived or defined as such by the contracting parties. It is remarkable that the apparent extensions of economic theory beyond the limits constituting the discipline have left intact the asylum of the sacred, apart from a few sacrilegious incursions. Gary S. Becker, for example, who was one of the first to take explicit account of the types of capital that are usually ignored, never considers anything other than monetary costs and profits, forgetting the nonmonetary investments (*inter alia*, the affective ones) and the material and symbolic profits that education provides in a deferred, indirect way, such as the added value which the dispositions produced or reinforced by schooling (bodily or verbal manners, tastes, etc.) or the relationships established with fellow students can yield in the matrimonial market (Becker 1964a).

3. *Symbolic capital,* that is to say, capital—in whatever form—insofar as it is represented, i.e., apprehended symbolically, in a relationship of knowledge or, more precisely, of misrecognition and recognition, presupposes the intervention of the habitus, as a socially constituted cognitive capacity.

4. When talking about concepts for their own sake, as I do here, rather than using them in research, one always runs the risk of being both schematic and formal, i.e., theoretical in the most usual and most usually approved sense of the word.

5. This proposition implies no recognition of the value of scholastic verdicts; it merely registers the relationship which exists in reality between a certain cultural capital and the laws of the educational market. Dispositions that are given a negative value in the educational market may receive very high value in other markets—not least, of course, in the relationships internal to the class.

6. In a relatively undifferentiated society, in which access to the means of appropriating the cultural heritage is very equally distributed, embodied culture does not function as cultural capital, i.e., as a means of acquiring exclusive advantages.

7. What I call the generalized Arrow effect, i.e., the fact that all cultural goods—paintings, monuments, machines, and any objects shaped by man, particularly all those which belong to the childhood environment—exert an educative effect by their mere existence, is no doubt one of the structural factors behind the 'schooling explosion,' in the sense that a growth in the quantity of cultural capital accumulated in the objectified state increases the educative effect automatically exerted by the environment. If one adds to this the fact that embodied cultural capital is constantly increasing, it can be seen that, in each generation, the educational system can take more for granted. The fact that the same educational investment is increasingly productive is one of the structural factors of the inflation of qualifications (together with cyclical factors linked to effects of capital conversion).

8. The cultural object, as a living social institution, is, simultaneously, a socially instituted material object and a particular class of habitus, to which it is addressed. The material object—for example, a work of art in its materiality—may be separated by space (e.g., a Dogon statue) or by time (e.g., a Simone Martini painting) from the habitus for which it was intended. This leads to one of the most fundamental biases of art history. Understanding the effect (not to be confused with the function) which the work tended to produce—for example, the form of belief it tended to induce—and which is the true basis of the conscious or unconscious choice of the means used (technique, colors, etc.), and therefore of the form itself, is possible only if one at least raises the question of the habitus on which it 'operated.'

9. The dialectical relationship between objectified cultural capital—of which the form *par excellence* is writing—and embodied cultural capital has generally been reduced to an exalted description of the degradation of the spirit by the letter, the living by the inert, creation by routine, grace by heaviness.

10. This is particularly true in France, where in many occupations (particularly the civil service) there is a very strict relationship between qualification, rank, and remuneration (translator's note).

11. Here, too, the notion of cultural capital did not spring from pure theoretical work, still less from an analogical extension of economic concepts. It arose from the need to identify the principle of social effects which, although they can be seen clearly at the level of singular agents—where statistical inquiry inevitably operates—cannot be reduced to the set of properties individually possessed by a given agent. These effects, in which spontaneous sociology readily perceives the work of 'connections,' are particularly visible in all cases in which different individuals obtain very unequal profits from virtually equivalent (economic or cultural) capital, depending on the extent to which they can mobilize by proxy the capital of a group (a family, the alumni of an elite school, a select club, the aristocracy, etc.) that is more or less constituted as such and more or less rich in capital.

12. Neighborhood relationships may, of course, receive an elementary form of institutionalization, as in the Bearn—or the Basque region—where neighbors, *lous besis* (a word which, in old texts, is applied to the legitimate inhabitants of the village, the rightful members of the assembly), are explicitly designated, in accordance with fairly codified rules, and are assigned functions which are differentiated according to their rank (there is a 'first neighbor,' a 'second neighbor,' and so on), particularly for the major social ceremonies (funerals, marriages, etc.). But even in this case, the relationships actually used by no means always coincide with the relationships socially instituted.

13. Manners (bearing, pronunciation, etc.) may be included in social capital insofar as, through the mode of acquisition they point to, they indicate initial membership of a more or less prestigious group.

14. National liberation movements or nationalist ideologies cannot be accounted for solely by reference to strictly economic profits, i.e., anticipation of the profits which may be derived from redistribution of a proportion of wealth to the advantage of the nationals (nationalization) and the recovery of highly paid jobs (see Breton 1964). To these specifically economic anticipated profits, which would only explain the nationalism of the privileged classes, must be added the very real and very immediate profits derived from membership (social capital) which are proportionately greater for those who are lower down the social hierarchy ('poor whites') or, more precisely, more threatened by economic and social decline.

15. There is every reason to suppose that socializing, or, more generally, relational, dispositions are very unequally distributed among the social classes and, within a given class, among fractions of different origin.

16. A 'full power to act and speak' (translator).

17. It goes without saying that social capital is so totally governed by the logic of knowledge and acknowledgment that it always functions as symbolic capital.

18. It should be made clear, to dispel a likely misunderstanding, that the investment in question here is not necessarily conceived as a calculated pursuit of gain, but that it has every likelihood of being experienced in terms of the logic of emotional investment, i.e., as an involvement which is both necessary and disinterested. This has not always been appreciated by historians, who (even when they are as alert to symbolic effects as E. P. Thompson) tend to conceive symbolic practices—powdered wigs and the whole paraphernalia of office—as explicit strategies of domination, intended to be seen (from below), and to interpret generous or charitable conduct as 'calculated acts of class appeasement.' This naively Machiavellian view forgets that the most sincerely disinterested acts may be those best corresponding to objective interest. A number of fields, particularly those which most tend to deny interest and every sort of calculation, like the fields of cultural production, grant full recognition, and with it the consecration which guarantees success, only to those who distinguish themselves by the immediate conformity of their investments, a token of sincerity and attachment to the essential principles of the field. It would be thoroughly erroneous to describe the choices of the habitus which lead an artist, writer, or researcher toward his natural place (a subject, style, manner, etc.) in terms of rational strategy and cynical calculation. This is despite the fact that, for example, shifts from one genre, school, or speciality to another, quasi-religious conversions that are performed 'in all sincerity,' can be understood as capital conversions, the direction and moment of which (on which their success often depends) are determined by a 'sense of investment' which is the less likely to be seen as such the more skillful it is. Innocence is the privilege of those who move in their field of activity like fish in water.

19. To understand the attractiveness of this pair of antagonistic positions which serve as each other's alibi, one would need to analyze the unconscious profits and the profits of unconsciousness which they procure for intellectuals. While some find in economism a means of exempting themselves by excluding the cultural capital and all the specific profits which place them on the side of the dominant, others can abandon the detestable terrain of the economic, where everything reminds them that they can be evaluated, in the last analysis, in economic terms, for that of the symbolic. (The latter merely reproduce, in the realm of the symbolic, the strategy whereby intellectuals and artists endeavor to impose the recognition of their values, i.e., their value, by inverting the law of the market in which what one has or what one earns completely defines what one is worth and what one is—as is shown by the practice of banks which, with techniques such as the personalization of credit, tend to subordinate the granting of loans and the fixing of interest rates to an exhaustive inquiry into the borrower's present and future resources.)

20. Among the advantages procured by capital in all its types, the most precious is the increased volume of useful time that is made possible through the various methods of appropriating other people's time (in the form of services). It may take the form either of increased spare time, secured by reducing the time consumed in activities directly channeled toward producing the means of reproducing the existence of the domestic group, or of more intense use of the time so consumed, by recourse to other people's labor or to devices and methods which are available only to those who have spent time learning how to use them and which (like better transport or living close to the place of work) make it possible to save time. (This is in contrast to the cash savings of the poor, which are paid for in time—do-it-yourself, bargain hunting, etc.) None of this is true of mere economic capital; it is possession of cultural capital that makes it possible to derive greater profit not only from labor-time, by securing a higher yield from the same time, but also from spare time, and so to increase both economic and cultural capital.

21. It goes without saying that the dominant fractions, who tend to place ever greater emphasis on educational investment, within an overall strategy of asset diversification and of investments aimed at combining security with high yield, have all sorts of ways of evading scholastic verdicts. The direct transmission of economic capital remains one of the principal means of reproduction, and the effect of social capital ('a helping hand,' 'string-pulling,' the 'old boy network') tends to correct the effect of academic sanctions. Educational qualifications never function perfectly as currency. They are never entirely separable from their holders: their value rises in proportion to the value of their bearer, especially in the least rigid areas of the social structure.

References

Becker, G. S. (1964a), *A Theoretical and Empirical Analysis with Special Reference to Education* (New York: National Bureau of Economic Research).
—— (1964b), *Human Capital* (New York: Columbia Univ. Press).
Bourdieu, P. (1982), 'Les rites d'institution', *Actes de la recherche en sciences sociales*, 43: 58–63.
Breton, A. (1962), 'The Economics of Nationalism', *Journal of Political Economy*, 72: 376–86.
Grassby, R. (1970), 'English Merchant Capitalism in the Late Seventeenth Century: The Composition of Business Fortunes', *Past and Present*, 46: 87–107.

7

Social Class and Pedagogic Practice

BASIL BERNSTEIN

I shall start this paper[1] with an analysis of the basic social relation of any pedagogic practice. In this analysis I shall distinguish between pedagogic practice as a cultural relay and pedagogic practice in terms of what that practice relays— in other words, pedagogic practice as a social form and as a specific content. I shall argue that the inner logic of pedagogic practice as a cultural relay is provided by a set of three rules, and the nature of these rules acts selectively on the content of any pedagogic practice. If these rules constitute what can be called the 'how' of any practice, then any particular 'how' created by any one set of rules acts selectively on the 'what' of the practice, the form of its content. The form of the content in turn acts selectively on those who can successfully acquire. I shall examine in some detail the social class assumptions and consequences of forms of pedagogic practice.

On the basis of the fundamental rules of any pedagogic practice I shall generate:

1. What are regarded as opposing modalities of pedagogic practice, usually referred to as conservative or traditional and progressive or child-centred.
2. What are regarded as oppositions within what is considered the same basic form. Here the opposition is between a pedagogic practice dependent upon the market place for its orientation and legitimation, a practice emphasizing the assumed relevance of vocational skills, and a pedagogic practice independent of the market place, claiming for itself an orientation and legitimation derived from the assumed autonomy of knowledge. It will be argued that the pedagogic practices of the new vocationalism and those of the old autonomy of knowledge represent a conflict between different elitist ideologies, one based on the class hierarchy of the market and the other based on the hierarchy of knowledge and its class supports.

The basic argument will be that whether we are considering the opposition between conservative and progressive or the opposition between market and knowledge-oriented pedagogic practice, present class inequalities are likely to be reproduced.

I shall start first with some thoughts about the inner logic of any pedagogic practice. A pedagogic practice can be understood as a relay, a cultural relay: a uniquely human device for both the reproduction and the production of culture. As I have said earlier, I shall distinguish between what is relayed, the contents, and how the contents are relayed. That is, between the 'what' and the 'how' of any transmission. When I refer to the inner logic of a pedagogic practice I am referring to a set of rules which are prior to the content to be relayed (see Figure 7.1).

The relationship basic to cultural reproduction or transformation is essentially the pedagogic relation, and the pedagogic relation consists of transmitters and acquirers. I shall examine the internal logic of this relationship. In fact, I consider the fundamental logic of any pedagogic relation.

I have drawn a distinction here between what I call the fundamental logic of the practice and the various practices to which this logic can give rise. This is rather similar to language, itself: a finite set

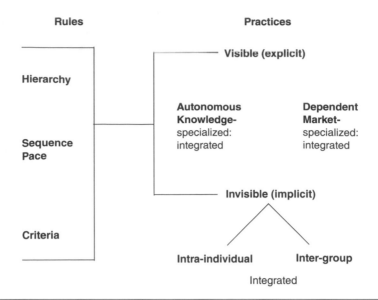

Figure 7.1 Pedagogic practices: generic forms and modalities. Whereas invisible pedagogies are always likely to relay integrated or embedded skills/subjects, visible pedagogies, especially of the autonomous type, are more likely to relay differentiated skills/subjects.

of rules which can generate a great number of other rule systems. I will examine some of the realizations of these practices and I will analyse the social class assumptions of these practices.

If we look at the relationship between transmitters and acquirers, I shall assert that this is essentially, and intrinsically, an asymmetrical relation. There may be various strategies for disguising, masking, hiding the asymmetry. For example, in certain modalities of practice the acquirer is perceived as a transmitter, and, perhaps, the transmitter appears to be the acquirer, but these are essentially arabesques. This may seem a very cynical view but we shall see whether it is of any value. Now it is the case that although this relation is intrinsically asymmetrical the realization of the asymmetry may be very complex.

The Rules of Pedagogic Practice as Cultural Relay

I shall propose that the essential logic of any pedagogic relation consists of the relationship essentially between three rules. And of these three rules,[2] the first is the dominant one. I would now like to outline concretely the three rules.

Hierarchical Rule

In any pedagogic relationship the transmitter has to learn to be a transmitter and the acquirer has to learn to be an acquirer. When you go to the doctor you have to learn how to be a patient. It is no good going to the doctor and saying, 'I feel really bad today, everything is really grey.' He says, 'Don't waste my time,' because he has many patients. 'Where is the pain? How long have you had it? What kind of pain is it? Is it acute? Is it chronic? Is it sharp? Is it persistent?' After a bit you learn how to talk to your doctor. He teaches you to be an acquirer. But how he teaches you is the function of a much more general set of forces which we shall go on to discover.

The acquirer, then, has to learn to be an acquirer and the transmitter has to learn to be a transmitter. The process of learning how to be a transmitter entails the acquiring of rules of social order, character, and manner which became the condition for appropriate conduct in the pedagogic relation. It is these rules which are a prerequisite of any enduring pedagogic relation. In any one such relation the rules of conduct may to different degrees permit a space for negotiation. These rules of conduct will here be called hierarchical rules which establish the conditions for order, character, and manner.

Sequencing Rules

Now if there is a transmission it cannot always happen at once. Something must come before and something must come after. If something comes before and after, there is a progression. If there is a progression, there must be sequencing rules. Every pedagogic practice must have sequencing rules, and these sequencing rules will imply pacing rules. Pacing is the rate of expected acquisition of the sequencing rules, that is, how much you have to learn in a given amount of time. Essentially, pacing is the time allowed for achieving the sequencing rules.

Criterial Rules

Finally there are criteria which the acquirer is expected to take over and to apply to his/her own practices and those of others. The criteria enable the acquirer to understand what counts as a legitimate or illegitimate communication, social relation, or position.

The internal logic of any pedagogic relation consists of hierarchical rules, sequential/pacing rules, criterial rules. We can distinguish, at another level, two more general rules. The hierarchical rules will be called the *regulative* rules and the other rules of sequence/pace criteria will be called instructional or *discursive* rules. The fundamental rule is the regulative one. Later on we shall see why this is the case.[3] Briefly, all education is intrinsically a moral activity which articulates the dominant ideology(ies) of dominant group(s). On the basis of these rules, I want to generate, to begin with, two different kinds of practices, and I shall do so on the basis of an examination of these rules.

In any teaching relation, the essence of the relation is to evaluate the competence of the acquirer. What you are evaluating is whether the criteria that have been made available to the acquirer have been achieved—whether they are regulative criteria about conduct, character, and manner, or instructional, discursive criteria: how to solve this problem or that problem, or produce an acceptable piece of writing or speech.

On the basis of the above rules of regulative and discursive order, I shall distinguish between two generic types or modalities of pedagogic practice. I must emphasize that these are types, and each can give rise to a range of practices, some of which will be discussed later in this paper.

Generating Modalities of Pedagogic Practice

Hierarchical Rules

If we take, first of all, the hierarchical rules, these rules can be explicit but they can also be implicit. If they are explicit, then the power relations in the relationship are very clear. The relationship is one of explicit subordination and superordination. This creates an explicit hierarchy. But a hierarchy need not necessarily be explicit. A hierarchy can be implicit. Let me give an example.

In 1968 the French took to the streets and the English studied a government report (Plowden, 1967) on primary education. The report was called *Children and their Primary Schools*—not 'Children and Primary Schools' or 'Primary Schools and Children'. In this book there were thirty-six pictures. If you look at those thirty-six photographs, there are children playing creatively by themselves: individual, productive play. There are pictures of children playing in groups, there are children in the school corridors and in the gardens surrounding the school, but it is difficult to find a teacher. This is the context created by an implicit hierarchy. The more implicit the hierarchy, the more difficult it is to distinguish the transmitter. We can define an implicit hierarchy as a relationship where power is masked or hidden by devices of communication. In the case of an implicit hierarchy, the teacher acts directly on the context of acquisition but indirectly on the acquirer. Thus hierarchy can be either explicit or implicit.

Sequencing Rules

These rules can be explicit. If they are explicit, then it means that children of 5 years of age are expected to develop particular competences, to behave in a particular way, and at 6 years of age they are expected to have different competences. Explicit rules regulate the development of the child, usually in terms of age. This means that the child is always aware of what her/his expected state of consciousness is supposed to be. He or she may not like it, but it is clear. Explicit sequencing rules construct the temporal project of the child. They construct temporal dislocations. These sequencing rules may be inscribed in syllabuses, in curricula, in behavioural rules, in rules of punishment and reward, and are often marked by transition rituals. However, sequencing rules can be implicit. Where sequencing rules are implicit the child initially can never be aware of his or her temporal project. Only the transmitter is aware of the temporal project of the child. We have a difference here. In the case of explicit sequencing rules, the child has some awareness of its temporal project; in the case of implicit sequencing rules only the teacher or the transmitter can be so aware.

We have to ask ourselves what is the basis of such a relationship, because if the child is not aware of his or her temporal project, then the child lives only in the present. When the sequencing rules are explicit, the child has some awareness of her/his temporal project although he or she lives in the past. The grammatical tenses of these pedagogic practices are opposed to each other. One child lives in the past although he or she can see his/her future, whereas the other child lives in the present of its own doings. Sequencing rules reveal what may be called the ideology of tense.

How does this come about? If sequencing rules are implicit, then they will be drawn from a range of theories. The theories that I am going to put forward here are not the only ones, but others will be structurally similar where they apply to children. The theories are set out in Figure 7.2. They construct a pedagogic *bricolage*.

If we look at these theories we can see that although they are very different, they have certain things in common. First, almost all the theories, with the exception of Gestalt, is a developmental theory. What is acquired has a meaning only in relation to a particular stage. (In the case of Freud there is the development from polymorphous perverse, the nirvana of babyhood, followed by oral, anal, phallic, and genital.) With one exception, all these theories are stage theories. Second, in every one of these theories the child is active in his or her own acquisition. Third, in all these theories the acquisition of the child cannot be readily modified by explicit public regulation, as learning is a tacit, invisible act. Fourth, in every one of these theories, the child's institutional and cultural biography is excluded. The theories are asociological. At most the child has a family. Fifth, in every one of these theories, except the ethological, the relationship between the transmitter and the acquirer or the parent and the child is such that the socializer is potentially if not actually dangerous. These theories tend to be critical of

	Stage	Active	Learning	Abstracted	Implicit Hierarchy
Piaget	1	2	3	4	5
Freud (non-Freudian)	1	2	3	4	5
Chomsky	1	2	3	4	5
Ethological theories of critical learning	1	2	3	4	—
Gestalt	—	2	3	4	5

Figure 7.2

the transmitter as an imposer of meaning. Every one of the theories, except the ethological, replaces domination by facilitation, imposition by accommodation.

The theories imply an implicit hierarchy. Now if you are going to apply this *bricolage* to the classroom as a teacher, or as a social worker, or as a counsellor, you have to have what is called a theory of reading. For in these theories the child is transformed into a text which only the transmitter can read. In other words, the teacher, the social worker, the psychotherapist is looking for certain signs, but the signs have meaning only to the teacher, and the child can never be aware of the meaning of its own signs, as their reading requires complex theories.

I was once in a classroom where a child was by himself. I happened to say that the child looked very unhappy, and the teacher said, 'Don't worry about that. He is just working through a problem.' The teacher, then, can read the child, and the teacher's behaviour to that child will depend on this reading, which in turn depends upon theories and upon how they have been transmitted, that is, recontextualized

Sequencing rules can be implicit or explicit. Where rules are implicit the acquirer initially can never know the meaning of her/his sign, as the meaning is derived from complex theories and their recontextualizing, and so available only to the transmitter.

Criterial Rules

Criteria can be explicit and specific. For example, in a school the child may be making some facsimile of a person, drawing a person, and the teacher comes along, looks at the drawing and says (it does not have to be repressive; explicit criteria do not have to be repressively realized), 'That's a lovely man, but he's only got three fingers,' or 'That's a very good house, but where is the chimney?' In other words, the pedagogy works by making available to the child what is missing in the product. Now if it works in this way, by showing what is missing in the product, the criteria will always be explicit and specific, *and the child will be aware of the criteria.* He or she may not like them, but they will be articulated. However, criteria can be implicit, multiple, and diffuse. Imagine we go to another classroom. The children have very big pieces of paper. A whole series of media are available through which their unique consciousness can be graphically realized. And the facilitator happens to glance at the image and says to the child, Tell me about it.' 'Oh, that's very exciting.'

In the case of implicit criteria, by definition, the child is not aware except in a very general way of the criteria she/he has to meet. It is as if this pedagogic practice creates a space in which the acquirer can create his/her text under conditions of apparently minimum external constraint and in a context and social relationship which appears highly supportive of the 'spontaneous' text the acquirer offers (Daniels, 1989).

We can now say that we have distinguished between pedagogic practices in terms of those which have explicit hierarchical rules, explicit sequencing/pacing rules, and explicit criteria and those with implicit hierarchical sequencing/pacing and criterial rules.[4]

Types of Pedagogic Practice: Visible and Invisible

I shall now define two generic types of pedagogic practice, as follows. If the rules of regulative and discursive order are explicit (hierarchy/sequence/pace) criteria, I shall call such a type a *visible* pedagogic practice (VP) and if the rules of regulative and discursive order are implicit, I shall call such a type an *invisible* pedagogic practice (IP).

Visible Pedagogies

A visible pedagogy (and there are many modalities) will always place the emphasis on the *performance* of the child, upon the text the child is creating and the extent to which that text is meeting the criteria.

BISHOP BURTON COLLEGE LIBRARY

Thus acquirers will be graded according to the extent that they meet the criteria. A visible pedagogy puts the emphasis on the external product of the child.

Visible pedagogies and their modalities will act to produce differences between children: they are necessarily stratifying practices of transmission, a learning consequence for both transmitters and acquirers. It is here worth adding that because a visible pedagogy has explicit rules of regulative and discursive order it does not mean that there are no tacit rules or messages, only that their meaning must be understood in the context of a visible pedagogy.

Invisible Pedagogies

In the case of an invisible pedagogy the discursive rules (the rules of order of instruction) are known only to the transmitter, and in this sense a pedagogic practice of this type is (at least initially) invisible to the acquirer, essentially because the acquirer appears to fill the pedagogic space rather than the transmitter. The concrete present of the acquirer is manifest rather than the abstract/abstracted past of the controlling discourse.

Invisible pedagogies are less concerned to produce explicit stratifying differences between acquirers because they are apparently less interested in matching the acquirer's text against an external common standard. Their focus is not upon a 'gradable' performance of the acquirer but upon procedures internal to the acquirer (cognitive, linguistic, affective, motivational) as a consequence of which a text is created and experienced. These *procedures of acquisition* are considered to be shared by all acquirers, although their realization in texts will create differences between acquirers.

But these differences do not signal differences in potential, as all acquirers are judged to share common procedures. Differences revealed by an invisible pedagogy are not to be used as a basis for comparison *between* acquirers, for differences reveal *uniqueness*. Thus whereas visible pedagogies focus upon an external gradable text, invisible pedagogies focus upon the procedures/competences which all acquirers bring to the pedagogic context. Invisible pedagogies are concerned to arrange that context to enable shared competences to develop realizations appropriate to the acquirer. Thus, in the case of invisible pedagogies, external noncomparable differences are produced by internal *commonalities*—that is, shared competences—whereas in the case of visible pedagogies, external *comparable* differences are produced by internal differences in potential. In short, invisible pedagogies emphasize acquisition—competence and visible pedagogies transmission—performance.[5]

These differences in emphasis between visible and invisible pedagogies will clearly affect both the selection and the organization of what is to be acquired, that is, the recontextualizing principle adopted to create and systematize the contents to be acquired and the context in which it is acquired.

Different theories of instruction in these two pedagogic types, which we illustrate in Figure 7.3 and, at the same time, show how modalities of the two types can be regarded as liberal, conservative, and radical practices.

Figure 7.3

In Figure 7.3 the vertical dimension refers to the object of change of the pedagogic practice. Thus the primary object may be to produce changes in the individual or the primary object may be to produce changes not in the individual but between social groups. The horizontal dimension refers to the focus of the pedagogic practice, which can be either upon the acquirer or upon the transmitter. Clearly the latter indicates a visible and the former an invisible pedagogy. If we take the top left-hand quadrant, intra-individual–acquisition, then this would indicate what is often regarded as 'progressive' pedagogic practice whose theories of instruction are likely to be drawn from those listed earlier. However, if we take the bottom left-hand quadrant, acquisition–intergroup, the primary object of this pedagogic practice is to produce changes *between* social groups, that is, how the acquirer comes to understand the relation between social groups and through this new appreciation change his/her practice. This would be a radical rather than a liberal–progressive practice, e.g., Freire and, through Freire, the pedagogy of liberation theology. It would also include neo-Marxist formulations such as those of Giroux (1989).

The top right-hand quadrant, intra-individual–transmission, is likely to select behaviourist or neo-behaviourist theories of instruction which, relative to those selected in the top left-hand quadrant, are often regarded as conservative. It is a matter of interest that this top right-hand quadrant is regarded as conservative but has often produced very innovative and radical acquirers. The bottom right-hand quadrant shows a radical realization of an apparently conservative pedagogic practice.

So far, then, we can see that these generic types can take either progressive, conservative, or radical modalities, and that theories of instruction will act selectively upon both the 'what' and 'how' of any pedagogic practice. Further, these different theories will act selectively upon what attributes of the acquirer become candidates for what labels. Finally, each theory will carry its own conditions of contestation, 'resistance', subversion.

I have proposed that it is important to distinguish between the fundamental grammar or ordering principles of a pedagogic practice and the forms of realization as pedagogic types. The ordering principles I have analysed as regulative (hierarchical) and instructional (selection, sequence/pace, and criteria). On the basis of this grammar I have generated two generic forms of pedagogic practice according to whether the ordering principles are explicit or implicit. These basic forms were shown to yield progressive, conservative, and radical modalities.

The next section will concentrate upon the social class assumptions of the generic types visible/invisible in their nonradical forms. We shall consider after this analysis two modalities of visible pedagogies, an autonomous modality and a market-oriented modality.

Social Class Assumptions of Pedagogic Practice

The fundamental proposition is that the same distribution of power may be reproduced by apparently opposing modalities of control. There is not a one-to-one relation between a given distribution of power and the modality of control through which it is relayed. In terms of this paper, pedagogic practices are cultural relays of the distribution of power. Although visible and invisible pedagogies are apparently opposing types, it will be shown that both carry social class assumptions. However, these social class assumptions vary with the pedagogic type. The class assumptions of visible pedagogies are different from the class assumptions of invisible pedagogies. These class assumptions carry consequences for those children who are able to exploit the possibilities of the pedagogic practices. The assumptions of a visible pedagogy are more likely to be met by that fraction of the middle class whose employment has a direct relation to the economic field (production, distribution, and the circulation of capital). Whereas the assumptions of an invisible pedagogy are more likely to be met by that fraction of the middle class who have a direct relation not to the economic field but to the field of symbolic control and who work in specialized agencies of symbolic control usually located in the public sector (see chapter 4). For both these fractions, education is a crucial means of cultural and economic reproduction, although perhaps less so for that fraction directly related to the economic field.[6]

Social Class Assumptions of Visible Pedagogies

Sequencing Rules

I shall start by looking at the sequencing rules of a visible pedagogy. In the case of a visible pedagogy the sequencing rules are explicit and mark the future of the child in very clear steps or stages. At 5 you should know and be this, at 6 you should know and be that, and at 7 you should know and be something else. Now it is quite clear that if a child comes to school at 5 and cannot meet the intitial requirements of the sequencing rules, it will have difficulty in meeting the requirements at 6. Gradually the child will fall further and further behind. Three strategies may be applied in this situation, or later in the life of the acquirer. Either a repair system will have to be introduced to cope with the children who have failed to meet sequencing requirements or the pacing rules will have to be relaxed so that the child is given more time to meet the requirements of the sequencing rules. Either strategy results in a stratification of acquirers. In the case of a repair system the stratification is explicit and public; in the case of relaxation of the pacing the stratification is implicit, and perhaps will not become explicit and public until later in the pedagogic life. A third strategy would be to maintain the pacing and sequencing rules but to reduce either the quantity or the quality of the contents to be acquired or both. All three strategies produce a more delicate system of stratification within an already stratifying pedagogic practice.

Early reading is crucial to a visible pedagogy and is an early requirement of the sequencing rules. Psychologists tell us that at a given age a child should be able to read. I am not certain I wholly accept this. The age by which a child should be able to read is a function of the sequencing rules of the pedagogic practice of the school. In the case of a visible pedagogy, it is crucial that a child reads early, and this for many reasons.

Once a child can read, the book is there, and the book is the textbook or its equivalent. Once a child can read, independent solitary work is possible. He/she is also gradually introduced into a nonoral form of discourse, the rules of which are often at variance with oral forms. It is not only that reading involves the acquisition of a new symbolic relay but that *what* is relayed is itself different from the content of oral forms. Further, school reading is in many cases different from nonschool reading. The difference is in what is relayed. In an important sense reading makes the child eventually less dependent upon the teacher and gives the acquirer access to alternative perspectives. Thus those children who are unable to meet sequencing rules as they apply to reading become more dependent upon the teacher and upon oral forms of discourse.

There is another aspect of sequencing rules which we should consider: the relation between the local, the here and now, the context-dependent, and the less local, the more distant, the more context-independent meanings. In pedagogic terms this refers to the acquisition of context-tied operations, on the one hand, and on the other to operations and understanding of principles and their application to new situations. In visible pedagogies there is usually a time interval between these different levels of discourse, in the sense that the local, context-dependent, context-tied operations come in the early stage of the pedagogic practice and the understanding and application of principles come at a later stage; the understanding of the principles of the principles even later. Visible pedagogies entail a distribution of expected age-related discourses.

However, if children cannot meet the requirements of the sequencing rules and are caught up in the strategies of the repair system, then these children, often the children of the lower working class (including other disadvantaged ethnic groups), are constrained by the local, context-dependent, context-tied skills; by a world of facticity. Children who can meet the requirements of the sequencing rules will eventually have access to the principles of their own discourse. These children are more likely to be middle class and are more likely to come to understand that the heart of discourse is not order but disorder, not coherence but incoherence, not clarity but ambiguity, and that the heart of discourse is the possibility of new realities.

We might ask ourselves, if this is the possibility of pedagogic discourse, why are the children of the dominant classes not demonstrating the possibilities of the discourses they have acquired? And the answer must be that socialization into a visible pedagogy tries, though not always successfully, to ensure that its discourse is safe rather than dangerous. In this way a visible pedagogy produces deformation of the children/students of both the dominant and the dominated social classes. In summary we can say that a visible pedagogy is likely to distribute different forms of consciousness according to the social class origin of acquirers. These different forms evolve from the sequencing rules.

Pacing Rules: Economy of Pedagogic Discourse

Pacing refers to the expected rate of acquisition, that is, the rate at which learning is expected to occur. Pacing is thus linked to sequencing rules and here refers to the rate at which the progression established by those rules is to be transmitted and acquired. Pacing rules, then, regulate the rhythm of the transmission, and this rhythm may vary in speed. Figure 7.4 illustrates pacing and sites of acquisition.

I shall propose that the schools' academic curriculum, if it is to be effectively acquired, always requires two sites of acquisition, the school and the home. Curricula cannot be acquired wholly by time spent at school. This is because the pacing of the acquisition is such that time at school must be supplemented by official pedagogic time at home, and the home must provide a pedagogic context and control of the pupil to remain in that context. There must be an official pedagogic discipline in the home. How does the school reproduce itself in the home? As the pupil gets older, he/she is expected to do more and more school work in the home, and the family will be expected to ensure that the pupil has time at home for this work and will also have effective control over the peer-group practices of the child. The work the pupil is expected to do at home is, of course, homework. The basis of homework is usually a textbook. But the textbook requires a context, an official pedagogic context in the home. That is, a space—a silent space—and this is not usually available in the homes of the poor. Nor is pedagogic time available for poor children, as often time is used to work for money—the curriculum practice of the street. Under these conditions there cannot be an effective second site of acquisition

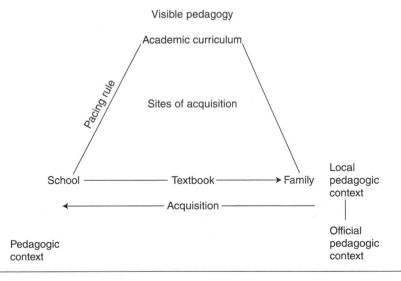

Figure 7.4

with an effective official pedagogic context and support. Without a second site, acquisition will not be possible, still less so as the child grows older. Failure becomes the expectation and the reality.

Where the catchment area of a school draws upon a lower working-class community it is likely, as we have seen, that the school will adopt strategies, or have strategies forced upon it, which will affect both the content and the pacing of the transmission. The content is likely to stress operations, local skills rather than the exploration of principles and general skills, and the pacing is likely to be weakened (Domingos, 1987). In this way children's consciousness is differentially and invidiously regulated according to their social class origin and their families' official pedagogic practice. In the case of a socially mixed catchment area where pupils are drawn from a variety of class backgrounds some schools, through a variety of strategies of stratification (sometimes including repetition), will stream (or 'set') pupils according to the school's estimate of their ability, and these different streams or sets will follow curricula varying in their content and/or pacing.

However, there is a more fundamental effect of strong pacing rules which affects the deep sociolinguistic rules of classroom communicative competence. With strong pacing, time is at a premium, and this regulates examples, illustrations, narratives which facilitate acquisition; regulates what questions may be put, and how many; regulates what counts as an explanation, both its length and its form. Further, strong pacing will tend to reduce pupils' speech and privilege teachers' talk, and this the pupils come to prefer, as time is scarce for the official pedagogic message. In this way the deep structure of pedagogic communication is itself affected. Pacing creates the rhythm of the communication, and rhythms of communication have different modalities. The rhythm of narrative is different from the rhythm of analysis. A strong pacing rule for the latter constructs a principle of communication very different from the inner structure of the communicative principle children use in everyday life. The dominant modality of human communication is not that of analysis but that of narrative. We tell each other stories. However, some families not only construct an official pedagogic context but also socialize their children into official pedagogic communication and the inner structure generated by its pacing rules: an inner structure which points towards analysis rather than narrative, non-linear rather than linear communicative competences. In this way the pacing rule not only affects the social relations of communication but regulates the inner logic of communication.

The strong pacing rule of the academic curriculum of the school creates the necessity of two sites of acquisition. It creates a particular form/modality of communication which does not privilege everyday narrative. In this structure children of the disadvantaged classes are doubly disadvantaged. There is no second site of acquisition and their orientation to language, narrative, is not privileged by the pedagogic communication of the school, either in form or in content, for only some narratives are permissible in school. Thus the pacing rule of the transmission acts selectively on those who can acquire the school's dominant pedagogic code, and this is a social class principle of selection. To weaken the pacing rule would require a change in the allocation of cultural capital and economic capital to the school. A change in cultural capital, because a weakened pacing rule sets up different classroom practice and communications which will require a change in the training of teachers and an increase in economic capital, because the transmission of the same information will now cost more. It is likely, however, that the costs of yearly repetition in some societies will most certainly be reduced, together with the costs of alienated youth. Currently the visible pedagogy of the school is cheap to transmit because it is subsidized by the middle-class family and paid for by the alienation and failure of children of the disadvantaged classes and groups.

We can now see that the pacing rule carries invisible social class assumptions which act selectively on those who can acquire the dominant pedagogic code of the school through the distributive consequences of the visible pedagogy's strong pacing and its regulation of the deep structure of sociolinguistic competences. Indeed, where pacing is strong we may find a *lexical* pedagogic code where one-word answers, or short sentences, relaying individual facts/skills/operations may be typical of the school class of marginal/lower working-class pupils, whereas a *syntactic* pedagogic code relaying relationships, processes, connections may be more typical of the school class of middle-class children, although even here pupil participation may be reduced.[7]

> We can regard pacing rules as regulating the economy of the transmission and so these rules become the meeting point of the material, discursive, and social base of the transmission.

It is important to point out that a visible pedagogy is not intrinsically a relay for the reproduction of differential school achievement among children from different social classes. It is certainly possible to create a visible pedagogy which would weaken the relation between social class and educational achievement. This may well require a supportive pre-school structure, a relaxing of the framing on pacing and sequencing rules, and a weakening of the framing regulating the flow of communication between the school classroom and the community(ies) the school draws upon. Such relaxation of the framing of a visible pedagogy raises the cost of the transmission and has crucial implications for teacher training and school management. An invisible pedagogy, as we shall see later, is likely to create a pedagogic code intrinsically more difficult, initially at least, for disadvantaged social groups (from the perspective of formal education) to read and to control.

I have discussed the social class assumptions of visible pedagogies only in respect to sequencing rule and pacing. The discussion of the social class assumptions of hierarchical rules will be deferred for purposes of exposition until the discussion of the social class assumptions of invisible pedagogies. I must point out that what has been analysed is the implicit ideological basis of the pedagogic relay itself, that is, the *bias in the relay* which acts selectively upon those who can acquire what is relayed. Clearly what is relayed, the instructional contents, the values these presuppose, and the standards of conduct, character, and manner which form the contents of the school's regulative discourse, carry cultural biases, including those of social class. These biases, the biases of what is relayed, are not the object of this analysis, as they are well documented in the literature.

Social Class Assumptions of an Invisible Pedagogy[8]

The class assumptions of an invisible pedagogy translate into cultural and economic prerequisites for the effective understanding and acquisition of this practice. I shall examine those assumptions with respect to the concept of space, the concept of time, and the concept of control. In the case of space and time I shall distinguish between economic and symbolic assumptions.

Space
Economic The material costs of the space of an invisible pedagogy relative to a visible pedagogy is high. For an invisible pedagogy presupposes movement on the part of the child—indeed, considerable freedom of movement. In a school class organized for a visible pedagogy the amount of space per child would be the size of the table or, later, a desk and chair. Under these conditions the school class can hold, and often does, a large number of acquirers. However, if the same space were to be organized for an invisible pedagogy most of the tables or desks would have to be removed to allow each child freedom of movement. But now it would not be possible to put the same number of children in the same space. The number would have to be reduced if the invisible pedagogy were to realize its potential. This reduction in the number of children necessarily increases the cost of the space. When the spatial requirement is translated into family space it is clear that the family cannot employ an invisible pedagogy where there are many members confined to a small space, as is the case with many working-class and lower working-class families, including, especially, disadvantaged families of minority ethnic groups. The spatial requirement is much more likely to be satisfied in the case of middle-class families.

Symbolic The rules whereby space is constructed, marked, and ordered contain implicit cognitive and social messages. In the case of a family operating with a visible pedagogy each room has its own function; within rooms objects may well have fixed positions, spaces may be reserved for special categories of person. There are strong explicit rules regulating the movement of objects, practices, communication from one space to another. Such space is strongly classified and pollution is necessarily visible. However, such strong classification can often provide privacy within its specialized boundaries. In general, this organization of space is predicated on a user rule: 'Leave the space as you find it'. Such a spatial grid carries cognitive and social messages.

However, in the case of a family operating an invisible pedagogy the spatial grid is very different. Relative to a visible pedagogy space it is more weakly marked. The rules regulating movements of objects, persons, practices, communications are less constraining. Meals may be provided on a cafeteria system. Living is more open-plan. Paradoxically, with greater freedom there is less privacy. If a visible pedagogy spatial grid is based on the fundamental rule that 'Things must be kept apart', with the rule of use 'Leave the space as you find it', then the spatial grid of an invisible pedagogy is based on the rule 'Things must be brought together', with the rule of use 'Make your own mark'. That is, the spatial grid of the invisible pedagogy facilitates, encourages individual representations in the sense of showing, revealing, individual representations. Cognitive and social messages are carried by such a space, and such is unlikely to be available and constructed by families disadvantaged by class or ethnicity.

Time
Economic If all children left school at 14 there would be no invisible pedagogies. An invisible pedagogy presupposes a long pedagogic life. Its relaxed rhythm, its less specialized acquisitions, its system of control (see later) entail a different temporal projection relative to a visible pedagogy for comparable acquisition. Indeed, this fact is explicitly taken into account by many middle-class families who favour this regime in the early years of their child's life before switching to a visible pedagogy at the secondary stage. Such favouring families often run a compensatory pedagogic programme dedicated to reading, writing, and counting whilst the child's creative potential may be facilitated by the invisible pedagogy of the infant school or pre-school.

Symbolic A child socialized by a familial visible pedagogy is involved in a particular symbolic projection in which time is punctuated by a series of dislocations in her/his treatment and expected behaviour. Time is symbolically marked as the child progresses through a series of statuses which define her/his relation not only to parents but also to the other siblings. The implicit theory of instruction held by parents which regulates their practice constructs age-specific communications/acquisitions. The child is developed in, and by, a particular construction of time.

However, in the case of an invisible pedagogy, the child is developed by, and is constructed in, a differently specialized construction of time. The child is constructed by implicitly held theories of instruction derived from the theories discussed earlier. This construction of time appears to give priority to the child's time/space, rather than to the time/space of the parents; to the concrete present of the child, and age statuses give way to the unique signs of the child's own constructed development. In this sense the structuring of the child's time is through a different temporal grid. Visible and invisible pedagogies construct different concepts of the child's development in time which may or may not be consonant with the concept of development held by the school.

There are some implications of a visible pedagogy which I shall develop here. Where the child moves through a series of specialized statuses in time, his/her conduct, achievement, or aspiration is relative to a particular status and the child is subject to normative criteria. He/she is not measured against himself/herself but only against those sharing a similar temporal category. From this point of view the child competes only with those in a similar temporal category. In this way competition is reduced, for jealousies, envious feelings, operates towards his/her peers. This is not to say that the child does not direct negative feelings towards other than his/her peers, but that he/she is aware, or can be made aware of, a distributive rule which privileges older children; a rule which is not personal but public.

In the case of an invisible pedagogy, because statuses are relatively more weakly marked, because of the more individualized or, better, personalized realizations expected, the child, by apparently competing only with her/himself, competes with everybody. This may well be the charm of criteria referencing. Parents relate to the child in terms of the child's apparently unique showings and representations. Here the child, despite the apparent democracy of the pedagogic regime, is placed in a more competitive relation, as comparisons are less likely to be age-graded. Thus jealousies, envious feelings, aspirations are likely to be less specifically focused and so more difficult for both the parents and the child to deal with. From a cognitive and from a social point of view, girls are less likely to be negatively constrained by invisible pedagogies than visible pedagogies. Conversely, for boys, under an invisible pedagogy practice, girls become successful competitors and a threat.

Control: Hierarchical Rules
Here I am concerned with how parents introduce and maintain principles of conduct, character, and manner—that is, concepts of social order, relation, and identity; in other words, with their regulative practice. In the case of a visible pedagogy the rules of social order are generally explicit and specific. The spatial and temporal grids provide an explicit structure, a grammar of proscriptions and prescriptions, and deviance is very visible. Once the child has acquired the implicit grammar of the spatial and temporal grids, the problems of control are relatively reduced. Clearly, they do not evaporate. If the child disobeys, then privileges are withdrawn and explicit rules are articulated. In the extreme, strategies of exclusion and physical punishment may be used. I would like it to be clear that visible pedagogies are not necessarily 'authoritarian' but they are certainly positional. Control functions to clarify, maintain, repair boundaries. However, in the case of invisible pedagogies we can ask, where does the control lie in a context of weakened spatial and temporal grids, of encouraged personalized representations, especially in a context where we could reasonably expect a greater potential for issues of control to arise?

I want to propose that in this apparently relaxed familial context control lies almost entirely in inter-personal communication: a form of communication which works round the areas of motivation and intentionality as read by the parents. The communication is multi-layered. In order to facilitate this multi-layering of communication a progressive weakening takes place of the classification between the inside of the child and the outside. The parents encourage the child to make more of his/her inside public and facilitate the process. More of the child's feelings, fantasies, fears, and aspirations are expected to be made public. The surveillance of the child is total. In this sense it is difficult for the child to hide and also difficult for the parents to. The communication process works to make the invisible visible, through language, and this may carry its own pathology.

In the case of a visible pedagogy we said that one of the strategies of control is exclusion but that this strategy carries difficulties in the case of an invisible pedagogy. For if the child is excluded (or as a strategy of self-defence excludes him/herself by withdrawing), then the communication process is weakened and so is the means of control. This gives the child a powerful strategy for controlling the parents by withdrawing, by excluding him/herself, by not being there, symbolically or physically. The parents must then develop strategies of retrieval in order to return the child symbolically or physically to the communication system. In this way the child acquires a particular elaborated variant of communication which gives rise to an elaborate repertoire of manipulative skills.

Invisible pedagogies give rise to procedures of control based upon multi-layered class patterns of communication necessary to support and promote their concept and practice of social order. And the construction of these communicative competences is likely to be class-based. Where these competences are not made available in the family the child is less likely to be self-regulating in school, according to the requirements of its invisible pedagogy practice, and is likely to misread both the practice and its pedagogic context.

I have argued that the assumptions of invisible pedagogies as they inform spatial, temporal, and control grids are less likely to be met in class or ethnically disadvantaged groups, and as a consequence the child here is likely to misread the cultural and cognitive significance of such a classroom practice, and the teacher is likely to misread the cultural and cognitive significance of the child.

We have focused upon different pedagogic sites in our analysis of the social class assumptions of visible pedagogies and invisible pedagogies in their generic form. In the case of visible pedagogies we focused upon the school and in the case of invisible pedagogies we focused upon the family. This is because the *surface* features of a visible pedagogy can be understood by all, as it is a standard pedagogic form, whether or not its underlying principles and practices are reproduced in the family. Thus it was necessary to analyse the underlying ordering principles of the official—that is, the school's —pedagogic practice in order to show that the ordering principles may militate against the acquisition of this practice by class or ethnically disadvantaged groups. In the case of invisible pedagogies we focused on the family to show the supporting domestic pedagogic practice required if the classroom context and practice were to be understood for their pedagogic significance.

What we find, as I have pointed out before, is rarely a pure form of an invisible pedagogy but rather an embedded pedagogic practice where the invisible pedagogy is embedded in a visible pedagogy:

$$\frac{\text{IP}}{\text{VP}}$$

Here —— indicates embedded. The specific specialized skills and attributes of a visible pedagogy are beneath the surface of an invisible pedagogy, or surface at special occasions. And this holds in the family. What is of interest is when the strong classification of a visible pedagogy emerges as a pedagogic form in itself or surfaces to interrupt an invisible pedagogy. It is clear that, even for ardent sponsors of invisible pedagogies, this practice is generally confined to the child's early years; certainly by the secondary level the demand is for a visible pedagogy, as it is this practice which leads to professional occupational placement. Given this situation, the socialization of a fraction of the middle class is perhaps unique as a modal type. We mean by modal that the form of socialization is not confined to individual families but is a publicly recognized form: a form in which the primary pedagogic so-cialization principles and practices are at variance with those of the secondary stage. Or where weak classification is embedded in a latent strong classification; and this, we suspect, has many complex consequences.

Whilst it is certainly not true to say that a visible pedagogy is a capitalist practice, it is the standard European pedagogic practice, in one form or another, of every elite secondary curriculum, whether in the East or the West. The strong classification of the visible pedagogy probably has its roots in the medieval university, in the major classification between the Trivium and the Quadrivium and in their sub-classifications, and the subordination of both to religion. The strong classification between mental and manual practice probably dates from the same period, when manual practice had its own specialized relays, either within the family or in specialized guilds, so creating the concept of the autonomous or abstract visible pedagogy. Such a visible pedagogy, autonomous with respect to control over its own practices, won its independence from the Church, but remained abstract in the sense that its discourse referred only to itself rather than to work. After gaining independence of the Church it became progressively regulated by the State. Whilst, in origin, the visible pedagogy as a relay is not itself a class product, *even though what it relayed was,* its institutionalization in either the private or the public sector led to a selective class-based acquisition.

In the case of the invisible pedagogy, certainly in the UK and probably elsewhere, the sponsors of this as a public form, its dissemination and construction as a practice, were members of that fraction of the middle class discussed earlier. Celia Jenkins (1989) has clearly shown that the members of the New Education Fellowship who were highly influential throughout the 1920s and 1930s in promoting and constructing the 'new education' were drawn almost entirely from professional agents of symbolic control functioning in specialized agencies of symbolic control. Those who opposed invisible pedagogies (other than pedagogues) were likely to be those members of the middle class whose work had a direct relation to the production, distribution, and circulation of capital.

The opposition between these fractions of the middle class is an opposition not over the distribution of power but over principles of social control. At economic and political levels the opposition is an opposition over the role of the State. On the whole the middle-class sponsors of invisible pedagogy support State intervention and the expansion of agents and agencies of symbolic control, and thus growth in public expenditure. For this is the ground and opportunity of their own reproduction and advancement, whereas the middle-class sponsors of visible pedagogy drawn from the economic sector and the entrepreneurial professions are opposed to growth in public expenditure. Thus there are opposing material and symbolic (discursive) interests.

We have so far discussed the class assumptions which act selectively on those who can achieve in visible and invisible pedagogies as generic types. We have earlier said that these generic types can generate a variety of modalities. We shall now consider two modalities of the visible pedagogy, modalities which are opposed to each other and which today are likely to be found in opposition in Europe and North and South America.

Autonomous and Market-Oriented Visible Pedagogies[9]

School systems and university systems are now more and more engaged in a struggle over what should be transmitted, over the autonomy of transmission, over the conditions of service of those who transmit, and over the procedures of evaluation of acquirers.

I shall conclude by looking, somewhat cursorily, at the present conflict between knowledge and market-oriented forms, that is, between 'autonomous' and 'dependent' forms of visible pedagogies. That is, between visible pedagogies justified by the intrinsic possibilities of knowledge itself and visible pedagogies justified by their market relevance. In a sense the autonomous visible pedagogy is both a sacred and a profane form, depending essentially upon one's position as either transmitter or acquirer. From an acquirer's point of view an autonomous visible pedagogy is instrumental to class placement through symbolic means. Yet it has the cover of the sacred. However, a market-oriented visible pedagogy is a truly secular form born out of the 'context of cost-efficient education', allegedly promoting relevant skills, attitudes, and technology in an era of large-scale chronic youth unemployment. The explicit rules of selection, sequence, pace, and criteria of a visible pedagogy readily translate into performance indicators of schools' staff and pupils, and a behaviourist theory of instruction readily realizes programmes, manuals, and packaged instruction. Specialization of curricula within a dominant market-oriented visible pedagogy allows for an almost perfect reproduction of the hierarchy of the economy within the school, or between schools (as in the case of 'magnet' schools), through the grading of curricula, e.g., managerial/administrative/business, through the various technological specializations, clerical, and imaginary trade apprenticeships for the lower working and marginal class groups. It is but a small step to encourage industry-based training and, as in Chile, State-sponsored privatized schools. Both autonomous and market-oriented visible pedagogies are relays of the stratification of knowledge, of social inequalities. However, the ideological base of the market-oriented visible pedagogy is more complex and, if I may be allowed, perhaps more sinister.

The autonomous visible pedagogy justifies itself by the intrinsic worthwhileness and value of the knowledge it relays and by the discipline its acquisition requires. Its arrogance lies in its claim to moral high ground and to the superiority of its culture, its indifference to its own stratification consequences, its conceit in its lack of relation to anything other than itself, its self-referential abstracted autonomy. The market-oriented visible pedagogy is ideologically a much more complex construction. It incorporates some of the criticism of the autonomous visible pedagogy, much of it originating from left-wing positions: criticism of the failure of the urban school, of the passivity and inferior status of parents, which combine to reduce their power over schools and teachers, of the boredom of working-class pupils and their consequent disruption of and resistance to irrelevant curricula, of assessment procedures which itemize relative failure rather than the positive strength of the acquirer. But it assimilates these criticisms into a new discourse: a new pedagogic Janus.

The explicit commitment to greater choice by parents and pupils is not a celebration of a participatory democracy but a thin cover for the old stratification of schools and curricula. New forms of assessment, profiling, criteria-referenced rather than norm-referenced assessment, allegedly to recognize and liberate individual qualities, allow of, and mark, greater control of assessment. At the same time periodic mass testing of pupils concentrates new distribution procedures for homogenizing acquisition and, at the same time, creates performance indicators of its effectiveness.[10] Vocationalism appears to offer the lower working class a legitimation of their own pedagogic interests in a manual-based curriculum, and in so doing appears to include them as significant pedagogic subjects, yet at the same time closes off their own personal and occupational possibilities.

The situation is indeed complex. At the same time as the economy is moving towards a greater concentration upon mergers and corporate growth, at a more micro level an entrepreneurial 'artisan' culture is being encouraged in the service sector. This is reflected in market-oriented visible pedagogies to develop imaginary apprenticeships into the skills for this function, e.g., decorating, plumbing, carpentry for the self-employed. Even the pedagogic regimes are mixed, drawing on features of invisible pedagogy, e.g., in the 'negotiation' of pupils' profiles, life skill programmes.[11] The new pedagogic discourse recontextualizes and thus repositions within its own ideology features of apparently oppositional discourses.[12]

The market-oriented visible pedagogy, at least in the UK, creates apparently greater local independence for, and competition between, schools and teachers, yet at the same time the schools and teachers are tied more directly to State regulation. And finally we can detect that the State is now operating on quite different principles with respect to the principles and practices of the economy and the principles and practices of specialized agencies/agents of symbolic control, especially education. In the economy privatization rules but competition is reduced as mergers proceed apace. As the State reduces its control, corporations and multinationals take up the vacated space. In the sector of the specialized agencies of symbolic control, especially in education, we see that privatization, the local autonomies of agencies, are there to encourage greater competition between units. Indeed, we might say that the major site of competition is not the economy in total but increasingly within the sector of publicly regulated symbolic control. Yet despite the greater competition within this sector it is subject to greater and more complex forms of State regulation. Thus the essential shift which appears to be taking place is the shift of State regulation from the economy to symbolic control. Yet State management of symbolic control is accomplished more and more by the exclusion of its own agents and their replacement by managers, administrators, industrialists of the economy.

The ideological message of a market-oriented visible pedagogy is less the regulation and realization of the pedagogy of the new 'relevance' than the new regulation and realization of symbolic control in the transition to capitalism's latest transformation: communications.[13]

Addendum

This paper is a revision of an earlier paper, 'Class and pedagogies: visible and invisible' (in *Class, Codes and Control*, vol. 3, revised edition 1977). It develops and extends the discussion of rules and their class assumptions and provides a more general model for generating types and modalities of pedagogic practices. Further, it includes a discussion of market-oriented pedagogies and speculations on their origin, function, and linkage to macro changes in the form of symbolic control. It does not, however, replace the earlier paper but extends and builds upon it. The paper does show that the basic underlying logic of this and other papers can deal with the question of content, as well as linking macro and micro levels of analysis.

In terms of the general classification and framing analysis, much of the focus of the paper in the discussion of specific pedagogic practices is upon framing rather than upon classification. It should be borne in mind that principles of classification are always invisibly present in any pedagogic practice in the sense that any context of that practice presupposes a relationship with other contexts, other pedagogic practices/communications, either within the institution or external to it. Further, principles of classification are visibly present within any pedagogic practice and are realized in the arrangement of acquirers, the distribution of tasks, and in the organizational features of the context. Thus principles of classification, as principles of framing, always have internal as well as external values.

Notes

1. This paper has benefited from seminars held at CIDE, Santiago, Chile, in 1985, and at the University of Valle, Cali, Colombia, in 1986. The present form arose out of an invitation from Adelphi University, New York, to deliver the Robert Finkelstein Annual Lecture, 1987. I am grateful to Dr Alan Sadovnik of Adelphi University for comments and discussion, and also to Celia Jenkins, of the Department of the Sociology of Education, University of London Institute of Education, whose Ph.D. thesis investigated the social class basis of progressive education in Britain.
2. For the purposes of this paper this logic has been reduced to three rules, but there is a fourth, a recontextualizing rule which creates the content to be transmitted. This is a complex matter, fully presented in chapter 5.
3. See chapter 5 for detailed analysis.
4. It is, of course, possible to have explicit hierarchical rules but degrees of implicitness of sequential/pacing rules, which indicate a weakening in the framing of these rules.
5. It is a matter of some interest that in the 1960s in the major disciplines of the human sciences, psychology, linguistics, and anthropology, the concept of competence underlined the structuralist theories of Piaget (child development), Chomsky (linguistics), and Lévi-Strauss (anthropology). Competence in all three theories refers to an in-built grammar. Chomsky's theory of syntax, Piaget's theory of the development and transformation of cognitive operations, Lévi-Strauss's theory of cultural assemblies and reassemblies are all competences triggered by interaction with non-culturally specific others. That is, competence arises out of two facilities, an in-built facility and an interactional facility. From this point of view competence-acquisition takes place, analytically speaking, at the level of the social, *not* the cultural, because acquisition is dependent not upon any cultural arrangement but upon *social* interaction.

    Competence theories, then, integrate the biological with the social, but both are disconnected from the cultural. Competence theories point to competence-acquisition as entailing active participation on the part of the acquirer. Indeed, competence-acquisition arises out of the creative possibilities of the acquirer in inferring rules (Chomsky) in the process of accommodation (Piaget) in *bricolage* (Lévi-Strauss). In a sense competence theories announce a fundamental democracy: all are equal in their acquisition, all actively participate in their acquisition, creativity is intrinsic to becoming social. Differences between individuals are then a product of culture. From this point of view competence theories may be regarded as critiques showing the disparity between what we are and what we become, between what we are capable of and our performance. However, this idealism is bought at a price: the price of severing the relation between power, culture, and competence, between meanings and the structures through which meanings become possible. The democracy of competence theories is a democracy removed from society.
6. An analysis of symbolic control, its agents, agencies, and its relation to the economic field may be found in Bernstein (1986), and set out in chapter 4. For empirical study of differences in the socialization of adolescents whose parents function in the field of symbolic control and the economic field see Holland (1986), Aggleton and Whitty (1985), and Cohen (1981).
7. It is important to point out that what we have called 'lexical' and 'syntactic' pedagogic practices are within the general thesis that the privileging code of the school is elaborated. We may now be finding that this code is officially suspended and replaced by a 'lexical' pedagogic practice relaying less the exploration of principles than context-specific operations which develop low-level skills. In the past, the suspension of an elaborated code with respect to groups of pupils, usually lower working-class, including racially disadvantaged groups, was not official policy but came about because of the context that teachers and pupils alike found themselves in.
8. King (1978 and elsewhere) criticizes the analysis of invisible pedagogy on the grounds that his empirical study of primary schools found no evidence of its existence. As has been pointed out here and in the original paper it is more likely that what will be found is an embedded pedagogic practice, the invisible embedded in the visible. The pure form is more likely to be found in the private sector. Invisible pedagogy was institutionalized under the name of *dialog-pedagogike* in Sweden in the 1970s. Empirical support for the practice of invisible pedagogy in middle-class families may be found in the references cited in note 5, and at the level of the classroom in Daniels (1988, 1989). An enquiry into different forms of special school organization, pedagogic practice, and pupil discrimination is to be found in *CORE* 12, 2. See also Jenkins (1989).

114 • Basil Bernstein

9. 'Autonomous' in the sense of independent is clearly *relative* to 'market-oriented' in the sense of dependent upon economy. Certainly in the United Kingdom (and, for that matter, elsewhere) all levels of the educational systems have for the past thirty years become more and more subject to central control. University research funding is now severely constrained both by the reduction in governmental funding (especially in the social sciences) and by governmental criteria regulating approved research. Market-oriented visible pedagogies indicate a shift of focus of central government, both with respect to the knowledge which is transmitted and with respect to the change in the controlling agents, which now include industrialists. This shift of focus involves not only the development of specialized curricula but also the development of specialized schools.

10. I am indebted to Patricia Broadfoot (1986) for these points.

11. The discussion of invisible pedagogies has occurred in a context where such a practice is dominant within the institution (e.g. family, primary school, pre-school). It has been noted that an invisible pedagogy is less likely to appear in a pure form in the public sector but more likely to be embedded in a visible pedagogy. However, it is possible that features of invisible pedagogy will be found as specialized practices within a predominantly visible pedagogy modality. Here such a specialized practice is likely to be particular to a part of the curriculum (e.g. life skills), addressed to a particular social group (e.g. disadvantaged class or ethnic groups), or may even form part of an assessment procedure. In general invisible pedagogies and/or 'integrated' pedagogic practices are more likely to be formed at primary level or, if at secondary level, associated with disadvantaged social groups as means of their social control. In general, shifts towards invisible pedagogies or similar 'progressive' practices which imply a weakening of classification and framing are more likely to occur in times of 'economic buoyancy'. Such practices are more expensive, both with respect to the training of the transmitters and with respect to the cost of the transmission, than visible pedagogies. In times of economic boom/growth the demand side is less powerful than the supply side, and as a consequence hierarchies may well take a more indirect, less explicit form as well as being less able to be as selective with respect to ideas, personnel, and interests. However, in times of slump and chronic unemployment demand is more powerful than supply, hierarchies may be expected to become more explicit and directive, more selective of ideas, personnel, and interests. As a consequence, in general, classification and framing relations are likely to strengthen in conjunction with stronger central control. However, as pointed out earlier, specialized invisible pedagogic practices are still likely to be inserted as devices of social control.

    In summary we could hypothesize that shifts in modal state pedagogic practices away from, or towards, weak classification and weak framing ('progressive' practices) are likely to be mediated by shifts in the economy which change the social basis of the influencing dominant agents of the state, the degree of explicitness of hierarchies, and the terms of supply of and demand for pedagogic practitioners. In the case of development/expansion of the economy, there is likely to be an increase in public expenditure on education, medical, and social services, and influencing dominant agents are likely to be drawn from agents of symbolic control specializing in agencies of symbolic control, whereas in the case of a downturn in the economy there is likely to be a reduction in public expenditure on education, medical, and social services, and influencing dominant agents of the state are likely to be drawn not from symbolic control but from the economic field.

12. Whilst it can be hypothesized that the more abstract the principles of the forces of division of labour then the more simple its social division of labour, because many of the lower (and increasingly the higher) functions are in information chains and feedback loops of the computer, it is also likely that, as the social division of labour of the economic field becomes both simplified and reduced, that of the field of symbolic control is likely to increase in complexity and size. Further, there is likely to be an attempt to develop an entrepreneurial service structure of the artesan type. Much of the vocational training of sections of the working class is directed towards this end.

13. The transition is linked to high levels of unemployment, changes in occupational functions and conditions, an increase in mergers, recurrent dangers of severe recession, which together may produce instabilities in the social order. The overall movement to greater state control in the field of symbolic control often announces itself through an ideology of the family and nation. This new individualism regulating the field of symbolic control contrasts sharply with the corporative potential of the communications revolution in the economic field.

References

Aggleton, P., and Whitty, G. (1985). 'Rebels without a cause? Socialization and subcultural sytle among children of the new middle classes', *Sociology of Education* 58, 1:60–72.

Bernstein, B. (1975). 'Class and pedagogies: Visible and invisible', in *Class, Codes and Control* 3: 116–56, London: Routledge; rev. in the 2nd ed., 1977.

Broadfoot, P. (1986). 'Whatever happened to inequality? Assessment policy and inequality: The UK experience', *British Journal of the Sociology of Education* 7, 2: 205–24.

Cohen, G. (1981). 'Culture and educational achievement', *Harvard Educational Review* 51, 2: 270–85.

Daniels, H.R.J. (1988). 'An enquiry into different forms of special school organization, pedagogic practice and pupil discrimination', C.O.R.E. 12, 2.

—— (1989). 'Visual displays as tacit relays of the structure of pedagogic practice', *British Journal of the Sociology of Edcuation* 10, 2: 123–40.

Giroux, H.A. (1989). *Schooling for Democracy*. London: Routledge.

Holland, J. (1986). 'Social class differences in adolescents' conception of the domestic and industrial division of labor', C.O.R.E. 10, 1.

Jenkins, C. (1989). 'The professional middle class and the origins of progressivism: A case study of new education fellowship, 1920–50,' ph.D. thesis, University of London.

Plowden Report. (1967). Children and their primary schools, report of the Central Advisory Council for Education (England), London: HMSO.

8

The Effects of Education as an Institution

JOHN W. MEYER

How does education affect society? The dominant view has it that the schools process individuals. They are organized networks of socializing experiences which prepare individuals to act in society. More direct macro-sociological effects have been given little attention. Yet in modern societies education is a highly developed institution. It has a network of rules creating public classifications of persons and knowledge. It defines which individuals belong to these categories and possess the appropriate knowledge. And it defines which persons have access to valued positions in society. Education is a central element in the public biography of individuals, greatly affecting their life chances. It is also a central element in the table of organization of society, constructing competencies and helping create professions and professionals. Such an institution clearly has an impact on society over and above the immediate socializing experiences it offers the young.

Recently, the traditional socialization view has been attacked with an argument which incorporates a more institutional conception of education, though in a very limited way. Education is seen as an allocating institution—operating under societal rules which allow the schools to directly confer success and failure in society quite apart from any socializing effects (e.g., Collins 1971; Bowles and Gintis 1976). Allocation theory leaves open the possibility that expanded educational systems have few net effects on society. The polemic controversy has obscured the fact that allocation theory (and institutional theory in general) has many unexplored implications for socialization theory and research; those implications are considered here. For instance, allocation theory suggests effects of expanded educational institutions both on those who attend and those who do not attend schools. It also can explain why completing a given level of schooling often matters much more in determining educational outcomes than do the features of the particular school attended.

But conventional allocation theory, while considering the institutional properties of educational systems, focuses mainly on the outcomes for individuals being processed. It tends to be assumed that education has no effect on the distribution of political, economic, and social positions in society. Allocation theory is thus a limited special case of a more general institutional theory—legitimation theory—which treats education as both constructing or altering roles in society and authoritatively allocating personnel to these roles. Modern educational systems involve large-scale public classification systems, defining new roles and statuses for both elites and members. These classifications are new constructions in that the newly defined persons are expected (and entitled) to behave, and to be treated by others, in new ways. Not only new types of persons but also new competencies are authoritatively created. Such legitimating effects of education transcend the effects education may have on individuals being processed by the schools. The former effects transform the behavior of people in society quite independent of their own educational experience.

In this paper, I develop the ideas of legitimation theory and propose comparative and experimental studies which could examine the effects of education on social structure, not simply on the individuals it processes. I move away from the contemporary view of educational organization as a production system constructing elaborated individuals. Modern education is seen instead as a system of institutionalized rites transforming social roles through powerful initiation ceremonies and as an agent transforming society by creating new classes of personnel with new types of authoritative knowledge.

The Traditional Socialization Model

Prevailing research on school effects is organized around a simple image of socialization in society: Schools provide experiences which instill knowledge, skills, attitudes, and values in their students. These students then have a revised and expanded set of personal qualities enabling them to demand more from, and achieve more in, the role structure of modern society. As the competence and orientation of the personnel of society are expanded and modernized, so society as a larger system is modernized and expanded.

Three general propositions are at issue here and make up a simple model, which is diagrammed in Figure 8.1:

Proposition 1 (*Socialization*). Schooled persons are socialized to expanded levels of knowledge and competence and expanded levels of modern values or orientations.

Proposition 2 (Socialization and Adult Competence). Early socialization to higher levels of knowledge, competence, and modern values or orientations creates higher levels of adult status and competence.

Proposition 3 (Individual Competence and Social Progress). The expansion of the number of skilled adults expands the complexity and wealth of society and social institutions.

Research on proposition 1 is rather clear-cut. Children and youth in schools learn a good deal more, and acquire more expanded social capacities than those not in school, even when background factors are controlled (see, e.g., Holsinger 1974; Plant 1965). The main problem in the research on this subject is the finding that the particular school students attend often seems to make little difference (see Jencks et al. [1972]; or the studies reviewed in Feldman and Newcomb [1969]). I return to this issue below; the point here is that something about participation in schools creates notable effects on all sorts of socialization—from knowledge to social values to status expectations.

Little direct empirical research has been done on proposition 3—the idea that changed people produce a changed social structure—though this kind of "demographic" explanation (Stinchcombe 1968) has been a main theme of sociological theories of social change. In recent decades some doubts have arisen, with a conservative fear that "overeducated" people create more social instability and breakdown than they do social development. There is no evidence of this, but the issue remains.

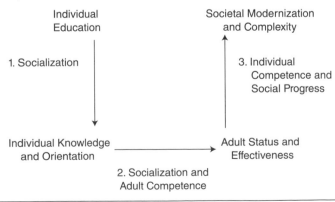

Figure 8.1 Traditional socialization theory.

Proposition 2 has been one source of doubt about the whole model. Traditional socialization theory in sociology (and child development research) becomes an adequate account of social structure only if (*a*) socialized qualities remain with the person with some stability over long periods of time, and (*b*) such qualities predict adult effectiveness in roles. But current research on personal qualities often suggests low autocorrelations over time (see the review by Mischel [1971]). Many empirical studies suggest that the personal qualities schooling creates do not effectively determine occupational success, once occupational entry has been obtained (see the polemic review by Berg [1971]). Even if socialized qualities have fair stability and offer fair predictive power, it is unlikely that the product of these effects (which amounts to a very low overall effect) explains the high correlation of education with adult status.

Thus, socialization theory, as an account of educational effects on society, has one area of success and two of failure. On the positive side, schooling does predict, with other variables held constant, many of the outcomes of socialization. On the negative side, many of the measurable socialization outcomes of schooling have little long-run staying power or predictive power.[1] Also on the negative side, variations among schools in their socialization programs show small effects on outcomes—if schools socialize through the immediate experiences they provide, schools providing different experiences should produce very different effects. The research literature provides little encouragement on this subject.[2]

Institutional Theories: Allocation Theory as a Limited Case

Traditional socialization theory defines education as an organized set of socializing experiences. It treats as peripheral the fact that modern educational systems are society-wide and state-controlled institutions. In discussions of socialization theory this property of educational settings barely appears (e.g., Wheeler 1966).

Partly in reaction to this limitation, but more in reaction to the empirical weakness of socialization theory and in polemic reaction to the earlier optimism about the socially progressive effects of education, allocation theories have been developed. It is argued that people in modern societies are allocated to adult roles on the basis of years and types of education, apart from anything they have learned in schools. Education is thus more a selector, sorter, and allocator than it is a socializer.

Education, in allocation theories, is a set of institutional rules which legitimately classify and authoritatively allocate individuals to positions in society. Allocation theories are limited in that they define only a few consequences of this system and consider effects mainly on the individuals being allocated, but they open up a broader range of institutional theories which are discussed below.

The power of the allocation idea arises from its obvious empirical validity. We all know that status positions in modern societies are assigned on the basis of education. Sometimes, as with civil service and professional positions (e.g., medicine, law, teaching), this is a matter of law. To teach in a high school one must have an educational credential. Whether one knows anything or not is less relevant. Often, rules about credentials are simply part of established organizational practice, as in the assignment of college and business-school graduates to managerial positions and of others to working-class jobs. Sometimes the whole process is informal, as in the inclination of juries and informal friendship groups to attend to the advice of their more educated members.

In any event, the relationship between education and social position—over and above socialization or learning—is quite direct. The line of research pursued by Blau and Duncan (1967) and Duncan, Featherman, and Duncan (1972) shows large direct effects of education on status attainment, sometimes with ability measures held constant. Education plays a direct causal role in occupational transition even late in the individual's career (Blau and Duncan 1967, chap. 5)—decades after any direct socialization effects must have decayed or become outmoded.

The basic idea is clear:

Proposition 4 (*Educational Allocation*). In modern societies, adult success is assigned to persons on the basis of duration and type of education, holding constant what they may have learned in school.

Educational allocation rules, that is, give to the schools social *charters* to define people as graduates and as therefore possessing distinctive rights and capacities in society (Meyer 1970a; see also Clark 1970). Thus the schools have power as an institutional system, not simply as a set of organizations processing individuals.

Impact of Allocation Rules on Socialization

The polemic contrast between socialization and allocation ideas—education as a socializing process versus education as a status competition—has concealed the fact that the two are not really inconsistent. Further, allocation theory offers interesting and useful extensions of traditional socialization ideas.

Assume that educational allocation rules in fact hold in society. Students and members of their social networks (e.g., parents, peers, teachers, and counselors) are informed members of society—not simply passive objects of educational production—and know these rules with some accuracy. Graduates, of course, experience the rules through the distinctive experiences and treatments they receive in society. Now if we assume a most elementary idea of social psychology, that people adapt and are adapted by others to their actual and expected experiences, two major propositions follow:

Proposition 5 (*Chartering*). Students tend to adopt personal and social qualities appropriate to the positions to which their schools are chartered to assign them.

Proposition 6 (*Lagged Socialization*). Adults tend to adopt qualities appropriate to the roles and expectations to which their educational statuses have assigned them.

These propositions argue that education functions for individuals as a set of initiation ceremonies of great and society-wide significance (Ramirez 1975; Garfinkel 1956). These ceremonies transform the futures and pasts of individuals, greatly enhancing their value in all sorts of social situations. On the basis of their education, individuals are expected to treat themselves, and others are expected to treat them, as having expanded rights and competencies. Given allocation rules, educational labels are of the greatest significance for the social identity of individuals.

Proposition 1 and proposition 5 parallel each other and in many instances overlap in accounting for the same findings. It is often unclear to what extent given socialization effects are generated by the immediate socializing situation in a given school and to what extent they are produced by the institutional authority in which the school is embedded.

However, proposition 5, in contrast to proposition 1, offers a direct explanation of the most puzzling general research paradox in the sociology of American education. The level of schooling achieved has substantial effects on all sorts of personal qualities. But outcome variations among schools—even though these schools differ greatly in structure and resources—are very small. This finding shows up in studies of college effects (Feldman and Newcomb 1969), high school effects, and effects at the elementary school level. If schools have their socializing effects as ritually chartered organizations (Meyer 1970a; Kamens 1971, 1974) rather than as organized collections of immediate socializing experiences, then all schools of similar ritual status can be expected to have similar effects. Since for many personnel assignment purposes all American high schools (or colleges) have similar status rights, variations in their effects should be small. But because all high schools are chartered to create "high school graduates"—a critical status in our society for college and occupational entry—all of them tend to produce marked effects on students. Proposition 5, in other words, argues that the most powerful socializing property of a school is its external institutional authority, derived from the rules of educational allocation, rather than its network of internal socializing experiences. Educators, who attend with great vigor to the accreditation of their schools, seem more aware of this process than do socialization researchers.

Thus, the educational contexts which vary substantially in the change and learning they produce in students do not usually include specific schools. They include contexts which are distinctively chartered:

1. Schooling per se. Life prospects (and hence changes in students) are vitally affected by being in an institution chartered as a school.
2. Type of school, when the types are differently chartered. Himmelweit and Swift (1969) and Kerckhoff (1975) show marked differences in outcomes for similar British students between grammar and secondary modern schools. American researchers have not looked for differences in expectations between initially similar students in general and vocational high schools. Some studies show distinct occupational effects of teachers, colleges, and engineering schools (Astin and Panos 1969).
3. Curriculum, when it is distinctively chartered. For instance, being in a college preparatory curriculum (in contrast to a vocational one) makes a considerable difference in the aspirations and expectations of American high school students (Alexander and Eckland 1975; see also Rosenbaum 1975).[3]

Proposition 6—the idea that education socializes adults by allocating them to expanded roles and role expectations—explains a second major paradoxical finding in the current sociology of education. The direct long-run effects of schools on graduates are thought to be rather moderate. But surveys of adults with regard to almost any dependent variable—attitudes, values, information, or participation—almost uniformly show that education plays a dominant role. For instance, Almond and Verba (1963) show with data on five countries that education is closely associated with political information, attitudes, and participation. Inkeles and Smith (1974) show the same result with data on six countries and are surprised to discover that the impact of education is much greater than that of work experience. Kohn's research (1969, and subsequently) shows exactly the same result, and again the author is surprised. But these findings make eminent sense. Educational allocation rules create a situation in which schooling is a fixed capital asset in the career of the individual, more durable than work or income, more stable than family life and relations, and less subject to market fluctuations than "real" property. Is it surprising that the attitudes and orientations of educated individuals continue to reflect such enhanced life prospects over long periods of time? They perceive these prospects and are surrounded by others who see them too.

Proposition 6 suggests that in explaining such long-run effects of education we do not need to look back to the details of the experience of socialization. Correlations between education and personal qualities can be maintained and increased by a structure or subsequent allocation which provides distinctive life experiences and anticipations for the educated. For instance, education can affect a person's sense of political efficacy by making him politically influential as well as by socializing him to a civic culture.

Further Implications of Allocation Theory

If taken seriously, and not simply used as a cynical critique of education, allocation theory would completely reorganize current research styles in the sociology of education. Allocation rules, unlike simple socialization effects, reign over both the students and the nonstudents, the educated and the uneducated, the graduates and those who never attended.

Research implication 1: Effects on nonstudents.—Let us examine the following hypotheses.

Hypothesis 1. The creation of social rules allocating status and competence to graduates leads to the socialization of students for expanded social roles.

Hypothesis 2. But such rules *lower* the prospects of nonstudents and, in a sense, desocialize them.

The more binding the allocation rules, the earlier and more convincingly are nonstudents committed to passive roles in society. This means that the society relying on credentials could well lower (below the previous floor) the modern competence of people of low education. Comparative contextual research is required to test this idea, since the independent variable is a property of the social system.

This argument has it that in a modern society education allocates its dropouts to failure. They (and their parents and friends) anticipate and adapt to this.

Hypothesis 3. Similarly, *subsequent* to the period of schooling, nongraduates are socialized through life experiences to the meaning of their failure just as graduates are socialized to the meaning of their success. The lagged differentials created by education should be greater the more firmly the principle of educational allocation is established.

Hypothesis 4. Those admitted to chartered educational organizations find their prospects enhanced even before attendance, while those rejected find their prospects lowered. They adapt their personal qualities in anticipation, even prior to attendance. These differentials should be greater the stronger the allocative position of the school.

For example, Benitez (1973) finds that students admitted to a national elite high school in the Philippines seem to gain in self-esteem and "competence" even before their socialization begins. Wallace's (1966) data suggest a similar interpretation.

Comparative research on effects such as these should help distinguish allocation theory from traditional socialization ideas.

Research implication 2: Aggregate effects.—A major implication of allocation theory is that inferences to the aggregate effects of education made from individual data on the basis of traditional socialization ideas are almost completely illegitimate. Researchers in the economics of education conventionally infer aggregate economic effects of education from income differentials between the educated and the less educated (see, e.g., the papers in Blaug 1968, 1969). It is assumed that these income differentials reflect real added value—the socialization gains of the educated. But if education is simply an allocation system, the gains of the educated may simply occur with equivalent losses for the uneducated. The expansion of education and educational allocation may have no effect on the aggregate product at all (Collins 1971).

Similarly, researchers on the political effects of education often infer that, because the educated occupy politically central positions, education must have helped create these positions (see the papers in Coleman 1965). But if education is simply a system of allocation, huge positional and attitudinal differences between the educated and the uneducated may exist with no aggregate effect at all. Igra (1976), in fact, shows (using Inkeles's data) that increases in the aggregate development of societies *lower* the political participation of individuals of given education (though the political information of individuals is found to be enhanced). Such "frog-pond effects" at lower levels of analysis are discussed by Davis (1966), Meyer (1970b), and Alexander and Eckland (1975).

The main arguments of allocation theory are added to those of socialization theory in Figure 8.2. Allocation ideas are discussed with some frequency in the current literature, though their implications for research remain little explored.

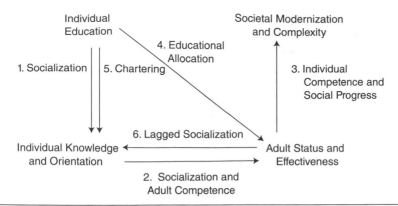

Figure 8.2 Allocation theory and its implications for socialization theory. (Pure allocation theory suggests that 3 is irrelevant. If a given set of adult competencies are simply allocated by education, no net societal gain in number of competent individuals need occur.)

The Limitations of Allocation Theory

Allocation theories, by conceiving of education as an institution, add a good deal to traditional socialization theory. But they do so in a very narrow way.

Education is seen in these theories as possessing its power because it is built into the rules and understandings which guide all sorts of personnel allocation processes in society. But its impact is considered only for those individuals being processed by the system—the students and nonstudents who are being sorted. And even this impact is denned in a limited way: these people are understood to respond only to their own role prospects as they are affected by education. Does the fact that all the other individuals around him are being magically transformed by powerful initiation ceremonies have no effect on a given student? And has it no effect on other members of society?

The problem here is that allocation theories ordinarily see education as allocating individuals to a fixed set of positions in society: a distribution of positions determined by other economic and political forces. Bowles and Gintis (1976) propose slight additional effects—education is thought to socialize people to accept as legitimate the limited roles to which they are allocated. Spence (1973) and Thurow (1975) see some marginal gains to society through more efficient selection by education. But the main development of allocation theory defines the *structure* of society as little affected by education.

Allocation theory, then, can be seen as a special case of a more general argument according to which education constructs and alters the network of positions in society in addition to allocating individuals to these positions. We simply need to abandon the assumption that the positions to which education allocates people cannot be built, expanded, and altered by education itself.

It is becoming more common to speak of education as legitimating the structure of modern society (Bowles and Gintis 1976), or of modern societies as in some essential way "schooled" (Illich 1971). If we want to understand the societal impact of education, not just its effects on the careers of individuals, we need to understand what this means.

The General Case: Legitimation Theory

Allocation theory is a special case of institutional theories of educational effects: it considers the effects of education as an institution (*a*) only on the individuals being processed and (*b*) with the structure of society held constant. We now turn to the general case: theories of the institutional impact of education on social structure itself—on the behavior of people throughout society.

Modern extended and institutionalized systems of education build into society certain rules which actors take for granted, know others take for granted, and incorporate in their decisions and actions.[4]

For instance, institutionalized educational systems create a situation in which social gatekeepers (e.g., personnel officers)—even if they read and believe Ivar Berg's book—nevertheless know that they must hire people on the basis of educational credentials.

Two closely related aspects of modern educational systems are relevant here as independent variables: (1) they are extended as systems of classification, categorizing entire adult populations by level and specialty; and (2) they are institutionalized, with their classifications often controlled by the state and enforced in daily life by rules about credentials written into law and applied in organizational practice. Almost everywhere, education is made compulsory and universal by national law, often in the national constitution (Boli-Bennett 1976). In most countries its structure is closely regulated by the nation-state (Ramirez 1973; Rubinson 1973).

Why does this occur? Whatever the economic origins of the process, the fact that it is usually accomplished and regulated by the state—unlike many aspects of economic development, which are left to individuals and subunits—suggests that its immediate origins lie in the political system: society as corporate organization (Swanson 1971) rather than as a system of exchange. *Formalized educational systems are, in fact, theories of socialization institutionalized as rules at the collective level.* The three core propositions used above to summarize traditional socialization theory *become* the structural basis of the educational system. Proposition 1—the idea that the schools teach critical skills and values—becomes institutionalized as the basic educational classification system: Education proceeds in a sequence (irreversible by ascriptive definition) from kindergarten through postdoctoral study and covers a defined series of valued substantive topics. The student is a "high school graduate" and has had compulsory units of history and English and mathematics. It is an institutionalized doctrine, since for many purposes one must treat the student as having acquired this knowledge by virtue of the units or credits completed, not by direct inspection. Proposition 2—the idea that schooled qualities are carried into adult effectiveness—is institutionalized in the basic rules for employing credentialled persons which dominate personnel allocation in modern society. If one hires an executive, a civil servant, or a teacher, one must inspect educational credentials—it is optional whether one inspects the person's competence. A teacher or a doctor who graduated from school in 1930 is still frequently treated as a socially and legally valid teacher or doctor. Proposition 3—the idea that educational allocation creates social progress—is institutionally embedded in our doctrines of progress: it consists of modernity, professionalization, and rationalization. The possession of the best certified and educated people is a main index of the advanced status of a hospital, a school, often a business organization, and indeed a society itself.

Educational systems themselves are thus, in a sense, ideologies. They rationalize in modern terms and remove from sacred and primordial explanations the nature and organization of personnel and knowledge in modern society. They are, presumably, the effects of the reorganization of modern society around secular individualism which is a main theme of Marx and Weber. Our problem here, however, is to discuss their effects.[5]

Legitimating Effects of Expanded and Institutionalized Education

Legitimating effects of education can be discussed in four general categories created by the intersection of two dichotomies. First, education functions in society as a legitimating *theory of knowledge* defining certain types of knowledge as extant and as authoritative. It also functions as a *theory of personnel*, defining categories of persons who are to be treated as possessing these bodies of knowledge and forms of authority.

Second, education validates both *elites* and *citizens*. Discussions of the legitimating function of education often emphasize only its role in supporting elites and inequality (e.g., Bowles and Gintis 1976; Carnoy 1972). But the overwhelmingly dominant kind of education in the modern world is

	Elite Education	Mass Education
Education as Theory of Knowledge	1. The Authority of Specialized Competence	3. The Universality of Collective Reality
Education as Theory of Personnel	2. Elite Definition and Certification	4. The Extension of Membership: Nation-building and Citizenship

Figure 8.3 Types of legitimating effects of education.

mass education (Coombs 1968), closely tied to the modern state and notion of universal citizenship (Marshall 1948; Bendix 1964; Habermas 1962).

These two distinctions define four types of legitimating effects of education, as specified in Figure 8.3. I discuss them in turn.

1. The Authority of Specialized Competence. Education does not simply allocate people to a fixed set of positions in society. It expands the authoritative culture and the set of specialized social positions entailed by this culture. Thus the creation of academic economics means that new types of knowledge must be taken into account by responsible actors. The creation of psychiatry means that former mysteries must now be dealt with in the social organization. The creation of academic programs in business management brings arenas of decision making from personal judgment, or luck, to the jurisdiction of rationalized knowledge. Social problems call for human-relations professionals (occasionally even sociologists). Safety or environmental problems call for industrial or environmental engineering.

The point here is that, quite apart from the immediate efficacy of these bodies of knowledge, they are authoritative and must be taken into account by actors at the risk of being judged negligent or irrational. The business manager who plans by the seat of his pants—unblessed by economic projections—has no excuse for ignoring the best advice. The political leader who sees social problems as beyond analysis or cure is reactionary and primeval. The emotionally disturbed person who rejects psychiatry is displaying irrationality.

Thus the knowledge categories of the educational system enter authoritatively into daily life. Mysteries are rationalized, brought under symbolic control, and incorporated into the social system. Society and its subunits are buffered from uncertainty (Thompson 1967):

> Proposition 7. The expansion (and institutionalization) of education expands the number of functions that are brought under social control and that responsible actors must take into account.[6]

2. Elite Definition and Certification. Education as an institution creates and defines particular categories of elite personnel. This has two aspects. (*a*) Education consists of allocation rules and initiation ceremonies designating which persons possess the authority and competence for various elite roles. This is the core idea of allocation theory. (*b*) But institutionalized education also defines the nature and authority of the elite roles themselves—helping to create the categories of personnel as well as to designate the particular occupants of these categories. In this way, expanded modern educational systems function as a personnel theory in society, justifying in modern cultural terms the expansion and specialization of modern elites.

Education, that is, not only creates "economic knowledge" which must be taken into account by rational actors. It is also a structure helping to create the role of economist, to justify economists' authority claims in society, and to define precisely who is an economist. Education thus creates, not only psychiatry, but psychiatrists; not only modern management ideology, but M.B.A.s. The rational actor must take into account medical knowledge and, to do so, he must consult a doctor. Thus, the modern organizational structure of society incorporates legitimated bodies of knowledge by incorporating the designated personnel.[7]

We take too narrow a view if we see this process as involving only a few specialized occupations. The most important rules concerning credentials are more general: the set of rules which connect the educational status of *college graduate* (and *high school graduate*) with all sorts of formal and informal elite positions. These rules define a generalized body of elite knowledge and specify its legitimate carriers.

It now becomes clear why views of educational allocation as "zero-sum"—allocating a fixed set of social statuses—are wrong. Education helps *create* new classes of knowledge and personnel which then come to be incorporated in society:

> Proposition 8. The expansion (and institutionalization) of education expands the number of specialized and elite positions in society. It defines and justifies their occupancy by particular people.[8]

The point here is that institutionalized education does more than simply allocate some to success and others to failure. The educated learn to claim specialized functions and to legitimate the specialized functions of others. The less educated learn that they are part of a social world of rights and duties elaborated far beyond the traditional community. This is one of the core meanings of the modern social status *citizen*.

3. The Universality of Collective Reality. Mass education creates a whole series of social assumptions about the common culture of society and thus expands the social meaning of citizenship, personhood, and individuality (modern ideas, all). It establishes a whole series of common elements for everyone.[9] (*a*) It creates the assumption of a national language or languages and defines universal literacy, (*b*) It reifies a given national history, (*c*) It constructs a common civic order—common heroes and villains, a common constitutional and political order with some shared cultural symbols and with legitimate national participation, (*d*) It validates the existence of a common natural reality through science and a common logical structure through mathematics and in this way constructs a myth of a common culture intimately linked to world society, (*e*) It constructs broad definitions of citizen and human rights as part of the modern world view.

Regardless of what people actually learn in school about their language and culture, nationally institutionalized mass education creates the assumptions of a national culture. For many purposes, both elite and citizen actors must take them into account.

> Proposition 9. The expansion (and institutionalization) of education expands the content and jurisdiction of the elements taken for granted as part of collective reality.

4. The Extension of Membership: Nation-Building and Citizenship. Beyond defining and extending national culture, mass education defines almost the entire population as possessing this culture, as imbued with its meanings, and as having the rights implied by it. Mass education defines and builds the nation (Marshall 1948; Bendix 1964). It allocates persons to citizenship—establishing their membership in the nation over and above various subgroups. And it directly expands the definition of what citizenship and the nation mean and what obligations and rights are involved. Mass education helps create a public: as education expands, ideas about public opinion as a vital force in society rise (Habermas 1962; Bergesen 1977). Individuals come to be defined as possessing the competencies and the moral orientations to participate in an expanded collective life:

> Proposition 10. Mass education expands the number of persons seen as possessing human and citizenship responsibilities, capacities, and rights. It also expands the prevailing definitions of these roles and their associated qualities.

In expanding both the meaning of citizenship and the set of persons who are seen as citizens, education plays a dual role. Certainly it opens up new possibilities for citizens—in particular, new claims for equality which can be made on society. It also, however, redefines individuals as responsible subordinate members (and agents) of the state organization, and opens them to new avenues of control and manipulation.

Research Designs in Legitimation Theory

Legitimation ideas propose societal effects of education. They can be studied in several ways.

1. Most directly, data comparing societies over time can be examined. For instance, is it true, in comparing societies, that those with expanded mass education tend to create sooner and more completely the welfare, policing, and participatory apparatuses of citizenship?
2. The same questions can be looked at with time-series data pertaining to a single society. For example, what has been the effect of the expansion of higher education in the United States, independent of other factors, on the number of types of professionals who have privileged status (as "expert witnesses") in the courts?
3. The same questions can be studied at the individual level as well. Legitimation theory argues for the effects of the extension and institutionalization of national educational systems on the judgments, perceived realities, and actions of *given* individuals—ordinary persons, rule makers, and critical social gatekeepers. Studies can therefore compare similar individuals in societies differing in educational structure. Do persons of given education, in more schooled societies, see personal and social problems as more likely to require educated expertise? Do they see, as I argued above, a larger number of social functions as requiring explicit (and undoubtedly educated) collective social management? Comparative survey research can help examine such questions.
4. It is also possible to approach these questions experimentally. Education, it is argued, restructures social reality for given individuals. To explore this, subjects can be confronted with hypothetical societies, similar in many respects but differing in the expansion and authority of education. Would subjects be more likely to propose to use economists and other social scientists to help with business or political planning if we describe for them a society in which elite education is highly developed and institutionalized? Subjects might even attribute authority to nonexistent professions if those are described as rooted in educational programs.

These research design approaches can all be used to deal with the following central empirical hypotheses of legitimation theory.

1. Basing a particular elite in the educational system helps create and expand its authority. One can study empirically the differential rise in societies of personnel workers, social scientists, physicians, or psychiatrists as these groups are affected by differential educational institutionalization. This can be done with comparative, survey, or experimental techniques.
2. More generally, expanded elite educational systems produce and support *more* and larger elites with jurisdiction over more social functions. We can test this hypothesis by seeing whether more problems requiring collective action are denned in societies with expanded elite education, and by seeing whether the management of such problems is more likely to be reserved to educated elites in such societies.
3. Mass education expands the national culture. Both elites and masses, in societies with more mass education, should be more likely to perceive widespread literacy, attention to public

problems, information, and involvement. This should hold true even when the actual levels of these variables are held constant. Mass education is an institution, and like all institutions creates forms of pluralistic ignorance: it supports the widespread social assumption of an informed and attentive public. In expanding the national culture, mass education also creates and expands the assumption of homogeneity. In societies with more mass education, both masses and elites should be found to perceive more common interests and ideas in the population and less conflict and diversity. This should hold even when actual diversity is held constant.

4. Mass education, similarly, expands citizenship, both in size and content. Elites, in societies with more mass education, should be found to perceive masses as making more demands, having more rights, and posing more threats than in other societies. Elites planning new regimes in such societies should be found to employ more strategies of control through mobilization rather than through traditional authoritarianism. They should also attend to the creation and manipulation of "public opinion." Mass education may be one of the elements supporting the modern "activist" version of the classic military coup and regime. Again, one can study such a process comparatively, with survey data, or experimentally (presenting subjects with hypothetical societies).

These research suggestions make clear the nature of legitimation effects: Modern educational systems formally reconstruct, reorganize, and expand the socially defined categories of personnel and of knowledge in society. They expand and rationalize the social realities that enter into the choices of the socialized and the unsocialized, the allocated and the unallocated. Education is, as has often been noted, a secular religion in modern societies: as religions do, it provides a legitimating account of the competence of citizens, the authority of elites, and the sources of the adequacy of the social system to maintain itself in the face of uncertainty.[10]

The Impact of Educational Legitimation on Allocation and Socialization

The socializing impact of education as an institution is discussed above (Propositions 5 and 6) in the review of the allocation theory version of the larger idea of legitimation. The intervening discussions make necessary two extensions in the arguments presented there:

1. It is now clear that rules of educational allocation are not simply arbitrary social constructions which happen to have power over people. These rules are part of the basic institutional ideology of modern society: they represent equity, progress, and technical sophistication. As part of a larger institutional system, that is, the rules of educational allocation are highly *legitimate*, not merely instances of the exercise of power. This legitimacy intensifies the operation of rules of educational allocation, and intensifies the effects of these rules on individuals being socialized and allocated:

Proposition 11. The more institutionalized the modern system of education, the more intensified the causal relationships of allocation and socialization.

Educational allocation rules become more common, and their socializing consequences increase in intensity, under conditions of high educational institutionalization. The lagged socialization of the allocated (Proposition 6) becomes, not simply an adaptation to their increased power, but an affirmation of their authority and an account of a legitimate moral biography. Similarly, the process by which students acquire chartered qualities (Proposition 5) takes on additional meaning because of its legitimacy. Students and nonstudents are learning more than their own futures. They are also learning that the practical categories and topics of education give legitimate meaning to these futures (see also Bowles and Gintis 1976). For instance, the college student learns a little sociology because he is taught it (traditional socialization) and because he knows graduates may be expected to know a bit about it (chartering). Both processes are intensified by the legitimating reality of sociology: students (and nonstudents) learn that it *exists* as a body of knowledge and a personnel category, entirely over and above their personal acceptance of the utility of the field. Thus students acquire their sociology with a dutiful passivity which reflects the understanding that whether or not they accept this discipline, their degrees—valid throughout society—will reflect so many units of sociology.

Thus the objectified moral authority of the schools—over and above their raw power—undoubtedly intensifies socialization over and above that found in routine *training* organizations (Bidwell and Vreeland 1963).

2. In broader versions of institutional theory than allocation ideas, the effects of education are no longer fixed in sum: education may expand and alter the role structure of society. This means that there is no reason to believe that the socializing effects of allocation rules would be fixed in sum as is implied by hypotheses 1–3 above, in "Further Implications of Allocation Theory." If education expands the status order, anticipatory gains for students and their socialization consequences do not need to be balanced by losses for nonstudents. The new roles being created can simply be added to the status structure and to the socialization process. More commonly, the creation of a given new elite role also creates expanded rights and duties for others. Thus the expansion of medical authority in modern societies involves creating and expanding the role of doctor. But other people do not simply become nondoctors—they become patients. Education expands roles and sets them into proper relation with the rest of the society.

Once institutionalized education is seen as a legitimating system—not just a mechanism for allocating fixed opportunities—it can have many net consequences on both allocation and socialization of people being processed, just as on the rest of society.

The Impact of Educational Legitimation on Educational Organizations

The legitimating effect of educational organizations—but also much of their socializing and allocating power—is derived from their highly institutionalized status in society. Operating at the institutional level as an authoritative theory of personnel and knowledge in society, the schools constitute a crucial ritual system: a system of initiation ceremonies (personnel) and of classifications of information (knowledge).

This makes it clear why schools often seem to act as ritual organizations, sacrificing "effectiveness" for classificatory rigidity (Meyer and Rowan 1975; Kamens 1977). Their larger social effectiveness (and their claim to resources) inheres precisely in this ritual structure: the apparatus of classes and levels and degrees and subjects. By emphasizing their formal ritual structures, schools maximize their links to their main source of authority, their main resources, and quite possibly their main effectiveness. Dramatizing their structures as socially legitimated and legitimating initiation ceremonies informs students (and others) both about the payoffs to which they can adapt and about the fact that those payoffs are highly proper, deriving from the core meaning and values of society (Clark 1970). Ritualism, thus, by the process stated in Proposition 11, reinforces the immediate effectiveness of schools in dealing with students.

Summary of legitimation theory.—Legitimation theory suggests two general ideas concerning the effects of schooling. First, institutionalized education, as a theory of personnel and knowledge, affects society directly, apart from the training and allocation of students. Second, institutionalized education creates and intensifies the individual effects of socialization and allocation. In Figure 8.4 these two main themes are added to the explanatory structure presented earlier.

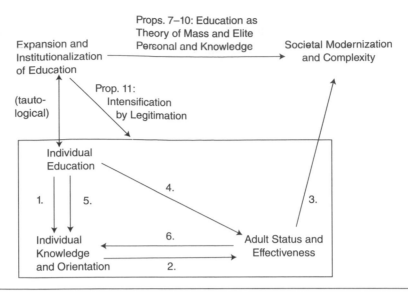

Figure 8.4 Legitimation effects of education.

Conclusion

Schools may teach people useful skills and values. Whether they do or not in particular cases, they certainly *allocate* people to positions of higher social status, and this affects the anticipations and socialization of the students (and nonstudents) as well as the experience and later socialization of the graduates (and nongraduates).

The allocating power of the schools is one aspect of their status as social institutions creating and validating categories of personnel and knowledge. The schools increase the number and legitimacy of these categories—far beyond levels possible with more primordial myths of the origins of personnel and knowledge—and thus expand the whole rationalized modern social structure. These legitimating effects of schools reconstruct reality for everyone—the schooled and the nonschooled alike. They also intensify the effects of allocating and socializing processes.

So a student is in a position of experiencing (*a*) the immediate socializing organization, (*b*) the fact that this organization has the allocating power to confer status on him, and (*c*) the broader fact that this allocation power has the highest level of legitimacy in society. The education he receives has a very special status and authority: its levels and content categories have the power to redefine him legitimately in the eyes of everyone around him and thus take on overwhelming ceremonial significance.

Research on such questions must examine the effects of education *as an institution*, considering effects of variables quite beyond the level of the classroom, the peer group, or the school as an organization. Either experimentally or with cross-societal (or time series) analyses, we need to consider the contextual effects of variations in the extension and institutionalization of education on the perspectives of students and nonstudents, graduates and nongraduates, citizens and elites. If education is a myth in modern society, it is a powerful one. The effects of myths inhere, not in the fact that individuals believe them, but in the fact that they "know" everyone else does, and thus that "for all practical purposes" the myths are true. We may all gossip privately about the uselessness of education, but in hiring and promoting, in consulting the various magi of our time, and in ordering our lives around contemporary rationality, we carry out parts in a drama in which education is authority.

Notes

1. Socialization researchers, of course, continue to pursue the grail, looking for new properties of individual socialization that are stable and that do effectively predict long-run success. The search has been going on for a long time,

2. A number of ideas have been suggested in defense of traditional theory: (1) we have not yet found or measured the relevant aspects of school structure; (2) schools tend to be random collections of teachers and thus to appear alike even though teaching is of great importance; (3) on the relevant properties—normative commitment and organization, or simply the time devoted to various topics—most schools in a country are very similar and thus have similar effects. I pursue a related, but more general, line below.

3. Intervening variables in all these effects would include the expectations of the students and those of their parents, teachers, counselors, and peers.

4. Actors may also internalize these rules as personal commitments, but this is less important—the critical aspect is that they internalize them as social facts and social realities (institutions which rely on personal beliefs, or even permit the question of personal beliefs to be relevant in social action, are less highly legitimated in important senses than are those which operate as realities).

5. The discussion which follows deals exclusively with the *effects* of institutionalized education on other aspects of society. Obviously, important causal effects also run the other way (see Meyer and Rubinson [1975] for a review). Empirically disentangling the reciprocal effects requires data on societies over time.

6. This assertion, incidentally, parallels an idea of Schumpeter (1950, chap. 12) about the way in which the intellectual optimism of modern capitalistic society generates its own institutionalization and destruction. The intellectuals rationalize more and more social functions, which are then brought under collective social and political control and removed from the market.

7. Imagine, for example, the consequences that would flow from the rise of routinely accredited university programs and degrees in astrology. Organizations would incorporate astrologers, the state would fund their programs and consult or incorporate them. Of course a justificatory literature would grow. The same basic processes have gone on with many occupational groups.

8. This proposition is impossible in conceptions of social status as simply a rank position, and thus as fixed in sum. But there is no reason to assume that the total amount of status (or for that matter power) in society is fixed. Independent of their ranks, statuses (and whole status distributions) may vary in the expansion of their substantive rights and powers. I have argued above that education expands the status rights attached to many positions in society, without necessarily altering the rank structure. This conception of status reflects Weber's original formulation.

9. I provide here a conventional list of the putative effects of mass education. But my argument is that, actual effects aside, they enter into social life as taken for granted assumptions. Many Americans are not literate in the national language. But we treat each other, expect elites to treat us, and organize our public life as if we all were. According to proposition 5, the existence of these effects as social assumptions greatly increases the likelihood that the schools actually produce them.

10. Modern education not only expands each society structurally; it also brings societies into closer organizational similarity with each other. Societies come to be made up of more and more similar elites—often in professional communication with each other—and masses with more and more shared social rights. This organizational homogeneity means that information—and exploitation—can proceed very rapidly. New ideas and techniques are not *alien*. They are the stock-in-trade of an already incorporated profession and can thus be adopted with less resistance. So, in the modern world, the presence of locally controlled, but organizationally similar, educational systems in almost all nation-states makes possible the rapid cultural penetration of techniques (and political revolution). And it makes possible new kinds of dependence (e.g., a "brain drain").

References

Alexander, K., and B. Eckland. 1975. "Contextual Effects in the High School Attainment Process." *American Sociological Review* 40 (June): 402–16.

Almond, G., and S. Verba. 1963. *The Civic Culture*. Princeton, N.J.: Princeton University Press.

Astin, A., and R. Panos. 1969. *The Educational and Vocational Development of College Students*. Washington, D.C.: American Council on Education.

Bendix, R. 1964. *Nation-Building and Citizenship*. New York: Wiley.

Benitez, J. 1973. "The Effect of Elite Recruitment and Training on Diffuse Socialization Outcomes." Doctoral dissertation, Stanford University.

Berg, I. 1971. *Education and Jobs*. Boston: Beacon.

Bergesen, A. 1977, "Political Witch Hunts: The Sacred and the Subversive in Cross-National Perspective." *American Sociological Review* 42 (April): 220–33.

Bidwell, C., and R. Vreeland. 1963. "College Education and Moral Orientations." *Administrative Science Quarterly* 8 (September): 166–91.

Blau, P. M., and O. D. Duncan. 1967. *The American Occupational Structure*. New York: Wiley.

Blaug, M., ed. 1968, 1969. *Economics of Education*. Baltimore: Penguin.

Boli-Bennett, J. 1976. "The Expansion of Constitutional Authority in Nation-States, 1870–1970: A Quantitative Assessment." Paper read at the annual meeting of the Pacific Sociological Association, San Diego, April. Mimeographed. Stanford, Calif.: Department of Sociology, Stanford University.

BISHOP BURTON COLLEGE
LIBRARY

Bowles, S., and H. Gintis. 1976. *Schooling in Capitalist America*. New York: Basic.

Carnoy, M., ed. 1972. *Schooling in a Corporate Society*. New York: McKay.

Clark, B. 1970. "The College as Saga: Historical Inquiry in the Sociology of Education." Paper read at the annual meeting of the American Sociological Association, Washington, D.C., August. Mimeographed. New Haven, Conn.: Department of Sociology, Yale University.

Coleman, J., ed. 1965. *Education and Political Development*. Princeton, N.J.: Princeton University Press.

Collins, R. 1971. "Functional and Conflict Theories of Educational Stratification." *American Sociological Review* 36 (December): 1002–18.

Coombs, P. 1968. *The World Educational Crisis*. New York: Oxford University Press.

Davis, J. A. 1966. "The Campus as a Frog Pond." *American Journal of Sociology* 72 (July): 17–31.

Duncan, O. D., D. L. Featherman, and B. Duncan. 1972. *Socioeconomic Background and Achievement*. New York: Seminar.

Feldman, K. A., and T. H. Newcomb. 1969. *The Impact of College on Students*. San Francisco: Jossey-Bass.

Garfinkel, Harold. 1956. "Conditions of Successful Degradation Ceremonies." *American Journal of Sociology* 61 (March): 420–24.

Habermas, J. 1962. *Structurwandel der Öffentlichkeit*. Koblenz: Neuwied.

Himmelweit, H., and B. Swift. 1969. "A Model for the Understanding of School as a Socializing Agent." Pp. 154–81 in *Trends and Issues in Developmental Psychology*, edited by P. Mussen, J. Langer, and M. Covington. New York: Holt, Rinehart & Winston.

Holsinger, D. 1974. "The Elementary School as Modernizer: A Brazilian Study." Pp. 24–46 in *Education and Individual Modernity in Developing Countries*, edited by A. Inkeles and D. Holsinger. Leiden: Brill.

Igra, A. 1976. "Social Mobilization, National Context, and Political Participation." Doctoral dissertation, Stanford University.

Illich, I. 1971. *Deschooling Society*. New York: Harper & Row.

Inkeles, A., and D. H. Smith. 1974. *Becoming Modern: Individual Change in Six Developing Countries*. Cambridge, Mass.: Harvard University Press.

Jencks, C., et al. 1972. *Inequality: A Reassessment of the Effect of Family and Schooling in America*. New York: Basic.

Kamens, D. 1971. "The College 'Charter' and College Size: Effects on Occupational Choice and College Attrition." *Sociology of Education* 44 (Summer): 270–96.

———. 1974. "Colleges and Elite Formation: The Case of Prestigious American Colleges." *Sociology of Education* 47 (Summer), 354–78.

———. 1977. "Legitimating Myths and Educational Organization: The Relationship between Organizational Ideology and Formal Structure." *American Sociological Review* 42 (April): 208–19.

Kerckhoff, A. C. 1975. "Patterns of Educational Attainment in Great Britain." *American Journal of Sociology* 80 (May): 1428–37.

Kohn, M. 1969. *Class and Conformity: A Study in Values*. Homewood, Ill.: Dorsey.

Marshall, T. H. 1948. *Citizenship and Social Class*. New York: Doubleday.

Meyer, J. 1970a. "The Charter: Conditions of Diffuse Socialization in Schools." Pp. 564–78 in *Social Processes and Social Structures*, edited by W. R. Scott. New York: Holt, Rinehart & Winston.

———. 1970b. "High School Effects on College Intentions." *American Journal of Sociology* 76 (July): 59–70.

———. 1973. "Theories of the Effects of Education on Civic Participation in Developing Societies." *SEADAG Papers Series*. New York: Asia Society.

Meyer, J., and B. Rowan. 1975. "Notes on the Structure of Educational Organizations." Paper read at the annual meeting of the American Sociological Association, San Francisco, August. Mimeographed. Stanford, Calif.: Department of Sociology, Stanford University.

Meyer, J., and R. Rubinson. 1975. "Education and Political Development." *Review of Research in Education*, vol. 3, pp. 134–62.

Mischel, W. 1971. *Introduction to Personality*. New York: Holt, Rinehart & Winston.

Plant, W. 1965. "Longitudinal Changes in Intolerance and Authoritarianism for Subjects Differing in Amount of College Education over Four Years." *Genetic Psychology Monographs* 72 (November): 247–87.

Ramirez, F. 1973. "Societal Corporateness and the Nationalization and Expansion of Educational Systems." Paper read at the annual meeting of the American Sociological Association, New York, August. Mimeographed. Stanford, Calif.: Department of Sociology, Stanford University.

———. 1975. "Creating Members: A Longitudinal Cross-national Analysis." Paper read at the Comparative and International Education Society meeting, San Francisco, March. Mimeographed. San Francisco: Department of Sociology, San Francisco State University.

Rosenbaum, J. 1975. "The Stratification of Socialization Processes." *American Sociological Review* 40 (February): 48–54.

Rubinson, R. 1973. "The Political Construction of Education: Conditions for the Creation of Membership in Political Society." Paper read at the annual meeting of the American Sociological Association, New York, August. Mimeographed. Stanford, Calif.: Department of Sociology, Stanford University.

Schumpeter, J. 1950. *Capitalism, Socialism and Democracy*. New York: Harper.

Spence, M. 1973. "Job Market Signalling." *Quarterly Journal of Economics* 87 (August): 355–75.

Stinchcombe, A. 1968. *Constructing Social Theories*. New York: Harcourt.

Swanson, G. 1971. "An Organizational Analysis of Collectivities." *American Sociological Review* 36 (August): 607–23.

Thompson, J. D. 1967. *Organizations in Action*. New York: McGraw-Hill.

Thurow, L. 1975. *Generating Inequality*. New York: Basic.

Wallace, W. L. 1966. *Student Culture: Social Structure and Continuity in a Liberal Arts College*. Chicago: Aldine.

Wheeler, S. 1966. "The Structure of Formally Organized Socialization Settings." In *Socialization after Childhood*, edited by O. G. Brian, Jr., and S. Wheeler. New York: Wiley.

PART **I**

Suggested Readings

Aronowitz, S., & Giroux, H. (1991). *Postmodern education: politics, culture and social criticism*. Minneapolis: University of Minnesota Press.

Bernstein, B. (1971). On the classification and framing of educational knowledge. In B. Bernstein, *Class, codes, and control: Vol. 1* (pp. 202–230) and *Class, codes, and control: Vol. 2* (1973b) (pp. 85–115). London: Routledge & Kegan Paul (Original published in M. F. D. Young (Ed.) *Knowledge and control: New directions for the sociology of education*, London: Collier-Macmillan.

Bernstein, B. (1977). Class and pedagogies: Visible and invisible (rev ed.). In B. Bernstein, *Class, codes and control: Vol. 3* (pp. 116–156). London: Routledge & Kegan Paul.

Bernstein, B. (1986). On pedagogic discourse. In J. G. Richardson (Ed.), *Handbook for theory and research in the sociology of education* (pp. 205–240). New York: Greenwood Press. (Revised and reprinted in B. Bernstein, 1990d, pp. 165–218.)

Bourdieu, P. (1973). Cultural reproduction and social reproduction. In R. Brown, (Ed.), *Knowledge, education, and cultural change* (pp. 71–112). London: Tavistock.

Bourdieu, P. (1973). *Outline of a theory of practice*. Cambridge, UK: Cambridge University Press.

Bourdieu, P. (1984). *Distinction: A social critique of the judgment of taste*. Cambridge, MA: Harvard University Press.

Bourdieu, P. (1986). The forms of capital. In J. G. Richardson (Ed). *Handbook of theory and research for the sociology of education*. New York: Greenwood Press, 1986, pp. 241–258

Bourdieu, P, & Passeron, J. C. (1977). *Reproduction in education, society and culture*. London: Sage.

Bowles, S., & Gintis, H. (1976). *Schooling in capitalist America*. New York: Basic Books.

Coleman, J. S. (1988). Social capital in the creation of human capital. *American Journal of Sociology*, *94*(Suppl.): S95–S120.

Coleman, J. S. (1990). *Foundations of social theory*. Cambridge: The Belknap Press of Harvard University Press.

Collins, R. (1971). Functional and conflict theories of educational stratification. *American Sociological Review, 36*(6), 1002–1019.

Collins, R. (1975). *Conflict sociology*. New York: Academic Press.

Collins, R. (1978). *The credential society*. New York: Academic Press.

Davies, S. (1995). Leaps of faith: Shifting currents in critical sociology of education. *American Journal of Sociology, 100*(6), 1448–1478.

Dreeben, R. (1994). The sociology of education: Its development in the United States. *Research in Sociology of Education and Socialization, 10.*

Durkheim, E. (1956). *Education and sociology*. New York: The Free Press.

Durkheim, E. (1962). *Moral education*. New York: The Free Press.

Durkheim, E. (1977). *The evolution of educational thought*. (P. Collins, Trans.) London: Routledge and Kegan Paul.

Giroux, H. (1981). *Ideology, culture and the process of schooling*. Philadelphia: Temple University Press.

Giroux, H. (1983). *Theory and resistance in education*. South Hadley, MA: Bergin & Garvey.

Giroux, H. (1991). *Postmodernism, feminism, and cultural politics: Redrawing educational boundaries*. Albany: SUNY Press.

Goffman, E. (1959). *The presentation of self in everyday life*. Garden City, NY: Doubleday.

Goffman, E. (1961a). *Asylums*. Garden City, NY: Doubleday.

Goffman, E. (1963a). *Stigma*. Englewood Cliffs, NJ: Prentice Hall.

Kingston, P. W. (2001). The unfulfilled promise of cultural capital theory. *Sociology of Education, 74* (Extra Issue), 88–99.

Marx, K. (1971). *The poverty of philosophy*. New York: International Publishers.

Marx, K., & F. Engels. (1947). *The German ideology*. New York: International Publishers (Original published 1846).

Meyer, J. (1977). The effects of education as an institution. *American Journal of Sociology, 83*(1), 55–77.

Meyer, J., & Rowan, B. (1977). The structure of educational organizations. In M. Meyer & Associates (Eds.), *Environments and organizations* (pp. 78–109). San Francisco: Jossey-Bass.

Meyer, J., & Rowan, B. (1978). Institutionalized organizations: Formal structure as myth and ceremony. *American Journal of Sociology, 83*, 340–363.

Parsons, T. (1959). The school as a social system. *Harvard Educational Review, 29*, 297–318.

Riehl, C. (2001). Bridges to the future: Contributions of qualitative research to the sociology of education. *Sociology of Education, 74* (Extra Issue), 115–134.

Rist, R. (1970). Student social class and teacher expectations: The self fulfilling prophecy in ghetto education. *Harvard Education Review, 40*, 411–451.

Rist, R. (1973). *The Urban school: Factory for failure*. Cambridge, MA: MIT Press.

Rist, R. (1977). On understanding the processes of schooling: The contributions of labeling theory. In Karabel, J., & Halsey, A. H. *Power and ideology in education* (pp. 292–305). New York: Oxford University Press.

Sadovnik, A.R. (1991). Basil Bernstein's theory of pedagogic practice: A structuralist approach. *Sociology of Education, 64*(1), 48–63.

Sadovnik, A. R. (1995). (Ed.) *Knowledge and pedagogy: The sociology of Basil Bernstein*. Norwood, NJ: Ablex.

Sadovnik, A. R. (1995). Postmodernism and the sociology of education: Closing the rift among scholarship, research, and practice. In George Noblit and William Pink (Eds.). *Continuity and contradiction: The futures of the sociology of education*. Cresskill, NJ: Hampton Press.

Swartz, D. (1997). *Culture and power: The sociology of Pierre Bourdieu*. Chicago: University of Chicago Press.

Weber, M. (1978). *Economy and society, Volumes 1 and 2*. (G. Roth & C. Wittich, Eds.) Berkeley: University of California Press.

Weber, M. The rationalization of education and training. In Arum, R. & Beattie, I. (Eds.) (2000). *The structure of schooling*. Mountain View, CA: Mayfield.

Wexler, P. (1987). *Social analysis: After the new sociology*. London: Routledge and Kegan Paul.

Wexler, P. (1996). *Holy sparks: Social theory, education, and religion*. New York: St. Martin's.

Young, M. F. D. (1971). *Knowledge and control: New directions for the sociology of education*, London: Collier-Macmillan.

School Organization and Processes: Teaching, Learning, and Curriculum

The readings in Part II examine school organization and processes and focus on the relationship among teaching, learning, and curriculum.

Chapter 9, "The Organizational Context of Teaching and Learning: Changing Theoretical Perspectives" by University of Wisconsin sociologist Adam Gamoran and his colleagues Walter Secada and Cora Marrett, provides an overview of different theoretical perspectives on the organization of teaching and learning.

Chapter 10, "Is There Really a Teacher Shortage" by University of Pennsylvania sociologist Richard Ingersoll, provides an analysis of the alleged teacher shortage and sociological explanations of teacher supply and demand. Ingersoll examines the organizational conditions of teacher work and how these relate to teacher shortages.

Chapter 11, "Whose Markets, Whose Knowledge" by University of Wisconsin educational theorist Michael Apple, provides a conflict perspective on the struggles over curriculum in the United States and how neo-conservatives and neo-liberals have dominated public discourse over the past two decades.

Questions for Reflection and Discussion

1. According to Gamoran and his colleagues, how do sociologists of education analyze the organizational contexts of teaching and learning? How do school organization and processes affect teaching and learning? If you were to reorganize your college or university to better educate its students, what insights from this article would you apply?

2. According to Richard Ingersoll, is there a teacher shortage? If there is, is the problem a supply problem or is it related to other factors inside schools? Based on his article, what policies would you implement to staff difficult to staff districts in urban and rural areas? What changes would you make in schools to increase retention of teachers?

3. How does Michael Apple view the organization and content of the school curriculum? Whose interests does he see reflected in what is taught? How does he see the role of different social, economic, political, and religious groups in the shaping of curriculum? How would functionalists respond to Apple's argument? How would Randall Collins?

9

The Organizational Context of Teaching and Learning

Changing Theoretical Perspectives

ADAM GAMORAN, WALTER G. SECADA, AND CORA B. MARRETT

Sociologists have a predilection for the collective. We are centrally concerned with social facts, characteristics of collectivities that give shape and motivation to individual action. Sociological research on schooling shares this interest in the collective. School resources, composition, climate, leadership, and governance, all collective attributes of schools, are often looked to as sources of influence on the outcomes of schooling for individual students.

Yet the study of school organization is marked more by failure than by success. It is especially significant that the most important contribution by sociologists to research on schooling—the famous Coleman Report of 1966—is also the most spectacular failure to connect the collective with the individual in an educational setting. Variation in school conditions was largely unrelated to differences in student outcomes, as school-level effects were dwarfed by the powerful influence of the home environment for student learning. Though policymakers drew implications from the positive impact on learning of the proportion of white students in a school, the effect of racial composition was small compared to the great importance of individual family background factors. This pattern of results, emphasizing the individual over the collective despite the sociologist's predilection for the opposite, was only to be expected given that over 80% of the variation in student learning occurs within schools, not between schools. If most of the variation in learning is internal to schools, then schoolwide characteristics cannot explain a large proportion of the variation in learning.

Despite these limitations, efforts to study school organization and student learning persist. School climate is a popular term for the normative environment of schools, and hundreds of studies have tried to document an association between climate and student learning (Anderson, 1982). Yet findings for school climate research have been weak and inconsistent, and recent authors, pointing to substantial variation within schools in perceived climate, have questioned whether the concept is meaningful (Pallas, 1988). Studies in the effective schools tradition also emphasized collective properties of schools, such as goals, leadership, and disciplinary environment (e.g., Edmonds, 1979). Although researchers have consistently reported associations between these conditions and students' achievement, this research tradition has been challenged for a lack of rigor and systematic focus in its investigations and a lack of attention to possible mechanisms through which school characteristics are supposed to influence student learning (Barr & Dreeben, 1983; Purkey & Smith, 1983).

More recent and empirically promising studies of schools and student learning also neglect important linkages. Research that documents the achievement advantages of Catholic schools has identified students' academic course taking as a key mechanism, but it is not clear whether this mechanism operates primarily at the individual or the collective level (Bryk, Lee, & Holland, 1993; Coleman &

Hoffer, 1987). A study of city high schools reported higher achievement in magnet schools than in comprehensive schools, but could not say what it was about magnet schools that led to higher achievement (Gamoran, 1996c). Research on restructured schools indicated that schoolwide restructuring may aid achievement, but many questions remain concerning what, exactly, is effective about restructuring and how school structure is linked with student learning (Lee & Smith, 1995, 1996, 1997; Newmann & Associates, 1996).

In this article, we respond to current limitations in the study of school organization and student learning. First, we take stock of research on school organization in greater detail. Second, we propose a new way of looking at the relation between the school's organizational context on the one hand, and the activities of teaching and learning on the other. Third, we present some different scenarios for teaching and learning activities and show how the organizational context of the school may play a different role in each case. Finally, we discuss the challenges of empirically verifying this new model of the organizational context of teaching and learning.

School Effects: From the Black Box to Nested Layers

Early studies of the impact of schools on student learning were exemplified by Coleman and colleagues' (1966) landmark research on equality of educational opportunity. Coleman and his colleagues estimated an economic production function in which student learning is an output that responds to various economic inputs such as expenditures, facilities, equipment, and background characteristics of teachers. In this model, the school is an unopened black box. What goes on inside the school—the production process itself—is not observed. If the production process were straightforward and predictable, the input–output production function would be a sensible way to study the impact of school resources. Yet the process of teaching and learning is complex and not fully routinized. Input–output studies do not reveal much about the effects of schools because so much depends on how the resources are used, and the use of resources is not included in the usual production function.

Scholars, educators, and politicians alike were surprised to discover that for the most part, variation in school resources bore little direct relation to variation in students' achievement, once background differences among students were taken into account (Coleman et al., 1966; Hodgson, 1975). This finding was reconfirmed in extensive reanalyses (Hanushek, 1994; Jencks et al., 1972; Mosteller & Moynihan, 1972). Most recently, a meta-analysis suggested that average resources do matter for student learning (Greenwald, Hedges, & Laine, 1996; see Hanushek, 1997, for a critique). Moreover in developing countries, where levels of resources such as trained teachers, textbooks, and facilities vary widely, the link between such resources and students' achievement tends to be stronger than it is in the United States and in other developed countries (Fuller, 1987; Fuller & Clarke, 1994; Heyneman & Loxley, 1983). In any case, it is clear that the relation between resources and outcomes is inconsistent—sometimes positive, sometimes negative, and sometimes absent—and the question of how to use resources effectively is much more important than whether average resources matter for average outcomes.

Opening the Black Box: The Nested Layers Approach

During the 1980s, sociologists of education began to open the black box of schools by studying the processes through which learning occurs. Bidwell and Kasarda (1980) distinguished between the effects of schools, the organizational context for teaching and learning, and schooling—the experiences students have in school that actually produce learning. According to this view, schools set the conditions for schooling, so that the influence of schools as organizations is always mediated by their impact on the schooling process. In this formulation, one understands the effects of schools by tracing the impact of school conditions on schooling activities and then by examining the connection between schooling activities and student learning.

Barr and Dreeben (1983) elaborated on this approach by exploring the organizational linkages among the different structural levels of school systems. In their view, outputs at one level of the organizational hierarchy (e.g., the school) become the inputs at the next level (e.g., the classroom). For example, school administrators allocate time to classroom teachers, make decisions within classrooms about how to use time, and instructional time allows teachers to cover the curriculum, which promotes student learning (Gamoran & Dreeben, 1986). This nested layers approach opened up the black box of schooling and focused attention on the technology of schooling, that is, the processes of teaching and learning within classrooms.

The theoretical foundation for the nested layers model was laid by Parsons (1963), who distinguished between the technical, managerial, and institutional levels of organization, and argued that influences tend to flow across adjacent levels. In Parsons' scheme, resource allocation was a managerial activity, and the outputs of this activity affected processes at the technical level, which in schools consists of teaching and learning. Barr and Dreeben (1983) provided concrete specification of resources allocated at the managerial level (time and materials) and activities occurring in the technical level (coverage of curricular content).

The notion of nested layers offered a valuable conceptual advance over previous work, and it has achieved some empirical success as well. Studies of the flow of resources, most notably time for instruction, show that allocations from the district and school to the classroom set constraints on teaching, which in turn influences student learning (Gamoran & Dreeben, 1986; Monk, 1992). In their analysis, Barr and Dreeben (1983) took advantage of the statistical technique of path analysis, widely known to sociologists since Blau and Duncan's (1967) seminal work on social stratification, but not previously used to examine the inner workings of school systems. Using a path model, Barr and Dreeben provided empirical documentation of the flow of resources and activities from school to classroom, from classroom to instructional group, and from group to individual student. The logic of path analysis is also evident in nested layers analyses by Alexander and Cook (1982), Rowan and Miracle (1983), Gamoran and Dreeben (1986), and others.

The nested layers model appears to have correctly identified the connections between resource allocation and the technology of teaching. However, efforts to examine a wider spectrum of school conditions have yielded inconsistent results for the nested layers model. For example, not all subjects and grade levels indicate that curricular allocations exert strong influences on student learning. Doyle (1992), summarizing the literature on the impact of curriculum on pedagogy, concluded that "curriculum is a weak force for regulating teaching" (p. 488). Although teachers tend to cover the topics reflected in the formal curriculum, they use their own discretion and may vary widely in teaching methods, in time devoted to various topics, in modes of assessment, and so on (Barr & Sadow, 1989; Freeman & Porter, 1989; Stodolsky, 1988). These findings derive from the United States, but in other countries where high-stakes tests are more closely linked to prescribed curricula, the effects of curricular allocations on teaching practices may be stronger (Stevenson & Baker, 1991; Gamoran, 1996a).

Moreover, researchers have had difficulty showing that features of schools other than resources allocated for instruction have any bearing on student learning. For example, Gamoran (1987) examined a range of high school characteristics in an attempt to identify organizational conditions that influence learning by setting the conditions for students' instructional experiences. Although Gamoran observed strong relations between instructional experiences (e.g., coursetaking) and achievement, these associations were largely unrelated to school characteristics (e.g., student body composition, availability of academic programs). Other studies of school effects have been similarly unsuccessful in tracing the influence of organizational conditions through instructional experiences to student learning (e.g., Gahng, 1993; Gamoran, Porter, & Gahng, 1995). Researchers have uncovered important effects of different types of schools, such as Catholic schools (Bryk et al., 1993; Coleman & Hoffer, 1987) and magnet schools (Gamoran, 1996c), but the organizational conditions that mattered tended to be aggregate indicators of students' instructional experiences, such as extensive academic coursetaking and orderly classrooms. Research on school types thus supports the conclusion that instructional conditions affect student learning but offers less evidence about organizational influences on instructional conditions.

Recent studies of schools and student learning have focused less on the organizational constraints of material resources and shifted the emphasis toward organizational structures and processes such as leadership, collaboration, and efficacy among educators in a school. This literature builds on the effective schools tradition (e.g., Edmonds, 1979; Purkey & Smith, 1983) that emphasized key conditions at the school level including goal consensus, high expectations for student learning, principal leadership, emphasis on basic skills, and monitoring of students' progress. Like the effective schools tradition, several recent studies show consistent associations between organizational conditions and student learning. For example, Bryk and Driscoll (1988) observed a strong positive association between students' achievement in mathematics and an index of school community—whether teachers worked together, whether the principal supported the teachers' work, and so on. Similarly, Lee and Smith (1995, 1996) showed that students' achievement is higher in high schools in which teachers perceive a greater sense of efficacy and responsibility for student learning and in schools where educators have engaged in restructuring activities, such as team teaching, changing the grouping structure, flexible scheduling, and so on.

This body of work, from research on effective schools to studies of restructuring, is limited by ambiguity in causal mechanisms and even in causal direction. If high expectations are associated with high achievement, for example, which causes which? Research on effective schools gave little attention to the actual mechanisms through which school conditions are translated into achievement. How were expectations elevated, goal consensus achieved, and so on, and how were these conditions linked to student learning? These questions were not addressed.

Current work has implicitly adopted the nested layers view as a conceptual framework. That is, the organizational context is assumed to influence student learning by constraining conditions for classroom instruction. In this framework, social conditions such as a strong sense of community promote adherence to an academic mission among teachers, which leads to enhanced teaching and greater learning. Despite the clearer conception of mechanisms, causal ambiguity remains problematic. For example, Lee and Smith (1996) argued that students achieve more when their teachers accept collective responsibility for students' learning. Lee and Smith supported their claim by showing an association between teachers' sense of responsibility and student learning. In fact, however, the causal process could run in the opposite direction: Teachers may be more apt to accept responsibility in schools where levels of learning are high.

In a study of mathematics reform, Adajian (1995) showed that teachers who participated in schoolwide professional communities engaged in more innovative mathematics teaching, including an emphasis on problem solving and on hands-on applications. This finding is consistent with the notion that a community of teachers encourages instructional innovation, which promotes greater learning. However, it is not clear from Adajian's cross-sectional data whether the professional community led to innovative teaching, or vice versa. Similarly, Lee and Smith (1997) interpreted their analysis of national data to indicate that high levels of academic coursetaking and instructional emphases on problem solving and on inquiry accounted for the benefits of restructured schools over traditionally structured schools. Yet an alternative hypothesis—that innovative instruction may lead to both school restructuring and better learning—cannot be dismissed.

Just as Barr and Dreeben (1983) took advantage of statistical advances in path analysis, current work on the relation between school conditions and student learning has also benefited from new statistical techniques, particularly multilevel modeling (or hierarchical linear modeling). The multilevel approach distinguishes group-level and individual-level effects more accurately than earlier regression methods (Bryk & Raudenbush, 1992; Goldstein, 1995). Multilevel modeling is a particularly elegant method for examining differences between groups in individual-level effects; for example, multilevel methods provide the best evidence that the effect of socioeconomic status on student learning is weaker in Catholic schools than in public schools (Bryk et al., 1993). This finding indicates that achievement is more equitably distributed in Catholic schools. However, the multilevel approach does not address the causal ambiguities of the nested layers model, nor does it offer any special benefits in the quest to identify the mechanisms through which school conditions influence student learning. On the contrary, multilevel analysts often specify individual or classroom conditions such as coursetaking and instruction as aggregate school conditions, missing the opportunity to link school conditions to student learning through the mechanism of individual or classroom-based academic experiences (Bryk et al., 1993; Lee & Smith, 1997).

The nested layers model operates well for instructionally specific resources such as time and materials and for clearly defined teaching activities such as content coverage. It seems particularly appropriate when there are clear norms about the salience of curricular topics, such as early reading instruction. It is not clear that the perspective can be applied to a broader range of school and/or classroom conditions.

The Loose-Coupling Alternative

Whereas Bidwell and Kasarda (1980) and Barr and Dreeben (1983) responded to the failure of the input–output model by specifying more carefully the technical connections between organizational resources, teaching practices, and student learning, other writers emphasized the general absence of tight connections within the school system organization. Earlier, Bidwell (1965) had recognized the structural looseness of schools, and writers such as Weick (1976) and Meyer and Rowan (1977, 1978) expanded this notion to suggest that the structural isolation of classrooms, the autonomy of teachers, and the relative absence of formal authority means that schools are loosely coupled organizations. In a loosely coupled system, decisions occurring in one segment of the organization do not reverberate in clearly patterned ways elsewhere. Thus, what occurs in one classroom may have little impact on another, and decisions made by the principal have only modest effects on what students actually experience (Weick, 1976). According to this view, schools are tightly coupled around symbolic designations such as who gets taught by whom but are loosely coupled on matters of core technology such as what gets taught in the classroom (Meyer & Rowan, 1978). Teaching practices are a result of teacher training and on-the-job socialization and are not affected much by schoolwide conditions such as resources, plans, or administrative decisions (Weick, 1982). Student learning is primarily a response to societal expectations rather than to particular school conditions or to classroom instruction (Meyer, 1977).

The reason schools are loosely coupled, according to this perspective, is that it is difficult to judge their effectiveness using a bureaucratic model of costs and outputs (Meyer & Rowan, 1977, 1978; Weick, 1976). Teaching is an uncertain technology: cause–effect relations are not well understood, and there is no consensus on the best teaching methods. Moreover, the goals of schooling are ambiguous and often conflicting, so it is hard to determine what standards to use for judging schools. Finally, the participants in schools change over time, adding further uncertainty to the complexities of teaching and the ambiguities of goals. Consequently, schools turn away from their technical cores (teaching and learning) and emphasize their symbolic attributes such as categories and certification. In schools, structures are detached from activities, and activities are disconnected from outcomes (Meyer & Rowan, 1978). A logic of confidence allows schools to appear to work when the symbolic trappings of grade-level structures, certified teachers, students progressing from grade to grade, and so on, are present (Meyer & Rowan, 1978). In this way schools avoid inspection of their technical cores and locus on legitimation in the wider society.

Metz (1989) and Hemmings and Metz (1991) provided evidence from a study of eight high schools that is strikingly consistent with the loose-coupling perspective. Despite substantial differences among the eight schools in the characteristics of their communities, all adopted the same set of structures and routines, from the arrangement of classrooms, to the organization of the curriculum, to the allocation of time. These outward attributes articulated each school's legitimacy as a "real school." Despite the similarities, students' experiences could differ dramatically from one school to the next, because students' schooling experiences bore little relation to the symbolic structural features of their schools. Moreover, the acceptance of a real school as an organizational framework limited consideration of alternate arrangements, even when the standard structures and processes were unsuccessful in promoting pupils' progress. According to Metz (1989),

> If one looks at students' learning simply as a technical system, it is quite remarkable to see situations where a technical process (or the social structure which frames it) is clearly not effective on a massive scale, but no one in the organization calls for developing alternative technical or structural approaches, (p. 79)

On the contrary, educators in schools with the least successful students were often the most insistent that their schools reflected the societal consensus on what high schools should look like.

If schools are loosely coupled, what keeps them coupled at all? How is work coordinated in a loosely coupled organization? First, as noted previously, some aspects of schools are tightly coupled: categories such as grade levels and teacher are closely monitored and used to arrange persons and positions (though not activities). Second, according to Weick (1982), teachers' common professional socialization helps coordinate work in schools. Weick argued that "even though (educators) don't communicate much with each other, they can still coordinate their actions because each person can anticipate accurately what the other person is thinking and doing" (1982, p. 675). In fact, common socialization may be the basis for the logic of confidence, that is, unexamined assumptions about who is doing what in their classrooms. For example, fourth-grade teachers may assume that third-grade teachers are introducing concepts on which they will build when they teach the same students in the following year. Similarly, teachers teaching the same subject area in different grades share a common disciplinary socialization that yields a coherent approach to teaching despite the absence of formal mechanisms of coordination (Rowan & Miskel, 1999; Stodolsky & Grossman, 1995). Shared views of subject matter probably reflect both socialization in teacher training programs and broader social definitions of subject-matter characteristics. Several writers have noted that teachers of mathematics and of foreign languages tend to see their subjects as sequentially organized in clear hierarchies, whereas language arts and social studies teachers have more flexible views of their subject matters (Gamoran & Weinstein, 1998; Loveless, 1994; Rowan, Raudenbush, & Cheong, 1993; Stodolsky & Grossman, 1995).

Meyer and Rowan (1978) acknowledged that loose coupling is probably more important in the United States than in many other countries because of the strong American tradition of decentralization and local control over education. Other countries typically have more centralized control over the curriculum, regulated through national testing, which results in tighter alignment between formal goals and outcomes than in the United States (Bishop, 1998). Formal inspections from central authorities, which rarely occur in the United States, may also serve to regulate the practice of teaching (Wilson, 1996). Thus, loose coupling as an explanatory framework may be more successful for the American case than elsewhere. Still, uncertainties that are inherent in teaching raise questions about the tightness of coupling even in more centralized educational systems than that of the United States (Benavot & Resh, 1998).

The loose-coupling model offers a strong challenge to the nested layers approach. Where nested layers is correct for the narrow conditions of resources and content coverage, could loose coupling prevail for other conditions of schooling, such as leadership, relations among teachers and between teachers and students, and so on? Loose coupling would account for the weak and inconsistent impact of school climate on teaching and on learning (Anderson, 1982). It would also explain why policy interventions often fail to reach the classroom, particularly in the United States (e.g., Pressman & Wildavsky, 1979). Further, as Meyer (1977) has argued, loose coupling is consistent with the finding of little variability between schools in student learning alongside substantial variability within schools. By and large, according to this view, schools operate similarly because they are focused on conformity to a common set of societal norms.

Moving beyond the nested layers model to confront the challenge of loose coupling requires a more nuanced analysis of the linkages between school conditions, teaching practices, and student learning. As a starting point, it is essential to rethink common assumptions about causal direction and change and to probe more deeply for the mechanisms that may connect the different elements of school organization.

Beyond Nested Layers

Building on the insights of Rowan (1990) and Newmann and Associates (1996), we suggest that the nested layers approach is limited by its assumption of a one-way relationship between organizational conditions and instructional practices. Rowan argued that when teaching is understood to be a complex, nonroutine activity, organizational support for innovation and success requires an organic relation between teaching practices and school organization, a connection that involves feedback and growth in both directions. The greater the recognition of the uncertainty and complexity of teaching, the more likely organic structures are to emerge. For example, teachers who recognize the complexities of teaching are more prone to form collegial networks for sharing information and mutual support. Rowan buttressed these claims with an insightful review of studies that indicated weak effects of collaboration and collegiality on teaching practices. Instead, organizational structures sometimes grew out of the demands of teaching. For example, Cohen, Deal, Meyer, and Scott (1979) observed that complex instructional tasks contributed to increased communication and teaming among teachers, but team teaching did not bring about complex instruction. Still, Rowan concluded that when collegial relations are intensive and embedded in a culture that emphasizes continuous improvement, the strength and quality of social relations among teachers may influence teaching practices. Although provocative, this conclusion was based on few cases, and Rowan found it difficult to provide evidence that relations among teachers substantially affect how they carry out their work in classrooms. In a subsequent empirical study, Rowan and his colleagues (1993) reported that the more teaching was viewed as a nonroutine activity, the greater the prevalence of organic management in the school. However, organic management did not result in greater amounts of ongoing learning among teachers.

Further support for the notion that organizational support for effective teaching may emerge from teachers' commitment to innovative instructional practices comes from Newmann and Associates' (1996) study of 24 highly restructured schools. This research began with the idea that there are levers at the school site that, when pressed, lead to better teaching and to more learning. What the investigators found, however, was more complex than a simple nested layers story. All 24 schools had innovative structural features, but few exhibited consistent evidence of exceptionally high-quality teaching and learning. The most successful schools were those in which educators were committed to intellectual quality in students' academic experiences and in which this commitment was the driving force behind organizational reforms. For example, teachers at Cibola High School were committed to disciplined inquiry and students' construction of knowledge. They used detracked classes to engage students in project work that resulted in high-quality instruction and high levels of learning. By contrast, teachers at Wallingford High School, who were also committed to detracking, had little notion of how their teaching might change in a detracked context. At Wallingford, researchers observed low-quality teaching and learning, mainly reflected in lectures and in a watered-down curriculum. Thus, detracking as a school organizational characteristic grew out of and supported a particular pedagogy in Cibola, whereas it was unrelated to instruction at Wallingford.

Similar conclusions emerged recently from another major study of school restructuring. Peterson, McCarthey, and Elmore (1996) reported that school structure had little consistent impact on teaching practices. Instead, teaching practices changed in response to teachers' learning, particularly when learning occurred in a community of educators. Teaching practices contributed to school conditions as much as the reverse. The authors concluded the following:

> Changing practice is primarily a problem of [teacher] learning, not a problem of organization. … School structures can provide opportunities for the learning of new teaching practices and new strategies for student learning, but structures, by themselves, do not cause learning to occur. … School structure follows from good practice not vice versa. (p. 149)

Our view of the organizational context of teaching and learning is more closely related to the nested layers model than to loose coupling. As in the nested layers view, and in contrast to loose coupling, we argue that student learning responds to instruction. This notion derives from research that documents the impact of variation in teaching on student learning, ranging from course-taking effects (Gamoran, 1987), to content coverage (Barr & Dreeben, 1983; Gamoran, Porter, Smithson, & White, 1997; Rowman & Miracle, 1983) to instructional coherence and teacher-student interaction (Gamoran, Nystrand, Berends, & LePore, 1995). Also consistent with the nested layers view, we expect that organizational resources affect student learning, but only as they are applied by teachers in classrooms. This aspect of our model has its foundation in research by Barr and Dreeben (1983; see also Gamoran & Dreeben, 1986). These studies showed that resources matter for learning when teachers apply resources in their classroom teaching. However, our model moves beyond the nested layers view in that we recognize that the relation between school conditions and classroom teaching may work in both directions and may shift over time. School conditions may respond to teaching practices, and teaching practices may be constrained or encouraged by their organizational context, as causal effects flow in both directions.

At the same time, our model draws from loose coupling the notion that teaching practices are influenced by professional socialization and training. As Peterson, McCarthey, and Elmore (1996) noted, teachers can learn to change their practice. This conclusion suggests that teachers not only respond to preservice training, as discussed by Weick (1982), but also to professional development that occurs on the job and that is a requirement for maintaining teaching certification in most states. In some cases professional development may be the sort of ritual activity that Meyer and Rowan (1978) recognized as important for legitimation but having little real significance for practice. In other cases, however, Peterson, Elmore, and McCarthey's findings suggest that professional development may result in meaningful change for teachers who participate.

Organizational Resources as the Context for Teaching and for Learning

Before elaborating on the role of professional development, we need to consider what aspects of school organization constitute salient contextual conditions for activities and outcomes. Prior research indicates that organizational resources constitute the most essential elements of the school's organizational context for teaching and for learning (Gamoran & Dreeben, 1986; Kilgore & Pendelton, 1993). We offer a broader conception of organizational resources than is found in most previous studies and as elaborated in the following sections. Resources emphasized by the input–output and the nested layers models are subsumed in our approach, and we also incorporate aspects of the school climate and school effectiveness traditions. Leadership, collaboration, and administrative support, as well as knowledge and skills, are all seen as types of resources that educators can draw on to improve their teaching. Hence, much of the past research on school effects is incorporated into our framework. However, our model does not include all aspects of school context. We focus on three categories of essential resources: material, human, and social. Other recent writers also point to the special salience of these conditions (Anderson, 1996; Newmann, 1998; Spillane & Thompson, 1997).

Material Resources

Despite inconsistent empirical support for the impact of expenditures on students' achievement, material resources constitute an important condition in the organizational context of teaching. Such resources include curriculum materials, equipment, and supplies; time available for teaching, planning and preparation; expenditures for personnel, particularly instructional staff; and the authority to expend funds for other purposes related to teaching and to learning. Material resources have no direct connection to learning because their impact depends on how they are used. Typically, educators at the school level have little discretion over the allocation of funds. According to the study of restructured schools, even when funding decisions are made at the school level, resources may not be used in ways that improve teaching (Newmann & Associates, 1996). However, some schools used resources in ways that improved instruction by allocating extra time for collaboration among teachers, by supporting professional development, and by providing tutoring sessions for students who needed extra help.

A variety of literatures support the conclusion that the effects of material resources are contingent on use. Resources devoted to instruction, not surprisingly, are more likely to pay off for student learning than resources directed in other ways (Newmann & Associates, 1996). Even when resources are allocated toward instructional needs, however, their benefits depend on how they are applied. Reducing class size, for example, may be the most common application of additional resources, yet a research literature consisting of hundreds of studies has yielded widely varying results. As Slavin (1989, 1990) has argued, reducing the number of students in a class is unlikely to yield any differences in student learning unless teachers are engaged in practices that are enhanced by working with fewer students at a time. When teachers carry out standard routines of lecture and recitation, it matters little whether there are 15, 20, or even 30 students in the class. Class size is likely to affect learning when instruction emphasizes more interactive involvement such as project work, extensive writing, and discussion, which may foster more intensive participation and feedback when there are fewer students at hand.

A similar argument can be made about time for instruction, another application of material resources. Generally, the research indicates that more time for teaching results in more learning for students (e.g., Brophy & Good, 1986). The implicit mechanism underlying the findings, as Barr and Dreeben (1983) explained, is a nested layers model: when teachers have more time available, they use it to cover the curriculum more extensively or in greater depth, and this yields enhanced learning for students. However, the pattern is not invariant. For example, when more time is allocated to first-grade teachers, they use it to advance their highest priority, the reading curriculum (Gamoran & Dreeben, 1986). They do not use additional time for other subjects, such as mathematics, science, or social studies (Gamoran, 1988). Thus time, a resource allocated by administrators to teachers, is an essential element in the context of first-grade reading instruction, but it has limited implications for first-grade teaching in other subjects. More generally, the impact of time as an organizational resource clearly depends on how that time is allocated by teachers within classrooms.

Because the impact of resources depends on how the resources are used, control over material resources is also an important consideration. According to one view, because teachers have the closest contact with students, they know best what resources are needed to meet students' needs. This perspective sees teachers as knowledgeable professionals and suggests that the greater teachers' control over the allocation of resources, the more effectively the resources will be used (Gamoran, Porter, &

Gahng, 1995). However, research to date has found little evidence for effects of teacher control over resources on teaching or learning (Park, 1998).

Human Resources

Some perspectives on schooling assume that differences among teachers in how they have been trained or in what they know have little to do with the effects of instruction on learning. Older notions of teacher-proof curricula (see Brophy & Good, 1986) have counterparts in the most extreme view of standards-based reform, which emphasizes standardized curricula as the key to successful teaching and student testing as the means of ensuring that the curriculum is taught (see Borman, Cookson, Sadovnik, & Spade, 1996). The input–output model of schooling similarly ignores the teaching process in considering the production of learning. These views are consistent with a highly bureaucratized model of schooling in which teachers adhere to standard procedures to maximize efficiency (e.g., Callahan, 1962).

Research evidence depicts teaching as an activity that, in some cases, is highly routinized. Jackson (1968) observed that teaching tends to be preactive, or scripted in advance, rather than reactive, or responsive to students. Many writers have documented the extent to which classroom life is dominated by teachers (e.g., Gamoran et al., 1995; Goodlad, 1984; McNeil, 1986). As loose-coupling theorists have shown, this attempted routinization has gaps—points at which teaching may or may not coincide with what students need for learning. Nonetheless, a logic of confidence allows teachers to proceed without being troubled by a mismatch between script and students (Hemmings & Metz, 1991; Meyer & Rowan, 1978).

Recent research on teaching, however, indicates that the logic of confidence does not always prevail and that teachers' knowledge makes a difference in the quality of instruction and, in particular, teachers' abilities to respond to students (Cohen, 1990). Drawing on findings from cognitive science, education researchers posit three types of knowledge that are essential for teaching: pedagogical knowledge, in which teachers know general strategies of teaching; content knowledge, what teachers know about their subject matters; and pedagogical content knowledge, the knowledge of how to teach a particular subject matter in a way that fosters students' understanding (Shulman, 1987). Following this argument, then, we propose that teachers' human resources—their knowledge, skills, and dispositions—constitute an important resource that may shape the quality of their teaching and their students' learning. Studies of teacher knowledge in specific areas of pedagogic content indicate that the implementation of a new instructional approach improves as teachers come to understand it more deeply (Tharp & Gallimore, 1988).

The emphasis on human resources implies a different model of change than that favored by a model focused on material resources. If human resources are important, then teacher development may be a central element of reform activities (Tharp & Gallimore, 1988). Given the high degree of teacher autonomy in the classroom, a perspective that emphasizes teachers' learning over material resources seems especially promising.

Principal leadership is another type of human resource found in schools. Research in the effective schools tradition emphasized leadership, but empirical corroboration for the salience of principal leadership for student learning is weak (Good & Brophy, 1986). A key limitation of this work is its failure to specify the mechanisms by which leadership may stimulate better learning. Current research on leadership emphasizes the principal's role in creating a community with a common purpose (Newmann & Associates, 1996). Successful principals provide a vision that sets forth a particular mission for the school and galvanizes commitment from teachers and from students. At the same time, the principal may be able to select staff members who accept the school's mission. In this way, a principal's leadership may result in a schoolwide instructional emphasis on common goals.

Interestingly, this view of leadership is more compatible with the loose-coupling model than with nested layers. Rather than viewing the allocation of resources as the key mechanism for the impact of leadership, as implied by the nested layers view, this perspective on leadership emphasizes its symbolic attributes, which are central to loose-coupling theory (Meyer & Rowan, 1978). Even though selecting staff is a technical activity, it has symbolic implications when acceptance of a common vision is a chief criterion for selection. According to loose coupling, structure and technical work are weakly connected, but rituals and symbols, including those that define the school's mission in the wider society, play an important role in pulling together and legitimizing the school in its social context. Following this view, principal leadership may affect the work of teachers by shaping a purpose for the school through selection of staff and articulation of a guiding vision.

Social Resources

Our argument about social resources comes neither from loose coupling nor from the nested layers model. Both views stress the isolation and autonomy of teachers within their classrooms, differing in that nested layers studies have shown that material resources allocated to classrooms and used by teachers can affect student learning (e.g., Gamoran & Dreeben, 1986). According to these perspectives there is little to be gained from collegiality among the faculty of a school, except perhaps the pleasures of a friendlier workplace. Similarly, these widely followed theories would lead one to expect few benefits of teacher participation in collective decisions about school policies. According to loose coupling, school policies simply have little relevance for what goes on in classrooms. According to the nested layers view, policy decisions are managerial activities whose impact occurs through the allocation of resources, regardless of how allocative decisions are made. For different reasons, neither perspective supposes that relations among teachers matter for instructional practices.

In contrast, an emerging literature about the social organization of schools suggests that under certain conditions, social relations among educators may profoundly influence teachers' classroom work and thereby affect student learning. As Rowan (1990) explained, when teaching is viewed as complex and interactive, dynamic and changing as opposed to routine, an organic system of management that relies on developing commitment rather than imposing controls may lead to more successful teaching and learning. Organic management means encouraging social relationships of trust, shared responsibility, collective decision making, and common values as mechanisms for bringing about change. When these activities are focused on student learning, they may indeed matter for instruction and for achievement (Newmann & Associates, 1996). Thus, aspects of the social environment of the school, including shared values, collaboration, and collective decision making, constitute social resources on which educators may draw to bolster their teaching.

At the same time, social resources may also emerge from experiences in the practice of teaching. Teachers who refrain from regarding instruction as a standardized, routine activity are faced with the uncertainties of finding successful ways of meeting students' needs. This uncertainty is always present in teaching, but typically it is obscured by the logic of confidence that promotes following prescribed routines that avoid being deflected by students' responses. Recognition of uncertainty may lead teachers to talk with one another—breaking down the usual isolation of teaching—as they search for better solutions to the problems of teaching and learning that appear in their classrooms. These discussions about instruction may strengthen the collective ties among teachers and teachers and in turn may help address their concerns about teaching.

Although Newmann and Associates' (1996) findings are consistent with the view that social resources matter for teaching, an alternate interpretation of the evidence cannot be rejected. Even when social relations among teachers emerge out of practical experience, these social relations may have little bearing on instruction because teachers are autonomous in their classrooms. Under this scenario, social relations would be a correlate of successful teaching but not a causal factor. Research to date cannot adjudicate among the alternative interpretations.

Professional community. One way of characterizing social resources in a school is as a professional community of educators. Several recent writers claim that a strong professional community provides the capacity for improving instruction and ultimately for enhancing student learning. Talbert and McLaughlin (1994) distinguished between professionalism and community: professionalism includes technical knowledge, an ethic of service, and commitment to the profession, and community refers to collaboration and continuous learning among teachers. Their view of professionalism is akin to our notion of human resources, except that they examine the collective, shared presence of technical knowledge, finding that teacher collaboration and learning promote a technical culture in the school. Newmann and Associates (1996) explored the contribution of professional community to authentic pedagogy, an instructional focus on disciplinary content, students' construction of knowledge, and relevance. Professional community, in their view, consists of shared purpose, a collective focus on student learning, collaboration, reflective conversations about teaching, and deprivatized practice (i.e., breaking the usual isolation of teaching by observing one another's teaching). They found more authentic pedagogy in schools with stronger professional communities. Secada and Adajian (1997), using a similar view of professional community but adding collective control over key decisions to the concept, provided a case study of an elementary school that illustrates how one schoolwide professional community helped teachers improve their teaching of mathematics.

Findings from studies of professional community are provocative, but several caveats are in order. First, the studies are based on small samples of schools. Second, particularly in the case of Newmann and Associates (1996), generalization from the evidence is difficult because the schools were selected especially for their unique features. Third, most studies of professional community have implicitly adopted the nested layers view that professional community enhances teaching and thereby improves learning; yet it is also possible that professional community is a by-product of enhanced teaching, rather than a stimulus. Secada and Adajian (1997) suggested that teachers' professional community and instructional practice may affect one another, but their empirical analysis was limited to one causal direction: the influence of professional community an instruction. Similarly, Louis, Kruse, and Marks (1996) acknowledged that the connections between social relations among teachers and classroom instruction are complex:

> [Our analysis] cannot prove that professional community causes teachers to engage in more authentic classroom practice. A skeptic could plausibly argue that teachers who are making efforts to increase authentic pedagogy are more likely to seek support for this difficult task from colleagues, thus creating professional community. (p. 184)

Social capital. We may also think of social resources in a school as a form of social capital. Social capital in a school refers to trust, expectations, shared understandings, and a sense of obligations that may characterize networks of relationships among educators (see Coleman. 1988 for a more general definition). In contrast to schools in which teachers work in isolation, teachers in some schools form relationships with one another around academic concerns of teaching and learning. These social networks constitute resources on which teachers can draw in their efforts to improve teaching (Kilgore & Pendelton, 1993). Collaboration, collegial relations, and opportunities for reflective discussion about teaching help build social capital. In such schools, teachers are likely to work together, even in the classroom; in this way, teaching becomes deprivatized and the typical isolation of teaching is overcome. Administrative support, such as advice and consultation about teaching and school policies, also builds social resources on which teachers can draw. Coleman (1988) explained that social capital can facilitate the development of human capital. In the case of schools, social capital among teachers helps them improve their knowledge and skills (i.e., their human capital) by providing a normative environment that encourages experimentation, offers a place to discuss uncertainties, and rewards improvement. This portrait differs substantially from the standard picture of schools in which teachers' activities are largely unseen by other adults and their unique contributions are unrecognized and unacknowledged.

More broadly, it is important to recognize the potential interplay between material, human, and social resources (which may also be termed economic, human, and social capital; see Spillane & Thompson, 1997). Just as social capital may promote human capital, teachers with particular knowledge and dispositions may be more likely to forge relations of social capital in the first place. Moreover, economic capital may be essential for developing both human and social capital, as teachers' learning and collaboration require infusions of time, materials, and expertise from outside the standard worklife of a school and its staff. Perhaps most important, economic resources devoted to teachers' professional development may stimulate both human and social capital as well as their interplay.

Professional Development of the Engine of Change

What is the basis for suggesting that professional development is a key mechanism for improving teaching? Surely many teachers would react to this claim with skepticism, as professional development is often regarded as a necessary job requirement without much connection to the actual work of teaching (Sparks & Loucks-Horsley, 1989). Much professional development, it seems, fails to influence practice. Workshops are typically isolated events, often unrelated to teachers' ongoing concerns. At best, a workshop is seen as useful if it provides a new tool for a teacher's toolkit—something that can be applied in an immediate and direct way (Fullan, 1991). This type of professional development does not result in meaningful change (Goldenberg & Gallimore, 1991), nor, we suspect, does it contribute to significant variation in teaching practices among teachers.

However, current research on teaching suggests an alternate possibility. Professional development that is sustained, coherent, collaborative, and reflective may lead to real changes in practice (Darling-Hammond & McLaughlin, 1996). Lieberman (1996) proposed an expanded view of professional development including direct learning through courses, through workshops, and through other avenues, informal learning in school through peer coaching, through sharing experiences, through conducting case studies, and the like, and informal learning outside of school through opportunities such as networks, partnerships, and collaboratives. According to Lieberman, "Teachers who engage in these new professional opportunities often find themselves in an exciting and powerful cycle: The more they learn, the more they open up to new possibilities and the more they seek to learn more" (pp. 189–190). Not all teachers follow this path, but those who do are profoundly influenced in their practice.

Professional development may influence organizational resources in two ways. First, it may contribute to teachers' knowledge, skills, and dispositions, that is, the human resources of a school. This is a common view of the benefits of professional development (e.g., Sparks & Loucks-Horsley, 1989), and it stands behind the regulations of many states that require teachers to participate in professional development in order to maintain their teaching licenses. Second, professional development may contribute to the social resources of a school, particularly if it is collaborative and reflective. When serious professional development is based in a school, it may help establish many of the features of a professional community, including collaboration, shared values, deprivatized practice, and reflective discussions about student learning. Thus, professional development has potential for building a school's capacity to create change in teaching and in learning (Darling-Hammond & McLaughlin, 1996; Little, 1986; Newmann & Associates, 1996; Tharp & Gallimore, 1988).

At the same time, organizational resources may affect the provision and nature of professional development. Professional development requires substantial funds, particularly if it is sustained over time and involves collaboration among teachers. Little (1986, 1990) showed that conditions for effective professional development are difficult to maintain, requiring time, leadership, and energy. Thus, the relation between organizational resources and professional development is dynamic, sometimes building momentum as noted by Lieberman (1996), but at other times faltering due to lack of resources (Little, 1990).

Not only do resources and professional development affect one another, but the impact of professional development on teaching probably depends in part on the level of resources available for implementation and for diffusion of new ideas and practices. Lotan, Cohen, and Morphew (1997) reported that teachers were more likely to engage in nonroutine behavior—a key outcome of their complex instruction professional development program—in schools where principals were more knowledgeable and supportive and where teachers obtained assistance in acquiring materials and supplies. Examining the persistence of a similar reform, Dahl (1997) found that new practices were more likely to be sustained over time when principals helped coordinate both material resources (supplies, equipment, and space) and social resources (teachers' opportunities to work together).

A key question for our formulation concerns the salience of the school's boundaries for changes in teaching and in learning. Our model assumes that resources that reach the school are of primary importance. This assumption is clearly appropriate for material and human resources because resources applied in the classroom are filtered through the school and through teachers. It is less clear whether the school is an especially important locus of social resources. If teachers find professional communities in other types of organizations or collaboratives, how much does the school really matter for their development as successful teachers? Although much of the research literature focuses on schoolwide professional communities (e.g., Newmann & Associates, 1996), it is clear from research on high schools that departments are the key organizational units (Little, 1990; Talbert, 1995). Consequently, it may be that departments rather than whole schools should be the focus of research on professional community. Middle and elementary schools, though not typically divided into departments, may have other types of subgroups in which professional communities are embedded. In addition, teacher networks that draw participants from many different schools may serve as important professional communities for some teachers (Newmann & Associates, 1996). Hence, there is no guarantee at any level that the boundaries of the professional community are the boundaries of the school.

Professional Development and Schoolwide Transformation

In some cases, professional development serves as a stimulus to change throughout a school. Humbolt Elementary School, one of the schools included in Newmann and Associates' (1996) study, joined a national organization for school reform after a few teachers became interested in its instructional approach. In-service participation by these teachers ultimately led to the adoption of a new approach by the entire school staff. In most cases, however, the schools that exhibited exceptionally high-quality teaching and learning were not so much transformed as established as new schools from the beginning. Change, moreover, was not seen as something that took place once but was regarded as a process of continuous improvement. At Careen Academy, an elementary school, key innovations included portfolio assessments, narrative reports on students' progress, and remaining with the same teacher for more than one year. Researchers concluded that "all three practices are works in progress, however, and teachers work continually to define and enrich them" (Newmann & Associates, 1996, p. 84). Similarly at Cibola High School, a teacher explained that"...every year we should get better. What we accepted as a minimum one year should be unsatisfactory the next year. It has to be that way. We have to ask for more every year. That's an ongoing thing, we'll never stop struggling over that" (Newmann & Associates, 1996, p. 131). In successful restructured schools, innovations were dynamic and adaptive, not static.

Professional development often played a key role in stimulating, supporting, and enhancing these changes. Careen Academy provides persuasive evidence of the power of professional development

(Newmann & Associates, 1996). Careen teachers participate in a summer institute lasting 1 to 3 weeks every year. They also attend four Saturday workshops, as well as a variety of activities outside the school district. Newmann and Associates (1996) also discovered that teachers were participating in three voluntary study groups on an ongoing basis. These activities contributed substantially to teachers' efforts in the classroom.

Despite these cases of wholescale development and change, other evidence indicates that most often, change efforts fall short of schoolwide transformation. Drawing on recent research, we have identified three other outcomes that commonly occur, even in the face of sustained, reflective professional development involving a number of teachers in a school: Teachers who favor change may find themselves in constant conflict with other actors in the school, due to others' resistance to change; they may compromise their ideals and moderate their teaching initiatives to avoid conflict (or adapt their technological efforts to accommodate existing circumstances); or they may create alternative structures within schools in which the new teaching practices may flourish, but not expand beyond the boundary of the alternate structure (e.g., a school-within-a-school). The outcome that finally emerges depends in part on the dynamic interplay between organizational resources and teaching practices. Research on school restructuring provides illustrations for these claims and draws attention to possible mechanisms through which the various outcomes may occur.

Constant conflict. In some cases, change efforts result in continual conflict within schools. Mechanisms that produce this conflict are varied. In Fremont High School, one of the highly restructured schools examined by Newmann and Associates (1996), a group of teachers attempted to eliminate low-level math classes and teach all students in mixed-ability classes within a subset of the school. These changes resulted in tension within the school, with teachers outside the group complaining that too much time was spent addressing affective needs and not enough was spent on academic concerns and arguing that students were not being prepared for upper division math courses. The same study found another example of constant conflict at Selway Middle School, a charter school led by a group of four teachers committed to authentic instruction. Although other teachers shared the ideal of authenticity, they resented the oligarchic control exercised by the four leading teachers and believed they had no voice in the policies and direction of the school.

In the first case, conflict occurred between two groups of teachers with competing ideas about the essential goals of math instruction and with differing views of the varied capabilities of students. In the second case, the conflict was also between groups of teachers, but it centered on control and governance issues rather than on a philosophy of teaching. In still other instances, conflict occurs between administrators and teachers or between teachers and parents. More generally, constant conflict seems to emerge under any one of three circumstances: when there are philosophical differences about what constitutes real teaching and learning; when there are competing preferences for the allocation of limited resources; or when teachers resist additional work necessary for teaching reforms. Actions that foment conflict include administrators' active opposition to change, restriction of resources to leaders of change processes, sabotage by antireform forces, and educators lining up external forces to oppose the sought-after changes.

Compromise and adaptation. Efforts to avoid internal conflict may lead to a second type of outcome, in which would-be reformers moderate their innovations as an adaptation to existing conditions. In some cases this means taking on the language of change without carrying out the activities of change. Researchers observed this situation in restructured schools where teachers "talked the talk" but did not "walk the walk"—that is, teachers spoke the rhetoric of reform but did not engage in innovative instructional practices (Gamoran, 1996b; Newmann & Associates, 1996). This outcome may result from a lack of training among teachers, from an assumption that desired changes cannot succeed, or

BISHOP BURTON COLLEGE
LIBRARY

as a consequence of pressure from other sources, such as district pressure to raise standardized test scores.

One may find that the adaptation response is an incremental step on the way toward long-term change. More commonly, however, our experience suggests that limited changes do not continue incrementally over the long term. Instead, once the boundaries of change are defined, further reforms in the same area of work do not occur.

Alternate structures. Sometimes teachers seeking change manage to avoid compromising their innovative approach to teaching and learning but are unable to diffuse their initiative to the entire school staff. In this circumstance the initiative often emerges as an alternate structure within a traditionally structured organization. An extreme example of this outcome was Island High School, in which every new idea seemingly resulted in a new structure. There were special programs for at-risk youth, for pregnant girls, for bilingual students, for low-achieving students, for technology-oriented students, and so on (Newmann & Associates, 1996). More commonly, a new initiative may result in a school-within-a-school that exists alongside and often in competition with the regular structure.

Why do innovative practices emerge through alternate structures instead of as transformations of existing institutions? Lack of organizational resources, particularly limited material and social resources, is the most likely reason. First, whereas special resources may be available for modest reforms, the new resources may be insufficient to encourage a more complete transformation. Second, teachers within schools are typically isolated from one another, separated by the boundaries of their classroom walls. They may lack opportunities to learn from one another and to teach one another. Communication among teachers around substantive issues is typically limited. Third, and probably most important, there is a strong norm of autonomy within schools, and it is considered inappropriate to criticize other teachers. Teachers are reluctant to question others' professional judgment, preferring to let others proceed as they have been and limiting the innovative practices to those who come to it on their own.

When outsiders see that reforms have been limited to alternate structures, they may take this result as a sign of the reform's failure. This perception may further inhibit growth or may lead to the reform's decline. Limitations on growth may also lead to a "circle the wagons" mentality among the leaders of change, a strong defense of a limited territory to keep the reform alive. These processes may tend to solidify the segmented character of school reforms, as Newmann and Associates (1996) observed at Island High School.

Examples of Teaching and Learning: Applying the Models

Thus far we have alluded to different views of teaching, but we have not provided many details. We noted, for example, that the uncertainties of teaching are often ignored in favor of standard routines, but sometimes uncertainties are recognized by teachers who may respond by attempting to increase their own knowledge. This example suggests that differences in conceptions of teaching may have consequences for the organizational context of teaching. That is, the aspect of the organizational context that is most salient may depend on one's conception of teaching. To explore this issue more fully, we describe three different approaches to teaching that we term teaching for understanding, conventional teaching, and core knowledge teaching. Each of these approaches calls into prominence different aspects of our dynamic model of the organizational context of teaching and learning.

Teaching for Understanding

According to Carpenter and Lehrer (1999), student understanding involves five interrelated forms of mental activity: constructing relationships, extending and applying knowledge, reflecting about experiences, articulating what one knows, and making knowledge one's own. By teaching for understanding, we mean instruction designed to stimulate these mental activities. A variety of writers have described such teaching as emphasizing students' construction of meaning and discovery of knowledge through active learning (e.g., Cohen, McLaughlin, & Talbert, 1993). Newmann and Associates (1996) had a similar concept in mind when they examined authentic pedagogy, which involves disciplined inquiry, student construction of knowledge, and relevance to students' lives beyond the school.

Teaching for understanding requires teachers to confront the uncertainties of teaching. As emphasized in loose-coupling theory, teaching is an ambiguous technology. Typically, this uncertainty is managed by focusing attention on the symbolic and ritual aspects of schooling and by avoiding inspection of the technical core. In teaching for understanding, however, the logic of confidence is not sufficient for managing uncertainty. These teachers are forced to go beyond scripted routines because they are faced with pressing questions about what students do or do not understand and what activities may improve understanding for particular students at a particular point in time. Teaching for understanding requires a means of managing uncertainty that recognizes and responds to questions rather than avoiding them. In response, teachers are likely to reach out to other teachers involved in similar efforts. Colleagues may provide moral support as well as practical suggestions. They may talk with one another, plan together, visit one another's classrooms, and so on—in short, they may begin to construct a professional community. Thus, a supportive social environment may emerge from efforts to teach for understanding. To flourish, however, this environment requires material resources, particularly time for collaboration, and human resources, some level of knowledge about fostering students' understanding, which may come from professional development. We propose that the relation between teaching for understanding and social resources in a school is dynamic, as the uncertainties of instruction, once recognized, provide the content of social relationships among educators, and these relationships in turn contribute to enhanced teaching for understanding. This conception is consistent with Bidwell, Frank, and Quiroz's (1997) finding that progressivist views of teaching are more prevalent in schools in which working conditions are more collegial.

Teaching for understanding may also call for another connection not previously recognized; feedback from student learning to teaching practices. Teachers who are focusing on students' understanding must adjust their activities in response to students' progress in learning. Thus, teaching for understanding forms a nexus between two dual processes: on the one side, the dynamic relation between teaching for understanding and social relations in the school, and on the other, a feedback loop between teaching and learning.

Conventional Teaching

By conventional teaching we mean teaching organized through a set pattern of lecture, recitation, and seatwork. This is not an abstracted ideal type; rather it accurately characterizes much of the teaching in American schools, particularly after the primary grades. A variety of studies have depicted this emotionally flat, teacher-dominated process (e.g., Goodlad, 1984). Nystrand (1997) described it as "monologic instruction," meaning that classroom life is essentially a monologue—even when students recite, they are following a script that has been laid down by the teacher. The flow of questions and answers follows a well-known pattern of initiation (teacher question), response by a student, and teacher's evaluation of the student's response (Mehan, 1979). In this type of instruction, even small-group work is prescribed by teachers (Nystrand, Gamoran, & Heck, 1993).

What are the key organizational contexts for conventional teaching? Here the flow tends to be one way, not dynamic. Consistent with the nested layers model, allocations of time and curricular materials are expected to influence teachers' coverage of curricular content. In contrast to teaching for understanding, social resources would have little impact on teachers' instructional practices. In conventional teaching, teachers work in isolation from one another, and issues of potential uncertainty are submerged beneath instructional routines. Consequently, there is little impetus for reflection about the substantive problems of teaching. Of course, teachers talk every day with their colleagues about the troubles of the job. These conversations, however, typically focus on administrative issues or on problems of specific students, rather than on new instructional approaches, on content questions, or on the intellectual quality of students' work (Newmann & Associates, 1996). We propose that the predominance of conventional teaching coupled with the marginal relevance of social resources for conventional teaching accounts for the inconsistent and generally weak effects of school-level social indicators such as collegiality and collaboration. Teachers' expectations and efficacy are exceptions to the pattern of weak school effects, but these apparent effects are better explained as responses to students' success rather than as determinants. For conventional teaching and social resources, loose coupling prevails.

Core Knowledge Teaching

Core knowledge teaching refers to teachers who emphasize the transmission of subject-matter knowledge from established authoritative sources to students. According to Hirsch (1993, 1996), this transmission of knowledge is the essential function of schooling. In contrast to teaching for understanding, where students construct meaning for themselves, core knowledge views meaning as residing outside students, within the subject matter itself. Core knowledge teaching also contrasts with conventional teaching in two important ways. First, core knowledge has explicit standards for what constitutes important knowledge (Hirsch, 1996). Second, core knowledge teaching emphasizes depth of knowledge to a much greater degree than in conventional teaching, which often introduces fragmented bits of information and ignores controversy and underlying linkages among issues (McNeil, 1986).

For core knowledge teachers, the key organizational resources are curricular materials and their own knowledge of the subject matter. Thus, material and human resources are more salient than social resources. One could imagine that core knowledge faculty might engage in substantive discussions of curricular content, and from these discussions might emerge a professional community of teachers, as in teaching for understanding. However, because the core knowledge curriculum is largely given, whereas students' understanding is highly uncertain, one would expect social relations among teachers to play a less prominent role in responding to and shaping instructional practices of core knowledge teaching as compared with teaching for understanding. Consistent with this view, Bidwell, Frank, and Quiroz (1997) reported no significant associations between the character of teachers' working relationships and their reported emphases on instructional rigor.

As in conventional teaching, we expect that student learning occurs in response to core knowledge teaching, without a meaningful feedback loop. Thus, teaching for understanding is the only case of those we have considered in which instruction responds significantly to student learning.

Conclusions: Toward a Research Agenda

In this article, we have both simplified and added complexity to conceptions of how the school as an organization provides a context for teaching and for learning. We simplified them by arguing that organizational resources are the most essential aspects of the organizational context. We subsume most of the conditions examined in previous research under our concept of resources, including such widely diverse conditions as time, materials, class size, knowledge, leadership, and collaboration. The focus on resources allowed us to trace the development of theoretical conceptions of school organization, from input–output notions, to nested layers, to our own model. In each of these perspectives, resources are the most salient features of the context of teaching and learning.

In simplifying it, we have left out some aspects of school organization. In particular, aspects of structure that are not merely a matter of resources are not found in our model. For example, structural differentiation into tracks and ability groups is usually not a matter of economic resources, yet it figures prominently as a context for teaching (Oakes, Gamoran, & Page, 1992). Interestingly, changes in differentiation policies often fail to bring about instructional improvements (Gamoran & Weinstein, 1998). Research in this area shows that structural differentiation is not an easy policy lever because of resistance to change and insufficient knowledge about teaching under new structural conditions (Wells & Serna, 1996). Indeed, research findings about structural differentiation are consistent with the general conclusions of Peterson and associates (1996), that structural conditions may facilitate teaching improvements but they are not the primary causal factors. Further research may help to specify more fully the importance of structure as a complement to resources (Newmann, 1998).

Composition of the student body is another organizational feature that does not figure prominently in our analysis. Composition, like structure, may be associated with differences in teaching and in learning but does not appear to be a driving force (Gamoran, 1992). An important question about composition is whether it operates as a contingency for organizational resources; that is, whether different types and levels of resources are needed to bring about similar changes in schools that differ in their student bodies. For example, is professional development of a certain type or quality necessary to improve teaching when the students are especially disadvantaged? This complication may also be addressed in future research.

Although we simplified it by leaving out some aspects of organization, in other ways our model is more complex than previous visions of schools and schooling because it recognizes the possibility of dynamic, multidirectional associations between organizational resources, teaching, and learning. Such complexity may not prevail in all cases, but it likely occurs in many of the reform efforts currently underway, which focus on teaching for understanding (Cohen et al., 1993), authentic pedagogy (Newmann & Associates, 1996), and dialogic instruction (Nystrand, 1997). Research on how these dynamic associations emerge is essential for learning how to provide a supportive context for new instructional approaches. Some combination of survey and qualitative research that monitors schools and districts over time is needed to trace the connections among resources, teaching, and learning.

The relation between teaching and its organizational context depends in part on what conception of teaching prevails. The importance of particular resources may also vary among and within educational systems in response to different or to changing conceptions of governance and accountability. For example, whereas loose coupling has been especially apparent in the United States until now, new accountability standards for what teachers teach and for what students learn may change the connections between allocations and outcomes. A question for future research is whether reform that emphasize new standards will be accompanied by tighter linkages between curricular allocation and students' performance, as envisioned in the nested layers view, or whether increases in professional development for teachers, rather than the pressures of curriculum and testing, may lead to changes in teaching. Yet another alternative is that longstanding norms in American education will be maintained, and educators will successfully resist pressures for greater accountability in the context of a persistently loosely coupled system. Cross-national research, as well as research that monitors trends within education systems over time, would shed light on these issues.

Research on the allocation and impact of resources has yielded clearer conclusions for some resources than for others. For some narrowly specified aspects of time, curriculum coverage, and student learning, the nested layers view has been sustained. Human resources such as teachers' knowledge also seem closely linked to teaching when teaching practices are carefully specified. Existing research offers less confidence about the impact of other human resources, such as leadership, or about social resources, particularly the relationships among educators. Research on these conditions is inconclusive, and we have argued that a more nuanced analysis of resource flows is necessary to identify their multidirectional effects.

An organization is a system of linked relationships, not simply a collection of individuals or of isolated categories. An organizational role, such as teacher, has meaning only when thought of in connection with some other role, such as student, principal, or parent. For this reason a sociological study of an organization calls for a study of relationships, centering on how relationships become ordered, how they change, and how they influence outcomes. What may prove intriguing across organizations are differences in the character of the linkages that prevail. A focus on relationships offers greater possibilities for understanding the context of teaching and learning, and thus for supporting the reform of teaching, than does a focus on the traits of organizational participants.

References

Adajian, L. B. (1995). *Teacher's professional community and the teaching of mathematics.* Unpublished doctoral dissertation, University of Wisconsin, Madison.

Alexander, K. L., & Cook, M. A. (1982). Curricula and coursework: A surprise ending to a familiar story. *American Sociological Review, 47,* 626–640.

Anderson, C. S. (1982). The search for school climate: A review of the research. *Review of Educational Research, 52,* 368–420.

Anderson, C. W. (1996). *Reform in teacher education as building systemic capacity to support the scholarship of teaching.* Paper presented at the International Workshop on Reform Issues in Teacher Education, Taipei, Taiwan.

Barr, R., & Dreeben, R. (1983). *How schools work.* Chicago: University of Chicago Press.

Barr, R., & Sadow, M. W. (1989). Influence of basal programs on fourth-grade reading instruction. *Reading Research Quarterly, 24,* 44–71.

Benavot, A., & Resh, N. (1998). *Diversity within uniformity: Conflicting pressures in the costruction of implemented school curricula.* Paper presented at the annual meeting of the American Sociological Association, San Francisco, California.

Bidwell, C. E. (1965). The school as a formal organization. In J. G. March (Ed.), *Handbook of organizations* (pp. 922–1022). Chicago: Rand McNally.

Bidwell, C. E., Frank, K. A., & Quiroz, P. A. (1997). Teacher types, workplace controls, and the organization of schools. *Sociology of Education, 70,* 285–307.

Bidwell, C. E., & Kasarda, J. D. (1980). Conceptualizing and measuring the effects of school and schooling. *American Journal of Education, 88,* 401–430.

Bishop, J. H. (1998). The effect of curriculum-based external exit exams on student achievement. *Journal of Economic Education, 29,* 171–182.

Blau, P. M., & Duncan, O. D. (1967). *The American occupational structure.* New York: Wiley.

Borman, K., Cookson, P., Sadovnik, A., & Spade, J. Z. (Eds., 1996). *Implementing federal legislation: Sociological perspectives on policy.* Norwood, NJ: Ablex.

Brophy, J., & Good, T. L. (1986). Teacher behavior and student achievement. In M. C. Wittrock (Ed.), *Handbook of research on teaching* (3rd ed., pp. 315–375). New York: Macmillan.

Bryk, A. S., & Driscoll, M. E. (1988). *The high school as community: Contextual influences, and consequences for students and teachers.* Madison, WI: National Center on Effective Secondary Schools.

Bryk, A. S., Lee, V. E., & Holland, P. B. (1993). *Catholic schools and the common good.* Cambridge, MA: Harvard University Press.

Bryk, A. S., & Raudenbush, S. W. (1992). *Hierarchical linear models.* Newbury Park, CA: Sage.

Callahan, R. (1962). *Education and the cult of efficiency.* Chicago: University of Chicago Press.

Carpenter, T. P., & Lehrer, R. (1999). Teaching and learning mathematics with understanding. In E. Fenneman & T. A. Romberg (Eds.), *Mathematics classrooms that promote understanding* (pp. 19–32). Mahwah, NJ: Lawrence Erlbaum.

Cohen, D. K. (1990). A revolution in one classroom: The case of Mrs. Oublier. *Educational Evaluation and Policy Analysis, 12,* 311–330.

Cohen, D. K., McLaughlin, M. W., & Talbert, J. E. (1993). *Teaching for understanding.* San Francisco, CA: Jossey-Bass.

Cohen, E. G., Deal, T. E., Meyer, J. W., & Scott, W. R. (1979). Technology and teaming in the elementary school. *Sociology of Education, 52,* 20–33.

Coleman, J. S. (1988). Social capital in the creation of human capital. *American Journal of Sociology, 94,* S95–S120.

Coleman, J. S., Campbell, E., Hobson, C., McPartland, J., Mood, A., Weinfield, F., & York, R. (1966). *Equality of educational opportunity.* Washington, DC: U.S. Government Printing Office.

Coleman, J. S., & Hoffer, T. (1987). *Public and private high schools: The impact of communities.* New York: Basic Books.

Dahl, R. (1997). Organizational factors and the continuation of a complex instructional technology. In E. G. Cohen & R. A. Lotan (Eds.), *Working for equity in heterogeneous classrooms: Sociological theory in practice* (pp. 260–274). New York: Teachers College Press.

Darling Hammond, L., & McLaughlin, M. W. (1996). Policies that support professional development in an era of reform. In *Teacher learning: New policies, new practices* (pp. 202–218). New York: Teachers College Press.

Doyle, W. (1992). Curriculum and pedagogy. In P. W. Jackson (Ed.), *Handbook of research on curriculum* (pp. 486–516). New York: Macmillan.

Edmonds, R. (1979). Effective schools for the urban poor. *Educational Leadership, 37,* 15–27.

Freeman, R. J., & Porter, A. C. (1989). Do textbooks dictate the content of mathematics instruction in elementary schools? *American Educational Research Journal, 26,* 403–421.

Fullan, M. G. (1991). *The new meaning of educational change.* New York: Teachers College Press.

Fuller, B. (1987). What school factors raise achievement in the Third World? *Review of Educational Research, 57,* 255–292.

Fuller, B., & Clarke, P. (1994). Raising school effects while ignoring culture? Local conditions and the influence of classroom tools, rules, and pedagogy. *Review of Educational Research, 64,* 119–157.

Gahng, T.-J. (1993). *A further search for school effects on achievement and intervening school experiences: An analysis of the Longitudinal Study of American Youth data.* Unpublished doctoral dissertation, University of Wisconsin, Madison.

Gamoran, A. (1987). The stratification of high school learning opportunities. *Sociology of Education, 60,* 135–155.

Gamoran, A. (1988). Resource allocation and the effects of schooling: A sociological perspective. In D. W. Monk & J. Underwood (Eds.). *Microlevel school finance: Issues and implications for policy* (pp. 207–232). Ninth Annual Yearbook of the American Educational Finance Association. Cambridge, MA: Ballinger.

Gamoran, A. (1992). Social factors in education. In M. Alkin (Ed.), *Encyclopedia of Educational Research* (6th ed., pp. 1222–1229). New York: Macmillan.

Gamoran, A. (1996a). Curriculum standardization and equality of opportunity in Scottish secondary education, 1984–1990. *Sociology of Education, 29,* 1–21.

Gamoran, A. (1996b). Goals 2000 in organizational perspective: Will it make a difference for states, districts, and schools? In K. Borman, P. Cookson, A. Sadovnik, & J. Z. Spade (Eds.), *Implementing federal legislation: Sociological perspectives on policy* (pp. 429–443). Norwood, NJ: Ablex.

Gamoran, A. (1996c). Student achievement in public magnet, public comprehensive, and private city high schools. *Educational Evaluation and Policy Analysis, 18,* 1–18.

Gamoran, A., & Dreeben, R. (1986). Coupling and control in educational organizations. *Administrative Science Quarterly, 31,* 612–632.

Gamoran, A., Nystrand, M., Berends, M., & LePore, P. C. (1995). An organizational analysis of the effects of ability grouping. *American Educational Research Journal, 32,* 687–715.

Gamoran, A., Porter, A. C., & Gahng, T.-J. (1995). Teacher empowerment: A policy in search of theory and evidence. In W. J. Fowler, B. Levin, & H. J. Walberg (Eds.), *Organizational Influences on Educational Productivity, Volume 5* (pp. 175–193). Greenwich, CT: JAI Press.

Gamoran, A., Porter, A. C., Smithson, J., & White, P. A. (1997). Upgrading high school mathematics instruction: Improving learning opportunities for low-income, low-achieving youth. *Educational Evaluation and Policy Analysis. 19,* 325–338.

Gamoran, A., & Weinstein, M. (1998). Differentiation and opportunity in restructured schools. *American Journal of Education, 106,* 385–415.

Goldenberg, C., & Gallimore, R. (1991, November). Changing teaching takes more than a one-shot workshop. *Educational Leadership, 49,* 69–72.

Goldstein, H. (1995). *Multilevel statistical models.* New York: Halsted Press.

Good, T. L., & Brophy, J. E. (1986). School effects. In M. C. Wittrock (Ed.), *Handbook of research on teaching* (3rd ed., pp. 570–602). New York: Macmillan.

Goodlad, J. (1984). *A place called school.* New York: McGraw-Hill.

Greenwald, R., Hedges, L., & Laine, R. D. (1996). The effects of school resources on student achievement. *Review of Educational Research, 66,* 361–396.

Hanushek, E. (1994). *Making schools work: Improving performance and controlling costs.* Washington, DC: Brookings.

Hanushek, E. (1997). Assessing the effects of school resources on student performance: An update. *Educational Evaluation and Policy Analysis, 19,* 141–64.

Hemmings, A., & Metz, M. H. (1991). Real teaching: How high school teachers negotiate societal, local community, and student pressures when they define their work. In R. N. Page & L. Valli (Eds.), *Curriculum differentiation: Interpretive studies in U.S. secondary schools* (pp. 91–112). Albany, NY: State University of New York Press.

Heyneman, S., & Loxley, W. (1983). The effects of primary-school quality on academic achievement across twenty-nine high- and low-income countries. *American Journal of Sociology, 88,* 1162–1194.

Hirsch, E. D. (1993). The core knowledge curriculum: What's behind its success? *Educational Leadership, 50,* 23–25.

Hirsch, E. D. (1996). *The schools we need and why we don't have them.* New York: Doubleday.

Hodgson, G. (1975). Do schools make a difference? In D. M. Levine & M. J. Bane (Eds.), *The inequality controversy* (pp. 24–44). New York: Basic Books.

Jackson, P. A. (1968). *Life in classrooms.* New York: Holt, Rinehart and Winston.

Jencks, C. L., Smith, M., Acland, H, Bane, M. J., Cohen, D. K., Gintis, H., Heyns, B., & Michelson, S. (1972). *Inequality: A reassessment of the effects of family and schooling in America.* New York: Basic Books.

Kilgore, S. B., & Pendelton, W. W. (1993). The organizational context of learning: Framework for understanding the acquisition of knowledge. *Sociology of Education, 66,* 63–87.

Lee, V. E., & Smith, J. B. (1995). Effects of high school restructuring and size on early gains in achievement and engagement. *Sociology of Education, 68,* 241–270.

Lee, V. E., & Smith, J. B. (1996). Collective responsibility for learning and its effects on gains in achievement for early secondary students. *American Journal of Education, 104,* 103–147.

Lee, V. E., & Smith, J. B. (1997). How high school organization influences the equitable distribution of learning in mathematics and science. *Sociology of Education, 70,* 128–150.

Lieberman, A. (1996). Practices that support teacher development: Transforming conceptions of professional learning. In *Teacher learning: New policies, new practices* (pp. 185–201). New York: Teachers College Press.

Little, J. W. (1986). Seductive images and organizational realities in professional development. In A. Lieberman (Ed.), *Rethinking school improvement* (pp. 26–45). New York: Teachers College Press.

Little, J. W. (1990). Conditions of professional development in secondary schools. In M. W. McLaughlin, J. E. Talbert, & N. Bascia, *The contexts of teaching in secondary schools: Teachers' realities* (pp. 187–223). New York: Teachers College Press.

Lotan, R. A., Cohen, E. G., & Morphew, C C. (1997). Principals, colleagues, staff developers: The case for organizational support. In E. G. Cohen & R. A. Lotan (Eds.), *Working for equity in heterogeneous classrooms: Sociological theory in practice* (pp. 223–239). New York: Teachers College Press.

Louis, K. S., Kruse, S. D., & Marks, H. M. (1996). Schoolwide professional community. In F. M. Newmann & Associates, *Authentic achievement: Restructuring schools for intellectual quality* (pp. 179–203). San Francisco, CA: Jossey-Bass.

Loveless, T. (1994). The influence of subject areas on middle school tracking policies. *Research in Sociology of Education and Socialization, 10,* 147–175.

McNeil, L. (1986). *Contradictions of control.* New York: Routledge & Kegan Paul.

Mehan, H. (1979). *Learning lessons: Social organization in the classroom.* Cambridge, MA: Harvard University Press.

Meyer, J. W. (1977). The effects of education as an institution. *American Journal of Sociology, 83,* 55–77.

Meyer, J. W., & Rowan, B. (1977). Institutionalized organizations: Formal structure as myth and ceremony. *American Journal of Sociology, 83,* 340–363.

Meyer, J. W., & Rowan, B. (1978). The structure of educational organizations. In M. Meyer & Associates, *Environments and organizations.* San Francisco, CA: Jossey-Bass.

Metz, M. H. (1989). Real school: A universal drama amid disparate experiences. *Politics of Education Association Yearbook, 1989,* 75–91.

Monk, D. H. (1992). Education productivity research: An update and assessment of is role in education finance reform. *Educational Evaluation and Policy Analysis, 14,* 307–332.

Mosteller, F. W., & Moynihan, D. P. (1972). *On equality of educational opportunity.* New York: Random House.

Newmann, F. M. (1998). How secondary schools contribute to academic success. In K. Borman & B. Schneider (Eds.), *The adolescent years: Social influences and educational challenges.* National Society for the Study of Education Yearbook 97:1. Chicago: University of Chicago Press.

Newmann, F. M., & Associates. (1996). *Authentic achievement: Restructuring schools for intellectual quality.* San Francisco, CA: Jossey-Bass.

Nystrand, M. (1997). *Opening dialogue.* New York: Teachers College Press.

Nystrand, M., Gamoran, A., & Heck, M. J. (1993). Using small groups for response to and thinking about literature. *English Journal, 82,* 14–22.

Oakes, J., Gamoran, A., & Page, R. N. (1992). Curriculum differentiation: Opportunities, outcomes, and meanings. In P. W. Jackson (Ed.), *Handbook of research on curriculum* (pp. 570–608). New York: Macmillan.

Pallas, A. (1988). School climate in American high schools. *Teachers College Record, 89,* 541–554.

Park, B. J. (1998). *Teacher empowerment and its effects on teachers' lives and student achievement in the U.S. high school.* Unpublished doctoral dissertation, University of Wisconsin, Madison.

Parsons, T. (1963). *Structure and process in modern societies.* Glencoe, IL: The Free Press.

Peterson, P. L., McCarthey, S. J., & Elmore, R. F. (1996). Learning from school restructuring. *American Educational Research Journal, 33,* 119–153.

Pressman, J. L., & Wildavsky, A. (1979). *Implementation* (2nd ed.). Berkeley, CA: University of California Press.

Purkey, S. C., & Smith, M. S. (1983). Effective schools: A review. *Elementary School Journal, 83,* 427–452.

Rowan, B. (1990). Commitment and control: Alternative strategies for the organizational design of schools. In C. Cazden (Ed.), *Review of Research in Education,* Vol., 16 (pp. 353–389). Washington, DC: American Educational Research Association.

Rowan, B., & Miracle, A. W., Jr. (1983). Systems of ability grouping and the stratification of achievement in elementary schools. *Sociology of Education, 56,* 133–144.

Rowan, B., & Miskel, C. (1999). Institutional theory and the study of educational organizations. In J. Murphy & K. S. Louis (Eds.), *Handbook of research in educational administration.* San Francisco, CA: Jossey-Bass.

Rowan, B., Raudenbush, S. W., & Cheong, Y. F. (1993). Teaching as a non-routine task: Implications for the management of schools. *Educational Administration Quarterly, 29,* 479–500.

Secada, W. G., & Adajian, L. B. (1997). Mathematics teachers' change in the context of their professional communities. In L. Fennema & B. S. Nelson (Eds.), *Mathematics teachers in transition* (pp. 193–219). Mahwah, NJ: Lawrence Erlbaum Associates.

Shulman, L. (1987). Knowledge and teaching: Foundations of the new reform. *Harvard Educational Review, 57,* 1–22.

Slavin, R. E. (1989). Class size and student achievement: Small effects of small classes. *Educational Psychologist, 24,* 99–109.

Slavin, R. E. (1990). Class size and student achievement: Is smaller better? *Contemporary Education, 62,* 6–12.

Sparks, D., & Loucks-Horsley, S. (1989). Five models of staff development for teachers. *Journal of Staff Development, 10,* 40–57.

Spillane, J., & Thompson, C. (1997). Reconstructing conceptions of local capacity: The local education agency's capacity for ambitious educational reform. *Educational Evaluation and Policy Analysis, 19,* 185–203.

Stevenson, D., & Baker, D. (1991). State control of the curriculum and classroom instruction. *Sociology of Education, 64,* 1–10.

Stodolsky, S. (1988). *The subject matters.* Chicago: University of Chicago Press.

Stodolsky, S., & Grossman, P. (1995). The impact of subject matter on curricular activity: An analysis of five academic subjects. *American Educational Research Journal, 32,* 227–249.

Talbert, J. E. (1995). Boundaries of teachers' professional communities in U. S. high schools: Power and precari-ousness of the subject department. In L. S. Siskin & J. W. Little (Eds.), *The subjects in question* (pp. 68–94). New York: Teachers College Press.

Talbert, J. E., & McLaughlin, M. W. (1994). Teacher professionalism in local school contexts. *American Journal of Education, 102*, 123–153.

Tharp, R. G., & Gallimore, R. (1988). *Rousing minds to life*. Cambridge, England: Cambridge University Press.

Weick, K. E. (1976). Educational organizations as loosely coupled systems. *Administrative Science Quarterly, 21*, 1–19.

Weick, K. E. (1982). Administering education in loosely coupled systems. *Phi Delta Kappan, 63*, 673–675.

Wells, A. S., & Serna, I. (1996). The politics of culture: Understanding local political resistance to detracking in racially mixed schools. *Harvard Educational Review, 66*, 93–118.

Wilson, T. P. (1996). *Reaching for a better standard*. New York: Teachers College Press.

10
Is There Really a Teacher Shortage?

RICHARD INGERSOLL

Few educational problems have received more attention in recent years than the failure to ensure that elementary and secondary classrooms are all staffed with qualified teachers. Severe teacher shortages, it is widely believed, are confronting our elementary and secondary schools. We have been warned repeatedly that "the nation will need to hire at least two million teachers over the next ten years" (e.g., National Commission on Teaching, 1997, pp. 15–16), and our teacher training institutions are simply not producing sufficient numbers of teachers to meet the demand. At the root of this school staffing crisis, according to the conventional wisdom, are two converging macro demographic trends—increasing student enrollments and increasing teacher turnover due to a "graying" teaching force. The resulting shortfalls of teachers, the argument continues, force many school systems to resort to lowering standards to fill teaching openings, inevitably resulting in high levels of underqualified teachers and lower school performance.

The prevailing policy response to these school staffing problems has been to attempt to increase the supply of teachers. In recent years a wide range of initiatives have been implemented to recruit new candidates into teaching. Among these are career-change programs, such as "troops-to-teachers," designed to entice professionals into mid-career switches to teaching and Peace Corps-like programs, such as Teach for America, designed to lure the "best and brightest" into understaffed schools. Some school districts have resorted to recruiting teaching candidates from overseas. Many states have instituted alternative certification programs, whereby college graduates can postpone formal education training and begin teaching immediately. Financial incentives, such as signing bonuses, student loan forgiveness, housing assistance, and tuition reimbursement have all been instituted to aid teacher recruitment (Hirsch, Koppich, & Knapp 2001; Feistritzer, 1997; Kopp, 1992). The "No Child Left Behind Act" passed in winter 2002 provides extensive federal funding for such initiatives.

Teacher shortages and subsequent teacher recruitment initiatives are not new to the K-12 education system. In the early and mid 1980s a series of highly publicized reports trumpeted an almost identical series of diagnoses and prescriptions (see, e.g., National Commission on Excellence in Education, 1983; Darling-Hammond, 1984; National Academy of Sciences, 1987; for reviews of this issue, see Boe & Gilford, 1992). Indeed, teacher shortages have been a cyclic threat for decades (Weaver, 1983).

Concern over teacher shortages in turn has spurred interest in empirical research on these issues, but until the past decade such efforts were limited by a lack of data. It was partly in order to address these data shortcomings that the U.S. Department of Education's National Center for Education Statistics conceived the Schools and Staffing Survey (SASS) and its supplement, the Teacher Followup Survey (TFS), beginning in the late 1980s (Haggstrom et al., 1988). This is now the largest and most comprehensive data source available on the staffing, occupational, and organizational aspects of schools.

Over the past decade I have undertaken a series of research projects using SASS/TFS to examine a range of issues concerned with teacher supply, demand, and quality (e.g., Ingersoll, 1995, 1999, 2001a, 2003b). In this report I will summarize what these data tell us about the realities of school staffing problems and teacher shortages. The theoretical perspective I adopt in my research is drawn from organizational theory and the sociology of organizations, occupations, and work. My operating premise is that in order to fully understand the causes and consequences of these social problems, it is necessary to examine them from the perspective of the organizations—the schools and districts—where these processes happen and within which teachers work. Employee supply, demand, and turnover are central issues in organizational theory and research. However, there have been few efforts to apply this theoretical perspective to understanding school staffing problems and policy. As I will show, by "bringing the organization back in," these school staffing problems are reframed from macro-level issues, involving inexorable societal demographic trends, to organizational issues, involving manipulable and policy-amenable aspects of particular schools. A close look at the data from this perspective, I argue, shows that the conventional wisdom concerning teacher shortages is largely a case of a wrong diagnosis and a wrong prescription.

The Data

As mentioned, the primary data source for this research is the nationally representative Schools and Staffing Survey (SASS) and its supplement, the Teacher Followup Survey (TFS), both conducted by the National Center for Education Statistics of the U.S. Department of Education. To date, four independent cycles of SASS have been completed: 1987–1988; 1990–1991; 1993–1994; 1999–2000. SASS is an unusually large survey. Each cycle of SASS administers survey questionnaires to a random sample of about 53,000 teachers, 12,000 principals, and 4,500 districts, representing all types of teachers, schools, districts, and all 50 states. In addition, one year later, the same schools are contacted again, and all those in the original teacher sample who had moved from or left their teaching jobs are given a follow-up second questionnaire to obtain information on their departures. This latter group, along with a representative sample of those who stayed in their schools, comprise the Teacher Followup Survey. The TFS sample contains about 7,000 teachers. Unlike most previous data sources on teacher turnover, the TFS is large, comprehensive, nationally representative, and includes the reasons teachers themselves give for their departures and a wide range of information on the characteristics and conditions of elementary and secondary schools. It is also unusual in that it does not solely focus on a particular subset of total separations, but includes all turnover: voluntary, involuntary, transfers, quits, retirements, etc. In this report, I present data from all four cycles of SASS and TFS (as of summer 2003, the 2000–2001 TFS had only been partially released by NCES and data presented here from that cycle are preliminary estimates).

Demand for Teachers Has Risen

What do the data tell us about school staffing problems and teacher shortages? The data show that the conventional wisdom on teacher shortages is correct in some respects. Consistent with shortage predictions, data from SASS and other NCES data sources show that demand for teachers has indeed increased in recent years. Since 1984, student enrollments have increased, most schools have had job openings for teachers, and the size of the teaching workforce (K-12) has increased, although the rate of these increases began to decline slightly in the late 1990s (Gerald & Hussar, 1998; Snyder & Hoffman, 2001, p. 11). Most importantly, many schools with teaching openings have experienced difficulties with recruitment. Overall, the data show that in the 1999–2000 school year, 58% of all schools reported at least some difficulty filling one or more teaching job openings, in one or more fields. However, the data also show that in any given field less than half of the total population of schools actually experienced recruitment problems (see Figure 10.1). For instance in 1999–2000, 54% of secondary schools had job openings for English teachers and about one half of these indicated they had at least some difficulty

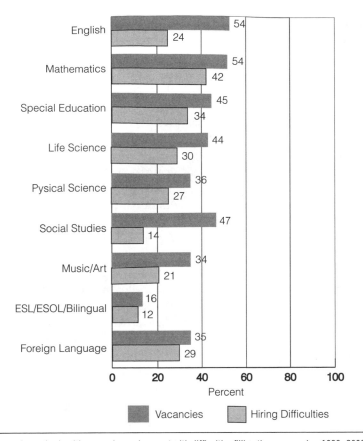

Figure 10.1 Percent secondary schools with vacancies and percent with difficulties filling those vacancies, 1999–2000.

filling these openings—representing one quarter of all secondary schools. Similarly, 54% of secondary schools had job openings for math teachers and about four fifths of these indicated they had at least some difficulty filling these math openings—representing about 40% of all secondary schools. Likewise, 45% of secondary schools had job openings for special education teachers and about three quarters of these indicated they had at least some difficulty filling these openings—representing 34% of secondary schools.[1]

How Adequate is the Supply of Teachers?

While demand has increased and many schools have had hiring difficulties, the data do not show, contrary to the conventional wisdom, that there is overall an insufficient supply of teachers being produced. National data on the overall supply of teachers trained, licensed, and certified each year are difficult to obtain. One source is NCES' Integrated Postsecondary Educational Data System (IPEDS). This source collects data on the numbers of post-secondary degree completions by field and by year. The IPEDS data indicate that, for example, at the end of the 1998–99 academic year, there were over 220,000 new recipients of education degrees at the undergraduate and graduate levels (IPEDS, 2001). But, the SASS data show that only about 86,000 of those hired for the following school year were drawn from this group of recent college graduates. Indeed, large proportions of those who train to become teachers do not ever become teachers. For example, data from the nationally representative 1993 Baccalaureate and Beyond Survey show that, of new recipients of bachelor's of education degrees who graduated in 1993, after one year out of college only 42% had taught and after four years out of college only 58% had taught. Many of those who decided not to pursue teaching indicated that they needed more education, or wanted another occupation (for a more detailed presentation of the B&B data, see Henke et al., 2000).

In short, the data appear to indicate that, overall, there are more than enough prospective teachers produced each year in the U.S. But, there are also some important limitations to these data. An overall surplus of newly trained teachers does not, of course, mean there are sufficient numbers of graduates produced in each field. A large proportion of education degree completions are in elementary education. The data are unclear on whether a sufficient quantity of teachers are produced each year in such fields as math, science, and special education.

But, on the other hand, the IPEDS database on degree completions underestimates the supply of newly qualified teachers because it does not include recipients of noneducation undergraduate degrees who also completed the requirements for certification. Moreover, newly qualified candidates, as counted in the IPEDS data, are only one source of new hires in schools. Far more of those newly hired into schools each year are from what is often referred to as the "reserve pool." These include delayed entrants—those who completed teacher training in prior years, but who have never taught, and re-entrants—former teachers who left teaching for a period to later return. The addition of these other types and sources of teachers could well mean that there are more than enough teachers produced each year.

However, from an organizational perspective, the key question is not whether the overall national supply of teachers is adequate or inadequate, instead it is which schools have staffing problems and teacher supply and demand imbalances. Even in the same jurisdiction, the degree of staffing problems varies greatly among different types of schools, and sites ostensibly drawing from the same teacher supply pool can have significantly different staffing scenarios. Some analysts have found, for example, that in the same metropolitan area in the same year some schools have extensive waiting lists of qualified candidates for their teaching job openings, while other nearby schools have great difficulty filling their teaching job openings with qualified candidates (National Commission on Teaching, 1997). Consistent with this, I have found in an analysis of variance of the SASS data that the variation in school hiring difficulties is far greater within, than between, states.[2] This suggests that to be fully understood imbalances between demand and supply must be examined at the level of the organization—an issue to which I return.

The Importance of Teacher Turnover for School Staffing Problems

There is another problem with the conventional wisdom on shortages. The data show that the demand for new teachers and subsequent staffing difficulties are not primarily due to student enrollment and teacher retirement increases, as widely believed, but these are largely due to teacher turnover—teachers moving from or leaving their teaching jobs—and most of this turnover has little to do with a graying workforce.

The TFS data show that teaching has a relatively stable annual turnover rate: 14.5% in 1988–89; 13.2% in 1991–92; 14.3% in 1994–95; 15.7% in 2000–2001 (see Figure 10.2). There are two types of total turnover included in Figure 10.2: movers—those who move to teaching jobs in other schools (often and hereafter referred to as teacher migration)—and leavers—those who leave the teaching occupation altogether (often and hereafter referred to as teacher attrition). Total teacher departures are fairly evenly split between them. Much of the existing research on teacher turnover does not include the former. Teacher cross-school migration is a form of turnover that does not decrease the overall supply of teachers because departures are simultaneously new hires. As a result, many assume that teacher migration does not contribute to the problem of staffing schools and to overall shortages. From a macro and system level of analysis, this is probably correct and for this reason educational

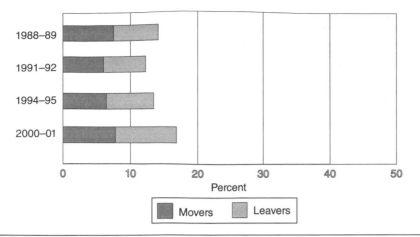

Figure 10.2 Percent annual teacher turnover.

researchers have often de-emphasized or excluded movers. However, from an organizational perspective and from the viewpoint of those managing at the school-level, movers and leavers have the same effect—in either case it results in a decrease in staff, which usually must be replaced. Hence, research on employee turnover in other occupations and organizations almost always includes both movers and leavers—and for this reason I include them here. As illustrated in Figure 10.2, adopting a system-level or an organizational-level of analysis makes a difference—if one excludes cross-school moves, total turnover would appear far less than it is—from the viewpoint of those managing schools.

One question that naturally arises concerns how rates of teacher turnover from schools compare to those in other organizations, occupations, and industries. There has never been much empirical research on this issue. In earlier work I compared the TFS data with data from one of the better known sources of information on employee turnover in a range of occupations and organizations, the Bureau of National Affairs (2002). This comparison showed that teaching has a slightly higher annual turnover rate than the nationwide level for total employee departures—which over the past decade averaged 11.9% annually (Ingersoll, 2001a). But, this comparison provided only a crude benchmark. The BNA data represent an organizational rate of employee turnover, which ostensibly includes the whole range of employees on the payroll—from clerical staff to senior management—within a given organization. Far more informative would be comparisons of *occupational* rates of turnover, i.e., how do rates of teacher turnover compare to those in other occupations? But, such data are difficult to obtain and suffer from serious issues of measure comparability (Price, 1977, 1997).[3] In more recent work I have found that, as one might expect, teaching has higher turnover than some higher-status professions (professors at 9.3%; technology and scientific professionals from 3.6% to 9.2%), about the same as other female semi-professions (nurses at 18%) and less turnover than some lower-status, lower-skill occupations (federal clerical workers at 30%).[4]

But, from an organizational perspective the key question is not whether teaching has higher or lower turnover than other occupations, but rather is teacher turnover a problem for schools themselves. The data indicate it is. There is a strong link between teacher turnover and the difficulties schools have adequately staffing classrooms with qualified teachers—as shown in Table 10.1 which presents data on the flows in and out of schools from all four cycles of the SASS/TFS data.

Reading down the column for the 1993–94 school year, for example, Table 10.1 indicates there were just under three million teachers in the K-12 education system that year, including both public and private schools. About 377,135 of these teachers entered their schools at the beginning of the 1993–94 school year. Of these, 192,550 had not taught the prior year. This latter group included newly

Table 10.1 Trends in Teacher Flows In and Out of Schools

	1987–88 School Year	1990–91 School Year	1993–94 School Year	1999–2000 School Year
1.) Total Teaching Force – during school year	2,630,335	2,915,774	2,939,659	3,451,316
2.) Total Hires - at beginning of school year	361,649	387, 807	377, 135	534, 861
A.) Entrants	178,344	191,179	192,550	232,232
B.) Movers from other schools	183, 305	196, 628	184, 585	302,629
3.) Total Departures – by following school year	390,731	382,879	417,588	539,778
A.) Movers to other schools	218,086	208,885	204,680	252,408
B.) Leavers from occupation	172,645	173,994	212,908	287,370
Retirees	35, 179	47, 178	50,242	NA

Notes:
- Entrants: includes new, delayed, and re-entrants. This refers to those who did not teach the prior year; some did teach in the past.
- These data are calculated at the level of the school. Hence, "hires" and "departures" refer to those newly entering or departing a particular school. "Movers" includes transfers among schools within districts. Reassignments within a school are not defined as hires or as departures.
- As of summer 2003, teacher retirement data for the 2000 school year were not yet available.

qualified candidates fresh out of college, delayed entrants who had completed their training in a prior year but had not previously taught, and re-entrants who had taught previously, stopped for a while and then returned. Another 184,585 of these hires to schools had moved from another school. By the following school year, 417,588 teachers had moved from or left their school jobs. Just under half of these departures—204,680—moved to other schools to teach. Another 212,908 left the occupation altogether. Of the latter, 50,242 were retirees.

Table 10.1 documents two important points. First, the data show that the demand for new teachers is not primarily due to student enrollment increases, nor to teacher retirement increases, but to pre-retirement teacher turnover. That is, most of the hiring of new teachers is simply to fill spots vacated by teachers who just departed. For instance, about 191,000 individuals entered teaching at the beginning of the 1990–91 school year. However, by the following school year 12 months later, about 174,000 teachers (equivalent to 91% of those just hired) left the occupation altogether. At the beginning of the 1993–94, three years later, about 192,500 teachers entered teaching, but by the following school year, about 213,000 (equivalent to 110% of those just hired) left the occupation. At the beginning of the 1999–00, six years later, about 232,000 teachers entered teaching, but by the following school year, about 287,000 (equivalent to 124% of those just hired) left the occupation.

Second, although teacher retirements have increased in recent years, they account for only a small portion of the above total turnover. For example, from 1994 to 1995 there were about 50,000 retirees, accounting for only 24% of the 213,000 leavers and only 12% of the total turnover of 417,588 during that period. In sum, the data show that the demand for new teachers, and subsequent staffing difficulties, is not primarily due to student enrollment increases, nor to teacher retirement increases, but to pre-retirement teacher turnover. That is, most of the hiring of new teachers is simply to fill spots vacated by teachers who just departed. And, most of those departing are not doing so because of gray hair.

The Revolving Door

It is also important to note that teaching is a relatively large occupation—it represents 4% of the entire civilian workforce. There are, for example, over twice as many K-12 teachers as registered nurses and five times as many teachers as either lawyers or professors (U.S. Bureau of the Census, 2002).[5] The

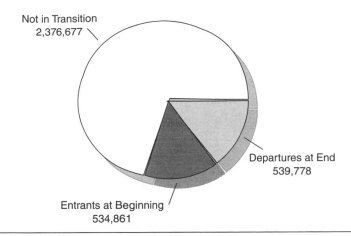

Not in Transition
2,376,677

Departures at End
539,778

Entrants at Beginning
534,861

Figure 10.3 Numbers of teachers in transition before, during, and after the 1999–2000 school year.

sheer size of the teaching force combined with its relatively high annual turnover means that there are large flows in, through, and out of schools each year. The image that these data suggest is one of a "revolving door,"—which I have tried to capture in Figure 10.3. It shows that for the 1999–2000 school year, 534,861 teachers entered schools, while by the following school year an even larger number—539,778—had moved from or left their schools.[6] Hence, in a 12-month period over one million teachers—almost a third of this relatively large workforce—were in job transition into, between, or out of schools. This revolving door is a major factor behind school staffing problems.

Table 10.1 and Figure 10.3 also provide a context to interpret the widely used statistic, introduced earlier, that the nation "will need to hire at least two million teachers over the next 10 years." This statistic was drawn from an NCES analysis (Gerald & Hussar, 1998; Hussar, 1998) that projected the numbers of teachers that would need to be hired from 1998 to 2008 in order to replace those who had left teaching and to account for student enrollment increases. These analyses themselves did not examine supply, nor changes in hiring needs over time. But, a wide variety of commentators, researchers, and policy makers have interpreted this statistic to mean that hiring two million new teachers is an unusually large number and assumed to be evidence that we face an alarmingly inadequate supply of new teachers being produced. A close look at the data reveals that neither is the case.

The Importance of Teacher Turnover for Organizations

Of course, not all teacher turnover is detrimental. There is an extensive research literature on employee turnover conducted by those who study organizations and occupations in general (e.g., Price 1977, 1989; Mueller & Price, 1990; Bluedorn, 1982; Halaby & Weakliem, 1989; Horn & Griffeth, 1995; Kalleberg & Mastekaasa, 1998; March & Simon, 1958; Mobley, 1982; Steers & Momday, 1981). On the one hand, researchers in this tradition have long held that a low level of employee turnover is normal and efficacious in a well-managed organization. Too little turnover of employees is tied to stagnancy in organizations; effective organizations usually both promote and benefit from a limited degree of turnover by eliminating low-caliber performers and bringing in "new blood" to facilitate innovation. Moreover, some job and career changes are, of course, normal and inevitable in any occupation. On the other hand, researchers in this tradition have also long held that high levels of employee turnover are both cause and effect of performance problems in organizations.

Organizational analysts have also noted that the consequences of employee turnover vary among different types of employees and among different types of organizations. Labor process analysts, for instance, have argued that a major issue, from the viewpoint of organizational management, is the extent to which the organization is, or is not, dependent on particular types of employees and, hence, vulnerable to the disruption caused by their turnover (e.g., Braverman, 1974; Burawoy, 1979; Edwards, 1979). For just this reason the issue of employee "substitutability," or the ease with which organizations can replace employees, is a central concern in organizational management and a central theme in organizational research. In this perspective, employee turnover is especially consequential for work that involves uncertain and nonroutine technologies and which requires extensive interaction among participants. Such organizations are often unusually dependent upon the commitment and cohesion of employees and, hence, especially vulnerable to turnover (e.g., Burns & Stalker, 1961; Kanter, 1977; Likert, 1967; Porter, Lawler & Hackman, 1975; Turner & Lawrence, 1964; Walton, 1980).

Schools are an example of this type of organization. Education theory and research have long shown that, while education is a mass "industry" involving large complex formal organizations, in important ways schools do not fit standard input-output, economic-production models in either theory or practice (Bidwell, 1965; Lortie, 1975; Ingersoll, 2003a). The "raw materials" in schools are children and youth; the "technology" of teaching and learning is often uncertain, ambiguous, and nonroutine; and the "product" is youngsters' growth. As a result while schools in some ways resemble economic-production organizations, in other ways they resemble another kind of institution altogether—the family. Student test outcomes are one of the important output functions of school production. But not surprisingly, similar to families the presence of a positive sense of community, belongingness, communication, and cohesion among members has long been held by education theory and research to be one of the most important indicators and aspects of effective schools (e.g., Durkheim, 1925/1961; Waller, 1932; Parsons, 1959; Grant, 1988; Coleman & Hoffer, 1987; Kirst 1989; Rosenholtz, 1989).

Hence, from an organizational perspective, some teacher turnover, especially of ineffective teachers, is necessary and beneficial. But from this perspective, turnover of teachers from schools is of concern not simply because it may be an indicator of sites of potential staffing problems and so-called teacher shortages, but because of its relationship to school cohesion and, in turn, performance. Moreover, from this perspective this relationship runs both directions. That is, high rates of teacher turnover are of concern not only because they may be an outcome indicating underlying problems in how well schools function, but also because they can be disruptive, in and of themselves, for the quality of school community and performance.

Some of these costs and consequences of turnover are more easily measured and quantified than others. In contrast to the corporate sector, however, there has been very little attention paid to the costs and consequences of employee turnover in education. One notable exception was a recent attempt to quantify the costs of teacher turnover in Texas—this study concluded these costs run into the hundreds of millions of dollars each year to the state. (Texas Center for Educational Research, 2000).

Teacher and School Differences in Turnover

The data also show that the revolving door varies greatly among different kinds of teachers and different kinds of schools. As found in previous research (Murnane et al., 1991; Huling-Austin, 1990; Hafner & Owings, 1991), the SASS data show that teaching is an occupation that loses many of its newly trained members very early in their careers—long before the retirement years. I used these data to provide a rough estimate of the cumulative attrition of beginning teachers from the occupation in their first several years of teaching. The data suggest that after just five years, between 40 and 50% of all beginning teachers have left teaching altogether, (see Figure 10.4).[7] Of course, not all of this attrition results in a permanent loss of teachers. One form of this revolving door is represented by temporary attrition—teachers who leave teaching but return in later years, as discussed earlier (also see Murnane et al., 1991). But again, from the viewpoint of those managing at the school-level, temporary and permanent attrition have the same effect—in either case it results in an immediate decrease in staff, which usually must be replaced.

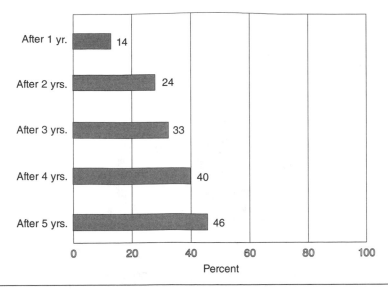

Figure 10.4 Beginning teacher attrition (cumulative percent teachers having left teaching occupation, by years of experience).

Annual teacher turnover also varies according to the teachers' main field. Math, science, and elementary special education teachers have higher rates of turnover, and social studies and English have lower rates (see Figure 10.5). Moreover, a number of studies have found that teachers with higher ability, as measured by test scores such as the SAT, the National Teacher Exam, and teacher licensure tests, are more likely to turn over (e.g., Weaver, 1983; Murnane et al., 1991; Schlecty & Vance, 1981; Stinebrickner, 2001; Henke et al., 2000).

The data also show that the revolving door varies greatly among different kinds of schools, as illustrated in Figure 10.6.[8] For example, high-poverty public schools have far higher turnover rates than

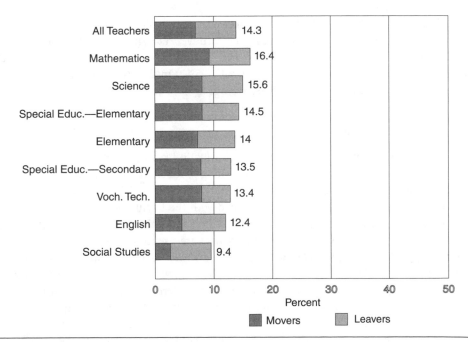

Figure 10.5 Percent annual teacher turnover, by field, 1994–95.

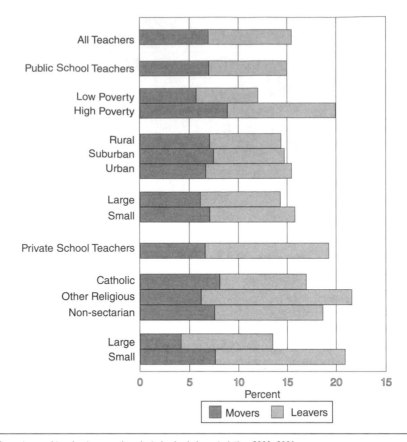

Figure 10.6 Percent annual teacher turnover, by selected school characteristics, 2000–2001.

do more affluent public schools. Urban public schools have slightly more turnover than do suburban and rural public schools. Private schools have higher turnover rates than public schools, but there are also large differences among private schools. On one end of the continuum lie larger private schools with among the lowest average turnover rate—about 13.5%. On the other end of the continuum lie smaller private schools with among the highest average levels—about 22%.

The Sources of Teacher Turnover

These data raise another important set of questions: why do teachers depart at relatively high rates and why are these rates so dramatically different among schools? To answer these questions I conducted multivariate statistical analyses of data from different cycles of SASS/TFS to determine which characteristics of teachers and schools are associated with the likelihood of teacher turnover, after controlling for background factors (Ingersoll, 2001b). I also examined data on the reasons teachers themselves give for their turnover. Such self-report data are useful because those departing are, of course, often in the best position to know the reasons for their turnover. But, such self-report data are also retrospective attributions, subject to bias and, hence, warrant caution in interpretation. Nevertheless, I found a great deal of consistency among these different types of data and from different cycles of the survey. The following section summarizes my principal findings. Along with the annual rates of turnover, Table 10.2 presents self-report data on teachers' reasons for both migration and attrition. In addition, for all teachers who departed because of job dissatisfaction, the bottom portion

Table 10.2 Percent Teacher Turnover and Percent Teachers Giving Various Reasons for Their Turnover, 1994–95.

	All	Movers	Leavers
Rates of Turnover	14.3	7	7.3
Reasons for Turnover			25
Retirement	13	–	8
School Staffing Action	20	34	44
Family or Personal	40	36	25
To Pursue other Job	27	29	25
Dissatisfaction	29	32	
Reasons for Dissatisfaction			
Poor Salary	54	49	61
Poor Administrative Support	43	51	32
Student Discipline Problems	23	22	24
Lack of Faculty Influence & Autonomy	17	18	15
Poor Student Motivation	15	12	18
No Opportunity for Professional Advancement	6	8	5
Inadequate Time to Prepare	6	5	6
Intrusions on Teaching Time	7	5	11
Class Sizes too Large	7	3	11

of the table presents data on the reasons for their dissatisfaction.[9] (definitions of these reasons can be found in the Appendix)

Contrary to conventional wisdom, retirement is not an especially prominent factor. The latter was listed by only 25% of leavers and 13% of total departures. School staffing cutbacks due to lay-offs, terminations, school closings, and reorganizations account for a larger proportion of turnover than does retirement. These staffing actions more often result in migration to other teaching jobs rather than leaving the teaching occupation altogether. But, the data also show that, overall, staffing actions, like retirement, account for only a small portion of total turnover from schools—about 20%.

A third category of turnover—that for personal reasons—includes departures for pregnancy, child rearing, health problems, and family moves. These account for more turnover than either retirement or staffing actions and they are probably common to all occupations and all types of organizations. The two final sets of reasons are directly related to the organizational conditions of teaching. Individually each of these categories accounts for more turnover than does retirement. Together these are the most prominent source of turnover. Almost half of all departures report as a reason either job dissatisfaction or the desire to pursue a better job, another career, or to improve career opportunities in or out of education.

Of those who depart because of job dissatisfaction, most often link their turnover to low salaries, lack of support from the school administration, student discipline problems, poor student motivation, and lack of teacher influence over decision-making. In general, similar kinds of dissatisfactions lie behind both teacher migration and teacher attrition. Interestingly, several factors stand out as *not major reasons* behind turnover, according to those who departed: large class sizes, intrusions on classroom time, and lack of planning time.

In sum, the data indicate that teachers depart their jobs for a variety of reasons. Retirement accounts for a relatively small number of total departures, a moderate number of departures are due to school staffing actions, a large proportion indicate they depart for personal reasons, and a large proportion also report they depart either because they are dissatisfied with their jobs or in order to seek better jobs or other career opportunities. I have found these reasons for turnover to be highly consistent across different types and cycles of the data, across different kinds of schools, and across different subsets of teacher turnover. These findings are important because of their policy implications. Unlike explanations that focus on external demographic trends "out there," these findings suggest there is a role "in here" for the internal organization and management of schools.

Implications for Policy

It is widely believed that shortfalls of teachers resulting primarily from two converging demographic trends—increasing student enrollments and increasing teacher retirements—are leading to problems staffing schools with qualified teachers and will, in turn, lower educational performance. In response school districts, states, and the federal government have developed a variety of recruitment initiatives designed to recruit more candidates into teaching.

However worthwhile these efforts may be, the data suggest that, alone, they will not solve school staffing problems. The data suggest that school staffing problems are not solely or even primarily due to teacher shortfalls resulting from either increases in student enrollment or increases in teacher retirement. In contrast, the data suggest that school staffing problems are to a large extent a result of a "revolving door"—where large numbers of teachers depart teaching for reasons other than retirement. From the framework of supply and demand theory, the data show that the problem is not primarily shortages, in the sense of an insufficient supply of teachers being recruited and trained. Some economists would still call this a shortage—in the technical sense that there is an inadequate quantity of teachers supplied—those willing to continue to offer their services at a given wage and given working conditions in given schools. This diagnostic and terminological distinction has crucial implications for prescription. It is also a distinction that is almost always overlooked in research and policy on the teacher shortage.

Supply and demand theory holds that where the quantity of teachers demanded is greater than the quantity of teachers supplied, there are two basic policy remedies: increase the quantity supplied or decrease the quantity demanded. The first approach—the traditionally dominant approach—is to increase the quantity of teachers supplied through recruitment. However, this analysis cautions that recruitment programs alone will not solve the staffing problems of schools if they do not also decrease turnover. States such as California, where class-size-reductions have strained the supply of new teachers pose exceptions. But, for just these reasons, California, like other states, must pay close attention to retention. In short, recruiting more teachers will not solve the teacher crisis if 40 to 50% of such teachers then leave within five years. The image that comes to mind is a bucket rapidly losing water because of holes in the bottom. Pouring more water into the bucket will not be the answer if the holes are not first patched.

Recruitment and other supply-side solutions may not only fail to solve the problem but could also make the situation worse. If recruitment strategies involve lowering teacher standards, or if the effect of increasing teacher supply is to deflate salaries or erode working conditions, then these measures may simply exacerbate the root factors behind school staffing problems.

This situation is analogous to aspects of management-labor conflict in industry. Critics of business practice argue that industrialists have long used labor supply recruitment as a strategy to undermine worker and union efforts to improve working conditions and wages (e.g. Braverman, 1974; Burawoy, 1979; Edwards, 1979). For example, by bringing in immigrant laborers from eastern and southern Europe at the turn of the 19th century, industrialists, the critics hold, were able to keep wages down, undermine union power, and increase profits. One of the downsides with this strategy, from a management perspective, is that it can decrease employee quality and increase employee turnover. Hence, one of the objectives behind the design of the assembly-line model of production used in industry was to increase the ease of substitutability and, hence, insulate the organization from disruption caused by employee turnover.

Similarly, social scientists have long characterized K-12 teaching as a lower status, easy-in/easy-out, high turnover occupation that has relied historically on recruitment, and not retention, to solve its staffing problems (e.g., Tyack, 1974; Lortie, 1975). Since the inception of the public school system in the late 19th century, teaching was socially defined and treated as a temporary line of work suitable for women, prior to their "real" career of child rearing. For men, teaching was socially defined as a stepping stone, prior to their "real" career in one of the male-dominated skilled blue-collar occupations or white-collar professions. Indeed, historically there was an ambivalence toward persistors in teaching, especially males—who had to account for why they continued to be "merely" a teacher. Low pre-service training standards and requirements, relatively unselective entry criteria, and front-loaded salaries that paid newcomers relatively high salaries compared to veterans all tended to favor recruitment over retention. Moreover, low pay, isolated job conditions, little professional autonomy, and a faint sense of a career ladder all undermined longer-term commitment to teaching as a career and profession. Attempts to upgrade the status of the occupation through more rigorous training and licensing standards or more selective entry gates often resulted in decreases in male entrants to teaching, who were more attracted to occupations with better rewards attached to rigorous standards (Strober & Tyack, 1980).

It appears that school districts continue to favor teacher recruitment strategies for many of the same reasons and with many of the same consequences. By widening the entry gate and increasing the quantity of teachers supplied, districts are able to control labor costs and, hence, control local property taxes. The downside of this strategy in schools, as in industry, is that it can decrease employee quality and increase employee turnover. Treating workers as interchangeable, expendable, low-skill workers cuts some expenses, but it is not cost-free. If turnover is at the root of school staffing problems and if the quality of the teaching job is a large factor behind turnover, then policies that further erode the low status of teaching, that undermine salary increases, or that undermine working conditions may simply backfire by increasing turnover.

In short, the data suggest that school staffing problems are rooted in the way schools are organized and the way the teaching occupation is treated and that lasting improvements in the quality and quantity of the teaching workforce will require improvements in the quality of the teaching job.

Conclusion: What is to Be Done?

How do schools improve the teaching job? Teachers themselves have offered some ideas. The 1994–95 TFS asked teachers who had moved from or left their teaching jobs since the prior year to suggest possible steps schools might take to encourage teachers to remain in teaching. Their responses are summarized in Figure 10.7.[10]

One strategy suggested by departed teachers to aid retention is *increasing salaries*, which are, not surprisingly, strongly linked to teacher turnover rates. But, salaries are not the only issue, which is important from a policy perspective because increasing overall salaries is expensive given the sheer size of the occupation.

Reduction of *student discipline problems* is a second factor frequently suggested by departed teachers. Multivariate analysis of the data also document that this factor is strongly tied to the rates of teacher turnover; again, not surprisingly, schools with more student misbehavior problems have more teacher turnover (Ingersoll, 2001b). But, the data also tell us that, regardless of the background and poverty levels of the student population, schools vary dramatically in their degree of student misbehavior.

One of the factors tied to both student discipline and teacher turnover is how much *decisionmaking influence* teachers themselves have over school policies that affect their jobs, especially those concerned with student behavioral rules and sanctions. In a separate multivariate analysis of data

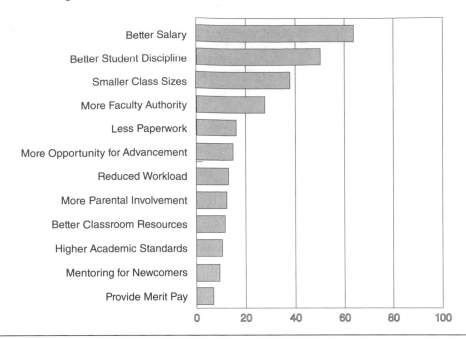

Figure 10.7 Of those teachers who moved from or left their jobs, percent giving various steps schools might take to encourage teachers to remain in teaching, 1994–95.

from SASS, I have found that, on average, teachers have little say in many of the key decisions that concern and affect their work, but schools where teachers are allowed more input into issues, such as student discipline in particular, have less conflict between staff and students and less teacher turnover (Ingersoll, 2003a). Increasing teacher decisionmaking power and authority is also, not surprisingly, suggested by teachers as a step to aid retention.

Class size reduction was also frequently suggested by teachers as a step to increase retention, although interestingly, it was not frequently given by departing teachers as one of the sources behind turnover related to dissatisfaction (Table 10.2).

Also surprising in Figure 10.7 is how few teachers suggested increasing support, such as *mentoring*, for new teachers as one of the main steps necessary for retention.

In a separate multivariate analysis of the 1999–2000 SASS data, we explored the impact of mentoring and induction programs on the turnover of new teachers. After controlling for the background characteristics of teachers and schools, we found a strong link between participation by beginning teachers in induction and mentoring programs and their likelihood of moving or leaving after their first year on the job (Smith & Ingersoll, 2003). The data showed that the predicted probability of turnover of first year, newly hired, inexperienced teachers, who did not participate in any induction and mentoring programs was 40% (see Figure 10.8). In contrast, after controlling for the background characteristics of teachers and schools, the turnover probability of beginning teachers who received what I labeled as "some" induction (had a helpful mentor from their same field; had common planning time with other teachers in their subject area; and had regularly scheduled collaboration with other teachers on issues of instruction) was 28%. Twenty-two percent of beginning teachers received just these three components. Finally, a very small number (less than 1% of beginning teachers in 1999–00) experienced what I label as a "full" induction experience that included the above three components, plus five more: participated in a general induction program; participated in a seminar for beginning teachers; had regular or supportive communication with their principal, other administrators, or department chair; participated in an external network; and had a reduced number of course preparations.

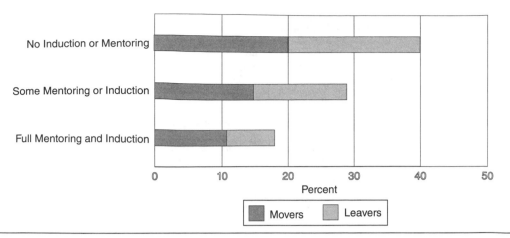

Figure 10.8 Percent turnover after first year of newly hired, inexperienced teachers, according to whether they participated in induction and mentoring programs, 2000–01.

Participation in these activities, collectively, had a very large and statistically significant impact—the probability of a departure at the end of their first year for those getting this package was less than half of those who participated in no induction activities.

It is important to recognize that none of these data suggests adopting any of the above steps will be inexpensive or easy. But, from the perspective of this analysis, the data suggest that schools are not simply victims of inexorable demographic trends and that there is a significant role for the management and organization of schools in both the genesis of, and the solution to, school staffing problems. The data suggest that improvements in the above aspects of the teaching job would contribute to lower rates of turnover, in turn, diminish school staffing problems and, hence, ultimately, aid the performance of schools.

Notes

1. The data on school hiring difficulties from the 1999–2000 SASS school questionnaire asked school officials "how difficult or easy it was to fill the vacancies for this school year" in each field. I counted as having "difficulty filling teaching vacancies" all those schools reporting either: "somewhat difficult," "very difficult," or "could not fill."
2. Using a one-way random effects ANOVA model, the data show that the variance component within states was 44 times the size of the variance component between states. Intraclass correlation = .022.
3. One example of a cross-occupational comparison that appears to have measurement shortcomings is an analysis of Baccalaureate and Beyond data by Henke et al. (2001). This analysis looked at beginning teacher attrition in comparison to other recent college grads. It followed 1993 grads who became teachers in the 1993–1994 year and then calculated how many of them were gone by April 1997. The analysis found an 18% rate of new teacher attrition for the three year span from April 1994 to April 1997. But the analysis did not appear to count all types of attrition. It appears that it only counted as attrition those who moved to full-time, nonteaching careers and jobs. It did not count those who went back to college, or those who left the workforce to, for example, do family caregiving. But other data, such as the SASS/TFS, tell us these other flows are substantial and are certainly counted as attrition in existing research. Not including them would make the overall attrition look smaller than it really is. Indeed, elsewhere in that report it appeared that 12% of new teachers left the full-time workforce for these other things; adding this 12% to the 18% attrition, the analysis did count, brings the B&B 3 year attrition rate to something close to 30% after three years—which is quite consistent with many other studies on beginning teacher attrition. It is unclear what this undercounting might mean for the cross-occupation comparisons made in the report, but it certainly casts doubt on them.
4. Data for professors are from a study sponsored by the American Association for University Professors (1989) and represent annual averages for the period from 1972 to 1989. (Ehrenberg et al. 1991) Data on technology and science professionals, such as engineers, research scientists, and software designers represent the 2000 year and are from Kochanski and Ledford (2001). Data for nurses are from the March 2000 National Sample Survey of Registered Nurses conducted by the American Hospital Association. Data for federal employees are from the Office of Personnel Management (2003).
5. The most recent data from the US Census Bureau are from 2001: 5,473,000 teachers/135,073,000 total workforce = 4.05%. "Teachers" include all Pre-K, K, Elementary, Secondary and Special education teachers. College and university instructors and professors are not counted as teachers. Counselors and librarians are not counted as teachers.

6. As in Table 10.1, the data in Figure 10.3 are calculated at the level of the school. Hence "hires" and "departures" refer to those newly entering or departing a particular school. "Movers" includes transfers among schools within districts. Reassignments within a school are not defined as hires or as departures.

7. I calculated these cumulative rates of beginning teacher attrition using preliminary data from the 2000–2001 TFS. The results are similar to what I've found using each of the other three cycles of the TFS—1988–89; 1991–92; 1994–95. It should be recognized that the data shown in Figure 10.4 are only a rough approximation. The SASS/TFS data do not follow a particular cohort of newly hired teachers to ascertain how many remain in teaching after five years. Instead I approximated the cumulative loss of beginning teachers by multiplying together the probabilities of staying in teaching for teachers with experience from 1 to 5 years, (i.e.. yr 1 probability of staying in teaching × yr. 2 probability × yr. 3 probability × yr. 4 probability × yr. 5 probability). These cumulative estimates also do not account for those who later re-enter teaching—which has been found to be as much as 25%.

8. In Figure 10.6, large schools are defined as those with 600 or more students; small schools are those with fewer than 300 students. High-poverty refers to schools with a poverty enrollment of 80% or more; low-poverty refers to schools with a poverty enrollment below 10%. Middle categories of size and poverty are omitted in the figure.

9. The data in Table 10.2 are from the 1994–95 TFS because the relevant data from the 2000–2001 TFS were not released as of summer 2003. Note that the column segments in Table 10.2 displaying percentages reporting various reasons for turnover each add up to more than 100%, because respondents could indicate up to three reasons for their departures. The same applies to the column segments displaying reasons for dissatisfaction. See Appendix for definitions of these reasons.

10. The data in Figure 10.7 are from the 1994–95 TFS, because the relevant data from the 2000–2001 TFS were not released as of summer 2003. Note that the estimates add up to more than 100%, because respondents could indicate up to three steps.

References

American Association of University Professors. (1989). The annual report on the economic status of the profession, 1988–89. *Academe, 75*(2), 3–74.

Bidwell, C. (1965). The school as a formal organization. In J. March (Ed.), *Handbook of organizations* (pp. 973–1002). Chicago, IL: Rand McNally.

Bluedorn, A. C. (1982). A unified model of turnover from organizations. *Human Relations, 35,* 135–153.

Boe, E., & Gilford, D. (1992). *Teacher supply, demand and quality.* Washington, DC: National Academy Press.

Braverman, Harry. (1974). *Labor and monopoly capitalism.* New York: Monthly Review Press.

Burawoy, Michael. (1979). *Manufacturing consent: Changes in the labor process under monopoly capitalism.* Chicago: University of Chicago Press.

Bureau of National Affairs. (2002). BNAs quarterly report on job absence and turnover. *Bulletin to Management.* Washington DC: Bureau of National Affairs.

Burns, T., & Stalker, G. M. (1961). *The management of innovation.* London: Tavistock.

Coleman, J., & Hoffer, T. (1987). *Public and private schools: The impact of communities.* New York: Basic.

Darling-Hammond, L. (1984). *Beyond the commission reports: The coming crisis in teaching.* Santa Monica, CA: Rand Corporation.

Durkheim, E. (1961/1925). *Moral education: A study in the theory and application of the sociology of education,* translated by E. K. Wilson and H. Schnurer. New York: Free Press.

Edwards, Richard. (1979). *Contested terrain.* New York: Basic Books.

Ehrenberg, R., Kasper, H., & Rees, D. (1991). Faculty turnover at American colleges and universities: Analyses of AAUP data. *Economics of Education Review, 10*(2) 99–110.

Feistritzer, E. (1997). *Alternative teacher certification: A state-by-state analysis (1997).* Washington, DC: National Center for Education Information.

Gerald, D., & Hussar, W. (1998). *Projections of education statistics to 2008.* Washington, DC: National Center for Education Statistics.

Grant, G. (1988). *The world we created at Hamilton High.* Cambridge, MA: Harvard University Press.

Hafner, A., & Owings, J. (1991). *Careers in teaching: Following members of the high school class of 1972 in and out of teaching* (NCES Report No. 91–470). Washington, DC: U.S. Department of Education, National Center for Education Statistics.

Haggstrom, G. W., Darling-Hammond, L., & Grissmer, D. (1988). *Assessing teacher supply and demand.* Santa Monica, CA: Rand Corporation.

Halaby, C., & Weakliem, D. (1989). Worker control and attachment to the firm. *American Journal of Sociology, 95,* 549–591.

Henke, R., Chen, X., & Geis, S. (2000). *Progress through the pipeline: 1992–93 college graduates and elementary/secondary school teaching as of 1997.* Washington, DC: National Center for Education Statistics.

Henke, R., Zahn, L & Carroll, D. (2001). *Attrition of new teachers among recent college graduates.* Washington, DC: National Center for Education Statistics.

Hirsch, E, Koppich, J., & Knapp, M. (2001). *Revisiting what states are doing to improve the quality of teaching: An update on patterns and trends.* Center for the Study of Teaching and Policy, University of Washington.

Hom, P., & Griffeth, R. (1995). *Employee turnover.* Cincinnati: South-Western Publishing.

Huling-Austin, L. (1990). Teacher induction programs and internships. In W. R. Houston (Ed.), *Handbook of research on teacher education.* Reston, VA: Association of Teacher Educators.

Hussar, W. (1998). *Predicting the need for newly hired teachers in the United States to 2008–09.* Washington, DC: National Center for Education Statistics.

Ingersoll, R. (1995). *Teacher supply, teacher qualifications and teacher turnover*. Washington, DC: National Center for Education Statistics.

Ingersoll, R. (1999). The problem of underqualified teachers in American secondary schools. *Educational Researcher, 28*, 26–37.

Ingersoll, R. (2001a). *Teacher turnover, teacher shortages and the organization of schools*. Center for the Study of Teaching and Policy, University of Washington.

Ingersoll, R. (2001b). Teacher turnover and teacher shortages: An organizational analysis. *American Educational Research Journal, 38*(3), 499–534.

Ingersoll, R. (2003a) *Who controls teachers' work?: Power and accountability in America's schools*. Cambridge, MA: Harvard University Press. <http://www.hup.harvard.edu/catalog/INGWHO.html>

Ingersoll, R. (2003b) Is there a shortage among mathematics and science teachers? *Science Educator 12*(1), 1–9.

Ingersoll, R. & Smith, T. (2003). The wrong solution to the teacher shortage. *Educational Leadership 60*(8), 30–33.

Integrated Postsecondary Educational Data System (IPEDS). (2001). *Data file*. Washington, DC: National Center for Education Statistics.

Kalleberg, A., & Mastekaasa, A. (1998). Organizational size, layoffs and quits in Norway. *Social Forces, 76*, 1243–73.

Kanter, R. (1977). *Men and women of the coloration*. New York: Basic.

Kirst, M. (1989). Who should control the schools? In T. J. Sergiovanni & J. Moore (Eds.), *Schooling for tomorrow*. Boston: Allyn and Bacon.

Kochanski, J. & Ledford, G. (2001). How to keep me—Retaining technical professionals. *Research-Technology Management*. May–June: 31–38.

Kopp, W. (1992). Reforming schools of education will not be enough. *Yale Law and Policy Review, 10*, 58–68.

Likert, R. (1967). *The human organization*. New York: McGraw-Hill.

Lortie, D. (1975). *School teacher*. Chicago: University of Chicago Press.

March, J., & Simon, H. (1958). *Organizations*. New York: Wiley.

Mobley, W. (1982). *Employee turnover: Causes, consequences and control*. Reading, MA: Addison-Wesley.

Mueller, C., & Price, J. (1990). Economic, psychological and sociological determinants of voluntary turnover. *Journal of behavioral economics, 19*, 321–335.

Murnane, R., Singer, J., Willett. J., Kemple, J., & Olsen, R. (Eds.). (1991). *Who will teach?: Policies that matter*. Cambridge, MA: Harvard University Press.

National Academy of Sciences. (1987). *Toward understanding teacher supply and demand*. Washington, DC: National Academy Press.

National Commission on Excellence in Education. (1983). *A nation at risk: The imperative for educational reform*. Washington, DC: Government Printing Office.

National Commission on Teaching and America's Future. (1997). *Doing what matters most: Investing in quality teaching*. New York: NCTAF.

Office of Personnel Management, (2003). *Central Personnel Data File (CPDF)*. Washington, DC: OPM. <http://www.opm.gov/feddata/index.asp>

Parsons, Talcott. (1959). The school class as a social system: Some of its functions in American society. *Harvard Educational Review 29*, 297–318.

Porter, L. W., Lawler, E. E., & Hackman, J. R. (1975). *Behavior in organizations*. New York: McGraw-Hill.

Price, J. (1977). *The study of turnover*. Ames: Iowa State University Press.

Price, J. (1989). The impact of turnover on the organization. *Work and Occupations, 16*, 461–473.

Price, J. (1997). Handbook of organizational measurement. *International Journal of Manpower*, 18: no. 4–6.

Rosenholtz, S. (1989). *Teacher's workplace: The social organization of schools*. New York: Longman.

Schlecty, P., & Vance, V. (1981). Do academically able teachers leave education? The North Carolina case. *Phi Delta Kappan, 63*, 105–112.

Smith, T., & Ingersoll, R. (2003). Reducing teacher turnover: What are the components of effective induction? Paper presented at the annual meeting of the American Educational Research Association, Chicago. IL.

Snyder, T., & Hoffman, C. (2001). *The digest of education*. Washington, DC: U.S. Department of Education, National Center for Education Statistics.

Steers, R. M., & Momday, R. T. (1981). Employee turnover and the post-decision accommodation process. In B. M. Shaw and L. L. Cummings (Eds.), *Research in organizational behavior*. Greenwich: JAI Press.

Stinebrickner, T. R. (2001). A dynamic model of teacher labor supply. *Journal of Labor Economics, 19*(1), 196–230.

Strober, M., & Tyack, D (1980). Why do women teach and men manage? *Signs, 5*, 499–500.

Texas Center for Educational Research. (2000). *The cost of teacher turnover*. Austin, TX: Texas State Board for Educator Certification.

Turner, A. N., & Lawrence, P. R. (1964). *Industrial jobs and the worker*. Cambridge, MA: Harvard University Press.

Tyack, D. (1974). *The one best system*. Cambridge, MA: Harvard University Press.

U.S. Bureau of the Census. (2002). *Statistical abstract* (117th Edition). Washington, DC: U.S. Department of Commerce.

Waller, W. (1932). *The sociology of teaching*. New York: Wiley.

Walton, R. E. (1980). Establishing and maintaining high commitment work systems. In J. Kimberly & R. Miles (Eds.), *The organization life cycle*. San Francisco: Jossey-Bass.

Weaver, T. (1983). *America's teacher quality problem: Alternatives for reform*. New York: Praeger Publishers.

11

Whose Markets, Whose Knowledge?

MICHAEL W. APPLE

...We have entered a period of reaction in education. Our educational institutions are seen as total failures. High dropout rates, a decline in "functional literacy," a loss of standards and discipline, the failure to teach "real knowledge" and economically useful skills, poor scores on standardized tests, and more—all these are charges leveled at schools. And all of these, we are told, have led to declining economic productivity, unemployment, poverty, a loss of international competitiveness, and so on. Return to a "common culture," make schools more efficient, more responsive to the private sector. Do this and our problems will be solved.

Behind all of these charges is an attack on egalitarian norms and values. Although hidden in the rhetorical flourishes of the critics, in essence "too much democracy"—culturally and politically—is seen as one of the major causes of "our" declining economy and culture. Similar tendencies are quite visible in other countries as well. The extent of the reaction is captured in the words of Kenneth Baker, former British Secretary of Education and Science in the Thatcher government, who evaluated nearly a decade of rightist efforts in education by saying, "The age of egalitarianism is over."[1] He was speaking decidedly positively, not negatively.

The threat to egalitarian ideals that these attacks represent is not usually made quite this explicitly, as they are often couched in the discourse of "improving" competitiveness, jobs, standards, and quality in an educational system that is seen as in total crisis. This discourse is clearly present today in "New Labour" in the United Kingdom and in similar policies in the United States. In all too many ways, both nations' educational policies continue trends established under earlier conservative (and sometimes supposedly "liberal") governments.

It would be simplistic, however, to interpret what is happening as only the result of efforts by dominant economic elites to impose their will on education. Many of these attacks do represent attempts to reintegrate education into an economic agenda. Yet they cannot be fully reduced to that, nor can they be reduced to being only about the economy. Cultural struggles and struggles over race, gender, and sexuality coincide with class alliances and class power.

Education is a site of struggle and compromise. It serves as a proxy as well for larger battles over what our institutions should do, whom they should serve, and who should make these decisions. And, yet, by itself it is one of the major arenas in which resources, power, and ideology specific to policy, finance, curriculum, pedagogy, and evaluation in education are worked through. Thus, education is both cause and effect, determining and determined. Because of this, no one article could hope to give a complete picture of this complexity. What I hope to do instead is to provide an outline of some of the major tensions surrounding education in the United States as it moves in conservative directions. A key word here is directions. The plural is crucial to my arguments, because, as I showed, there are multiple and at times contradictory tendencies within the rightist turn.

Although my focus in this article is largely internal, it is impossible to understand current educational policy in the United States without placing it in its international context. Thus, behind the stress on higher standards, more rigorous testing, education for employment, and a much closer relationship between education and the economy in general, and so on, was the fear of losing in international competition and the loss of jobs and money to Japan, Mexico, and increasingly now the "Asian Tiger" economies such as China and elsewhere (although this has been mediated by the economic upheavals still being experienced in parts of Asia).[2] In the same way, the equally evident pressure in the United States to reinstall a (selective) vision of a common culture, to place more emphasis on the "Western tradition," on religion, on the English language, and similar emphases are deeply connected to cultural fears about Latin America, Africa, and Asia. This context provides a backdrop for my discussion.

The rightward turn has been the result of the successful struggle by the right to form a broad-based alliance. This new alliance has been so successful in part because it has been able to win the battle over common sense.[3] That is, it has creatively stitched together different social tendencies and commitments and has organized them under its own general leadership in issues dealing with social welfare, culture, the economy, and as we shall see in this article, education. Its aim in educational and social policy is what I called "conservative modernization."[4]

This alliance contains four major elements. Each has its own relatively autonomous history and dynamics, but each has also been sutured into the more general conservative movement. These elements include neoliberals, neoconservatives, authoritarian populists, and a particular fraction of the upwardly mobile professional and managerial new middle class. I pay particular attention to the first two of these groups here since they—especially neoliberals—are currently in leadership in this alliance to "reform" education. However, in no way do I want to dismiss the power of the latter two groups, and I return to them in later chapters.

Neoliberalism: Schooling, Choice, and Democracy

Neoliberals are the most powerful element within the alliance supporting conservative modernization. They are guided by a vision of the weak state. Thus, what is private is necessarily good and what is public is necessarily bad. Public institutions such as schools are "black holes" into which money is poured—and then seemingly disappears—but which do not provide anywhere near adequate results. For neoliberals, one form of rationality is more powerful than any other—economic rationality. Efficiency and an "ethic" of cost-benefit analysis are the dominant norms. All people are to act in ways that maximize their own personal benefits. Indeed, behind this position is an empirical claim that this is how *all* rational actors act. Yet, rather than being a neutral description of the world of social motivation, this is actually a construction of the world around the valuative characteristics of an efficiently acquisitive class type.[5]

Underpinning this position is a vision of students as human capital. The world is intensely competitive economically, and students—as future workers—must be given the requisite skills and dispositions to compete efficiently and effectively.[6] Furthermore, any money spent on schools that is not directly related to these economic goals is suspect. In fact, as "black holes," schools and other public services as they are currently organized and controlled waste economic resources that should go into private enterprise. Thus, for neoliberals, not only are public schools failing our children as future workers, but like nearly all public institutions they are sucking the financial life out of this society. Partly this is the result of "producer capture." Schools are built for teachers and state bureaucrats, not "consumers." They respond to the demands of professionals and other selfish state workers, not the consumers who rely on them. The increasingly virulent attacks on teachers unions and professional associations by the right is but the tip of the iceberg here.

The idea of the "consumer" is crucial here. For neoliberals, the world in essence is a vast supermarket. "Consumer choice" is the guarantor of democracy. In effect, education is seen as simply one more product like bread, cars, and television.[7] By turning it over to the market through voucher and choice plans, education will be largely self-regulating. Thus, democracy is turned into consumption practices. In these plans, the ideal of the citizen is that of the purchaser. The ideological effects of this position are momentous. Rather than democracy being a *political* concept, it is transformed into a wholly *economic* concept. The message of such policies is what might best be called "arithmetical particularism," in which the unattached individual—as a consumer—is deraced, declassed, and degendered.[8]

The metaphors of the consumer and the supermarket are actually quite apposite here. For just as in real life, there are individuals who indeed can go into supermarkets and choose among a vast array of similar or diverse products. And there are those who can only engage in what can best be called "postmodern" consumption. They stand outside the supermarket and can only consume the image.

The entire project of neoliberalism is connected to a larger process of exporting the blame from the decisions of dominant groups onto the state and onto poor people. After all, it was not the government that made the decisions to engage in capital flight and to move factories to those nations that have weak or no unions, fewer environmental regulations, and repressive governments. And it was not working-class and poor communities that chose to lose those jobs and factories, with the loss of hope and schools and communities in crisis that were among the results of these decisions. And it was neither of them who chose to lay off millions of workers—many of whom had done rather well in school—because of mergers and leveraged buyouts, trends that have again become more pronounced.

With their emphasis on the consumer rather than the producer, neoliberal policies need also to be seen as part of a more extensive attack on government employees. In education in particular, they constitute an offensive against teacher unions that are seen to be much too powerful and much too costly. Neoliberal policies, although they may not have been created as a conscious attack on women, need to be interpreted as part of a longer history of attacks on women's labor, as the vast majority of teachers in the United States—as in so many other nations—are women.[9]

Varied policy initiatives have emerged from the neoliberal segments of the new hegemonic alliance. Most have centered on either creating closer linkages between education and the economy or placing schools themselves into the market. The former is represented by widespread proposals for "school to work" and "education for employment" programs, and by vigorous cost-cutting attacks on the "bloated state." The latter initiative is no less widespread and is becoming increasingly powerful. It is represented by both national and state-by-state proposals for voucher and choice programs.[10] These include providing public money for private and religious schools (although these are highly contested proposals). Behind this is a plan to subject schools to the discipline of market competition.[11] Such "quasi-market solutions" are among the most divisive and hotly debated policy issues in the entire nation, with important court cases concerning funding for private or religious schools through voucher mechanisms having been decided or now being closely watched.[12]

Some proponents of "choice" argue that only enhanced parental "voice" and choice will provide a chance for "educational salvation" for minority parents and children.[13] Moe, for instance, claims that the best hope for the poor to gain the right "to leave bad schools and seek out good ones" is through an "unorthodox alliance."[14] Only by allying themselves with Republicans and business—the most powerful groups supposedly willing to transform the system—can the poor succeed, a set of arguments I shall take up and critically analyze later.

...Growing empirical evidence indicates that the development of "quasi-markets" in education has led to the exacerbation of existing social divisions surrounding class and race.[15] There are now increasingly convincing arguments that while the supposed overt goal of voucher and choice plans is to give poor people the right to exit public schools, among the ultimate long-term effects may be the increase of "white flight" from public schools into private and religious schools and the creation of the conditions where affluent white parents may refuse to pay taxes to support public schools that are more and more suffering from the debilitating effects of the fiscal crisis of the state. The result is even more educational apartheid, not less.[16]

In his own review of evidence from the U.S. experience, Whitty argues that although advocates of choice assume that competition will enhance the efficiency and responsiveness of schools, as well as give disadvantaged children opportunities that they currently do not have, this may be a false hope. These hopes are not now being realized and are unlikely to be realized in the future "in the context of broader policies that do nothing to challenge deeper social and cultural inequalities." As he goes on to say, "Atomized decision-making in a highly stratified society may appear to give everyone equal opportunities but transforming responsibility for decision-making from the public to the private sphere can actually reduce the scope for collective action to improve the quality of education for all."[17]

This position is ratified by Henig, who states that "the sad irony of the current education-reform movement is that, through overidentification with school choice proposals, the healthy impulse to consider radical reforms to address social problems may be channeled into initiatives that further erode the potential for collective deliberation and collective response."[18] When this effect is coupled with the fact that such neoliberal policies in practice may reproduce traditional hierarchies of class, race, and gender, these proposals should give us serious pause.[19]

There is a second variant of neoliberalism. This one *is* willing to spend more state and/or private money on schools, if and only if schools meet the needs expressed by capital. Thus, resources are made available for "reforms" and policies that further connect the education system to the project of making our economy more competitive. Two examples can provide a glimpse of this position. In a number of states, legislation has been passed that directs schools and universities to make closer links between education and the business community. In the state of Wisconsin, for instance, all teacher education programs had to include identifiable experiences on "education for employment" for all of its future teachers; and all teaching in the public elementary, middle, and secondary schools of the state had to include elements of education for employment in its formal curricula.[20]

The second example is seemingly less consequential, but in reality it is a powerful statement of the reintegration of educational policy and practice into the ideological agenda of neoliberalism. I am referring here to Channel One, a for-profit television network that is now being broadcast into schools enrolling over 40 percent of all middle and secondary school students in the nation (many of these schools are financially hard-pressed given the fiscal crisis, even though some states are currently experiencing slightly better budgets). In this "reform," schools are offered a "free" satellite dish, two VCRs, and television monitors for each of their classrooms by a private media corporation. They are also offered a free news broadcast for these students. In return for the equipment and the news, all participating schools must sign a three- to five-year contract guaranteeing that their students will watch Channel One every day.

This agreement sounds relatively benign. However, not only is the technology "hardwired" so that *only* Channel One can be received but also *mandatory advertisements* for major fast food, athletic wear, and other corporations are broadcast along with the news, which students—by contract—also must watch. Students, in essence, are sold as a captive audience to corporations. Because, by law, these students must be in schools, the United States is one of the first nations in the world to consciously allow its youth to be sold as commodities to those many corporations willing to pay the high price of advertising on Channel One to get a guaranteed (captive) audience.[21] Thus, under a number of variants of neoliberalism not only are schools transformed into market commodities, but so too now are our children.[22]

The attractiveness of conservative policies in education rests in large part on major shifts in our common sense—about what democracy is, about whether we see ourselves as possessive individuals ("consumers"), and ultimately about how we see the market working. Underlying neoliberal policies in education and their social policies in general is a faith in the essential fairness and justice of markets. Markets ultimately will distribute resources efficiently and fairly according to effort. They ultimately will create jobs for all who want them. They are the best possible mechanism to ensure a better future for all citizens (consumers).

Because of this, we of course must ask what the economy that reigns supreme in neoliberal positions actually looks like. Far from the positive picture painted by neoliberals in which technologically advanced jobs will replace the drudgery and the under- and unemployment so many people now experience if we were to only set the market loose on our schools and children, the reality is something else again. Unfortunately, markets clearly are as powerfully destructive as they are productive in people's lives.[23]

Let us take as a case in point the paid labor market to which neoliberals want us to attach so much of the education system. Even with the growth in proportion in high-tech-related jobs, the kinds of work that are and will be increasingly available to a large portion of the American population will not be highly skilled, technically elegant positions. Just the opposite will be the case. The paid labor market will increasingly be dominated by low-paying, repetitive work in the retail, trade, and service sectors. This is made strikingly clear by one fact. More cashier jobs will be created by the year 2005 than jobs for computer scientists, systems analysts, physical therapists, operations analysts, and radio-logic technicians *combined*. In fact, it is projected that 95 percent of all new positions will be found in the service sector. This sector broadly includes personal care, home health aides; social workers (many of whom are now losing or have lost their jobs because of cutbacks in social spending); hotel and lodging workers; restaurant employees; transportation workers; and business and clerical personnel. Furthermore, eight of the top ten individual occupations that will account for the most job growth in the next ten years include the following: retail salespersons, cashiers, office clerks, truck drivers, waitresses/waiters, nursing aides/orderlies, food preparation workers, and janitors. The majority of these positions obviously do not require high levels of education. Many of them are low-paid, non-unionized, temporary, and part-time, with low or no benefits. And many are dramatically linked to, and often exacerbate, the existing race, gender, and class divisions of labor. These trends are predicted to continue.[24] This is the emerging economy we face, not the overly romantic picture painted by neo-liberals who urge us to trust the market.

Neoliberals argue that making the market the ultimate arbiter of social worthiness will eliminate politics and its accompanying irrationality from our educational and social decisions. Efficiency and cost-benefit analysis will be the engines of social and educational transformation. Yet among the ultimate effects of such "economizing" and "depoliticizing" strategies is actually to make it ever harder to interrupt the growing inequalities in resources and power that so deeply characterize this society. Nancy Fraser illuminates the process in the following way:

> In male dominated capitalist societies, what is "political" is normally defined contrastively against what is "economic" and what is "domestic" or "personal." Here, then, we can identify two principal sets of institutions that depoliticize social discourses: they are, first, domestic institutions, especially the normative domestic form, namely the modern restricted male-headed nuclear family; and, second, official economic capitalist system institutions, especially paid workplaces, markets, credit mechanisms, and "private" enterprises and corporations. Domestic institutions depoliticize certain matters by personalizing and/or familializing them; they cast these as private-domestic or personal-familial matters in contradistinction to public, political matters. Official economic capitalist system institutions, on the other hand, depoliticize certain matters by economizing them; the issues in question here are cast as impersonal market imperatives, or as "private" ownership prerogatives, or as technical problems for managers and planners, all in contradistinction to political matters. In both cases, the result is a foreshortening of chains of in-order-to relations for interpreting people's needs; interpretive chains are truncated and

prevented from spilling across the boundaries separating the "domestic" and the "economic" from the political.[25]

This very process of depoliticization makes it very difficult for the needs of those with less economic, political, and cultural power to be accurately heard and acted on in ways that deal with the true depth of the problem. For Fraser, this outcome occurs because of what happens when "needs discourses" get retranslated into both market talk and "privately" driven policies.

For our purposes here, we can talk about two major kinds of needs discourses: oppositional and reprivatization discourses. *Oppositional* forms of needs talk arise when needs are politicized from below and are part of the crystallization of new oppositional identities on the part of subordinated social groups. What was once seen as largely a "private" matter is now placed into the larger political arena. Sexual harassment, race and sex segregation in paid labor, and affirmative action policies in educational and economic institutions provide examples of "private" issues that have now spilled over and can no longer be confined to the "domestic" sphere.[26]

Reprivatization discourses emerge as a response to the newly emergent oppositional forms and try to press these forms back into the "private" or the "domestic" arena. They are often aimed at dismantling or cutting back social services, deregulating "private" enterprise, or stopping what are seen as "runaway needs." Thus, reprivatizers may attempt to keep issues such as, say, domestic battery from spilling over into overt political discourse and will seek to define it as purely a family matter. Or they will argue that the closing of a factory is not a political question but instead is an "unimpeachable prerogative of private ownership or an unassailable imperative of an impersonal market mechanism."[27] In each of these cases, the task is to contest both the possible breakout of runaway needs and to depoliticize the issues.

In educational policy in the United States, there are a number of clear examples of these processes. The state of California provides a well-known instance. A binding referendum that prohibited the use of affirmative action policies in state government, in university admission policies, and so on was passed overwhelmingly as reprivatizers spent an exceptional amount of money on an advertising campaign that labeled such policies as "out of control" and as improper government intervention into decisions involving "individual merit." The California referendum has spawned similar, and quite controversial, initiatives in other states. Voucher plans in education—where contentious issues surrounding whose knowledge should be taught, who should control school policy and practice, and how schools should be financed are left to the market to decide—offer another prime example of such attempts at "depoliticizing" educational needs. Finally, giving primary responsibility over the definition of important "work skills" to the private sector—an act that evacuates the possibility of criticism of the ways work is actually constructed, controlled, and paid—enables a definition of work both as a "private" matter and as purely a technical choice to go unchallenged. All these examples show the emerging power of reprivatizing discourses.

A distinction that is useful here in understanding what is happening in these cases is that between "value" and "sense" legitimation.[28] Each signifies a different strategy by which powerful groups or states legitimate their authority. In the first (value) strategy, legitimation is accomplished by actually giving people what may have been promised. Thus, the social democratic state may provide social services for the population in return for continued support. That the state will do this is often the result of oppositional discourses gaining more power in the social arena and having more power to redefine the border between public and private.

In the second (sense) strategy, rather than providing people with policies that meet the needs they have expressed, states and/or dominant groups attempt to *change the very meaning* of the sense of social need into something that is very different. Thus, if less powerful people call for "more democracy" and for a more responsive state, the task is not to give "value" that meets this demand, especially when it may lead to runaway needs. Rather, the task is to change what actually *counts* as democracy. In the case of neoliberal policies, democracy is now redefined as guaranteeing choice in an unfettered market. In essence, the state withdraws. The extent of acceptance of such transformations of needs and needs discourses shows the success of the reprivatizers in redefining the borders between public and private again and demonstrates how a people's common sense can be shifted in conservative directions during a time of economic and ideological crisis.

Neoconservatism: Teaching "Real" Knowledge

Although neoliberals largely are in leadership in the conservative alliance, I noted that the second major element within the new alliance is neoconservatism. Unlike the neoliberal emphasis on the weak state, neoconservatives are usually guided by a vision of the strong state. This is especially true surrounding issues of knowledge, values, and the body. Whereas neoliberalism may be seen as being based in what Raymond Williams would call an "emergent" ideological assemblage, neoconservatism is grounded in "residual" forms.[29] It is largely, though not totally, based in a romantic appraisal of the past, a past in which "real knowledge" and morality reigned supreme, in which people "knew their place," and where stable communities guided by a natural order protected us from the ravages of society.[30]

Among the policies being proposed under this ideological position are mandatory national and statewide curricula, national and statewide testing, a "return" to higher standards, a revivification of the "Western tradition," patriotism, and conservative variants of character education. Yet underlying some of the neoconservative thrust in education and in social policy in general is not only a call for "return." Behind it as well—and this is essential—is a fear of the "Other," fears that have been exacerbated and often cynically employed for political purposes and used to drive wedges between religious traditions since the tragedy of September 11. This is expressed in its support for a standardized national curriculum, its attacks on bilingualism and multiculturalism, and its insistent call for raising standards.[31]

That the neoconservative emphasis on a return to traditional values and "morality" has struck a responsive chord can be seen in the fact that among the best-selling books in the nation during the past decade was William Bennett's *The Book of Virtues*.[32] Bennett, a former Secretary of Education in a conservative Republican administration, has argued that for too long a period of time, "We have stopped doing the right things [and] allowed an assault on intellectual and moral standards." In opposition to this, we need "a renewed commitment to excellence, character, and fundamentals."[33] Bennett's book aims at providing "moral tales" for children to "restore" a commitment to "traditional virtues" such as patriotism, honesty, moral character, and entrepreneurial spirit. Such positions not only have entered the common sense of society in quite influential ways but also have provided part of the driving force behind the movement toward charter schools. These schools have individual charters that allow them to opt out of most state requirements and develop curricula based on the wishes of their clientele. Although in theory there is much to commend in such policies, all too many charter schools have become ways through which conservative religious activists and others gain public funding for schools—and home schooling—that would otherwise be prohibited such support.[34]

Behind much of the neoconservative position is a clear sense of loss—a loss of faith, of imagined communities, of a nearly pastoral vision of like-minded people who shared norms and values and in which the "Western tradition" reigned supreme. It is more than a little similar to Mary Douglas's discussion of purity and danger, in which what was imagined to exist is sacred and "pollution" is feared above all else.[35] We/they binary oppositions dominate this discourse and the culture of the "Other" is to be feared.

This sense of cultural pollution can be seen in the increasingly virulent attacks on multiculturalism (which is itself a very broad category that combines multiple political and cultural positions),[36] on the offering of schooling or any other social benefits to the children of "illegal" immigrants and even in some cases to the children of legal immigrants, in the conservative English-only movement, and in the equally conservative attempts to reorient curricula and textbooks toward a particular construction of the Western tradition.

In this regard, neoconservatives lament the "decline" of the traditional curriculum and of the history, literature, and values it is said to have represented.[37] Behind this worry is a set of historical assumptions about "tradition," about the existence of a social consensus over what should count as legitimate knowledge, and about cultural superiority.[38] Yet it is crucial to remember that the "traditional" curriculum whose decline is lamented so fervently by neoconservative critics "ignored most of the groups that compose the American population whether they were from Africa, Europe, Asia, Central and South America, or from indigenous North American peoples."[39] Its primary and often exclusive focus was typically only on quite a narrow spectrum of those people who came from a small number of northern and Western European nations, in spite of the fact that the cultures and histories represented in the United States were "forged out of a much larger and more diverse complex of peoples and societies." The mores and cultures of this narrow spectrum were seen as archetypes of "tradition" for everyone. They were not simply taught, but taught as superior to every other set of mores and culture.[40]

As Lawrence Levine reminds us, a selective and faulty sense of history fuels the nostalgic yearnings of neoconservatives. The canon and the curriculum have never been static. They have always been in a constant process of revision, "with irate defenders insisting, as they still do, that change would bring with it instant decline."[41] Indeed, even the inclusion of such "classics" as Shakespeare within the curriculum of schools in the United States came about only after prolonged and intense battles, ones that were the equal of the divisive debates over whose knowledge should be taught today. Thus, Levine notes that when neoconservative cultural critics ask for a "return" to a "common culture" and "tradition," they are oversimplifying to the point of distortion. What is happening in terms of the expansion and alteration of official knowledge in schools and universities today "is by no means out of the ordinary; certainly it is not a radical departure from the patterns that have marked the history of [education]—constant and often controversial expansion and alteration of curricula and canons and incessant struggle over the nature of that expansion and alteration."[42]

Of course, such conservative positions have been forced into a kind of compromise in order to maintain their cultural and ideological leadership as a movement to "reform" educational policy and practice. A prime example is the emerging discourse over the history curriculum—in particular the construction of the United States as a "nation of immigrants."[43] In this hegemonic discourse, everyone in the history of the nation was an immigrant, from the first Native American population who supposedly trekked across the Bering Strait and ultimately populated North, Central, and South America, to the later waves of populations who came from Africa, Mexico, Ireland, Germany, Scandinavia, Italy, Russia, Poland, and elsewhere, to finally the recent populations from Asia, Latin America, Africa, and other regions. Although it is true that the United States is constituted by people from all over the world—and that is one of the things that makes it so culturally rich and vital—such a perspective constitutes an erasure of historical memory. For some groups came *in chains*, with massive numbers of death in the Middle Passage, and were subjected to state-sanctioned slavery and apartheid for hundreds of years. Others suffered what can only be called bodily, linguistic, and cultural destruction.[44]

This said, however, it does point to the fact that although the neoconservative goals of national curricula and national testing are pressed for, they are strongly mediated by the necessity of compromise. Because of this, even the strongest supporters of neoconservative educational programs and policies have had to also support the creation of curricula that at least partly recognize "the contributions of the Other."[45] This is partly because there is an absence of an overt and strong national department of education and a tradition of state and local control of schooling. The "solution" has been to have national standards developed "voluntarily" in each subject area.[46] Indeed, the example I gave earlier about history is one of the results of such voluntary standards.

Because it is the national professional organizations in these subject areas—such as the National Council of Teachers of Mathematics (NCTM)—that are developing such national standards, the standards themselves are compromises and thus are often more flexible than those wished for by neo-conservatives. This very process does act to provide a check on conservative policies over knowledge. However, this should not lead to an overly romantic picture of the overall tendencies emerging in educational policy. Leadership in school "reform" is increasingly dominated by conservative discourses surrounding "standards," "excellence," "accountability," and so on. Because the more flexible parts of the standards have proven to be too expensive to actually implement and have generated consider-able conservative backlash,[47] standards talk ultimately functions to give more rhetorical weight to the neoconservative movement to enhance central control over "official knowledge" and to "raise the bar" for achievement. The social implications of this in terms of creating even more differential school results are increasingly worrisome.[48]

Yet it is not only in such things as the control over legitimate knowledge where neoconservative impulses are seen. The idea of a strong state is also visible in the growth of the regulatory state as it concerns teachers. There has been a steadily growing change from "licensed autonomy" to "regulated autonomy" as teachers' work is more highly standardized, rationalized, and "policed."[49] Under condi-tions of licensed autonomy, once teachers are given the appropriate professional certification they are basically free—within limits—to act in their classrooms according to their judgment. Such a regime is based on trust in "professional discretion." Under the growing conditions of regulated autonomy, teachers' actions are now subject to much greater scrutiny in terms of process and outcomes.[50] Indeed, some states in the United States not only have specified the content that teachers are to teach but also have regulated the only appropriate methods of teaching. Not following these specified "appropriate" methods puts the teacher at risk of administrative sanctions. Such a regime of control is based not on trust, but on a deep suspicion of the motives and competence of teachers. For neoconservatives it is the equivalent of the notion of "producer capture" that is so powerful among neoliberals. For the former, however, it is not the market that will solve this problem, but a strong and interventionist state that will see to it that only "legitimate" content and methods are taught. And this will be policed by statewide and national tests of both students and teachers. The imprint of these kinds of commitments are thoroughly visible in such policies as No Child Left Behind.

I have claimed elsewhere that such policies lead to the "deskilling" of teachers, the "intensification" of their work, and the loss of autonomy and respect. This is not surprising, as behind much of this conservative impulse is a clear distrust of teachers and an attack both on teachers' claims to compe-tence and especially on teachers' unions.[51]

The mistrust of teachers, the concern over a supposed loss of cultural control, and the sense of dangerous "pollution" are among the many cultural and social fears that drive neoconservative policies. However, as I noted earlier, underpinning these positions as well is often an ethnocentric, and even racialized, understanding of the world. Perhaps this can be best illuminated through the example of Herrnstein and Murray's volume, *The Bell Curve*.[52] In a book that sold hundreds of thousands of copies, the authors argue for a genetic determinism based on race (and to some extent gender). For them, it is romantic to assume that educational and social policies can ultimately lead to more equal results, since differences in intelligence and achievement are basically genetically driven. The wisest thing policy makers can do would be to accept this and plan for a society that recognizes these biological differences and does not provide "false hopes" to the poor and the less intelligent, most of whom will be black. Obviously, this book has reinforced racist stereotypes that have long played a considerable part in educational and social policies in the United States.[53]

Rather than seeing race as it is—as a fully *social* category that is mobilized and used in different ways by different groups at different times[54]—positions such as those argued by Herrnstein and Murray provide a veneer of seeming scientific legitimacy for policy discourses that have been discredited intellectually many times before. The sponsored mobility given to this book, in which it is reported that the authors received large sums of money from neoconservative foundations to write and publicize the volume, speaks clearly not only to the racial underpinnings of important parts of the neoconservative agenda but also to the power of conservative groups to bring their case before the public.

The consequences of such positions are not only found in educational policies, but in the intersection of such policies with broader social and economic policies, where they have been quite influential. Here too we can find claims that what the poor lack is not money, but both an "appropriate" biological inheritance and a decided lack of values regarding discipline, hard work, and morality.[55] Prime examples here include programs such as "Learnfare" and "Workfare" in which parents lose a portion of their welfare benefits if their children miss a significant number of school days or in which no benefits are paid if a person does not accept low-paid work, no matter how demeaning or even if child care or health care are not provided by the state. Such policies reinstall earlier "workhouse" policies that were so popular—and so utterly damaging—in the United States, Britain, and elsewhere.[56]

I have spent much of my time in this section documenting the growing power of neoconservative positions in educational and social policy in the United States. Neoconservatives have forged a creative coalition with neoliberals, a coalition that—in concert with other groups—is effectively changing the landscape on which policies are argued out. Yet, even given the growing influence of neoliberal and neoconservative policies, they would be considerably less successful if they had not also brought authoritarian populist religious fundamentalists and conservative evangelicals under the umbrella of the conservative alliance. It is to this group that we now turn.

Authoritarian Populism: Schooling as God Wanted It

Perhaps more than in any other major industrialized nation, it is not possible to fully understand educational politics in the United States without paying a good deal of attention to the "Christian Right." It is exceptionally powerful and influential, beyond its numbers, in debates over public policy in the media, education, social welfare, the politics of sexuality and the body, religion, and so on. Its influence comes from the immense commitment by activists within it, its large financial base, its populist rhetorical positions, and its aggressiveness in pursuing its agenda. "New Right" authoritarian populists ground their positions on education and social policy in general in particular visions of biblical authority, "Christian morality," gender roles, and the family. The New Right sees gender and the family, for instance, as an organic and divine unity that resolves "male egoism and female selflessness."

As Hunter puts it:

Since gender is divine and natural…there is [no] room for legitimate political conflict…. Within the family women and men—stability and dynamism—are harmoniously fused when undisturbed by modernism, liberalism, feminism, and humanism which not only threaten masculinity and femininity directly, but also [do so] through their effects on children and youth…. "Real women," i.e., women who know themselves as wives *and* mothers, will not threaten the sanctity of the home by striving for self. When men or women challenge these gender roles they break with God and nature; when liberals, feminists, and secular humanists prevent them from fulfilling these roles they undermine the divine and natural supports upon which society rests.[57]

In the minds of such groups, public schooling thus is *itself* a site of immense danger. In the words of the conservative activist Tim LaHaye, "Modern public education is the most dangerous force in a child's life: religiously, sexually, economically, patriotically, and physically."[58] This is connected to the New Right's sense of loss surrounding schooling and the family.

> Until recently, as the New Right sees it, schools were extensions of home and traditional morality. Parents could entrust their children to public schools because they were locally controlled and reflected Biblical and parental values. However, taken over by alien, elitist forces, schools now interpose themselves between parents and children. Many people experience fragmentation of the unity between family, church, and school as a loss of control of daily life, one's children, and America. Indeed, [the New Right] argues that parental control of education is Biblical, for in God's plan, the primary responsibility for educating the young lies in the home and directly in the father.[59]

It is exactly this sense of "alien and elite control," the loss of biblical connections, and the destruction of "God-given" family and moral structures that drives the authoritarian populist agenda. It is an agenda that is increasingly powerful, not only rhetorically, but in terms of funding and in conflicts over what schools should do, how they should be financed, and who should control them. This agenda includes, but goes beyond, issues of gender, sexuality, and the family. It extends as well to a much larger array of questions about what is to count as "legitimate" knowledge in schools. And in this larger arena of concern about the entire corpus of school knowledge, conservative activists have had no small measure of success in pressuring textbook publishers to change what they include and in altering important aspects of state educational policy on teaching, curriculum, and evaluation. This is crucial, as in the absence of an overt national curriculum, the commercially produced *textbook*—regulated by individual state's purchases and authority—remains the dominant definition of the curriculum in the United States.[60]

The power of these groups is visible, for example, in the "self-censorship" in which publishers engage. For instance, under conservative pressure a number of publishers of high school literature anthologies have chosen to include Martin Luther King's "I Have a Dream" speech, but *only* after all references to the intense racism of the United States have been removed.[61] At the level of state curriculum policy, this is very visible in the textbook legislation in, say, Texas, which mandates texts that stress patriotism, obedience to authority, and the discouragement of "deviance."[62] Because most textbook publishers aim the content and organization of their textbooks at what will be approved by a small number of populous states that in essence approve and purchase their textbooks *statewide*, this gives states such as Texas (and California) immense power in determining what will count as "official knowledge" throughout the entire country.[63]

Thus, in concert with neoconservative elements within the conservative alliance, authoritarian populist religious activists have had a substantial influence on curriculum policy and practice. For them, only by recentering issues of authority, morality, family, church, and "decency" can schools overcome the "moral decay" so evident all around us.[64] Only by returning to inerrantist understandings of biblical teachings and fostering (or mandating) a climate in schools where such teachings are given renewed emphasis can our culture be saved.[65]

Although a number of states and school systems have been able to create mechanisms that deflect some of these pressures, the bureaucratic nature of many school systems and of the local and regional state in general has actually produced the conditions where parents and other community members who might otherwise disagree with the New Right ideologically are convinced to join them in their attacks on the content and organization of schooling.[66]

Although authoritarian populist struggles over curriculum and texts have been growing rapidly, this mistrust of public schools has also fueled considerable and intense support among them for neoliberal policies such as voucher and choice plans. The New Right, as a largely populist assemblage, has some very real mistrust of the motives and economic plans of capital. After all, such rightist populists have themselves experienced the effects of downsizing, layoffs, and economic restructuring. However, even given their partial insights into the differential effects of global competition and economic restructuring, they see in proposals for educational marketization and privatization a way in which they can use such "reforms" for their own purposes. Either through reduced school taxes, through tax credits, or through the allocation of public money to private and religious schools, they can create a set of schools organized around the more moral "imagined communities" they believe have been lost.[67] I take this up in more detail later on.

This search for the reconstitution of imagined communities points to one of the effects of reprivatization talk on the politics surrounding educational policy. In the process of denying the legitimacy of oppositional claims, reprivatization discourses may actually tend to politicize the issues even more. These issues become even more a part of public, not "domestic," contestation. This paradox—reprivatization talk may actually lead to further public discussion of breakaway needs—does not always lead to victories by oppositional groups such as feminists, racially subjected peoples, or other disempowered groups, however. Rather, such politicization can in fact lead to the growth of new social movements and new social identities whose fundamental aim is to push breakaway needs back into the economic, domestic, and private spheres. New, and quite conservative, coalitions can be formed.

This is exactly what has happened in the United States, where a set of reprivatizing discourses "in the accents of authoritarian populism" has made creative connections with the hopes and especially the fears of a range of disaffected constituencies and has united them into a tense but very effective alliance supporting positions behind reprivatization.[68] And this could not have been done if rightist groups had not succeeded in changing the very meaning of key concepts of democracy in such a way that the Christian Right could comfortably find a place under the larger umbrella of the conservative alliance.

The Professional and Managerial New Middle Class: More Testing, More Often

Although I speak somewhat more briefly about them here because of their relatively limited—but rapidly growing—power, there is a final group that provides some of the support for the policies of conservative modernization. This is a fraction of the professional new middle class that gains its own mobility within the state and within the economy based on the use of technical expertise. These are people with backgrounds in management and efficiency techniques who provide the technical and "professional" support for accountability, measurement, "product control," and assessment that is required by the proponents of neoliberal policies of marketization and neoconservative policies of tighter central control in education.

Members of this fraction of the upwardly mobile professional and managerial new middle class do not necessarily believe in the ideological positions that underpin the conservative alliance. In fact, in other aspects of their lives they may be considerably more moderate and even "liberal" politically. However, as experts in efficiency, management, testing, and accountability, they provide the technical expertise to put in place the policies of conservative modernization. Their own mobility *depends* on the expansion of both such expertise and the professional ideologies of control, measurement, and efficiency that accompany it. Thus, they often support such policies as "neutral instrumentalities," even when these policies may be used for purposes other than the supposedly neutral ends to which this class fraction is committed.[69]

Because of this situation, it is important to realize that a good deal of the current emphasis in schools on high-stakes testing, on more rigorous forms of accountability, and on tighter control is not totally reducible to the needs of neoliberals and neoconservatives. Rather, part of the pressure for these policies comes from educational managers and bureaucratic offices who fully believe that such control is warranted and "good." Not only do these forms of control have an extremely long history in education, but tighter control, high-stakes testing, and (reductive) accountability methods provide more dynamic roles for such managers, a point I noted earlier. These policies enable such actors to engage in a moral crusade and enhance the status of their own expertise.

Yet, in a time when competition for credentials and cultural capital is intense, the increasing power of mechanisms of restratification such as the return of high levels of mandatory standardization also provides mechanisms that enhance the chances that the children of the professional and managerial new middle class will have *less competition* from other children. Thus, the introduction of devices to restratify a population enhances the value of the credentials that the new middle class is more likely to accumulate, given the stock of cultural capital it already possesses.[70] I am not claiming that this is necessarily intentional, but creating such devices does *function* to increase the chances for mobility by middle-class children who depend not on economic capital but on cultural capital for advancement.

In such a situation, I believe that this group is not immune to ideological shifts to the right. Given the fear generated by the attacks on the state and on the public sphere by both neoliberals and neoconservatives, this class fraction is decidedly worried about the future mobility of its children in an uncertain economic world. Thus, they may be drawn more overtly to parts of the conservative alliance's positions, especially those coming from the neoconservative elements that stress greater attention to traditional "high-status" content, greater attention to testing, and a greater emphasis on schooling as a stratifying mechanism. This can be seen in a number of states where parents of this class fraction are supporting charter schools that will stress academic achievement in traditional subjects and traditional teaching practices. Where the majority of members of this class grouping will align in the future in the debates over policy remains to be seen. Given their contradictory ideological tendencies, it is possible that the right will be able to mobilize them under conditions of fear for the future of their jobs and children.[71]

Conclusion

Because of the complexity of educational politics in the United States, I have devoted most of this article to an analysis of the conservative social movements that are having a powerful impact on debates over policy and practice in education and in the larger social arena. I have suggested that conservative modernization in education is guided by tense coalition forces, some of whose aims partly contradict others.

The very nature of this coalition is crucial. It is more than a little possible that the alliance underpinning conservative modernization can overcome its own internal contradictions and can succeed in radically transforming educational policy and practice. Thus, although neoliberals call for a weak state and neoconservatives demand a strong state, these very evident contradictory impulses can come together in creative ways. The emerging focus on centralized standards, content, and tighter control paradoxically can be the first and most essential step on the path to marketization through voucher and choice plans.

Once statewide or national curricula and tests are put in place, comparative school-by-school data will be available and will be published in a manner similar to the "league tables" on school achievement published in England. Only when there is standardized content and assessment can the market be set free, since the "consumer" can then have "objective" data on which schools are "succeeding" and which schools are not. Market rationality, based on "consumer choice," will ensure that the supposedly good schools will gain students and the bad schools will disappear. This assemblage is embodied in many of the impulses behind No Child Left Behind, for example.

...But let me say here that one of these effects is that when the poor "choose" to keep their children in under-funded and decaying schools in the inner cities or in rural areas (given the decline and expense of urban mass transportation, poor information, the absence of time, and their decaying economic conditions, to name but a few of the realities), *they* (the poor) will be blamed individually and collectively for making bad "consumer choices." Reprivatizing discourses and arithmetical particularism will justify the structural inequalities that will be (re)produced here. In this way, as odd as it may seem, neoliberal and neoconservative policies, ones ultimately supported by authoritarian populists and even by many members of the professional middle class, that are seemingly contradictory may mutually reinforce each other in the long run.[72]

Yet, although I have argued that the overall leadership in educational policy is exercised by this alliance, I do not want to give the impression that these four elements under the hegemonic umbrella of this coalition are uncontested or are always victorious. This is simply not the case. As a number of people have demonstrated, scores of counterhegemonic programs and possibilities exist at the local level throughout the United States. Many institutions of higher education, schools, and even entire school districts have shown remarkable resiliency in the face of the concerted ideological attacks and pressures from conservative restorational groups. And many teachers, academics, community activists, and others have created and defended educational programs that are both pedagogically and politically emancipatory.[73]

Indeed, we are beginning to see cracks in the alliance's power in unanticipated ways. For example, a growing number of students in elementary, middle, and secondary schools are actively refusing to take the mandatory tests that many states have introduced. This action has been supported by groups of teachers, administrators, parents, and activists.[74] Clearly, things are bubbling up from below the surface whose effects will be "interesting" to say the least.

Having said this, however, it is important to note the obstacles in creating the conditions for large-scale movements to defend and build progressive policies. We need to remember that there is no powerful central ministry of education in the United States. Teachers' unions are relatively weak at a national level (nor is there any guarantee that teachers' unions always act progressively). There is no consensus about an "appropriate" progressive agenda in educational policy here, as there is a vast multiplicity of compelling (and unfortunately at times competing) agendas involving race/ethnicity, gender, sexuality, class, religion, "ability," and so on. Thus, it is structurally difficult to sustain long-term national movements for more progressive policies and practices.

Because of this, most counterhegemonic work is organized locally or regionally. However, there currently are growing attempts at building national coalitions around what might best be called a "decentered unity." Organizations such as the National Coalition of Educational Activists and those centered around "Rethinking Schools" are becoming more visible nationally.[75] None of these movements have the financial and organizational backing that stands behind the neoliberal, neoconservative, and authoritarian populist groups. None have the ability to bring their case before the "public" through the media and through foundations in the ways that conservative groups have been able to do. And none have the capacity or the resources to quickly mobilize a large base of nationally directed membership to challenge or promote specific policies in the ways that the members of the alliance can.

Yet, in the face of all of these structural, financial, and political dilemmas, the fact that so many groups of people have not been integrated under the alliance's hegemonic umbrella and have created scores of local examples of the very possibility of difference shows us in the most eloquent and lived ways that educational policies and practices do not go in any one unidimensional direction. Even more important, these multiple examples demonstrate that the success of conservative policies is never guaranteed. This is crucial in a time when it is easy to lose sight of what is necessary for an education worthy of its name.

Notes

1. Madeleine Arnot, "Schooling for Social Justice," unpublished paper, University of Cambridge, Department of Education, 1990.
2. William Greider, *One World, Ready or Not* (New York: Simon & Schuster, 1997).
3. See Michael W. Apple, *Cultural Politics and Education* (New York: Teachers College Press, 1996) and Michael W. Apple, *Official Knowledge*, 2d ed. (New York: Routledge, 2000).
4. I am drawing upon Roger Dale, "The Thatcherite Project in Education," *Critical Social Policy* 9 (winter 1989/1990): 4–19. Because of the size and complexity of the United States, I cannot focus on all the policy issues and initiatives now being debated or implemented. For further descriptions, see the chapters on policy research in William Pink and George Noblit, eds., *Continuity and Contradiction: The Futures of the Sociology of Education* (Cresskill, NJ: Hampton Press, 1995).
5. Apple, *Cultural Politics and Education* and Ted Honderich, *Conservatism* (Boulder: Westview Press, 1990).
6. Given the current emphasis on this by neoliberals, it may be the case that while Bowles and Gintis's book on the relationship between education and capitalism, *Schooling in Capitalist America*, was reductive, economistic, and essentializing when it first appeared in 1976, oddly it may be more accurate today. See Samuel Bowles and Herbert Gintis, *Schooling in Capitalist America* (New York: Basic Books, 1976). For criticism of their position, see Michael W. Apple, *Teachers and Texts* (New York: Routledge, 1988); Michael W. Apple, *Education and Power*, 2d ed. (New York: Routledge, 1995); and Mike Cole, ed., *Bowles and Gintis Revisited* (New York: Falmer Press, 1988).
7. See Michael W. Apple, *Ideology and Curriculum*, 3rd ed. (New York: RoutledgeFalmer, 2004).
8. Stephen Ball, *Education Reform* (Philadelphia: Open University Press, 1994) and Apple, *Cultural Politics and Education*.
9. Apple, *Teachers and Texts*, 31–78 and Sandra Acker, "Gender and Teachers' Work," in *Review of Research in Education, Volume 21*, ed. Michael W. Apple (Washington, DC: American Educational Research Association, 1995), 99–162. A number of the larger gender implications of neoliberalism in education and the economy can be seen in Jacky Brine, *Under-Educating Woman: Globalizing Inequality* (Philadelphia: Open University Press, 1992) and Madeleine Arnot, Miriam David, and Gaby Weiner, *Closing the Gender Gap: Postwar Education and Social Change* (Cambridge, England: Polity Press, 1999).
10. John Chubb and Terry Moe, *Politics, Markets, and America's Schools* (Washington, DC: The Brookings Institution, 1990). See also, Ernest House, *Schools for Sale* (New York: Teachers College Press, 1998).
11. See the discussion of these arguments in Kristen L. Buras and Michael W. Apple, "School Choice, Neoliberal Promises, and Unpromising Evidence," *Educational Policy* 19 (July 2005): 550-564.
12. See Amy Stuart Wells, *Time to Choose* (New York: Hill & Wang, 1993); Jeffrey Henig, *Rethinking School Choice* (Princeton, NJ: Princeton University Press, 1994); Kevin Smith and Kenneth Meier, eds., *The Case Against School Choice* (Armonk, NY: M. E. Sharpe, 1995); Bruce Fuller, Elizabeth Burr, Luis Huerta, Susan Puryear, and Edward Wexler, *School Choice: Abundant Hopes, Scarce Evidence of Results* (Berkeley and Stanford: Policy Analysis for California Education, University of California at Berkeley and Stanford University, 1999); and John F. Witte, *The Market Approach to Education* (Princeton, NJ: Princeton University Press, 2000).
13. Geoff Whitty, "Creating Quasi-Markets in Education," in *Review of Research in Education, Volume 22*, ed. Michael W. Apple (Washington, DC: American Educational Research Association, 1997), 17. See also Chubb and Moe, *Politics, Markets, and America's Schools* and Gary Rosen, "Are Schools Vouchers Un-American?" *Commentary* 109 (February 2000): 26–31.
14. Quoted in Whitty, "Creating Quasi-Markets in Education," 17.
15. See, for example, Geoff Whitty, Sally Power, and David Halpin, *Devolution and Choice in Education* (Philadelphia: Open University Press, 1998) and Hugh Lauder and David Hughes, *Trading in Futures: Why Markets in Education Don't Work* (Philadelphia: Open University Press, 1999).
16. See Apple, *Cultural Politics and Education*, especially Chapter 4, for a description of the ways in which many current social and educational policies often widen racial gaps.
17. Whitty, "Creating Quasi-Markets in Education," 58.
18. Henig, *Rethinking School Choice*, 22.
19. See Whitty, "Creating Quasi-Markets in Education," Lauder and Hughes, *Trading in Futures*, and Apple, *Cultural Politics and Education*.
20. Many times, however, these initiatives are actually "unfunded mandates." That is, requirements such as these are made mandatory, but no additional funding is provided to accomplish them. The intensification of teachers' labor at all levels of the education system that results from this situation is very visible. On the history of education for employment, see Herbert Kliebard, *Schooled to Work: Vocationalism and the American Curriculum, 1876–1946* (New York: Teachers College Press, 1999). For clear and thoughtful analyses of other effects on higher education, see Geoffrey White, ed., *Campus, Inc.* (Amherst, NY: Prometheus Books, 2000) and Sheila Slaughter and Larry L. Leslie, *Academic Capitalism* (Baltimore, MD: Johns Hopkins University Press, 1997).
21. For further discussion of the powerful forces of commercialism in schools, see Alex Molnar, *School Commercialism* (New York: Routledge, 2005).
22. I have engaged in a much more detailed analysis of Channel One in Apple, *Official Knowledge*, 89–112. See also Alex Molnar, *Giving Kids the Business* (Boulder: Westview Press, 1996). A good example as well is provided by financially troubled ZapMe!, which gives free computer equipment in return for demographic information on children in schools. Of course, there is a history of resistance to things such as Channel One. UNPLUG, a student-led group, has been in the forefront of contesting the commercialization of schools. Further, as I discuss in my final chapter, both conservative and progressive groups have joined forces to act against Channel One.

23. Apple, *Cultural Politics and Education,* 68–90 and Greider, *One World, Ready or Not.*
24. Ibid. See also, Christopher Cook, "Temps Demand a New Deal," *The Nation,* 27 March 2000, pp.13–19.
25. Nancy Fraser, *Unruly Practices* (Minneapolis: University of Minnesota Press, 1989), 168.
26. Ibid., 172. See also the discussion of how gains in one sphere of social life can be "transported" into another sphere in Samuel Bowles and Herbert Gintis, *Democracy and Capitalism* (New York: Basic Books, 1986) and Apple, *Teachers and Texts.* On the history of such positions in health care, see Sandra Opdycke, *No One Was Turned Away* (New York: Oxford University Press, 1999).
27. Fraser, *Unruly Practices,* 172.
28. Roger Dale, *The State and Education Policy* (Philadelphia: Open University Press, 1989).
29. For further discussion of residual and emergent ideological forms, see Raymond Williams, *Marxism and Literature* (New York: Oxford University Press, 1977).
30. See Allen Hunter, *Children in the Service of Conservatism* (Madison: University of Wisconsin, Institute for Legal Studies, 1988) and Apple, *Cultural Politics and Education.*
31. See, for example, E. D. Hirsch Jr., *The Schools We Need and Why We Don't Have Them* (New York: Doubleday, 1996). For an insightful critique of Hirsch's position, see Kristen L. Buras, "Questioning Core Assumptions: A Critical Reading of E. D. Hirsch's *The Schools We Need and Why We Don't Have Them,*" *Harvard Educational Review* 69 (spring 1999): 67–93. See also Susan Ohanian, *One Size Fits Few: The Folly of Educational Standards* (Portsmouth, NH: Heinemann, 1999).
32. William Bennett, *The Book of Virtues* (New York: Simon & Schuster, 1994).
33. William Bennett, *Our Children and Our Country* (New York: Simon & Schuster, 1988), 8–10.
34. See Amy Stuart Wells, *Beyond the Rhetoric of Charter School Reform* (Los Angeles: University of California at Los Angeles, Graduate School of Education and Information Studies, 1999).
35. Mary Douglas, *Purity and Danger* (London: Routledge, 1966).
36. See, for example, Cameron McCarthy and Warren Crichlow, eds., *Race, Identity, and Representation in Education* (New York: Routledge, 1994).
37. See, for example, Diane Ravitch, *Left Back* (New York: Simon and Schuster, 2000). See my response to Ravitch in Michael W. Apple, "Standards, Subject Matter, and a Romantic Past," *Educational Policy* 15 (May 2001):7–36.
38. This is treated in greater depth in Apple, *Ideology and Curriculum.*
39. Lawrence Levine, *The Opening of the American Mind* (Boston: Beacon Press, 1996), 20.
40. Ibid.
41. Ibid., 15. See also Apple, *Ideology and Curriculum* and Herbert Kliebard, *The Struggle for the American Curriculum,* 2d ed. (New York: Routledge, 1995).
42. Levine, *The Opening of the American Mind,* 15.
43. Catherine Cornbleth and Dexter Waugh, *The Great Speckled Bird* (New York: St. Martin's Press, 1995).
44. For a counternarrative on the history of the United States, see Howard Zinn, *A People's History of the United States* (New York: HarperCollins, 1999). See also Howard Zinn, *The Howard Zinn Reader* (New York: Seven Stories Press, 1997) and Howard Zinn, *The Future of History* (Monroe, ME: Common Courage Press, 1999).
45. This is often done through a process of "mentioning" where texts and curricula include material on the contributions of women and "minority" groups but never allow the reader to see the world through the eyes of oppressed groups. Or as is the case in the discourse of "we are all immigrants," compromises are made so that the myth of historical similarity is constructed at the same time as economic divides among groups grow worse and worse. See Apple, *Official Knowledge,* 42–60.
46. Diane Ravitch, *National Standards in American Education* (Washington, DC: The Brookings Institution, 1995).
47. In the face of concerted criticism, the NCTM recently has officially voted to return to more of an emphasis on traditional mathematical concerns and methods of teaching. See Anemona Hartocollis, "Math Teachers Back Return of Education to Basic Skills," *The New York Times,* 15 April 2000, p. A16.
48. This is discussed in more detail in Michael W. Apple, *Power, Meaning, and Identity* (New York: Peter Lang, 1999) and Apple, *Cultural Politics and Education.* See also Ohanian, *One Size Fits Few.*
49. This distinction is developed in more depth in Dale, *The State and Education Policy.*
50. For a detailed critical discussion of the effects of this on curricula, teaching, and evaluation, see Linda McNeil, *Contradictions of School Reform* (New York: Routledge, 2000).
51. See Apple, *Education and Power;* Apple, *Teachers and Texts;* and Acker, "Gender and Teachers' Work." Clear gender and class antagonisms are at work here, ones that have a long history. Analyses of the ways in which race intersects with these dynamics and helps construct the history and labor process of teaching has been somewhat less developed. However, the ongoing work of Michelle Foster and Michael Fultz is quite helpful in this regard.
52. Richard Herrnstein and Charles Murray, *The Bell Curve* (New York: Free Press, 1994).
53. See Michael Omi and Howard Winant, *Racial Formation in the United States,* 2d ed. (New York: Routledge, 1994) and Steven Selden, *Inheriting Shame* (New York: Teachers College Press, 1999). Selden's book in particular demonstrates how very prevalent constructions of race were in a wide range of educational policies and practices, including many programs and individuals whose participation in, say, the popular eugenics movement is little known.
54. Ibid. See also Richard Dyer, *White* (New York: Routledge, 1997) and Cornel West, *Race Matters* (New York: Vintage Books, 1994).
55. Rebecca Klatch, *Women of the New Right* (Philadelphia: Temple University Press, 1987). For criticism of some of these positions, and especially those espoused by Herrnstein and Murray, see Joe Kincheloe, Shirley Steinberg, and Aaron D. Gresson, eds., *Measured Lies* (New York: St. Martin's Press, 1996).
56. For further discussion of this, see Apple, *Cultural Politics and Education,* 11–13.
57. Hunter, *Children in the Service of Conservatism,* 15.

58. Quoted in Ibid., 57.
59. Ibid.
60. The power of the text and its contradictory impulses have been detailed in Apple, *Teachers and Texts* and Apple, *Official Knowledge*. For more discussion of the ways in which struggles over the textbook help mobilize conservative activists, see Apple, *Cultural Politics and Education*, 42–67.
61. Delfattore, *What Johnny Shouldn't Read*, 123.
62. Ibid., 139.
63. The history and influence of the state's role in defining official knowledge and in textbooks is developed in much more depth in Apple, *Teachers and Texts* and Apple, *Official Knowledge*. See also Cornbleth and Waugh, *The Great Speckled Bird*.
64. See Alexandra S. Dimick and Michael W. Apple, "Texas and the Politics of Abstinence-Only Textbooks," *Teachers College Record*, May 02, 2005.
65. See Delfattore, *What Johnny Shouldn't Read*; Ralph Reed, *After the Revolution* (Dallas: Word Publishing, 1996); and Fritz Detwiler, *Standing on the Premises of God* (New York: New York University Press, 1999).
66. Anita Oliver and I provide an analysis of a concrete instance of this in Apple, *Cultural Politics and Education*, 42–67.
67. Although he limits himself to a discussion of the nation as an "imagined community," I am extending Benedict Anderson's metaphor to include religious communities as well since many of the attributes are the same. See Benedict Anderson, *Imagined Communities* (New York: Verso, 1991).
68. Fraser, *Unruly Practices*, 172–73.
69. Basil Bernstein makes an important distinction between those fractions of the new middle class who work for the state and those who work in the private sector. They may have different ideological and educational commitments. See Basil Bernstein, *The Structuring of Pedagogic Discourse* (New York: Routledge, 1990). For more on the ways "intermediate" classes and class fractions operate and interpret their worlds, see Erik Olin Wright, ed., *The Debate on Classes* (New York: Verso, 1998); Erik Olin Wright, *Classes* (New York: Verso, 1985); Erik Olin Wright, *Class Counts* (New York: Cambridge University Press, 1997); and Pierre Bourdieu, *Distinction* (Cambridge: Harvard University Press, 1984).
70. See Bourdieu, *Distinction;* Pierre Bourdieu, *Homo Academicus* (Stanford: Stanford University Press, 1988); and Pierre Bourdieu, *The State Nobility* (Stanford: Stanford University Press, 1996).
71. A combination of the work of Bernstein, Wright, and Bourdieu would be useful in understanding this class. A satirical, but still interesting, analysis of a segment of this class can be found in the work of the conservative commentator David Brooks. See David Brooks, *Bobos in Paradise* (New York: Simon & Schuster, 2000).
72. See Apple, *Cultural Politics and Education*, 22–41.
73. See especially Michael W. Apple and James A. Beane, eds., *Democratic Schools* (Alexandria, VA: Association for Supervision and Curriculum Development, 1995); Michael W. Apple and James A. Beane, eds., *Democratic Schools: Lessons from the Chalk Face* (Buckingham, England: Open University Press, 1999); and Gregory Smith, *Public Schools That Work* (New York: Routledge, 1993). Also of considerable interest here is the work on detracking and educational reform by Jeannie Oakes. See Jeannie Oakes, Karen H. Quartz, Steve Ryan, and Martin Lipton, *Becoming Good American Schools* (San Francisco: Jossey-Bass, 2000).
74. See Jacques Steinberg, "Blue Books Closed, Students Boycott Standardized Tests," *The New York Times,* 13 April 2000, pp. A1, A22. It remains to be seen whether this will grow. It is also unclear whether children of the poor and culturally and economically disenfranchised will participate widely in this. After all, affluent children *do* have options and can compensate for not having tests scores. This may not be the case for the children of those this society calls the "Other."
75. See, for example, the journal *Rethinking Schools*. It is one of the very best indicators of progressive struggles, policies, and practices in education. Information can be gotten from Rethinking Schools, 1001 E. Keefe Avenue, Milwaukee, WI 53212, USA or via its Web site at <www.rethinkingschools.org>.

BISHOP BURTON COLLEGE
LIBRARY

Suggested Readings

Anyon, J. (1980). Social class and the hidden curriculum of work. *Journal of Education, 162*, 67–92.

Apple, M. W. (1978). *Ideology and curriculum*. Boston: Routledge and Kegan Paul.

Apple, M. W. (1992). The text and cultural politics. *Educational Researcher, 21*(7): 4–11, 19.

Apple, M. W. (1993). *Official knowledge: Democratic education in a conservative age*. New York: Routledge.

Biddle, B., Good, T., & Goodson, I. Eds. (1996). *International handbook of teachers and teaching*. Amsterdam: Kluwer Academic Publishers.

Bidwell, C. E. (1965). The school as a formal organization. In J. G. March (Ed.), *Handbook of research on organizations* (pp. 972–1018). Chicago: Rand McNally.

Binder, A. (2002). *Contentious curricula: Afro-centrism and creationism in American public schools*. Princeton, NJ: Princeton University Press.

Bryk, A., Lee, V. E., & Holland, P. B. (1993). *Catholic schools and the common good*. Cambridge, MA: Harvard University Press.

Cohen, E. G. (1994a). *Designing group work: Strategies for the heterogeneous classroom*. New York: Teachers College Press.

Cohen, E. G. (1994b). Restructuring the classroom: Conditions for productive small groups. *Review of Educational Research, 64*, 1–35.

Cohen, E. G., Lotan, R., & Leechor, C. (1989). Can classrooms learn? *Sociology of Education, 62*, 75–94.

Dreeben, R. (1968). *On what is learned in school*. Boston: Addison-Wesley.

Dworkin, A. G. (1985). *When teachers give up: Teacher burnout, teacher turnover, and their impact on children*. Austin, TX: Hogg Foundation for Mental Health and Texas Press.

Dworkin, A. G. (1987). *Teacher burnout in the public schools: Structural causes and consequences for children*. Albany: SUNY Press.

Gamoran, A., & Dreeben, R. (1986). Coupling and control in educational organizations. *Administrative Science Quarterly, 31*, 612–632.

Goodson, I. (1992). *Studying teachers' lives*. London: Routledge.

Goodson, I. (1993). *School subjects and curriculum change* (3rd ed.). London, New York and Philadelphia: Falmer Press.

Ingersoll, R. M. (1994). Organizational control in secondary schools. *Harvard Educational Review, 64*, 150–172.

Ingersoll, R. (1999). The problem of under-qualified teachers in American secondary schools. *Educational Researcher, 28*, 26–37.

Ingersoll, R. (2001). Teacher turnover and teacher shortages. *American Educational Research Journal, 38*(3), 499–534.

Ingersoll, R. (2003). *Who controls teachers' work?: Power and accountability in America's schools*. Cambridge, MA: Harvard University Press.

Johnson, S. M. (1990). *Teachers at work*. New York: Basic Books.

Lee, V. E., Dedrick, R. F., & Smith, J. B. (1991). The effect of the social organization of schools on teachers: Self-Efficacy and satisfaction. *Sociology of Education, 64*, 190–208.

Lesko, N. (2001). *Act your age! A cultural construction of adolescence*. New York: Routledge.

Lortie, D. (1975). *School teacher: A sociological study*. Chicago: University of Chicago Press.

Lubeck, S. (1985). *Sandbox society: An ethnographic comparison*. London: Falmer.

Maher, F., & Tetrault, M. T. (1994). *The feminist classroom*. New York: Basic.

McFarland, D. (2001). Student resistance: How formal and informal organization of classrooms facilitate everyday forms of student deviance. *American Journal of Sociology, 107*, 612–678.

McLaughlin, M., & Little, J. W. (Eds.). (1993). *Teachers work: Individuals, colleagues, and contexts*. New York: Teachers College Press.

McLaughlin, M. W., & Talbert, J. E. (1993a). *Contexts that matter for teaching and learning*. Stanford, CA: Center for Research on the Context of Secondary School Teaching.

McLaughlin, M. W., & Talbert, J. E. (1993b). How the world of students and teachers challenges policy coherence. In S. H. Fuhrman (Ed.), *Designing coherent education policy: Improving the system*. San Francisco: Jossey-Bass.

McLaughlin, M. W., & Talbert, J. E. (2006). *Building school-based teacher learning communities*. Teachers College Press, 2006.

Metz, M. H. (1978). *Classrooms and corridors*. Berkeley, CA: University of California Press.

Metz, M. H. (1990). How social class differences shape teachers work. In M. W. McLaughlin, J. E. Talbert, & N. Bascia (Eds.), *The contexts of teaching in secondary schools. Teachers realities*. New York: Teachers College Press.

Meyer, J. W., Kamens, D., Benavot, A., Cha, Y. K., & Wong, S. Y. (1992). *School knowledge for the masses: World models and national primary curriculum categories in the twentieth century.* London: Falmer.

Schneider, B., & Bryk, A. (1996). *Social trust: A moral resource for school improvement.* Chicago: Center for School Improvement.

Schneider, B., & Stevenson, D. (1999). *The ambitious generation: America's teenagers, motivated but directionless.* New Haven, CT: Yale University Press.

Semel, S. F. (1996). "Yes, but...": Multiculturalism and the reduction of educational inequality. *Teachers College Record, 98*(1), 153–177.

Semel, S. F., & Sadovnik, A. R. (1999). *"Schools of tomorrow," schools of today: What happened to progressive education.* New York: Peter Lang.

Stevenson, D., & Baker, D. (1991). State control of the curriculum and classroom instruction. *Sociology of Education, 64,* 1–10.

Whitty, G. (1985). *Sociology and school knowledge.* London: Metheun.

Wong, S. L. (1991). Evaluating the content of textbooks: Public interests and professional authority. *Sociology of Education, 64,* 11–18.

Weick, K. (1976). Educational organizations as loosely-coupled systems. *Administrative Science Quarterly, 21,* 1–19.

PART **III**

International Education

The readings in Part III examine issues in comparative and international education. The purpose of international comparisons is to explore the similarities and differences among different national systems of education in order to see to what extent there are universal processes of educational formation or to what extent schools reflect specific national cultures and characteristics.

Chapter 12, "The Political Construction of Mass Schooling: European Origins and Worldwide Institutionalization" by Stanford University sociologist Francisco Ramirez and Emory University sociologist John Boli, provides an application of institutional theory to the development of mass schooling internationally. The authors examine the relationship between mass schooling, democracy, and civil society.

Chapter 13, "Marketization and Privatization in Mass Education Systems" by University of London sociologist Geoff Whitty and Cardiff University sociologist Sally Power, examines the movements worldwide toward the use of markets and privatization in education and the debates over these processes.

Chapter 14, "Nation Versus Nation: The Race to Be the First in the World" by Pennsylvania State sociologists David P. Baker and Gerald LeTendre, examines the worldwide competition to become first in the international student achievement rankings. They apply institutional theory to analyze the politics of competition, the similarities and differences among national educational systems, and the problems with the current rankings frenzy.

Questions for Reflection and Discussion

1. How do institutional theorists such as Ramirez and Boli explain the development of mass educational systems throughout the world? What would Bowles and Gintis say about their explanation? What would Randall Collins say?
2. What do Whitty and Power say about the effect of markets and privatization in education? What would Michael Apple say about these processes? How would Ramirez and Boli explain privatization of education as opposed to the continued development of mass public school systems?
3. How do Baker and LeTendre explain the competition to become ranked first on international tests? How would functionalist and conflict theorists explain this worldwide phenomenon?

12

The Political Construction of Mass Schooling

European Origins and Worldwide Institutionalization

FRANCISCO O. RAMIREZ AND JOHN BOLI

INTRODUCTION

During the late eighteenth and nineteenth centuries, national states constructed mass schooling systems that eventually came to encompass their entire populations of children. State authorization, sponsorship, funding, and control of mass education first developed in Western Europe (Collins 1977) and later became a central feature of a highly institutionalized model of national development throughout the world (Ramirez and Boli 1982). And yet, most comparative studies of education almost entirely overlook the historical origins of state systems of schooling (see the papers in Altbach, Arnove, and Kelly 1982; Kazamias 1977; Eckstein and Noah 1969), thereby ignoring the sociological significance of the successful institutionalization of this social innovation.

We examine the European origins and worldwide institutionalization of the state system of mass schooling. Our main objective is to account for the rise and legitimation of nation-states' compelling interest in mass education. We explicitly do not purport to explain the early expansion of primary school enrollments, though studies of this process are interesting in their own right (see, for instance, Craig and Spear 1983).[1] Some existing studies seek to explain early cross-national *differences* in the linkages between the state and education, such as variations in the degree of centralized control over education (Archer 1979), but we focus on transnational *similarities* in the institutional character of state educational systems. These similarities include ideological acceptance of particular goals for mass education, the adoption of compulsory school laws and constitutional provisions affirming a state interest in mass education, and the formation of national educational ministries and bureaus.

Our starting point is the observation that the development of the state's compelling interest in education was not solely a response to the needs of an industrializing economy, to class or status conflicts, nor to unique historical conjunctures in particular countries, such as the character of the central bureaucracy in Prussia (Rosenberg 1958), the revolutions and reactions in France (Gontard 1976), the power of the peasantry in Sweden (Warne 1929), or the extension of the franchise to the working classes in England (Jones 1977). These internal, societal-level factors were indeed important in shaping the particular characteristics of the various state educational systems. Our concern, however, lies in understanding the universality of state schooling: Why was the social innovation of mass state-sponsored education adopted in virtually every Western European country in the "long" nineteenth century, from Prussia (1763) to Belgium (1914), despite great variation in societal characteristics and histories?

To make sense of this phenomenon, we need to consider the broader civilizational network within which these nation-states operated. This is not an entirely novel idea: Cohen (1970, 1979) has argued that state-sponsored mass schooling systems can emerge only in a civilizational network of nation states competing with one another, and Reisner (1922) has argued that state action in the educational domain is an outcome of European competitive processes. Here, we want to back up these views with a review of the historical evidence for a number of European countries and then develop a theoretical explanation for this phenomenon.

Our view is that European states became engaged in authorizing, funding, and managing mass schooling as part of an endeavor to construct a unified national polity (cf. Ringer 1977; Bendix 1964). Within such a polity, individuals were expected to find their primary identification with the nation, and it was presumed that state power would be enhanced by the universal participation of citizens in national projects. We show that in some cases, a military defeat or a failure to keep pace with industrial development in rival countries stimulated the state to turn to education as a means of national revitalization to avoid losing power and prestige in the interstate system. In other cases, when a nation moving toward a position of first rank in the system was challenged by rivals attempting to block its rise through military alliances and economic exertions, mass schooling was adopted as a means of achieving more comprehensive mobilization to assure continued success in the system. External challenges of these sorts were important stimuli to state action in education, not least because they exacerbated the costs associated with internal obstacles to national development and success, including such factors as the power of the clergy, state- or class-based privileges, and subunit political autonomy (Ringer 1977).

But why should mass education be invoked as a means of enhancing national unity and ensuring national success in the interstate system? Competitive rivalries and crises of national integration in prior eras had not led to the call for state-sponsored mass schooling. Nor is it correct to assume that the adoption of compulsory mass education so effectively enhanced the position of a nation-state within the broader world system that it generated imitative behavior. State interest in mass education was shaped by the political construction of mass education, that is, by its *perceived institutional character* rather than by the actual effects of compulsory mass education on nation-state structures.[2] Thus, our task is to explain why the extension of schooling to the masses through a compulsory state-sponsored system became a plausible and ultimately irresistible response to challenges from the external environment.

The explanation we develop involves two general ideas:

1. The nation-states of Europe adopted state educational systems because this organizational strategy was the course of action most consistent with *the developing Western European model of a national society*. We view this model as a set of institutionalized definitions of reality that operated as a symbolic universe (Berger and Luckman 1966) assigning meaning and legitimacy to some entities, organizational forms, and courses of action while making others unintelligible and unsupportable. The movement toward a closer union between states and schools proceeded despite sometimes profound opposition, because a state educational system increasingly became what a national society must develop when faced with challenging or adverse circumstances. The latter were increasingly interpreted not just as national crises but also as opportunities for a more comprehensive nation-building effort. Hence, the European model of a national society in the nineteenth century facilitated the establishment and success of state educational systems despite the many extinction pressures associated with the "liability of newness" (Freeman, Carroll, and Hannan 1983). As this model of the nation-state has become further institutionalized in the twentieth century, new nation-state candidates have increasingly adopted the expected educational goals and organizational forms that demonstrate the authenticity of their nation-building

projects within the established system of nation-states (cf. DiMaggio and Powell 1983; Meyer and Rowan 1977).

2. The European model of a national society emerged primarily as the product of three much-discussed and related *transformations in European culture, polity, and economy*: the Reformation and Counter-Reformation, the construction of the national state and the interstate system, and the triumph of the exchange economy. These transformations in the larger environment produced a model of the national society that emphasized both the primacy of the socializable individual (Berger, Berger, and Kellner 1973) and the ultimate authority and national responsibility of the state (Grew 1984). Thus, we contend that the union of states and schools as a nation-building process was imposed by the larger environment on its subunit states. Because the world today continues to reflect these basic features of the European experience, the European model of a nation-state is now writ worldwide. A state educational system has therefore become an institutional imperative for contemporary nation-states.

The task of this paper is to develop these ideas into a coherent explanation of the construction and institutionalization of the state educational system. First, we briefly examine the historical record, centering our discussion on five economically less developed European states—Prussia, Austria, Denmark, Sweden, and Italy—and then considering state-school linkages in the two most developed and dominant nineteenth-century powers—England and France.[3] We show that state educational systems did not originate in the most dominant countries, contrary to the widespread assumption that educational innovations inevitably start there and diffuse to less developed or less powerful countries. Rather, the most dominant powers were able to resist the systemwide pressures favoring mass education and cling to the older organizational forms associated with their earlier success in the system, even though such resistance could prove disadvantageous in the long run.

The second section of the paper develops our explanation. Focusing on Europe as a whole, we identify five institutionalized legitimating myths that underlie the European model of a national society and that justified the extension of schooling to the children of the masses and the takeover of schooling by the state. We then briefly discuss the environmental forces that shaped these legitimating myths and produced the national society model that came to dominate in nineteenth-century Europe.[4]

We conclude by briefly discussing comparative research findings that illustrate the contemporary relevance of our explanatory argument, showing that the political construction of mass schooling is a worldwide institutional undertaking legitimated by what has become the world model of a national society.

State Education Efforts to 1900: Historical Sketches

Less Developed and Less Dominant Countries

The earliest regulation proclaiming universal, compulsory education appeared in the German state of Weimar in 1619 (Thut and Adams 1964). In other countries where compulsory education was instituted early on, the rule was applied only to a very restricted class of persons, e.g., to the samurai warrior elite in Tokugawa, Japan (Dore 1964). Our historical review begins with Prussia, where the Weimarian ambition was first put into practice on a wide scale. Throughout this discussion, we rely on sources specific to each country and on Flora's (1983) dates for the various stages in the development of mass schooling and compulsory education.

Prussia. In the seventeenth century, both England and the United Provinces made great strides in economic development while the German areas stagnated (Cipolla 1974). But during this period, the relatively insignificant Electorate of Brandenburg developed into the state of Prussia, which became the nucleus of modernization of the German national state, a process completed in 1871 (see the analysis by Rosenberg [1958]). In the 1700s, Prussia was essentially a "state without a nation"; i.e., it had a strong and centralized bureaucracy that oversaw a highly fragmented polity dominated by local interests. The Prussian problem lay in creating a nation to match its state.

The starting point for examining educational development in Prussia is 1716, when Frederick William I made attendance at village schools compulsory for all children not otherwise provided with instruction. The phrase "not otherwise provided" is important; this directive was not aimed at the children of the elite, for they had private tutors or attended the Gymnasium. In 1763, Frederick II (Frederick the Great) reiterated the earlier order for compulsory education in a famous directive, "General Regulations for Village Schools" (Cubberley 1920). He pledged some financial aid from the state, which resulted in a modest increase in formal schooling in parts of Prussia.

What influenced Frederick the Great to initiate efforts in education? Marriott and Robertson (1915) argue that Frederick, following a military model of governance, tried to unify Prussia through state-directed education. All children were taught to identify with the state and its goals and purposes rather than with local polities (estates, peasant communities, regions, etc.). The timing of Frederick's regulations is highly significant: They were issued at the end of the Seven Years War, in which Prussia and England fought newly allied Austria and France. Although Prussia won the war, victory came only at great cost: enormous loss of life, exhaustion of the state treasury, and devastation of the economy. Moreover, Prussia was still surrounded by hostile enemies. Frederick faced a severe national crisis, largely because of the obdurate unwillingness of the German nobility to form a coherent territorially based national polity. Education became the means of reconstruction and renewal.

Prussia went through much the same experience only forty years later, this time on the losing end. Napoleon's triumph over the Prussians at Jena in 1806 destroyed a large part of the Prussian army and subjected Prussia to heavy French influence. The humiliating Treaty of Tilsit, imposed on Prussia by Napoleon, provoked a strong national revival movement that was epitomized by Fichte's lectures delivered in 1807 in Berlin, *Addresses to the German Nation* (Boyd and King 1975). Fichte called for patriotism to the German nation, even though that nation had yet to coalesce fully, and stressed education as the means to that end. He claimed that universal, state-directed, compulsory education would teach all Germans to be good Germans and would prepare them to play whatever role—military, economic, political—fell to them in helping the state reassert Prussian power (Marriott and Robertson 1915).

Conditions were ripe for Fichte's words to have effect. Almost immediately, a Bureau of Education was established within the Ministry of the Interior; ten years later, a separate Department of Education was created in the Ministry of Religion, Education, and Public Health. Between 1817 and 1825, under the direction of Baron von Altenstein, state administration of education was established (Rowlinson 1974). Taxes were imposed to finance the school system, and every Land was required to establish local primary and folk schools. State certification of primary school teachers and the establishment of state normal schools to provide teacher training followed later (Reisner 1922).

Some of the designers of the Prussian system were liberal reformers, but Prussian officialdom was extremely skeptical of providing the masses with too much schooling or with schooling that was too classical. Frederick the Great had clearly expressed the prevailing sentiment: "We do not confer upon the individual or upon society any benefit when we educate him beyond the bounds of his social class and vocation, give him a cultivation which he cannot make use of, and awaken in him pretensions and needs which his lot in life does not allow him to satisfy" (quoted in Reisner 1922, pp. 143–44). The reification of social divisions in Prussia went hand in hand with the reflexive association of education with religion. In 1848, when an assembly of teachers at Tivoli (near Berlin) recommended the establishment of a secular educational ministry, the government response was extremely negative: Religious instruction was more important than pedagogical theory (Alexander 1918). But two years after the Franco-Prussian War, a more unified German polity removed from the clergy the authority to inspect the schools. In 1906 the primary school system was reorganized, giving the state greater and more direct responsibility for financing education (Anderson 1970).

Some aspects of the union of state and schools in Prussia are undoubtedly unique to the German national experience, but two features of this process stand out. First, the state attempted to use mass schooling to create a more unified national citizenry and thereby consolidate state power both within the nation and relative to other national states, as enunciated explicitly by Fichte. Second, the union was sparked by a clear challenge to Prussia's position in the European state system—its defeat at the hands of the French after a period during which Prussia had managed gradually to increase its international stature and power. Prussia saw its rise in the European system blocked. Its response was state-controlled education, and the system it constructed would later be widely cited as an important element of Prussian (German) success in the state system.

Austria. In 1774, under Joseph II, Austria passed a universal compulsory education law. This law was clearly copied after Frederick the Great's work and was sparked by the dissolution of the Society of Jesus, which had controlled most of Austrian education until that time (Papanek 1962). This first effort to link schools with the state was conditioned by the defeat of Austria in the Seven Years War (1756–1763). But the full development of a system of national education was frustrated by the reactionary politics that swept Austria in the aftermath of the French Revolution and the Napoleonic era. The return of the Jesuits in 1814 ushered in an era of religious resurgence in educational matters, and after a period of state control during which the religious authorities gradually exerted more and more influence over the schools, the state signed a concordat with the Pope in 1855, returning full control to the Church.

The definitive movement toward a state educational system in Austria was triggered by Prussia's defeat of Austria in 1866 (Papanek 1962). The 1867 constitution was intended to reform Austrian government and revitalize its national power; to accomplish this nation-building goal, schools were delivered firmly into state control. Complete separation of schools from the Church was instituted in the following year. A compulsory education law followed in 1869. This movement toward the unification of schools and state took place despite vigorous opposition from a papacy that viewed state-directed education as an evil by-product of modernity.

If Prussia was upwardly mobile in the European state system between 1700 and 1870, Austria travelled the same road in reverse. The Napoleonic Wars affected Prussia and Austria in opposite ways. For Prussia, military defeat and political humiliation paved the way for the nationalization of public education; for Austria, the same experience led to a renewed commitment to the symbolic foundation of the empire—the Church (Rokkan 1980). Only after Bismarck successfully divided the moribund empire and confronted Austria with a powerful and unified Germany did Austria go the route of national state construction. At that historical juncture (1867–1868), the process of tying mass education to the state in Austria no longer differed greatly from that in Prussia. In both cases, mass public education was adopted as a means of improving national competitiveness in the interstate system.

Denmark and Sweden. Credit for the first state-managed system of compulsory mass schooling is often assigned to Denmark (Bendix 1964). As early as 1721, Frederick IV sought to build a system of schools in the royal domains, and his son Christian VI extended those efforts toward a genuine national system. But Christian could not muster the necessary resources; thus, the royal law of 1739 calling for compulsory schooling was largely a symbolic gesture that could not be realized in practice (Warne 1929). The breakthrough in forging the link between the state and education was made in 1789 under Frederick VI through the establishment of a Grand School Commission. This commission did not finish its work until 1814, when its report led to the passage of a law that set the foundations of the modern Danish school system; the specifications included compulsory education for children between the ages of seven and fourteen (Boje, Borup, and Rützebeck 1932).

Denmark's experience in establishing a state-controlled school system resembles that of Austria more than Prussia. Denmark had been a major European power in the seventeenth century, despite its small size. By 1800, however, Denmark's demise was an indisputable fact, and the loss of Norway to Sweden in 1809 symbolized its fall all too well. Denmark was prime for the appearance of its Fichte, and it found one in the person of N.F.S. Grundtvig, a clergyman who between 1807 and 1814 became the prime advocate of education as a means for Denmark to regain its spiritual and national strength (Vibaek 1964). After passage of the law of 1814, Denmark proceeded rapidly with the construction of a national system.

The development of the Swedish state educational system was influenced by changes in Sweden's position in the European system. Sweden was a major European power under Gustav Adolf in the seventeenth century, but its empire lasted only a short time as Prussia, England, and Russia struggled for control of the Baltic, enlisting Sweden and Denmark as subordinate powers in various alliances. Sweden experienced severe difficulties following several military defeats in the eighteenth century, but the conditions necessary to evoke a call for salvation through education had not yet developed in European culture. Hence, though a number of educational proposals were made before the nineteenth century, most of them were offered by reform theologians whose only concern was for religious instruction. In the middle and late eighteenth century, liberal reformers proposed educational measures to democratize the state and help Sweden regain its Great Power status, but they were defeated in the Riksdag by a coalition of the aristocracy and clergy, who feared that education would make the peasants rebellious (Warne 1929).

Sweden's involvement in the Napoleonic Wars produced further difficulties. Sweden lost Finland to Russia in 1809, receiving Norway from Denmark as a consolation prize. The ensuing upheaval resulted in a new constitution, and further turmoil and uncertainty led the Swedes to invite Jean Bernadotte, one of Napoleon's generals, to take the throne in 1810. At the same time, bourgeois liberals led a movement to develop mass schooling to provide national unity and purpose. Their efforts were defeated by the reactionary politics of the aristocracy, clergy, and new king and by the unwillingness of the peasantry to foot the bill for an educational system (Jansson 1948).

The end of the Napoleonic Wars found Sweden definitively reduced to a second-rank power. Two developments resulted. First, there was a great cultural revitalization movement, both in literature and in primarily popular religious movements. The leading figure in this movement was Esaias Tegner, Sweden's greatest poet, who (before a change of heart in the 1830s) strongly advocated the establishment of universal elementary education to unify and strengthen Sweden (Stomberg 1931). Second, a period of liberal reform swept Sweden in the 1830s and 1840s, inspired largely by the recurring revolutions in France and impeded less by aristocratic reaction in Sweden than elsewhere because of the rising power of the bourgeois class (Carlsson and Rosén 1961). Motivated partly by the desire to uplift the Swedish nation and partly by the perceived need for an educated populace in the monetarized economy that Sweden had begun to develop, the liberals pushed through a school reform bill in 1842 that founded a state system of elementary schools throughout the country. The primary model for the Swedish effort was Denmark's rapidly growing school system, but frequent reference was also made to Prussian educational progress. The 1842 law was followed in later decades by further bills that made education truly universal, and the Swedish system became in turn a model for other countries because of its efficiency and effectiveness.

In Sweden, the crisis brought about by the Napoleonic Wars was quite acute, but it did not immediately generate a state educational system, despite efforts in that direction. Detailed study of this period in Swedish history suggests that it was the resistance of the relatively powerful and independent peasantry (in conjunction with the usual resistance of the clergy and aristocracy) that slowed the movement toward state-controlled education. In any case, by mid-century, the Swedish mass schooling system was well established.

Italy. Italy constitutes a complicated case. The country's political fate was controlled by the European core powers, and national unification was not achieved until relatively late (1860). The northern Italian states were both economically and politically more developed than those in the south and more closely involved with European culture and politics. Hence, the drive for independence and unification came mostly from the north. Typically, movements in France were imitated in northern Italy, but the multiplicity of political units and the lack of an integrating national polity prevented these movements from developing effectively.

The first serious calls for state-directed schooling came in 1796, when Austria's counterattack on France seemed likely to quench the Revolution. Inspired directly by their French counterparts, the Italian Jacobins seized on education as the means to mobilize the people. They urged the construction of a secular state-operated system throughout the country (Woolf 1979), but, like the Revolution in Italy, the various proposals offered in this period came to very little.

Throughout the first half of the nineteenth century, Italian liberals and radicals organized for reform or revolution but were defeated by reactionary rulers backed by one or more of the major powers and, in the educational sphere, by the ever-present Church. Conditions favorable to Italian independence and unification finally appeared after the Crimean War, when it became clear that the balance of power formalized in the Concert of Europe had broken down (Woolf 1979). The independence movement rapidly gained strength, and by 1857, revolts, coups d'etat, and civil war raged throughout the country. In 1859, in this climate of extreme political turmoil and struggle for national entity and identity, an educational reform law was passed in Piedmont under the sponsorship of Gabrio Casati, the first Minister of Public Instruction. The law established a complete state system of education, from elementary through university level, and drastically limited the role of the Church (Tannenbaum 1974). After 1860, the law was gradually applied to the unified territories, and by 1877, the legal framework for a national system of compulsory public education was in place.

In Italy, the lag between ideological commitments to education and the implementation of organizational structure was unusually great, consistent with the ineffectiveness and fragmentation of the Italian state throughout most of its history. Thus, though the educational system was quite effectively instituted in some of the northern areas by 1880, very little was accomplished in the south before 1900, and centralizing reforms in 1904 and 1911 were necessary to begin to make the system truly universal in scope (Tannenbaum 1974). Even with these reforms, Italian elementary education developed relatively slowly until after World War II.

The Italian case offers an illuminating variant in which the state's effort in education was almost anticipatory: The Piedmontese state strove to build a national educational system even before national unification had been achieved. It was thus in the midst of its effort to enter the European state system as a unified entity that Italy initiated state-sponsored mass education. Like Prussia, Italy was upwardly mobile in the system, and education was seen as a means of increasing Italian power and prestige.

The Dominant European Powers: France and England

The dominant powers in the period up to 1850 were France and England. In France, education under the *ancien régime* consisted mainly of secondary schools run by the religious orders for the middle and upper classes. Mass schooling, to the extent that it existed, was restricted to religious instruction, and the schools were run by the Catholic Church, though they were nominally under the authority of the king. In this respect, the educational situation in England was quite similar; the principle of state supremacy over all ecclesiastical affairs (and, by implication, over the schools) had been established under Elizabeth I in the Acts of Supremacy and Unification (Thut and Adams 1964). In fact, however, these educational institutions functioned as voluntary associations with little input from the state.

Elites were their principal clientele, and the education of poor children was left to philanthropy until well into the nineteenth century.

France. The movement toward a state-managed system of compulsory primary education commenced earlier in France than in England. The Constitution of 1791 called for the establishment of a system of free public instruction common to all citizens. A series of education proposals—by Tallyrand (1791), Condorcet (1792), Lepelletier de Saint Fargeau (1793)—failed to translate the 1791 constitutional mandate into organizational reality (Furet and Ozouf 1977), and the cycle of revolution/reform/reaction that followed the Revolution prevented the permanent establishment of a national system until relatively late.

The importance of nationalizing education was not lost on Napoleon as he rose to power. In 1805 he wrote,

> Of all political questions, that [of education] is perhaps the most important. There cannot be a firmly established political state unless there is a teaching body with definitely recognized principles. If the child is not taught from infancy that he ought to be a republican or a monarchist, a Catholic or a free-thinker, the state will not constitute a nation; it will rest on uncertain and shifting foundations; and it will be constantly exposed to disorder and change. (Quoted in Reisner 1922, p. 35)

No clearer statement of the relationship of education to the formation of a national state could have been made. But in practice, Napoleon ignored primary education, concentrating instead on developing secondary and higher education, especially the Lycées and the Grandes Ecoles, with the objective of producing an effective elite to operate the military and governmental apparatus (Lynch 1974). Napoleon was still operating in accordance with the older European model of society; in his time, mass education had not yet become an ideological and social imperative. We argue, however, that he would have directed much more attention to primary schooling if he had come to power in 1850 rather than 1800.

After the defeat of Napoleon, the Church regained centrality in educational matters only to have its influence reduced anew after 1830, during the constitutional monarchy of Louis Philippe. The first serious attempt to organize a national system of primary education was generated by a law of 1833; under the direction of Guizot, an educational system, strongly influenced by the Cousin report on the Prussian primary educational-system, was established (Gontard 1976). The plan called for the establishment of schools in all but the smallest communes, state aid for poor communes, normal schools throughout the nation, and the relegation of religious instruction to an optional activity. These democratizing and secularizing trends were halted, once again, by the reaction that followed the Revolution of 1840 and the regime of Louis Napoleon in 1852. Primary school teachers in particular were targeted for repression, because they had become a vocal political force calling for free, universal, and compulsory education for the whole of France. Many teachers were dismissed, and clerical control over education was again enhanced (Lynch 1974).

The final round of the cycle occurred after the humiliating defeat by Prussia in 1870 and the establishment of the Third Republic a year later. Public debate quickly focused on primary education as a means of national renewal; one popular expression current in France at the time was that the Franco-Prussian War had been "won by the Prussian schoolmaster" (Reisner 1922). The political reconstruction of French schools rapidly became a symbol of the Third Republic. By 1881, with Jules Ferry as Minister of Public Instruction, a universal, free, compulsory primary school system had been established, and within five years of that date, very extensive state control of the educational system had been achieved (Furet and Ozouf 1977).

France offers us a fairly pure example of the nation-building perspective on education. Early demands for state involvement in elementary education were made within the context of an intense effort to reconstruct the French national polity. Identification with the national polity was achieved through the Revolution and the Napoleonic Wars, during which France found itself pitted against all of Western and Central Europe. Broadly based nationalistic sentiment, the modern alchemy through which many different individuals become one with the interests and purposes of the state, was practically invented in France during this era. But the embodiment of nationalism in education was frustrated in France by the frequent swings between revolution and reaction that occurred between 1815 and 1870. It took a decisive defeat at the hands of a unifying Germany to complete in France the nation-building project that finally resulted in a genuine national system of mass education.

England. England managed to avoid the violent revolutionary upheavals that rocked France in the eighteenth and nineteenth centuries. But the movement toward state-sponsored mass education was inhibited by the very success of England's navy and merchants in the world economy. Schooling developed slowly in private hands, and classical liberal restraints on state action kept the state out of education much longer in England than elsewhere. Hence, it is not surprising that the first attempt to extend public aid to parochial schools for the masses (the Whitehead Bill of 1807) was defeated in the House of Lords. The principle of voluntarism that had shaped the private, religious, elitist schools of England would not be easily overturned, especially in light of the global success to which it was believed these schools had contributed (Jones 1977). Though these sectarian, mostly Anglican, schools were nominally under the authority of the Crown, there was virtually no state "interference" in the schools until 1833.

The reform of 1833 was part of the liberalization process that opened Parliament to the English bourgeoisie. It was limited to a program of state grants to the schools administered by national voluntary societies that were closely tied to the churches (Jones 1977). In a short time, the Anglican educational society had won out over its Nonconformist counterpart and had gained control of most of the grants, helping to block extensive state control of the schools.

But events in the 1860s altered the situation. First, further political reform began to enfranchise the working classes (1867), and a new Liberal-Labor alliance argued strongly for compulsory mass education. The full democratization of the political realm was seen as inevitable, and education was increasingly regarded as a means to civilize the lower classes so as to "avoid anarchy" (Robert Lowe's phrase, quoted in Jones [1977, p. 50]), i.e., to teach the lower classes proper behavior in the political arena. This line of thought was more prominent in England than elsewhere, but it was also promoted in France (Furet and Ozouf 1977).

Second, the rise of Germany and the United States threatened British industrial supremacy. By 1867, Bismarck's project to unify Germany had yielded the Confederation of North German States, a brief stopping point on the way toward a fully unified Germany in 1871, and Germany's rise to major power status was accomplished. The triumph of the North in the American Civil War similarly represented a clear challenge to British world supremacy by cutting the advantageous trade relationships Britain had enjoyed with the South (Moore 1966) and by signalling that a more cohesive United States would take a more aggressive role in the world economy, especially with respect to Latin America. The threat to British dominance was clearly acknowledged both at home and abroad (Jones 1977).

A waning of national confidence was clearly reflected in the British reaction to the 1867 Paris Exhibition, a world's fair at which English products compared unfavorably with those of other countries (Royal Society of Arts 1867). The Exhibition was widely interpreted as marking the end of unchallenged British superiority in the development and manufacture of goods. As a result of all these developments, there arose a clamor for education both to improve British workmanship and to achieve greater national cohesion in order to compete in the larger system. The consequent Elementary Education (Forster) Act of 1870 mandated the provision of schooling, though it stopped short of decreeing compulsory education. A decade later, compulsory education was instituted nationwide. But it was not until 1902, when both Germany and the United States had outdistanced England in a number of dimensions of industrial production (Temin 1966), that the dual educational system (church and state schools) was unified and the role of the churches was effectively ended.

Although the law of 1902 was significant in some fundamental respects (for example, primary and secondary education were placed under a common educational authority), it did not elevate the Board of Education into a national ministry. Instead, the law created a system of local educational authorities through which much of the governance of the school system would take place. Not until 1944 did England establish a national ministry as the central educational authority. By then, the radical demise of British economic, political, and military power was conspicuous, and the United States had emerged as the new dominant power in the world.

England provides an instructive example of the limits on the power of the European model of a national society to affect the behavior of states. Because it was the dominant world power, England could exercise greater freedom from the constraints imposed by the model—constraints that bound less powerful nations more exactly. Less dominant nations that were highly integrated into the European interstate system, such as Denmark and Prussia, conformed to the model more fully to establish their legitimacy and to mobilize their populations to compete in the system.

The Political Construction of Mass Education: European Origins

Why were state educational systems constructed throughout Europe in the late eighteenth and nineteenth centuries? Our brief historical sketches reveal that, despite much variation in level of industrialization, class structure, and political regime, the ideological and organizational responses of the various countries to challenges to state power were strikingly similar. The typical response encompassed the following elements: declaration of a national interest in mass education, legislation to make schooling compulsory, creation of a state educational ministry or department, and establishment of state authority over existing and new schools.

To understand this largely uniform response, we consider Europe as a whole, first discussing five institutionalized legitimating myths that had important implications for state-sponsored mass education. We then examine how the European model of a national society was shaped by three major transformations in European social structure and culture: the Reformation and Counter-Reformation, the rise of the national state and the interstate system, and the establishment of the exchange economy. We argue that the European states adopted a state educational system as part of a nation-building process imposed on them by the larger environment within which they competed. The state educational system became a sensible, and even imperative, organizational undertaking because it was broadly legitimated by the dominant model of a national society. The latter, in turn, was derived from and bolstered by the major transformations we shall discuss.

The European Model of a National Society

Of the many legitimating myths that arose and became institutionalized in Western Europe in the modern era, five are of primary importance for our understanding of the process by which mass schooling became a necessary part of the response to external challenges to state power. They include the legitimating myths of (1) the individual, (2) the nation as a society made up of individuals, (3) progress, (4) childhood socialization as the key to adult character, and (5) the state as guardian of the nation and guarantor of progress.

By the nineteenth century, the individual had clearly become the primary unit of action and the fundamental source of value in society, replacing the more corporate units (the family, clan, region, etc.) that had primordial importance in earlier times. Closely associated with the primacy of the individual was the institutionalized definition of the nation as an aggregate of individuals. The nation was not to be identified with the reigning household or the dominant families. Hence, national development presupposed individual development; national revitalization required individual revitalization. Moreover, national and individual development were defined as goals that could be realistically attained. Confidence in realizing a better future was at the heart of the reigning myth of progress (Nisbet 1980; Ferraroti 1985). This ideology led to a stronger emphasis on and preoccupation with the next generation—that is, with the children.

While national development was contingent on individual development, individual development itself hinged on childhood experience. This assumption presupposed continuity of personality throughout the life cycle ('the child is father to the man'), the malleability of the individual child, and the feasibility of explicit intervention in the development of the child. All of this has been referred to as the eighteenth-century discovery of socialization theory (Sommerville 1982).

This set of interrelated myths linked the development of children to the national interest: Good, loyal, and productive children would become good, loyal, and productive adults who in the aggregate would produce a better, stronger, and more developed national society. It was therefore important that children be systematically exposed to the appropriate socializing influences so that they would develop appropriate values.

The undertaking of this mandate has been discussed as a process of maintaining the social order (Dreeben 1969); thus, mass schooling was presumed to be charged with much the same mandate given to initiation ceremonies in stateless societies (Van Gennep 1960). But the myth of progress altered the mandate significantly: The emerging systems of mass schooling were expected not only to preserve the social order but also to *create the new national society*, that is, to make progress possible. The latter was expected to be accomplished via the production of the new man. Unlike initiation ceremonies, which enjoy only a generically conservative charter, the emerging systems of mass schooling were designed to achieve unity *and progress*.[5]

What agency was to assume ultimate responsibility for the socialization of children? The welfare of children had previously fallen under the authority of the family and, in some circumstances (e.g., extreme poverty or abandonment), the established churches. But once the welfare of children was linked to the national interest, the pertinent question became, What agency or organization most legitimately exercised original jurisdiction over the national domain? (See Swanson 1971.) The European model of a national society clearly allocated this jurisdiction to the state. The national interest was increasingly identified with the interests of the nation-state; in fact, the latter was expected to give substance and direction to this interest (Grew 1984). Since the national welfare was believed to be influenced by the character instilled in the nation's children, the state was impelled to play a role in the socialization of children.

The creation and intensification of the links between states and schools made sense after these myths were institutionalized in European society. These myths explain, in turn, why a range of military, political, and economic setbacks came to be classified as crises requiring national revitalization or as opportunities for upwardly mobile nation building. Given the progressive orientation to the future, national revitalization frequently centered on the establishment of a more effective school system. Given the allocation of responsibility for the nation to the state, the union of state and schools loomed large in the national revitalization movement. Thus, a state system of mass schooling became the favored strategy in the process of nation building and citizenship development (Marshall 1948; Bendix 1964, 1978) and in the homogenization of the masses (Collins 1977, 1979).[6]

Postulating the European model of a national society facilitates our understanding of the strong insistence on state control over education in this period. The nineteenth century has been depicted as both the "century of the child" (Sommerville 1982; Hughes and Klemm 1907) and the "age of nationalism" (Kohn 1962). These two seemingly unrelated depictions are in fact complementary. The words of La Chalotais, a French Republican spokesman, in 1763 capture the essence of the matter: "I claim the right to demand for the Nation an education that will depend upon the State alone; because it belongs essentially to it; because every nation has an inalienable and imprescriptible right to instruct its members; and finally, because the children of the State should be educated by the members of the State" (quoted in Bendix 1964, p. 110).

This sentiment became quite common in the nineteenth century as clerical control over education was effectively challenged throughout most of Europe. Mass schooling became national schooling, and state authority over national education became the rule. In our time, the postulation of a similar model now writ worldwide helps us understand why differences in sixth-grade scores on standard-ized math or science tests lead to the formation of national educational commissions and the sober rhetoric of "a nation at risk" (National Commission on Excellence in Education 1983).

Social Transformations and Development of the European Model

Institutionalized definitions of reality are grounded in the common experiences of a people (Berger and Luckman 1966). The European model of a national society reflected and codified the experiences associated with the three major transformations of culture, polity, and economy. These transformations are complex and interrelated, and we cannot escape some degree of arbitrariness in our attempt to sort out the effects of each transformation from those of the others in the exposition that follows.

The Reformation and Counter-Reformation

The contribution of the Reformation and Counter-Reformation to the union of states and schools was threefold. First, the survival of the reform movements marked the beginning of the decline of the Catholic Church's cultural hegemony in Europe. Secular powers no longer felt compelled to seek the legitimacy bestowed by the blessing of the Church. The religious movements also desacralized one another ('the whore of Rome,' 'the Protestant heathen'), thereby weakening the monopoly of all religious organizations over legitimation symbols and eventually enabling the secular powers to bypass religious authority entirely in proclaiming their legitimacy. The Reformation and Counter-Reformation thus increased the authority of national states over their populations and legitimated the authority of the interstate system (and its subunit states) over European society as a whole, creating a secular substitute for the overarching Church. The religious conflicts thus gave rise to political developments that ultimately generated the institutionalized myth of the state as the guardian of the nation.

The second important ramification of the religious movements was ontological. The Protestant em-phasis on a personal relationship with God as the only means to salvation strengthened the primordial status and authority of the individual. Though individualism had earlier roots in medieval Europe (Morris 1972), the focus on the individual became much more accentuated after the Reformation (Weber 1958). The concern with education as an implication of this emphasis is easy to trace: Personal salvation required familiarity with the word of God; thus, to become a true Christian, literacy was essential (cf. Bagley 1937). The reformers expended much energy translating the Bible into vernacular languages to enhance its accessibility to all individuals (Bainton 1956), and their publication of huge numbers of pamphlets and catechetical tracts suddenly provided reading material on a broad basis, greatly stimulating literacy (Cipolla 1969).

The third outcome of the religious movements was the rapid rise of concern for childhood social-ization, leading to the production of child-rearing manuals and sermons on children (Jolibert 1981). Stereotypes about Puritans notwithstanding, this early work on children was clearly progress-oriented; the earlier views of childhood, which ranged from an immodest indifference to a preoccupation with childhood innocence as a limited and fragile good that needed to be shielded from worldly assault, were replaced by the more optimistic view that children had an innate capacity for goodness that could be expanded through appropriate nurturance.

The Catholic counterattack largely embraced the individualistic and socialization ideologies implicit in the Protestant perspective (Sommerville 1982; Aries 1962). Spearheading the Counter-Reformation, the Society of Jesus, in its founding charter (1540), committed itself to work for the education of children. Moreover, Jesuit pedagogy involved an unprecedented degree of emphasis on individual learning and character formation (Durkheim 1937; Jolibert 1981). The internal states of individual children, not merely their external observance of rule and ritual, preoccupied the Jesuits and other "children-oriented" religious orders, such as the Order of Notre Dame (1628) and the Brothers of the Christian Schools (1684).

To summarize, the experiences of the reform and counter-reform movements generated myths that legitimated the primacy of individuals, the significance of childhood and childhood socialization, and the expanded authority of the state. The overarching authority of the Church was sharply diminished; it was replaced by the legitimacy and authority of more delimited social entities, in particular, the individual and the emerging national state. Both the individual and the national state were "empowered to act" in a more complete way than before, and the mobilization of individuals under state aegis became a legitimate means of pursuing the myth of progress.

The Rise of National States and the Interstate System

Much recent scholarship on the origins and development of national states in Western Europe (e.g., Lubasz 1964; Anderson 1974; Tilly 1975) has broadened our understanding of the obstacles to state building. It is evident that the major stumbling block in early state-building efforts was the pervasive authority and influence of the Church (Tierney 1964). For a millennium after the collapse of Rome, the Church was the dominant organization in Europe (Strayer 1970), and the Church both generated and monopolized the cultural symbols of legitimation that loosely integrated the European civilizational network. Within this frame, attempts by secular powers to carve for themselves spheres of original jurisdiction were inevitably thwarted. The religious wars of the fifteenth and sixteenth centuries helped the states greatly by weakening Church authority and diminishing Church resources.

The emerging state structures did not merely react against the authority of the Church. State organization was strongly aided by the Church's example of both administrative structure and claims to original sovereignty (Meyer 1980). Absolutist monarchical authority claims were secular copies of earlier Church authority (e.g., the doctrine of divine right). In the nineteenth century, states altered these authority claims by justifying them on behalf of "the nation" (Bendix 1978; Dyson 1980) and by tempering them with considerations of the rights of individuals—a legacy of the Reformation and the Enlightenment. The nineteenth-century national states were thus creatures molded both by the historical experience of Church authority and by the Reformation and Counter-Reformation.

The national states were also strongly influenced by the emerging political character of Europe, that is, by the crystallization of a European interstate system in the absence of a European political center. The religious wars led to a decline in the authority of the Church and to the erosion of the power of the Hapsburg dynasty, but the dominant European powers of the seventeenth and eighteenth centuries failed to create a political center around which Europe could be integrated. Europe was left without its prior basis for loose integration, i.e., Latin Christendom, and without a secular replacement.

However, Europe did not degenerate into an anarchic environment within which states preyed on one another in a totally unrestricted way. Instead, a new form of political structure arose: the interstate system, a set of actors and institutional rules, agreements, and conventions that validated the original sovereignty and organizational structure of the emerging national states (Ruggie 1983) and acted as a powerful constraint on the behavior of states (cf. Krasner 1983; Thomas and Meyer 1986). The interstate system evolved from a loose collection of centralizing monarchies that espoused divine-right ideologies to a highly interdependent set of national states that invoked "the nation" as the overriding justification for state action. It provided each state with a recipe for state building and its leaders with a more or less common vocabulary for articulating the national interest. As a result, state purposes and structures became strikingly uniform from the nineteenth century onwards (Boli-Bennett 1979; Grew 1984). Transforming the masses into national citizens became a standardized feature of the state-orchestrated nation-building process; utilizing state-sponsored mass schooling to achieve this political end became a routinely accepted modus operandi (Ramirez and Boli 1982).

The Rise of the Exchange Economy

In conjunction with these religious and political transformations, Europe underwent massive change in the social organization of its productive activities in the long sixteenth century. This change has been analyzed as the demise of social economy and the rise of market society (Polanyi 1944) and more recently as the emergence of the European capitalist economy (Wallerstein 1974). The new economy of exchange greatly increased the fiscal powers of the state through the taxation of commercial transactions (Lubasz 1964). It also led to legal and institutional changes—the development of contract law, the expansion of private property relations, the creation of a labor market that separated peasants from the constraints and protections of traditional serfdom and leaseholding arrangements, etc.—that were facilitated by, and in turn accelerated, the processes of individuation associated with the religious movements discussed earlier. Increasingly, the economic organization of Europe invested individuals with both the authority to conduct their own productive activities and the responsibility to support the state financially. Given the competitiveness of an economically integrating Europe, the productivity and loyalty of individuals became a central concern of state authorities.

In a related development, the entry of the educated bourgeois classes into state bureaucracies as professional administrators (Fischer and Lundgreen 1975; Rosenberg 1958) led to an increase in the social value of secular education. With the embourgeoisement of much of European society during the nineteenth century (Ellul 1967), the significance of schooling as a general means of occupational success and social mobility became broadly institutionalized.[7] In this way, there arose an economic and social ideology that supported universal education and that complemented the political ideology of state-directed schooling for purposes of national progress. Though this "human capital" theory of progress, which facilitated linkages between the state and school, originated among the bourgeoisie, the bourgeois classes fought against the expansion of schooling in the late nineteenth century (Archer 1979; Moraze 1957). However, the economic success of the bourgeoisie so greatly aided the organizational and extractive powers of the state that it was unable to contain the drive toward universal public education. The expanded state educational system was thus as much an unintended consequence of the success of the bourgeoisie as the initial ties between state and school were unplanned effects of the triumph of the Reformation.

The Political Construction of Mass Education: Worldwide Institutionalization

The world in the twentieth century remains economically integrated but politically decentralized. But as we have noted, the absence of a world state cannot be equated with the absence of worldwide understandings and conventions that legitimate some forms of social development and undermine others. A striking feature of the world in the last century has been the dramatic rise in the authority and power of the national state and the sharp increase in the civil, political, and social rights of individuals (Boli-Bennett 1981). The national state and the individual are strongly institutionalized entities within world culture, linked to one another through the institution of citizenship. The latter, in turn, presupposes an institutionalized and expanded state educational system.

Hence, the European model of a national society has evolved into a world model that strongly influences the behavior of states and societies. The extension of the world institutional framework to all territories and peoples has been achieved, standardizing the basic parameters of social ontology, purpose, and value throughout the world. Though cultural differences among national societies persist, it is increasingly taken for granted that all peoples must be organized into national units, that states must control those units, that economic development and social justice are attainable goals reflecting the highest purposes of humanity, that the state must play a central role in society if those purposes are to be realized, and that an expanded, state educational system is essential to individual and national progress. Therefore, it has become increasingly unthinkable for nation-state subunits of the world system to organize themselves in any way inconsistent with the world model.

Postulating this world model of a national society facilitates our understanding of the following research findings:

1. More recently independent states create educational ministries (Adams and Farrell 1967) and compulsory education laws (Ramirez and Boli 1982) more rapidly, symbolizing a more rapid union of states and schools.[8]

2. States are devoting an increasing proportion of funds to education and are taking a greater role in financing mass education (Inkeles and Sirowy 1983) and in regulating school admission policies, curricula, and examination structures (Ramirez and Rubinson 1979).[9]

3. Primary school enrollments in virtually all countries have rapidly expanded since the end of World War II, regardless of economic resources or political structure (Meyer et al. 1977), and this expansion has occurred faster in public schools than in private schools (World Bank 1980).

4. National and individual development have emerged as the most legitimate objectives of mass schooling (Fiala and Gordon 1986), replacing such objectives as the preservation of status distinctions, the maintenance of indigenous cultural values, and the protection of regional or subgroup interests—the types of objectives that motivated social development in earlier models of society. The emphasis on national development is clearly reflected in educational policy statements (Inkeles and Sirowy 1983), and the primacy of the individual, as distinguished from both class- and sex-related distinctions, is indicated by the nearly universal adoption of the comprehensive school and the tremendous increase in the female share of primary education (Craig 1981).

5. The quantity and quality of school-based socialization of the individual has increased. This is indicated by a great increase in the mean length of compulsory schooling during this century (Williamson and Fleming 1977) and by a universal decrease in the student/teacher ratio, symbolizing the commitment to more individualized instruction (Inkeles and Sirowy 1983).

6. The use of educational reform as an important solution to challenges to national power and prestige in the interstate system has been further institutionalized. Note the wave of educational reform triggered in the U.S. by the Soviet launching of Sputnik and, more recently, the reform generated by the growing fear of "Japan, incorporated." Other developed countries, in response to military and industrial challenges, have also used educational reform as an element of national revitalization strategies. Less developed countries have been equally enthusiastic in embracing education as a key component of their nation-building movements (Coleman 1965), more as part of their effort to attain legitimacy in the larger system than as a way of challenging for a leading position.

This perspective also helps us understand why certain states—namely, nineteenth-century England and the twentieth century United States—did not assume complete control of mass education as a tool for political mobilization. As the dominant world powers, these countries have been freer to operate at variance with the established model of national mobilization, in the familiar process whereby only those at the top of a power structure can safely deviate from convention. We find, however, that when England lost its dominant position after World War I, it also began to conform much more fully to the state-directed model of educational development. We can expect much the same sort of

214 • Francisco O. Ramirez and John Boli

change in the United States in coming decades as its position as world leader comes more and more into question.

In less powerful countries, national commitments to mass schooling are more certainly imposed by the world model; indeed, such commitments are supported directly by transnational organizations such as the United Nations and the World Bank. No matter how impoverished or fragmented, every candidate national society must present itself to the world as one committed to establishing a system of mass schooling. It must provide formal access to mass schooling for all its citizens, and schooling must be rationalized around national development and individual growth goals. The production of the ideal citizen/worker is expected to have high priority on the national agenda, and the national state is held primarily responsible for this process of refining and channeling human capital.

The European model of a national society has become so deeply institutionalized as a world model that crises of the sort that occurred in the nineteenth century are no longer necessary to generate the union of states and schools. Instead, the state-formation process itself is now a sufficient condition to induce the newly independent state to devote a large proportion of its effort to constructing a secular, compulsory mass educational system. As the world model changes, we can expect to find changes in states' involvement in education as well, but in the foreseeable future, it is hard to imagine conditions (other than large-scale catastrophe) under which the insistence on state-sponsored socialization for purposes of individual and national development would be seriously weakened.

Notes

1. To some extent, more general arguments originally formulated to explain the expansion of educational systems can also be applied to the problem of state control of education: modes and levels of industrial and urban development (Katz 1968), types and degrees of class or status-group conflict (Collins 1979; Bowles and Gintis 1976), kinds of political regimes (Bendix 1964), etc.
2. We are indebted to the anonymous reviewer who suggested that we explicitly acknowledge that the state interest in mass education was stimulated not by the inherently efficacious character of mass education but by its putative institutional character.
3. Our neglect of the U.S. is motivated by two factors:
   (1) the U.S. was not well integrated into the interstate system until very late, so that our arguments about the system's importance in stimulating state-sponsored education do not apply to the U.S. in the nineteenth century;
   (2) for a variety of reasons, the central state has played a relatively weak role in education in the U.S. A different explanation must be invoked to account for the nature of the educational system here (see the very general argument developed in Boli, Ramirez, and Meyer [1985]). However, in the postwar period, our argument applies rather well even to the U.S. See footnote 6.
4. We use the terms *institutionalized definitions of reality* and *institutionalized legitimating myths* interchangeably throughout this paper, though we recognize the distinction between the cognitive and normative dimensions of the legitimation process. For an extended explication of a conceptualization of legitimation that emphasizes the extent to which both knowledge and values are socially constructed, see Berger and Luckmann (1966, pp. 92–128).
5. Both social order and cultural reproduction theories assume that mass schooling plays only a generically conservative role in society (e.g., Dreeben 1969; Bourdieu and Passeron 1970). The functionalist orientation of social order theories is well known, but Archer (in press) has convincingly argued that the same analytical orientation characterizes cultural reproduction theories. In social order theories, mass schooling "functions" to maintain social order; in cultural reproduction theories, it maintains elite rule or class dominance. Elsewhere, we have assessed the theoretical shortcomings and evidentiary problems associated with both mainstream and critical functionalist explanations of the rise of mass education (Boli et al. 1985). Suffice it to reiterate that historically, social order and class dominance have been maintained through all sorts of exclusionary and repressive mechanisms that appear to differ from the distinctively universalistic, politically incorporative, and progress-oriented mandate of mass schooling.
6. In the U.S., mass education has historically been more closely linked to the ideology of national character than to the organization of the state (Tyack 1966). Mass education is more a consequence of populist movements (Meyer et al. 1979) and status competition among ethnic groups (Collins 1979) than an outcome of state directives (see also Richardson 1986). The peculiarly decentralized character of the American state has recently been the object of much analysis (Skocpol 1980; for a discussion that specifically deals with the loose ties between state and class and the consequences for education, see Rubinson [1986]). Note, however, that a stronger state role in education was initiated after the Civil War as an attempt to integrate the South into the national polity (Bullock 1970). Expansion of state activity in education has proceeded in recent decades as well. Ideologically, the state education system in the U.S. has developed in the same direction as that in other countries, but organizationally, the level of "coupling" continues to be relatively loose.
7. We believe that status conflict theories (e.g., Collins 1979) correctly describe how varying groups attempt to use the educational system to promote their values, to advance their members, and either to retain their position of dominance or to

challenge the dominant elite. However, this perspective does not explain how mass schooling became institutionalized in the first place; it assumes that the educational realm is an important arena for group competition and social control processes without clarifying the political construction of the educational realm, that is, the agreed-upon meaning and value of mass schooling. This paper focuses on the institutionalization of mass schooling by examining the legitimating myths that facilitated its development and by considering the large-scale transformations that generated these legitimating myths. In doing so, we clarify the conditions under which the educational realm becomes the realm for competitive processes, though we emphasize competition between nation-states instead of within nation-states, since most of the literature is restricted to the latter.

8. The date of independence measure is taken from Banks (1975); the dates of compulsory education laws are found in the *World Survey of Education Handbooks* (UNESCO 1955, 71) and in Flora (1983).

9. State control over mass schooling was measured via a content analysis of detailed descriptions of educational systems reported in the *World Survey of Education Handbooks*. Seven variables capturing the degree to which the state monopolized control were coded. Over one hundred countries were classified according to this index of state control over mass schooling.

References

Adams, Don, and Joseph P. Farrell. 1967. *Education and Social Development*. Syracuse: Center for Development Education, Syracuse University.

Alexander, Thomas. 1918. *The Prussian Elementary Schools*. New York: Macmillan.

Altbach, Philip, Robert Arnove, and Gail Kelley. 1982. *Comparative Education*. New York: Macmillan.

Anderson, Eugene N. 1970. "The Prussian Volksschule in the Nineteenth Century." Pp. 261–79 in *Entstehung und Wandel der Modernen Gesellschaff*, edited by Gerhard A. Ritter. Berlin: de Gruyter.

Anderson, Perry. 1974. *Lineages of the Absolutist State*. London: New Left Books.

Archer, Margaret S. 1979. *Social Origins of Educational Systems*. Beverly Hills: Sage.

———. In press. "The Neglect of the Educational System by Bernstein and Bourdieu." *European Journal of Sociology*.

Aries, Philippe. 1962. *Centuries of Childhood*. New York: Vintage.

Bagley, William C. 1937. *A Century of the Universal School*. New York: Macmillan.

Bainton, Roland H. 1956. *The Reformation of the Sixteenth Century*. Boston: Beacon.

Banks, Arthur S. 1975. *Cross-National Time Series Data Archive*. Binghamton: Center for Comparative Political Research, SUNY-Binghamton.

Bendix, Reinhard. 1964. *Nation Building and Citizenship*. New York: Wiley.

———. 1978. *Kings or People: Power and the Mandate to Rule*. Berkeley: University of California Press.

Berger, Peter, Brigitte Berger, and Hansfried Kellner. 1973. *The Homeless Mind*. New York: Random House.

Berger, Peter, and Thomas Luckman. 1966. *The Social Construction of Reality*. Garden City, NY: Doubleday.

Boje, Andreas, Ernest Borup, and Holger Rützebeck. 1932. *Education in Denmark*. London: Oxford University Press.

Boli, John, Francisco O. Ramirez, and John W. Meyer. 1985. "Explaining the Origins and Expansion of Mass Education." *Comparative Education Review* 29:145–70.

Boli-Bennett, John. 1979. "The Ideology of Expanding State Authority in National Constitutions, 1870–1970." Pp. 222–37 in *National Development and the World System*, edited by John W. Meyer and Michael T. Hannan. Chicago: University of Chicago Press.

———. 1981. "Human Rights or State Expansion? Cross-national Definitions of Constitutional Rights, 1870–1970." Pp. 173–93 in *Global Human Rights: Public Policies, Comparative Measures, and NGO Strategies*, edited by Ved Nanda, James Scarritt, and George Shepard. Boulder. Westview.

Bourdieu, Pierre, and J. C. Passeron. 1970. *La Reproduction*. Paris: Editions de Minuit.

Bowles, Samuel, and Herbert Gintis. 1976. *Schooling in Capitalist America*. New York: Basic Books.

Boyd, William, and Edmund J. King. 1975. *The History of Western Education*. 11th ed. London: Adam and Charles Black.

Bullock, Henry Allen. 1970. *A History of Negro Education in the South*. New York Praeger.

Carlsson, Sten, and Jerker Rosén. 1961. *Svensk Historia, Vol. 2: Tiden Efter 1718*. Stockholm: Svenska Bokförlaget.

Cipolla, Carlo M. 1969. *Literacy and Development in the West*. Harmondsworth: Penguin.

———. 1974. "Introduction." Pp. 7–13 in *Fontana Economic History of Europe, Vol. 4: The Sixteenth and Seventeeth Centuries*. Glasgow: Collins.

Cohen, Yehudi. 1970. "Schools and Civilizational Systems." Pp. 55–147 in *The Social Sciences and the Comparative Study of Educational Systems*, edited by Joseph Fischer. Scranton, PA: International Textbook.

———. 1979. "The State System, Schooling, and Cognitive and Motivational Patterns." Pp. 103–40 in *Social Forces and Schooling*, edited by Nobuo Shimahara and Adam Scrupski. New York: McKay.

Coleman, James S. 1965. *Education and Political Development*. Princeton: Princeton University Press.

Collins, Randall. 1977. "Some Comparative Principles of Educational Stratification." *Harvard Educational* Review 47:1–27.

———. 1979. *The Credential Society: A Historical Sociology of Education and Stratification*. New York: Academic Press.

Craig, John. 1981. "The Expansion of Education." *Review of Research in Education* 9:151–210.

Craig, John, and Norman Spear. 1983. "Explaining Educational Expansion: An Agenda for Historical Research." Pp. 133–60 in *The Sociology of Educational Expansion: Take-Off, Growth, and Inflation in Educational Systems*, edited by Margaret S. Archer. Beverly Hills: Sage.

Cubberley, Ellwood P. 1920. *Readings in the History of Education*. Boston: Houghton Mifflin.

DiMaggio, Paul J., and Walter W. Powell. 1983. "The Iron Cage Revisited: Institutional Isomorphism and Collective Rationality in Organizational Fields." *American Sociological Review* 48:147–60.

Dore, Ronald. 1964. *Education in Tokugawa Japan*. Berkeley: University of California Press.
Dreeben, Robert. 1969. *On What is Learned in School*. Reading, MA: Addison-Wesley.
Durkheim, Emile. 1937. *L'Evolution pédagogique en France*. 2 vols. Paris: Felix Alcan.
Dyson, K. 1980. *The State Tradition in Western Europe*. New York: Oxford University Press.
Eckstein, Max, and Hans Noah. 1969. *Scientific Investigations in Comparative Education*. New York: Macmillan.
Ellul, Jacques. 1967. *Metamorphose du bourgeois*. Paris: Calmann-Levy.
Ferraroti, Franco. 1985. *The Myth of Inevitable Progress*. Westport, CT: Greenwood.
Fiala, Robert, and Audri Gordon. 1986. "Educational Ideology and the World Educational Revolution, 1950–1970." Unpublished paper, Department of Sociology, University of New Mexico.
Fischer, Wolfram, and Peter Lundgreen. 1975. "The Recruitment and Training of Administrative and Technical Personnel." Pp. 456–561 in *The Formation of National States in Western Europe*, edited by Charles Tilly. Princeton: Princeton University Press.
Flora, Peter. 1983. *State, Economy, and Society in Western Europe, 1815–1975*. 2 vols. Frankfurt: Campus Verlag.
Freeman, John, Glenn R. Carroll, and Michael T. Hannan. 1983. "The Liability of Newness: Age Dependency in Organizational Death Rates." *American Sociological Review* 48:692–710.
Furet, François, and Jacques Ozouf. 1977. *Lire et ecrire: L'Alphabetisation des Français de Calvin a Jules Ferry*. Paris: Editions de Minuit.
Gontard, Maurice. 1976. *Les Ecoles primaires de la France bourgeoise (1833–1875)*. 2d ed. Toulouse: Institut National de Recherche et de Documentation Pedagogiques.
Grew, Raymond. 1984. "The Nineteenth Century European State." Pp. 83–120 in *Statemaking and Social Movements: Essays in History and Theory*, edited by Charles Bright and Susan Harding. Ann Arbor: University of Michigan Press.
Hughes, James, and L.R. Klemm. 1907. *Progress of Education in the Century*. Toronto: Linscott.
Inkeles, Alex, and Larry Sirowy. 1983. "Convergent and Divergent Trends in National Educational Systems." *Social Forces* 62:303–34.
Jansson, Göte. 1948. *Tegner och Politiken* Uppsala: Almquist and Wiksells.
Jolibert, Bernard. 1981. *L'Enfance au XVIIe siecle*. Paris: Librairie Philosophique J. Vrin.
Jones, Donald K. 1977. *The Making of the Education System, 1851–81*. London: Routledge and Kegan Paul.
Katz, Michael B. 1968. *The Irony of Early School Reform: Educational Innovation in Mid-Nineteenth Century Massachusetts*. Cambridge, MA: Harvard University Press.
Kazamias, Andreas M., ed. 1977. "The State of the Art" (Special issue). *Comparative Education Review* 21 (2, 3).
Kohn, Hans. 1962. *The Age of Nationalism*. New York: Harper and Row.
Krasner, Steven D. 1983. *International Regimes*. Ithaca: Cornell University Press.
Lubasz, Heinz. 1964. *The Development of the Modern State*. New York: Macmillan.
Lynch, James. 1974. "Myth and Reality in the History of French Education." Pp. 1–19 in *The History of Education in Europe*, edited by T.G. Cook. London: Methuen.
Marriott, J.A.R., and G. Grant Robertson. 1915. *The Evolution of Prussia*. London: Oxford University Press.
Marshall, T.H. 1948. *Citizenship and Social Class*. New York: Doubleday.
Meyer, John W. 1980. "The World Polity and the Authority of the Nation-State." Pp. 109–37 in *Studies of the Modern World-System*, edited by Albert J. Bergesen. New York: Academic Press.
Meyer, John W., Francisco O. Ramirez, Richard Rubinson, and John Boli-Bennett. 1977. "The World Educational Revolution, 1950–1970." *Sociology of Education* 50:242–58.
Meyer, John W., and Brian Rowan. 1977. "Institutionalized Organization: Formal Structure as Myth and Ritual." *American Journal of Sociology* 83:340–63.
Meyer, John W., David Tyack, Joane P. Nagel, and Audri Gordon. 1979. "Public Education as Nation-Building in America." *American Journal of Sociology* 85:978–86.
Moore, Barrington. 1966. *Social Origins of Dictatorship and Democracy: Lord and Peasant in the Making of the Modern World*. Boston: Beacon.
Moraze, Charles. 1957. *Les Bourgeois Conquerants, XIXe siecle*. Paris: Armand Colin.
Morris, Colin. 1972. *The Discovery of the Individual, 1050–1200*. London: SPCK.
National Commission on Excellence in Education. 1983. *A Nation at Risk*. Washington, DC: National Commission on Excellence in Education.
Nisbet, Robert. 1980. *History of the Idea of Progress*. New York: Basic Books.
Papanek, Ernst. 1962. *The Austrian School Reform*. Westport, CT: Greenwood.
Polanyi, Karl. 1944. *The Great Transformation*. Boston: Beacon.
Ramirez, Francisco O., and John Boli. 1982. "Global Patterns of Educational Institutionalization." Pp. 15–38 in *Comparative Education*, edited by Philip Altbach, Robert Arnove, and Gail Kelley. New York: Macmillan.
Ramirez, Francisco O., and Richard Rubinson. 1979. "Creating Members: The Political Incorporation and Expansion of Public Education." Pp. 72–84 in *National Development and the World System*, edited by John W. Meyer and Michael T. Hannan. Chicago: University of Chicago Press.
Reisner, Edward. 1922. *Nationalism and Education Since 1789*. New York: Macmillan.
Richardson, John. 1986. "Historical Sequences and the Origins of Common Schooling in the American States." Pp. 35–63 in *Handbook of Theory and Research for the Sociology of Education*, edited by John Richardson. New York: Greenwood.
Ringer, Fritz K. 1977. *Education and Society in Modern Europe*. Bloomington: Indiana University Press.
Rokkan, Stein. 1980. "Territories, Centres, and Peripheries: Toward a Geoethnic-Geoeconomic-Geopolitical Model of Differentiation Within Western Europe." Pp. 163–204 in *Center and Periphery: Spatial Variation in Politics*, edited by J. Gothmann. Beverly Hills: Sage.

Rosenberg, Hans. 1958. *Bureaucracy, Aristocracy, and Autocracy: The Prussian Experience, 1660–1815*. Boston: Beacon.

Rowlinson, William. 1974. "German Education in a European Context." Pp. 21–35 in *The History of Education in Europe*, edited by T.G. Cook. London: Methuen.

Royal Society of Arts. 1867. *Reports of Artisans Selected by a Committee Appointed by the Council of the Society of Arts to Visit the Paris Universal Exhibition, 1867*. London: Bell and Daldy.

Rubinson, Richard. 1986 "Class Formation and Schooling in the United States." *American Journal of Sociology*, forthcoming.

Ruggie, John G. 1983. "Continuity and Transformation in the World Polity: Toward a Neorealist Synthesis." *World Politics* 36:261–85.

Skocpol, Theda. 1980. "Political Response to Capitalist Crisis: Neo-Marxist Theories of the State and the Case of the New Deal." *Politics and Society* 10:155–201.

Sommerville, John. 1982. *The Rise and Fall of Childhood*. Beverly Hills: Sage.

Stomberg, Andrew W. 1931. *A History of Sweden*. New York: Macmillan.

Strayer, Joseph. 1970. *On the Medieval Origins of the Modern State*. Princeton: Princeton University Press.

Swanson, Guy. 1971. "An Organizational Analysis of Collectivities." *American Sociological Review* 36:607–23.

Tannenbaum, Edward R. 1974. "Education." Pp. 231–53 in *Modern Italy: A Topical History Since 1861*, edited by Edward R. Tannenbaum and Emiliana P. Noether. New York: New York University Press.

Temin, Peter. 1966. "The Relative Decline of the Steel Industry, 1880–1913." Pp. 140–55 in *Industrialization in Two Systems: Essays in Honor of Alexander Gerschenkron*, edited by H. Rosovsky. New York: Wiley.

Thomas, George M., and John W. Meyer. 1986. "The Expansion of the State." *Annual Review of Sociology* 10, in press.

Thut, I.N., and Don Adams. 1964. *Educational Patterns in Contemporary Societies*. New York: McGraw-Hill.

Tierney, Brian. 1964. *The Crisis of Church and State, 1050–1300*. Englewood Cliffs: Prentice-Hall.

Tilly, Charles. 1975. *The Formation of National States in Western Europe*. Princeton: Princeton University Press.

Tyack, David. 1966. "Forming the National Character." *Harvard Educational Review* 36:29–41.

UNESCO. 1955–71. *World Survey of Education Handbook*. 5 vols. Geneva: United Nations.

Van Gennep, Arnold. 1960. *The Rites of Passage*. Chicago: University of Chicago Press.

Vibaek, Jens. 1964. *Danmarks Historie, Volume 10: Reform og Fallit, 1784–1830*. Copenhagen: Politikens Forlag.

Wallerstein, Immanuel. 1974. *The Modern World System*. Vol. 1. New York: Academic Press.

Warne, Albin. 1929. *Till Folkskolans Förhistoria i Sverige*. Stockholm: Svenska Kyrkans Diakonistyrelsens Bokförlag.

Weber, Max. 1958. *The Protestant Ethic and the Spirit of Capitalism*. Translated by Talcott Parsons. New York: Scribner's.

Williamson, J.B., and J.J. Fleming. 1977. "Convergence Theory and the Social Welfare Sector: A Cross-National Analysis." *International Journal of Comparative Sociology* 18:242–53.

Woolf, Stuart. 1979. *A History of Italy, 1700–1860: The Social Constraints of Political Change*. London: Methuen.

World Bank. 1980. *Education: Sector Policy Paper*. Washington, DC: International Bank for Reconstruction and Development.

13
Marketization and Privatization in Mass Education Systems

GEOFF WHITTY AND SALLY POWER

In many parts of the world, there have been attempts to move away from the "one best system" of state funded and state provided education. Recent reforms have sought to dismantle centralized bureaucracies and create in their place devolved systems of schooling with increased emphasis on parental choice and competition between increasingly diversified types of schools. These reforms are often seen to be leading to an increasing "marketization" and "privatization" of education. The first part of this paper seeks to locate these changes in broader developments in welfare policy and considers whether marketization and privatization are part of the same policy constellation or represent distinctive tendencies. Sections 2 and 3 look at the form and effects of these reforms within three countries—England and Wales, New Zealand and the USA. In the light of these effects, the final part of the paper considers whether and how we might move beyond marketization and privatization to revitalize mass education systems.

1. Marketization and Privatization of Welfare

Although the terms marketization and privatization are frequently used, sometimes interchangeably, to describe recent changes in welfare provision, they are often only loosely defined. In connection with privatization, for instance, Donnison (1984, p. 45) argues that "its meaning is at best uncertain and often tendentious." Indeed, he goes so far as to claim that it is little more than the invention of political journalists designed "not to clarify analysis but as a symbol ... to dramatise a conflict and mobilise support." However, while such terms are clearly politically embedded, exploration of their constituent elements and distinctive features provides a useful framework to analyze the scale and nature of welfare restructuring.

At its simplest level, the organization of welfare can be represented in terms of the relationship between sources of funding and provision (Figure 13.1). Klein (1984, p. 14) suggests that "the 'pure' model of comprehensive state welfare" has been located in Cell 1. This is especially true of most (though not all) mass education systems, where both funding and provision have traditionally been located firmly in the public sector.

However, this presents rather too static a picture to capture the complex processes involved in recent reforms in education and other aspects of welfare (Whitty, 1984). Analyses by Heald (1983) and Murphy et al. (1998) show that privatization is a multi-faceted set of processes rather than a straightforward movement out of Cell 1 into Cell 4. Their work suggests that it could thus entail one or more of the following shifts away from the "pure" welfare state model:

	FINANCE (FUNDING)		
PRODUCTION		**Public**	**Private**
(PROVISION)	Public	1	2
	Private	3	4

Figure 13.1 Modes of welfare provision and funding (after Klein, 1984).

- charging for public services previously paid for out of taxation (Klein's Cell 2)
- letting the private sector run a service that continues to be paid for out of taxation (Cell 3)
- selling public services and transferring their functions to the private sector (Cell 4)
- deregulating the private sector or liberalizing arrangements that previously prevented the private sector from competing with state-provided services (Cells 3/4 competing with Cells 1/2).

Similarly, for Le Grand and Robinson (1984, p. 6), privatization is broadly defined and may involve a decline in state provision, a reduction of state subsidies and more deregulation, as well as straightforward transfer of services from the public to the private sectors. It is possible to see examples of all these processes within recent education reforms. For example, Pring (1987) has suggested that, under the Thatcher government in Britain, there was an increase in the purchasing at public expense of educational services provided in private schools, contracting out of services (such as school meals and cleaning) to private providers, an increasing requirement upon parents in public schools to pay for services (such as music tuition in schools) that had hitherto sometimes been provided free at the point of consumption and the introduction of student loans into the higher education system. Pring argues that, when seen in conjunction with an ever-increasing impoverishing of the public sector, the latter is in danger of becoming merely residual provision for those who cannot afford to "go private."

Nevertheless, if we look strictly at the issue of funding, or even at provision in most countries, it is difficult to argue that education has been privatized on any significant scale. In many cases, marketization might be a better metaphor for what has been happening. In relation to welfare, marketization most often refers to the development of "quasi-markets" in state funded and/or state provided services. Most commentators see quasi-markets in education as involving a combination of parental choice and school autonomy, together with a greater or lesser degree of public accountability and government regulation. These kinds of reforms have been particularly evident in many mass education systems, including those discussed later in this paper, Levačić (1995) suggests that the distinguishing characteristics of a quasi-market for a public service are "the separation of purchaser from provider and an element of user choice between providers." She adds that a quasi-market usually remains highly regulated, with the government controlling "such matters as entry by new providers, investment, the quality of service (as with the national curriculum) and price, which is often zero to the user" (p. 167). The lack of a conventional cash nexus and the strength of government intervention distinguish quasi-markets from the idealized view of a "free" market, though few contemporary markets in any field are actually free from government regulation and many of them involve some element of overt or covert subsidy.

Burchardt et al. (1999) have recently sought to build some of these considerations into a more complicated map of welfare provision (which we have adapted in Figure 13.2). Based on a "wheel of welfare", it shows different combinations of public and private provision, public and private finance, and public and private decision-making. Onto this, they map various directions of movement out of the "all public" sector characterized by public provision, public finance, and public decision (similar to Klein's Cell 1). These movements include outright privatization, contracting out, the marketing of public services, the introduction of user charges and the use of vouchers. Oddly, in our view, they

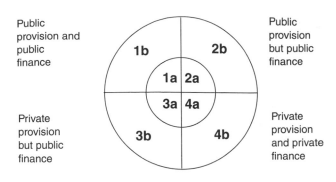

Public provision and public finance

1b

2b

Public provision but public finance

1a **2a**

3a **4a**

Private provision but public finance

3b

4b

Private provision and private finance

KEY:

Inner Circle — public decision
1a	eg 'pure public' services
2a	eg publicly provided services paid for by user charges
3a	eg contracted-out services purchased by the state
4a	eg contracted-out services paid for by consumer

Outer Circle — private decision
1b	eg publicly provided services bought with vouchers
2b	eg publicly provided services bought by individuals
3b	eg privately provided services bought with voucher, tax reliefs or grants
4b	eg 'free market' services

Figure 13.2 Classification of public and private welfare activity (after Burchardt et al., 1999).

include quasi-markets as well as the conventional welfare state in their "all public" segment, when the advantage of their model over Klein's is that it potentially allows one to distinguish between the two by including a segment that entails public funding and provision but private decision-making, as entailed in many examples of marketization.

Burchardt et al. (1999) also show that, in relation to educational expenditure in England, there was a reduction between 1979/80 and 1995/96 from 66% to 52% in the proportion of expenditure falling within the public provision/public finance/public decision-making sector. However, it seems likely that the bulk of the reduction (and certainly the doubling of free-market services from 8% to 18%) fell outside the compulsory phase of education. There was a small increase in contracted out services (from 23% to 25%), although, as Butcher (1995, p. 112) has pointed out, these probably involved "mainly technical and ancillary services." There would also appear to have been a significant increase in the purchase of privately provided services with state finance, but the amount involved is small (only from 3% to 5%). More significantly, there has been some movement within state education "out from the 'all public' sector into the privately-decided sector" (p. 27), yet Burchardt et al. (1999) themselves claim that "practical constraints" on parental decision-making outweigh their "theoretical freedom" and thus keep most education within the "all public" sector of their model (p. 11). Thus, although their analysis does show clearly that education remains firmly within the public sector in most respects, our own view is that they underestimate the extent to which educational decision-making has been "privatized" in the ideological sense.

In considering privatization and marketization in Australia, Marginson (1993) usefully warns us against seeing the two processes as inextricably linked. For example, it is possible to have privatization without marketization. Indeed, state subsidies to the private sector may actually protect it from market forces. On the other hand, marketization of the state sector may make resort to the private sector less attractive to some parents. However, although there may be tensions between privatization and marketization, they are more likely to complement rather than compete with each other. As Marginson (1993) himself points out, while "privatization does not in itself constitute market relations, it creates a potentially favourable environment for market activity" (p. 178).

Similarly, even where quasi-markets are confined to public sector providers, it is possible to argue that some aspects of marketization contribute to privatization in an ideological if not a strictly economic sense. These might include:

BISHOP BURTON COLLEGE
LIBRARY

- fostering the belief that the private sector approach is superior to that traditionally adopted in the public sector
- requiring public sector institutions to operate more like those in the private sector
- encouraging private (individual/family) decision-making in place of bureaucratic fiat.

The growing influence of private sector organizations as consultants in public provision can itself contribute to a change in the ethos of the sector, while Young (1986) even points to the greater involvement of the voluntary sector in publicly funded welfare provision as an aspect of privatization. The growth of quasi-autonomous institutions operating with devolved budgets and competing for clients in the market place, with or without significant private and voluntary sector involvement, certainly constitutes a change in the prevailing character of the welfare state in many countries.

Thus, even those reforms that merely foster competition between public sector providers may move provision away from the tradition welfare state model, while technically remaining within Klein's Cell 1 (Figure 13.1) and Burchardt et al.'s "public" domain (top left-hand quadrant in Figure 13.2). However, while they might strictly be regarded as elements of marketization, they could also be considered a prelude to privatization. Many critics of devices like devolved budgeting, internal markets, and cost-center accounting have seen them in these terms. "Half-way houses" between state and private sectors, such as self-governing state schools, have been seen as examples of what is sometimes termed "creeping privatization," as might a state sector education voucher scheme.

Even though it is clear that, notwithstanding the rhetoric of the advocates and critics of recent reforms, all mass education systems we know of still fall within Archer's (1984) definition of "state education systems," this does not mean that the growth of marketization, together with elements of privatization, has not had a significant impact on the nature of such systems. It is to this issue that we now turn, initially looking at recent policy changes in three countries and then exploring their effects.

2. Privatization and Marketization in Three Countries

This part of the paper will outline some of the policies of privatization and marketization that have developed in recent years in England and Wales, New Zealand, and the USA. It will look at policies that directly involve the private sector and those that seek to create quasi-markets in public education. We shall thus be concerned with measures that claim to enhance opportunities for choice among state schools[1] and those that use public funds to extend choice into the private sector. Often linked to such policies are moves to devolve various aspects of decision-making from regional and district offices to individual schools and permit those schools to market themselves in distinctive ways.

In England and Wales, prior to the 1980s, the vast majority of children were educated in state schools maintained by democratically elected local education authorities (LEAs) which exercised political and bureaucratic control over their schools but also often provided them with considerable professional support. There was, however, more diversity than is often acknowledged, especially through the inclusion of voluntary schools (mainly Anglican and Catholic) within the state sector. There was also a significant and influential private sector catering for about 7% of children of compulsory school age. Nevertheless, after the Conservative victory at the 1979 election, the Thatcher and Major governments set about trying to break what they saw as the LEA monopoly of public schooling through the provisions of a series of Education Acts passed in the 1980s and early 1990s.

Although the introduction of the National Curriculum and its associated system of testing can be seen as a centralizing control, most of the measures have been designed to enhance parental choice and transfer responsibilities from LEAs to individual schools. The earliest of these include the Assisted Places Scheme, part of the 1980 Education Act, which provided public funding to enable academically able children from poor homes to attend some of the country's elite private schools (see Edwards et al.,

1989; Fitz et al., 1989). Subsequently, the government sought to create new forms of state schools outside the influence of LEAs. City technology colleges (CTCs) were intended to be new secondary schools for the inner city, with a curriculum emphasis on science and technology and run by independent trusts with business sponsors (Walford and Miller, 1991; Whitty et al., 1993). The grant-maintained schools policy, which was included in the 1988 Education Reform Act, enabled existing state schools to "opt out" of their LEAs after a parental ballot and run themselves with direct funding from central government (Fitz et al., 1993). More recent legislation has permitted schools to change their character by varying their enrolment schemes, encouraged new types of specialist schools and made it possible for some private schools to "opt in" to the state system (Edwards and Whitty, 1997; Walford, 1995).

Local Management of Schools (LMS) has given those schools that have remained with their LEAs more control over their own budgets and day-to-day management, receiving funds determined by the number and ages of their students. Open enrolment allows state schools to attract as many students as possible, at least up to their physical capacity, instead of being kept to lower limits or strict catchment areas (or zones) in order that other schools could remain open. When introduced in 1988, this was seen as the necessary corollary of per capita funding in creating a quasi-market in education. In some respects, it was a "virtual voucher" system (Sexton, 1987), which was expected to make all schools more responsive to their clients and either become more effective or go to the wall.

The range of policies introduced in England and Wales thus included some "privatizing" measures, such as the Assisted Places Scheme, but the major changes are better regarded as examples of marketization. It is possible to argue that the sort of privatization entailed within the Assisted Places Scheme suppressed marketization within the private sector by protecting private schools from the full brunt of market forces. Indeed, some of the schools that sought to join the Scheme were considered economically vulnerable and one in Wales had to close before it could admit its first assisted place holders (Whitty et al., 1998). On the other hand, the marketization of the public sector through schemes such as LMS and open enrolment, by making the public sector more like the private, may have reduced the distinctive nature of private schools. Taken together, though, the reforms encourage a process of privatization in the ideological sense if not the strictly economic one.

Similar reforms in New Zealand were introduced by a Labour government, albeit one that had enthusiastically embraced monetarism and "new public management" techniques in the mid-1980s (Wylie, 1995). They were subsequently given a more explicitly marketizing thrust by the National Party government elected in 1990. The reforms led to a shift in the responsibility for budget allocation, staff employment, and educational outcomes from central government and regional educational boards to individual state schools. Schools were given boards of trustees that have effective control over their enrolment schemes, with even lighter regulation than in England. However, Wylie (1994) argues that some aspects of the New Zealand reforms "offer a model of school self-management which is more balanced than the English experience." This is because, at least initially, they put "a great emphasis on equity … on community involvement … on parental involvement [and on] partnership: between parents and professionals" (p. xv). Furthermore, neither the costs of teacher salaries nor of some central support services were devolved to individual school budgets, though there have subsequently been moves in this direction. Only 3% of New Zealand schools were in a pilot scheme for "bulk funding" (or devolution of 100% of their funding including teachers' salaries), but a "direct funding" option was opened up to all schools in 1996. Alongside these reforms, national curriculum guidelines were introduced but these were less detailed and prescriptive than the English model and paid more attention to minority ethnic interests. More recently, the extension of publicly-funded choice into the private sector has begun with the introduction of Targeted Individual Entitlements, the New Zealand equivalent of the Assisted Places Scheme, which has led to claims that "it marks the start of a move towards a voucher system in which schools compete for parents' education dollar" (Wellington Evening Post, 28/9/95).

In the USA, the limited role of the federal government in relation to education makes it harder to generalize about the nature and provenance of policies designed to enhance parental choice and devolve decision-making to individual public schools. The more significant decisions are taken at state and district levels. While a few states, such as Minnesota, have statewide choice plans, many initiatives have been more local. Wells (1993) demonstrates the huge variety in origins and likely effects of the various choice plans that have been mooted or implemented in the U.S. over the past few years. Similarly, American specialist or "focus" schools have very different origins and purposes (Raywid, 1994; Hill et al., 1990). They include long-standing specialty schools, such as the Boston Latin School and New York's highly academic Stuyvesant High School, magnet schools associated with desegregation plans, alternative schools, sometimes based on progressive pedagogic principles, and private Catholic schools. The nature of the quasi-autonomous charter schools that are currently being established in many states and the extent of site-based management within school districts also varies considerably (Wohlstetter et al., 1995).

Devolution and choice in the U.S. enlists significant support from progressive forces, particularly amongst those representing ethnic groups who have felt particularly shortchanged by public education (e.g. Wells et al., 1996). The mixed evidence about the efficacy and effects of desegregation and magnet schools in the 1980s (Blank, 1990; Moore and Davenport, 1990) has sometimes led to the conclusion that enhanced parental voice and choice, rather than more concerted political intervention, will provide the best chance of educational salvation for minority parents and their children. Moe (1994) goes so far as to claim that the best hope for the poor to gain the right "to leave bad schools and seek out good ones" is through an "unorthodox alliance" with "Republicans and business ... who are the only powerful groups willing to transform the system" (p. 33). For this reason, some aspects of the current reform agenda have developed a populist appeal well beyond the coteries of conservative politicians or even the white populations to which they are usually expected to appeal. This is true, for example, of the state-funded private school voucher scheme introduced for students from poor families in Milwaukee, Wisconsin (Witte et al., 1994).

The delegitimation of bureaucratic and political control in of education in the USA (Chubb and Moe, 1990) also points to the complex ways in which marketization and privatization may be connected. While the states and the districts have retained significant powers, the reforms have facilitated an increase in privately-managed schools. This fall, the Edison Project will have 48 schools in its scheme. Edison, a for-profit private company, contracts with districts to take over public schools and is anticipated to see a growth in revenue from the current $68 million to $126 million in 1999 (Henry, 1998). In addition, individual charter schools appear to be using their quasi-autonomous status to enhance their funding basis. Many ask parents to invest substantial amounts of time and money as a condition of their child's attendance (Diandra and Corwin, 1994).

Thus, while the reforms have different aspects in different countries, they all display common tendencies towards limited privatization alongside more extensive marketizing policies that promote institutional autonomy and devolve decision-making down to the institution and the individual, so that the boundary between what is public and what is private becomes less clear. The blurring of this boundary was supposed to revitalize mass education systems through making all schools more effective and more responsive. We now go on to consider the limited evidence that is available about the actual effects of recent policies in our three countries.

3. Initial Research Evidence

This part of the paper will review some of the evidence that is so far available concerning the progress and effects of these marketization and privatization policies in England and Wales, New Zealand and the USA. Advocates of these policies argue that they will lead to increased diversity of provision and more efficient and effective schools. Some proponents, notably Moe (1994) in the USA and Pollard (1995) in the UK, have argued that such reforms will bring particular benefits for families from disadvantaged communities, who have been ill-served by more conventional arrangements. However, critics suggest that, even if they enhance efficiency, responsiveness, choice and diversity (and even that, they say, is questionable), such policies will almost certainly increase inequality between schools.

In England and Wales, there seems to be little evidence that choice policies are fostering horizontal diversity in schooling. Glatter et al. (1997) found no evidence of greater diversity of provision, except where there was specific government funding for specialist schools, but rather a tendency towards greater uniformity. However, although some other commentators have suggested that the reforms might even strengthen hierarchies (Walford and Miller, 1991), Glatter and his colleagues found no significant movement in the traditional hierarchy of types of school had yet taken place.

With regard to claims that the reforms will lead to more effective use of resources, there is little to suggest that any gains have been substantial. In England, a national study conducted by Birmingham University and funded by National Association of Head Teachers was generally positive about the impact of LMS but conceded that direct evidence of the influence of self-management on learning was "elusive." The team's initial survey (Arnott et al., 1992) showed that the vast majority of head teachers agreed with the statement that "local management allows a school to make more effective use of its resources." However, a majority also felt that meetings were being taken up by administrative issues that lessened their attention to students' learning. They were thoroughly divided on the question of whether "children's learning is benefiting from local management." Thus, it was rather unclear to what their concept of greater effectiveness actually related.

The results cited here came mainly from head teacher respondents, whose authority has been greatly enhanced by the self-management reform. It may be significant that the relatively few classroom teachers who were interviewed by the Birmingham research team were far more cautious about the benefits of LMS for student learning and overall standards. An independently funded study (Levačić, 1995) found head teachers generally welcomed self-management even where their school had lost resources as a result of it, while classroom teachers were skeptical about its benefits even in schools which had gained in resources. Levačić concludes that, although local management enhances cost-efficiency, there is "a lack of strong theoretical argument and empirical evidence" to show that it improves the quality of teaching and learning, as claimed by the government (Levačić, 1995, p. xi).

In the final report of the Birmingham study (Bullock and Thomas, 1994), relatively more head teachers claimed improvements in student learning, but significantly these seem to be associated with increased funding rather than self-management per se. While the Birmingham team concluded that self-management was broadly a successful reform, they argued that more evidence was needed on the relationship between resourcing levels and learning outcomes. This seems particularly important in that the schools most affected by budgetary difficulties, and therefore least likely to report a positive impact on students' learning, were often found to be those with students from disadvantaged backgrounds.

The Birmingham study echoes some of the concerns expressed by Le Grand and Bartlett (1993) in their study of quasi-markets in social policy. Bartlett (1993) points out that, although parental choice has been increased by open enrolment, "the door is firmly closed once a school [is full]. And by encouraging an increasingly selective admissions policy in [over-subscribed] schools open enrolment may have the effect of bringing about increased opportunities for cream-skimming and hence inequality." Furthermore, he found that "those schools which faced financial losses under the formula funding system tended to be schools which drew the greatest proportion of pupils from the most disadvantaged section of the community" (Bartlett, 1993). Thus, whatever gains may have emerged from the reforms in terms of efficiency and responsiveness to some clients, there are serious concerns about their implications for equity.

The danger of "cream skimming" is clearly demonstrated in an important series of studies from King's College, London, on the operation of quasi-markets. In an early study, Bowe et al. (1992) suggested that schools were competing to attract greater cultural capital and thus hoping for higher yielding returns. Subsequently, Gewirtz et al. (1995) have shown schools seeking students who are "able," "gifted," "motivated and committed," and middle class, with girls and children with South Asian backgrounds being seen as particular assets in terms of their potential to enhance test scores. The least desirable clientele include those who are "less able," have special educational needs, especially emotional and behavioral difficulties, as well as children from working class backgrounds and boys, unless they also have some of the more desirable attributes.

There is certainly evidence that some schools discriminate against children with special educational needs and it is hard to see how this can be avoided without public intervention. Bartlett (1993) argues that, only if the market price varies with the needs of the client will this not happen. In other words, funding formulae need to be weighted to give schools an incentive to take more expensive children. The current premium paid for children with special educational needs may not be enough, if it makes the school less popular with clients who, although bringing in less money, bring in other desirable attributes. Bowe et al. (1992) and Vincent et al. (1995) give examples of schools making just this sort of calculation.

The academically able are the "cream" that most schools seek to attract. Such students stay in the system longer and thus bring in more money, as well as making the school appear successful in terms of its test scores and hence attractive to other desirable clients. Glennerster (1991) suggests that, given the opportunity, most schools will want to become more selective because taking children who will bring scores down will affect their overall market position. In this situation, those *schools* that are in a position to choose often seek to identify their success with an emphasis on traditional academic virtues and thus attract those students most likely to display them. Many of the first schools to opt out and become grant maintained were selective, single sex and with traditional sixth forms and this gave the sector an aura of elite status (Fitz et al., 1993). Some grant maintained comprehensive schools have reverted to being overtly academically selective, and Bush et al. (1993) suggested that 30% of the grant maintained "comprehensive" schools they investigated were now using covert selection. In addition, grant maintained schools have been identified as amongst those with the highest rates of exclusion of existing students and amongst the least willing to cater for students with special educational needs (Feintuck, 1994). Recent research by Levačic and Hardman (1999) also reveals that the examination results of these schools rose as the proportion of socio-economically disadvantaged children within them declined. To that extent grant maintained schools can hardly claim to have increased parental choice across the board (see Power et al., 1994).

Similar concerns have been voiced about the Assisted Places Scheme (Edwards et al., 1989). This "contracting out" to the private sector of places for academically able but disadvantaged students has benefited only a small proportion of students. Yet, the Scheme has endorsed the superiority of the private sector and diminished the number of academically able students in the public sector (Fitz et al., 1989). And, because uptake of places is dependent upon the awareness of individual parents, relatively few of its beneficiaries come from the kinds of background featured in public justifications for the policy.

Walford (1992) argues that, while choice will lead to better quality schooling for some children, the evidence so far suggests that it will "discriminate in particular against working class children and children of Afro-Caribbean descent" (p. 137). Smith and Noble (1995) also conclude from the evidence that English choice policies are further disadvantaging already disadvantaged groups. Although schools have always been socially and racially segregated to the extent that residential segregation exists, Gewirtz et al. (1995) suggest that choice may well exacerbate this segregation by extending it into previously integrated schools serving mixed localities. Their research indicates that working class children and particularly children with special educational needs are likely to be increasingly "ghettoized" in poorly resourced schools.

Although, it could be argued that the English education system is unusual in being dominated by an elite private sector and a tendency towards selective education, these processes also appear to be occurring in the other countries. The Smithfield Project, a major government-funded study of the impact of choice policies in New Zealand, suggests that much the same sort of social polarization is taking place there (Lauder et al., 1994; Waslander and Thrupp, 1995). In another New Zealand study (Fowler, 1993), schools located in low socio-economic areas were found to be judged negatively because of factors over which they had no influence, such as type of intake, location, and problems perceived by parents as linked to these. Wylie (1994) too has noted that schools in low-income areas there are more likely to be losing students to other schools. If we could be sure that their poor reputation was deserved, this might be taken as evidence that the market was working well with effective schools reaping their just rewards. But, as in England, judgements of schools tend to be made on social grounds or narrow academic criteria and with little reference to their overall performance or even their academic effectiveness on value-added measures (Gewirtz et al., 1995). Meanwhile, the current funding regime makes it extremely difficult for schools in disadvantaged areas to break out of the cycle of decline. Wylie's study of the fifth year of self-managing schools in New Zealand (Wylie, 1994) identified schools in low-income areas, and schools with high Maori enrolments, as experiencing greater resource problems than others.

Wylie (1994, 1995) reports that marketizing measures have led to state schools paying more attention to the attractiveness of physical plant and public image than to changes to teaching and learning other than the spread of computers. They have also led to increased attention to the information about school programs and children's progress that reaches parents, changes which "are clearly not without value in themselves." But she also notes that "they do not seem able to counter or outweigh factors affecting school rolls which lie beyond school power, such as local demographics affected by employment, ethnicity, and class" (Wylie, 1995, citing Gordon, 1994; Waslander and Thrupp, 1995). Such research suggests that many of the differences between schools result from factors largely beyond the control of parents and schools, except the power of advantaged parents and advantaged schools to further enhance their advantage and thus increase educational inequalities and social polarization. These findings have very recently been challenged by Gorard and Fitz (1998a,b) who have claimed that the tendency towards increased polarization in both England and Wales and New Zealand may have been merely an initial effect of marketization policies and that social polarization has actually been reduced in subsequent years. Educational polarization, however, has been confirmed in the case of England by Her Majesty's Chief Inspector of Schools (HMCI, 1998) and, despite some outstanding exceptions, schools located in contexts of multiple disadvantage have overall levels of performance well below the national average and tend to be relatively ineffective at boosting students' progress (Gray, 1998).

In the USA, despite the association of public school choice with racial desegregation, there are considerable concerns about the equity effects of recent attempts to enhance choice, especially as there is no clear evidence to date of a positive impact on student achievement. What evidence there is about the effects of choice policies on student achievement and equity continues to be at best inconclusive (Plank et al., 1993), despite claims by choice advocates that "the best available evidence" shows that parental choice improves the education of all children, especially low income and minority students' (Domanico, 1990).

Even some of the more positive evidence from controlled choice districts, such as Cambridge (Rossell and Glenn, 1988) and Montclair (Clewell and Joy, 1990), which seemed to show gradual overall achievement gains, is now regarded by Henig (1994) as methodologically flawed making it difficult to attribute improvements to choice per se. Furthermore, although choice has not always led to resegregation, as its critics feared, improvements in the racial balance of Montclair and Cambridge schools were most noticeable during periods of strong government intervention. Henig goes on to argue that the much vaunted East Harlem "miracle" (Fliegel and Macguire, 1990) has "escaped any serious effort at controlled analysis" even though it has had a special role "in countering charges that the benefits of choice programs will not accrue to minorities and the poor" (p. 142). Not only have the apparently impressive gains in achievement now leveled off or even been reversed, it is impossible to be sure that the earlier figures were not merely the effect of schools being able to choose students from higher socio-economic groups from outside the area or, alternatively, of the empowerment of teachers.

The American evidence with regard to private school choice is also contentious, but relevant to our concerns in view of current demands for an extension of the use of public funds to permit students to attend private schools. Much of the controversy centers on the various interpretations of the data from Coleman's high school studies (Coleman et al., 1982) and, in particular, the work of Chubb and Moe (1990). Henig (1994) argues that small advantage attributed to private schools is a product of the methodology used. Lee and Bryk (1993) also suggest the evidence as presented does not support Chubb and Moe's conclusions. Nevertheless, Bryk et al. (1993) claim on the basis of their *own* work that Catholic schools do impact positively on the performance of low income families but they attribute this at least as much to an ethos of strong community values antithetical to the marketplace as to the espousal of market forces.

Witte's evaluation of the controversial Milwaukee privatizing experiment, which enables children from poor families to choose private schools at public expense, concludes in its fourth year report that "in terms of achievement scores ... students perform approximately the same as M[ilwaukee] P[ublic] S[chool] students." However, attendance of choice children is slightly higher and parental satisfaction has been high. For the schools, "the program has generally been positive, has allowed several to survive, several to expand, and contributed to the building of a new school" (Witte et al., 1994). Yet neither Witte's own conclusions nor Greene and Peterson's (1996) rather more positive reworking of the data can be used to sustain some of the more extravagant claims made both for and against this type of program. It is a small and narrowly targeted program and certainly not, of itself, a sufficient basis upon which to judge the likely effects of a more thoroughgoing voucher initiative.

The Milwaukee program overall has not hitherto been oversubscribed and, although students are self-selected, the schools involved have not been in a position to exercise choice. Elsewhere, the combination of oversubscription and self-selection in explaining apparent performance gains through private school choice suggest that equity is a major issue as it is in England and New Zealand. Smith and Meier (1995) use existing data to test the school choice hypothesis and conclude that "competition between public and private schools appears to result in a cream skimming effect" and that there is no reason to expect that the same will not happen with enhanced public school choice.

4. Moving Beyond Privatization and Marketization

In general, the system-wide effects of recent reform measures do not seem yet to demonstrate the positive outcomes envisaged by their leading proponents. In making this claim, we are, of course, generalizing from the evidence available. We would not wish to deny that there are instances where reforms to public education systems have made a positive difference to the educational experiences of students and teachers. The Kura Kaupapa Maori in New Zealand and some of the "alternative" U.S. charter schools provide examples where self-determination by communities and professionals has brought about innovative and potentially empowering educational environments. However, there are doubts as to the sustainability of such programs and about the extent to which they can be attributed to marketizing and privatizing measures rather than other changes in modes of provision and governance. Moreover, these innovative instances need to be set alongside a prevailing pattern of educational conservatism and consolidated hierarchies both within and between schools.

It could be argued that it is the contradictions and tensions between the policies that impede their effectiveness. Commentators from the radical right see the answer as moving still further towards more genuinely marketized and even fully privatized forms of education provision. Indeed, some advocates of market forces have argued that the indifferent performance of the reforms so far is merely evidence that they have not gone far enough. For example, a government Minister responsible for the introduction of the Assisted Places Scheme in England used our own research (Edwards et al., 1989) showing that it had failed to attract many working class students as a basis for arguing in favour of a fully-fledged voucher scheme (Boyson, 1990). Similarly, Moe's (1994) only major criticism of the British reforms was that the government had "created an open enrolment system in which there is very little to choose from, because the supply of schools is controlled by the LEAs." In order to free up the supply side, he suggested that all schools should become autonomous. Tooley (1996) favours an even more deregulated system and the abandonment of a centrally prescribed curriculum.

Much of the support for moving further towards decentralizing education provision derives from the alleged benefits of existing private provision. However, as we discussed earlier, the evidence with regard to private school choice is contentious. Even if we accept that some children who currently attend state schools might benefit from private education, there is little to suggest that extending opportunities to attend private schools more widely would benefit all groups equally. Witte et al. (1995) have undertaken an analysis of the current social composition of private and public schools in Wisconsin and conclude that "an open-ended voucher scheme would clearly benefit households that are more affluent than the average household in Wisconsin." They go on to say that, although some might believe that making vouchers available to everyone would open up private schools to the poor, the opposite argument seems equally plausible. With more money available, private schools that cannot currently afford to select, such as some of the inner city private schools in the Milwaukee choice experiment, could become more selective. The already highly selective schools could then maintain their advantage by demanding add-on payments in addition to vouchers.

Some on the right argue that these processes are inevitable in a system that is only partly privatized. Tooley (1995) claims that the potential of markets in education cannot be properly assessed by looking at the effects of quasi-markets, or what he prefers to term "so-called" markets. In his own vision of *Education Without the State* (Tooley, 1996) he argues that we need a "one tier private system" and that parents and students should be free to determine the kind of schooling they feel suits them best. He envisages lowering the school leaving age and providing every student with a "lifelong individual fund for education" which they would then be able to spend when and where they saw fit.

Tooley rightly reminds us of the equity failings of democratic systems. And, of course, empirical research on current systems does not, indeed in principle could not, show that total deregulation would not have beneficial effects. Yet, most of the available evidence does seem to suggest that going further in the direction of marketization and privatization would be unlikely to yield overall improvements in the quality of education and might well have damaging equity effects. Even Chubb and Moe (1990), who argue that equality is better "protected" by markets than any political institutions, concede that choice of school in a democracy cannot be unlimited or entirely unregulated. So, despite the rhetoric that suggests that devolution and choice takes educational decision-making out of politics, key decisions about goals and frameworks will still need to be made in the broader political arena.

The need to provide a better balance between consumer rights and citizen rights in education, while recognizing the desirability of some facets of choice and devolution, has led in England to proposals to put a greater degree of democratic control back in the picture. In particular, there has been recent discussion around how to revive democratic involvement and accountability at local level as a counter-balance to the market and the strong central state. For example, Pryke (1996) remarks that, "despite the experiments to let schools do their own thing"—and he believes this has gone further in England than anywhere else in the world—"the great majority of them, and parents, have recognised the need for a body to act for them as a community of schools" (p. 21). Similarly, Brighouse (1996), Birmingham's senior education officer, who argues that an atomized market will create chaos and "put further distance between the educational and social haves and the educational and social have-nots," says that "there needs to be a local agency aware of school differences, sensitively working with each school, securing equity and setting a climate for a drive towards ever higher standards" (p. 11). Responding to the question as to why such bodies should be democratically accountable, he suggests that in matters of education provision "there is a need to balance various and sometimes conflicting needs and priorities (including) the needs of very different communities within, for example, a modern city" and that difference and equity can best be seen to be held in balance in an openly democratic forum (p. 14).

Part of the challenge for those adopting this view must be to move away from atomized decision-making to the reassertion of collective responsibility without recreating the very bureaucratic systems whose shortcomings have helped to legitimate the recent tendency to treat education as a private good rather than a public responsibility. While choice policies are part of a social text that helps to create new subject positions which undermine traditional forms of collectivism, those forms of collectivism themselves failed to empower many members of society, including women and minority ethnic groups. We need to ask how we can use the positive aspects of choice and autonomy to facilitate the development of new forms of community empowerment rather than exacerbating social differentiation. As Henig (1994) says of the USA, "the sad irony of the current education-reform movement is that, through over identification with school-choice proposals rooted in market-based ideas, the healthy impulse to consider radical reforms to address social problems may be channeled into initiatives that further erode the potential for collective deliberation and collective response" (p. 222). Some reform proposals, such as Cookson's (1994) "educational trust funds" and Atkinson's (1994) "educational enterprises," seem superficially to have similarities with neo-liberal policies of marketization and privatization. However, they are articulated with a rather different political agenda and could potentially make a positive contribution to the enhancement of social justice in education.

In seeking out ways of responding to this challenge, many have looked with enthusiasm to Britain where the New Labour government seems to be drawing on critiques of both traditional social democratic forms and neo-liberal market forms to develop a so-called "Third Way" in which there are no fixed preconceptions about what form of either provision or funding is best. The judgement is apparently to be made entirely on the basis of "what works." It is therefore possible to find, for example, in its proposed Education Action Zones (DFEE, 1997), both a reassertion of collective responsibility for educational provision and a readiness to consider the active involvement of private (even "for profit") companies in its delivery. And, although the government has abandoned the Assisted Places Scheme in order to uphold its commitment to "benefit the many, not the few," it has sought to bring private and state schools into closer partnership. It is, of course, too early to say what the effects of these policies will be—many are still being formulated. However, while the Third Way may offer an alternative to either vehement advocacy or rejection of marketization and privatization, there is already some concern about the coherence of New Labour's reforms (Whitty, 1998) and the extent to which marketization and privatization will continue unabated under the new more fashionable discourse of mutuality and partnership.

Note

1. In the remainder of the paper, we use the term "state schools" to describe publicly funded and publicly provided schools in England and New Zealand and the term "public schools" to describe such schools in the USA.

References

Archer, M., 1984. *Social Origins of Educational Systems*. Sage, London.

Arnott, M., Bullock, A., Thomas, H., 1992. Consequences of local management: an assessment by head teachers'. Paper presented to the ERA Research Network, 12 February.

Atkinson, D., 1994. Radical Urban Solutions. Cassell, London.

Bartlett, W., 1993. Quasi-markets and educational reforms. In: Le Grand, J., Bartlett, W. (Eds.) *Quasi-Markets and Social Policy*. Macmillan, London.

Blank, R., 1990. Educational effects of magnet high schools. In: Clune, W.H., Witte, J.F. (Eds.) *Choice and Control in American Education*, vol. 2. Falmer Press, London.

Bowe, R., Ball, S., Gold, A., 1992. *Reforming Education and Changing Schools*. Routledge, London.

Boyson, R., 1990. Review of Edwards et al. (1989a). *Times Higher Education Supplement*, 18 May.

Brighouse, T., 1996. *A Question of Standards: The Need for a Local Democratic Voice*. Politeia, London.

Bryk, A.S., Lee, V.E., Holland, P.B., 1993. *Catholic Schools and the Common Good*. Harvard University Press, Cambridge.

Bullock, A., Thomas, H., 1994. *The impact of local management of schools: final report*. Birmingham, University of Birmingham.

Burchardt, T., Hills, J., Propper, C., 1999. *Private Welfare and Public Policy*. Joseph Rowntree Foundation, York.

Bush, T., Coleman, M, Glover, D., 1993. *Managing Autonomous Schools*. Chapman, London.

Butcher, T., 1995. *Delivering Welfare: The Governance of Social Services in the 1990s*. Open University Press, Milton Keynes.

Chubb, J., Moe, T., 1990. *Politics, Markets and Americas Schools*. Brookings Institution, Washington.

Clewell, B.C., Joy, M.F., 1990. *Choice in Montclair, New Jersey*. ETS, Princeton.

Coleman, J.S., Hoffer, T., Kilgore, S., 1982. *High School Achievement: Public, Catholic and Private Schools*. Basic Books, New York.

Cookson, P.W., 1994. *School Choice: The Struggle for the Soul of American Education*. Yale University Press, New Haven.

DfEE, 1997. *Excellence in Schools* (White Paper). HMSO, London.

Diandra, M.C., Corwin, R.G., 1994. *Vision and Reality: A First Year Look at California's Charter Schools*. Southwest Regional Laboratory, Los Alamitos, CA.

Domanico, R.J., 1990. Restructuring New York Citys public schools: the case for public school choice. *Education Policy Paper #3*, New York, Manhattan Institute for Policy Research.

Donnison, D., 1984. *The Politics of Poverty*. Robertson, Oxford.

Edwards, T., Whitty, G., 1997. Specialisation and selection in secondary education. *Oxford Review of Education* 23, 5–15.

Edwards, T., Fitz, J., Whitty, G., 1989. *The State and Private Education: An Evaluation of the Assisted Places Scheme*. Falmer Press, London.

Feintuck, M., 1994. *Accountability and Choice in Schooling*. Open University Press, Milton Keynes.

Fitz, J., Edwards, T., Whitty, G., 1989. The assisted places scheme: an ambiguous case of privatization. *British Journal of Educational Studies* 37 (3), 222–234.

Fitz, J., Halpin, D., Power, S., 1993. *Grant Maintained Schools: Education in the Marketplace*. Kogan Page, London.

Fliegel, S., Macguire, J., 1990. *Miracle in East Harlem: The Fight for Choice in Public Education*. Random House, New York.

Fowler, M., 1993. *Factors influencing Choice of Secondary Schools*. University of Canterbury, Christchurch.

Gewirtz, S., Ball, S.J., Bowe, R., 1995. *Markets, Choice and Equity*. Open University Press, Milton Keynes.

Glatter, R., Woods, P.E., Bagley, C., 1997. Diversity, differentiation and hierarchy. In: Glatter, R. Jr (Ed.) *Choice and Diversity in Schooling: Perspectives and Prospects*. Routledge, London.

Glennerster, H., 1991. Quasi-markets for education? *Economic Journal* 101, 1268–1276.

Gorard, S., Fitz, J., 1998a. The more things change ... the missing impact of marketisation. *British Journal of Sociology of Education* 19 (3), 365–376.

Gorard, S., Fitz, J., 1998b. Under starters orders: the established market, the Cardiff study and the Smithfield project. *International Studies in Sociology of Education* 8 (3), 299–314.

Gordon, L., 1994. "Rich" and "poor" schools in Aotearoa. *New Zealand Journal of Educational Studies* 29 (2), 113–125.

Gray, J., 1998. *The contribution of educational research to school improvement*. Professorial Lecture, Institute of Education, University of London.

Greene, J., Peterson, P., 1996. School choice data rescued from bad science. *Wall Street Journal* 14 August.

Heald, D., 1983. *Public Expenditure: Its Defence and Reform*. Robertson, Oxford.

Henig, J.R., 1994. *Rethinking School Choice: Limits of the Market Metaphor*. Princeton University Press, Princeton.

Henry, T., 1998. Edison Project adds more schools, funds. *USA Today*, 27 May, D7.

Hill, P.T., Foster, G.E., Gendler, T., 1990. *High Schools with Character*. Rand, Santa Monica.

HMCI, 1998. *Secondary Education 1993–97: A review of secondary schools in England*. OFSTED, London.

Klein, R., 1984. Privatization and the welfare state. *Lloyds Bank Review* (January), 12–29.

Lauder, H., Hughes, D., Waslander, S., Thrupp, M., McGlinn, J., Newton, S., Dupuis, A., 1994. The creation of market competition for education in New Zealand, Smithfield Project, Wellington, Victoria University of Wellington.

Lee, V.E., Bryk, A.S., 1993. Science or policy argument? In: Rasell, E., Rothstein, R. (Eds.) *School Choice: Examining the Evidence*. Economic Policy Institute, Washington, DC.

Le Grand, J., Bartlett, W. (Eds.), 1993. *Quasi-Markets and Social Policy*. Macmillan, London.

Le Grand, J., Robinson, R. (Eds.), 1984. *Privatization and the Welfare State*. Allen & Unwin, London.

Levaçic, R., 1995. *Local Management of Schools: Analysis and Practice*. Open University Press, Milton Keynes.

Levaçic, R., Hardman, J., 1999. The performance of grant maintained schools in England: an experiment in autonomy. *Journal of Education Policy* 14 (2), 185–212.

Marginson, S., 1993. *Education and Public Policy in Australia*. Cambridge University Press, Cambridge.

Moe, T., 1994. The British battle for choice. In: Billingsley, K.L. (Ed.), *Voices on Choice: The Education Reform Debate*. Pacific Institute for Public Policy, San Francisco.

Moore, D., Davenport, S., 1990. School choice: the new improved sorting machine. In: Boyd, W., Walberg, H. (Eds.) *Choice in Education*. McCutchan, Berkeley, CA.

Murphy, J., Gilmer, S.W., Weise, R., Page, A., 1998. *Pathways to Privatization in Education*. Ablex, Greenwich, CT.

Plank, S., Schiller, K.S., Schneider, B., Coleman, J.S., 1993. Effects of choice in education. In: Rasell, E., Rothstein, R. (Eds.) *School Choice: Examining the Evidence*. Economic Policy Institute, Washington, DC.

Pollard, S., 1995. *Schools, Selection and the Left*. Social Market Foundation, London.

Power, S., Fitz, J., Halpin, D., 1994. Parents, pupils and grant maintained schools. *British Educational Research Journal* 20 (2), 209–226.

Pring, R., 1987. Privatization in education. *Journal of Education Policy* 2 (4), 289–299.

Pryke, R., 1996. Positioning the LEA in LEArning. *Education Journal* 6, 21.

Raywid, M.A., 1994. *Focus schools: a genre to consider*. Urban Diversity Series No. 106, Columbia University, ERIC Clearinghouse on Urban Education, New York.

Rossell, C.H., Glenn, C.L., 1988. The Cambridge controlled choice plan. *Urban Review* 20 (2), 75–94.

Sexton, S., 1987. Our Schools—A Radical Policy. Institute of Economic Affairs, Education Unit, Warlingham.

Smith, K.B., Meier, K.J., 1995. *The Case Against School Choice: Politics, Markets and Fools*. Sharpe, Armonk, NY.

Smith, T., Noble, M., 1995. *Education Divides: Poverty and Schooling in the 1990s*. Child Poverty Action Group, London.

Tooley, J., 1995. Markets or democracy? A reply to Stewart Ranson. *British Journal of Educational Studies* 43 (1), 31–34.

Tooley, J., 1996. *Education without the State*. Institute of Economic Affairs, London.

Vincent, C., Evans, J., Lunt, I., Young, P., 1995. Policy and practice: the changing nature of special educational provision in schools. *British Journal of Special Education* 22 (1), 4–11.

Walford, G., 1992. Educational choice and equity in Great Britain. *Educational Policy* 6 (2), 123–138.

Walford, G., 1995. *Educational Politics: Pressure Groups and Faith-based Schools*. Avebury, Aldershot.

Walford, G., Miller, H., 1991. *City Technology College*. Open University Press, Milton Keynes.

Waslander, S., Thrupp, M., 1995. Choice, competition and segregation: an empirical analysis of a New Zealand secondary school market 1990–1993. *Journal of Education Policy* 10 (1), 1–26.

Wells, A.S., 1993. *Time to Choose: America at the Crossroads of School Choice Policy*. Hill & Wang, New York.

Wells, A.S., Grutzik, C, Carnochan, S., 1996. The multiple meanings of the US charter school reform: exploring the politics of deregulation. Paper presented at the British Educational Research Association Annual Conference, University of Lancaster.

Whitty, G., 1984. The "privatization" of education. *Educational Leadership* 41 (7), 51–54.

Whitty, G., 1998. New labour, education and disadvantage. *Education and Social Justice* 1 (1), 2–8.

Whitty, G., Edwards, T., Gewirtz, S., 1993. *Specialisation and Choice in Urban Education: The City Technology College Experiment*. Routledge, London.

Whitty, G., Power, S., Edwards, T., 1998. The assisted places scheme: its impact and its role in privatization and marketization. *Journal of Education Policy* 13 (2), 237–250.

Witte, J.F., Thorn, C.A., Pritchard, K.M., Claibourn, M., 1994. Fourth year report: Milwaukee Parental Choice Program, Department of Public Instruction, Madison.

Witte, J.F., Thorn, C.A., Pritchard, K.A., 1995. *Private and Public Education in Wisconsin: Implications for the Choice Debate*. University of Wisconsin, Madison.

Wohlstetter, P., Wenning, R., Briggs, K.L., 1995. Charter schools in the United States: the question of autonomy. *Educational Policy* 9 (4), 331–358.

Wylie, C., 1994. *Self Managing Schools in New Zealand: The Fifth Year*. New Zealand Council for Educational Research, Wellington.

Wylie, C, 1995. Contrary currents: the application of the public sector reform framework in education. *New Zealand Journal of Educational Studies* 20 (2), 149–164.

Young, S., 1986. The nature of privatization in Britain 1979–85. *Western European Politics* 9, 235–252.

14

Nation versus Nation

The Race to Be the First in the World

DAVID P. BAKER AND GERALD LETENDRE

This article leaves the world of how schools operate and turns to the politics of how schools change across nations. Public reaction to results from international school achievement tests in many nations has heightened awareness about educational competition with other nations. For example, in the mid-1990s, after the first set of TIMSS results became public, the United States went into a kind of soul searching about its mathematics and science curricula nationwide. The release of the more recent international study on OECD nations called PISA led Germany into a national education crisis. Around the world, countries are using the results of international tests as a kind of academic Olympiad, serving as a referendum on their school system's performance. Even though these tests were never designed to assess the overall performance of an entire school system, nations and even subnational educational authorities now regularly use them for competitive assessment.

The story here is about why there is so much focus on educational problems, inventing of solutions, and implementing them across systems of schooling in nations. As with our other tales, we find a common trend among nations, one of constantly tinkering and adjusting schooling to improve achievement, social fairness, and satisfy the numerous stakeholders in formal education.

By way of illustration of the dynamics of this trend, we focus on the case of mathematics and science curricular reform policy in the United States after the first TIMSS results were released the mid-1990s, since it continues to have major implications for education policy in this nation even today. We describe how, in the middle of the last decade, American policy makers embraced an image of the international competitiveness of the nation's mathematics and science test scores that led to a rationale for curricular reform. We then present some of our own analyses of this image with the TIMSS data, and show how *underwhelming* the empirical case really was for these curricular reforms in the United States. Our analyses suggest that if there had been more thorough appreciation of how complicated the empirical relationship is between quality of curricula in nations and level of achievement of students, a more balanced set of reforms might have been developed from TIMSS. We then speculate on the institutional nature of educational reform cycles in nations and worldwide.

From Comparison to Competition to Reform

National school systems seem always to be in the shop for repairs, or for what educators boldly like to call "reforms." In an interesting volume on *The Impact of TIMSS on the Teaching and Learning of Mathematics and Science*, twenty-nine national experts report on the effect the release of TIMSS test scores results had on educational policy in particular nations (Robitaille, Beaton, and Plomp, 2000). One is struck by constant reference to the need for nations to improve mathematics. Each nation has its own story of how TIMSS brought a particular problem to light that needs to be fixed and is now being addressed in this way or that. Remarkably, this is as true for the top-scoring nations as it is for low-performing ones. For example, high-scoring South Korea sees a national gender difference in mathematics that it says needs fixing, and even top-scoring Singapore manages to admit that there is "room for improvement" in mathematics and science education.

Modern systems of public mass schooling appear to travel a continuous cycle of identifying problems, constructing solutions, and implementing new reforms, only then to start the process all over again. But this description is too orderly for what really takes place; instead, most of the time reform cycles are running at different speeds around various parts of the system all at the same time. There is simultaneously much problem identifying, solution seeking, and reform implementing happening throughout educational systems. International comparative data have often been the spark to set off a cycle of this kind. National educational crises start as easily as the common cold spreads—the right sneeze in public, so to speak, and the cycle begins.

Even though continuous reform is common in all national education systems, discussion about educational problems, solutions, and implementation takes on a particularly national tone and image. Educational problems are often discussed as though they are truly unique to a particular nation, needing unique solutions made chiefly from homegrown ideas, spread through a unique national process of implementation of solutions, all operating within a national polity made up of indigenous political enemies and champions of any particular educational reform.

But even a cursory look across nations defies the image of struggling with one's own unique problems and solutions. Although cycles of problem identification and reform are national in the simplest sense, their overall volume across nations is so large that it is likely a world trend. Furthermore, it looks irrational as a solely national enterprise; for example, top-performing nations in past international mathematics and science studies launch into reforms as frequently as do poor-performing nations, sometimes deciding on reforms that take high- and low-performing nations back toward each other without even recognizing it![1] As the TIMSS volume on national reaction illustrates, a national ministry is never heard publicly proclaiming that everything is just rosy in the nation's education system and there is no need to fix anything. To do so is political suicide, and politicians know it, since they believe in the centrality of the educational process as much as the rest of society.

In our times, educational reform is perpetual and self-reaffirming. There is remarkably little cynicism about the educational reform cycle in society; it is widely and strongly believed in. Given this, we wonder if there is not a larger institutional logic behind reform that would explain the continuous high volume in nation after nation.

The Policy Trap

Several years ago with colleagues we wrote a paper entitled "The Policy Trap," about how misinterpretation stemming from rushed and underdeveloped analyses of international test results trapped nations into misidentifying problems and aiming reform issues in less-than-productive directions (LeTendre and others, 2001). The American reaction to TIMSS on a policy level illustrates this interesting phenomenon.

To simplify and make a long story short, an initial set of reasonably good academic Olympiad standings for the United States in the TIMSS fourth grade sample were dashed by internationally mediocre eighth grade results reported some time after the fourth grade results. The main message for American education policy makers that emerged from the highly publicized results was that the mathematics and science curricula had to be raised to international standards if America's educational achievement level were to also rise internationally. Comparison of what American students learned from elementary grades to middle and high school scores was disheartening and widely covered in

TABLE 14.1 Estimated Increase Between Fourth and Eighth Grades on Science and Math

Nation	Science	Nation	Math
Iran	234	Thailand	168
Thailand	220	Singapore	159
Kuwait	213	Iceland	149
Singapore	210	Japan	148
Israel	179	New Zealand	146
Hungary	175	Hong Kong	141
Portugal	165	Norway	138
Czech Republic	164	Korea	137
Slovenia	164	Czech Republic	135
Greece	161	Iran	134
Cyprus	154	Canada	133
Netherlands	150	England	130
Norway	150	Israel	128
Ireland	149	Greece	128
England	149	Hungary	127
Iceland	148	Slovenia	127
New Zealand	147	Kuwait	125
Hong Kong	142	Australia	121
Japan	140	Austria	119
Austria	138	Ireland	116
Scotland	133	Portugal	115
Latvia	130	Scotland	115
Canada	130	Cyprus	108
Australia	127	Latvia	105
U.S.A.	113	Netherlands	103
Korea	105	U.S.A.	93

Source: Martin and others 1997.

the national media. For example, Table 14.1 shows an estimate of what students from a number of nations learn from fourth to eighth grade. The United States is at the bottom of the international rankings of how much mathematics is learned by eighth grade, although the American eighth grade mean is among average-performing nations. Results of this kind, coupled with the heated-up interest in the idea that mathematics and science education even at the most elementary level leads to national economic well-being, quickly kicked off a major cycle of problem identifying, solution inventing, and reform implementing in the United States. What happened next is what created the education policy trap we have observed in other nations as well: celebration of a solution waiting for a problem.

For some time now in the United States, mathematics and science educators have thought that what is taught across public schools in the nation is not too demanding a curriculum, and that more rigorous and better-implemented curricular materials would improve national achievement. Dating back to the 1960s' "new math" era and even before during the Sputnik crisis, there has been a long-standing wish on the part of mathematics and science curricular specialists in the United States to get a real chance at improving, strengthening, and standardizing curricula throughout the nation. This venerable interest in reform of American mathematics and science curricula was in the mid-1990s the solution waiting for a problem to attach itself to, and the media buzz about the "slump" in the TIMSS results from fourth to eighth grades became this problem—and a politically perfect one at that.

Educational reform cycles seem to occur most rapidly in the United States when there is a pending sense of educational doom (Cross, 2003). From Sputnik through the report *Nation at Risk* to the first release of the TIMSS results decades later, nothing seems to spell doom in American education quite like internationally inadequate mathematics and science education. In fact, this is probably the case in most nations.

Policy analysts and makers quickly seized on the idea that U.S. math and science curricula were "broken" and that this was the chief cause of the nation's slump in achievement compared internationally. Major national and local mathematics and science forces, such as the National Science Foundation, the U.S. Department of Education, nongovernmental organizations of curricular expert professional associations, state Departments of Education, and some local school districts, were all ready to spring into action upon hearing about this problem. Of course, they had the solution already in mind: curricular reform.

The mobilization of the American education establishment over mathematics and science curricula reform was primed by two well-established ideas about the educational performance of the nation and its economic well-being that had been widely disseminated in the media and even in scholarly works since publication of *A Nation at Risk,* in 1983. One idea was that the level of achievement of a nation in technical fields such as mathematics and science is directly linked to the nation's economic productivity. For example, two decades of concern over failing economic competition led to the national "economic threat" from superior East Asian (Japan, South Korea) national educational achievements. The other idea was that American public mass schooling was failing the nation as a producer of technically capable future workers. Both of these ideas were powerful in terms of policy, even though research on them suggests that national economic productivity is far more complicated than a one-to-one link with the performance of the school system.

By the time the TIMSS results were released in the mid-1990s, these ideas were already driving the highly ambitious federal government's "GOALS 2000" reforms. The GOALS legislation contained little in the way of concrete plans for improving education, but it laid out a clear set of lofty (if unrealistic) ambitions. The United States was to become "first in the world" in math and science by the year 2000; this was actually a goal borrowed from the George H. Bush administration. GOALS 2000 implicitly made the nation's performance on international tests a referendum on the quality of the entire educational system and promulgated the belief that a higher ranking was indicative of greater national economic competitiveness.

Note both the rhetoric of anticipation of an educational problem waiting to be solved as well as a dramatic call to reform schooling—in a press release from a powerful NGO interested in American science production. It is illustrative of the kind of statements made throughout this period:

The American Association for the Advancement of Science (AAAS) is saddened but not surprised by the disappointing scores of U.S. high school seniors in the Third International Mathematics and Science Study (TIMSS), released today by the Department of Education.

"As a country dependent on science and technology, we must see this poor performance as a call to action," said Richard Nicholson, AAAS's executive officer. "AAAS urges every community across the nation to launch into a forthright discussion about the implications of these scores and how we can improve the current system of education in science and mathematics. It will take a concerted effort by all of us—schools, parents, industry, government, and science communities—to ensure that future results are much more encouraging."

February 24, 1997—Washington, D.C, AAAS Press Release

The politics behind this case of educational reform in the United States turned on two main assumptions. First, the American mathematics and science curricula were indeed broken and in need of reform as compared to other nations. Second, if we managed to fix our broken curricula we would improve the nation's educational competitiveness internationally.

Broken Curricula?

Influential reports, using past and current international data to evaluate the state of the American mathematics and science curricula, portray in dramatic terms an image of broken national mathematics and science curricula, including "a broken spiral," "an underachieving curriculum," "splintered," and "a mile wide and an inch deep" (McKnight, Crosswhite, and Dossey, 1987; Schmidt, McKnight, and Raizen, 1997). In the immediate post-TIMSS environment in the United States, the latter image—namely, that a pressing national educational problem is its "mile wide and an inch deep" mathematics and science curricula, was the main message. This image really took hold as being an identifiable problem easily described in media and accepted among influential stakeholders interested in American science and technology production. The American mathematics and science curricula at the eighth and twelfth grade levels in the 1990s were thought to cover too many topics in too superficial a manner to ensure effective learning among the nation's students. The solution, of course, was already known—reform the curricula—but how to get this across to the broad spectrum of policy makers in the highly localized American educational system?

Mathematics and science curricular experts, among them William Schmidt, the chief author of many influential and official American TIMSS reports, led a media campaign, often with the support of the National Science Foundation, to spread the broken mathematics and science curricula message throughout the nation. Here, for example, is how Schmidt and a colleague describe the broken curricula image in 1997: "These results [from TIMSS] point out that U.S. education in the middle grades is particularly troubled; the promise of our fourth-grade children (particularly in science) is dashed against the undemanding curriculum of the nation's middle schools" (Valverde and Schmidt, p. 60).

But were the U.S. mathematics and science curricula truly broken, as in being a mile wide and an inch deep? If they were broken and then fixed, would American achievement be likely to improve compared to other nations? To foreshadow a bit, neither of these key assumptions driving American policy about the mathematics and science curricula reform since the release of the initial TIMSS results is supported by the very data that are often attributed in identifying the problem in the first place.

Assessing National Curricula: Breadth, Depth, and Repetition

An abundance of international data on curriculum and what happens to it in the classroom from the 1980s onward has taken the curricular theorist out of the classroom and into the world of nations and politics. For example, many important past ideas about curriculum tended to be about classroom processes, such as the idea of a "hidden curriculum," or the things that get taught unintentionally during the classroom process (see Bowles and Gintis, 1976; Eckert, 1989; Goldman and McDermott, 1987). Even Bruner's influential ideas (1962) about effective spiraling curriculum were conceived in terms of a teacher who anchors her material around key concepts and then spirals upward as she goes through the year. Cross-national surveys, particularly the IEA-type data sets (like TIMSS), which have always been designed with considerable input from curricular experts, expanded the image of how the whole curricular process works in a nation beyond just the content or very micro ideas about teaching. It is taken for granted that curricula are organized at several levels in a nation, each level with its own name.

On the first level are national curricular guidelines and national textbooks representing the *intended* or *ideal* national curriculum. On the next level is the national *implemented* curriculum, which is what is actually taught in the nation's classrooms. Last, the national *achieved* curriculum is what is actually learned by a nation's students from the intended curriculum. An expanded notion of a nation's curriculum and the flow of international data increased policy makers' interest in international comparisons of achievement, as well as curricular explanations for any cross-national differences.

Most countries in the world create national curriculum guidelines and use standardized textbooks regarding what should be taught in their schools. In this respect, the United States is notable in lacking any national curricula or guidelines. Intended curricula in the United States are only partially the domain of individual states, with a large amount of the control of content residing at the district or even the school level. This administrative arrangement certainly contributes to the belief among American curricular experts that a lack of formal standardization in intended curricula, as well as localized and hence perhaps weak quality control over the implemented curricula in the nation's classrooms, is the cause of the nation's mediocre eighth grade and twelfth grade mathematics and science compared to many other nations.

But these strongly held beliefs among American educators have never really been put to an empirical test at the cross-national level. Our TIMSS analysis project colleague and educational psychologist Erling Boe, in a policy brief in 2001, describes the astonishing lack of evidence about the relationship between national characteristics and national achievement, including the intended and implemented curricula, in the official American TIMSS reports that caused such concern about the image of broken mathematics and science curricula in the first place:

It is not surprising, therefore, that a critic of TIMSS (Bracy, 2000, p. 5) could claim legitimately, four years after the first release of data, that publications issued by the U.S. Department of Education had not offered any explanations about which differences in national education systems have produced the differences in observed achievement. In fact, none of the official reports of TIMSS findings issued to date have contained a quantified bivariate relationship between any specific predictor variable and any national-level achievement score, nor has there been publication of any multivariate models of national differences in math or science achievement. This observation applies to all of the many reports issued [by] the TIMSS. [Boe and others, 2001, pp. 1–2]

Boe's observations are all the more ironic because the TIMSS study was specifically designed to examine claims like those of the broken American curricula argument. Consequently, using the TIMSS data for what they were partially intended for, we investigate the characteristics of the implemented American eighth grade mathematics curriculum to see if it is indeed "broken" in comparison to curricula in other nations. Then we refer to the Boe report's results about the relationship between national curricular characteristics and national achievement. Our example here is limited to just mathematics, but we find roughly the same empirical situation exists for the science curriculum as well.

In keeping with the metaphoric image of "mile wide and inch deep" put forth by American mathematics curricular experts, we examine the "breadth," "depth," and repetition (broken spiraling) of the curriculum implemented in American classrooms as compared to other nations.

Simply measured, breadth is the number of topics covered in a school year and depth is the time spent on each topic. The mile-wide-and-inch-deep image suggested American teachers try to cover too many topics, and it is often thought that if a teacher covers too much content this robs emphasis and detracts from achievement. Similarly, if too many topics are repeated there is no upward spiral of learning of mathematics concepts at a more advanced level.

Nations where teachers cover a lot of topics could be said to have a broad curriculum. So is it true that the United States has an extremely broad mathematics curriculum?

As shown in Table 14.2, the average American eighth grade teacher teaches between seventeen and eighteen mathematics topics during the eighth grade. Although the U.S. average is among those nations with broader curricula, one could hardly call it extremely broad. Most nations have relatively broad curricula; for example, high-scoring South Korea has an average of more than nineteen topics. There are only eight relatively "narrow streams" in the world of national mathematics curricula captured by these TIMSS nations. Overall, most nations are quite similar in the number of topics taught in eighth grade mathematics.

TABLE 14.2 Math Breadth for the Implemented Curriculum: Average Number of Math Topics Taught in 1994

Country	Math Breadth Mean	Coefficient of Variation for Math Breadth
Hungary	21.6	0.36
Greece	19.8	0.27
New Zealand	19.5	0.52
Korea	19.4	0.36
Australia	18	0.57
Slovenia	17.59	0.47
U.S.A.	**17.51**	**0.68**
Portugal	17.5	0.38
Canada	16.8	0.64
Spain	16.7	0.56
Lithuania	16.2	0.67
Romania	16.1	0.73
Belgium (Flemish)	15.9	0.47
Iran, Islamic Rep.	15.9	0.7
Colombia	15.6	0.61
Slovak Rep.	15.6	0.6
Hong Kong	15.5	0.54
Netherlands	15.3	0.61
Singapore	15.2	0.3
Belgium (French)	14	0.6
Switzerland	13.9	0.79
Austria	13.8	0.58
Germany	13.7	0.8
Iceland	13.6	0.7
Czech Rep.	13.2	0.72
Israel	11.1	0.58
Latvia	11	0.73
Sweden	10.4	0.85
Russian Federation	9.5	0.07
Thailand	7.18	1

Note: Nations in same shaded area have averages that are statistically similar.
Source: TIMSS 1995.

The second column shows an indicator of how similar or dissimilar teachers within a given country are in terms of how many mathematics topics they teach in a school year. There is some variation within many nations. For example, Greece has the least variation among teachers (.27), meaning that most teachers cover about the average of nearly twenty topics. In the United States, at .68, some teachers cover fewer topics and some teachers cover more topics than the national average of 17.5 in the school year. But this level of variation in the United States is neither very large in absolute terms nor the largest among these nations.

If we carry on with the analogy of the river that proved so useful in making the case for curricular reform among American policy makers, the U.S. curricular stream is no wider than most countries, but it has many channels and backwaters. U.S. students, depending on their teacher, may experience a broad or narrow range of topics. Conversely, students in nations such as Greece and Singapore receive a more uniformly broad mathematics curricula over the eighth grade year.

Much of the variation in the exposure to mathematics topics in classrooms arises from processes within nations more than processes between nations. To be precise, about 70 percent of the variation we see among these nations in terms of the breadth of the math curriculum from classroom to classroom comes from within the countries themselves, leaving only 30 percent being between the nations. Most cover a lot of topics, and in many nations the amount of topics varies some from teacher to teacher.

TABLE 14.3 Math Repetition for the Implemented Curriculum: Average Topics Taught in the Past Year and 1994

Country	Math Repetition Mean	Coefficient of Variation for Math Repetition
Singapore	14.4	0.35
Romania	10.8	0.89
Hungary	10.3	0.88
Lithuania	9.3	0.8
Slovak Rep.	8.8	0.85
Slovenia	8.4	0.84
Iran, Islamic Rep.	8.3	0.97
Spain	6.7	0.98
Austria	6.5	0.96
Portugal	6.4	0.95
Germany	6.1	1.18
Greece	6	1.11
Israel	6	0.92
Korea	5.7	1.2
Russian Federation	5.7	0.08
Czech Republic	5.5	1.14
Latvia	5.3	0.98
U.S.A.	5.1	**1.46**
Hong Kong	4.9	1.33
Netherlands	4.9	1.33
Australia	4.6	1.43
Colombia	4.6	1.34
Belgium (Flemish)	4.4	1.25
Canada	4.2	1.67
Switzerland	4.1	1.31
Belgium (French)	3	1.38
New Zealand	3	2.01
Iceland	2.3	2.01
Sweden	1.8	2.34
Thailand	…	…

Source: TIMSS 1995.

If the average implemented curriculum in most nations is broad, what about depth? As just one indicator of depth, we find that the average amount of instructional time given to topics did not vary greatly across these nations, and again the American implemented mathematics curriculum as a whole is not extremely shallow in its coverage. At the same time, the average American eighth grade mathematics teacher is not more prone to topic repetition than other nations' teachers are, at least not to the extent that it might create the broken spiral described in the broken curriculum literature. Actually, as Table 14.3 shows, the average U.S. teacher is less repetitious than the average teacher across the whole TIMSS sample.

So it would appear that if the implemented American eighth grade mathematics curriculum is broken, it is no more broken than in most other nations. Although there is cross-national variation on these characteristics of the curriculum, the United States is not extreme in any sense. This leads to the next question: What if nations are able to have narrower, deeper, and less repetitious mathematics intended and implemented curricula, would this mean higher national achievement?

National Curricula and National Achievement

Boe and colleagues (2001) examined this question in great detail. They looked at achievement both across the full mathematics test given by TIMSS as well as with several types of subscores that focus on several parts of mathematics achievement. They studied characteristics of the national intended curriculum using special curricular data over several grades (Schmidt, McKnight, and Raizen, 1997; Schmidt and others, 1997), as well as other curricular data. As a supplement to the Boe report, we analyzed measures of the implemented curricula broadness, depth, and repetition described earlier (national averages and within-nation variation).

In all of these analyses, on a range of characteristics of national intended and implemented curricula in both mathematics and science, virtually *no* national qualities of curricula are related to any of a range of indicators of national achievement in eighth grade. High-performing nations are not more likely to have curricula with a particular set of characteristics in terms of both intended content and implementation in the classroom. Whether it is for the full mathematics and science tests or focused subscores, or for indicators of the intended or implemented curricula, there is no pattern of association between the qualities of national curricula and national achievement. The only exception is a moderate relationship between the coverage of algebra in nations and the cross-national level of algebra achievement.

So does this mean that curriculum is not important in the schooling process? Clearly not, but given the widely held belief that the curriculum plays a primary role in driving the national achievement level, these findings may astound some. How can they be explained?

One answer might be that curriculum really isn't important in producing the national level of achievement; another might be that the TIMSS curricular data were so flawed as to be unable to show this relationship. But we find little evidence to support either interpretation. Schmidt and others (2001) find significant correlations between curricula subtopics taught and achieved *within nations* (not among countries)—suggesting, as one would expect, that if students were not taught something they tended not to get problems of that type right on the TIMSS achievement test. Also, the TIMSS data were collected under rigorous scientific standards, so we doubt they could be so flawed as to be "hiding" major relationships between national curricula and achievement. Rather, a more global view of national curricula and national achievement helps to explain these results.

Assuming that if students are not taught something they tend to know less about it than ones who are taught, what would account for this lack of across-national association between curricula and achievement? Let's consider the intended curriculum first.

A plausible answer seems to be that every country in the TIMSS intends for its students to learn roughly the same knowledge base in mathematics and science, significantly reducing cross-national variation in the intended curriculum. A convergence of curricula means that the curricular content of eighth grade mathematics and science from one nation to the next is not large. In fact, research on historical curricular trends shows precisely this; national intended curricula continue to converge on similar content over time and across nations (see, for example, Benavot and others, 1991; McEneaney and Meyer, 2000). There has come to be much greater homogeneity in terms of recognized core knowledge—content for curricula—at least through the end of primary schooling across nations. Although nations vary with regard to the emphasis they place on numerous subtopics in the intended curriculum, virtually all nations teach mathematics and science with an increasingly standard notion of the essence and components of these subjects. In the elementary years, most students worldwide are exposed to core concepts, so it is understandable that there is no association between intended curriculum and achievement across nations. Even the one set of cross-national associations there is (those between algebra curriculum and achievement) is for a relatively distinct subtopic of mathematics that nations either do or do not teach in eighth grade. This case demonstrates what would be the case with the TIMSS data if there were significant differences in what nations intended to teach.

This isomorphic-curricular argument also explains why cross-national differences in implementation of curricula are not related to cross-national differences in achievement. We suspect there is not really much difference across nations in average implementation, particularly as compared to variation within nations. As we pointed out, considerably more variation in implemented curricula occurs among classes within nations than among nations. No nation—and certainly not the United States from the perspective of the TIMSS data—appears to have a wildly broken curriculum in terms of its average implementation. Finally, purely curricular-based reasons for national differences in achievement have been questioned for some time on the grounds that a host of curricular processes show only minor differences across nations and tend not to be significantly related to achievement (see Stevenson and Baker, 1996; see Valverde and others, 2002, for an opposite argument).

Institutionalized Policy Reform

What is interesting here beyond the specifics of this case of international educational competition and curricular reform is not just that our analysis finds little evidence for characterizing American curricula as broken, or that we find almost no evidence of an association between characteristics of national curricula and national level of achievement. Instead, the whole case illustrates how relatively easy it is for modern education systems to jump on a reform cycle. During the years that this American case unfolded, few seriously questioned the veracity of the two main assumptions about the broken American curricula and their role in national achievement. The cycle was easily launched and then wrapped in the scantiest of real evidence; there was a long-standing solution waiting for a problem, and this led to reform.

Although it may be too early to assess the long-run impact of curricular reforms in mathematics and science in the United States, we suspect that the general ideas stemming from the TIMSS case will have a significant effect on American educational policy at the national, state, and local levels for some time to come. Educational reform never happens in a vacuum; there is always some connection to past reforms, and each has some imprint on future ones. We wonder what those who will look back on the Bush administration's No Child Left Behind legislation will say about its connection to the ideas stirred up by the mathematics and science curricular reform issues of the 1990s.

Was it wrong after the release of the TIMSS initial results to be concerned about the nation's curriculum, or to have wanted to improve it to match the best in the world, or to want to try moving teachers to implement curricula in a more effective way? Of course not. Along with other professional educators, we would encourage any nation to implement the best curriculum that can be designed, and to continuously monitor it and make improvements where possible.

What we have described here is not some sort of scandal; quite the opposite. It was the result of multiple good intentions of many powerful stakeholders in educational policy in the United States. Everyone involved had the best of intentions of improving the nation's schools. We doubt that even timely, in-depth analyses of curricula and national achievement showing some of the flaws and overstatements in the original assumptions, as we show here, would have deterred this exuberant outbreak of mathematics and science curricular reform in the United States. There was just too much anticipation of the solution of reform in these areas for too long a time. What is most likely the cost of this laserlike focus on curricular reform was a chance to discuss a number of other educational problems in the United States that are identifiable with the TIMSS data—resource inequality and disadvantaged students discussed . . . being notable.

The American case is just one of many that illustrate a similar process about educational reform. We began this article with the image of a reform-crazed educational world, which often uses studies like TIMSS to adopt solutions and new approaches to prevailing concerns about a nation's schools in general. So how can we make sense of this from a more global perspective? We have already suggested that it is not just a process by which education is considered useful and everyone wants the best they can find. If this were so, it would be hard to explain why even top-performing nations are about equally prone to cycles of reform as are nations with poorer performance.

There are two productive ways to think about an educational world dripping with the political motivation for finding problems, creating solutions, and enacting reforms. One is about how education is a sector made up of many formal organizations constantly mixing with the realpolitik of social policy within a nation. The second is on a deeper institutional level, about what education has come to represent in society.

Educational Reform as an Organizational Product

As an institution, mass schooling in every nation is made up of a dense population of formal organizations of stakeholders in contrast to, say, the institution of the family, which comprises informal organizations. Schools, local education units, ministries of education, NGOs of professional educators, teachers' unions, and so forth are cast into a thick web of formal organizations, all of which have an interest and some influence in producing educational policy. As such, the institutional ideas behind education shape organizational behavior as much as they do the behavior of individuals participating in these organizations (Meyer and Jepperson, 2000). But how organizations behave is somewhat different from how individuals do, and this difference plays a role in producing the high volume of educational reform.

A relatively new and important school of thought about the interaction between formal organizations and the characteristics of the institutional sector they are in suggests some useful ways to think about constant worldwide educational reform. Observers of formal organizations from a neoinstitutional perspective (Richard Scott, John Meyer, Brian Rowan, and others) show us how constrained and even ritualistic organizations can be by the institutionalized world of common meaning and appropriate actions that they function in (Powell and DiMaggio, 1991).

As an organization, a school behaves more as the people within it think a school should behave than it does according to some unique rationalized plan of action. This is also true for governmental agencies, unions, and NGOs of all types within the educational sector. Certainly, formal organizations are bureaucracies and there are considerable rationalized processes within them, but formal organizations also conform to institutional ideas as to what they should be rational about and even how to be rational.

Taking this idea a step further, a fellow theoretical traveler of this viewpoint and organizational theorist, James March, finds that organizational processes such as problem identification, solution finding, and implementing are themselves ritualized to a degree. He convincingly argues that in real organizations, particularly large ones, each of these activities runs in a separate stream within the organization and generally does not occur in the order one would assume. Hence, organizational solutions wait for the right problems, methods of implementation wait for the right solution to spread, and so forth (March and Olsen, 1979). One needs only to ask an astute older colleague in a large organization about the history of computerization and its effect on the organization's integrating this technology to hear stories of solutions waiting for and trying to find problems, or technology waiting for applications, or implementation strategies looking for solutions to distribute, and so forth.

An insightful way to think about the American TIMSS case, as well as similar reform activity in other nations, is not to attribute the reform cycle to the actions of just one or even a few organizations (a ministry, or a union, or even the statistical branch of a ministry that helps produce studies like TIMSS). Instead, attribute the actions to a web of numerous organizations, all of which in one way or another take part in the production of problems, solutions, and implementation strategies.

As we have described, a legacy of reaction to past international studies and the image of a problematic American mathematics curriculum led expert groups of mathematics educators, federal mathematics and science policy makers, and so forth to be receptive to a curricular interpretation of the United States's placing in the academic Olympiad of TIMSS even though this interpretation is not well supported by other parts of the TIMSS data set. In the mid-1990s, use of the TIMSS international scores was really just the spark, much as Sputnik and *Nation at Risk* functioned for earlier reform cycles. The web of organizations was loaded like a compressed spring aimed at a reform cycle; American performance on international tests (which in study after study is usually in the midrange, and rarely extremely bad) released this reform energy.

The point is that institutions like education, comprising to a high degree webs of formal organizations all producing streams of problems, solutions, and implementation, are capable of generating intense motivation for collective rationalized action aimed at a specific target. For example, American organizations such as the AAAS or the NSF, made up of high-profile experts and given the public charter to monitor and recommend ways to improve American technology and science, can generate collective motivation to look for solutions, find problems, and rally around implementation of reforms. Never do we see such an organization in the United States make a public statement that all is fine with its charge.

Certainly nations differ in the exact nature in which educational policy is made and reform is started. Nations with stronger centralized political parties organize approaches to reform differently from the American system of education with its highly disconnected, localized governance system. Such political-structure variation across nations probably has some relationship to the frequency of reform cycles across them. For example, the United States, with its very high ratio of educational organizations (other than schools) to students, yields a nation often primed for reform (Tyack and Cuban, 1995). Some other nations may have slightly less frequent rounds of reform, but overall the process we describe leads to considerable reform activities worldwide. Last of all, there is evidence to suggest that, as with the case here, use of external information from other nations is more frequent when policy debates are about highly contested issues (Steiner-Khamsi, 2002; Schriewer, 1990).

Reform as an Institutional Value

The image of reform as an institutionalized value helps us think about educational policy reform as a worldwide experience that stems directly from the institutional character of mass schooling. We have discussed the power of education in modern society as an institution, how central it has become to so many important things about the future of our children and our nations. We have shown how as an institution it surpassed even the vital role of the family in many aspects of childrearing and the passing down of advantage to future generations. For better or worse, mass schooling is among a relatively small number of central institutions in modern society, and our tales so far have documented some of the things that are happening worldwide in this powerful institution. Yet when we try to explain the world trend of educational reform, we encounter a paradox.

As sociologists have long pointed out, when institutions reach their height of power and influence on human behavior, they organize meanings and norms that are highly resistant to change. However, constant educational reform seems to move in the opposite direction. The powerful institution of mass schooling appears entirely open to change.

One way out of this paradox is to suggest that reform really doesn't change much; what occurs is merely surface change, while the main values of the institution remain stable underneath. Certainly there is some truth in this image, and we don't want to equate all reform with major institutional change. Yet as various histories of educational reform in the United States have shown, reform often does lead to profound institutional change (Tyack and Cuban, 1995). Reform is not necessarily always trivial or faddish.

Perhaps a better way out of the paradox is to consider how the tendency for continuous reform cycles is built into the institutional fabric of education. Institutional theorist Meyer has thought the most about this aspect of mass schooling. In a provocative chapter (in a book celebrating the academic career of David Tyack) titled "Reflections on Education as Transcendence," he discusses how the institutional origins of mass schooling are strikingly religious in form (Meyer, 2000). This no doubt sounds like a strange thing to say about public schooling, which usually meticulously separates out religious beliefs from public instruction. But Meyer is not referring to the teaching of religion; rather, he refers to the idea that in its institutional form mass education takes on religious-like power in modern society. He points out that schooling's mission to transmit major knowledge about how the world works and its ability to transform students into "educated adults" in a universalistic fashion gives the institution transcendental qualities. It is not that public mass schooling is about religion; instead, it has powerful institutional components that make it like a religion in modern society.

Reform gets built into core values about education in modern society. The word *reform* itself, of course, derives from the idea of reforming the universal Catholic Church. Not radical restructuring but constant reform gives the institution a certain dynamic power. It is not static; it is open to some change, to the flexible exercising of basic institutional ideas in developing a better school system. This quality of schooling is what drives so much reform.

Its power as an institution is in large part derived from the belief held by many in modern society that schooling is a key component in producing the good society. Technically, morally, and civically, education is called upon to provide the masses with the right stuff to form a productive, just, and orderly world. When social problems arise, the call for an educational solution is not far behind. A powerful modern ideology is that society itself is a project, and one of the fundamental parts of the project is to use education to achieve society. Seen this way, it is no wonder that reform to improve the basic ideas, goals, and operation of mass schooling is nearly continuous and publically welcomed—exactly as it appears to be across so many nations.

Note

1. Compare, for example, how Japan, after scoring high in international studies in the 1980s, took to heart interpretations of its results that suggested too much emphasis was placed on basic computational skills and then sought reforms that put more high-order thinking in the mathematics curricula, while the United States, after scoring in the middle of the pack, sought reform for more basic skills as an interpretation of how to "catch up" with Japan.

References

Boe, E., Barkanic, G., Shin, S., May, H., Leow, C., Singleton, C., Zeng, G., and Borouch, R. *Correlates of National Differences in Mathematics and Science Achievement: Evidence from TIMSS.* (Data Analysis Report, 2001-DARI.) Philadelphia: Center for Research and Evaluation in Social Policy, University of Pennsylvania.

Bowles, S., and Gintis, H. *Schooling in Capitalist America.* New York: Basic Books, 1976.

Bracy, G. "The TIMSS 'Final Year' Study and Report: A Critique." *Educational Researcher*, 2000, 29, 4-10.

Bruner, J. *On Knowing: Lessons for the Left Hand.* New York: Antheneum, 1962.

Cross, C. *Political Education: National Policy Comes of Age.* New York: Teachers College Press, 2003.

Eckert, P. *Jocks and Burnouts.* New York: Teachers College Press, 1989.

Goldman, S., and McDermott, R. "The Culture of Competition in American Schools." In G. Spindler (ed.), *Education and Cultural Progress.* Prospect Heights, Ill.: Waveland Press, 1987.

LeTendre, G., Akiba, M., Goesling, B., Wiseman, A., and Baker, D. "The Policy Trap: National Educational Policy and the Third International Math and Science Study." *International Journal of Educational Policy, Research and Practice*, 2000, 2 (1), 45-64.

March, J., and Olsen, J. *Ambiguity and Choice in Organizations.* Bergen, Norway: Universitetsforgalet, 1979.

McKnight, C., Crosswhite, F., and Dossey, J. *The Underachieving Curriculum: Assessing U.S. Mathematics from an International Perspective.* Champaign, Ill.: Stipes, 1987.

Meyer, J. "Reflections on Education as Transcendence." In L. Cuban and D. Shipps (eds.) *Reconstructing the Common Good in Education.* Stanford, Calif.: Stanford University Press, 2000.

Meyer, J., and Jepperson, R. "The 'Actor' of Modern Society: The Cultural Construction of Social Agency." *Sociological Theory*, 2000, 18(1), 100-120.

Powell, W., and Dimaggio, P. *The New Institutionalism in Organizational Analysis.* Chicago: University of Chicago Press, 1991.

Robitaille, D., Beaton, A., and Plomp, J. *The Impact of TIMSS on the Teaching and Learning of Mathematics and Science.* Vancouver, B.C.: Pacific Education Press, 2000.

Schmidt, W., McKnight, C., and Raizen, S. *A Splintered Vision: An Investigation of U.S. Science and Mathematics Education.* Lansing, Mich.: National Research Center for the Third International Mathematics and Science Study, Michigan State University, 1997.

Schmidt, W., McKnight, C., Valverde, G., Houang, R., and Wiley, D. *Many Visions, Many Aims: A Cross-National Investigation of Curricular Intentions in School Mathematics.* Norwell, MA.: Kluwer Academic, 1997.

Schriewer, J. "The Method of Comparison and the Need for Externalization: Methodological Criteria and Sociological Concepts." In J. Schriewer and B. Holmes (eds.) *Theories and Methods in Comparative Education.* Bern, Switzerland: Lang, 1990.

Steiner-Khamsi, G. "Re-Territorializing Educational Import." In A. Novoa and M. Lawn (eds.) *Fabricating Europe: The Formation of an Education Space.* London: Kluwer Academic, 2002.

Tyack, D., and Cuban, L. *Tinkering Toward Utopia: A Century of Public School Reform.* Cambridge, Mass.: Harvard University Press, 1995.

Valverde, G., and Schmidt, W. "Refocusing U.S. Math and Science Education." *Issues in Science and Technology,* 1997, 14, 60-66.

PART III
Suggested Readings

Archer, M. S. (1979). *Social origins of educational systems*. Beverly Hills: Sage.

Arnot, M., & Dillabough, J. (2000) *Challenging democracy: International perspectives on gender, education and citizenship.* NewYork: Routledge.

Baker, D. P. (1993). Compared to Japan, the U.S. is a low achiever...really: New evidence and comment on Westbury. *Educational Researcher, 22*, 18–26.

Baker, D. P. (1994). In comparative isolation: Why comparative research has so little influence on American Sociology of Education. In Aaron M. Pallas (Ed.), *Research in sociology of education and socialization* (Vol. 10, pp. 53–70). Greenwich CT: JAI Press.

Baker, D. P., & LeTendre, G. (2005). *National differences, global similarities*. Stanford, CA: Stanford University Press.

Benavot, A. (1992). Educational expansion and economic growth in the modern world, 1913–1985. In B. Fuller & R. Rubison (Eds.), *The political construction of education*. New York: Praeger.

Boli, J., Ramirez, F., & Meyer, J.W. (1985). Explaining the origins and expansion of mass education. *Comparative Education Review, 29*, 145–170.

Bradley, K., & Ramirez, F. (1996). World polity and gender parity: Women's share of higher education, 1965–1985. *Research in Sociology of Education*. JAI Press.

Collins, R. (1977). Some comparative principles of educational stratification. *Harvard Educational Review, 47*(1), 1–27.

Cookson, P. W., & Persell, C. H. (1986). English and American residential schools: A comparative study of the reproduction of elites. *Comparative Education Review, 30*, 260–270.

Cookson, P. W., Sadovnik, A. R., & Semel, S. F. (1992). *International handbook of educational reform*. Westport, CT: Greenwood.

Cummings, W. K. (2003). *The institutions of education*. Oxford: Symposium Books.

Kerckhoff, A. C. (2001). Education and social stratification process in comparative perspective. *Sociology of Education, 74* (Extra Issue), 3–18.

Kerckhoff, A. C., & Everett, D. D. (1986). Sponsored and contest education pathways in Great Britain and the United States. In A. C. Kerckhoff (Ed.), *Research in sociology of education and socialization: Vol. 6*, (pp. 133–163). Greenwich, CT: JAI Press.

Lewis, C. (1995). *Educating mind and heart: Rethinking the roots of Japanese education*. London: Cambridge University Press.

Meyer, J., Ramirez, F. O., Rubinson, R., & Boli, J. (1977). The world educational revolution, 1950–1970. *Sociology of Education, 50*, 242–258.

Ogbu, J. U. (1978). *Minority education and caste*. New York: Academic Press.

Ramirez, F., & Boli, J. (1987). The political construction of mass schooling: European origins and worldwide institutionalization. *Sociology of Education, 60,* 2–17.

White, M. (1987). *The Japanese educational challenge*. New York: The Free Press.

Whitty, G., & Power, S. (2000). Marketization and privatization in mass education systems. *International Journal of Educational Development, 20*.

Higher Education

Following World War II, access to higher education in the United States expanded. During the 1960s, liberal educational reformers demanded that groups historically denied access to higher education, such as African Americans, Latinos, women, and the working class, be given increased opportunities for postsecondary education. Compensatory higher education programs and affirmative action became institutionalized, but were challenged by conservatives who argued that opening access debased the meritocratic functions of higher education by lowering standards to many unqualified and underprepared students. Today, although the percentage of students attending postsecondary schools in the United States is the highest in the world, there remains disagreement as to whether this expansion represents actual democratization or an expansion of secondary stratification to postsecondary education. Functionalists argue that the development of mass higher education reflects an increase in democratic access; conflict theorists argue that as more students attended higher education institutions, working-class and minority students tended to attend two-year institutions, middle-class students to attend four-year public institutions, and upper-middle class and upper-class students to attend elite private institutions. The following articles examine important issues and trends in higher education in the United States and provide empirical evidence regarding this debate.

Chapter 15, "Changes in Access to Higher Education in the United States, 1980–1992" by Bryn Mawr College sociologist David Karen, analyzes changes in admissions to higher education in the last decades of the twentieth century. He examines the effects of demands for the democratization of higher education by providing increased access to marginalized groups and attempts by privileged groups to maintain their competitive advantages.

Chapter 16, "It's Not Enough to Get Through the Open Door: Inequalities by Social Background in Transfer from Community Colleges to Four-Year Colleges" by Teachers College Columbia University sociologist Kevin Dougherty and American Institutes for Education researcher Gregory S. Kienzl, examines whether or not two-year colleges have provided access for their mainly working-class and minority populations to four-year colleges and universities. This chapter tests functionalist and conflict theories of higher education, the former arguing that community colleges provide increased access for educational and social mobility and the latter arguing that they extend and reproduce social class reproduction to higher education.

Chapter 17, "College-for-All: Do Students Understand What College Demands?" by Northwestern University sociologist James E. Rosenbaum, examines the effects of open admissions policies and the ideology that everyone should and can go to college. He argues that high school counselor, teacher, and student beliefs that you do not have to work hard to get into some college have deleterious effects on working-class and minority students, who find themselves under prepared for the rigors of a college education.

Questions for Reflection and Discussion

1. According to Karen, how did access to higher education in the United States change in the 1980s? Do you think these changes represented an increase in opportunity for groups historically denied access or the shift upward of secondary education stratification?

2. According to Dougherty and Kienzl, have community colleges provided significant opportunities for low-income and minority groups to transfer to four-year colleges? If not, why do you think this has been the case? Should two-year colleges function as feeders to four-year colleges or should they have a more vocational function, preparing students for jobs when they graduate?

3. What does Rosenbaum argue are the effects of a "college for all" ideology? Do you think all students should go to college? Do you think standards for admission to college should be higher?

4. How would functionalist, conflict theorists, and institutional theorists explain the processes described in the three articles on higher education? How would Bowles and Gintis and Randall Collins differ? Do you think that standards have been lowered and the prestige of a college degree has been debased over the past two decades?

15
Changes in Access to Higher Education in the United States, 1980–1992

DAVID KAREN

Any discussion of the transition from high school to college in the United States must include recognition of the uniqueness of the U.S. higher education "system." As Ben-David (1971) noted three decades ago, it is only in the broadest sense that we can call the set of institutions that make up the U.S. higher education sector a "system." Distinctions can be made between two-year and four-year colleges, public and private, historically black and historically white, colleges and universities, and so forth. Institutions of higher education vary in their governance structures, market positions, and organizational fields. Although it may be appropriate to discuss a *given* state's "system" of public higher education, we would then be faced with 50 systems to take into account, without beginning to account for the private institutions. Indeed, the National Center for Public Policy and Higher Education's report, *Measuring Up 2000: The State-by-State Report Card for Higher Education* (2001) indicated radically different profiles of high school graduation and college participation by state and large differences on these measures by race and income within states.

This situation differs radically from that of other advanced industrial societies, in which the central state plays a much larger role and in which admission is often determined almost solely by a standardized test, usually administered early in a student's educational career. The process of matching students to institutions is much more fluid in the United States, as befits a society that emphasizes its commitment to equality of opportunity.

The lack of central coordination in U.S. postsecondary education provides many points of access through many channels. It is even possible to enter a postsecondary program without a high school diploma, thus clearly underlining the openness of the U.S. educational system and, presumably, the U.S. social structure even to late bloomers. This situation contrasts radically with European systems in which one's particular track in high school (often determined before high school) becomes the ticket to one's specific place in the tertiary educational system. Indeed, in Europe, as well, there is a much tighter connection than in the United States between specific educational credentials and occupational outcomes, and these "credential tracks" are locked in at an earlier age (see Kerckhoff 1995). At the same time, as Bidwell and Quiroz (1991) pointed out, there is much greater "client power" or opportunity in U.S. schools than elsewhere for families of high socioeconomic status (SES) to intervene in the less standardized, less bureaucratized, and decentralized U.S. context. So, while the United States ostensibly provides a plethora of opportunities for higher education even to those who have struggled in the secondary system, it also tends to advantage the already advantaged within that system. An additional, monumental difference is that in Europe, most postsecondary programs are free of charge (even though *some* countries impose tuition charges), whereas in the United States, the payment of a nondiscounted tuition at top-tier private institutions is possible only for those at the top of the income distribution (Mortenson 2000).

This unusual combination of higher educational opportunities and constraints leads to a situation in which the United States appears to hold open the possibility of some kind of postsecondary education for all, while it generally makes it less likely that those from low-SES backgrounds (and other subordinate groups) will take advantage of it and more likely that those from high-SES backgrounds will do so. Coupled with the highly stratified nature of the system of higher education, characterized by a diffuse but unmistakable set of connections between high-prestige institutions and high-prestige careers, it becomes possible for a set of institutions that are ostensibly geared toward providing equality of opportunity actually to reproduce inequality. In his review of "Institutional Arrangements and Stratification Processes in Industrial Societies," Kerckhoff (1995) argued that compared to other advanced industrial societies, the United States, thanks to the highly differentiated set of higher education institutions and the lack of a direct or specific link between educational credentials and the labor market, provides greater possibilities for social mobility. At the same time, he recognized the greater likelihood that family resources will affect students' educational opportunities, which would *reduce* the possibilities for social mobility in the United States. These conflicting pressures lead to a greater opaqueness in the status transmission process, which more effectively legitimates these resulting inequalities (Brint and Karabel 1989). It should also be remembered that the inequality in access to highly remunerative careers is a much higher-stakes issue in the United States than in countries whose social welfare sector is more highly developed and where a social safety net is in place (cf. Brint and Karabel 1989).

Stratification in the Higher Education Sector

For the United States, then, compared to other advanced industrial societies, it is much more important to attend to institutional stratification *within* the higher education sector. Whereas in Europe, it would be appropriate to focus on the accumulation of educational credentials that are connected to specific labor market outcomes, in the United States, we must look at the differentiation that occurs among postsecondary institutions. Indeed, this research focus has increased over the years. From studies that have found that community college attenders receive less income and occupational bang for their educational buck than do four-year college attenders (Dougherty 1987; Lavin and Hyllegard 1996) to those that have showed positive socioeconomic and other outcomes for those who attend prestigious institutions (discussed later), the evidence seems clear that, as Trow (1984:149) stated, "[t]he advantages of elite institutions are so overwhelming that they create what is for them (but not for the rest of higher education or the larger society) a kind of 'virtuous circle' in which advantage begets advantage."

A range of studies has shown effects of various aspects of college selectivity and resources on socioeconomic and other outcomes (Feldman and Newcomb 1969; Karabel and McClelland 1989; Kingston and Lewis 1990; Pascarella, Smart, and Stoecker 1989; Sewell 1971; Smart 1986, 1988; Smart and Pascarella 1986; Solmon 1975; Tsui 1998; Useem and Karabel 1986; Wise 1975). Collectively, these studies have found that where one goes to college can have effects on one's future education, occupation (including one's rank within an occupation, e.g., how high the corporate ladder one ascends), and income, as well as on various nonsocioeconomic outcomes, such as tolerance, civic participation, and happiness. More recent analyses of the effect of college selectivity and other characteristics on the socioeconomic outcomes of alumni have demonstrated consistently positive effects on further education, occupation, and income. The most comprehensive of such analyses (Bowen and Bok 1998) found positive effects of selectivity on a variety of outcomes (e.g., income and life satisfaction) even among a restricted group of selective institutions. Using data on college attenders, both early and in midcareer, for instance, Bowen and Bok showed that attendance at more selective institutions was positively related to socioeconomic outcomes. Presumably, if their sample had included nonselective four-year institutions, the effects of selectivity, net of background variables, would have been even stronger. A report from the National Center for Education Statistics (NCES 2000b) analyzed data from a follow-up of the High School and Beyond (HSB) 1980 sophomore cohort and concluded that a variety of college characteristics—including selectivity, availability of certain majors, region, and expenditures—contributed to increased earnings in the early careers of college graduates (though differently for men and women, and not all college characteristics had similar effects).[1]

In this context, it becomes critical to assess the degree to which access to the different sectors of higher education is fairly distributed. After all, the U.S. commitment to equality of opportunity is rooted, at least in part, in the notion that anyone can attend college. If, however, the most selective sectors of higher education are disproportionately available only to the already advantaged and are connected to the most rewarded positions in the society, then we must examine carefully the degree to which a vehicle that is ostensibly organized for social mobility may actually undermine its realization.

A key point of this article is that it matters *where* one goes to college. As the number of places in higher education expands, there can be large increases in the *amount* of education any given group attains without any change in its relative position in the educational hierarchy. One needs to gain access to higher-status institutions to increase one's *relative* educational mobility. The aggregate data on higher education enrollments by sector reveal one obvious change: Women have not only decreased their concentration in the two-year sector but have (on the basis of various published reports in the *Chronicle of Higher Education)* increased their access to elite institutions as well. In terms of how different racial groups have distributed themselves, it appears that there has been a degree of stability over the past decade. There is some evidence that students of color have become more concentrated in the two-year sector than whites have, but this is not an overwhelming trend. Similarly, there has been a slight tendency for this pattern among students from low versus high socioeconomic backgrounds (see NCES 1997b:219).

Much research on the high school-to-college transition has focused simply on the characteristics of high school graduates that most likely lead to college *attendance*. In an important study, however, Hearn (1991) found that 1980 high school graduates who attended college and were from historically excluded groups were less likely to attend higher-status institutions, net of other variables. I used this study as a baseline for the current work. In their comprehensive review of access to higher education, Baker and Vélez (1996) suggested that the traditional focus on social class background and academic ability needs to be expanded to include gender and race, especially with respect to destination within higher education. Davies and Guppy (1997) examined college destinations of individuals who were aged 14–21 in 1979 with data from the National Longitudinal Survey of Youth. They found that SES is a significant predictor, net of other background factors and ability, of college selectivity. They also found that men, net of other background factors, are more likely to attend more-selective colleges than are women, although this effect was not significant after ability was controlled. In general, Davies and Guppy replicated the results of Hearn's (1991) analyses of the college destinations of the 1980 HSB cohort.

Two questions are relevant here:

1. How have these processes changed, if at all, in recent years?
2. How can we understand the processes by which such sorting occurs?

Linking Students to Colleges

Bourdieu's work (1977, 1984; Bourdieu and Passeron 1977) suggested that important, institutionally based matching processes occur that link a person's social origin (broadly conceived) with her or his destination within education and, ultimately, in the social structure. At the same time that individuals are setting their sights on a range of potentially reachable social destinations or developing a set of realistic expectations for the future, there are strong pressures that allocate individuals into particular places on the socioeconomic transmission belt. At the level of the individual, this adjustment of aspirations to what is in the realm of the possible occurs through what Bourdieu (1977, 1984; see also Bourdieu and Passeron 1977) called *habitus*. According to Swartz (1997:104), habitus "represents a sort of deep-structuring cultural matrix that generates self-fulfilling prophecies according to different class opportunities." So, as high school students begin to think about specific postsecondary options, their behaviors should reflect their semiconscious assessments of the probabilities of specific outcomes. These assessments, evident perhaps in students' test-taking and college application behaviors, will vary on the basis of students' social location of origin. From a Bourdieuan point of view, they would reflect one's dispositions toward the future that are based on the totality of one's social location, including such criteria as gender, race, and region, as well as class characteristics like economic, cultural, and social capital. One would expect, then, that students from noncollege backgrounds would be more likely to aspire to, apply to, and attend relatively nonselective postsecondary institutions (and thus submit relatively few applications, since success from any given application is high), while those whose parents have advanced degrees would be more likely to aspire to, apply to, and attend highly selective colleges and universities (Karen 1988; McDonough 1997).

The key question here is this: What happens to these matching processes during periods of the expansion of higher education? Between 1970 and 1996, higher education enrollments increased by 66 percent, from 8.6 million to 14.3 million students (NCES 2000a: 127). This increase was accompanied by a shift in the gender representation of students and in the type of institution attended. In 1970, 59 percent of the students were male, and only 27 percent of enrollments were in two-year institutions; by 1996, men represented only 44 percent of enrollments, and two-year institutions had expanded to enroll 38 percent of students. Considering the magnitude of this change, one must ask whether, in addition to women, other groups that previously had been disproportionately excluded from higher education, such as students of color and working-class students, were able to make inroads into higher education and whether, given the disproportionate expansion of the two-year sector, their enrollments were concentrated at the bottom of the higher education hierarchy. I previously showed (Karen 1991, 1998) that although there were changes in the distribution of women and students of color within higher education through 1976, the distribution since then indicates a leveling off of the inroads that students of color made in top-tier institutions, while women continued to increase their representation in these institutions. Students from working-class backgrounds, however, did not shift their relative place within the higher educational hierarchy. I argued that subordinate groups' political mobilization or the lack thereof was a prime cause of this pattern.

At the same time, since 1976, there has been notable political mobilization by dominant groups (i.e., countermobilization) to maintain their relative exclusivity in elite higher education. Through fiscal crises (and the attendant cuts in support for social programs),[2] direct changes in the availability of financial aid at the institutional level (e.g., changes away from need-blind admissions), attacks on social welfare policy, and the lack of enforcement of and then active attacks on affirmative action policies, the countermobilization has been intense, especially in the 1990s (Lavin 2000). To the extent that institutions increasingly use high-stakes tests for admission and base financial aid on "merit," rather than need (e.g., Hope grants), we have a formula for further excluding low-income students from the most selective institutions.

As I explain later, the focus of this article is on the college enrollment patterns of 1980 and 1992 high school graduates. Between 1980 and 1992, the college enrollment rates of 16–24 year olds who had graduated from high school in the previous 12 months increased 25 percent (from 49.3 percent to 61.7 percent), even as the number of enrollments declined by 100,000.[3] As more of a graduating cohort enters postsecondary education, what can we expect in terms of how they will distribute themselves among institutions of higher education?

Competing Explanations for College Destinations

During this period of expansion, then, we did not see, as a functionalist status-attainment orientation (e.g., Blau and Duncan 1967) might predict, strong movement toward a more equal distribution of underrepresented groups across the spectrum of higher education institutions. In fact, Blossfeld and Shavit (1993:22) turned the expectation of such modernization theorists on its head, concluding their summary of cross-national studies of educational attainment by stating that educational "expansion actually facilitates to a large extent the *persistence* [italics added] of inequalities in educational opportunity." Whether by increasing the size of the nonelite sector of higher education for working-class students or simply by allowing greater expansion of the sectors populated largely by the elite, Hout, Raftery, and Bell (1993) noted that one can have a large increase in the size of the postsecondary education sector of a given society but still maintain inequalities in educational access and attainment between dominant and subordinate groups. In the United States, Hout et al. maintained, it appears that we follow this "typical" pattern of "maximally maintained inequality" (MMI).[4] Indeed, as I noted earlier, the pressures to maintain the elite in elite institutions and the expansion of the bottom tier for new entrants have been apparent in the United States. As long as the elite has not reached a saturation point in their access to elite higher education (say, above 90 percent), it is possible for an MMI regime to be retained.

With respect to access to different levels of selectivity of higher education, it is plausible to hypothesize that subordinate groups had three different experiences in the 1980–92 period:

1. greater opportunities for subordinate groups and *declining inequality*, since the whole pie expanded à la the modernization theorists; or
2. MMI, as implied by Hout et al. (1993), because of the expansion of the higher-tier institutions for elite students and the expansion of the lower-tier institutions for nonelite students; or
3. persisting inequality, which is due, in this case, to political mobilization (i.e., countermobilization) of dominant groups.

The fundamental distinction, obviously, is whether inequality is declining or persisting (option 1 versus 2 and 3), and it is necessary to understand, between options 2 and 3, whether the explanation for this persisting inequality is due to MMI or political mobilization.

Later, I discuss how one may distinguish between options 2 and 3. In any case, between 1980 and 1992, the larger political context experienced no large jolts, so perhaps one can see more clearly the overall trends in the access policies of institutions of higher education and how subordinate groups reacted to a countermobilization offensive.

Plan of Analysis

In my study, I examined the data set of the National Education Longitudinal Study of 1988 (NELS:88) to see what factors are most influential in predicting college destinations (defined by selectivity) for a group of high school graduates. Specifically, I replicated Hearn's (1991) analyses of HSB to determine what changed with respect to destination within higher education in the 1980–92 period. By looking at individual-level data, I could sort out not only how the college population changed but how, net of other variables, each factor changed between 1980 and 1992 in its association with the dependent variable. My focus was on how social background and academic variables interact to affect the college destinations of high school graduates. As I noted earlier, Bowen and Bok (1998) found strong effects of the selectivity of colleges on future educational, occupational, and income attainments, as well as on community involvement and life satisfaction, even in a survey that was limited to selective institutions. According to NELS (NCES 1997a:iv), "three quarters of all 1992 high school graduates enrolled in some type of postsecondary institution by 1994." With this kind of mass infusion into postsecondary education of a cohort of high school graduates and strong effects on outcomes of institutional selectivity, it is critical to assess which factors determine where particular students go to college.

Although the entire process leading to particular destinations is interesting both theoretically and practically, I was interested in understanding analytically a key set of predictors (hence, the model may be considered underspecified). I attempted to tease out the degree to which the 1980–92 period was one of increased meritocracy (a greater effect of academic variables) and/or continued ascription regarding access of subordinate groups (a greater effect of social origins). This period is a useful one to study, since it represents 12 years of continuous Republican control of the White House. Although it did not correspond entirely to the period of cutbacks in funding for higher education (which began in 1977), it was a relatively stable period with respect to both domestic politics (the Reagan-Bush years) and the continual downgrading of funding of higher education in the context of fiscal crisis (see Karen 1991, 1998; Mortenson 2000). At the same time, it witnessed a shift toward women's greater participation in higher education,[5] such that some consider that women are no longer disadvantaged in access to college (e.g., Kleinfeld 1999). Similarly, some have argued (e.g., D'souza 1991) that affirmative action is no longer necessary because historical wrongs in the exclusion of blacks from higher education have been righted.

Following Hearn (1991), I split the independent variables between background socioeconomic-ascriptive characteristics and academic attributes of the individual student. Race-ethnicity, gender, and family resources (parents' education, income, and number of siblings) represent the nonacademic influences on college destinations. The academic influences that I examined included high school grades, tested ability, academic versus nonacademic track, various extracurricular activities, and educational expectations. These are, to the extent possible, the same variables that Hearn used in his analysis of HSB. In addition, in an expanded model, I added a number of variables that helped flesh out my conceptualization of both social background and academic influences on college destination. For the former, I added a series of dummy variables to represent locale and type of high school (rural, urban, and suburban, private and public) and two household-resources variables that, I expected, tap various forms of advantage for the student. For the latter, I included one variable—number of institutions applied to—that is a good indicator of a student's orientation to the higher education field and reflects one's individual habitus (Bourdieu 1977, 1984; Bourdieu and Passeron 1977) with respect to a possible college destination. Although academic with respect to its content, I hope that this variable taps the student's comprehension of the higher education *field*[6] (Bourdieu 1984) as well as its interaction with the influence of the student's social background, broadly conceived.

The question that I posed is this: Who goes where to college? I focused on the initial destinations in college for those who graduated high school and relatively soon began college. Of course, this focus means that I severely limited the potential effects of social background, since any effects that social background has on high school graduation and college attendance are ignored. In some ways, I set up a limited test of the "meritocracy" hypothesis. Once I let social background exert all its effects on *whether* people graduate from high school and *whether* they attend college, I asked whether, among those who do attend college, social background continues to have consequences on *where* they go. One may expect that at that relatively embedded point in one's educational career, one's purely academic attributes would take over as singularly determinant, as Stolzenberg (1994) found for graduate students. Yet Hearn's (1990, 1991, 1992) previous work suggested that the meritocratic hypothesis was, at best, overstated. I assess whether we have moved closer to a fully open society as I compare the college destinations of the 1980 and 1992 seniors. I am especially interested in the degree to which there were declines in the importance of social background on college destination. In an open society, where one goes to college, with its attendant benefits for further socioeconomic outcomes, would not be dependent on one's race, class, or gender.

DATA

NELS is a nationally representative sample of eighth graders in 1988 who were followed every two years through 1994. This survey, then, yields information about the transition to higher education from high school. When most of the sample was in the 12th grade, the sample was "freshened" to create a nationally representative sample of high school seniors. In his analysis of HSB, Hearn (1991) examined those seniors from the 1980 cohort who attended some institution of higher education within one year of graduation. In this article, for comparison purposes, I focus on high school graduates from the NELS sample who attended some postsecondary institution by June 1993. After completing the strict comparisons, I introduce a more detailed model that includes some additional variables that derive from my theoretical perspective.

In this analysis, I focus on all NELS respondents who were in the third (i.e., 1994) follow-up, who responded fully to the relevant questions, and who graduated from high school and attended college by June 1993. I used data on students and institutions from the Restricted-Use NELS Data Files and Electronic Codebook CD-ROM. These data were supplemented by data on selectivity from the Higher Education Research Institute. Weighted data were used, with significance tests based on relative weights (i.e., Weight/Average weight)[7] so that sample size was retained for the purposes of inference.[8] Variables were coded, to the extent possible, in exactly the same way as Hearn (1991) did and are presented in Appendix A; for descriptive statistics and the correlation matrix for these variables, see Appendices B and C. The sample consisted of white, black, and Hispanic students (following Hearn).[9]

Although Hearn (1991) examined both selectivity and expenditures per student in his assessment of the relative roles of ascribed and achieved characteristics on college entry, since the latest findings from NCES (2000b) indicated that expenditures per student is much less important for student outcomes than is selectivity, I focus only on the selectivity of the institution, on the basis of standardized test scores.[10] The selectivity data are not optimal because I used 1983 selectivity data for those who entered college in 1992.[11] Given the relative stability of institutional stratification (Clark 1983), however, this probably did not bias my results in any important way.

Findings

NELS High School Graduates

To replicate Hearn's (1991) work regarding selectivity, I regressed selectivity of institution on the following variables in two blocks (see Table 15.1):

1. dummy variables for black, Hispanic, and female; mother's and father's education; total family income; and number of siblings
2. the same variables plus test composite; grades; high school track; dummy variables for participation in journalism, drama, academic or preprofessional clubs, and school government; and educational expectations.

Regressing selectivity on the social background variables (Table 15.1) explains 16.4 percent of the variance. Blacks are less likely to attend selective institutions, net of other factors. Controlling for the other variables in the equation, Hispanics and women, on the other hand, attend institutions that are as selective as whites and men, respectively. Except for the number of siblings, the socioeconomic variables all have effects on the selectivity of the institution attended. Father's education has the strongest effect, followed by income and mother's education.

Some interesting changes in these effects occurred when I entered the academic variables, which doubles the percentage of variance explained (to 32 percent). The most interesting effect is that net of

Table 15.1 Comparison of HSB and NELS

	Background Factors Only				Full Model			
	HSB Metric Coefficient	NELS Metric Coefficient	HSB Standardized Coefficient	NELS Standardized Coefficient	HSB Metric Coefficient	NELS Metric Coefficient	HSB Standardized Coefficient	NELS Standardized Coefficient
Black	-5.85	**-6.80**	-0.12***	**-0.15***	-3.19	**-2.39**	-0.06***	**-0.05****
Hispanic	-3.29	**0.57**	-0.07***	**0.01**	-0.20	**1.38**	0.00	**0.03**
Female	-1.52	**-0.09**	-0.06***	**0.00**	-0.92	**-1.35**	-0.04*	**-0.05***
Father's education	0.59	**1.45**	0.13***	**0.21***	0.23	**0.86**	0.05**	**0.12***
Mother's education	0.47	**0.55**	0.09***	**0.07***	0.30	**0.26**	0.06***	**0.03**
Parental income	0.80	**1.26**	0.11***	**0.16***	0.51	**1.02**	0.07***	**0.13***
Number of siblings	-0.25	**-0.17**	-0.03	**-0.02**	0.03	**-0.08**	0.00	**-0.01**
Tested ability					0.39	**0.39**	0.25***	**0.25***
High school grades					0.73	**1.76**	0.08***	**0.18***
High school track					2.63	**-0.42**	0.11***	**-0.01**
High school student government					1.57	**-0.09**	0.06***	**0.00**
High school departmental or preprofessional club					-0.45	**0.74**	-0.02	**0.03**
High school journalism					0.53	**1.84**	0.02	**0.06***
High school drama or debate					-0.17	**0.79**	0.00	**0.03**
Educational expectations					1.06	**1.14**	0.14***	**0.09***
Constant	83.51	**81.22**			51.05	**44.56**		
R^2			0.10	**0.17**			0.27	**0.33**
Adjusted R^2				0.16				0.32

Note: NELS data in bold face; Hearn's HSB data in regular print.
*$p <= .05$, **$p <= .01$, ***$p <= .001$.

all other variables, women are significantly less likely than men to attend selective colleges. It appears, then, that families persist in investing more heavily in their sons' educations than in their daughters', after academic factors are controlled (Davies and Guppy 1997). Mother's education is insignificant in this expanded equation, while income and father's education have relatively equal effects on selectivity. Among the academic variables, the test composite and grades have the strongest effect by far on selectivity, with the test composite having an effect almost 40 percent greater than grades. Students who participate in journalism and have higher educational expectations also tend to go to more selective institutions.

The strong effects of test composite and grades on the dependent variable lend support to the notion that access to college is meritocratically based. At the same time, the social background factors alone produce an R^2 that is approximately 50 percent of the size of the R^2 of the full model. This finding suggests that for a cohort of students who were in high school a full quarter century after the Higher Education Act of 1965, which was designed to equalize opportunities for higher education, where one goes to college continues to be dependent on one's circumstances of birth. In particular, it is interesting that even as women have become less concentrated in two-year institutions, they still end up in less selective institutions of higher education once academic variables are controlled.

Comparison to 1980 High School Graduates When I compared Hearn's (1991) findings to the ones for 1980–92, what did I find? Overall, I found much the same story of certain meritocratic tendencies, coupled with strong evidence of the continuing effects of social background.[12] In the HSB and NELS data, each of the selectivity equations has an R^2 of a similar magnitude.

Looking first at the social background effects on selectivity (see Table 15.1), as opposed to Hearn (1991), who found that blacks and Hispanics (relative to whites) and females (relative to males) were less likely to attend the more selective institutions, I found that blacks were the only one of the three groups who attended less-selective institutions, net of other background factors, and that this tendency was stronger in the more recent cohort. Although the number of siblings was insignificant in both cohorts, father's education and family income each had much stronger effects on selectivity in the more recent cohort, and mother's education was of a similar magnitude in each cohort. Comparing the selectivity findings of HSB and NELS in the full models (see Table 15.1), I found that blacks and females continued to be less likely than whites and males, respectively, to attend the most selective institutions in 1980–92. Although the effect of mother's education disappeared, the effects of father's education and parental income approximately doubled between the two cohorts, indicating an overall increase in the effects of socioeconomic background.

Looking at the academic variables, I found some interesting differences between the cohorts. First, I should note a *noneffect*: Being in the academic track appears to have no effect on selectivity in the NELS cohort, whereas it was a relatively strong predictor in the HSB cohort Although further analyses need to be conducted to understand this finding, it is probably a function of the lack of variance in this variable: Fully 85 percent of my college-going sample was in the academic track (compared to 61 percent in Hearn's 1991 HSB sample). This finding raises questions, of course, about whether tracking, during the period between HSB and NELS increased effects on *whether* people went to college. Second, though tested ability had similar effects across cohorts, grades more than doubled in magnitude[13] and educational expectations declined by one third. Finally, for reasons that I cannot explain using these data, participation in student government was the only student activity that was a significant factor in the HSB data, while participation in school journalism emerged as the lone significant extracurricular participation variable in the NELS data.[14]

The results of this comparison can be summarized by pointing to the continued and increased relative effects of background—especially of father's education and parental income—on the selectivity of institutions between 1980 and 1992, even after academic variables have been taken into account. One

BISHOP BURTON COLLEGE
LIBRARY

way of examining this comparison is to look at the ratio of the R^2 of the background model to the full models. In the HSB data, the ratio was . 37, whereas in the NELS data, it was .51. Obviously, this finding suggests an increase in the role of ascription in the portion of the college-matching process that I can explain.[15] The continued negative effect for females (in both cohorts) is notable, especially given the overall gross changes in the distribution of female enrollments across sectors of higher education. The selectivity data suggest that all other things being equal, blacks continued to attend less-selective institutions than did whites in the 1980–92 period. The factors associated with countermobilization (e. g., fiscal crisis, cutbacks in financial aid, and anti-affirmative action judicial decisions and rhetoric) that I noted earlier certainly could have produced this outcome.

The Expanded Model In a preliminary way, I attempted to expand our understanding of the effects of both certain academic and nonacademic variables on where people go to college by adding a number of variables to my models (see Table 15.2). To block 1, I added two weighted scales of household resources, as well as dummy variables for types of schools. To block 2, I added a variable for number of institutions applied to, to get a better sense of a student's orientation to college beyond a basic measure of educational expectations.

The household resources scales were constructed using variables from NELS that asked about various possessions in the home, ranging from encyclopedias and books to a dishwasher and VCR. Using factor analysis, I constructed a "household educational resources capital measure" and a "household appliance capital" measure.[16] The idea here is that these resources may have different kinds of effects on college destinations. Household appliance capital, especially insofar as it is not correlated with my household educational capital measure ($r = -.185$), may indicate just how much the family is disinclined to expend scarce resources on specifically educational goods. Of course, both of them were examined to see whether they flesh out some of the unmeasured effects of social background. Similarly, dummy variables for urban and rural schools were inserted to gauge their effects relative to the modal suburban school, while a private school dummy variable was inserted to tap into another form of family advantage.

My inclusion of a student's number of college applications in the block of academic variables reflects my sense that the educational expectations variable does not sufficiently tap a student's understanding of the educational landscape and of her or his orientation to it. By including the student's number of college applications, I specifically took into account the student's sense of the degree to which higher education is a structured field that is laden with inequalities in access to scarce resources.[17] At the same time, as Appendix A indicates, this variable includes values ranging only from 0 to 3, so that I did not overly bias my results in the direction of a strong relationship between a higher number of applications and higher selectivity.

When I regressed selectivity on the new variables (Table 15.2), I found that R^2 is increased by almost 2 percentage points with the addition of the variables in block 1 and by almost 3 percentage points with the addition of the one variable to block 2. Both these additions are statistically significant.

Comparing the expanded block 1 to its original version, I found no large changes in the effects of the original variables on selectivity. Among the newly included variables, the dummies for rural school and private school are significant, while the measures of appliance capital and educational capital and the dummy variable for urban schools are not. Students who attend rural schools tend to go to less selective institutions, whereas students who go to private schools tend to go to more selective institutions. When I added the original block 2 variables, I found that, as with the original model, blacks and females tend to go to less-selective institutions. The other variables maintained their relative weight and significance or nonsignificance.

The number of institutions applied to turned out to be an important variable, with a standardized coefficient equal to the size of high school grades and over three fourths the size of test scores. Though

Table 15.2 Regression for Institutional Selectivity

	Model 1		Model 2		Model 3		Model 4	
	Metric Coefficient	Standardized Coefficient	Metric Coefficient	Standardized Coefficient	Metric Coefficient	Standardized Coefficient	Metric Coefficient	Standardized Coefficient
Black	-7.12	-0.14***	-8.08	-0.16***	-3.55	-0.07***	-4.22	-0.09***
Hispanic	0.93	0.02	-0.24	0.00	1.03	0.02	1.36	0.02
Female	-0.23	-0.01	-0.23	-0.01	-1.34	-0.05**	-1.27	-0.05**
Father's education	1.33	0.19***	1.30	0.19***	0.77	0.11***	0.66	0.10***
Mother's education	0.80	0.10***	0.76	0.10***	0.48	0.06**	0.43	0.06**
Parental income	1.29	0.16***	1.20	0.14***	0.97	0.12***	0.81	0.10***
Number of siblings	-0.27	-0.03	-0.33	-0.04	-0.09	-0.01	-0.07	-0.01
Appliance capital	-0.71	-0.04	-0.60	-0.03	-0.46	-0.03		
Educational capital	-0.35	-0.02	-0.72	-0.04	-0.69	-0.04		
Urbanicity of school	0.76	0.03	0.13	0.00	0.16	0.01		
Rural school	-2.04	-0.08***	-2.06	-0.08***	-1.64	-0.06**		
Private school	2.65	0.09***	2.06	0.07***	1.82	0.06**		
Tested ability	0.44	0.26***	0.40	0.24***				
High school grades	1.78	0.17***	1.89	0.18***				
High school track	0.05	0.00	-0.19	-0.01				
High school student government	-0.27	-0.01	-0.43	-0.01				
High school departmental or preprofessional club	0.41	0.02	0.32	0.01				
High school drama or debate	0.62	0.02	0.44	0.01				
High school journalism	1.34	0.05*	0.95	0.03				
Educational expectations	1.10	0.08***	0.84	0.06**				
Number of postsecondary schools applied to	3.53	0.19***						
R^2	.17 (R^2)		.19 (R^2)		.34 (R^2)		.38 (R^2)	
	.17 (adjusted R^2)		.18 (adjusted R^2)		.34 (adjusted R^2)		.37 (adjusted R^2)	

it reduced the size of the effect of educational expectations, it did so only to a limited extent. The remaining variables did not change to any notable extent, except for high school journalism, which became insignificant.

Discussion

Although there are differences between the samples and measures used (see note 12), I believe it is useful to make some tentative comparisons between the HSB and NELS cohorts with respect to the factors that appear to be the most determinant of where people go to college. As Hearn (1991:167) argued regarding HSB, "the primary direct influences on college destinations are academically based: test scores, high school grades, academic track, extracurricular involvements, and educational expectations." This is a good general summary of the NELS findings except for the inclusion of academic track, which was not significant in the present study. While this finding lends support to claims by those who argue that openness and opportunity are the watchwords of the decentralized, relatively uncoordinated U.S. higher education system, the fact that women were found consistently (in both data sets) to attend less-selective institutions than men, controlling for all other factors, certainly disputes this notion. And claims that we have reached a race-blind society are belied by the finding (in both data sets) that net of other factors, being black is associated with attending less-selective institutions. Perhaps most telling with respect to the issue of openness and opportunity is that even with these samples restricted to college-goers and with much social selection already having taken place, there were, in both cohorts, direct effects of the key social background variables (especially family income and father's education) on the dependent variables, even after the academic variables were controlled.

The question remains as to how the changes that occurred between 1980 and 1992 can be explained. Returning to the three possible explanations suggested earlier, it seems clear that the increase in the number of places in postsecondary education did not lead to any major amelioration of the subordinate groups' relative exclusion from the more selective institutions, as suggested by the modernization hypothesis (option 1). Of the remaining explanations (options 2 and 3), which agree that inequality has *persisted,* how can the continued negative effects of being female and/or black and/or of lower socioeconomic origins on selectivity be explained? In previous work (Karen 1991), I argued that political mobilization by subordinate groups was able to upset the "usual" slotting of social groups into their historic places within higher education. This mobilization led, during the period preceding 1977, to a change in where blacks and women attended college, as they moved into the more selective institutions. Students from lower socioeconomic backgrounds, who did not mobilize, maintained their place at the bottom of the system. After 1977, political mobilization by dominant groups (countermobilization) resulted in a leveling out of the percentage of spaces in selective institutions that went to minority groups.[18] Though this countermobilization did not affect women (dominant groups did not want to subvert their daughters' opportunities!), I suggested that the institutionalization, through affirmative action offices, of race-conscious admissions enabled institutions to maintain their commitments (though not to increase them) to subordinate ethnic-racial groups even in the face of opposition. Women's continued success in gaining admission to selective institutions (in terms of percentages) while still being relatively disadvantaged in the admissions process (i.e., the negative weights in the equations) may reflect their relatively better high school grades and higher scores on other academically based variables. Of course, the continued exclusion of those from lower socioeconomic groups would be part and parcel of the ratcheting up of the countermobilization.

Although this pattern is certainly consistent with option 3, MMI (option 2) should not be discounted. It very well explains the relatively strong effects of social origins on where one attends college and is consistent with the large expansion of the two-year college sector. Since the thrust of this explanation is based more on SES (though Hout et al. 1993 did examine gender) and does not include the selectivity of institutions, its direct explanatory relevance to race and gender in the current context is unclear. It is also not clear how this explanation would have worked during the period preceding this countermobilization, when women's and blacks' enrollments were increasing disproportionately at highly selective institutions (Karen 1991). Indeed, even as it conforms to some of my findings, the MMI hypothesis may be couched at too general a level for the examination of these questions. The comparative framework within which Hout et al. proposed the MMI hypothesis allowed me to consider processes of change in the allocation of higher education in much broader terms. The peculiarities of the U.S. higher education landscape and the role of race in stratification processes (which Hout et al. did not consider), however, make it difficult to draw conclusions at a comparative level.

Focusing on the NELS data, I added a number of variables that, I expected, would flesh out my understanding of the allocation of students to higher education. A somewhat surprising finding was that my household resource variables did not have significant effects on college destination. At the same time, I found that locale/type of high school tended to be associated with college destination in the expected directions, with private schools being positively associated and rural schools being negatively associated with higher-selectivity institutions. My inclusion of the number of institutions applied to is an important elaboration of the educational expectations variable. Both variables are academically based, in the sense that they are related specifically to a student's education, but both are rooted in the student's larger social context of ambition, especially her or his social background. Number of institutions applied to may be the best one-variable proxy for a student's higher educational habitus, and, as such, it has strong and consistent effects on college destination.[19] Its pattern of correlations with other social background variables suggests that it, indeed, adds something new to the conceptualization of habitus.

Although institutions of higher education have had to deal with reductions in federal grant dollars for students since the mid-1970s, which arguably have affected where students go to college (Karen 1991, 1998), more recent attacks on affirmative action have also affected where people go to college. In California, for example, where Proposition 209, which, among other things, outlawed affirmative action in admissions to public institutions, the representation of blacks and Hispanics at the two flagship universities declined precipitously after its implementation (Karabel 1999). My findings suggest that if the goal of public policy is to realize the aspirations of the Higher Education Act of 1965 to equalize opportunities for access to higher education, higher education affirmative action policies for people of color, women, and low-income families ought, if anything, to be ratcheted up. I found that even *within* higher education, a place where the meritocratic values of faculty and administrators should have the strongest effect, the persistent effects of social background are present. Obviously, if the United States wishes to increase the representation of students of color and of poor students in colleges and universities, then the nets need to be cast more widely so that a greater diversity of people and talents can be brought into the widest range of institutions. Not only must institutions reward a broader range of talents, but, to the extent that they do rely on traditional criteria for admissions, they must implement them fairly. And they must do so *now* so as not to exacerbate, in the current political context, the inequities I found in the early 1990s data.

Notes

1. This NCES study looked at institutional expenditures per full time-equivalent enrollment on instruction and, separately, on student services, broadly conceived. Neither type of expenditure had a significant effect on women's earnings, and only instructional expenditures had a small significant effect on men's earnings. By contrast, selectivity had significant effects on earnings for both men and women.

2. Mortenson (2000) reported that the maximum Pell Grant award was able to pay for the highest percentage of institutional charges in 1976 and, except for a blip around 1980 (before the cuts by the Reagan administration), declined thereafter. The decline stemmed somewhat during the Clinton years. Still, the award "today buys about half as much higher education

as it did at the end of the 1970s" (p. 41). The most recent data suggest that federal and state aid for higher education has not kept up with the costs of higher education, making college even more unaffordable. The National Center for Public Policy and Higher Education's recent report summarized five national trends this way: "Our conclusion regarding the affordability of a college or university education is this: Americans are losing ground" (2002:9).

3. These data were taken from Table 187 in NCES (2000c:215). Although there were fewer high school graduates and, subsequently, fewer college attenders in 1992 than in 1980, the higher education sector as a whole expanded by almost 2.4 million students (NCES 2000c:Table 176, p. 203).

4. Hout et al. (1993) contributed their article to an edited collection that focused on comparative work. So as to maximize comparability, they omitted race-ethnicity variables. Although this may have been a reasonable decision for comparative purposes, their nonrace/ethnicity version of MMI as pertaining to the United States is severely handicapped.

5. In 1972, 53 percent of the male high school graduates enrolled in college the October after they completed high school, compared to 46 percent of the female high school graduates. By 1998, the 7 percentage point difference favored females: 69 percent to 62 percent (NCES 2000c:215).

6. In this context, a Bourdieuan notion of field implies an understanding of the relationships that exist among institutions of higher education as they compete for greater resources. It would include an understanding of their competition for desired students, as well as their placement of alumni in desired positions.

7. F3QWT was the specific weight used. Thanks to Aurora D'Amico and Ralph Lee of NCES for their patient assistance in helping with questions about weighting.

8. Following Hearn (1991), I did not made any adjustments for design effects in this article.

9. Future research will focus on Asian Americans and ethnicity-SES interactions.

10. In previous versions of this article, I included expenditures per student as a dependent variable. Although there were some differences, the results did not differ radically from those obtained for selectivity. These results are available from me on request

11. The Higher Education Research Institute has not updated this information. For each institution, the average SAT score of entering students is the selectivity measure used.

12. In presenting these comparisons, I caution against any overinterpretation. Besides issues of measurement error and differences in sample composition, there may be some other unaccounted-for differences that may skew these results. Therefore, I make only broad claims about the differences in these results.

13. Note that grades were taken from transcript data in the NELS study, a likely source of the increase.

14. I could certainly speculate that leadership and writing ability are qualities that are rewarded by highly selective colleges.

15. If anything, this comparison underestimates the relative contribution of background factors, since the greatest increase in precision in the equations came from using transcript grades in NELS, which should provide a boost for the academic variables in NELS relative to the self-reports that Hearn used with HSB.

16. Specifically, the household cultural capital measure is a weighted combination of the following possessions variables: place to study, daily newspaper, magazines, encyclopedia, atlas, dictionary, typewriter, and computer. The household appliance capital measure is a weighted combination of dishwasher, dryer, washing machine, microwave, VCR, and own bedroom. The difference between Bourdieu's use of *capital* in his larger theory and my shorthand label for various household resources should be obvious.

17. In an earlier work (Karen 1988), I argued that one should examine closely the status and selectivity of the institutions applied to so as to assess better the social context of a student's ambition, the student's knowledge of the higher education field, and her or his habitus. Although I do not wish to imply that the number of institutions applied to should have the same causal status as the other variables in the equation, I do want it to reflect, in some way, the student's understanding of the higher education landscape.

18. These percentages had been rising through 1976 (Karen 1991).

19. For a detailed discussion of habitus and the college application process, see McDonough (1997).

References

Baker, Therese L., and William Vélez. 1996. "Access to and Opportunity in Postsecondary Education in the United States: A Review." *Sociology of Education* 69 [extra issue]:82–101.

Ben-David, Joseph. 1971. *American Higher Education: Directions Old and New*. New York: McGraw-Hill.

Bidwell, Charles E., and Pamela A. Quiroz. 1991. "Organizational Control in the High School Workplace: A Theoretical Argument." *Journal of Research on Adolescence* 1:211–29.

Blau, Peter, and Otis Dudley Duncan. 1967. *The American Occupational Structure*. New York: Free Press.

Blossfeld, Hans-Peter, and Yossi Shavit. 1993. *Persistent Inequality: Changing Educational Attainment in Thirteen Countries.*, Boulder, CO: Westview Press.

Bourdieu, Pierre. 1977. "Cultural Reproduction and Social Reproduction." Pp. 487–511 in *Power and Ideology in Education*, edited by Jerome Karabel and A. H. Halsey. New York: Oxford University Press.

———. 1984. *Distinction: A Social Critique of the judgment of Taste*. Cambridge, MA: Harvard University Press.

Bourdieu, Pierre, and Jean-Claude Passeron. 1977. *Reproduction: In Education, Society, and Culture*. Beverly Hills, CA: Sage.

Bowen, William C, and Derek Bok. 1998. *The Shape of the River: Long-Term Consequences of Considering Race in College and University Admissions*. Princeton, NJ: Princeton University Press.

Brint, Steven, and Jerome Karabel. 1989. *The Diverted Dream: Community Colleges and the Promise of Educational Opportunity in America, 1900–1985*. New York: Oxford University Press.

Clark, Burton R. 1983. *The Higher Education System*. Berkeley: University of California Press.

Davies, Scott, and Neil Guppy. 1997. "Fields of Study, College Selectivity, and Student Inequalities in Higher Education." *Social Forces* 75:1417–38.

Dougherty, Kevin. 1987. "The Effects of Community Colleges: Aid or Hindrance to Socioeconomic Attainment?" *Sociology of Education* 60:86–103.

D'souza, Dinesh. 1991. *Illiberal Education: The Politics of Race and Sex on Campus.* New York: Free Press,

Feldman, Kenneth, and Theodore Newcomb. 1969. *The Impact of College on Students* (Vol. 1). San Francisco: Jossey-Bass.

Hearn, James C. 1990. "Pathways to Attendance at Elite Colleges." Pp. 121–45 in *The High Status Track: Studies of Elite Schools and Stratification,* edited by Paul W. Kingston and Lionel S. Lewis. Albany: State University of New York Press.

———.1991. "Academic and Nonacademic Influences on the College Destinations of 1980 High School Graduates." *Sociology of Education* 64:158–71.

———. 1992. "Emerging Variations in Postsecondary Attendance Patterns: An Investigation of Part-Time, Delayed, and Non-degree Enrollment." *Research in Higher Education* 33:657–87.

Hout, Michael, Adrian E. Raftery, and Eleanor O. Bell. 1993. "Making the Grade: Educational Stratification in the United States, 1925–1989." Pp. 25–50 in *Persistent Inequality: Changing Educational Attainment in Thirteen Countries,* edited by Hans-Peter Blossfeld and Yossi Shavit Boulder, CO: Westview Press.

Karabel, Jerome. 1999. "The Rise and Fall of Affirmative Action at the University of California." *Journal of Blacks in Higher Education* 25:109–12.

Karabel, Jerome, and Katherine E. McClelland. 1989. "Occupational Advantage and the Impact of College Rank on Labor Market Outcomes." *Sociological Inquiry* 57:323–47.

Karen, David. 1988. "Who Applies Where to College." Paper presented at the annual meeting of the American Educational Research Association, New Orleans.

———. 1991. "The Politics of Class, Race, and Gender Access to Higher Education in the United States, 1960–1986." *American Journal of Education* 99:208–37.

———. 1998. "Diversity in Access to Higher Education: Changes from the 1960s to the 1990s by Race, Class, and Gender." Paper presented at the annual conference of the Eastern Sociological Society, Philadelphia.

Kerckhoff, Alan C. 1995. "Institutional Arrangements and Stratification Processes in Industrial Societies." *Annual Review of Sociology* 21:323–347.

Kingston, Paul W., and Lionel S. Lewis, eds. 1990. *The High-Status Track: Studies of Elite Schools and Stratification.* Albany: State University of New York Press.

Kleinfeld, Judith. 1999. "The Real Gender Gap in Schools and Colleges." *The Public Interest* 134:3–20.

Lavin, David E. 2000. "Policy Change and Access to 2- and 4-Year Colleges: The Case of the City University of New York." *American Behavioral Scientist* 43:1139–58.

Lavin, David E., and David Hyllegard. 1996. *Changing the Odds: Open Admissions and the Life Chances of the Disadvantaged.* New Haven, CT: Yale University Press.

McDonough, Patricia. 1997. *Choosing Colleges.* Albany: State University of New York Press.

Mortenson, Thomas G. 2000. "Poverty, Race, and the Failure of Public Policy: The Crisis of Access in Higher Education." *Academe* 86:38–43.

National Center for Education Statistics. 1997a. *Access to Postsecondary Education for the 1992 High School Graduates* (NCES 98–105). Washington, DC: U.S. Government Printing Office.

———. 1997b. The *Condition of Education* (NCES 97–388). Washington, DC: U.S. Government Printing Office.

———. 2000a. *The Condition of Education 2000* (NCES 2000–062). Washington, DC: U.S. Government Printing Office.

———. 2000b. *College Quality and the Earnings of Recent College Graduates* (NCES 2000–043). Washington, DC: U.S. Government Printing Office.

———. 2000c. *Digest of Education Statistics 1999* (NCES 2000–031). Washington, DC: U.S. Government Printing Office.

National Center for Public Policy and Higher Education. 2001. *Measuring Up 2000: The State-by-State Report Card for Higher Education.* Available on-line at http://measuringup2000.highereducation.org

———. 2002. *Losing Ground: A National Status Report on the Affordability of American Higher Education.* Available on-line at http://www.highereducation.org/reports/losing_ground/ar.shtml

Pascarella, Ernest, John C. Smart, and Judith Stoecker. 1989. "College Race and the Early Status Attainment of Black Students." *Journal of Higher Education,* 60:82–107.

Sewell, William H. 1971. "Inequality of Opportunity for Higher Education." *American Sociological Review* 36:793–809.

Smart, John C. 1986. "College Effects on Occupational Status Attainment." *Research in Higher Education* 24:73–93.

———. 1988. "College Influences on Graduates' Income Levels." *Research in Higher Education* 29:41–59.

Smart, John C, and Ernest T. Pascarella. 1986. "Socioeconomic Achievements of Former College Students." *Journal of Higher Education* 57: 529–49.

Solmon, Lewis C. 1975. "The Definition of College Quality and Its Impact on Earnings." *Explorations in Economic Research* 2:537–87.

Stolzenberg, Ross M. 1994. "Educational Continuation by College Graduates." *American journal of Sociology* 99:1042–77.

Swartz, David. 1997. *Culture and Power. The Sociology of Pierre Bourdieu.* Chicago: University of Chicago Press.

Trow, Martin. 1984. "The Analysis of Status." Pp. 132–64 in *Perspectives on Higher Education: Eight Disciplinary and Comparative Views,* edited by Burton R. Clark. Berkeley: University of California Press.

Tsui, Lisa. 1998. "The Effects of Gender, Education, and Personal Skills Self-Confidence on Income in Business Management." *Sex Roles: A journal of Research* 38:363–73.

Useem, Michael, and Jerome Karabel, 1986. "Pathways to Top Corporate Management." *American Sociological Review* 51:184–200.

Wise, David A. 1975. "Academic Achievement and Job Performance." *American Economic Review* 65:350–66.

16

It's Not Enough to Get Through the Open Door

Inequalities by Social Background in Transfer from Community Colleges to Four-Year Colleges

KEVIN J. DOUGHERTY AND GREGORY S. KIENZL

From the beginning of the community college, one of its fundamental missions has been to facilitate the attainment of baccalaureate degrees by providing the early stages of a baccalaureate education and aiding transfer to four-year colleges (Brint and Karabel 1989; Cohen and Brawer 2003; Dougherty 1994). This role not only continues today but also promises to become increasingly important (Dougherty 2002; Wellman 2002).

But during the years between 1960 and 1990, the transfer mission was eclipsed. Community colleges shifted their attention to expanding occupational education and continuing education, and transfer rates declined (Brint and Karabel 1989; Dougherty 1994; Dougherty and Bakia 2000). For example, among students entering community college right out of high school, the rate of transfer to four-year colleges within four years of entering college dropped from 29% for those entering community college in 1972 to 20% for those entering community college in 1980 (Grubb 1991, 202).[1]

However, in the last 10 years, interest in the transfer function has strongly revived. The reasons are various. State governments have encouraged students eligible for the state universities to begin at community colleges and then transfer to four-year colleges because this saves the states considerable money at a time when university enrollments have been sharply rising but state finances have been badly battered by a stagnant economy (Dougherty 2002; Ignash and Townsend 2001; Mercer 1992; Wellman 2002, 4). For example, during the first decade of the new millennium, college enrollments are projected to increase 21% in California, 12% in Texas, 26% in Florida, and 20% in North Carolina (Wellman 2002, 4). Moreover, community college transfer attracted the attention of policy makers in states such as California and Texas, where affirmative action in admissions had been outlawed, but universities hoped to retain a diverse student body (Hebel 2000). Finally, advocates, scholars, and policy makers concerned about issues of social stratification have highlighted the importance of transfer, noting that minority and working-class students are increasingly relying on community colleges for access to the baccalaureate[2] because of sharply rising four-year college tuition, stagnating need-based student aid,[3] slumping incomes for less advantaged families, and the reduction of remedial education in public four-year colleges (Callan 2003; Dougherty 2002, 315–33; Lumina Foundation 2005; McPherson and Schapiro 1998, 44–46; McPherson and Schapiro 1999, 6–7, 19–24; Wellman 2002, 4–7; Young 2002).

In focusing on transfer, we are not suggesting that other outcomes of the community college are not important. Certainly, many students enter the community college interested not in transfer but in acquiring short-term training or a terminal degree, whether a certificate or an associate's degree. And in fact, students do secure valued outcomes other than transfer. For students who entered community colleges in 1995–1996, 10% had secured a certificate, and 16% had received a terminal associate's degree by June 2001 (Berkner, Ho, and Cataldi 2002, 12). And these degrees do bring significant payoffs: compared with high school graduates with similar social and academic characteristics, terminal associate degree holders enjoy a 15%–30% income advantage, and certificate degree holders a 5%–15% advantage (Grubb 2002; Kane and Rouse 1999; Kienzl 2004; Marcotte et al. 2005).

Yet transfer still remains important. Many students enter the community college with the expectation of achieving at least a baccalaureate degree. For example, an analysis of the National Education Longitudinal Study of the 8th Grade in 1988 (NELS: 88) found that among those students who graduated from high school in 1992 and entered a community college within the subsequent two years, 63% stated that they were aiming at a baccalaureate degree or higher (Hoachlander, Sikora, and Horn 2003, 10). This figure is echoed by an analysis of the most recent Beginning Postsecondary Students Longitudinal Study (BPS:96), which found that, among first-time college students entering public two-year colleges in 1995–1996, 78% planned for at least a bachelor's degree (Kojaku and Nunez 1998, 7). Clearly, there is reason to question how firm and realistic these high educational ambitions are, but they cannot simply be dismissed.[4] Moreover, there is strong warrant for community college entrants to pursue a baccalaureate degree. Although some holders of terminal occupational degrees, such as nursing, can secure incomes that exceed those of certain baccalaureate degree holders, the fact remains that on average, baccalaureate degrees still confer significantly higher economic returns than do terminal associate degrees or certificates. On average, with all other things being equal, baccalaureate degree holders enjoy a 30%–40% advantage in yearly income over high school graduates, considerably higher than the income advantage for the average terminal associate degree or certificate holder (Grubb 2002; Kane and Rouse 1999; Kienzl 2004).

This renewed importance of transfer raises the question of how equitably transfer opportunities are distributed by student background. The answer to this question carries major implications for state policies that encourage more baccalaureate aspirants to begin college at community colleges. If major differences exist in transfer rates by social background, the pursuit of equal access cannot stop simply with getting minority and working-class baccalaureate aspirants into the community college. It is also important to make sure that students have an equal chance to transfer.[5]

Review of the Literature

Transfer has been the subject of a considerable amount of study over the years.[6] The research literature is dominated by institutional studies that examine the transfer rate for a particular community college. However, a fair number of studies of national data sets exist: Velez and Javalgi's 1987 analysis of the National Longitudinal Survey of the High School Class of 1972 (NLS-72); Lee and Frank's 1990 study of High School and Beyond (HS&B); Grubb's 1991 study of both NLS-72 and HS&B; Surette's 2001 analysis of the National Longitudinal Survey of Youth (NLSY); the studies by McCormick (1997) and Bradburn, Hurst, and Peng (2001) of the Beginning Postsecondary Students Longitudinal Study (BPS:90) of 1989–1994; and the studies by Hoachlander, Sikora, and Horn (2003) of NELS:88 and the Beginning Postsecondary Students Longitudinal Study of 1995–1996 (BPS:96).

The studies of the NLS-72, HS&B, and NLSY found that for students entering community colleges in the early 1970s and early 1980s, socioeconomic status (SES), race-ethnicity, and gender all significantly affected transfer rates. Students who were female, black, or had lower-SES parents were significantly less likely to transfer than were students with the obverse characteristics (Lee and Frank 1990; Surette 2001; Velez and Javalgi 1987).

Despite the quality of these national studies, there is good reason for further analysis. For one, these studies are restricted to the 1970s and 1980s, yet the question remains as to whether the patterns found hold for the 1990s. During the late 1980s and 1990s, major efforts were made to raise the transfer rate, particularly for minority and lower-SES students. For example, the Ford Foundation sponsored the Urban Community College Transfer Opportunity Program, and several states, such as California and Florida, put extra resources into enhancing transfer rates (Dougherty 1994, 254–60; Ford Foundation 1988). Moreover, the 1990s witnessed a shift in college-going rates by gender, with women eclipsing men.

In addition, the earlier studies ignored the impact of variations in age. The surveys used by earlier studies focused on students entering college right out of high school, thus disallowing any examination of the transfer rates of students who delayed their college entrance by two or more years. Yet, the issue of the impact of age differences on transfer rates has become quite important as increasing numbers of older people enter college. To be sure, many are not first-time college entrants but returning college students. Still, many first-time college entrants are of nontraditional age. For example, among first-time college students entering community college in 1995–1996, 26% were 24 years of age and older (Kojaku and Nunez 1998, 7). Evidence that age is likely to be associated with differences in transfer comes from the Transfer and Retention of Urban Community College Students, an ongoing study of transfer in the Los Angeles Community College District. The project has found significant differences by age in transfer preparation—that is, in the taking of state-designated courses designed to prepare students for transfer (Hagedorn et al. n.d.).

All these reasons suggest the desirability of studying transfer patterns during the 1990s, particularly using data sets that allow us to examine older first-time college entrants. Two national longitudinal surveys allow us to do this. The National Educational Longitudinal Study of the 8th Grade (NELS:88) is a long-term follow-up of students who were in the eighth grade in 1988. They were subsequently followed through the year 2000. A key advantage of NELS:88 is the availability of college transcripts, which allows us to precisely measure college attendance and track transitions between postsecondary institutions. The main limitation of the NELS:88—that it cannot capture the experience of older first-time college students—is rectified by the Beginning Postsecondary Students Longitudinal Study of 1989–90 (BPS:90), which examines first-time college students of any age who entered college in 1989 and were followed up in 1994.

The data on transfer rates in the BPS:90 sample have been ably analyzed by McCormick (1997) and Bradburn, Hurst, and Peng (2001). However, neither study provides a full-blown multivariate analysis of the impact of student background on transfer. McCormick analyzed the impact of SES, gender, and age (but not race), controlling for educational aspirations, college enrollment status (full time or part time), college GPA, receipt of financial aid, and overall satisfaction with the first institution (43). These are good variables to control, but many are also left out, including racial-ethnic background, high school academic performance, marital and parental status at time of college entry, working during college, and college major. Hence, a more extensive analysis of the impact of social background on transfer and the mechanisms by which that impact is transmitted is needed.

Research Questions and Methods

The previous considerations prompted us to ask two research questions.

1. To what degree do transfer rates vary by student social background, and how have those patterns changed over time?
    Previous studies have found that SES, race-ethnicity, and gender all significantly affect transfer rates (Lee and Frank 1990; Velez and Javalgi 1987). However, these studies analyzed data from the 1970s and the 1980s (NLS-72 and HS&B, respectively). We investigated whether in the 1990s, with the renewal of interest in and support for transfer, inequality of transfer by class, race, and gender changed in its extent or form. Moreover, we also investigated the impact of a variable that those earlier studies could not examine: age.

2. How are the effects of social background transmitted?
   In this article, we focus on the impact of three sets of mediating variables: precollege personal characteristics (academic preparation in high school and educational and occupational aspirations); external demands as the student enters college (marital and parental status, extent and intensity of work, and enrollment status); and experiences during college (major or college program, degree of academic and social integration into the college).

Data

For this study, we analyzed two national data sets: the National Education Longitudinal Study of the 8th Grade (NELS: 88) and the Beginning Post-secondary Students Longitudinal Study (BPS:90). Both focus on students entering college around the same time, but they bring different strengths to this analysis. NELS:88 gives us a larger sample of community college entrants, a better measure of SES (see below), and a better set of variables that measure precollege academic preparation. However, because NELS:88 focuses on younger students, it did not allow us to examine the impact of age on transfer. Moreover, it lacks measures of academic and social integration during college. BPS:90 rectified both omissions by examining students of any age who are entering college in 1989–1990 and by providing a large number of academic and social integration variables. By analyzing these data sets together, we can get a much better sense of the extent of the impact of social background on transfer and the means by which that impact is exerted.

In the case of NELS:88, we focused on students who first entered a community college in the period between 1992 (when most of the respondents would have graduated from high school) and 1994. This allowed for a few delayers to be eligible for our analysis. All students in our NELS:88 sample responded to the 1990, 1992, 1994, and 2000 follow-ups. In the case of BPS:90, we focused on students who entered a community college in 1989 and had responded to the 1992 and 1994 follow-ups. These data sets are described in the appendix.

Dependent Variable

Our dependent variable is *transfer status*. It is a binary variable that measures whether community college entrants transferred to a four-year college at any point after their initial year in postsecondary education (PSE). For BPS:90, we used the student's primary postsecondary institution in the 1989–1990 academic year to anchor our analysis, and we restricted our sample to those stating that they attended a public two-year college as their primary institution in their first year. For the next five years, students were asked to identify their primary institution each year. If a student indicated attendance at a four-year college during any year subsequent to 1989, the student is considered to have transferred. In a small number of cases, community college students may have reported attending a four-year college and then switching back to a two-year school. We still consider them as having transferred to a four-year college. For NELS:88, we relied on transcript information to identify initial postsecondary entry and subsequent transitions between institutions. To be counted as having transferred in our NELS:88 analysis, a student's referent institution must be a public two-year college, and transfer credits must be observed on the student's four-year college transcript. Community college students who were simultaneously enrolled in a four-year college were not regarded as transfer students unless the intensity of their four-year attendance dominated in terms of credits earned in that period. Overall, students in BPS:90 had five years to transfer to a four-year college, while students in NELS:88 had, at most, eight years.

We examined the transfer status of all community college entrants, with no restriction pertaining to intentions. Much discussion has gone into what is the appropriate denominator for any measure of transfer. Many community college advocates have correctly pointed out that many students enter the community college with no intention to transfer, or if they state such an intention, it is only weakly and unrealistically held. Hence, they have called for calculating transfer rates only for those who have clearly established potential to transfer. One frequently used formula is to restrict the denominator of calculations of transfer rates to those who have accumulated 12 or more credits within four years of entering community college (Bradburn, Hurst, and Peng 2001; Cohen and Brawer 2003, 56).

Such restrictions of the denominator introduced some important distortions of analysis. First, they failed to consider as transfer eligible many students who do indeed end up transferring. For example, Bradburn and Hurst found that in the Beginning Postsecondary Students Longitudinal Study of 1989–94, 45% of those who had transferred by 1994 did not meet the 12-credit criterion proposed by Cohen and Brawer (Bradburn, Hurst, and Peng 2001, 123). Another problem with restricting the denominator to purportedly transfer-oriented students is that it hinders our ability to measure the importance of factors that affect transfer. Focusing on students with, say, baccalaureate aspirations or certain patterns of course taking hinders our ability to examine how powerfully educational aspirations or certain course-taking patterns shape whether students transfer. Moreover, measures that build transfer propensity into the denominator suggested that transfer propensity is a trait that students bring into community college and one that cannot be changed; this undercuts awareness of the possibility and desirability of changing that incoming propensity, such as by "warming up" student motivation to transfer. For all these reasons, we chose to examine the transfer status of all community college entrants regardless of incoming characteristics. We could then explicitly bring into the analysis the question of the relationship between transfer propensity and having a certain level of educational aspirations upon entering college.

Independent Variables

We examined the impact on transfer of four sets of independent variables:

- Social background: SES, race-ethnicity, gender, age
- Other precollege personal characteristics: Academic preparation in high school, educational and occupational aspirations
- External demands as the student enters college: Marital and parental status at the time of college entrance, extent and intensity of work
- Experiences during college: Enrollment status, major or college program, degree of academic and social integration into the college

Our focus is on the social background variables. In addition to establishing their total unique effects, we are interested in how much of this effect is indirect—transmitted through or mediated by the other variables in the model.

Social Background Our analysis of the impact of social background on transfer rates spotlights four background characteristics:

- Socioeconomic status (SES): In the case of NELS:88, this is an index combining the education, occupations, and incomes of parents. The scale is in centiles. Because of major deficiencies in the SES index available in BPS:90,[7] we instead use family income, in log form, and the educational level of the parent with the most education. Parental education is measured in the form of five dummy variables: less than high school, high school graduate only, some college, baccalaureate degree recipient, post-baccalaureate training.
- Gender: Binary variable, female = 1, male = 0.
- Race and ethnicity: Binary variables for black, Hispanic, and Asian backgrounds that compare the transfer rates for students of these backgrounds with those for white students. No Asian American students were in our BPS:90 community college sample.

- Age: Age at first enrollment in college, coded as four binary variables at the following intervals: 16–18, 19–20, 21–30, and 31+.

Much of the impact of social background on transfer is indirect, operating through other intervening or mediating variables. In this article, we focus on three sets of mediating variables.

Other Precollege Personal Characteristics
- Academic preparation coming out of high school: In the case of NELS:88, we used scores on reading and math tests taken in the 12th grade. The scale is in centiles. Unfortunately, BPS:90 does not have test score data for most respondents, so instead we used four other binary variables: self-rating of academic ability; whether students received a regular diploma; and whether students took remedial math or reading in college. The self-rating of academic ability was based on whether students rated themselves above average in academic ability "compared with the average person of your age."
- Educational aspirations: For both NELS.88 and BPS:90, we used a binary variable indicating whether the respondent aspired to a baccalaureate degree or higher.
- Occupational aspirations: For NELS:88, we used two variables indicating whether the respondent aspired to a professional or managerial occupation or to a lower white-collar or skilled blue-collar job. The comparison group is those aspiring to unskilled or semiskilled blue-collar jobs. Unfortunately, because a comparable question was not asked in the BPS:90 survey, we could not construct a comparable set of variables for BPS:90 and therefore relied on a single binary variable. However, as presently coded, the highest levels of occupational expectations in both data sets are roughly analogous.

External Demands as Students Enter College Students vary considerably regarding the extent of outside demands—including family obligations and work—that they encounter as they enter college. We hypothesize that the lower these demands, the more likely students are to transfer, either because they are less likely to drop out of higher education without a credential or because they are less likely to immediately work and not pursue a baccalaureate degree if they receive a subbaccalaureate credential.

- Marital status: For both NELS.88 and BPS:90, we used whether the respondent was single, never married, at the time of college entrance. Married, separated, and divorced people were put in the excluded category. We are hypothesizing that single never-married people have fewer family obligations that may impede prolonged education or deter moving to a four-year college.
- Parental status: For both NELS:88 and BPS:90, this is defined as whether the respondent was childless at the time of college entrance. Respondents who had a child prior to college entrance were put in the excluded category.
- Work involvement during college: We hypothesize that students are more likely to transfer if they have fewer work obligations during college, either because those obligations reflect income demands incompatible with staying in college or because they provide a competing alternative to obtaining a baccalaureate degree. In both NELS:88 and BPS:90, we used a measure of work intensity that indexes the average number of hours a student worked during those weeks that he or she was working. It takes the form of three dummy variables: *no work, working 20 hours or less,* and *working between 21 and 39 hours* (NOWORK, HRSLTPT, HRSPT). The excluded category is *working 40 hours or more* (HRSFT).

Experiences During College It is not just the characteristics and experiences that students bring to college that may affect transfer but also their experiences during college. Hence, we looked at a variety of collegiate experiences. One that many observers have pointed to is the major or college program that students choose. It has been argued that students majoring in vocational subjects are considerably less likely to transfer to four-year colleges (Brint and Karabel 1989; Dougherty 1994). Moreover, because dropout interferes with transfer, we examined several different variables that have been found to affect college persistence. In particular, we focused on full-time enrollment and degree of academic and social integration into the college. The data on these within-college experiences are considerably richer in BPS:90 than NELS:88, so we rely more on the former data set at this point.

Unfortunately, we cannot capture with NELS:88 or BPS:90 data a number of other variables that have been identified as having a considerable impact on the likelihood of transfer. These include the extent to which a student's community college is highly vocationalized, its degree of commitment to transfer, whether students are accepted by four-year colleges into their preferred programs and campuses, how many credits are accepted for transfer, and how much financial aid would-be transfer students receive from four-year colleges (Dougherty 1994, 2002).

Enrollment status We hypothesize that students are more likely to persist in college and therefore are more likely to transfer the closer to full-time their student status. Full-time enrollment both betokens fewer external demands and perhaps shows a stronger commitment to college, but it also strengthens students' academic and social integration by making students more available to the academic and social influence of faculty and fellow students. In the analysis, our enrollment status variable is dichotomous, indicating whether a student was enrolled full time.

Major We hypothesize that students' majors or programs in the community colleges will affect the likelihood of transfer through differential exposure to faculty and staff who urge and facilitate transfer to four-year colleges and by shaping students' degrees of academic and social integration. In the case of NELS:88, we coded students' sell–reported major as academic, vocational, or undecided,[8] with undecided being the reference category. Unfortunately, because of peculiarities in the BPS:90 variables, we could not isolate those who were undecided. Hence, we simply coded students as academic or vocational, with the latter serving as the reference category.

Academic integration Drawing on the work of Tinto (1993) and Braxton (2000), we used several measures of a student's integration into the academic life of his or her community college during the first year of college. These include the student's GPA (as a measure of successful integration) and several measures of conditions facilitative of a commitment to the academic life: whether students talked to their academic advisors (RTALKADV), talked about academic matters with faculty outside of class (RTALKFAC), attended career related lectures (RLECTURI), and had academic contact with students in the form of participation in study groups (RSTDYGRP). In all cases, these variables were coded in binary form—that is, whether students have had the experiences in question. These measures are available only in BPS:90.

Social integration We used several different measures of students' social integration into the social life of their community colleges during the first year. These measures include whether students had informal contact with faculty outside of class (CONTACT), participated in school clubs (CLUBS), had campus friendship ties as marked by going places with friends from school (GOPLACES), and used student assistance programs on campus, such as counseling, remediation, and health programs (CENTERS). These variables, all coded in binary form, are available only in BPS:90.

See Table 16.1 for the means and standard deviations of these and other variables used in the analysis.

We estimated the impact of these characteristics on transfer via a set of logistic regressions. This set of regressions is described in Table 16.2. As can be seen, the baseline equation—Model 0—regresses transfer status on each of the four social background variables by themselves. In Model 1, we then put in all four social background variables together to give us the total unique effect of each background variable. In succeeding equations, we added various possible mediating variables, thus allowing us to explore the indirect effects of social background on transfer.

Table 16.1 Sample Means and Standard Deviations from Beginning Postsecondary Student Longitudinal Survey (BPS:90) and National Education Longitudinal Survey of 1988 (NELS:88)

Variable label	BPS:90		NELS:88	
	Mean	SD	Mean	SD
Outcome				
Transferred to four-year college	0.221	0.415	0.378	0.485
Social Background				
Female	0.512	0.500	0.503	0.500
Socioeconomic status [*x100*]			0.530	0.255
Parents with less than high school education	0.135	0.342		
Parents with high school education [*ref*]	0.377	0.485		
Parents with some college/AA	0.212	0.409		
Parents with BA education	0.179	0.384		
Parents with more than BA education	0.097	0.296		
Family income in 1988 (log)	10.016	0.983		
Black, not Hispanic	0.087	0.283	0.087	0.282
Hispanic	0.118	0.322	0.138	0.345
Asian	—	—	0.038	0.191
16 to 18 years old [*ref*]	0.439	0.497		
19 to 20 years old	0.243	0.429		
21 to 30 years old	0.186	0.390		
31 years old and higher	0.131	0.338		
High School Preparation				
12th-grade math test score [*x100*]			0.494	0.241
12th-grade reading test score [*x100*]			0.494	0.255
Received high school diploma	0.923	0.266		
No remedial math in PSE	0.889	0.314		
No remedial reading in PSE	0.896	0.305		
Above-average academic ability [*compared with others*]	0.242	0.429		
Educational Aspirations				
Aspire to complete at least a BA degree	0.705	0.457	0.708	0.455
Occupational Aspirations				
Working-class occupational expectation [*ref*]			0.034	0.182
Lower-middle-class occupational expectation			0.404	0.491
Upper-middle-class occupational expectation			0.562	0.496
Expected occupation requires at least a BA degree	0.302	0.459		
Family Status				
Single, not married	0.753	0.432	0.553	0.497
Did not have a child	0.808	0.394	0.627	0.484
Work Involvement during First PSE Year				
Did not work in first year in college	0.173	0.378	0.142	0.349
Worked 20 hours or less during first year in college	0.178	0.383	0.213	0.409
Worked 21–39 hours during first year in college	0.343	0.475	0.347	0.476
Worked 40 hours or more during first year in college [*ref*]	0.306	0.461	0.298	0.458
Enrollment Status				
Exclusively full-time enrollment during first year in college	0.482	0.500	0.779	0.415
Program of Study				
Academic major	0.345	0.476	0.325	0.469
Occupational major	0.655	0.476	0.196	0.397
Did not declare a major	—	—	0.479	0.500

(*Continued*)

Variable label	BPS:90		NELS:88	
	Mean	SD	Mean	SD
Academic Integration				
GPA in first year of college is mostly As and Bs	0.320	0.467		
Contact with advisor	0.720	0.449		
Academic contact with faculty	0.703	0.457		
Attend career events	0.435	0.496		
Study group participation	0.542	0.499		
Social Integration				
Informal faculty contact	0.473	0.500		
Campus club member	0.193	0.395		
Do things with friends on campus	0.693	0.462		
Use of student services	0.200	0.400		
Number of observations	653		2,660	

Source: Beginning Postsecondary Student Longitudinal Survey (2003) and National Education Longitudinal Survey (2003).
Note: Authors' calculations. PSE = postsecondary education.

These potential mediating variables were added in an order dictated by our judgment regarding where they fall in a causal sequence connecting social background with transfer. If the addition of one of these potential variables substantially reduces the coefficient for a background variable, we know that new variable is carrying part of the influence on transfer of that background variable.

Regression Method

Because our dependent variable is binary, we estimated the impact of these variables on transfer by means of logistic regression. The logistic model is

$$\text{prob}(y = 1) = \text{logit}(X\beta i) = \frac{e^{X\beta i}}{1 + e^{X\beta i}}$$

where y is the outcome variable, transfer to a four-year college, and X is a vector of social background and educational characteristics. Unlike ordinary least squares (OLS) regression, the coefficient of a logistic regression cannot be interpreted as the probability of attaining a positive outcome—that is, the marginal effect on the dependent variable from a one-unit increase in the independent variables. Thus, in logistic regression, a separate calculation is made of the marginal effect. It is expressed as

$$[\text{prob}(y = 1)][1 - \text{prob}(y = 1)]\hat{\beta} i$$

and is usually reported at the mean values of the explanatory variables. This statistic is shown along with the regression coefficient, allowing a more straightforward interpretation of the impacts of the independent variables.

Findings

The Impact of Social Background

Our analysis of transfer in the 1990s using NELS:88 and BPS:90 arrived at findings about the impact of social background on transfer that both converge with and diverge from studies of transfer in the 1970s and 1980s, using the National Longitudinal Survey of the High School Class of 1972 (Velez and Javalgi 1987) and High School and Beyond (Cabrera, LaNasa, and Burkum 2001; Lee and Frank 1990).

Table 16.2 Description of Determinants Tested by Logistic Regression

Determinants	Model 0	Model 1	Model 2	Model 3	Model 4	Model 5	Model 6	Model 7
Social Background	X							
Socioeconomic status		X	X	X	X	X	X	X
Race/ethnicity		X	X	X	X	X	X	X
Gender		X	X	X	X	X	X	X
Age*		X	X	X	X	X	X	X
Other Precollege Traits								
High school preparation		X	X	X	X	X	X	X
Educational aspirations			X	X	X	X	X	X
Occupational aspirations			X	X	X	X	X	X
External Demands at College Entrance								
Marital status				X	X	X	X	X
Parental status				X	X	X	X	X
Average hours worked				X	X	X	X	X
College Experiences								
Full-time attendance						X	X	X
Major							X	X
Academic contact with faculty*								X
Talk with advisor*								X
Attend career events*								X
Join study groups*								X
Informal faculty contact*								X
Campus club member*								X
Student service use*								X
Friends on campus*								X

*Variables only available for BPS:90.
Note: Model 0 regresses transfer status on each of the background variables singly. Model 1 does so with all the background variables in at the same time.

In particular, we found, as did earlier studies, a very strongly significant impact of parental SES. We also found a powerful impact of age, a variable that the earlier studies could not address because of the nature of their data sets. However, unlike earlier studies, we did not find a statistically significant impact of gender and race-ethnicity on transfer rates.

The Impact of Socioeconomic Status Our analysis of NELS:88 and BPS:90 found that in the 1990s, as in earlier decades, the SES of the parents of students was strongly and significantly associated with whether those students transferred to four-year colleges. As can be seen in Models 0 and 1 in Tables 16.3 and 16.4, SES has a sizable and statistically significant impact on transfer rates, both before and after controlling for gender, race-ethnicity, and age. For example, in the NELS:88 analysis—comparing students who are in the top and bottom 10% in SES (87th and 16th percentiles, respectively) but of the same race, gender, and age—the gap in transfer rate is 45 percentage points (55% vs. 10%).

The Impact of Age A major benefit of analyzing the Beginning Postsecondary Students Longitudinal Study (BPS:90) is that it allowed us to examine the impact of age. Unlike NELS:88 and its predecessors (HS&B and NLS-72), BPS:90 is not built around the evolving experiences of a particular age cohort, whether 8th graders, 10th graders, or 12th graders. Rather, BPS:90 focuses on all students entering college for the first time in a given year, regardless of age.[9] Hence, it allows us to analyze students who are first entering college at much more advanced years than the traditional college-age students

Table 16.3 Determinants of Transfer to Four-Year College: Logistic Regression Analysis of National Education Longitudinal Study of 1988 (NELS:88) Data

								Results from Models						
	Model 0		Model 1		Model 2		Model 3		Model 4		Model 5		Model 6	
Variable label	Coef (std err)	dy/dx	Coef (std err)	dy/dx	Coef (std err)	dy/dx	Coef (std err)	dy/dx	Coef (std err)	dy/dx	Coef (std err)	dy/dx	Coef (std err)	dy/dx
Social Background														
Socioeconomic status [x100]	2.629** (0.286)	0.637	2.602** (0.290)	0.633	2.254** (0.363)	0.563	2.100** (0.375)	0.516	2.146** (0.396)	0.528	2.127** (0.415)	0.501	2.256** (0.460)	0.525
Female	(0.139)	-0.056	-0.030 (0.143)	-0.007	0.179 (0.166)	0.045	0.206 (0.192)	0.051	0.256 (0.198)	0.063	0.275 (0.206)	0.065	0.265 (0.214)	0.062
Race and Ethnicity														
Black, not Hispanic	-0.578 (0.375)	-0.127	-0.134 (0.371)	-0.032	0.283 (0.455)	0.070	0.334 (0.390)	0.080	0.549 (0.347)	0.129	0.364 (0.323)	0.082	0.678* (0.336)	0.143
Hispanic	-0.220 (0.272)	-0.051	0.116 (0.228)	0.028	0.420 (0.274)	0.104	0.230 (0.301)	0.056	0.390 (0.330)	0.093	0.493 (0.317)	0.109	0.746* (0.354)	0.156
Asian	0.528 (0.344)	0.130	0.465 (0.383)	0.115	0.116 (0.482)	0.029	-0.159 (0.612)	-0.039	-0.255 (0.633)	-0.063	-0.336 (0.678)	-0.081	-0.343 (0.542)	-0.082
High School Preparation														
12th-grade math test score [x100]					2.517** (0.416)	0.629	2.297** (0.455)	0.564	2.314** (0.476)	0.569	2.234** (0.486)	0.526	2.300** (0.496)	0.535
12th-grade reading test score [x100]					0.054 (0.419)	0.013	-0.226 (0.457)	-0.056	-0.489 (0.473)	-0.120	-0.339 (0.461)	-0.080	-0.515 (0.514)	-0.120
Educational Aspiration														
Aspire to complete at least a BA degree							0.948** (0.209)	0.233	0.919** (0.221)	0.226	0.945** (0.226)	0.230	0.773** (0.239)	0.187
Occupational Aspirations														
Lower-middle-class occup expectation							0.368 (0.438)	0.089	0.369 (0.388)	0.090	0.290 (0.432)	0.067	0.263 (0.452)	0.060
Upper-middle-class occup expectation							0.778 (0.424)	0.191	0.699 (0.375)	0.172	0.583 (0.421)	0.139	0.503 (0.440)	0.119
Family Status														
Single, not married									0.229 (0.206)	0.056	0.248 (0.220)	0.059	0.248 (0.218)	0.058
Did not have a child									0.871** (0.264)	0.214	0.882** (0.280)	0.213	0.777** (0.273)	0.187

(Continued)

Table 16.3 (Continued)

Results from Models

Variable label	Model 0 Coef (std err)	Model 0 dy/dx	Model 1 Coef (std err)	Model 1 dy/dx	Model 2 Coef (std err)	Model 2 dy/dx	Model 3 Coef (std err)	Model 3 dy/dx	Model 4 Coef (std err)	Model 4 dy/dx	Model 5 Coef (std err)	Model 5 dy/dx	Model 6 Coef (std err)	Model 6 dy/dx
Work Involvement during First PSE Year														
Did not work									0.521 (0.335)	0.12	0.446 (0.340)	0.100	0.396 (0.376)	0.088
Worked 20 hours or less									1.135** (0.226)	0.259	1.059** (0.225)	0.229	0.864** (0.239)	0.188
Worked 21 to 39 hours									0.689** (0.232)	0.164	0.621** (0.238)	0.141	0.493* (0.243)	0.111
Enrollment Status														
Exclusively full-time enrollment											0.642** (0.224)	0.157	0.614* (0.240)	0.149
Program of Study														
Academic student													1.337** (0.250)	0.301
Occupational student													-0.394 (0.292)	-0.094
Constant			-1.897 (0.203)		-3.092 (0.275)		-3.879 (0.479)		-5.083 (0.490)		-5.475 (0.576)		-5.627 (0.622)	
Pseudo-R²			0.072		0.116		0.158		0.212		0.217		0.280	
Number of observations			2,574		2,052		1,705		1,631		1,523		1,523	

Source: National Education Longitudinal Survey of 1988 (2003). Authors' calculations.
Note: Coefficients marked with a single asterisk (*) are significant at the 5% level; double asterisk (**) at the 1% level. PSE = post-secondary education.

analyzed by previous studies of transfer. Analyzing BPS:90, we found that age does have a major impact on transfer. Controlling for other background characteristics, students who are older than 18 when they enter community college are significantly less likely to transfer, with the size of this negative age effect increasing as students get older. For example, students entering community college between ages 21 and 30 are 15% less likely to transfer, and students aged 31 and older are 20% less likely to transfer than are students entering college below age 19 (see Model 1 in Table 16.4).

This finding is of great importance given the growing number of students who are first entering college well after they leave high school. Although community colleges have made major efforts to facilitate the success of older students, the fact remains that they are much less likely to transfer than are younger students. This begs the question of why; this question will be addressed when we turn to analyzing the factors that transmit the influence of the social background variables on transfer.

The Impacts of Race-Ethnicity and Gender Unlike studies of transfer in the 1970s and 1980s (Lee and Frank 1990, 190; Velez and Javalgi 1987, 86), we did not find that race-ethnicity has a statistically significant impact on transfer rates in the 1990s. To be sure, compared with whites, blacks and Hispanics are less likely to transfer, and Asians are more likely to transfer. For example, in NELS:88, the transfer rates for blacks and Hispanics are, respectively, 13 and 5 percentage points lower than for whites, while that for Asians is 13 points higher (see Model 0 in Table 16.3).

However, unlike the case for data from the 1970s and 1980s, these differences are not statistically significant. Regardless of whether other background variables are controlled, blacks, Hispanics, and Asians do not demonstrate statistically significant differences in transfer rates compared with whites (see Models 0 and 1 in Tables 3 and 4). However, there is an important caveat to this finding in the case of blacks. As we note next, if we compare blacks and whites with similar educational aspirations (and high school academic preparation), the black-white gap in transfer rates grows sharply, becoming statistically significant in the BPS:90 analysis.

In the case of gender, earlier studies of transfer using national data sets found that males had a significantly higher transfer rate than females (Lee and Frank 1990, 184, 190; Velez and Javalgi 1987, 85, 88). For example, analyzing NLS-72, Velez and Javalgi found that in the 1970s, males were 18% more likely to transfer than females, even after controlling for differences in social background, academic preparation, and aspirations. However, using data from the 1990s, although we did find that women are still less likely to transfer (a gap of six percentage points), this gender gap is much smaller than before and no longer statistically significant. Gender is no longer strongly associated with transfer, whether before or after controlling for SES, race-ethnicity, and age (see Models 0 and 1 in Tables 16.3 and 16.4).

That we diverge from previous studies in not finding statistically significant impacts of race and gender on transfer rates could be attributed to peculiarities of the data that we used. However, it is noteworthy that the lack of significant impact showed up in both data sets that we analyzed. Moreover, it is important to note that the impact of race and gender on transfer was weaker in data from the 1980s (Lee and Frank 1990) compared with the 1970s data (Velez and Javalgi 1987). This suggests that a major temporal shift has occurred in the impact of race and gender to the point that they have ceased to play a major role in affecting the magnitude of transfer. This temporal shift could be due to the major efforts in the 1980s and 1990s to reduce race and gender gaps in college access and success. However, because those efforts were also directed toward reducing the social class gap in transfer, it is puzzling that the class gap remains large and statistically significant.[10]

How Are Social Background Effects Transmitted?

It is not enough to document that social class and age have a significant impact on transfer. It is important to determine how that impact is exerted. To that end, we look at three sets of possible mediating variables.

Table 16.4 Determinants of Transfer to Four-Year College: Logistic Regression Analysis of Beginning Postsecondary Student Longitudinal Survey (BPS:90) Data

	Results from Models															
	Model 0		Model 1		Model 2		Model 3		Model 4		Model 5		Model 6		Model 7	
Variable Label	Coef (std err)	dy/dx	Coef (std err)	dy/dx	Coef (std err)	dy/dx	Coef (std err)	dy/dx	Coef (std err)	dy/dx	Coef (std err)	dy/dx	Coef (std err)	dy/dx	Coef (std err)	dy/dx
Social background																
Family income in 1988 (log)	0.428** (0.127)	0.073	0.111 (0.099)	0.018	0.095 (0.109)	0.015	0.104 (0.111)	0.014	0.034 (0.117)	0.004	0.023 (0.115)	0.003	0.261 (0.160)	0.026	0.259 (0.170)	0.024
Parents with less than high school education	-1.414** (0.522)	-0.174	-1.041 (0.567)	-0.129	-0.930 (0.586)	-0.114	-0.899 (0.598)	-0.098	-0.903 (0.622)	-0.094	-1.006 (0.649)	-0.100	-0.121 (0.641)	-0.012	-0.055 (0.679)	-0.005
Parents with some college/AA	0.253 (0.258)	0.044	0.163 (0.289)	0.027	0.212 (0.302)	0.034	0.119 (0.314)	0.017	-0.023 (0.330)	-0.003	-0.113 (0.331)	-0.014	0.177 (0.454)	0.019	0.264 (0.486)	0.026
Parents with BA education	0.412 (0.262)	0.075	0.149 (0.276)	0.024	0.134 (0.281)	0.021	-0.094 (0.299)	-0.013	-0.191 (0.305)	-0.024	-0.254 (0.298)	-0.031	0.203 (0.376)	0.021	0.077 (0.409)	0.007
Parents with more than BA education	1.367** (0.345)	0.291	0.990** (0.367)	0.193	0.906* (0.375)	0.170	0.457 (0.396)	0.071	0.261 (0.420)	0.037	0.250 (0.414)	0.035	0.456 (0.528)	0.053	0.355 (0.554)	0.037
Female	-0.067 (0.184)	-0.012	0.157 (0.220)	0.025	0.253 (0.229)	0.039	0.299 (0.235)	0.041	0.490 (0.256)	0.065	0.538* (0.258)	0.070	0.700* (0.309)	0.072	0.715* (0.332)	0.067
Race and Ethnicity																
Black, not Hispanic	-0.588 (0.382)	-0.087	-0.546 (0.418)	-0.075	-0.546 (0.425)	-0.073	-0.971* (0.468)	-0.101	-1.057* (0.474)	-0.103	-1.089* (0.475)	-0.103	-2.303** (0.702)	-0.121	-2.432** (0.699)	-0.112
Hispanic	-0.006 (0.283)	-0.001	0.078 (0.349)	0.013	0.114 (0.395)	0.018	0.012 (0.388)	0.002	-0.014 (0.401)	-0.002	0.132 (0.432)	0.018	0.136 (0.580)	0.014	0.314 (0.566)	0.032
Age at First College Entrance																
19 to 20 years old	-0.847** (0.268)	-0.112	-0.759** (0.270)	-0.108	-0.692* (0.285)	-0.096	-0.703* (0.284)	-0.086	-0.681* (0.278)	-0.080	-0.658** (0.277)	-0.076	-0.286 (0.363)	-0.027	-0.295 (0.381)	-0.026
21 to 30 years old	-1.550** (0.381)	-0.173	-1.174** (0.413)	-0.147	-1.072* (0.429)	-0.133	-0.965* (0.433)	-0.107	-0.222 (0.492)	-0.028	-0.118 (0.507)	-0.015	0.049 (0.665)	0.005	-0.101 (0.685)	-0.009
31 years old and higher	-2.634** (0.539)	-0.222	-2.295** (0.706)	-0.204	-2.530** (0.735)	-0.207	-2.108** (0.778)	-0.166	-0.208 (1.032)	-0.026	0.007 (1.087)	0.001	0.807 (1.043)	0.103	0.496 (1.185)	0.054

	(1) b (SE)	(1) β	(2) b (SE)	(2) β	(3) b (SE)	(3) β	(4) b (SE)	(4) β	(5) b (SE)	(5) β	(6) b (SE)	(6) β
High School Preparation												
Above average academic ability [compared with others]	0.758** (0.257)	0.130	0.622* (0.278)	0.094	0.636* (0.289)	0.093	0.673* (0.289)	0.097	0.275 (0.309)	0.029	0.209 (0.336)	0.020
Received high school diploma	1.092 (0.692)	0.124	1.166 (0.723)	0.113	0.669 (0.753)	0.072	0.692 (0.713)	0.073	0.635 (0.920)	0.052	1.918 (1.208)	0.097
No remedial math in PSE	-0.815* (0.350)	-0.150	-0.774 (0.425)	-0.128	-0.992* (0.427)	-0.167	-1.008* (0.430)	-0.167	-1.099* (0.535)	-0.150	-1.298* (0.532)	-0.174
No remedial reading in PSE	0.784 (0.482)	0.099	0.799 (0.512)	0.088	0.870 (0.524)	0.091	0.685 (0.542)	0.073	0.934 (0.699)	0.071	0.985 (0.671)	0.068
Educational Aspirations												
Aspire to complete at least a BA degree			2.213** (0.460)	0.230	2.270** (0.519)	0.225	2.280** (0.519)	0.220	2.664** (0.598)	0.192	2.805** (0.613)	0.184
Occupational Aspirations												
Expected occup requires at least a BA degree			0.093 (0.219)	0.013	0.075 (0.231)	0.010	-0.021 (0.234)	-0.003	0.238 (0.284)	0.025	0.180 (0.287)	0.017
Family Status												
Single, not married					0.564 (0.561)	0.066	0.607 (0.570)	0.069	0.797 (0.808)	0.068	0.891 (0.869)	0.068
Did not have a child					1.702* (0.764)	0.156	1.711** (0.796)	0.153	1.857* (0.864)	0.123	1.864 (0.977)	0.115
Work Involvement during First PSE Year												
Did not work							0.590 (0.446)	0.089	0.401 (0.602)	0.056	0.321 (0.617)	0.032
Worked 20 hours or less							0.596 (0.380)	0.089	0.445 (0.523)	0.050	0.434 (0.547)	0.045
Worked 21 to 39 hours							0.357 (0.392)	0.049	0.258 (0.519)	0.027	0.590 (0.544)	0.059
Enrollment Status												
Exclusively full-time enrollment									0.553 (0.364)	0.056	0.790* (0.375)	0.074
Program of Study												
Academic student									0.651* (0.282)	0.071	0.705* (0.293)	0.072

(Continued)

Table 16.4 (Continued)

	Model 0		Model 1		Model 2		Model 3		Model 4		Model 5		Model 6		Model 7	
Variable Label	Coef (std err)	dy/dx	Coef (std err)	dy/dx	Coef (std err)	dy/dx	Coef (std err)	dy/dx	Coef (std err)	dy/dx	Coef (std err)	dy/dx	Coef (std err)	dy/dx	Coef (std err)	dy/dx
Academic Integration																
GPA in first year of college is mostly As and Bs															0.397 (0.350)	0.039
Contact with advisor															-0.038 (0.460)	-0.004
Academic contact with faculty															-0.306 (0.435)	-0.030
Attend career events															-0.419 (0.319)	-0.038
Study group participation															0.762* (0.347)	0.068
Social Integration																
Informal faculty contact															0.312 (0.339)	0.029
Campus club member															0.290 (0.377)	0.029
Do things with friends on campus															-0.579 (0.502)	-0.060
Use of student services															-0.243 (0.383)	-0.021
Constant			-1.969 (1.027)		-3.127 (1.483)		-5.032 (1.535)		-6.359 (1.783)		-6.387 (1.774)		-10.414 (2.321)		-11.762 (2.719)	
Pseudo-R²			0.111		0.138		0.206		0.227		0.233		0.262		0.299	
Number of observations			588		570		539		506		502		382		356	

Source: Beginning Postsecondary student Longitudinal survey (2003). Authors' calculations.
Note: Coefficients marked with a single asterisk (*) are significant at the 5% level; double asterisk (**) at the 1% level. PSE = post-secondary education.

- Other precollege personal characteristics: Academic preparation in high school, educational and occupational aspirations
- External demands as students enter college: Marital and parental status at the time of college entrance, and extent and intensity of work
- Experiences during college: Enrollment status, major or college program, degree of academic and social integration into the college

As we show next, we found that these variables, with the notable exception of most of the academic and social integration variables, do substantially mediate the impact of social background on transfer.

Precollege Academic Traits We examined three sets of precollege characteristics that might mediate the impact of social background on transferring: academic preparation in high school and educational and occupational aspirations before college entrance. Models 2 and 3 in Tables 16.3 and 16.4 summarize the impact of adding these variables to the baseline social background equation. A sharp decrease in the coefficient of a background variable as another variable (such as educational aspirations) was added indicates that the new variable plays a major role in transmitting the impact of the background variable on transfer.[11]

Academic preparation coming out of high school. Our analysis found that transfer in the 1990s continued the pattern of earlier decades of transfer being strongly affected by degree of academic preparation coming out of high school (Cabrera et al. 2001, 22, 24; Lee and Frank 1990, 190; Velez and Javalgi 1987, 88). Moreover, we also found that academic preparation plays a major role in mediating the impact of social background on transfer.

As mentioned, NELS:88 provided us with the best measures of academic preparation coming out of high school. We found that a student's score on the NELS:88 12th-grade math test has a strong impact on transfer likelihood, though reading test scores do not. In the case of BPS:90, test scores were not available for most respondents, so we used four variables to measure academic preparation: self-rating of academic ability; whether a student received a regular diploma; and whether a student took remedial math or reading in college. We found that a self-rating as *above average* in academic ability has a strongly significant positive impact on transfer. Surprisingly, however, we also found that taking remedial math increases transfer likelihood. Two possible causes could be at work. Those taking remedial math may benefit from skill improvement and therefore transfer potential. Alternatively, those taking remedial math—because a considerable element of self-selection is involved (Perin and Charron, forthcoming)—may also be those who are more motivated to begin with to achieve greater academic success and thus transfer.

The addition of academic preparation coming out of high school sharply reduces the impact of the social background variables, indicating that a considerable part of the impact of social background on transfer is indirect, operating through differences in precollege academic preparation. For example, in the NELS:88 analysis, when high school test scores are added to the social background variables, the coefficient of SES drops 15%, that of Black background drops 80%, and that of Hispanic background drops 76% (see Models 1 and 2 in Table 16.3). Clearly, a considerable part of the impact of class and racial-ethnic background on transfer is due to differences in academic preparation coming out of high school.

However, differences in high school academic preparation seem to play little role in accounting for the impact of age on transfer. In the BPS:90 analysis, we found minimal drops in the effect of the age variables when we controlled for the four high school preparation variables (see Model 2 in Table 16.4). We should not put undue weight on this finding given that the measures of academic preparation that we used in the BPS:90 analysis are less than ideal. For example, the four academic preparation variables in BPS:90 mediate much less of the influence of the SES variables (family income and parental education) on transfer than do the test score variables in NELS:88. Still, it is striking that the addition of the academic preparation variables in BPS:90 causes a much smaller drop in the coefficients for age than for the BPS.90 SES and race variables.

Educational aspirations. Educational aspirations continued in the 1990s to have the same strong impact on transfer that they did in the 1970s and 1980s (Cabrera et al. 2001, 22, 24; Lee and Frank 1990, 190; Velez and Javalgi 1987, 190). In both NELS:88 and BPS:90, educational aspirations have a large and statistically significant impact even when social background and high school academic preparation are controlled (see Model 3 in Tables 16.3 and 16.4).

Differences in educational aspirations play a key role in mediating the impact of social background on transfer. For example, in NELS:88, the addition of educational aspirations drops the coefficient for SES by another 24%. And in BPS:90, the coefficient for the oldest age group (31 and older) drops 18%, though the other coefficients for the other age variables are much less affected (see Model 3 in Tables 16.3 and 16.4).

But if class and age inequality in transfer is in part due to associated differences in educational aspirations, the opposite is the case with race. Controlling for educational aspirations does not reduce the coefficient for the black background variable but sharply increases it. In fact, in the BPS:90 analysis, the black background variable becomes statistically significant. This suggests that educational aspirations work as a suppressor variable for blacks. That is, the negative impact of black background on transfer is kept from being as big as it might otherwise be because blacks have higher educational aspirations than whites of similar social class, gender, and age.[12] But once that aspirational advantage is nullified by controlling for educational aspirations, the negative impact on transfer of being black becomes considerably larger.

Occupational aspirations. Occupational aspirations do not have a statistically significant impact on transfer in either NELS:88 or BPS:90. As a result, occupational aspirations mediate very little of the impact of SES, race-ethnicity, or age on transfer.

External Family and Work Demands as Students Enter College We have hypothesized that students are more likely to transfer if they encounter fewer external demands, whether from work or family, as they enter college. In Model 4, we add three sets of variables: marital status, parental status, and degree of involvement with work. To ease interpretation, we measured the variables in terms of the hypothesized absence of external demands—that is, we are comparing single to ever-married people; those without children to those with children; and those who do not work or work part time to those who work full time.

Being single does not have a significant impact on transfer in either NELS:88 and BPS:90. However, being childless at time of college entry has a substantially large, positive effect in both BPS:90 and NELS:88 (see Model 4 in Tables 16.3 and 16.4).

Not working or working fewer than 40 hours a week proves to have a positive impact on transfer in NELS:88 and BPS:90, but this impact is statistically significant only in NELS:88 (see Model 4 in Tables 16.3 and 16.4). Curiously, in NELS:88, though not BPS:90, working fewer than 20 hours a week has a more positive impact on transfer than not working at all.

The family status and work intensity variables substantially mediate the impact of age on transfer. In BPS:90, controlling for these variables reduces the coefficient of the age 21 to 30 variable by 78% and of the 31 years and older variable by 90%. However, the picture is less clear with regard to SES. Controlling for the external demands variables reduces the impact of family income in BPS:90 by 67%, and it substantially reduces two of the three dummy variables pertaining to students with parents with more than a high school education. But in NELS:88, controlling for the external demands variables actually increases the coefficient for SES.

Experiences During College Our three sets of measures of collegiate experiences proved to have quite mixed effects. Enrolling in an academic major proved to have a positive and significant impact on transfer. In the case of enrollment status, being enrolled full-time increased the probability that a student would transfer, with the impact being statistically significant in NELS:88 but not BPS:90. Finally, almost all the measures of academic and social integration in the BPS:90 analysis proved statistically insignificant.

Enrollment status As expected, the closer to full time a student's enrollment, the more likely he or she is to transfer. This is clearly seen in the NELS:88 analysis, in which the size of the effect is large and statistically significant. In the BPS:90 analysis, however, the magnitude of the effect is roughly half that of NELS:88, and the variable just missed being significant at the 5% level (see Model 5 in Tables 16.3 and 16.4).

Enrollment status mediated a significant portion of the impact of black background (in NELS:88 but not BPS:90) and being age 21 and older in BPS:90, as evidenced by the sharp drops in the coefficients for these variables when enrollment status was controlled (see Models 5 and 4 in Tables 16.3 and 16.4).

Major Enrolling in an academic program had a positive and significant impact (at the 0.05 level) in both NELS:88 and BPS:90. In NELS:88, the comparison group was those students who had not declared a major in the first year of college. In BPS:90, the comparison was occupational students because we were not able to isolate those students who did not have a major (see Model 6 in Tables 16.3 and 16.4).

Differences in college major appear to play a significant role in transmitting the impact of race and age on transfer. Controlling for students' college major sharply reduces the negative coefficients for those age 19 and older in BPS:90. However, choice of college major does not seem to be a significant channel through which socioeconomic background affects transfer. Controlling for major actually slightly increases the SES coefficient in NELS:88 and has inconsistent impacts on the various SES variables in BPS:90.

That enrolling in an academic program has a positive impact on transfer is important because the argument has been made that enrolling in an occupational major is no barrier to transfer. This is true if one means that it is not an absolute barrier, but it still remains an important *relative* barrier, reducing the probability that students will transfer.

Academic and Social Integration The academic and social integration variables proved to have very little impact on transfer between community colleges and four-year colleges in BPS:90. (These variables were not available in NELS.) Only one, involvement in a study group with other students, had a statistically significant impact. Moreover, several of the variables, such as academic contact with an advisor and with faculty members, had signs opposite to what we expected. Their impact on transfer was negative when we had expected positive impacts (see Model 7 in Table 16.4).

The weak effect and sometimes unexpected signs of the academic and social integration variables may be attributable to their positive impact on two different sets of students: students who go on to transfer and students who persist long enough to acquire a subbaccalaureate degree but then do not transfer. Greater contact with a faculty member or advisor may increase the persistence of both groups but promote the transfer of only the first group. Such a spread of effects across the transfer-nontransfer divide would considerably weaken the impact of the integration variables on transfer likelihood.[13]

Whatever the case, controlling for the academic and social integration variables did not affect the coefficients for the SES, race, and age variables in any clear pattern.

Summary and Conclusions

Our analysis of the National Education Longitudinal Study of the 8th Grade (NELS: 88) and the Beginning Postsecondary Students Longitudinal Study (BPS:90) arrives at findings that both validate and break with previous studies. As with earlier studies, we found that the likelihood of transfer is strongly affected by parental SES. Students whose parents have higher incomes, more advanced education, and more prestigious and remunerative jobs have a very large and statistically significant advantage in transfer over less socioeconomically favored students. A significant portion of class advantage is transmitted through differences between more or less well-off students in precollege academic preparation and educational aspirations. However, even after controlling for these differences—and differences in occupational aspirations, marital and parental status at time of college entry, enrollment status, and college major—most of the impact of socioeconomic background on transfer is still left unexplained (about 85% in NELS:88 but less in BPS:90).

With regard to race and ethnicity, we found that in the 1990s, as in the 1970s and 1980s, blacks and Hispanics had lower transfer rates than did whites and Asians. However, our study breaks with earlier studies (Lee and Frank 1990, 190; Velez and Javalgi 1987, 86) in finding that this racial-ethnic disparity is not statistically significant, particularly if we compare black and Latino students with whites of similar gender, age, and above all, SES. But there is an important caveat to be made: when we control for educational aspirations, the black-white gap in transfer rates widens considerably, becoming statistically significant in the case of BPS:90, though not of NELS:88. Blacks have higher educational aspirations than whites of the same socioeconomic background, which serves to mitigate the negative impact of being black on transfer, keeping the black disadvantage smaller than it would otherwise be.

Another key difference from studies of transfer in the 1970s and 1980s is that we did not find powerful effects of gender on transfer rates in the 1990s. Although women are slightly less likely to transfer, that difference is no longer statistically significant both before and after controlling for other background differences.

These differences in findings about the impacts of race and gender between our study of transfer in the 1990s and earlier studies of transfer in the 1980s and 1970s could be an artifact of differences in data quality or analytic technique, but we doubt this. The patterns that we found hold across two different data sets: NELS:88 and BPS:90. Moreover, transfer in the 1980s appears to have been less affected by gender and race-ethnicity than was transfer in the 1970s (Cabrera et al. 2001; Lee and Frank 1990; Velez and Javalgi 1987). Moreover, a host of programs were initiated in the 1980s to reduce class and race differences in transfer (Dougherty, 1994, 254–60; Ford Foundation 1988). Hence, we believe that the absence of statistically significant gender and race/ethnic effects that we found in Models 0 and 1 of our analyses most probably reflects temporal changes in the impact on transfer of these social background characteristics rather than artifacts of data quality or analysis technique.

Another key difference between our findings and those from studies of transfer patterns in the 1970s and 1980s is that we have been able to analyze the impact of age, a variable that earlier studies were unable to study because of the age restrictions built into the cohort structure of the NLS-72 and HS&B longitudinal surveys (Cabrera et al. 2001; Lee and Frank 1990; Velez and Javalgi 1987). We found that age at college entry has a very powerful impact on transfer. Older college entrants, especially if they are over 30 years of age, are much less likely to transfer than students who enter college right out of high school. Differences in academic preparation among different age groups seem to explain little of the age gap in transfer.[14] This gap is explained mostly by differences by age in educational aspirations (particularly for those 21 and older at college entrance), external demands (particularly having children),[15] enrollment status, and college major.

That differences in social background, particularly SES, powerfully affect whether students transfer is of great concern, especially in light of the increasing role being given to community colleges as gateways to the baccalaureate. This inequality in transfer argues that it is not enough to get baccalaureate aspirants to the community college's open door. It is also necessary to ensure equality of opportunity for community college success (Lumina Foundation 2005). To reduce or even eliminate differences in transfer rate according to social background, we need to investigate the precise channels by which social background affects transfer processes.

We have seen that differences in high school academic preparation,[16] educational aspirations,[17] having children, and college major play an important role in mediating class, age, and racial-ethnic differences in transfer. Still, we are far from exhausting our analysis of these mediating processes. We need to learn more about how precisely having children reduces the likelihood of transfer. Moreover, even with all the mediating variables that we have analyzed, most of the impact of social class on transfer is left unexplained in NELS:88. To fill in this uncharted territory, future analyses need to examine the impact of institutional variables that we have not been able to capture in our analysis of the NELS:88 and BPS:90 data—for example, the extent to which a student's community college is committed both in word and deed to transfer; the readiness with which students are accepted by four-year colleges into their preferred programs and campuses; how many credits are accepted for transfer; and how much financial aid would-be transfer students receive from four-year colleges (Dougherty, 1994, 2002).

Although much analysis remains to be done before we fully understand why inequality of opportunity in transfer exists between community colleges and four-year colleges, we already have leads that policy makers should pursue. Clearly, we need to continue to improve high school preparation not only to ensure equality of access to college but also equality of opportunity within college (Dougherty 1996; Gladieux and Swail 2000; Rosenbaum 2001; Rothstein 2004). We also need to reduce the gap in aspirations at matriculation between community college entrants who are high and low in SES and younger and older in age (McDonough 1997; Terenzini, Cabrera, and Bernal 2001). In addition, we need to find ways to reduce the transfer gap between occupational majors and academic majors. Key in this regard is finding ways of providing better transfer counseling to occupational majors and making it easier for them to secure admission, financial aid, and credit acceptance at four-year colleges (Dougherty 2002, 326–27).

Appendix
Description for Data Tests Used

National Education Longitudinal Study of the 8ᵗʰ Grade

(NELS:88)

NELS:88/2000 began with a nationally representative sample of eighth graders in 1988 and followed them up in 1990, 1992, 1994, and 2000. For the baseline data, questions were asked of students and their parents, teachers, and high school principals, and data such as high school transcripts were collected from school records. All dropouts were retained in the study. The 1992 follow-up occurred when most sample members were in the second term of their senior year. At that point, the NELS:88 sample was freshened by adding more respondents in order to represent the high school class of 1992, allowing trend comparisons to the high school classes of 1972 and 1980 that were studied in the National Longitudinal Survey of the High School Class of 1972 (NLS-72) and High School and Beyond (HS&B). The postsecondary transcript-based version of NELS:88/2000 allowed us to look more accurately at which colleges students entered, the college courses and program choices that students made, and transfer rates among colleges. Overall, there were more than 12,000 observations in the NELS:88 sample, but the size of the public two-year college sample is 2,660.

Beginning Postsecondary Students Survey

Based on the 1990 National Postsecondary Student Aid Study (NPSAS:90), the Beginning Postsecondary Students Longitudinal Study (BPS:90) consisted of first-time beginners (FTBs) who enrolled in a postsecondary institution at any time between July 1, 1989, and June 30, 1990. The NPSAS:90 design involved a multistage probability sample of students enrolled in postsecondary institutions. To be eligible for participation in NPSAS:90, a postsecondary institution was required to satisfy several conditions. During the 1989–1990 academic year, the institution must have offered an educational program for persons who have completed secondary education; an academically, occupationally, or vocationally oriented program of study; access to persons other than those employed by the institution; more than just correspondence courses; and at least one program lasting at least three months or 300 contact hours. A student was NPSAS:90-eligible if he or she was enrolled in an eligible institution during the 1989–1990 academic year for one or more of the following purposes: taking course(s) for credit; participating in a degree or formal award program of at least three months' duration; and taking part in a vocationally specific program of at least three months' duration. Students were excluded regardless of whether they satisfied the above conditions if they enrolled solely in a high school program at an eligible postsecondary institution, enrolled only in correspondence courses or programs of less than three months' duration, or were taking courses only for remedial or avocational purposes without receiving credit.

Initially, the BPS:90 began with around 7,200 students of all ages entering college for the first time in fall 1989. These students were then followed up in spring 1994. Complete demographic and enrollment information up to and including the 1994 follow-up is available for 83% of the sample. Data restrictions, such as institution miscodings, reduce the sample to roughly 5,600 observations. Our analysis is focused on those students who entered public two-year colleges in fall 1989. As our measure of college entered, we used the colleges that students identified as their primary institution. This yielded a sample of 653 first-time community college students.

Notes

1. Grubb analyzed the National Longitudinal Survey of the High School Class of 1972 (NLS-72) and the High School and Beyond Survey (HSB). The NLS-72 questioned 19,001 high school seniors nationwide in spring 1972 and followed them up in the fall of 1973, 1974, 1976, 1979, and 1986. The HSB study followed 10,583 high school graduates in 1982, 1984, and 1986 (Green, Duggoni, and Ingels 1995).
2. In 1981, the proportion of college entrants entering community colleges was 44.6% among students with family incomes below $20,000 and 41.4% among those with family incomes between $20,000 and $30,000. For the same groups (using inflation-adjusted constant dollars) in 1998, the percentages were 46.7% and 43.1%, respectively. At the same time, the proportion entering community colleges dropped sharply for all those with family incomes above $30,000. For example, among those with family incomes between $60,000 and $100,000 (in 1981 dollars), the proportion dropped from 31.2% to 25.7% (McPherson and Schapiro, 1999, 22–23).
3. In fiscal years 2002 and 2003, tuition at public four-year colleges rose by 10%, while state need-based aid rose only 7% (Callan 2003, 3A; Young 2002).
4. For example, in the BPS:96, only 37% of the community college entrants said that their primary purpose was transfer to a four-year college (Hoachlander, Sikora, and Horn 2003, 13). At the same time, it is important to keep in mind that even students who are focused on acquiring job skills or subbaccalaureate credentials may still harbor the desire to eventually acquire a bachelor's degree. Among BPS:96 students who had a primary intention of receiving a subbaccalaureate degree, 19% also planned to transfer (15).
5. But even if there is no difference by social background in transfer rates, there would still be the problem that baccalaureate aspirants who enter community colleges are less likely to eventually receive bachelor's degrees than comparable students (in background, high school record, and educational and occupational aspirations) entering four-year colleges. For more on this, see Dougherty (1994, 2002).
6. For reviews of the literature on the extent and determinants of transfer, see Dougherty (1994, 2002) and Pascarella and Terenzini (2005).
7. The socioeconomic variable in BPS:90 includes a measure for family income that takes a radically different form according to the student's dependency status. For students who are financially dependent on their parents, the family income value plugged in is that of the parents. But for students who are financially independent, the family income value plugged in is their own. As a result of this specification, the SES variable that emerges behaves quite oddly, showing no impact on transfer rates.

8. One of the benefits of NELS:88 is the availability of students' postsecondary transcripts, which are supposedly less prone to recall and other reporting errors inherent in self-reported information. However, there is one potential problem with using transcripts, and this drawback is magnified for community college students. Students with abbreviated or incoherent enrollment spells or who attended college but did not attain a degree, which regrettably are commonly at public two-year colleges, are coded as "nonmajors" since their program of study could not be determined clearly from transcripts.

9. It should be noted that the BPS:90 data set does exclude students in noncredit remedial and avocational programs—that is, it excludes students who are not taking courses for credit, not enrolled in a degree or formal award program of more than three months' duration, or not taking an occupational program of more than three months' duration (Bradburn, Hurst, and Peng 2001, 2).

10. One of our reviewers raised the interesting question of whether the disappearance of the gender gap in transfer rates is due to the fall in male transfer as much or more than it is due to a rise in the female transfer rate. Unfortunately, we cannot answer this question without having access to the transfer rates for each gender. We have them from our analysis of the 1990s, but the studies of transfer in the 1970s and 1980s that we have consulted do not provide gender breakdowns. However, if the gender dynamics of transfer over the last 20 years are the same as the gender dynamics of college access (U.S. National Center for Education Statistics 2002, 225), then one could argue that the erasure of the gap has been primarily due to a rise in women's transfer rates rather than in a decline in men's. A reviewer also raised the question of whether our null finding was due to the fact that, unlike previous studies, ours also controlled for age, which is correlated with gender. However, this is unlikely to be the cause of our divergence from previous studies; we did not control for age in our analysis of NELS:88 and also found a nonsignificant impact of gender in that analysis.

11. However, a sharp decrease in the coefficient of a variable may not necessarily be significant if, as in the case of gender, the baseline effect was not large to begin with.

12. When we regress educational aspirations in NELS:88 on race (black and Hispanic dummy variables), both variables are positive, though only the black variable is statistically significant. And when we control for SES, gender, and age, the coefficients stay positive and become even larger and statistically significant. This shows the degree to which blacks especially have an aspirational advantage over whites of similar social class and gender. In saying this, we do not want to gainsay the powerful argument that this aspirational advantage lies more in idealistic hopes for education than in realistic plans for securing it (Mickelson 1990). Still, it is noteworthy that controlling for these attitudes strongly changes the impact of race on transfer rates.

13. We checked to see if the small coefficients and sometimes surprising signs of these variables might be due to a high degree of collinearity. However, the highest correlation between any two academic or social integration variables was 0.39, and most correlations were well below this, with the average being around 0.17.

14. The tentative tone of our conclusion is due to the measures of academic preparation that we had available in BPS:90 not being as good as we would like and put a limit on how strongly we can say that academic preparation plays little role in accounting for age differences in transfer.

15. This is certainly the case for students in the "21 to 30" and "over 30" age groups. Not surprisingly, having children explains much less of the negative impact on transfer of being age 19 to 20 simply because most students of that age do not have children. But for older students, being a parent is much more common and imposes a myriad of obstacles—presumably of desire, time, energy, money and locational flexibility—that make it difficult to pursue a baccalaureate degree.

16. Differences in academic preparation coming out of high school play an important role in explaining class and race differences in transfer but seemingly not age differences.

17. Differences in educational aspirations play an important role in explaining class and age differences in transfer, but race does not appear to have an impact.

References

Berkner, Lutz, Shirley Ho, and Emily Forrest Cataldi. 2002. *Descriptive summary of 1995–96 Beginning Postsecondary Students: Six years later. Statistical analysis report.* NCES 2003-151. Washington, DC: National Center for Education Statistics.

Bradburn, Ellen M., David G. Hurst, and Samuel Peng. 2001. Community college transfer rates to 4-year institutions using alternative definitions of transfer. *Education Statistics Quarterly* 3 (3): 119–25.

Braxton John M., ed. 2000. *Reworking the student departure puzzle.* Nashville, TN: Vanderbilt University Press.

Brint, Steven G., and Jerome B. Karabel. 1989. *The diverted dream: Community colleges and the promise of educational opportunity in America, 1900–1985.* New York: Oxford University Press.

Cabrera, Alberto F., Steven M. LaNasa, and Kurt R. Burkum. 2001. *Pathways to a four-year degree: The higher education story of one generation.* University Park, PA: Center for the Study of Higher Education, Pennsylvania State University.

Callan, Patrick. 2003. A different kind of recession. *National Crosstalk.* http://www.highereducation.org/crosstalk/ct0103/front. shtml (accessed November 21, 2005). Cohen, Arthur M., and Florence B. Brawer. 2003. *The American community college.* 4th ed. San Francisco: Jossey-Bass.

Dougherty, Kevin J. 1994. *The contradictory college: The conflicting origins, outcomes, and futures of the community college.* Albany: State University of New York Press.

Dougherty, Kevin J. 1996. Opportunity to learn standards: A sociological critique. Special issue. *Sociology of Education* 68: 40–65.

Dougherty, Kevin J. 2002. The evolving role of the community college: Policy issues and research questions. In *Higher education: Handbook of theory and research*, ed. John Smart and William G. Tierney, 295–348. Dordrecht, Netherlands: Kluwer.

Dougherty, Kevin J., and Marianne Bakia. 2000. Community colleges and contract training. *Teachers College Record* 102: 197–243.

Ford Foundation. 1988. *An assessment of Urban Community Colleges Transfer Opportunities Program. The Ford Foundation's Second Stage Transfer Opportunity Awards. Final report.* New York: Ford Foundation. ERIC ED 293573.

Gladieux, Lawrence, and W. Scott Swail. Beyond access: Improving the odds of college success. *Phi Delta Kappan 81:* 688–92.

Green, Patricia, Bernard L. Duggoni, and Steven J. Ingels. 1995. *Trends among high school seniors, 1972–1992. National Educational Longitudinal Study of 1988.* NCES 95380. Washington, DC: National Center for Education Statistics.

Grubb, W. Norton. 1991. The decline of community college transfer rates: Evidence from National Longitudinal Surveys. *Journal of Higher Education 62:* 194–217.

Grubb, W. Norton. 2002. Learning and earning in the middle, part I: National studies. *Economics of Education Review 21:* 299–321.

Hagedorn, Linda Serra, Hye Sun Moon, Scott Cypers, William E. Maxwell, and Jaime Lester, n.d. *Transfer between community colleges and four-year colleges: The all-American game.* Los Angeles: Transfer and Retention in Urban Community College Students, University of Southern California. http://www.usc.edu/dept/education/truccs/Papers/baseball.pdf (accessed November 21, 2005).

Hebel, Sara. 2000. States without affirmative action focus on community-college transfers. *Chronicle of Higher Education 46* (38): A35–37.

Hoachlander, Gary, Anna C. Sikora, and Laura Horn. 2003. *Community college students: Goals, academic preparation, and outcomes.* NCES 2003–164. Washington, DC: National Center for Education Statistics.

Ignash, Jan, and Barbara Townsend. 2001. Statewide transfer and articulation policies. In *Community colleges: Policy in the future context,* ed. Barbara Townsend and Susan Twombly, 173–92. Westport, CT: Ablex.

Kane, Thomas J., and Cecilia R. Rouse. 1999. The community college: Educating students at the margin between college and work. *Journal of Economic Perspectives 13* (1): 63–84.

Kienzl, Gregory S. 2004. *The triple helix of education and earnings: The effect of schooling, work, and pathways on the economic outcomes of community college students.* PhD diss., Teachers College, Columbia Univ.

Kojaku, Lawrence K., and Anne-Marie Nunez. 1998. *Descriptive summary of 1995–96 Beginning Postsecondary Students.* NCES 1999–030. Washington, DC: National Center for Education Statistics.

Lee, Valerie, and Kenneth Frank. 1990. Student characteristics that facilitate the transfer from two-year to four-year colleges. *Sociology of Education 63:* 178–93.

Lumina Foundation for Higher Education. 2005. *Achieving the dream: Colleges count,* http://www.luminafoundation.org/grants/atdfaqs.html (accessed November 21, 2005).

Marcotte, David E., Thomas Bailey, Carey Borkoski, and Greg S. Kienzl. 2005. The returns of a community college education: Evidence from the National Education Longitudinal Survey. *Educational Evaluation and Policy Analysis 27:* 157–75.

McCormick, Alex. 1997. *Transfer behavior among Beginning Postsecondary Students 1989–94,* NCES 97–266. Washington, DC: National Center for Education Statistics.

McDonough, Patricia. 1997. *Choosing colleges: How social class and schools structure opportunity.* Albany: State University of New York Press.

McPherson, Michael S., and Morton O. Schapiro. 1998. *The student aid game.* Princeton, NJ: Princeton University Press.

McPherson, Michael S., and Morton O. Schapiro. 1999. *Reinforcing stratification in American higher education: Some disturbing trends.* Stanford, CA: National Center for Postsecondary Improvement.

Mercer, Joye. 1992. States turn to community colleges as route to bachelor's degree as 4-year campuses fate tight budgets and overcrowding. *Chronicle of Higher Education,* May 6.

Mickelson, Roslyn Arlin. 1990. The attitude-achievement paradox among black adolescents. *Sociology of Education 63:* 44–61.

Pascarella, Ernest T., and Patrick T. Terenzini. 2005. *How college affects students,* 2nd ed. San Francisco: Jossey-Bass.

Perin, Dolores, and Carolyn Charron. Forthcoming. "Lights just click on every day": Academic preparedness and remediation in community colleges. In *Defending the community college equity agenda,* ed. Thomas Bailey and Vanessa Smith Morest. Baltimore: Johns Hopkins University. Press.

Rosenbaum, James E. 2001. *Beyond college for all: Career paths for the forgotten half.* New York: Russell Sage Foundation.

Rothstein, Richard. 2004. Class and the classroom. *American School Board Journal 191* (10): 17–21.

Surette, Brian J. 2001. Transfer from two-year to four-year college: An analysis of gender differences. *Economics of Education Review 20:* 151–63.

Terenzini, Patrick T, Alberto F. Cabrera, and Elena M. Bernal. 2001. *Swimming against the tide: The poor in American higher education.* New York: College Board.

Tinto, Vincent. 1993. *Leaving college: Rethinking the causes and cures of student attrition.* 2nd ed. Chicago: University of Chicago Press.

United States National Center for Education Statistics. 2002. *Digest of education statistics, 2002.* Washington, DC: Government Printing Office.

Velez, William, and Rajshekhar G. Javalgi. 1987. Two-year college to four-year college: The likelihood of transfer. *American Journal of Education 96:* 81–94.

Wellman, Jane V. 2002. *State policy and community college-baccalaureate transfer.* San Jose, CA: National Center for Public Policy and Higher Education.

Young, Jeffrey. 2002. Public-college tuition jumps at highest rate in 10 years. *Chronicle of Higher Education,* October 22.

17
College-for-All
Do Students Understand What College Demands?

JAMES E. ROSENBAUM

Sociology has long tried to discover the ways disadvantaged backgrounds harm youth. While human capital theory in economics attributes such problems to deficiencies in individuals' ability or motivation, sociology looks at the ways societal factors block opportunity. However, reality is likely to be more complex. Societal factors do sometimes pose explicit barriers; but explicit barriers are relatively ineffective because they are so obviously unjust, readily seen, and easily attacked. Ambiguous opportunities and unclear requirements may be far more important in blocking mobility than explicit barriers (Cicourel and Kitsuse, 1963; Rosenbaum, 1978, 1989). Clark (1960) showed that the ambiguous mission of community colleges seemed to offer access to four-year colleges when, in fact, these institutions "cooled out" aspirations as students gradually realized that college was not appropriate for their abilities.

In the decades since Clark's study, community colleges have grown enormously. While four-year college enrollment roughly doubled between 1960 and 1990, public community college enrollment increased five-fold in the same period—from 200,000 to over 1,000,000 (U.S. Department of Health, Education, and Welfare, 1992, Table 169). In turn, college opportunities have dramatically increased. While 45.1% of high school graduates entered some postsecondary institution in 1960, over 62% did in 1993. Moreover, community colleges initiated open-admissions policies and remedial courses to reduce the academic barriers to college; and the Associate of Arts (AA) degree has increased in value in the labor market so that students do not need a BA to get an economic benefit from attending community college (Brint and Karabel, 1989; Grubb, 1992, 1993, 1995). Community colleges have increased access to an economically valued degree.

Have these changes created an easy route to college success, or do they merely confuse students so that they fail to prepare themselves appropriately? Studies since Clark's have continued to find substantial college attrition (Grubb, 1989) and have focussed on the factors that redirect students' plans (Karabel, 1986). Yet, rather than focus on the cooling-out process in community colleges, one must remember that "cooling out" is just the institutional mechanism for dealing with failure—not the original cause.

Clark took the term "cooling out" from Goffman's (1952) analysis of confidence swindles. The key to a swindle is to give "marks" confidence that they will gain a valuable reward at very little cost and then lure them to an "easy success" strategy. That is why a "mark" willingly hands over something of value to a swindler, and people pay for "snake oil" remedies that offer high expectations for a small price. Marks only realize that their expectations were mistaken at a later time, after the person who encouraged the expectation is no longer present.

This paper contends that the high level of community-college dropout arises because high schools offer vague promises of open opportunity for college but fail to specify the actual requirements for successful degree completion. Like Goffman's confidence schemes, students are promised college for very little effort. Lured by the prospect of easy success, students choose easy curricula and low efforts. Just as some high schools implicitly offer students an undemanding curriculum in return for non-disruptive behavior (Sedlak, Wheeler, Pullin, and Cusick, 1986), many high schools enlist students' cooperation by telling them that college is the only respectable goal and that it is easily attainable by all. Rather than community-college failure arising from an overt barrier in community colleges, the seeds of failure in community colleges may arise much earlier—when youth are still in high school.

In the current era, many high schools encourage the "college-for-all" norm which states that all students can and should attend college but which fails to tell students what they must do to attain this goal (Rosenbaum, Miller, and Krei, 1996). The college-for-all norm (CFA) is a variant of "the contest mobility norm" which says that opportunity for upward mobility should always stay open (Turner, 1960). This norm encourages youth to retain ambitions of advancement as long as possible, but it ignores barriers that limit youths' careers (Rosenbaum, 1975, 1976, 1986).

Americans are rightly proud of the CFA norm. It discourages schools from tracking students prematurely, and it encourages high expectations in youth. It argues for better instruction in schools, especially schools serving low-income youth. Without this norm, society might give up on raising the educational achievement of the most disadvantaged youth.

While it is not meant to be deceptive, the CFA norm can inadvertently encourage a deception that hurts many youth, including the disadvantaged youth it is meant to help. The CFA norm encourages all students to plan on college regardless of their past achievement. To avoid discouraging students, the CFA norm avoids focussing on requirements; but, in the process, it fails to tell students what steps they should take and does not warn them when their low achievements make their college plans unlikely to be attained. While such encouragement helps younger children, it may mislead students in their later years of high school.

Thus, while 70.9% of high school seniors in the class of 1982 planned to get college degrees, half of 12th-grade students lacked basic 9th-grade math and verbal skills (Murnane and Levy, 1997), and only about half of college entrants completed a college degree (Resnick and Wirt, 1996). The completion rate from two-year colleges is even worse. For the 1980 graduates enrolled full time in two-year public colleges in October 1980, less than 40% (38.8%) completed any degree (AA or higher) by 1986, and the rates were only 15.2% for the substantial numbers (about 25%) who were enrolled part time (U.S. Department of Health, Education, and Welfare, 1992, table 287). Students rarely attained their college plans. For the 1980 graduates who planned less than four years of college (but more than a certificate), less than 20% (19.9%) attained a college degree (AA or higher) in the next six years (U.S. Department of Health, Education, and Welfare, 1992, Table 286).

This has not always been true. The dropout rate from public two-year colleges increased sharply after 1972 (49.6% in 1980 vs. 36.0% in 1972, Grubb, 1989, Table 2). One reason for these disappointing outcomes is that school officials do not warn students about potential problems. Rather than acting as gatekeepers as they did in earlier decades (Rosenbaum, 1976), guidance counselors now urge all students to attend college but rarely warn poorly prepared students that they will have difficulty completing a degree (Rosenbaum, Miller, and Krei, 1996). Rather than hurting students by posing obstacles to their plans, counselors may now be hurting students by not informing them of potential obstacles they will face later on.

Contrary to Karabel's (1986) interpretation of community colleges as institutions which mislead students, Goffman's model suggests that deception is earlier, more subtle, and often in a different location. Indeed, "marks" go along with a swindle because their hopes are initially "heated up" to unrealistic expectations, and "cooling out" is only done late in the process. Thus, rather than focus on the "cooling out" process, one needs to examine why youth have unrealistically high expectations—the precipitating conditions for why "cooling out" is required.

This paper asserts that information is central to this process. If high school students are informed that they are poorly prepared for community college, they can either increase their efforts to prepare themselves or revise their plans to be more realistic. In either case, "cooling out" is unneeded, and youths' plans will be less likely to fail.

High schools probably do not intentionally deceive students. Rather, many schools have well-intentioned practices of raising students' expectations; but these practices may have unintended consequences. High schools encourage college plans for all students, even poorly achieving students whose subsequent failure is highly predictable even before they enter community colleges. Yet, students do not anticipate their probable failure, and they do not take actions to prepare themselves for their goals.

Such a mechanism is more subtle than the one Karabel describes. Poor information allows many students to have high hopes, to use their high school experiences poorly, and thus to seem to be personally responsible for their failures—in precisely the way that human capital theory describes. By the time students enter community college, their eventual outcomes are largely determined. Community colleges cannot be blamed for the poor preparation of their entrants. Yet, the high schools which poorly convey information about requirements are not a visible target. Indeed, they are praised for encouraging students to have "high expectations."

The above description suggests that students' perceptions of college requirements are key to their efforts in high school and to their college attainments. It can be posed as a model with several elements:

1. Many seniors believe they can attain college plans with low high school achievement.
2. Students with these beliefs, including college-bound students, exert little effort in high school.
3. Such beliefs are partly correct—students can enter college even if they have low achievement.
4. High school achievement predicts degree completion, but students' plans do not anticipate this relationship.
5. High school achievement predicts much of the lower attainment and disappointed plans of disadvantaged students.
6. Students with low high school achievement get less economic payoff for college degrees.

This paper takes these contentions as hypotheses and presents analyses to test them empirically. The analyses support these hypotheses and pose serious challenges to current practices. This paper concludes that shielding high school seniors from the realities of college demands and allowing them to hold unrealistic plans is not a kindness. It is a deception which prevents students from taking actions to improve their achievement or to revise their plans and make better use of high school. Students with unrealistic plans should be so informed. They should be encouraged to increase their efforts or to develop backup plans and preparation.

Data and Methods

This report is based on three kinds of data. First, students' perceptions are described using detailed interviews of a nonrandom sample of high school seniors in two high schools. Second, students' views are systematically analyzed using a survey administered to a random sample of 2,091 seniors classes in 12 high schools across the Chicago metropolitan area during 1992–94. The schools and sample are diverse in ethnicity and SES backgrounds and are described in detail elsewhere (Rosenbaum and Roy, 1996).

Third, students' outcomes are assessed using the recent release of the 12-year follow-up of the High School and Beyond 1980 sophomores (National Center for Educational Statistics, 1983). This national sample was first surveyed in 1980 (when respondents were sophomores) and subsequently resurveyed in 1982, 1984, 1986, and 1992. Of the original 14,825 sophomores in 1980, the survey obtained responses from 95.1% in 1982 ($n = 14,102$), and 85.3% in 1992 ($n = 12,640$). This survey provides a unique opportunity for a long-term study of the determinants of educational attainments. This paper studies the outcomes for the individuals responding in both the 1982 and 1992 surveys.

Many Seniors Believe They Can Attain College Plans with Low High School Achievement

Economic theory is a good model of our rational common sense assumptions. For instance, human capital theory explains students' achievement using two factors: students' inherent capabilities and their efforts to invest in themselves. The theory says students will invest in themselves and exert effort in school because they know there is a societal payoff.

While it is widely assumed that students believe that school efforts have a payoff, this assumption is rarely examined. Do students believe that school effort and achievement are relevant and helpful in improving their future careers? Of course teachers tell this to students, but it is clearly in teachers' own self-interest to convince students of their own importance. As parents and teachers often notice, one of the less convenient aspects of adolescence is the cognitive capacity that enables them to doubt what they are told.

Stinchcombe (1965) hypothesized that many students believed that school was not relevant to their future careers and that students' school efforts were determined, not only by their internal motivation, but also by their perceptions of schools' future relevance. While economists assume that incentives exist and are seen, Stinchcombe suggests this may not be true for work-bound students. Unfortunately, while Stinchcombe provided an intriguing model, his small sample and bivariate analyses (on a card sorter in the precomputer age) were too simple for a convincing test.

To examine these ideas, a nonrandom sample of 50 students was interviewed about how they thought about the relevance of school. Consistent with the dictum, "the more things change, the more they stay the same," these interviews in 1993 found similar sentiments to those Stinchcombe found 30 years previously. Many students reported that school was not relevant to their future careers. Yet something had changed. While Stinchcombe found that only work-bound students expressed these beliefs in 1960, these sentiments were also expressed by college-bound students in 1993. Many students who planned to attend college reported that high school achievement was not relevant to their future careers. Their comments suggested that the vast expansion of community colleges over the past 30 years contributed to their views. One student noted, "High school doesn't really matter..., because...junior college is not such a big deal to get into" (#42). Another said, "If you could apply yourself [in junior college], you'd get better grades" [regardless of how you did in high school] (#27). Many students agreed with the student who saw the "two-year college as another chance for someone who's messed up in high school" (#39). This second chance was also viewed as making high school effort less relevant. As one student said in explaining why he does not try hard in high school, "I think college is much more important than high school" (#16).

To examine Stinchcombe's hypotheses more systematically, survey items were constructed which reflected two aspects of individuals' perceptions of schools' relevance: whether students believed that high school education had relevance for their future success (hereafter "future relevance") and whether students believed that there was no penalty if they had poor school performance (hereafter "no penalty" attitude). The first variable refers to students' belief that high school can help their future careers; the second refers to beliefs that bad school performance (even if possibly relevant) is not necessarily a barrier to attaining their future careers.[1]

Surveys were recently administered to 2,091 high school seniors enrolled in 12 city and suburban high schools in a large, Midwestern metropolitan area. Just as Stinchcombe found, the survey found that many students doubted school's future relevance. This was not only true for work-bound students. Almost as many college-bound students held such beliefs. On five-point scales ranging from "strongly agree" to "strongly disagree," our analyses found that 30–40% of students did not agree with such statements as, "My courses give me useful preparation I'll need in life" (39.3% for whole sample, for college-bound respondents, 37.2%), "School teaches me valuable skills" (29.7%, college 28.2%), and "Getting a good job depends on how well you do at school" (36.6%, college 36.5%). We summed to create a scale for "future relevance."

Similar patterns appear for items concerned with lack of penalty for poor high school grades. Almost 46% of students agree with the item "Even if I do not work hard in high school, I can still make my future plans come true" (45.9%, college 44.3%). While educators want students to believe that students with bad grades rarely get college degrees or good jobs, many students disagree with the first point (regarding graduation from two-year colleges, 40.7% for whole sample, college 41.2%) and almost as many disagree with the second (getting good jobs after high school, 37.9%, college 32.9%). Most surprisingly, despite many campaigns against dropping out of high school, over 40% of seniors do not disagree with the statement "People can do OK even if they drop out of high school" (43.7%, college 40.8%). Apparently, many students see no penalty to their planned careers if they do not have high school diplomas, good grades, and work hard in school. We summed these latter items to create a scale for "no penalty."

The two scales of "future relevance" and "no penalty" are correlated, but the correlation is far from perfect ($r = .30$). Students who plan to get a college degree have a somewhat higher sense of schools' "future relevance," and a lesser sense that there is "no penalty" if they do poorly in high school, than students without college plans, but the difference is small (about 1/3 of a standard deviation). Moreover, these beliefs vary substantially within such groups, and the variation is similar within both groups (standard deviations of .61–65).

Students with These Beliefs Exert Little Effort in High School

While there is nothing wrong with students having optimistic hopes, we would be concerned if students responded to these beliefs by reducing their efforts. This section examines: what factors may determine future relevance and no penalty beliefs, what factors may determine students' school efforts, and whether these beliefs mediate the potential influence of other factors on students' school efforts and may have independent influences on students' school efforts.

The antecedents of future relevance and no penalty beliefs are first examined. The survey asked three or more items relating to locus of control, parent support, teacher help, school help, peer pro-school influences, and peer anti-school (rebellion) influences. Items were factor analyzed and scales were constructed. All had alpha coefficients over .70. The survey also asked about respondents' race, ethnicity, parents' education and occupation, and gender (for details, see Rosenbaum and Roy, 1996).

First, OLS regression analyses show that both future relevance and no-penalty are strongly explained by parent support for school, teacher help, and personal locus of control. Peers and low-SES studies also have significant coefficients but gender and being Black do not (Table 17.1, columns 1 and 2).

Second, we examine the antecedents of students' school effort. Effort is measured by a scale combining students' reports of their behaviors (how much time they spend on homework) and three other items: I just do enough to pass my classes, I try to do my best in school, I only work in school if I'm worried about failing (each coded on a five-point scale from "strongly agree" to "strongly disagree").

As in previous research (Kandel and Lesser, 1972), these analyses find that students' school efforts are explained by parent, peer, and school variables (Table 17.1, column 3). Males and having low-SES have negative coefficients, but ethnicity has no influence. Students' locus of control has a large and significant effect.

Table 17.1 Determinants of Future Relevance, No Penalty, and Effort (Standardized Coefficients)

	Future Relevance	No Penalty	Effort (step 1)	Effort (step 2)
Parental support for school	.1702**	−.2786**	.2795**	.2128**
Rebellious peers	−.0576*	.0943**	−.1369**	−.1143**
Pro-school peers	.0949**	−.0217	.1157**	.0979**
Locus of control	.1253**	−.1655**	.2060**	.1627**
Female	−.0411	−.0149	.1051**	.1094**
Low SES	−.0439*	.0828**	−.0554*	−.0366
Black	.0344	−.0202	.0006	−.0076
Hispanic	.0526*	−.0391	−.0370	−.0510*
Asian	.0660**	−.0030	−.0043	−.0149
Teacher help	.2822**	.0510*	.0893**	.0530*
School help	.1310**	−.0441	.0564**	.0300
Future relevance				.1550**
No penalty belief				−.1448**
R-squared (adjusted)	.2446	.1710	.2947	.3393

n = 2,091, * = p< .05, ** = p < .01

However, when future relevance and no-penalty are added to the analysis, we find that they mediate much of the potential influence of parents, school help, teacher help, and locus of control and reduce the negative coefficient of SES to nonsignificance. In contrast, their addition has relatively little effect on the influence of the two peer variables (see column 4). After controlling for other factors, future relevance and no-penalty also have significant independent effects on effort (standardized coefficients of .155 for future relevance, −.145 for "no penalty," column 4). Thus, these beliefs have significant and independent associations with effort, perhaps indicating strong effects in reducing students' school efforts.

These findings have implications for theory and practice. Theoretically, this study supports Stinchcombe's hypothesis. Students vary in whether they see school as relevant to their future lives, and this variable is strongly associated with their school efforts. In addition, this study identifies a second measure—the "no penalty" belief—and shows that both beliefs have significant, independent relationships with school effort.

These results imply that some youth have misread the American emphasis on opportunity. While Americans want society to provide "second chances" to youth, Stevenson and Stigler (1992) warn that youth might misinterpret this to mean that school failures never matter and effort is not needed. This study finds that many youth see little penalty to avoiding school work and little payoff to high school, and these beliefs may justify their poor effort in high school.

Of course, it is possible that causality goes in the other direction—that individuals rationalize their poor effort by denying future relevance. However, these views, whether beliefs or rationalizations, are held by 40% of students so they are not just the problems of a few individuals. Indeed, since guidance counselors do not challenge these beliefs, part of the problem arises from school practices (Rosenbaum, Miller, and Krei, 1996). Even if these views arise as rationalizations, they are not effectively challenged by schools and represent misconceptions that encourage a continuing cycle of further low effort.

Students Can Enter College Even If They Have Low Achievement

Are students wrong when they say school achievement is not relevant to their futures? Community colleges are frequently seen as "second chance" institutions for those who have done poorly before, offering open admissions, low tuition, and remedial courses. In some community college departments, remedial courses may be 40% of the courses offered. Over 40% of freshmen at public two-year colleges take one or more years of remedial coursework just to acquire the same skills they did not learn in high school (National Center for Educational Statistics, 1995).

Although sociologists have produced extensive research showing that grades are strongly related to college attendance (e.g., Kerckhoff and Campbell 1977; Porter, 1974), much of this research is based on studies from the 1960s and 1970s. Yet, college admissions have changed a great deal since 1960. As noted, the five-fold growth of community colleges has dramatically increased opportunities to go to college, and fewer students are likely to face barriers to access to college.

Moreover, community colleges have initiated open-admissions policies and remedial courses to reduce the academic barriers to college. In the past, college admission standards compelled lower-achieving students to confront their unrealistic college plans. While college admission standards were a severe barrier to college for low-achieving students in 1960, admission standards are now practically nonexistent in community colleges. For example, Illinois high school graduates can attend a community college even if they have Ds and no college-prep courses (after age 21, even a diploma is not required). In addition, a full array of remedial courses have been devised to provide high-school-level curricula in the community colleges in order to improve students' chances of success (Brint and Karabel, 1989; Dougherty, 1994; Grubb and Kalman, 1994). Open admissions policies and remedial courses have removed some academic barriers to college entrance.

Are students correct in the belief that high school performance is not relevant to their educational outcomes? The High School and Beyond data indicate that poor high school performance does not prevent college attendance. Even students with low grades (Cs or lower) can attend college. Indeed, 27% of students enrolling in two-year colleges had low grades in high school. That is only slightly less than the proportion of students with low grades who did not enroll in any postsecondary education (30%). Obviously, low grades are not a barrier to enrolling in two-year colleges. College-bound students who think high school effort is irrelevant to their future plans are partly correct—high school grades are not an obstacle to enrollment in two-year colleges.

High School Achievement Predicts Degree Completion, but Students' Plans Do Not Anticipate This Relationship

Having found that many students believe high school achievement is not relevant and, indeed, that many students with low grades can enter two-year colleges, one must wonder whether these students are correct that high school achievement is not relevant to college attainment. Or do these beliefs lead students to make plans which they will be unable to realize? This section of the paper addresses these questions with simple percentages, and the next section uses multivariate analyses.

These analyses emphasize grades because all students know their grades, so students could use this knowledge if they chose to do so. But do they choose to do so? Because most people have had a few teachers who gave arbitrary or unfair grades, grades are often dismissed as erroneous and irrelevant. Yet, knowledge of scale construction suggests that averaging grades eliminates random ideosyncracies and might make grade averages a meaningful indicator. This section examines whether students' cumulative grade point averages in high school predict college outcomes.

Our analyses of the High School and Beyond data find that many students with college plans fail to attain college degrees, and high school grades strongly predict which students fail at their college plans. Of the 12,475 seniors with complete information on plans, grades, and educational attainment, 8,795 (70.5%) planned to get a college degree (AA or higher) in their senior year in high school. Many seniors (4,103 of the 12,475) had low grades (Cs or lower), yet 50.8% of those with low grades still planned to get a college degree ($n = 2,086$).

However, low grades have a strong impact on actual educational attainment. Among all seniors with college plans, 40.3% succeed in getting a college degree (AA or higher) in the 10 years after high school (Table 17.2a). By comparison, low high school grades cut students' chances in half—only 19.6% of seniors with low grades attained their college plans.

Table 17.2 Percentage of Seniors With College Plans Who Complete College Degrees Within 10 Years

Table 17.2a. Percentage of Seniors with College Plans (AA or higher) Who Complete at Least an AA

Average high school grades	As	Bs	Cs or lower	Total
Percent attaining AA or higher	69.5	43.2	19.2	40.3
N	2007	4702	2086	8795

Table 17.2b. Percentage of Seniors with BA Plans Who Succeed in Completing at least a BA Degree

Average high school grades	As	Bs	Cs or lower	Total
Percent attaining BA or higher	70.7	46.6	20.5	49.5
N	1668	2944	916	5528

Table 17.2c. Percentage of Seniors with AA Plans Who Succeed in Completing at an AA

Average high school grades	As	Bs	Cs or lower	Total
Percent attaining AA or higher	46.6	27.1	12.6	23.9
N	339	1758	1170	3267

Note. The data displayed represent 1992 degree attainment figures for High School and Beyond respondents who were seniors in 1982.

Of all the seniors planning to get a BA or higher ($n = 5,528$), 49.5% succeed in getting that degree (Table 17.2b). However, students with As have a 70.7% chance of getting a BA or higher, and those with Bs have a 46.6% chance. Students planning BAs who have a C average or less ($n = 916$) achieve BA degrees at less than half the rate of all students with BA plans (49.5% > 20.5%). It might also be noted that 73% of those with poor grades do little homework—less than an hour per week, and low homework time decreases their BA chances to only 11%.

Since the AA is a shorter and perhaps easier degree than a BA, one might expect that students planning to get AA degrees are more likely to be successful. That is not the case. Seniors who plan to get an AA degree succeed less often than those planning a BA. Of the 3,267 seniors who plan to get an AA degree, only 23.9% succeed in getting a college degree (AA or higher) in the next 10 years; and of those with low grades (Cs or lower), only 12.6% do (Table 17.2c). The success rates are even lower for those with low grades who did little homework ($n = 248$; $p = 8\%$). Recall that these tables report students' college-degree outcomes, based only on their high school grades, and giving youth 10 years to attain any college degree (AA or higher).

Why do over half of seniors with low grades believe they can attain college degrees? Perhaps "social promotion" practices in high schools, which automatically promote students each year to the next grade regardless of their achievement, may encourage this belief. Similarly, open admissions at community colleges may contribute to this belief. Seeing these two practices, which award attainments without requiring academic achievement, students may infer a similar view of college degrees—as an award for putting in time that does not require academic achievement. This may also suggest that students view school as a credentialing process rather than a human-capital-building process.

Ironically, although colleges offering AA degrees are more accessible than BA colleges to students with low grades, the AA degree is not necessarily more available to them. Students with AA plans have lower success rates than students with BA plans, both because students with AA plans are twice as likely to have low grades and because their chances of getting the degree are very slim if they have low grades (12.6%). Multivariate analyses indicate that grades and homework time explain most of this differential success rate between those with BA and AA plans (Rosenbaum and Miller, 1998).

Newspaper stories sometimes report that students who got As in high school actually lack the academic skills to do well in college. This may explain our findings that only half (49.5%) of students with As in high school complete an AA degree or higher (although low SES seems to be more important than low test scores in explaining these failures). Yet, newspapers rarely consider the other issue, that students with Cs in high school have very little chance of completing a college degree, and their plans do not seem to recognize these risks.

In sum, many students report that they plan to get a college degree even though they have poor academic achievement. Yet, in fact, low grades predict much lower chances of attaining a degree. Within the High School and Beyond data, over 80% of students with low grades who planned to get a college degree failed to do so, and the failures were even greater for those planning an AA degree. Even without making any causal inferences, the strong predictive power of high school grades is important—it tells seniors how to place their bets. While students are correct that they can enter a college with low grades, they are usually mistaken in thinking that they can complete the degree. Their poor success rates make these outcomes a real long shot, not something students should be counting on.

High School Achievement Predicts Much of the Lower Attainment and Disappointed Plans of Disadvantaged Students

While the strong predictive power of high school grades tells seniors how to place their bets, do grades really predict educational attainment after controlling for other factors? If students want to raise their chances, they need to know whether to focus on improving grades, homework time, or track placement; and they may be worried that their future attainment is predestined by their social background (SES, ethnicity, gender) or intelligence (as test scores are sometimes interpreted). Policy makers also need to know to what extent grades or other factors predict the lower outcomes and disappointed plans of disadvantaged students.

Regression analysis is a good way to examine these issues. It allows researchers to look at simple gross associations between background characteristics and attainment and then to examine the mediating and independent predicting power of other factors such as high school achievement. We ran a series of OLS regressions on the High School and Beyond cohort who graduated in 1982 and were followed through 1992. The survey had 8,969 respondents who provided information for all variables in our model.

Our basic analyses made use of five dependent variables: students' cumulative grade point averages (Grades), tested achievement (Test), homework time (HW), educational plans (EdPlan), and educational attainment (EdYears). The first four were based on information gathered in the students' senior year, 1982; educational attainment constituted the number of years of students' educational attainments in 1992. Our independent variables included social background variables (Black, Hispanic, female, and a cumulative index of parents' SES computed in the High School and Beyond file), region of the U.S. (South, West, and Northeast regions, with the Midwest as the comparison), and school variables (private school, general, and vocational tracks, with college track as the comparison). Subsequent analyses concerned with plans and educational attainment added grade point average, tested achievement, and homework time as additional independent variables.

These analyses revealed several effects. First, Blacks, Hispanics, and low-SES students have lower grades and achievement test scores (Table 17.3, columns 1 and 3). If these coefficients indicate influences, they are partly mediated by track and private schools (columns 2 and 4). But even after controls are entered, Blacks, Hispanics, and low SES youth have lower grades and test scores.

Second, SES and being Black are associated with homework time, although in different directions (column 5), and the SES relationship is only partly diminished after controls are entered (column 6). While low-SES youth spend less time on homework than high-SES youth, Blacks spend significantly more time on homework than Whites (Hispanics spend about the same as Whites). Despite potential concerns because homework time is self-reported, Fordham and Ogbu's (1986) findings would predict that Blacks would underreport school effort (to avoid being seen as "acting White"), and these analyses find the opposite (Fordham and Ogbu's prediction was also not supported in Cook and Ludwig's, 1997, analysis). If homework time turns out to be an important predictor of educational attainment, then it may account for problems of low-SES students but is not likely to do so for Blacks.

Table 17.3 Regression Analyses for the Predictions of Grades, Tests, Homework, Educational Plans, and Attainment

	1 Grades	2 Grades	3 Test	4 Test	5 HW	6 HW	7 EdPlan	8 EdPlan	9 EdPlan	10 EdYears	11 EdYears	12 EdYears
SES	.207*	.163*	.368*	.295*	.223*	.164*	.450*	.378*	.240*	.386*	.324*	.201*
Black	-.141*	-.150*	-.212*	-.202*	.055*	.060*	.096*	.094*	.159*	-.023*	-.026*	.050*
Hispanic	-.110*	-.115*	-.201*	-.187*	-.007	.002	-.013	-.008	.060*	-.059*	-.045*	.024*
Female	.178*	.176*	-.037*	-.041*	.179*	.174*	.035*	.031*	-.014	.013	.007	-.040*
South		.020		-.055*		-.060*		-.014	.012		-.023*	-.008
West		.047*		-.007		-.017		.014	.013		-.058*	-.064*
NE		-.073*		.037*		.002		-.015	-.017		.038*	.045*
Private		-.021		.059*		.092*		.061*	.028*		.075*	.056*
Vocational		-.164		-.221*		-.119*		-.206*	-.098*		-.176*	-.075*
General		-.173		-.178*		-.172*		-.211*	-.104*		-.184*	-.085*
Test									.288*			.236*
GPA									.126*			.221*
HW									.200*			.105*
R^2(adj)%	12.2	16.1	27.2	33.5	7.8	12.1	19.6	25.3	41.2	16.5	22.1	36.3
n	8969	8969	8969	8969	8969	8969	8969	8969	8969	8969	8969	8969

Note. Standardized coefficients are presented. * = $p < .05$

Third, low-SES youth have lower educational plans, but Blacks have higher plans than Whites (column 7). These results remain after controls are entered for track and private schools (column 8). The SES relationship declines after controlling for grades, tests, and homework time, but the positive association for Blacks increases (column 9). Blacks have even higher plans than others with similar achievement, as previous research has noted (Jencks et al., 1972).

Fourth, Black, Hispanic, and low-SES youth have lower educational attainment (column 10). These relationships are only slightly altered after controls for track and private schools (column 11). However, these relationships are largely mediated by grades, test scores, and homework time. Indeed, when grades, test scores, and homework time are added to the analysis, the SES relationship declines substantially (from .324 to .201), although it remains statistically significant and the Black and Hispanic coefficients actually reverse and become significantly positive (column 12). Thus, students' grades, homework time, and tested achievement explain a significant part of the lower attainment of low-SES students, and Black and Hispanic students have higher attainments than Whites with similar achievement.

Finally, by adding seniors' plans to the regression, the analyses can discover which high school information predicts the disappointing attainments of disadvantaged students many years later (see Table 17.4). Since a few students (8.4%) attained more than they planned, they are removed from the analyses in Table 17.4, leaving 8,117 students in the analyses.[2] As a result, Table 17.4 shows the factors predicting which students' attainments fall short of their plans—explaining discrepancies between the 31.5% of students who attained their senior-year plans and the 60.1% who attained one or more years less than they planned. The analyses found that low-SES, Black, and Hispanic students had significantly lower attainments than they had planned (Table 17.4, column 1). However, when variables for school achievement and effort were added, the ethnic variables became insignificant and the SES coefficient became smaller (Table 17.4, column 3). Apparently, the disappointments of Black and Hispanic students are entirely predictable from their lower achievement and effort in high school.

Indeed, students' plans do not take sufficient account of their achievement. Over 58% (.142/.244) of the relationship between test scores and attainment and 78% (.173/.221) of the relationship between grades and attainment remain after controlling for plans (Table 17.4, columns 2 and 3). Less than half of these relationships are mediated by plans. Thus, consistent with the cross-tabular analyses (displayed

Table 17.4 Regression Analyses for the Predictions of Educational Attainment: All Students, Whites and Blacks

	1	2	3	4	5	6	7
	EdYears	EdYears	EdYears	EdYears	EdYears	EdYears	EdYears
SES	.154*	.211*	.127*	.213*	.113*	.225*	.190*
Black	−.072*	.050*	−.008				
Hispanic	−.035*	.032*	.011				
Female	.002	−.032*	−.025*	−.048*	−.031*	.055*	.024
South	−.006	.002	−.002	−.002	−.003	−.073	−.076*
West	−.060*	−.059*	−.064*	−.066*	−.069*	−.040	−.037
NE	.041*	.041*	.046*	.046*	.052*	.012	.011
Private	.031*	.045*	.031*	.047*	.033*	.019	.008
Vocational	−.083*	−.083*	−.044*	−.089*	−.047*	−.012	.000
General	−.089*	−.093*	−.052*	−.097*	−.052*	−.044	−.024
Test		.244*	.142*	.227*	.118*	.228*	.175*
Grades		.221*	.173*	.214*	.170*	.224*	.196*
HW		.119*	.050*	.114*	.040*	.071*	.043
Plans	.483*		.354*		.383*		.201*
R2(adj)%	40.3	38.3	45.4	38.1	46.0	27.2	30.0
n	8117	8117	8117	5014	5014	996	996

Note. Standardized coefficients are presented. * = $p < .05$ Analyses cases where EdYears is less than or equal to EdPlans.

in Table 17.2), we conclude that, even after controls, seniors' college plans vastly underestimate how much their grades and test scores predict their ultimate educational outcomes.

It is noteworthy that the female coefficient on educational attainment, which is virtually zero in the early regressions (Table 17.3, column 10), becomes significantly negative after controlling for achievement (column 12). Apparently, women have roughly the same educational attainments as males, but their attainments are still below what they would be if their previous achievement were the only determinant. Females have higher grades and homework time than males (but slightly lower test scores, see Table 17.3, columns 1–6), so there should be some concern about why their attainments are lower than their achievement would predict.

Finally, while the above analyses look at simple additive effects of ethnicity, one might still wonder if some of the factors in our model have different coefficients for Blacks and Whites. One indication of bias is when Blacks get less benefit from their achievements than Whites. In the 1970s, Porter (1974) found that Blacks received less gain in educational attainment from their high school grades than did Whites. Our regression analyses for educational attainment run separately for Whites and Blacks find that grades have about the same coefficients for both (Table 17.4, columns 4 and 6—betas .224 and .214), and the same is true for test scores (.228 and .227) but slightly larger coefficients for Whites than for Blacks (.114 vs .071) when it comes to homework.[3] Thus, Blacks get roughly the same gain in attainment for increases in their test scores and grades as Whites, although they get slightly less gain for increases in their homework time. Apparently, the old pattern of discrimination in which Blacks got lower attainment benefits for increasing their grades is no longer the case. Indeed, SES, test scores, and grades are somewhat stronger predictors of attainment for Blacks than for Whites (Table 17.4, columns 5 and 7).

In sum, these results indicate that SES, ethnicity, private schools, and track are related to attainment; but grades, test scores, and homework time also have effects which tend to mediate much of the relationship between disadvantaged backgrounds and attainment. However, there are indications that many students do not realize how much high school achievement predicts future attainment. While all students probably know their grades, their plans underestimate the extent that their grades predict their later attainment—and this is true for both Black and White students. Indeed, grades are the single best predictor of the ways attainment falls short of plans, and this predictability is somewhat larger for Blacks than for Whites. If students could focus on changing one set of attributes in high school to make their plans come true, they should improve those associated with their grades.[4,5]

Thus, these analyses suggest that students are overly complacent about the ease of getting a college degree. Many students have plans that have little chance of succeeding because their plans underestimate the relationship between high school achievement and later attainment. This is particularly true for Blacks, Hispanics, and low-SES students whose attainments fall short of their plans. These disappointments are largely predicted by their high school achievements (Table 17.4, columns 1 and 3). It seems likely that these students might work harder if they realized the future relevance of their high school achievement.

Students with Low High School Achievement Get Less Economic Payoff to College Degrees

Despite these odds, some students with low high school grades get college degrees. Do they get the same earnings payoff from college as students with better grades? While Murnane, Willett, and Levy (1995) have shown additive wage payoffs of educational attainment and achievement (measured by test scores), the present analyses examine whether college degrees have lower payoffs for those with lower achievement, which is operationalized by high school grades since it more clearly indicates achievement (rather than ability) and is known by all students. The above model is used to explain the 1991 earnings of the same High School and Beyond cohort, adding dummy variables for educational attainment (AA representing those who had received the AA but no higher; BA representing those

Table 17.5 Regression Analyses for the Predictions of Earnings

	Ln(Earnings)	Ln(Earaings)
SES	.101*	.101*
Black	.040	.041
Hispanic	.026	.025
Female	−.299*	−.299*
South	−.032*	−.032*
West	−.036	−.036
NE	.097*	.099*
Private	.043*	.045*
Vocational	−.030	−.031
General	−.027	−.026
Test	.003*	.003*
Grades	.034*	.025*
HW	−.004	−.004
AA	.101*	.155*
BA	.145*	.166*
MA	−.096*	−.112*
AALoGPA		−.227*
BALoGPA		−.123*
MALoGPA		.022
c	9.657	9.695
R^2(adj.)%	13.2	13.5

Note Nonstandardized coefficients are presented.
* = p< .05 N = 8,413

who had earned the BA but no higher degree; and MA representing those who had earned an MA or higher degrees). By taking the log of annual earnings as the dependent variable, unstandardized coefficients can be interpreted as percentage increases in earnings, so these tables report unstandardized coefficients. Thus, in the first step of the analysis, the High School and Beyond data indicate that youth who earn AA and BA degrees report 10.1% and 14.5% higher earnings, respectively, than those without a degree (Table 17.5, column 1).

To see if students with low grades get the same benefits from those degrees, these analyses create a new dummy variable (AA-LoGPA) for people who got an AA degree and had low grades in high school (AA-LoGPA equals 1 if a person has an AA degree and high school grades of C or lower, 0 otherwise.), and similar variables for BA-LoGPA and MA-LoGPA. Adding these three variables into the regression, the analyses find that youth who had low high school grades got less earnings advantage for their college degrees (Table 17.5, column 2). To figure the payoff to BAs for students with Cs, the coefficients for BA and BA-LoGPA are added, so the payoff to a BA degree is 4.3% (.166 −.123 = .043), and the payoff to an AA degree is −7.2%, less than if they had not gotten the degree (.155 − .227 = −.072). While the average student gets strong earnings benefits from BA and AA degrees, students with low grades get much smaller earnings benefits from a BA degree and lower earnings from an AA degree than from no degree.[6] Previous studies have found that poor grades predict lower earnings for young adults who have only a high school diploma (Miller, 1997; Rosenbaum, Miller, and Roy, 1996). These results indicate that low grades also substantially reduce the payoffs to college degrees (cf. also Rosenbaum and Miller, 1998).

Conclusion

These analyses help elucidate the problem of disadvantaged youth. Simple gross analyses find that low-SES, Black, and Hispanic students have lower educational attainment. However, the SES coefficient declines, and the ethnic disadvantages actually reverse and become advantages when achievement variables are entered. Thus, Blacks and Hispanics have significantly higher educational attainment than Whites with the same level of high school achievement. In addition, high school grades and test scores predict many of the cases where disadvantaged youth have lower attainment than they had planned.

Looking at these results, some might blame disadvantaged youth for their failures; but another interpretation is more plausible. Students' plans are what they think they can expect in the future, and their plans are likely to influence their high school efforts. In finding that students' plans do not take sufficient account of the influence of grades on their ultimate educational attainment, one can infer that students do not realize how much high school achievement affects their actual prospects. This is consistent with the future relevance and "no penalty" beliefs noted earlier. These results may indicate that schools fail to provide clear information to these youth which is consistent with what is known about counselors' advising practices (Rosenbaum, Miller, and Krei, 1996).

What is the harm in letting students have "high expectations?" Perhaps these plans are just dreams that make students a little happier and do them little harm. As noted, guidance counselors say they do not want to disappoint young people and so they encourage all students to attend college, even students with low achievement.

Consistent with this interpretation, Manski (1989) has proposed that many youth begin community college as an "experiment," a low-cost way to discover whether they can make it in college. But is it really low cost? Manski analyzes the process from the viewpoint of a student who is already in a community college, noting that his analysis does not consider students before they enter college.

However, there are opportunity costs to any decision, and this "experiment" has some large opportunity costs to students while they are still in high school. Should students with more than an 80% chance of failing at college place *all* their bets on their college experiment? Or would it be prudent for such students to hedge their college bets?

A first opportunity cost of the college-for-all norm is that students' high expectations may inadvertently encourage them to see high school as irrelevant and thus to make poor use of high school. Our interviews and survey of high school seniors indicate that 40% of students with college plans believe that high school is irrelevant. Postponing the key test for whether one is "college-bound" until after high school may inadvertently tell students that high school achievement is not important.

A second opportunity cost of the college-for-all norm is that it may lead to a lack of effort. Human capital theory posits that people invest effort in improving their capabilities if they believe better outcomes will result. But if they believe they can get the same outcomes without added effort, they will not make the effort. If students realize that their low high school grades will be associated with blocked college plans, they might increase their efforts in high school. Yet High School and Beyond data indicate that a large majority (78.0%) of poorly achieving high school students with college plans do less than an hour a day of homework, and many (25.3%) do less than an hour in a whole week. These High School and Beyond students exert little effort, even though they have low grades (which predict an 80% failure rate). Moreover, guidance counselors let these students hold unrealistic plans because they wish to encourage "high expectations" and "second chances" (Rosenbaum, Miller, and Krei, 1996). Students are not told what level of high school achievement is needed to succeed in community college, and they are lulled into a complacency that leaves them unprepared for getting college degrees.

The third opportunity cost of the college-for-all norm is that students with little prospect for getting a college degree will fail to get vocational training. Encouraging poorly achieving students to delay their work preparation until they see the results of their college "experiment" makes it likely that they will make poor use of vocational preparation in high school, which has been shown to improve earnings (Campbell, Basinger, Dauner, and Parks, 1986; Kang and Bishop, 1986; Rosenbaum, 1996).

Indeed, students with poor grades are less likely to be in vocational courses if they have college plans than if they are not planning college (Rosenbaum, unpublished analyses), and many students with low probability of success in college have no backup plans or training. Similarly, many public schools (such as those in Chicago) have reduced or ended their vocational programs because they expect all students to delay their vocational decisions until they get to college.

Although Manski did not consider it, there is an even more inexpensive experiment to help students infer their readiness for college—high school. If the CFA norm did not focus so much on getting everyone into college, then high schools could tell students their realistic chances of attaining college degrees. If students realized that high school achievement is the first "experiment," and this "experiment" has strong predictive power, then students with poor grades would either revise their plans downwards, or they might try to correct bad habits that lead to poor achievements.

Protecting students' high expectations when they are unwarranted is not a kindness; it is a deception. Failing to challenge students to examine the plausibility of their college plans has serious opportunity costs—it prevents them from seeing the importance of high school, it prevents them from taking the additional efforts that might make their plans more likely to come true, and it prevents them from preparing for alternative outcomes. When some seniors have high school records that make their college plans highly likely to fail, schools' protection of their "high expectations" is not a kind gesture. It looks a lot more like the confidence scheme that Goffman describes, distracting the "mark" from taking other constructive actions.

Unfortunately, students understand very well the *short-term* consequences of their high school efforts—they are minor. But they assume that this means that high school achievement and effort are irrelevant and that there will be no penalty if they do badly in high school. They believe they can postpone their efforts until they get into college, and their plans will work out fine.

Students' misperceptions may arise from their limited knowledge about older cohorts. High school students can see the college enrollment of last year's seniors more easily than the college completion of much older students, and they can more easily identify with the students a year older than themselves who enter college than with the 28-year-olds who never finished the degree. As a result, perceptions are likely to be distorted. Students easily perceive college enrollment, for which high school achievements are irrelevant, but they have difficulty seeing college completion, for which high school achievements are highly relevant. Under such circumstances, students' perceptions will not improve unless policy action is taken.

Policy Implications

The community college system and its open admissions policies are rightfully a source of pride. They have created new opportunities for large numbers of youth. However, open admissions may inadvertently contribute to students' complacency. Students with low grades may not realize that they have very poor prospects of getting a degree or earnings benefits from that degree.

High schools are partly responsible for such delusions. Our research suggests that high school guidance counselors believe that open admission means that they do not have to discourage students' college expectations. They believe that "high expectations" should be encouraged, and they report that they get complaints from parents and principals if they try to discourage unrealistically high plans (Rosenbaum, Miller, and Krei, 1996). Counselors' practices may help explain why students hold these views.

While policy has focussed on opening college admissions, it has not devoted similar effort to providing clear information about community colleges (Orfield, 1997; Paul, 1997, Rosenbaum, Miller, and Krei, 1997). Indeed, many schools push the college-for-all (CFA) norm, which lulls students into a complacency, which ultimately is unwarranted. High school grades could inform students about their likelihood of attaining a college degree, but this fact is hidden from students' awareness, and perhaps even teachers' and counselors' awareness.

To return to Goffman's model, the CFA norm is highly misleading and does great harm to youth. It offers big promises to students without warning that few low-achieving students will get a college degree. Indeed, it leaves many youth worse off than before, keeping them in the dark about actual requirements so they fail to take suitable actions to prepare themselves to accomplish their plans. It also harms youth as they waste time, energy, and money on a college experience they are ill prepared to handle and that is likely to lead to failure, low self-esteem, and misused opportunities in high school. While high school counselors brag about their college enrollment rates, students will blame themselves for the failure that they did not anticipate but which was highly predictable.

The CFA norm also has big impact on policies and practices in schools. An example can be seen in the Chicago public schools in the early 1990s when Superintendent Argie Johnson urged all of the city's high schools to stress college goals. She closed or withdrew resources from many vocational programs. Even the famous Chicago Vocational School began stressing that its goal was no longer vocational, but college. Meanwhile, the Chicago schools had low achievement levels, many of their graduates lacked the academic skills needed to take college-credit courses in the city college, and the degree completion rates at the city colleges were very low. The superintendent's urging that more students attend college was politically popular because it fit the CFA norm. It stressed "high expectations," but it may have led to increased failure.

This is not to urge that one abandon "high expectations" entirely or scrap open admissions policies. But three other reforms are warranted.

First, high schools should provide more complete information on community-college success rates as a function of students' grades, test scores, and homework time. This could be aided by a universally recognized test of achievement (not aptitude or intelligence), either statewide (such as Illinois's IGAP achievement test) or national (such as Clinton's proposal for national proficiency examinations). Even if such tests are not available, grades can be used. While the grades from individual teachers are highly imperfect, grade point averages have strong predictive power. Schools and society should be stressing their importance to students. Students need to realize that "open admissions" does not mean that high school achievement is irrelevant.

Second, linkages between high schools and colleges may help improve high school students' understanding of college requirements. By seeing that many college students must repeat high school classes, high school students will learn that they can work hard now, or next year they can repeat the same class and pay tuition for it. Several recent reforms seek to improve coordination of high school and college programs which may help students see the future relevance of their current courses (e.g., tech-prep, 2 + 2 programs, and career academies; see Berryman and Bailey, 1992; Stern, Finkelstein, Stone, Latting, and Dornsife, 1995).

Finally, students must be prepared for backup career options if their college plans are unlikely to succeed. While schools can encourage all students to aim for college, this should not be an excuse to cut vocational programs. Research indicates that after controls for test scores, vocational education graduates are 10–15% more likely to be in the labor force and are paid 8–9% more than graduates of academic programs (Campbell et al., 1986; Kang and Bishop, 1986; Rosenbaum, 1996).[7] Even if students plan to attend community college, low success rates at these colleges suggest that backup plans would be prudent, particularly for students with low grades. Over 80% of such students fail to get a degree and lose time, tuition, and self-confidence in the process. After they drop out of college, they enter the labor market without the vocational skills or preparation that they might have gotten if they had not been taken in by the college-for-all rhetoric.

Notes

1. Somewhat similar beliefs have been shown to influence students' achievements (Mickelson, 1990); but since achievement is influenced by many factors besides motivation, this study has chosen to focus on the determinants of effort (cf. also Steinberg, 1996, for an excellent overview).
2. Since one would not be concerned about the disappointment of very high plans, analyses were also run using recoded versions of plans and attainments in which values higher than BA were recoded to be the same as BA = 16. This recode does not alter results very much so those results are not reported.
3. Similar results are obtained on the full sample of 8,969 individuals not shown here.
4. What determines grades? Bowles and Gintis (1976) have suggested noncognitive components which are not supported in some other studies (Bills, 1983; Rosenbaum and Kariya, 1989, 1991). Miller and Rosenbaum (1998) pursue this question in greater detail.
5. Logit analyses were also run to see the determinants of who got AA or higher versus the high school graduates who got less than an AA. Using the same independent variables as the regression, the results indicate virtually the same conclusions as the above linear regression: grades, test scores, and homework all have significant influences, with grades having the largest influence. Grades have even larger influence than test scores in explaining disappointed plans. Similar findings occur in explaining who got BA or higher, although the grade influence is even greater. These tables are not reported because the results are virtually the same as those reported here.
6. Youth who did not complete high school are removed from this analysis so the constant represents all youth with high school diplomas but no college degrees. Note that the Malogpa coefficient is not significant and only 22 (4%) of MA students had low high school grades.
7. Kane and Rouse (1995) find that students get some economic benefit from the college credits they earn, even if they do not complete college degrees. However, these benefits may depend on whether the courses were vocational and on particular fields (Grubb, 1995). If the economic benefits of college courses (without a degree) arise from the vocational preparation they offer, then vocational courses in high schools or nondegree programs could possibly provide similar benefits. It is possible that the economic value of isolated college credits comes because individuals seek specific job-relevant courses, perhaps because of a job they already hold or one they know is available. Employers in some fields (tool and die, machining, etc.) require employees to obtain a few specific courses but not a certificate or degree (Rosenbaum and Binder, 1996).

    Moreover, for many students, the economic benefits of some college are negligible. Kane and Rouse (1995, p. 602) found that "40% [of two-year college dropouts] completed fewer than a semester's worth of credits" and a large number completed none, so the economic benefits of college entry were minimal for these students. Given that most of these students probably expected to get college degrees, they surely got much less academic and economic benefit from college than they anticipated and experienced relatively large psychological costs.

References

Berryman, Susan E. and Bailey, Thomas R. (1992). *The double helix: Education and the economy*. New York: Teachers College Press

Bills, David (1983). Social reproduction and the Bowles-Gintis thesis of a correspondence between school and work settings. *Research in sociology of education and socialization*. Greenwood, CT: JAI.

Bowles, Samuel and Gintis, Herbert (1976). *Schooling in capitalist America*. New York: Basic Books.

Brint, Steven and Karabel, Jerome (1989). *The diverted dream*. New York: Oxford University Press.

Campbell, Paul B., Basinger, K.S., Dauner, M.B., and Parks, M.A. (1986). *Outcomes of vocational education*. Columbus, OH: Ohio State University, National Center for Research in Vocational Education.

Cicourel, Aaron V. and Kitsuse, John I. (1963). *The educational decision-makers*. Indianapolis: Bobbs Merrill.

Clark, Burton (1960). The "cooling out" function in higher education. *American Journal of Sociology*, 65, 569–576.

Cook, Philip J. and Ludwig, Jens (1997). Weighing the burden of "acting White": Are there race differences in attitudes toward education? *Journal of Policy Analysis and Management*, 16(2), 256–278.

Dougherty, Kevin J. (1994). *The contradictory college*. Albany, NY: SUNY Press.

Fordham, Signithia and Ogbu, John (1986). Black students' school success: Coping with the burden of "acting White." *The Urban Review*, 18(3), 176–206.

Goffman, Erving (1952, November). Cooling the mark out: Some aspects of adaptation to failure. *Psychiatry*, 15, 451–163.

Grubb, W. Norton (1989). Dropouts, spells of time, and credits in postsecondary education. *Economics of Education Review*, 8(1), 49–67.

Grubb, W. Norton (1992). Postsecondary education and the sub-baccalaureate labor market. *Economics of Education Review*, 11(3), 225–248.

Grubb, W. Norton (1993). The varied economic returns of postsecondary education. *Journal of Human Resources*, 28(2), 265–282.

Grubb, W. Norton (1995). Response to comment. *Journal of Human Resources*, 30(1), 222–228.

Grubb, W. Norton and Kalman, Judy (1994, November). Relearning to earn. *American Journal of Education*, 103, 54–93.

Jencks, Christopher L., Smith, Smith, Acland, Henry, Bane, Mary Jo, Cohen, David K., Gintis, Herbert, Heyns, Barbara, and Michaelson, Stephan (1972). *Inequality*. New York: Basic Books.

Kandel, Denise and Lesser, Gerald (1972). *Youth in two worlds: United States and Denmark*. New York: Jossey-Bass.

Kane, Thomas and Rouse, Cecilia E. (1995). Labor-market returns to two- and four-year college. *American Economic Review,* 85(3), 600–614.

Kang, Suk and Bishop, John (1986). The effect of curriculum on labor market success. *Journal of Industrial Teacher Education,* 133–148.

Karabel, Jerome (1986) Community colleges and social stratification in the 1980s. In L.S. Zwerling (Ed.), *The community college and its critics.* San Francisco: Jossey-Bass, pp. 13–30.

Kerckhoff, Alan C. and Campbell, Richard T. (1977). Black-White differences in the educational attainment process. *Sociology of Education,* 50(1), 15–27.

Manski, Charles F. (1989). Schooling as experimentation. *Economics of Education Review,* 8(4), 305–312.

Mickelson, Roslyn. (1990, January). The attitude-achievement paradox among Black adolescents. *Sociology of Education,* 63, 44–61.

Miller, Shazia (1997). *Shortcut: High school grades as a signal of human capital.* Paper presented at the annual meeting of the American Sociological Association, Toronto.

Miller, Shazia and Rosenbaum, James (1998). *What do grades mean?* Unpublished manuscript, Northwestern University, Institute for Policy Research.

Murnane, Richard, Willett, John B., and Levy, Frank (1995). The growing importance of cognitive skills in wage determination. *Review of Economics and Statistics,* 77(2), 251–266.

Murnane, Richard and Levy, Frank (1997). *Teaching the new basic skills.* New York: The Free Press.

National Center for Educational Statistics (1983). *High school and beyond: 1980 senior cohort first follow-up (1982): Data file user's manual.* Chicago: National Opinion Research Center.

National Center for Educational Statistics (1983). *High school and beyond: Data file user's manual.* Chicago: National Opinion Research Center.

National Center for Educational Statistics (1995). *Remedial education at higher education institutions.* Washington, DC: U.S. Department of Education.

Orfield, Gary (1997). Going to work: Weak preparation, little help. In Kenneth K. Wong (Ed.), *Advances in educational policy* (Vol. 3). Greenwood, CT: JAI Press, pp. 3–32.

Paul, Faith (1997). Negotiated identities and academic program choice. In Kenneth K. Wong (Ed.), *Advances in educational policy* (Vol. 3). Greenwood, CT: JAI Press, pp. 53–78.

Porter, James N. (1974, June). Race, socialization and mobility in educational and early occupational attainment. *American Sociological Review,* 39, 303–316.

Resnick, Lauren B. and Wirt, John G. (1996). The changing workplace. In Lauren B. Resnick and John G. Wirt (Eds.), *Linking school and work.* San Francisco: Jossey Bass, pp. 1–22.

Rosenbaum, James E. (1975). The stratification of socialization processes. *American Sociological Review,* 40(1), 48–54.

Rosenbaum, James E. (1976). *Making inequality.* New York: Wiley.

Rosenbaum, James E. (1978). The structure of opportunity in school. *Social Forces,* 57, 236–256.

Rosenbaum, James E. (1986). Institutional career structures and the social construction of ability. In G. Richardson (Ed.), *Handbook of theory and research for the sociology of education.* Westport, CT: Greenwood Press, pp. 139–171.

Rosenbaum, James E. (1989). Organizational career systems and employee misperceptions. In Michael Arthur, Douglas T. Hall, and Barbara Lawrence (Eds.), *Handbook of career theory.* New York: Cambridge University Press, pp. 329–353.

Rosenbaum, James E. (1996, Summer). Policy uses of research on the high school-to-work transition. *Sociology of Education,* Summer, pp. 102–122.

Rosenbaum, James E. and Kariya, Takehiko (1989). From high school to work: Market and institutional mechanisms in Japan. *American Journal of Sociology,* 94(6), 1334–1365.

Rosenbaum, James E. and Kariya, Takehiko (1991). Do school achievements affect the early jobs of high school graduates in the United States and Japan? *Sociology of Education,* 64, 78–95.

Rosenbaum, James E. and Binder, Amy (1997, January). Do employers really need more educated youth? *Sociology of Education,* 70, 68–85.

Rosenbaum, James E. and Miller, Shazia (1998). The earnings payoff to college degrees for youth with poor high school achievement. ˙ Unpublished manuscript, Northwestern University, Institute for Policy Research.

Rosenbaum, James E., Miller, Shazia, and Krei, Melinda (1996, August). Gatekeeping in an era of more open gates. *American Journal of Education,* 104, 257–279.

Rosenbaum, James E., Miller, Shazia, and Krei, Melinda (1997). What role should counselors have? In Kenneth K. Wong (Ed.), *Advances in educational policy* (Vol. 3). Greenwood, CT: JAI Press, pp. 79–92.

Rosenbaum, James E. and Roy, Kevin (1996, April). Trajectories for success in the transition from school to work. Paper presented at the annual meeting of the American Educational Research Association, New York.

Rosenbaum, James E., Miller, Shazia, and Roy, Kevin (1996, August). Long-term effects of high school grades and job placements. Paper presented at the annual meeting of the American Sociological Association, New York.

Sedlak, Michael W., Wheeler, Christopher W., Pullin, Diane C., and Cusick, Phillip A. (1986). *Selling students short.* New York: Teachers College Press.

Steinberg, Lawrence (1996). *Beyond the classroom.* New York: Simon and Shuster.

Stern, David, Finkelstein, Neal, Stone, James, Latting, John, and Dornsife, Carolyn (1995). *School to work: Research on programs in the United States.* Washington and London: Falmer Press.

Stevenson, Harold W. and Stigler, James W. (1992). *The learning gap.* New York: Simon and Shuster.

Stinchcombe, Arthur L. (1965). *Rebellion in a high school.* Chicago: Quadrangle.

Turner, Ralph (1960). Sponsored and contest mobility and the school system. *American Sociological Review,* 25, 855–867.

U.S. Department of Health, Education, and Welfare (1992). *Digest of educational statistics.* Washington, DC: U.S. Government Printing Office.

PART IV
Suggested Readings

Allen, W. R. (1988). Black students in U.S. higher education: Toward improved access, adjustment and achievement. *Urban Review, 20,* 165–88.

Allen, W. R., Epps, E.G., & Haniff, N. Z. (1991). *College in Black and white: African American students in predominantly white and historically Black public universities.* Albany: SUNY Press.

Allen, W. R. (1992). The color of success: African American college student outcomes at predominantly white and historically Black public colleges and universities. *Harvard Educational Review, 62,* 26–44.

Bok, D., & Bowen, D. G. (1998). *The shape of the river.* Princeton, NJ: Princeton University Press.

Bradley, K. (2000). The incorporation of women into higher education: Paradoxical outcomes. *Sociology of Education, 73*(1), 1–18.

Brint, S., & Karabel, J. (1989). *The diverted dream: Community colleges and the promise of educational opportunity, 1900–1985.* New York: Oxford University Press.

Canada, K., & R. Pringle. (1995). The role of gender in college classroom interactions: a social context approach. *Sociology of Education, 68,* 3, 161–186.

Conley, D. (2001) Capital for college: Parental assets and postsecondary schooling. *Sociology of Education, 74,* 59–71.

Dougherty, K. J. (1997). Mass education: What is its impetus? What is its impact? *Teachers College Record, 99,* 66–72.

Dougherty, K. J. (1991). The community college at a crossroads: The need for structural reform. *Harvard Educational Review, 61,* 311–336.

Dougherty, K. J. (1994). *The contradictory college: The conflicting origins, impacts, and futures of the community college.* Albany: SUNY.

Dougherty, K. J., & Kienzl, G. S. (2006). It's not enough to get through the open door: Inequalities by social background in transfer from community colleges to four-year colleges. *Teachers College Record, 108,* 3, 452–487

Jacobs, J. A. (1995). Gender and academic specialties: Trends among recipients of college degrees in the 1980s. *Sociology of Education* 68, 81–98.

Karabel, J. (1972). Community colleges and social stratification. *Harvard Educational Review, 42,* 521–562.

Karabel, J. (2005). *The chosen: The hidden history of admission and exclusion at Harvard, Yale, and Princeton.* New York: Houghton-Mifflin.

Karen, D. (1990). Toward a political-organizational model of gate-keeping: The case of elite colleges. *Sociology of Education, 63,* 227–240.

Karen, D. (1991a). Achievement and ascription in admission to an elite college: A political-organizational analysis. *Sociological Forum, 6,* 349–380.

Karen, D. (1991b). Politics of race, class, and gender: Access to higher education in the United States, 1960–1986. *American Journal of Education, 99,* 208–237.

Karen, D. (2002). Changes in access to higher education in the United States: 1980–1992. *Sociology of Education, 75,* 191–210.

Lavin, D., Alba, R., & Silberstein, D. (1981). *Right versus privilege: The open admissions experiment at City University of New York.* New York: Basic.

Lavin, D., & D. Hyllegard. (1996). *Changing the odds: Open admissions and the life chances of the disadvantaged.* New Haven, CT.: Yale.

Lee, V. E. (1985). *Access to higher education: The experience of Blacks, Hispanics, and low socio-economic status whites.* Washington DC: Division of Policy Analysis and Research, American Council on Education.

Lee, V. E., & Frank, K. A. (1990). Students' characteristics that facilitate the transfer from two-year to four-year colleges. *Sociology of Education, 63,* 178–93.

Maher, F., & Tetrault, M. K. (2006). *Diversity and privilege in the academy.* New York: Routledge.

Massey, D. (2003). *The source of the river: The social origins of freshmen at America's selective colleges and universities.* Princeton, NJ: Princeton University Press.

McDonough, P. (1997). *Choosing colleges: How social class and schools structure opportunity.* Albany: SUNY Press.

Miller-Bernal, L. (1993). Single sex versus coeducational environments: A comparison of women students' experiences at four colleges. *American Journal of Education, 102*(1), 23–54.

Miller-Bernal, L. (1999). *Separate by degree: Women students' experiences in single-sex and coeducational colleges*. New York: Peter Lang.

Miller-Bernal, L., & Poulson, S. (2004). *Going coed: Coeducation at formerly men's college, 1950–2000*. Nashville: Vanderbilt University Press.

Miller-Bernal, L., & Poulson, S. (2006). *Challenged by Coeducation: Women's colleges since the 1960s*. Nashville, TN: Vanderbilt University Press.

Persell, C. H., Catsambis, S., & Cookson, P. W. (1992). Differential asset conversion: class and gender pathways to selective colleges. *Sociology of Education, 65*, 208–225.

Persell, C. Hodges, Sophia C., & Cookson, P. W. Jr. (1992). Family background, school type, and college attendance: A conjoint system of cultural capital transmission. *Journal of Research on Adolescence, 2*, 1–23.

Pincus, F. (1980). The false promises of the community college. *Harvard Educational Review, 50*, 332–361.

Riordan, C. (1992). Single- and mixed- gender colleges for women: Educational, attitudinal, and occupational outcomes. *Review of Higher Education, 15*, 327–446.

Rosenbaum, J. (1998). College-for-all: Do students understand what college demands? *Social Psychology of Education, 2*, 50–85.

Sadovnik, A. R. (1994). *Equity and excellence in higher education*. New York: Peter Lang Publishers.

Tierney, W. (1997). The parameters of affirmative action: Equity and excellence in the academy. *Review of Educational Research, 67*(2), 165–196.

PART V

Education and Inequality

The relationship between education and inequality has been a central concern of the sociology of education for the past forty years. Sociologists of education have examined the effects of schooling on life chances and economic outcomes, as well as the effects of race, social class, ethnicity, and gender on academic achievement. Sociological research has consistently found that family background strongly affects educational achievement, with students from higher socioeconomic backgrounds achieving at higher levels than students from lower socioeconomic backgrounds and White and Asian American students achieving at higher levels than African American, Latino, and Native American students. In addition, although women have reduced the achievement gap with men, male students still outperform women in mathematics and science, while women outperform men in reading and language arts. Moreover, women have higher high school and college graduation rates; and boys have significantly higher rates of special education placement. However, sociologists disagree about the causes of these achievement gaps and policy makers disagree about what should be done to reduce them.

A central question for sociologists of education concerns the factors that explain educational achievement and achievement gaps. Sociologists examine both school and nonschool factors to explain educational inequality. School factors include curriculum and pedagogy, teacher quality, school funding, tracking and ability grouping, school leadership, and other school level variables. Nonschool factors include poverty, community, family involvement, peer group interactions, genetic differences in intelligence (a highly controversial theory), and health and environmental factors (for a detailed discussion see Riordan, 2003; Sadovnik, Cookson, & Semel, 2006, chapter 9). Although some sociologists stress school factors and others stress nonschool factors, it appears that the interaction of both sets of factors explain differences in educational achievement among groups. The following articles examine these complex issues.

Chapter 18 includes a debate on the functions, effects, and desirability of placing students according to ability or differentiating curriculum for different groups of students, commonly referred to in the United States as tracking. "Tracking: From Theory to Practice" by University of Notre Dame sociologist Maureen Hallinan examines the unintended consequences of tracking and the need to eliminate tracking where it is dysfunctional and improve it where required. "More than Misplaced Technology: A Normative and Political Response to Hallinan on Tracking" by UCLA sociologist Jeannie Oakes provides a critical response to Hallinan that argues for the elimination of tracking. Following these essays, both authors respond to each other's arguments.

Chapter 19, "Invisible Inequality: Social Class and Childrearing in Black Families and White Families" by University of Maryland sociologist Annette Lareau, examines the relationship between social class, family and schooling. Through a comparison of middle-class and working-class families, Lareau analyzes how different patterns of childrearing education affect social and educational outcomes. Based on a multi-year ethnographic study of Black and White working-class and middle-class families, Lareau describes two different forms of childrearing and their differential effects on children from different social classes.

Chapter 20, "Collective Identity and the Burden of Acting White in Black History, Community and Education" by the late University of California, Berkeley, anthropologist John Ogbu, presents an overview of his controversial theory that Black students often have low educational achievement and attainment due to their perception that academic achievement is a characteristic of being White.

Chapter 21, "Burden of Acting Neither White Nor Black: Asian American Identities and Achievement in Urban Schools" by Rutgers University sociologist Jamie Lew, applies Ogbu's theory to Asian American students.

Chapter 22, "The Help-Seeking Orientation of Latino and non-Latino Urban High School Students: A Critical-Sociological Investigation" by UCLA sociologist Ricardo Stanton-Salazar and colleagues Lisa Chavez and Robert Tai, examines the role of social capital in the education of Latino high school students.

Chapter 23, "What Do We Know About the Effects of Single-Sex Schools in the Private Sector?: Implications for Public Schools" by Providence College sociologist Cornelius Riordan, examines the effects of single-sex schooling in private schools and suggests the policy implications for public schools.

Questions for Reflection and Discussion

1. What are the functions of tracking? Based on the essays by Hallinan and Oakes, do you believe tracking based on ability (ability grouping) or curriculum tracking (different curricula for different groups of students) is a reasonable way of organizing instruction? What do you think Hallinan and Oakes would say about gifted and talented programs and advanced placement courses? Do you think all students should receive the same curriculum and teaching methods? Do you think Oakes's recommendation of heterogeneous classes for all students is practical? Do you think the problem is tracking or the way students are sorted and selected into tracks? Would a tracking system be fair if it were based on merit alone, rather than other factors, such as race, social class, ethnicity, or gender? Is this possible? Finally, should students with learning problems or disabilities be tracked into separate special education classes or included in heterogeneous classes?

2. According to Lareau, how do working-class and middle-class family childrearing practices differ? Based on this article, do you think that working-class parents care less about their children's education? Do you think one form of childrearing practice is better than the other? Which do you think is a more powerful determinant of school achievement, social class or race?

3. According to Ogbu, why do Black students achieve at lower levels than White students? What do you think of his theory about the burden of acting White? Does Lew's research support Ogbu's theory when applied to Asian American students? According to Lew, how do race and social class interact to explain Asian American student achievement?

4. According to Stanton Salazar and his colleagues, what is the role of social capital in helping Latino students to succeed in school? Does their research support Bourdieu's theories of social and cultural capital?

5. According to Riordan, what are the lessons from single-sex schools that should be implemented in public schools? Do you think there should be single-sex classes in public schools or single-sex public schools? Do you think these violate Title IX, which prohibits discrimination in public schools based on gender? If so, why? If not, why not?

6. Based on the articles in this section, which do you think are more important in explaining achievement gaps, school or nonschool factors? Why?

References

Riordan, C. (2003). *Equality and achievement: An introduction to the sociology of education* (2d ed.). Saddle River, NJ: Prentice Hall.

Sadovnik, A. R., Cookson, P. W., & Semel, S. F. (2006). *Exploring education: An introduction to the foundations of education* (3rd ed.). Needham Heights, MA: Allyn and Bacon.

18
Tracking
From Theory to Practice

MAUREEN T. HALLINAN

and

More than Misplaced Technology
A Normative and Political Response to Hallinan on Tracking

JEANNIE OAKES

Tracking: From Theory to Practice

Maureen T. Hallinan

The term *tracking* refers to the practice of assigning students to instructional groups on the basis of ability. Originally, secondary school students were assigned to academic, general, or vocational tracks, with the courses within those tracks designed to prepare students for postsecondary education or careers. More recently, these track categories have been replaced by course levels, with students typically being assigned to advanced, honors, regular, or basic courses. These course levels continue to be referred to as tracks, with the regular and higher-level courses loosely equivalent to the academic track and the basic and lower courses loosely equivalent to the general and vocational tracks. Most secondary and junior high or middle schools track students for English and mathematics, and many schools track for social studies, science, language, and other courses. Tracking is an organizational practice whose aim is to facilitate instruction and to increase learning. The theory of tracking argues that tracking permits teachers to tailor instruction to the ability level of their students. A good fit between a student's ability and the level of instruction is believed to maximize the effectiveness and efficiency of the instructional process. Thus, tracking is meant to promote cognitive development; it is not designed to influence or modify students' social or emotional growth.

The practice of tracking is currently a topic of intense debate. The concern focuses on two issues pertaining to the effectiveness and equity of tracking. The first is whether tracking is more effective in promoting students' learning than are other methods of grouping. The second is whether all students benefit from tracking to the same degree.

The tracking debate is fed by conjectures and assumptions about the way tracking operates and how it affects students. Among these beliefs are that track placement is determined primarily by academic criteria, that tracks are strictly homogeneous with respect to ability, that track assignments tend to be permanent, that tracking has a negative effect on the self-esteem of low-ability students, that low-ability students are difficult to teach because they are not highly motivated to learn, and that tracking limits the college options of low-track students.

Research on Tracking

A number of fairly rigorous empirical studies, including both surveys and case studies, have provided information about how students are assigned to tracks and about the effects of track levels on students' learning. The findings of these studies are consistent with some of the commonly held beliefs about tracking, but contradict others. Empirical research supports the following conclusions about tracking.

Assignment to Tracks

1. In practice, the assignment of students to tracks is based not only on academic considerations, which would lead to strictly homogeneous groupings, but on nonacademic factors. Academic factors that influence track placement are grades, scores on standardized tests, teachers' and counselors' recommendations, prior track placement, and course prerequisites. Nonacademic considerations include course conflicts, cocurricular and extracurricular schedules, work demands, and teacher and curricular resources. A reliance on nonacademic factors increases the heterogeneity of ability groups and leads to overlapping ability distributions in adjacent tracks.
2. Schools vary in the constellation of factors on which they rely to assign students to tracks and in the weight they attach to each factor. As a result, track assignments are dependent, in part, on the schools that students attend.
3. Track assignments tend to be less permanent than is commonly believed. It is not uncommon for a student to change tracks during a school year and from one school year to the next. The flexibility of track assignments varies by school, by subject, and by grade level.
4. A greater proportion of minority and low-income students are assigned to the lower tracks. When academic achievement is controlled, the race-ethnicity and income effect on track assignment decreases, but does not disappear.
5. Higher social status is associated with placement in a higher track. The importance of track level for social status differs across schools.

Effects of Tracking

1. The quantity and quality of instruction increases with the level of the track. The curriculum and related instructional materials are more interesting and engaging in higher tracks. The amount of time spent on instruction, as opposed to administrative and disciplinary tasks, is greater in higher tracks. The relationship between track level and instructional characteristics differs among schools.
2. Students in high-ability tracks learn more and at a faster pace than do those in lower-ability tracks.
3. Tracking provides no advantage over heterogeneous grouping with respect to the achievement of students in the middle-ability range.

These conclusions indicate that tracking, as currently practiced, tends to be both inequitable and, at least for some students, ineffective. Tracking provides fewer learning opportunities for low-ability students than for those with higher ability. Since low ability is related to race, ethnicity, and socioeconomic status, tracking discriminates against students in these demographic categories. The disadvantages of tracking for low-ability students perpetuate the effects of background characteristics on achievement. Tracking also disadvantages lower-ability students by conveying on them lower social status. Differences among schools in the effectiveness and equity of tracking place additional constraints on access to learning opportunities for some students, usually those of lower ability.

In general, empirical research seems to provide the rationale for eliminating tracking as an organizational and pedagogical practice. However, the decision to detrack a school may be premature and unwarranted. To evaluate the effectiveness and equity of tracking in an effort to determine how it can be improved, rather than eliminated, it is necessary to examine its intended and unintended consequences.

Tracking as an Organizational Practice

Tracking is a way of organizing a student body. The intended purpose of tracking is to increase the effectiveness and efficiency of instruction. If tracking operated according to theory, students at all ability levels and from all backgrounds would learn more in tracked classes than in untracked ones. However, tracking produces unintended consequences that impede the attainment of its goal. Some of these consequences are inherent in the nature of tracking, whereas others are due to the failure of tracking practice to reflect tracking theory. These consequences make tracking less effective and less equitable than intended.

The task of an educational administrator who is faced with a decision about tracking is twofold: to determine whether the practice of tracking can be made more consistent with the theory and to ascertain whether negative features that are inherent in tracking can be outweighed by other school policies and practices. If the answer to these questions is affirmative, then it is reasonable to retain tracking, so teachers and students can benefit from the positive effects of the practice.

Modifying Negative Consequences

Segregation. One unintended negative consequence of tracking is the way it segregates students by race or ethnicity and socioeconomic status. Since academic achievement is related to students' background, minority and low-income students are disproportionately assigned to lower tracks. Even if the quality of instruction were the same across tracks, this segregating effect would concern educators and parents.

Although the segregation produced by tracking may be unavoidable, its negative effects can be countered by integrating students in their untracked classes and in other school activities. Ensuring that students spend a large part of their school day in integrated settings should lessen the negative effects of assignment to a small number of segregated classes. Furthermore, school authorities can create a school atmosphere that is intolerant of racism and that strongly supports positive social relations among different ethnic and racial groups.

Low social status. A second negative feature of tracking is its effects on students' social status. Tracking typically leads to a social hierarchy based on track level and academic performance. Students who are assigned to the lower tracks are apt to receive less respect from their peers and to be assigned lower status in the academic hierarchy. Lower status can have negative consequences for learning by decreasing a student's motivation and effort. In addition, rewards typically are given to higher-track students, which could further discourage or alienate lower-track students.

To counter the negative social dynamics created by tracking, school authorities need to create structures and methods to support the social and emotional experiences of lower-track students. Restructuring the reward system to broaden the bases for social recognition and respect is one way to enhance the status of low-track students.

Heterogeneous tracks. A third negative consequence of tracking results from the failure of authorities to create strictly homogeneous tracks. In practice, track levels are rarely as homogeneous as they could be. In most cases, the distribution of achievement in one track overlaps, to a surprising degree, with the distribution in adjacent tracks. Typically, students at the high end of the distribution in one track have higher achievement than do those at the low end of the distribution in the next higher track.

The degree of heterogeneity among students in a track affects teachers' ability to direct instruction to the students' ability levels. Thus, the failure of students to benefit from tracking may be due partly to the failure of schools to create homogeneous tracks.

Moreover, students develop cognitively at different rates. Even when a track structure is homogeneous at the beginning of a school year, students' different rates of growth introduce heterogeneity into the tracks during the school year. When students' track placements are permanent, either across a school year or for longer periods, allowance is not made for the heterogeneity that arises from these differential rates of growth. Heterogeneity becomes greater with time, creating a wider departure from the conditions under which tracking is expected to be effective.

What is needed is a flexible tracking policy that allows for reassignments to preserve the homogeneity of tracks. Empirical data show that track assignments in many secondary schools are flexible, both across and within school years. However, changes in tracks are often made to accommodate a student's participation in other school activities, rather than for academic reasons. These changes usually create greater heterogeneity in tracks.

Frequent reassignments of students to tracks to increase the homogeneity of tracks are desirable. Periodic evaluations of the distribution of achievement in tracks and a policy of reassigning students to different tracks, when appropriate, should ensure a good fit between students' abilities and the level of instruction.

Slower achievement of students in low tracks. The most serious, unintended negative effect of tracking is the slower growth in achievement of students in low tracks. This effect is caused, in part, by instructional inadequacies in the lower tracks. Instruction in many low tracks can be characterized by uninteresting lessons and instructional materials, by teachers' low expectations and standards for their students' performance, by low standards or teachers' performance, and by a significant number of interruptions in instruction owing to disciplinary problems.

Educational authorities have the ability to modify each of these characteristics of instruction in lower tracks. Teachers can provide more interesting instructional materials without going beyond the students' level of comprehension. They also can alter their assumptions about the learning potential of low-ability students. Recent research on the multiple facets of intelligence, as well as new developments in learning theory that have identified different learning styles, should be helpful in this regard. Teachers can raise their expectations and requirements for students' performance. Principals can devise reward systems that are aimed at improving teachers' instruction, and teachers can provide rewards that motivate students to study. The school can consistently and publicly acknowledge the accomplishments of students in all academic tracks. Principals and counselors can devise methods of dealing with disciplinary problems without infringing on the teachers' instructional time.

Negative social psychological consequences. In addition, negative social psychological processes occur in lower tracks that further jeopardize learning for lower-ability students. These processes link a student's assignment to a lower track to his or her self-esteem and social status. Students are likely to view their assignments to low tracks as evidence that teachers have a low regard for their academic abilities and as an indication that they cannot be successful in school and should not aspire to go to college. This inference leads to a loss of self-confidence and decreases their motivation to achieve academically. Discouragement usually results in students' detachment from learning and often leads to disruptive behavior or withdrawal. This negative cycle tends to be self-perpetuating.

Change or intervention can occur at any point in the negative social psychological processes that interfere with learning. The principal and faculty of a school can make a determined effort to communicate a positive message about the meaning of different track levels. Teachers can increase the academic demands they place on lower-track students and challenge these students to achieve. They can offer students frequent opportunities to succeed and provide tangible and public rewards for success and improvement. The school can adhere to a policy of flexible track assignments, motivating students to work harder to advance to higher tracks if they so choose. In short, educators can forestall or reverse the negative social psychological dynamics that often accompany placements in low tracks by fostering a more positive attitude about track placement and students' potential. When accompanied by improved instruction in the lower tracks, this attitude adjustment should generate social psychological processes that encourage, rather than obstruct, learning in the lower tracks.

A common reaction to these unintended negative consequences of tracking is to call for the abandonment of tracking as an educational practice. A more tempered response would be to improve the way tracking is practiced, so it better fits the ideal, and to counter students' negative cognitive, social psychological, or behavioral responses to being tracked. The negative effect of tracking on integration in schools can be reduced by a committed effort to eliminate racism in a school and by avoiding segregation in nontracked classes and other school activities.

Objective versus Subjective Criteria

The effectiveness and equity of tracking are also influenced by the way students are assigned to track levels. Schools differ in the criteria they use to determine students' placements in tracks. Within a school, differences also occur in the criteria for assigning students to different track levels.

Assignments to tracks that are based strictly on objective, academic criteria, such as standardized test scores, academic grades, and prerequisites for courses, produce the most academically homogeneous groups. When more arbitrary criteria are applied, such as counselors' and teachers' recommendations, parents' and students' preferences, and schedule conflicts with other academic courses or with cocurricular and extracurricular activities, tracks tend to be more heterogeneous.

Secondary schools seem to use more objective criteria in assigning students to higher tracks and more arbitrary criteria in assigning students to lower tracks. This tendency creates greater homogeneity in the upper tracks, implying that students who are assigned to the upper tracks enjoy a more optimal instructional environment than do those assigned to the lower tracks. Although subjective criteria may yield a more accurate assessment of students' potential than may objective measures, they usually do not because limitations on counselors' time leads to cursory evaluations, resulting in inappropriate assignments.

Schools differ in the criteria on which they base their decisions on track placements. Some schools rely heavily on objective measures; others use indicators of a student's improvement. Whether a school makes track placements on the basis of absolute, relative, or self-mastery standards has a direct impact on the track level to which a student is assigned. Differences in criteria among schools represent one way that tracking can transmit unequal learning opportunities to students.

School-district administrators, principals, and counselors establish their schools' criteria for placing students in tracks. Their challenge is to determine the most effective and equitable set of criteria to ensure the success of tracking. Most criteria that are defined at the district level are based on objective measures of ability or achievement, usually grades and standardized test scores. These are suitable measures generally, assuming that they correlate with students' ability, because they tend to create a fair degree of within-track homogeneity. Nevertheless, modifications of and exceptions to these criteria may be required to reduce heterogeneity further.

Although the use of objective measures of achievement as criteria for track placements increases the homogeneity of tracks, it creates other problems. Standardizing criteria for achievement results in the assignment of disproportionately fewer students to the upper tracks than to the lower tracks in some schools. Research has found that schools in which a small number of students qualify for admission to advanced tracks tend to lower their standards for admission to those tracks to increase the number of students in the advanced courses to a desire level. Thus, criteria for track placements may have to be defined at the school, rather than the district, level to take the characteristics of a school's population into account. Under these circumstances, careful counseling is called for when students change from one school to another.

A more serious consequence of standardizing criteria for admission to tracks and of basing admission primarily on objective measures of achievement is related to the equity of tracking. Administrators avoid setting objective criteria because doing so results in the assignment of fewer minority students to the higher tracks and disproportionately more minority students to the lower tracks. Since most administrators deplore this segregative aspect of tracking, they tend to prefer less objective measures of ability. To resolve this dilemma, it is necessary to compromise between the two desired goals of effectiveness and equity. In addition, however, schools need to make systematic, concerted efforts to improve the performance of low-ability students, so these students can meet the criteria for admission to higher tracks.

Conclusion

Tracking clearly has many shortcomings. Some of them, such as its segregative aspect and its effects on students' social status, are difficult to eliminate. However, schools have a number of opportunities to reduce these negative effects of tracking by ensuring that nontracked classes and other school activities are integrated and by expanding the bases of social status to include nonacademic talents.

Other shortcomings of tracking result not from the organizational technique itself, but from the way tracking is practiced in schools. Efforts to reform the practice should be directed toward improving the quantity and quality of instruction at all track levels, particularly the lower ones, to eliminate the instructional disadvantages of tracking that some students experience. Schools also need to guard against lessening the motivation of lower-track students by providing support mechanisms and reward systems for all students, including those in the lower tracks.

Finally, to ensure that tracking works as intended, great care is needed in making initial track assignments and in permitting students to change tracks when their original placements are no longer appropriate. Improving the fit of track assignments is a complex task. It requires school authorities to choose criteria that are valid measures of students' abilities and that reduce the likelihood of inappropriate placements. In the design of a student's schedule, track placement must take priority over other scheduling considerations. However, deviation from a rigid admissions policy is appropriate if it attains another objective, such as the integration of tracks, without having a major negative effect on the homogeneity of tracks.

In general, many of the criticisms leveled against tracking can be avoided by improving, rather than eliminating, tracking. The compelling advantage of retaining tracking, at least in certain subjects, is that it facilitates instruction and learning. The many teachers who favor tracking have concluded, from pedagogical experience, that teaching heterogeneously grouped students without additional resources, such as teacher aides and supplementary material, is a formidable task. Moreover, the outcome of detracking in less-than-ideal circumstances may be as unsatisfactory as that of tracking that is not practiced according to principle. If educators are willing to put serious efforts into creating a tracking system that attempts to maximize effectiveness and equity, the results should benefit students at all levels of ability.

More than Misapplied Technology: A Normative and Political Response to Hallinan on Tracking

Jeannie Oakes

After responding to tracking advocates' distortions of the research, I am gratified to see that Maureen Hallinan has the facts straight. But, then again, Hallinan cannot be said to be an advocate of tracking or can she? As a critic of tracking, she offers a reasonable definition of tracking, correctly identifies its explicit purposes, rightly recounts the widespread assumptions about how tracking works and how it affects students, and accurately summarizes research findings on the way students are assigned to tracks and tracking's actual effects on learning. Hallinan concludes her review of the research, as most other scholars do, by saying that the evidence on tracking adds up to a rationale for eliminating the practice, particularly since lower ability is associated with race, ethnicity, and social-class status, and, tracking, thereby, places low-status students at a considerable educational disadvantage. So far, so good.[1]

At this point in Hallinan's essay, something odd happens. She offers conclusions and a rationale that are indistinguishable from the new generation of tracking *advocates*. Hallinan asserts that it is not only premature, but likely to be unwarranted, to consider "detracking" schools! Like supporters of tracking, few of whom argue that tracking is currently done well, she contends that "a more tempered response" to the overwhelmingly negative evidence is for schools to make tracking practice more consistent with tracking theory and to balance the inherently negative features of tracking with countervailing policies and practices.

I find the disjuncture between Hallinan's review of the evidence and the implications she draws astonishing. Having spent the past three years studying 16 racially mixed secondary schools that have taken the tracking research seriously and responded with "detracking" reforms, my own conclusions depart dramatically from Hallinan's.[2] In what follows, I juxtapose Hallinan's position with my own thinking about tracking, which is based partly on the experiences of these and other schools.

Hallinan argues that tracking is essentially an organizational technique with intended and unintended consequences. Tracking's unintended consequences, she contends, are what impede tracking's intended goal of enabling students at all levels to learn more than they would in mixed-ability classes. Some of these unintended consequences are inherent in tracking, whereas others represent the failure of implementation—that is, schools do not properly enact tracking theory. This line of argument treats tracking itself as a disembodied practice, a technical matter that is far more a product of organizational structure than of the humans who enact it. It also renders tracking susceptible to tinkering—that is, to fixing the technology without altering its structural and cultural underpinnings.

In striking contrast, my work finds the structure of tracking to be embedded in cultural and political contexts, replete with good intentions, bad intentions, and messy human decision making. Consequently, I have come to believe that attempts to understand tracking apart from its normative and political content are sorely inadequate. For example, Hallinan characterizes the debate about tracking as a concern with issues of effectiveness and equity in relation to cognitive outcomes—learning. The folks who are working to detrack the schools I am studying would agree, but they also view tracking as being centrally concerned with students' life chances, including the transfer of social, economic, and political privilege, and racial and social-class discrimination.

Most educators cannot imagine tracking as a technical, neutral organizational practice that is unrelated to personal, societal, or vocational purposes. Tracking in real schools is connected to a deeply held conviction that schools are expected to contribute to a wide array of goals, only some of which are strictly cognitive, and the specific form that tracking takes reflects educators' efforts to juggle all these goals. It is no accident, for example, that students in lower-track academic classes are nearly always simultaneously being given vocational or child care training or are taught a general curriculum that is designed to prepare them for responsible citizenship and personal growth.

The history of tracking exemplifies schools' efforts to address social, personal, and workforce needs, as well as cognitive ones. At the turn of the century, G. Stanley Hall's notions about the proclivities and emotional needs of adolescents provided the intellectual underpinnings for giving most students a more practical, nonscholarly secondary school curriculum. At about the same time, Lewis Terman proclaimed that even though minority students could not be expected to have the mental capacity to master abstractions, they were well suited to separate classes that could train them to be "efficient workers." In 1908 the superintendent of Boston's schools supported tracking by heralding the new "sorting function" of schools. No more than a decade later, the National Association of Manufacturers and the

AFL-CIO added their support because tracking enabled schools to act as sites for non-partisan job training. Each of these individuals and groups may be said to have been acting on good intentions.

Asserting the good intentions of educators and the neutrality of tracking as an organizational technology, Hallinan softens the evidence about the disproportionately negative impact of tracking on low-income students and minority students. She argues that the racial and social-class segregation that occurs may be inevitable, given the unfortunate coincidence of "low ability" with low-income and minority status, but that the diminished outcomes that accompany this segregation are unintended consequences. Hallinan bases this latter judgment partly on her confidence that the only "correct" purpose of tracking—to foster cognitive development—is the only operational purpose and partly on her conviction that the well-documented negative effects of tracking result from educators' failure to enact its theory faithfully (in ways that benefit students in all tracks). Hallinan then contends that tracking's segregative effects can be counterbalanced by mixing students by race and social class in their untracked classes and by creating a nonracist school atmosphere. She claims that tracking's lamentable impact on students' social status—including low-track students' diminished motivation and effort—can be circumvented if schools alter their reward structures in ways that extend higher status to low-track students. She asserts that the educational discrepancies among tracks can be remedied with a beefed-up low-track curriculum.

Hallinan's ameliorative strategies are recognized by educators who are grappling with tracking's negative consequences as tried-and-false methods of the past. First, they see that few students miss the clear status message carried by racially identifiable tracking in high-status academic classes. Even if lower-status classes and extracurricular activities are more evenly mixed racially, students and adults in all but the most extraordinary schools have their stereotypes and prejudices reinforced by racially identifiable high- and low-track classes. Educators who have tried know the limits—even impossibility—of creating a climate of intolerance for racism and for the promotion of positive inter-group relations, as long as school structures institutionalize racist conceptions of intellectual capacity. A school may become calmer around racial issues with human relations efforts, but it cannot embody egalitarianism or social justice without deeper changes in tracking structures and the norms and political relations these structures enact.

Nearly all educators are well aware that low-track students consistently have lower-quality opportunities to learn than do their peers in higher tracks. They also recognize that these differences are not appropriate modifications of curriculum and instruction to differences in the abilities of students in various groups, but that they take the form of gross inequalities in access to knowledge, instructional resources, and well-qualified teachers. Many educators have spent their careers trying to beef up the low-track curriculum, to adopt a more positive disposition toward the capacities of low-track students, and to alter the reward systems that work against these students. These educators would undoubtedly find insulting the suggestion that an "attitude adjustment" (Hallinan's phrase) would enable them to be persuasive in communicating a positive message about the meaning of different track levels and would effectively cancel out low-track students' accurate perceptions that schools have a low regard for their abilities and prospects for success in school.

In addition to salutary efforts to integrate students, to enhance low-track students' feelings of worth outside tracked classrooms, and to improve the low-track curriculum, Hallinan suggests that tracking could be vastly improved if educators more faithfully enacted tracking theory by making tracks more homogeneous. To accomplish this greater uniformity within tracks, she recommends two changes. First, schools should base track assignments on the most "objective" measures of ability and achievement. Second, schools should employ more flexible placement practices, such as frequent reassessments and reassignments to other tracks.

Hallinan is absolutely correct when she asserts that most tracks are not highly homogeneous ability groups; the ranges of ability in tracks are wide and, in many schools, overlap considerably with those in other tracks. Where she goes wrong is in suggesting that this phenomenon results from a faulty application of technology—sloppy assessment or failure to account for students' differential rates of growth. And her recommendation for reassessment and reassignment ignores the political realities of tracking.

Track assignments stem from more than the cognitive criteria and the structural constraints (such as scheduling conflicts and limited resources) that Hallinan lists. Although these factors are important, there is consistent evidence that background factors, including the discriminatory placement of minority students in low tracks, also come into play. Neither the negative impact of minority status nor discriminatory placement practices are obvious in analyses of large-scale survey data, particularly when the data are aggregated across school systems. Such analyses tend to obscure between-system differences in track assignments resulting from the composition of the student population in the schools. And their measures are usually too gross to detect differential placement practices within schools.

Let me explain this a bit more. Senior high schools in low-income, high-minority communities are similar in structure to those in White and wealthy suburban areas. That is, in both types of communities the schools strive to be "comprehensive" and to offer both college preparatory and non-college preparatory programs and courses. Teachers and students in both settings have no difficulty pointing out which programs are designed for high-, average-, and low-ability students. However, such communities and schools are not so similar in how well students score on traditional measures of academic ability and achievement. Differences in the typical "ability" composition of schools (with students in White and wealthy schools scoring higher, on average) mean that many minority students attending schools in predominantly minority communities demonstrate ability levels—as measured by test scores—that would not be high enough to qualify them for academic tracks in whiter and wealthier communities. However, because their schools need to fill a requisite number of academic track "slots," some of these students are enrolled in the academic tracks at their schools. Consequently, when data about two such communities are aggregated, one finds a pattern of track placement that appears to give a slight advantage to African American students (after controlling for ability) of being assigned to academic tracks. This aggregation can mask considerable discrimination against minority students in high-track placements in both such systems.

When analyses of the relationship among race, ability, and placements within particular schools and school systems are performed, a different understanding results. For example, I recently analyzed the relationship between race and track placement (controlling for achievement) within schools in five medium-size city school systems with racially mixed student populations.[3] In each of these schools and systems, I found clear evidence of discriminatory placements, with Whites and Asians considerably (and statistically significantly) more likely to be placed in academic classes than comparably achieving African American and Latino students. In these systems the average achievement of African American and Latino students was lower than that of Whites and Asians. However, substantial discrimination against even high-scoring minorities skewed the racial composition of classes beyond what would have been the case had track placements been made by an unfailingly strict adherence to achievement as the criteria.

When one looks carefully at such systems, one finds that much of the heterogeneity within tracks comes about precisely because powerful parents are able to secure high-track placements for their unqualified children. This represents a type of political pressure that is not likely to respond to appeals to fairness. When a status preference exists, savvy parents of high socioeconomic status (SES) will use their considerable political capital on behalf of their children. Lower SES and minority students, whose ascribed characteristics work against them in their initial track placements, tend to have families who are precluded from such political maneuvering by their ignorance of schools' frequent acquiescence to parental pressure or by their timidity about exercising such pressure. Parents of students who are currently in the higher tracks would surely resist the reassignment of their children to lower tracks with even greater vehemence than they resist the dismantling of the track system itself.

Within schools, factors related to students' race and social class shape educators' perceptions of appropriate class placements. Educators value being able to exercise their professional judgment to make exceptions to rigid tracking practices for students who "work hard but don't test well," for those whose parents promise to provide support with private tutoring, and so on. The fact that such students are disproportionately White and middle class will do little to persuade educators that such exceptions are not "fair."

In the end, Hallinan's suggestions simply beg the question, arguing that schools can solve the inequities of tracking by solving the inequities of tracking—as if the norms, politics, and practices of schools are pieces of separate games to be played independently. My work has persuaded me that the inequalities of tracking are nothing other than the normative and political guises of tracking itself.

Hallinan argues that if tracking were fixed, it could benefit students at all ability levels. But, she also acknowledges that there is no empirical evidence that such benefits accrue. I can only speculate, based on years and years of discussion with advocates of tracking, why Hallinan resists "detracking" as a way to confront the problems of tracking. These reasons often include (1) a wish to circumvent comprehensive changes in other school regularities that schools must make when they move to heterogeneous ability grouping (such as changing staffing patterns, redistributing resources, reconceptualizing the curriculum and instruction, restructuring grading practices, and more), (2) a wish to avoid scrutiny of long-standing norms underlying schools' definition and evaluations of intelligence and learning (including such constructs as high-, average-, and low ability), and (3) a wish to avoid the often-nasty political contentiousness (not the least of which is the threat of "bright flight") that "detracking" reforms often bring. It may also be the case that Hallinan, like some other social scientists, believes that her role is simply to observe social phenomena without altering them and thus takes a highly conservative stance on reform.

I have come to believe, from studying educators as they struggle firsthand with detracking reforms (many with surprising success), that heterogeneity, in itself, may be the necessary lever to ensure that low-status students have access to a high-quality curriculum, teachers, and learning experiences—to say nothing of seats next to their advantaged White peers and the increased status that comes with them. Furthermore, although tracking places a *disproportionate* burden on low-income, minority children, the group that is *numerically* most affected by tracking are low- and middle-SES White children who are identified as something other than "high track." As long as students view themselves as "low," and they are concentrated in classes where teachers expect them to act as such, rich, multidimensional educational opportunities are unlikely to come their way.

Without a doubt, "detracking" is an extraordinary reform to undertake, and those in schools that are attempting it would be the first to agree. Yet, these educators believe, often with firsthand experience that is backed by a growing body of research, that they can teach all students well. Together. And, as dramatic as it may seem, they also believe that it is their professional and moral obligation to try.

Further Thoughts on Tracking

Maureen T. Hallinan

To have a meaningful discussion, it is necessary to define tracking and detracking. Tracking, or homogeneous grouping, is the organization of students for instruction, based on their ability and achievement. The practice is based on the belief that it promotes learning by providing a good fit between the level of instruction and students' learning needs. *Detracking*, or heterogeneous grouping, is the arrangement of students for instruction into groups that include students with a wide range of abilities. The rationale for detracking is the belief that cognitive diversity can be an effective teaching technique.

Both tracking and detracking, as Oakes notes, occur in a specific normative and political milieu. The school milieu can support the positive features of a school's organizational structure and promote learning, or it can undermine the pedagogical effectiveness of an organizational structure and obstruct learning. Typically, it is the school's climate and political and social agenda, not the practice of tracking or detracking, that accounts for a school's success or failure.

Most of the negative consequences of tracking can be attributed to a school environment that fails to provide the support needed to make tracking effective. Tracking itself is not designed to be a political tool, nor is it meant to influence the normative climate of a school. To assert that tracking is a failure because it is associated with a set of negative norms or a discriminatory political or social climate is a misplaced criticism. A tracked school's failure to provide students with equal opportunities to learn is not due to tracking, but to the absence of the school's commitment to equality. The negative impact of the segregation created by tracking is caused by the failure to embed tracking in an atmosphere that would counter this situation.

Remedying the deficiencies of tracking requires improving the social and political fabric of the school. It may involve changing teachers' and students' attitudes and behaviors, altering the reward structure of the school, and reorganizing the curriculum. It also may require modifying teachers' philosophies of education and political persuasions. The resulting positive school climate will enable students to take advantage of the benefits of tracking to increase their academic achievement.

When Oakes and others advocate detracking, they usually imply more than heterogeneous grouping. Proponents of detracking describe schools that have an ideal social and political climate. They refer to the use of pedagogical techniques that support lower-ability students, a curriculum that is tailored to a child's learning needs, the employment of teacher aides to assist teachers, diverse curricular assignments and projects, and an underlying respect for various manifestations of intelligence. These descriptions place heterogeneous grouping in a culture and political climate that is nondiscriminatory and that aims to accommodate the unique learning needs of each student. It is likely that this positive normative climate and support structure, rather than heterogeneous grouping, is responsible for the success of detracked schools. Homogeneous grouping may be equally effective in the same kind of environment, whereas heterogeneous grouping may be less successful than tracking in schools with a negative social climate.

The results of empirical research on the effects of ability and nonability groups on students' learning underscore the importance of separating a grouping practice from the environment in which it is practiced to evaluate its effectiveness. The studies show that the major differences between homogeneously and heterogeneously grouped schools lies in the variance, rather than the mean, of the student achievement distribution. On average, students do equally well in grouped and ungrouped instructional arrangements. But in ability grouped schools, the high-ability students tend to learn more, and the low-ability students tend to learn less than in heterogeneously grouped schools. This consistent finding implies either that ability grouping is inherently detrimental to low-ability students (and advantageous to high-ability students) or that intervening factors modify the effects of ability grouping on students who differ in ability. Both survey and ethnographic data indicate the latter.

The intervening factors that researchers identify as reducing the effectiveness of tracking for low-ability students undoubtedly are reflections of a school's normative, social, and political climate. Consequently, it is likely that a school's context, rather than its grouping practices, should be the object of reform. Replacing tracking with detracking without changing the climate of the school is unlikely to improve students' learning. On the other hand, changing a school's climate may eliminate the need to abandon tracking.

Critics of tracking seem to suggest that tracking exists only in schools that at least tolerate discrimination and inequality. Those who remain cautious about abandoning tracking note that studies of detracking seem to be conducted only in schools that are strongly dedicated to equal opportunity for all students. What is needed is rigorous empirical research on the effects of homogeneous and heterogeneous grouping in schools that vary in the several dimensions of school context to determine the impact of the organization of students on learning.

One More Thought

Jeannie Oakes

Forty years ago this month, the Supreme Court ruled that school segregation was unconstitutional because separate is *inherently* unequal. It was clear to the Warren Court that in the 60 years since *Plessy*, school segregation had proved to be neither a neutral practice nor one that was separable from the negative racial norms and the discriminatory political context in which it was embedded. The Court recognized that the practice of racial separation was both a cause and an effect of a social climate of discrimination and inequality. By *definition*, racial segregation existed in communities that at least tolerated discrimination and inequality, and, in contrast, those communities that voluntarily initiated school desegregation were places committed to equal opportunity for all students. Thus, the Court did not rule that the harms of segregation could be remedied by changing philosophies or political persuasions. Neither did it ask Kenneth Clark to repeat his doll studies on Black and White children in communities with more positive racial climates to assess whether the negative responses he obtained from Black children stemmed from the practice of segregation itself or from the absence of a commitment to equality in their communities. The *Brown* ruling recognized that, although for convenience and analysis, sociologists may talk about structures, norms, and politics as components of society, these components are not distinct or separable.

Tracking is partly, but not only, about race. Whereas African American and Latino children disproportionately wind up in lower-track classes, most of the children who are disadvantaged by tracking are poor and working-class Whites. The segregative mechanism of tracking, at least ostensibly, is ability. However, like racial segregation, tracking builds inequalities into schools that both devalue and materially disadvantage those groups who are least able to defend themselves. Ability, like race, is a social construction that leads schools to define and treat children from powerless groups—Black, Brown, and White—as expendable. Thus, like racial segregation, tracking carries with it class-based damage that can neither be avoided nor compensated for. Tracking's supporters, much like opponents of the *Brown* ruling, argue otherwise, claiming that separate could be equally effective if school and classroom environments were good. They ask that institutionalized segregation by ability be left in place because the real culprits are attitudes, behaviors, reward structures, philosophies, political persuasions, culture, and normative climate. I find little to support their position, either in the empirical evidence or in principle

Notes

1. Hallinan's piece rests heavily on empirical studies, but none are cited. For a comprehensive review of this literature, see Jeannie Oakes, Adam Gamoran, and Reba N. Page, "Curriculum Differentiation: Opportunities, Outcomes, and Meanings," in Philip Jackson, ed., *Handbook of Research on Curriculum* (New York: Macmillan, 1992). Although several later studies have added to this data base, they have not altered its fundamental conclusions.
2. Ten of these schools are currently participating in a three-year study, Beyond Sorting and Stratification: Creating Alternatives to Tracking in Racially-Mixed Secondary Schools, which I codirect at UCLA with Amy Stuart Wells under the sponsorship of the Lilly Endowment. The other six are part of a larger sample of schools that I am studying, under the sponsorship of the Carnegie Corporation of New York, that are attempting to reform the middle grades. Because both studies are still in progress, I offer only preliminary reflections about these schools here.
3. See Jeannie Oakes, Molly Selvin, Lynn Karoly, and Gretchen Guiton, *Educational Matchmaking: Academic and Vocational Tracking in Comprehensive High Schools* (Santa Monica, CA: RAND, 1992); and Jeannie Oakes, reports prepared in conjunction with two recent federal desegregation cases, *People Who Care v. Rockford Illinois Public Schools* and *Vasquez v. San Jose Unified School District*, 1993

19
Invisible Inequality
Social Class and Childrearing in Black Families and White Families

ANNETTE LAREAU

In recent decades, sociological knowledge about inequality in family life has increased dramatically. Yet, debate persists, especially about the transmission of class advantages to children. Kingston (2000) and others question whether disparate aspects of family life cohere in meaningful patterns. Pointing to a "thin evidentiary base" for claims of social class differences in the interior of family life, Kingston also asserts that "class distinguishes neither distinctive parenting styles or distinctive involvement of kids" in specific behaviors (p. 134).

One problem with many studies is that they are narrowly focused. Researchers look at the influence of parents' education on parent involvement in schooling *or* at children's time spent watching television *or* at time spent visiting relatives. Only a few studies examine more than one dynamic inside the home. Second, much of the empirical work is descriptive. For example, extensive research has been done on time use, including patterns of women's labor force participation, hours parents spend at work, and mothers' and fathers' contributions to childcare (Hertz and Marshall 2001; Jacobs and Gerson 1998; Menaghan 1991). Time parents spend with children also has been examined (Bianchi 2000; Bianchi and Robinson 1997; Marsiglio 1991; Presser 1989; Zick and Bryant 1996), as well as patterns of children's time use (Hofferth and Sandberg 2001b; Juster and Stafford 1985; Sandberg and Hofferth 2001). But these works have not given sufficient attention to the meaning of events or to the ways different family contexts may affect how a given task is executed (but see Daley 2001; Rubin 1976; Thorne 2001).

Third, researchers have not satisfactorily explained how these observed patterns are produced. Put differently, *conceptualizations* of the *social processes* through which families differ are underdeveloped and little is known about how family life transmits advantages to children. Few researchers have attempted to integrate what is known about behaviors and attitudes taught inside the home with the ways in which these practices may provide unequal resources for family members outside the home. A key exception is the work by Kohn and colleagues (e.g., Kohn and Schooler 1983), where the authors argue that middle-class parents value self-direction while working-class parents place a premium on "conformity to external authority." These researchers did not investigate, however, how parents go about translating these beliefs into actions.

Fourth, little is known about the degree to which children adopt and enact their parents' beliefs. Sociologists of the family have long stressed the importance of a more dynamic model of parent-child interaction (Skolnick 1991), but empirical research has been slow to emerge (but see Hess and Handel 1974). Ethnographers' efforts to document children's agency have provided vivid but highly circumscribed portraits (Shehan 1999; Waksler 1991), but most of the case studies look at only one social class or one ethnic group. Moreover, ethnographers typically do not explicitly examine how social class advantages are transmitted to children.

I draw on findings from a small, intensive data set collected using ethnographic methods. I map the connections between parents' resources and their children's daily lives. My first goal, then, is to challenge Kingston's (2000) argument that social class does not distinguish parents' behavior or children's daily lives. I seek to show empirically that social class does indeed create distinctive parenting styles. I demonstrate that parents differ by class in the ways they define their own roles in their children's lives as well as in how they perceive the nature of childhood. The middle-class parents, both white *and* black, tend to conform to a cultural logic of childrearing I call "concerted cultivation." They enroll their children in numerous age-specific organized activities that dominate family life and create enormous labor, particularly for mothers. The parents view these activities as transmitting important life skills to children. Middle-class parents also stress language use and the development of reasoning and employ talking as their preferred form of discipline. This "cultivation" approach results in a wider range of experiences for children but also creates a frenetic pace for parents, a cult of individualism within the family, and an emphasis on children's performance.[1]

The childrearing strategies of white and black working-class and poor parents emphasize the "accomplishment of natural growth."[2] These parents believe that as long as they provide love, food, and safety, their children will grow and thrive. They do not focus on developing their children's special talents. Compared to the middle-class children, working-class and poor children participate in few organized activities and have more free time and deeper, richer ties within their extended families. Working-class and poor parents issue many more directives to their children and, in some households, place more emphasis on physical discipline than do the middle-class parents. These findings extend Kohn and Schooler's (1983) observation of class differences in parents' values, showing that differences also exist in the *behavior* of parents *and* children.

Quantitative studies of children's activities offer valuable empirical evidence but only limited ideas about how to conceptualize the mechanisms through which social advantage is transmitted. Thus, my second goal is to offer "conceptual umbrellas" useful for making comparisons across race and class and for assessing the role of social structural location in shaping daily life.[3]

Last, I trace the connections between the class position of family members—including children—and the uneven outcomes of their experiences outside the home as they interact with professionals in dominant institutions. The pattern of concerted cultivation encourages an *emerging sense of entitlement* in children. All parents and children are not equally assertive, but the pattern of questioning and intervening among the white and black middle-class parents contrasts sharply with the definitions of how to be helpful and effective observed among the white and black working-class and poor adults. The pattern of the accomplishment of natural growth encourages an *emerging sense of constraint*. Adults as well as children in these social classes tend to be deferential and outwardly accepting in their interactions with professionals such as doctors and educators. At the same time, however, compared to their middle-class counterparts, white and black working-class and poor family members are more distrustful of professionals. These are differences with potential long-term consequences. In a historical moment when the dominant society privileges active, informed, assertive clients of health and educational services, the strategies employed by children and parents are not equally effective across classes. In sum, differences in family life lie not only in the advantages parents obtain for their children, but also in the skills they transmit to children for negotiating their own life paths.

Methodology

Study Participants

This study is based on interviews and observations of children, aged 8 to 10, and their families. The data were collected over time in three research phases. Phase one involved observations in two third-grade classrooms in a public school in the Midwestern community of "Lawrenceville."[4] After conducting observations for two months, I grouped the families into social class (and race) categories based on information provided by educators. I then chose every third name, and sent a letter to the child's home asking the mother and father to participate in separate interviews. Over 90 percent of parents agreed, for a total of 32 children (16 white and 16 African American). A black graduate student and I interviewed all mothers and most fathers (or guardians) of the children. Each interview lasted 90 to 120 minutes, and all took place in 1989–1990.

Phase two took place at two sites in a northeastern metropolitan area. One school, "Lower Richmond," although located in a predominantly white, working-class urban neighborhood, drew about half of its students from a nearby all-black housing project. I observed one third-grade class at Lower Richmond about twice a week for almost six months. The second site, "Swan," was located in a suburban neighborhood about 45 minutes from the city center. It was 90 percent white; most of the remaining 10 percent were middle-class black children.[5] There, I observed twice a week for two months at the end of the third grade; a research assistant then observed weekly for four more months in the fourth grade.[6] At each site, teachers and parents described their school in positive terms.[7] The observations took place between September 1992 and January 1994. In the fall of 1993, I drew an interview sample from Lower Richmond and Swan, following the same method of selection used for Lawrenceville. A team of research assistants and I interviewed the parents and guardians of 39 children. Again, the response rate was over 90 percent but because the classrooms did not generate enough black middle-class children and white poor children to fill the analytical categories, interviews were also conducted with 17 families with children aged 8 to 10. (Most of these interviews took place during the summers of 1996 and 1997.)[8] Thus, the total number of children who participated in the study was 88 (32 from the Midwest and 56 from the Northeast).

Family Observations

Phase three, the most intensive research phase of the study, involved home observations of 12 children and their families in the Northeast who had been previously interviewed (see Table 19.1).[9] Some themes, such as language use and families' social connections, surfaced mainly during this phase. Although I entered the field interested in examining the influence of social class on children's daily lives, I incorporated new themes as they "bubbled up" from the field observations. The evidence presented here comes mainly from the family observations, but I also use interview findings from the full sample of 88 children where appropriate.[10]

Nine of the 12 families came from the Northeastern classroom sample. The home observations took place, one family at a time, from December 1993 to August 1994. Three 10-year-olds (a black middle-class boy and girl and a white poor boy) who were not part of the classroom sample were observed in their homes during the summer of 1995.[11]

The research assistants and I took turns visiting the participating families daily, for a total of about 20 visits to each home, often in the space of one month.[12] The observations went beyond the home: Fieldworkers followed children and parents as they participated in school activities, church services and events, organized play, visits to relatives, and medical appointments. Observations typically lasted three hours, but sometimes much longer (e.g., when we observed an out-of-town funeral, a special extended family event, or a long shopping trip). Most cases also involved one overnight visit. We often carried tape recorders and used the audiotapes for reference in writing field notes. Writing field notes usually required 8 to 12 hours for each two- or three-hour home visit. Participating families each were paid $350, usually at the end of the visits.

We worked in teams of three. One field-worker visited three to four times per week; another visited one to two times per week; and I visited once or twice per week, except for the two families for which I was lead fieldworker. The research teams' composition varied with the race of the family. Two white graduate students and I (a middle-aged white woman) visited the white families; for the black families,

Table 19.1 Frequency Distribution of Children in the Study by Social Class and Race

Social Class	White	Black	Total
Middle class [a]	18	18	36
	(Garrett Tallinger)	(Alexander Williams)	
	(Melanie Handlon)	(Stacey Marshall)	
Working class [b]	14	12	26
	(Billy Yanelli)	(Tyrec Taylor)	
	(Wendy Driver)	(Jessica Irwin)[c]	
Poor[d]	12	14	26
	(Karl Greeley)	(Harold McAllister)	
	(Katie Brindle)	(Tara Carroll)	
Total sample	44	44	88

Note: The names in each cell of the table indicate the children selected to take place in the family-observation phase of the study.
[a] Middle-class children are those who live in households in which at least one parent is employed in a position that either entails substantial managerial authority or that draws upon highly complex, educationally certified skills (i.e., college-level).
[b] Working-class children are those who live in households in which neither parent is employed in a middle-class position and at least one parent is employed in a position with little or no managerial authority and that does not draw on highly complex, educationally certified skills. This category includes lower-level white-collar workers.
[c] An inter-racial girl who has a black father and a white mother.
[d] Poor children are those who live in households in which parents receive public assistance and do not participate in the labor force on a regular, continuous basis.

the teams included one white graduate student, one black graduate student, and me. All black families with male children were visited by teams that included a black male fieldworker. A white male field-worker observed the poor family with the white boy; the remaining white field workers were female. Team members met regularly to discuss the families and to review the emerging analytic themes.

Our presence altered family dynamics, especially at first. Over time, however, we saw signs of adjustment (e.g., yelling and cursing increased on the third day and again on the tenth). The children, especially, seemed to enjoy participating in the project. They reported it made them feel "special." They were visibly happy to see the fieldworkers arrive and reluctant to let them leave. The working-class and poor black boys were more comfortable with the black male field-workers than with the white female ones, especially at first.[13] Overall, however, family members reported in exit interviews that they had not changed their behavior significantly, or they mentioned very specific alterations (e.g., "the house got cleaner").

A Note on Class

I undertook field observations to develop an intensive, realistic portrait of family life. Although I deliberately focused on only 12 families, I wanted to compare children across gender and race. Adopting the fine-grained differentiations characteristic of current neo-Marxist and neo-Weberian empirical studies was not tenable.[14] Further limitations were imposed by the school populations at the sites I selected. Very few students were children of employers or of self-employed workers. I decided to focus exclusively on those whose parents were employees. Authority in the workplace and "credential barriers" are the criteria most commonly used to differentiate within this heterogeneous group. I assigned the families to a working-class or middle-class category based on detailed information that each of the employed adults provided about the work they did, the nature of the organization that employed them, and their educational credentials. I also included a category traditionally excluded from class groupings: families not involved in the labor market. In the first school I studied, many children were from households supported by public assistance. Omitting them would have restricted the scope of the study arbitrarily.[15]

The three class categories conceal important internal variations. The Williams family (black) and the Tallinger family (white) have very high incomes, both in excess of $175,000; the median income among the middle-class parents was much lower.[16] Income differences among the middle-class families were not associated with differences in childrearing methods. Moreover, no other data in the study showed compelling intraclass divisions. I consider the use of one term—middle class—to be reasonable.

Concerted Cultivation and Natural Growth

The interviews and observations suggested that crucial aspects of family life *cohered*. Within the concerted cultivation and accomplishment of natural growth approaches, three key dimensions may be distinguished: the organization of daily life, the use of language, and social connections. ("Interventions in institutions" and "consequences" are addressed later in the paper.) These dimensions do not capture all important parts of family life, but they do incorporate core aspects of childrearing (Table 19.2). Moreover, our field observations revealed that behaviors and activities related to these dimensions dominated the rhythms of family life. Conceptually, the organization of daily life and the use of language are crucial dimensions. Both must be present for the family to be described as engaging in one childrearing approach rather than the other. Social connections are significant but less conceptually essential.

All three aspects of childrearing were intricately woven into the families' daily routines, but rarely remarked upon. As part of everyday practice, they were invisible to parents and children. Analytically, however, they are useful means for comparing and contrasting ways in which social class differences shape the character of family life. I now examine two families in terms of these three key dimensions. I "control" for race and gender and contrast the lives of two black boys—one from an (upper) middle-class family and one from a family on public assistance. I could have focused on almost any of the other 12 children, but this pair seemed optimal, given the limited number of studies reporting on black middle-class families, as well as the aspect of my argument that suggests that race is less important than class in shaping childrearing patterns.

Table 19.2 Summary of Differences in Childrearing Approaches

Dimension Observed	Childrearing Approach	
	Concerted Cultivation	Accomplishment of Natural Growth
Key elements of each approach	Parent actively fosters and assesses child's talents, opinions, and skills	Parent cares for child and allows child to grow
Organization of daily life	Multiple child leisure activities are orchestrated by adults	Child "hangs out" particularly with kin
Language use	Reasoning/directives Child contestation of adult statements Extended negotiations between parents and child	Directives Rare for child to question or challenge adults General acceptance by child of directives
Social connections	Weak extended family ties Child often in homogenous age groupings	Strong extended family ties Child often in heterogeneous age groupings
Interventions in institutions	Criticisms and interventions on behalf of child Training of child to intervene on his or her own behalf	Dependence on institutions Sense of powerlessness and frustration Conflict between childrearing practices at home and at school
Consequences	Emerging sense of entitlement on the part of the child	Emerging sense of constraint on the part of the child

Developing Alexander Williams

Alexander Williams and his parents live in a predominantly black middle-class neighborhood. Their six-bedroom house is worth about $150,000.[17] Alexander is an only child. Both parents grew up in small towns in the South, and both are from large families. His father, a tall, handsome man, is a very successful trial lawyer who earns about $125,000 annually in a small firm specializing in medical malpractice cases. Two weeks each month, he works very long hours (from about 5:30 A.M. until midnight) preparing for trials. The other two weeks, his workday ends around 6:00 P.M. He rarely travels out of town. Alexander's mother, Christina, is a positive, bubbly woman with freckles and long, black, wavy hair.[18] A high-level manager in a major corporation, she has a corner office, a personal secretary, and responsibilities for other offices across the nation. She tries to limit her travel, but at least once a month she takes an overnight trip.

Alexander is a charming, inquisitive boy with a winsome smile. Ms. Williams is pleased that Alexander seems interested in so many things:

> Alexander is a joy. He's a gift to me. He's very energetic, very curious, loving, caring person, that, um...is outgoing and who, uh, really loves to be with people. And who loves to explore, and loves to read and...just do a lot of fun things.

The private school Alexander attends[19] has an on-site after-school program. There, he participates in several activities and receives guitar lessons and photography instruction.

Organization of daily life Alexander is busy with activities during the week and on weekends (Table 3). His mother describes their Saturday morning routine. The day starts early with a private piano lesson for Alexander downtown, a 20-minute drive from the house:

> It's an 8:15 class. But for me, it was a tradeoff. I am very adamant about Saturday morning TV. I don't know what it contributes. So...it was...um...either stay at home and fight on a Saturday morning [laughs] or go do something constructive....Now Saturday mornings are pretty booked up. You know, the piano lesson, and then straight to choir for a couple of hours. So, he has a very full schedule.

Ms. Williams's vehement opposition to television is based on her view of what Alexander needs to grow and thrive. She objects to TV's passivity and feels it is her obligation to help her son cultivate his talents.

Sometimes Alexander complains that "my mother signs me up for everything!" Generally, however, he likes his activities. He says they make him feel "special," and without them life would be "boring." His sense of time is thoroughly entwined with his activities: He feels disoriented when his schedule is not full. This unease is clear in the following field-note excerpt. The family is driving home from a Back-to-School night. The next morning, Ms. Williams will leave for a work-related day trip and will not return until late at night. Alexander is grumpy because he has nothing planned for the next day. He wants to have a friend over, but his mother rebuffs him. Whining, he wonders what he will do. His mother, speaking tersely, says:

> You have piano and guitar. You'll have some free time. [Pause] I think you'll survive for one night. [Alexander does not respond but seems mad. It is quiet for the rest of the trip home.]

Alexander's parents believe his activities provide a wide range of benefits important for his development. In discussing Alexander's piano lessons, Mr. Williams notes that as a Suzuki student,[20] Alexander is already able to read music. Speculating about more diffuse benefits of Alexander's involvement with piano, he says:

I don't see how any kid's adolescence and adulthood could not but be enhanced by an awareness of who Beethoven was. And is that Bach or Mozart? I don't know the difference between the two! I don't know Baroque from Classical—but he does. How can that not be a benefit in later life? I'm convinced that this rich experience will make him a better person, a better citizen, a better husband, a better father—certainly a better student.

Ms. Williams sees music as building her son's "confidence" and his "poise." In interviews and casual conversation, she stresses "exposure." She believes it is her responsibility to broaden Alexander's worldview. Childhood activities provide a learning ground for important life skills:

Sports provide great opportunities to learn how to be competitive. Learn how to accept defeat, you know. Learn how to accept winning, you know, in a gracious way. Also it gives him the opportunity to learn leadership skills and how to be a team player....Sports really provides a lot of really great opportunities.

Table 19.3 Participation in Activities Outside of School: Boys

Boy's Name/Race/Class	Activities Organized by Adults	Informal Activities
Middle Class		
Garrett Tallinger (white)	Soccer team Traveling soccer team Baseball team Basketball team (summer) Swim team Piano Saxophone (through school)	Plays with siblings in yard Watches television Plays computer games Overnights with friends
Alexander Williams (black)	Soccer team Baseball team Community choir Church choir Sunday school Piano (Suzuki) School plays Guitar (through school)	Restricted television Plays outside occasionally with two other boys Visits friends from school
Working Class		
Billy Yanelli (white)	Baseball team	Watches television Visits relatives Rides bike Plays outside in the street Hangs out with neighborhood kids
Tyrec Taylor (black)	Football team Vacation Bible School Sunday school (off/on)	Watches television Plays outside in the street Rides bikes with neighborhood boys Visit relatives Goes to swimming pool
Poor		
Karl Greeley (white)	Goes to swimming pool Walks dogs with neighbor	Watches television Plays Nintendo Plays with siblings
Harold McAllister (black)	Bible study in neighbor's house (occasionally) Bible camp (1 week)	Visits relatives Plays ball with neighborhood kids Watches television Watches videos

Alexander's schedule is constantly shifting; some activities wind down and others start up. Because the schedules of sports practices and games are issued no sooner than the start of the new season, advance planning is rarely possible. Given the sheer number of Alexander's activities, events inevitably overlap. Some activities, though short-lived, are extremely time consuming. Alexander's school play, for example, requires rehearsals three nights the week before the opening. In addition, in choosing activities, the Williamses have an added concern—the group's racial balance. Ms. Williams prefers that Alexander not be the only black child at events. Typically, one or two other black boys are involved, but the groups are predominantly white and the activities take place in predominantly white residential neighborhoods. Alexander is, however, part of his church's youth choir and Sunday School, activities in which all participants are black.

Many activities involve competition. Alex must audition for his solo performance in the school play, for example. Similarly, parents and children alike understand that participation on "A," "B," or "All-Star" sports teams signal different skill levels. Like other middle-class children in the study, Alexander seems to enjoy public performance. According to a field note, after his solo at a musical production in front of over 200 people, he appeared "contained, pleased, aware of the attention he's receiving."

Alexander's commitments do not consume *all* his free time. Still, his life is defined by a series of deadlines and schedules interwoven with a series of activities that are organized and controlled by adults rather than children. Neither he nor his parents see this as troublesome.

Language use Like other middle-class families, the Williamses often engage in conversation that promotes reasoning and negotiation. An excerpt from a field note (describing an exchange between Alexander and his mother during a car ride home after summer camp) shows the kind of pointed questions middle-class parents ask children. Ms. Williams is not just eliciting information. She is also giving Alexander the opportunity to develop and practice verbal skills, including how to summarize, clarify, and amplify information:

> As she drives, [Ms. Williams] asks Alex, "So, how was your day?"
> Alex: "Okay. I had hot dogs today, but they were burned! They were all black!"
> Mom: "Oh, great. You shouldn't have eaten any."
> Alex: "They weren't *all* black, only half were. The rest were regular."
> Mom: "Oh, okay. What was that game you were playing this morning?..."
> Alex: "It was [called] 'Whatcha doin?'"
> Mom: "How do you play?"
> Alexander explains the game elaborately—fieldworker doesn't quite follow. Mom asks Alex questions throughout his explanation, saying, "Oh, I see," when he answers. She asks him about another game she saw them play; he again explains.... She continues to prompt and encourage him with small giggles in the back of her throat as he elaborates.

Expressions of interest in children's activities often lead to negotiations over small, home-based matters. During the same car ride, Ms. Williams tries to adjust the dinner menu to suit Alexander:

> Alexander says, "I don't want hot dogs tonight."
> Mom: "Oh? Because you had them for lunch."
> Alexander nods.
> Mom: "Well, I can fix something else and save the hot dogs for tomorrow night."
> Alex: "But I don't want any pork chops either."
> Mom: "Well, Alexander, we need to eat something. Why didn't you have hamburgers today?"
> Alex: "They don't have them any more at the snack bar."

Mom asks Alexander if he's ok, if he wants a snack. Alexander says he's ok. Mom asks if he's sure he doesn't want a bag of chips?

Not all middle-class parents are as attentive to their children's needs as this mother, and none are *always* interested in negotiating. But a general pattern of reasoning and accommodating is common.

Social connections Mr. and Ms. Williams consider themselves very close to their extended families. Because the Williams's aging parents live in the South, visiting requires a plane trip. Ms. Williams takes Alexander with her to see his grandparents twice a year. She speaks on the phone with her parents at least once a week and also calls her siblings several times a week. Mr. Williams talks with his mother regularly by phone (he has less contact with his stepfather). With pride, he also mentions his niece, whose Ivy League education he is helping to finance.

Interactions with cousins are not normally a part of Alexander's leisure time. (As I explain below, other middle-class children did not see cousins routinely either, even when they lived nearby.) Nor does he often play with neighborhood children. The huge homes on the Williams's street are occupied mainly by couples without children. Most of Alexander's playmates come from his classroom or his organized activities. Because most of his school events, church life, and assorted activities are organized by the age (and sometimes gender) of the participants, Alexander interacts almost exclusively with children his own age, usually boys. Adult-organized activities thus define the context of his social life.

Mr. and Ms. Williams are aware that they allocate a sizable portion of time to Alexander's activities. What they stress, however, is the time they *hold back*. They mention activities the family has chosen *not* to take on (such as traveling soccer).

Summary Overall, Alexander's parents engaged in concerted cultivation. They fostered their son's growth through involvement in music, church, athletics, and academics. They talked with him at length, seeking his opinions and encouraging his ideas. Their approach involved considerable direct expenses (e.g., the cost of lessons and equipment) and large indirect expenses (e.g., the cost of taking time off from work, driving to practices, and foregoing adult leisure activities). Although Mr. and Ms. Williams acknowledged the importance of extended family, Alexander spent relatively little time with relatives. His social interactions occurred almost exclusively with children his own age and with adults. Alexander's many activities significantly shaped the organization of daily life in the family. Both parents' leisure time was tailored to their son's commitments. Mr. and Ms. Williams felt that the strategies they cultivated with Alexander would result in his having the best possible chance at a happy and productive life. They couldn't imagine themselves *not* investing large amounts of time and energy in their son's life. But, as I explain in the next section, which focuses on a black boy from a poor family, other parents held a different view.

Supporting the Natural Growth of Harold McAllister

Harold McAllister, a large, stocky boy with a big smile, is from a poor black family. He lives with his mother and his 8-year-old sister, Alexis, in a large apartment. Two cousins often stay overnight. Harold's 16-year-old sister and 18-year-old brother usually live with their grandmother, but sometimes they stay at the McAllister's home. Ms. McAllister, a high school graduate, relies on public assistance (AFDC). Hank, Harold and Alexis's father, is a mechanic. He and Ms. McAllister have never married. He visits regularly, sometimes weekly, stopping by after work to watch television or nap. Harold (but not Alexis) sometimes travels across town by bus to spend the weekend with Hank.

The McAllister's apartment is in a public housing project near a busy street. The complex consists of rows of two- and three-story brick units. The buildings, blocky and brown, have small yards enclosed by concrete and wood fences. Large floodlights are mounted on the corners of the buildings, and wide concrete sidewalks cut through the spaces between units. The ground is bare in many places; paper wrappers and glass litter the area.

Inside the apartment, life is humorous and lively, with family members and kin sharing in the daily routines. Ms. McAllister discussed, disdainfully, mothers who are on drugs or who abuse alcohol and do not "look after" their children. Indeed, the previous year Ms. McAllister called Child Protective Services to report her twin sister, a cocaine addict, because she was neglecting her children. Ms. McAllister is actively involved in her twin's daughters' lives. Her two nephews also frequently stay with her. Overall, she sees herself as a capable mother who takes care of her children and her extended family.

Organization of daily life Much of Harold's life and the lives of his family members revolve around home. Project residents often sit outside in lawn chairs or on front stoops, drinking beer, talking, and watching children play. During summer, windows are frequently left open, allowing breezes to waft through the units and providing vantage points from which residents can survey the neighborhood. A large deciduous tree in front of the McAllister's apartment unit provides welcome shade in the summer's heat.

Harold loves sports. He is particularly fond of basketball, but he also enjoys football, and he follows televised professional sports closely. Most afternoons, he is either inside watching television or outside playing ball. He tosses a football with cousins and boys from the neighboring units and organizes pick-up basketball games. Sometimes he and his friends use a rusty, bare hoop hanging from a telephone pole in the housing project; other times, they string up an old, blue plastic crate as a makeshift hoop. One obstacle to playing sports, however, is a shortage of equipment. Balls are costly to replace, especially given the rate at which they disappear—theft of children's play equipment, including balls and bicycles, is an ongoing problem. During a field observation, Harold asks his mother if she knows where the ball is. She replies with some vehemence, "They stole the blue and yellow ball, and they stole the green ball, and they stole the other ball."

Hunting for balls is a routine part of Harold's leisure time. One June day, with the temperature and humidity in the high 80's, Harold and his cousin Tyrice (and a fieldworker) wander around the housing project for about an hour, trying to find a basketball:

We head to the other side of the complex. On the way…we passed four guys sitting on the step. Their ages were 9 to 13 years. They had a radio blaring. Two were working intently on fixing a flat bike tire. The other two were dribbling a basketball.
Harold: "Yo! What's up, ya'll."
Group: "What's up, Har." "What's up? "Yo."
They continued to work on the tire and dribble the ball. As we walked down the hill, Harold asked, "Yo, could I use your ball?"
The guy responded, looking up from the tire, "Naw, man. Ya'll might lose it."

Harold, Tyrice, and the fieldworker walk to another part of the complex, heading for a makeshift basketball court where they hope to find a game in progress:

No such luck. Harold enters an apartment directly in front of the makeshift court. The door was open….Harold came back. "No ball. I guess I gotta go back."

The pace of life for Harold and his friends ebbs and flows with the children's interests and family obligations. The day of the basketball search, for example, after spending time listening to music and looking at baseball cards, the children join a water fight Tyrice instigates. It is a lively game, filled with laughter and with efforts to get the adults next door wet (against their wishes). When the game winds down, the kids ask their mother for money, receive it, and then walk to a store to buy chips and soda. They chat with another young boy and then amble back to the apartment, eating as they walk. Another afternoon, almost two weeks later, the children—Harold, two of his cousins, and two children from the neighborhood—and the fieldworker play basketball on a makeshift court in the street (using the fieldworker's ball). As Harold bounces the ball, neighborhood children of all ages wander through the space.

Thus, Harold's life is more free-flowing and more child-directed than is Alexander Williams's. The pace of any given day is not so much planned as emergent, reflecting child-based interests and activities. Parents intervene in specific areas, such as personal grooming, meals, and occasional chores, but they do not continuously direct and monitor their children's leisure activities. Moreover, the leisure activities Harold and other working-class and poor children pursue require them to develop a repertoire of skills for dealing with much older and much younger children as well as with neighbors and relatives.

Language use Life in the working-class and poor families in the study flows smoothly without extended verbal discussions. The amount of talking varies, but overall, it is considerably less than occurs in the middle-class homes.[21] Ms. McAllister jokes with the children and discusses what is on television. But she does not appear to cultivate conversation by asking the children questions or by drawing them out. Often she is brief and direct in her remarks. For instance, she coordinates the use of the apartment's only bathroom by using one-word directives. She sends the children (there are almost always at least four children home at once) to wash up by pointing to a child, saying one word, "bathroom," and handing him or her a washcloth. Wordlessly, the designated child gets up and goes to the bathroom to take a shower.

Similarly, although Ms. McAllister will listen to the children's complaints about school, she does not draw them out on these issues or seek to determine details, as Ms. Williams would. For instance, at the start of the new school year, when I ask Harold about his teacher, he tells me she is "mean" and that "she lies." Ms. McAllister, washing dishes, listens to her son, but she does not encourage Harold to support his opinion about his new teacher with more examples, nor does she mention any concerns of her own. Instead, she asks about last year's teacher, "What was the name of that man teacher?" Harold says, "Mr. Lindsey?" She says, "No, the other one." He says, "Mr. Terrene." Ms. McAllister smiles and says, "Yeah. I liked him." Unlike Alexander's mother, she seems content with a brief exchange of information.

Social connections Children, especially boys, frequently play outside. The number of potential playmates in Harold's world is vastly higher than the number in Alexander's neighborhood. When a field-worker stops to count heads, she finds 40 children of elementary school age residing in the nearby rows of apartments. With so many children nearby, Harold could choose to play only with others his own age. In fact, though, he often hangs out with older and younger children and with his cousins (who are close to his age).

The McAllister family, like other poor and working-class families, is involved in a web of extended kin. As noted earlier, Harold's older siblings and his two male cousins often spend the night at the McAllister home. Celebrations such as birthdays involve relatives almost exclusively. Party guests are not, as in middle-class families, friends from school or from extra-curricular activities. Birthdays are celebrated enthusiastically, with cake and special food to mark the occasion; presents, however, are not offered. Similarly, Christmas at Harold's house featured a tree and special food but no presents. At these and other family events, the older children voluntarily look after the younger ones: Harold plays with his 16-month-old niece, and his cousins carry around the younger babies.

The importance of family ties—and the contingent nature of life in the McAllister's world—is clear in the response Alexis offers when asked what she would do if she were given a million dollars:

Oh, boy! I'd buy my brother, my sister, my uncle, my aunt, my nieces and my nephews, and my grandpop, and my grandmom, and my mom, and my dad, and my friends, not my friends, but mostly my best friend—I'd buy them all clothes...and sneakers. And I'd buy some food, and I'd buy my mom some food, and I'd get my brothers and my sisters gifts for their birthdays.

Summary In a setting where everyone, including the children, was acutely aware of the lack of money, the McAllister family made do. Ms. McAllister rightfully saw herself as a very capable mother. She was a strong, positive influence in the lives of the children she looked after. Still, the contrast with Ms. Williams is striking. Ms. McAllister did not seem to think that Harold's opinions needed to be cultivated and developed. She, like most parents in the working-class and poor families, drew strong and clear boundaries between adults and children. Adults gave directions to children. Children were given freedom to play informally unless they were needed for chores. Extended family networks were deemed important and trustworthy.

The Intersection of Race and Class in Family Life

I expected race to powerfully shape children's daily schedules, but this was not evident (also see Conley 1999; Pattillo-McCoy 1999). This is not to say that race is unimportant. Black parents were particularly concerned with monitoring their children's lives outside the home for signs of racial problems.[22] Black middle-class fathers, especially, were likely to stress the importance of their sons understanding "what it means to be a black man in this society" (J. Hochschild 1995). Mr. Williams, in summarizing how he and his wife orient Alexander, said:

[We try to] teach him that race unfortunately is the most important aspect of our national life. I mean people look at other people and they see a color first. But that isn't going to define who he is. He will do his best. He will succeed, despite racism. And I think he lives his life that way.

Alexander's parents were acutely aware of the potential significance of race in his life. Both were adamant, however, that race should not be used as "an excuse" for not striving to succeed. Mr. Williams put it this way:

I discuss how race impacts on my life as an attorney, and I discuss how race will impact on his life. The one teaching that he takes away from this is that he is never to use discrimination as an excuse for not doing his best.

Thus far, few incidents of overt racism had occurred in Alexander's life, as his mother noted: Those situations have been far and few between....I mean, I can count them on my fingers.

Still, Ms. Williams recounted with obvious pain an incident at a birthday party Alexander had attended as a preschooler. The grandparents of the birthday child repeatedly asked, "Who is that boy?" and exclaimed, "He's so dark!" Such experiences fueled the Williams's resolve always to be "cautious":

We've never been, uh, parents who drop off their kid anywhere. We've always gone with him. And even now, I go in and—to school in the morning—and check [in]....The school environment, we've watched very closely.

Alexander's parents were not equally optimistic about the chances for racial equality in this country. Ms. Williams felt strongly that, especially while Alexander was young, his father should not voice his pessimism. Mr. Williams complained that this meant he had to "watch" what he said to Alexander about race relations. Still, both parents agreed about the need to be vigilant regarding potential racial problems in Alexander's life. Other black parents reported experiencing racial prejudice and expressed a similar commitment to vigilance.

Issues surrounding the prospect of growing up black and male in this society were threaded through Alexander's life in ways that had no equivalent among his middle-class, white male peers. Still, in fourth grade there were no signs of racial experiences having "taken hold" the way that they might as Alexander ages. In terms of the number and kind of activities he participated in, his life was very similar to that of Garrett Tallinger, his white counterpart (see Table 19.3). That both sets of parents were fully committed to a strategy of concentrated cultivation was apparent in the number of adult-organized activities the boys were enrolled in, the hectic pace of family life, and the stress on reasoning in parent-child negotiations. Likewise, the research assistants and I saw no striking differences in the ways in which white parents and black parents in the working-class and poor homes socialized their children.

Others (Fordham and Ogbu 1986) have found that in middle school and high school, adolescent peer groups often draw sharp racial boundaries, a pattern not evident among this study's third- and fourth-grade participants (but sometimes present among their older siblings). Following Tatum (1997:52), I attribute this to the children's relatively young ages (also see "Race in America," *The New York Times,* June 25, 2000, p. 1). In sum, in the broader society, key aspects of daily life were shaped by racial segregation and discrimination. But in terms of enrollment in organized activities, language use, and social connections, the largest differences between the families we observed were across social class, not racial groups.

Differences in Cultural Practices Across the Total Sample

The patterns observed among the Williams and McAllister families occurred among others in the 12-family subsample and across the larger group of 88 children. Frequently, they also echoed established patterns in the literature. These patterns highlight not only the amount of time spent on activities but also the quality of family life and the ways in which key dimensions of childrearing intertwine.

Organization of Daily Life

In the study as a whole, the rhythms of family life differed by social class. Working-class and poor children spent most of their free time in informal play; middle-class children took part in many adult-organized activities designed to develop their individual talents and interests. For the 88 children, I calculated an average score for the most common adult-directed, organized activities,[23] based on parents' answers to interview questions.[24] Middle-class children averaged 4.9 current activities ($N = 36$), working-class children averaged 2.5 activities ($N = 26$), and poor children averaged 1.5 ($N = 26$).[25] Black middle-class children had slightly more activities than white middle-class children, largely connected to more church involvement, with an average of 5.2 ($N = 18$) compared with 4.6 activities for whites ($N = 18$). The racial difference was very modest in the working-class group (2.8 activities for black children [$N = 12$] and 2.3 for white children [$N = 14$]) and the poor group (1.6 activities for black children [$N = 14$] and 1.4 for white children [$N = 12$]). Middle-class boys had slightly more activities than middle-class girls (5.1 versus 4.7, $N = 18$ for both) but gender did not make a difference for the other classes. The type of activity did however. Girls tended to participate in dance, music, and Scouts, and to be less active in sports. This pattern of social class differences in activities is comparable to other, earlier reports (Medrich et al. 1982). Hofferth and Sandberg's (2001a, 2000b) recent research using a representative national sample suggests that the number of children's organized activities increases with parents' education and that children's involvement in organized activities has risen in recent decades.

The dollar cost of children's organized activities was significant, particularly when families had more than one child. Cash outlays included paying the instructors and coaches who gave lessons, purchasing uniforms and performance attire, paying for tournament admission and travel to and from tournaments, and covering hotel and food costs for overnight stays. Summer camps also were expensive. At my request, the Tallingers added up the costs for Garrett's organized activities. The total was over $4,000 per year. Recent reports of parents' expenditures for children's involvement in a single sport (e.g., hockey) are comparably high (Schemari 2002). Children's activities consumed time as well as money, co-opting parents' limited leisure hours.

The study also uncovered differences in how much time children spent in activities controlled by adults. Take the schedule of Melanie Handlon, a white middle-class girl in the fourth grade (see Table 19.4). Between December 8 and December 24, Melanie had a piano lesson each Monday, Girl Scouts each Thursday, a special Girl Scout event one Monday night, a special holiday musical performance at school one Tuesday night, two orthodontist appointments, five special rehearsals for the church

Table 19.4 Participation in Activities Outside of School: Girls

Girl's Name/Race/Class	Activities Organized by Adults	Informal Activities
Middle Class		
Melanie Handlon (white)	Girl Scouts	Restricted television
	Piano	Plays outside with neighborhood kids
	Sunday school	Bakes cookies with mother
	Church	Swims (not on swim team)
	Church pageant	Listens to music
	Violin (through school)	
	Softball team	
Stacey Marshall (black)	Gymnastics lessons	Watches television
	Gymnastic teams	Plays outside
	Church	Visits friends from school
	Sunday school	Rides bike
	Youth choir	
Working Class		
Wendy Driver (white)	Catholic education (CCD)	Watches television
	Dance lessons	Visits relatives
	School choir	Does housework
		Rides bike
		Plays outside in the street
		Hangs out with cousins
Jessica Irwin (black father/ white mother)	Church	Restricted television
	Sunday school	Reads
	Saturday art class	Plays outside with neighborhood
	School band	kids
		Visit relatives
Poor		
Katie Brindle (white)	School choir	Watches television
	Friday evening church group	Visits relatives
	(rarely)	Plays with Barbies
		Rides bike
		Plays with neighborhood kids
Tara Carroll (black)	Church	Watches television
	Sunday school	Visits relatives
		Plays with dolls
		Plays Nintendo
		Plays with neighborhood kids

Christmas pageant, and regular Sunday commitments (an early church service, Sunday school, and youth choir). On weekdays she spent several hours after school struggling with her homework as her mother coached her step-by-step through the worksheets. The amount of time Melanie spent in situations where her movements were controlled by adults was typical of middle-class children in the study.

The schedule of Katie Brindle, a white fourth-grader from a poor family, contrasts sharply, showing few organized activities between December 2 and 24. She sang in the school choir. This involved one after-school rehearsal on Wednesdays; she walked home by herself after these rehearsals. Occasionally, Katie attended a Christian youth group on Friday nights (i.e., December 3). Significantly, all her activities were free. She wanted to enroll in ballet classes, but they were prohibitively expensive. What Katie did have was unstructured leisure time. Usually, she came home after school and then played outside with other children in the neighborhood or watched television. She also regularly visited her grandmother and her cousins, who lived a few minutes away by bus or car. She often spent weekend nights at her grandmother's house. Overall, Katie's life was centered in and around home. Compared with the middle-class children in the study, her life moved at a dramatically less hectic pace. This pattern was characteristic of the other working-class and poor families we interviewed.

In addition to these activities, television provided a major source of leisure entertainment. All children in the study spent at least some free time watching TV, but there were differences in when, what, and how much they watched. Most middle-class parents we interviewed characterized television as actually or potentially harmful to children; many stressed that they preferred their children to read for entertainment. Middle-class parents often had rules about the amount of time children could spend watching television.[26] These concerns did not surface in interviews with working-class and poor parents. Indeed, Ms. Yanelli, a white working-class mother, objected to restricting a child's access to television, noting, "You know, you learn so much from television." Working-class and poor parents did monitor the content of programs and made some shows off-limits for children. The television itself, however, was left on almost continuously (also see Robinson and Godbey 1997).

Language Use

The social class differences in language use we observed were similar to those reported by others (see Bernstein 1971; Hart and Risley 1995; Heath 1983). In middle-class homes, parents placed a tremendous emphasis on reasoning. They also drew out their children's views on specific subjects. Middle-class parents relied on directives for matters of health and safety, but most other aspects of daily life were potentially open to negotiation: Discussions arose over what children wore in the morning, what they ate, where they sat, and how they spent their time. Not all middle-class children were equally talkative, however. In addition, in observations, mothers exhibited more willingness to engage children in prolonged discussions than did fathers. The latter tended to be less engaged with children overall and less accepting of disruptions (A. Hochschild 1989).

In working-class and poor homes, most parents did not focus on developing their children's opinions, judgments, and observations. When children volunteered information, parents would listen, but typically they did not follow up with questions or comments. In the field note excerpt below, Wendy Driver shares her new understanding of sin with the members of her white working-class family. She is sitting in the living room with her brother (Willie), her mother, and her mother's live-in boyfriend (Mack). Everyone is watching television:

Wendy asks Willie: "Do you know what mortal sin is?"
Willie: "No."
Wendy asks Mom: "Do you know what mortal sin is?"
Mom: "What is it?"

Wendy asks Mack: "Do you know what it is?"

Mack: "No."

Mom: "Tell us what it is. You're the one who went to CCD [Catholic religious education classes]."

Wendy: "It's when you know something's wrong and you do it anyway."

No one acknowledged Wendy's comment. Wendy's mother and Mack looked at her while she gave her explanation of mortal sin, then looked back at the TV.

Wendy's family is conversationally cooperative, but unlike the Williamses, for example, no one here perceives the moment as an opportunity to further develop Wendy's vocabulary or to help her exercise her critical thinking skills.

Negotiations between parents and children in working-class and poor families were infrequent. Parents tended to use firm directives and they expected prompt, positive responses. Children who ignored parental instructions could expect physical punishment. Field notes from an evening in the home of the white, working-class Yanelli family capture one example of this familiar dynamic. It is past 8:00 P.M. Ms. Yanelli, her son Billy, and the fieldworker are playing *Scrabble*. Mr. Yanelli and a friend are absorbed in a game of chess. Throughout the evening, Billy and Ms. Yanelli have been at odds. She feels Billy has not been listening to her. Ms. Yanelli wants her son to stop playing *Scrabble*, take a shower, and go to bed.

Mom: "Billy, shower. I don't care if you cry, screams."

Billy: "We're not done with the *Scrabble* game."

Mom: "You're done. Finish your homework earlier." That evening, Billy had not finished his homework until 8:00 P.M. Billy remains seated.

Mom: "Come on! Tomorrow you've got a big day." Billy does not move.

Mom goes into the other room and gets a brown leather belt. She hits Billy twice on the leg.

Mom: "Get up right now! Tomorrow I can't get you up in the morning. Get up right now!"

Billy gets up and runs up the steps.

Ms. Yanelli's disciplinary approach is very different from that of the middle-class parents we observed. Like most working-class and poor parents we observed, she is directive and her instructions are nonnegotiable ("Billy, shower" and "You're done."). Using a belt may seem harsh, but it is neither a random nor irrational form of punishment here. Ms. Yanelli gave Billy notice of her expectations and she offered an explanation (it's late, and tomorrow he has "a big day"). She turned to physical discipline as a resource when she felt Billy was not sufficiently responsive.[27]

Social Connections

We also observed class differences in the context of children's social relations. Across the sample of 88 families, middle-class children's involvement in adult-organized activities led to mainly weak social ties. Soccer, photography classes, swim team, and so on typically take place in 6 to 8 week blocks, and participant turnover rates are relatively high. Equally important, middle-class children's commitment to organized activities generally pre-empted visits with extended family. Some did not have relatives who lived nearby, but even among those who did, children's schedules made it difficult to organize and attend regular extended-family gatherings. Many of the middle-class children visited with relatives only on major holidays.[28]

Similarly, middle-class parents tended to forge weak rather than strong ties. Most reported having social networks that included professionals: 93 percent of the sample of middle-class parents had a friend or relative who was a teacher, compared with 43 percent of working-class parents and 36 percent of poor families. For a physician friend or relative, the pattern was comparable (70 percent versus 14 percent and 18 percent, respectively).[29] Relationships such as these are not as deep as family ties, but they are a valuable resource when parents face a challenge in childrearing.

Working-class and poor families were much less likely to include professionals in their social networks but were much more likely than their middle-class counterparts to see or speak with kin daily. Children regularly interacted in casually assembled, heterogeneous age groups that included cousins as well as neighborhood children. As others have shown (Lever 1988), we observed gender differences in children's activities. Although girls sometimes ventured outside to ride bikes and play ball games, compared with boys they were more likely to stay inside the house to play. Whether inside or outside, the girls, like the boys, played in loose coalitions of kin and neighbors and created their own activities.

Interactions with representatives of major social institutions (the police, courts, schools, and government agencies) also appeared significantly shaped by social class. Members of white *and* black working-class and poor families offered spontaneous comments about their distrust of these officials. For example, one white working-class mother described an episode in which the police had come to her home looking for her ex-husband (a drug user). She recalled officers "breaking down the door" and terrifying her eldest son, then only three years old. Another white working-class mother reported that her father had been arrested. Although by all accounts in good spirits, he had been found dead in the city jail, an alleged suicide. Children listened to and appeared to absorb remarks such as these.

Fear was a key reason for the unease with which working-class and poor families approached formal (and some informal) encounters with officials. Some parents worried that authorities would "come and take [our] kids away." One black mother on public assistance interviewed as part of the larger study was outraged that school personnel had allowed her daughter to come home from school one winter day without her coat. She noted that if *she* had allowed that to happen, "the school" would have reported her to Child Protective Services for child abuse. Wendy Driver's mother (white working-class) complained that she felt obligated to take Wendy to the doctor, even when she knew nothing was wrong, because Wendy had gone to see the school nurse. Ms. Driver felt she had to be extra careful because she didn't want "them" to come and take her kids away.[30] Strikingly, no middle-class parents mention similar fears about the power of dominant institutions.

Obviously, these three dimensions of childrearing patterns—the organization of daily life, language use, and social connections—do not capture all the class advantages parents pass to their children. The middle-class children in the study enjoyed relatively privileged lives. They lived in large houses, some had swimming pools in their backyards, most had bedrooms of their own, all had many toys, and computers were common. These children also had broad horizons. They flew in airplanes, they traveled out of state for vacations, they often traveled an hour or two from home to take part in their activities, and they knew older children whose extracurricular activities involved international travel.

Still, in some important areas, variations among families did *not* appear to be linked to social class. Some of the middle-class children had learning problems. And, despite their relatively privileged social-class position, neither middle-class children nor their parents were insulated from the realities of serious illness and premature death among family and friends. In addition, some elements of family life seemed relatively immune to social class, including how orderly and tidy the households were. In one white middle-class family, the house was regularly in a state of disarray. The house was cleaned and tidied for a Christmas Eve gathering, but it returned to its normal state shortly thereafter. By contrast, a black middle-class family's home was always extremely tidy, as were some, but not all, of the working-class and poor homes. Nor did certain aspects of parenting, particularly the degree to which mothers appeared to "mean what they said," seem linked to social class. Families also differed with respect to the presence or absence of a sense of humor among individual members, levels of anxiety, and signs of stress-related illnesses they exhibited. Finally, there were significant differences in

BISHOP BURTON COLLEGE
LIBRARY

temperament and disposition among children in the same family. These variations are useful reminders that social class is not fully a determinant of the character of children's lives.

Impact of Childrearing Strategies on Interactions with Institutions

Social scientists sometimes emphasize the importance of reshaping parenting practices to improve children's chances of success. Explicitly and implicitly, the literature exhorts parents to comply with the views of professionals (Bronfenbrenner 1966; Epstein 2001; Heimer and Staffen 1998). Such calls for compliance do not, however, reconcile professionals' judgments regarding the intrinsic value of current childrearing standards with the evidence of the historical record, which shows regular shifts in such standards over time (Aries 1962; Wrigley 1989; Zelizer 1985). Nor are the stratified, and limited, possibilities for success in the broader society examined.

I now follow the families out of their homes and into encounters with representatives of dominant institutions—institutions that are directed by middle-class professionals. Again, I focus on Alexander Williams and Harold McAllister. (Institutional experiences are summarized in Table 2.) Across all social classes, parents and children interacted with teachers and school officials, healthcare professionals, and assorted government officials. Although they often addressed similar problems (e.g., learning disabilities, asthma, traffic violations), they typically did not achieve similar resolutions. The pattern of concerted cultivation fostered an *emerging sense of entitlement* in the life of Alexander Williams and other middle-class children. By contrast, the commitment to nurturing children's natural growth fostered an *emerging sense of constraint* in the life of Harold McAllister and other working-class or poor children. (These consequences of childrearing practices are summarized in Table 19.2.)

Both parents and children drew on the resources associated with these two childrearing approaches during their interactions with officials. Middle-class parents and children often customized these interactions; working-class and poor parents were more likely to have a "generic" relationship. When faced with problems, middle-class parents also appeared better equipped to exert influence over other adults compared with working-class and poor parents. Nor did middle-class parents or children display the intimidation or confusion we witnessed among many working-class and poor families when they faced a problem in their children's school experience.

Emerging Signs of Entitlement

Alexander Williams's mother, like many middle-class mothers, explicitly teaches her son to be an informed, assertive client in interactions with professionals. For example, as she drives Alexander to a routine doctor's appointment, she coaches him in the art of communicating effectively in healthcare settings:

> Alexander asks if he needs to get any shots today at the doctor's. Ms. Williams says he'll need to ask the doctor.... As we enter Park Lane, Mom says quietly to Alex: "Alexander, you should be thinking of questions you might want to ask the doctor. You can ask him anything you want. Don't be shy. You can ask anything."
> Alex thinks for a minute, then: "I have some bumps under my arms from my deodorant."
> Mom: "Really? You mean from your new deodorant?"
> Alex: "Yes."
> Mom: "Well, you should ask the doctor."

Alexander learns that he has the right to speak up (e.g., "don't be shy") and that he should prepare for an encounter with a person in a position of authority by gathering his thoughts in advance.

These class resources are subsequently *activated* in the encounter with the doctor (a jovial white man in his late thirties or early forties). The examination begins this way:

Doctor: "Okay, as usual, I'd like to go through the routine questions with you. And if you have any questions for me, just fire away." Doctor examines Alex's chart: "Height-wise, as usual, Alexander's in the ninety-fifth percentile."
Although the physician is talking to Ms. Williams, Alexander interrupts him:

Alex: "I'm in the what?" Doctor: "It means that you're taller than more than ninety-five out of a hundred young men when they're, uh, ten years old."
Alex: "I'm not ten."
Doctor: "Well, they graphed you at ten...they usually take the closest year to get that graph."
Alex: "Alright."
Alexander's "Alright" reveals that he feels entitled to weigh-in with his own judgment.

A few minutes later, the exam is interrupted when the doctor is asked to provide an emergency consultation by telephone. Alexander listens to the doctor's conversation and then uses what he has overheard as the basis for a clear directive:

Doctor: "The stitches are on the eyelids themselves, the laceration?...Um...I don't suture eyelids...um...Absolutely not!...Don't even touch them. That was very bad judgment on the camp's part....[Hangs up.] I'm sorry about the interruption."
Alex: "Stay away from my eyelids!"

Alexander's comment, which draws laughter from the adults, reflects this fourth grader's tremendous ease interacting with a physician.

Later, Ms. Williams and the doctor discuss Alexander's diet. Ms. Williams freely admits that they do not always follow nutritional guidelines. Her honesty is a form of capital because it gives the doctor accurate information on which to base a diagnosis. Feeling no need for deception positions mother and son to receive better care:

Doctor: Let's start with appetite. Do you get three meals a day?"
Alex: "Yeah."
Doctor: "And here's the important question: Do you get your fruits and vegetables too?"
Alex: "Yeah."
Mom, high-pitched: "Ooooo...."
Doctor: "I see I have a second opinion." [laughter]
Alex, voice rising: "You give me bananas and all in my lunch every day. And I had cabbage for dinner last night."
Doctor: "Do you get at least one or two fruits, one or two vegetables every day?"
Alex: "Yeah."
Doctor: "Marginally?"
Mom: "Ninety-eight percent of the time he eats pretty well."
Doctor: "OK, I can live with that...."

Class resources are again activated when Alexander's mother reveals she "gave up" on a medication. The doctor pleasantly but clearly instructs her to continue the medication. Again, though, he receives accurate information rather than facing silent resistance or defiance, as occurred in encounters between healthcare professionals and other (primarily working-class and poor) families. The doctor acknowledges Ms. Williams's relative power: He "argues for" continuation rather than directing her to execute a medically necessary action:

> Mom: "His allergies have just been, just acted up again. One time this summer and I had to bring him in."
> Doctor: "I see a note here from Dr. Svennson that she put him on Vancinace and Benadryl. Did it seem to help him?"
> Mom: "Just, not really. So, I used it for about a week and I just gave up." Doctor, sitting forward in his chair: "OK, I'm actually going to argue for not giving up. If he needs it, Vancinace is a very effective drug. But it takes at least a week to start...."
> Mom: "Oh. OK...."
> Doctor: "I'd rather have him use that than heavy oral medications. You have to give it a few weeks...."

A similar pattern of give and take and questioning characterizes Alexander's interaction with the doctor, as the following excerpt illustrates:

> Doctor: "The only thing that you really need besides my checking you, um, is to have, um, your eyes checked downstairs."
> Alex: "Yes! I love that, I love that!"
> Doctor laughs: "Well, now the most important question. Do you have any questions you want to ask me before I do your physical?"
> Alex: "Um.... only one. I've been getting some bumps on my arms, right around here [indicates underarm]."
> Doctor: "Underneath?"
> Alex: "Yeah."
> Doctor: "OK.... Do they hurt or itch?"
> Alex: "No, they're just there."
> Doctor: "OK, I'll take a look at those bumps for you. Um, what about you—um ..."
> Alex: "They're barely any left."
> Doctor: "OK, well, I'll take a peek.... Any questions or worries on your part? [Looking at the mother]
> Mom: "No.... He seems to be coming along very nicely."[31]

Alexander's mother's last comment reflects her view of him as a project, one that is progressing "very nicely." Throughout the visit, she signals her ease and her perception of the exam as an exchange between peers (with Alexander a legitimate participant), rather than a communication from a person in authority to his subordinates. Other middle-class parents seemed similarly comfortable. During Garrett Tallinger's exam, for example, his mother took off her sandals and tucked her legs up under her as she sat in the examination room. She also joked casually with the doctor.

Middle-class parents and children were also very assertive in situations at the public elementary school most of the middle-class children in the study attended. There were numerous conflicts during the year over matters small and large. For example, parents complained to one another and to the teachers about the amount of homework the children were assigned. A black middle-class mother whose daughters had not tested into the school's gifted program negotiated with officials to have the girls' (higher) results from a private testing company accepted instead. The parents of a fourth-grade boy drew the school superintendent into a battle over religious lyrics in a song scheduled to be sung as part of the holiday program. The superintendent consulted the district lawyer and ultimately "counseled" the principal to be more sensitive, and the song was dropped.

Children, too, asserted themselves at school. Examples include requesting that the classroom's blinds be lowered so the sun wasn't in their eyes, badgering the teacher for permission to retake a math test for a higher grade, and demanding to know why no cupcake had been saved when an absence prevented attendance at a classroom party. In these encounters, children were not simply complying with adults' requests or asking for a repeat of an earlier experience. They were displaying an emerging sense of entitlement by urging adults to permit a customized accommodation of institutional processes to suit their preferences.

Of course, some children (and parents) were more forceful than others in their dealings with teachers, and some were more successful than others. Melanie Handlon's mother, for example, took a very "hands-on" approach to her daughter's learning problems, coaching Melanie through her homework day after day. Instead of improved grades, however, the only result was a deteriorating home environment marked by tension and tears.

Emerging Signs of Constraint

The interactions the research assistants and I observed between professionals and working-class and poor parents frequently seemed cautious and constrained. This unease is evident, for example, during a physical Harold McAllister has before going to Bible camp. Harold's mother, normally boisterous and talkative at home, is quiet. Unlike Ms. Williams, she seems wary of supplying the doctor with accurate information:

> Doctor: "Does he eat something each day—either fish, meat, or egg?"
> Mom, response is low and muffled: "Yes."
> Doctor, attempting to make eye contact but mom stares intently at paper: "A yellow vegetable?"
> Mom, still no eye contact, looking at the floor: "Yeah."
> Doctor: "A green vegetable?" Mom, looking at the doctor: "Not all the time." [Fieldworker has not seen any of the children eat a green or yellow vegetable since visits began.]
> Doctor: "No. Fruit or juice?"
> Mom, low voice, little or no eye contact, looks at the doctor's scribbles on the paper he is filling out: "Ummh humn."
> Doctor: "Does he drink milk everyday?" Mom, abruptly, in considerably louder voice: "Yeah."
> Doctor: "Cereal, bread, rice, potato, anything like that?"
> Mom, shakes her head: "Yes, definitely." [Looks at doctor.]

Ms. McAllister's knowledge of developmental events in Harold's life is uneven. She is not sure when he learned to walk and cannot recall the name of his previous doctor. And when the doctor asks, "When was the last time he had a tetanus shot?" she counters, gruffly, "What's a tetanus shot?"

Unlike Ms. Williams, who urged Alexander to share information with the doctor, Ms. McAllister squelches eight-year-old Alexis's overtures:

> Doctor: "Any birth mark?"
> Mom looks at doctor, shakes her head no.
> Alexis, raising her left arm, says excitedly: "I have a birth mark under my arm!"
> Mom, raising her voice and looking stern: "Will you cool out a minute?" Mom, again answering the doctor's question: "No."

Despite Ms. McAllister's tension and the marked change in her everyday demeanor, Harold's whole exam is not uncomfortable. There are moments of laughter. Moreover, Harold's mother is not consistently shy or passive. Before the visit begins, the doctor comes into the waiting room and calls

Harold's and Alexis's names. In response, the McAllisters (and the fieldworker) stand. Ms. McAllister then beckons for her nephew Tyrice (who is about Harold's age) to come along *before* she clears this with the doctor. Later, she sends Tyrice down the hall to observe Harold being weighed; she relies on her nephew's report rather than asking for this information from the healthcare professionals.

Still, neither Harold nor his mother seemed as comfortable as Alexander had been. Alexander was used to extensive conversation at home; with the doctor, he was at ease initiating questions. Harold, who was used to responding to directives at home, primarily answered questions from the doctor, rather than posing his own. Alexander, encouraged by his mother, was assertive and confident with the doctor. Harold was reserved. Absorbing his mother's apparent need to conceal the truth about the range of foods he ate, he appeared cautious, displaying an emerging sense of constraint.

We observed a similar pattern in school interactions. Overall, the working-class and poor adults had much more distance or separation from the school than their middle-class counterparts. Ms. McAllister, for example, could be quite assertive in some settings (e.g., at the start of family observations, she visited the local drug dealer, warning him not to "mess with" the black male fieldworker).[32] But throughout the fourth-grade parent-teacher conference, she kept her winter jacket zipped up, sat hunched over in her chair, and spoke in barely audible tones. She was stunned when the teacher said that Harold did not do homework. Sounding dumbfounded, she said, "He does it at home." The teacher denied it and continued talking. Ms. McAllister made no further comments and did not probe for more information, except about a letter the teacher said he had mailed home and that she had not received. The conference ended, having yielded Ms. McAllister few insights into Harold's educational experience.[33]

Other working-class and poor parents also appeared baffled, intimidated, and subdued in parent-teacher conferences. Ms. Driver, who was extremely worried about her fourth-grader's inability to read, kept these concerns to herself. She explained to us, "I don't want to jump into anything and find it is the wrong thing." When working-class and poor parents did try to intervene in their children's educational experiences, they often felt ineffectual. Billy Yanelli's mother appeared relaxed and chatty in many of her interactions with other adults. With "the school," however, she was very apprehensive. She distrusted school personnel. She felt bullied and powerless. Hoping to resolve a problem involving her son, she tried to prepare her ideas in advance. Still, as she recounted during an interview, she failed to make school officials see Billy as vulnerable:

> Ms. Yanelli: I found a note in his school bag one morning and it said, "I'm going to kill you... you're a dead mother-f-er...." So, I started shaking. I was all ready to go over there. [I was] prepared for the counselor.... They said the reason they [the other kids] do what they do is because Billy makes them do it. So they had an answer for everything.
> Interviewer: How did you feel about that answer?
> Ms. Yanelli: I hate the school. I hate it.

Working-class and poor children seemed aware of their parents' frustration and witnessed their powerlessness. Billy Yanelli, for example, asserted in an interview that his mother "hate[d]" school officials.

At times, these parents encouraged their children to resist school officials' authority. The Yanellis told Billy to "beat up" a boy who was bothering him. Wendy Driver's mother advised her to punch a male classmate who pestered her and pulled her ponytail. Ms. Driver's boyfriend added, "Hit him when the teacher isn't looking."

In classroom observations, working-class and poor children could be quite lively and energetic, but we did not observe them try to customize their environments. They tended to react to adults' offers or, at times, to plead with educators to repeat previous experiences, such as reading a particular story, watching a movie, or going to the computer room. Compared to middle-class classroom interactions, the boundaries between adults and children seemed firmer and clearer. Although the children often resisted and tested school rules, they did not seem to be seeking to get educators to accommodate their own *individual* preferences.

Overall, then, the behavior of working-class and poor parents cannot be explained as a manifestation of their temperaments or of overall passivity; parents were quite energetic in intervening in their children's lives in other spheres. Rather, working-class and poor parents generally appeared to depend on the school (Lareau 2000a), even as they were dubious of the trustworthiness of the professionals. This suspicion of professionals in dominant institutions is, at least in some instances, a reasonable response.[34] The unequal level of trust, as well as differences in the amount and quality of information divulged, can yield unequal *profits* during a historical moment when professionals applaud assertiveness and reject passivity as an inappropriate parenting strategy (Epstein 2001). Middle-class children and parents often (but not always) accrued advantages or profits from their efforts. Alexander Williams succeeded in having the doctor take his medical concerns seriously. Ms. Marshall's children ended up in the gifted program, even though they did not technically qualify. Middle-class children expect institutions to be responsive to *them* and to accommodate their individual needs. By contrast, when Wendy Driver is told to hit the boy who is pestering her (when the teacher isn't looking) or Billy Yanelli is told to physically defend himself, despite school rules, they are not learning how to make bureaucratic institutions work to their advantage. Instead, they are being given lessons in frustration and powerlessness.

Why Does Social Class Matter?

Parents' economic resources helped create the observed class differences in childrearing practices. Enrollment fees that middle-class parents dismissed as "negligible" were formidable expenses for less affluent families. Parents also paid for clothing, equipment, hotel stays, fast food meals, summer camps, and fundraisers. In 1994, the Tallingers estimated the cost of Garrett's activities at $4,000 annually, and that figure was not unusually high.[35] Moreover, families needed reliable private transportation and flexible work schedules to get children to and from events. These resources were disproportionately concentrated in middle-class families.

Differences in educational resources also are important. Middle-class parents' superior levels of education gave them larger vocabularies that facilitated concerted cultivation, particularly in institutional interventions. Poor and working-class parents were not familiar with key terms professionals used, such as "tetanus shot." Furthermore, middle-class parents' educational backgrounds gave them confidence when criticizing educational professionals and intervening in school matters. Working-class and poor parents viewed educators as their social superiors.

Kohn and Schooler (1983) showed that parents' occupations, especially the complexity of their work, influence their childrearing beliefs. We found that parents' work mattered, but also saw signs that the experience of adulthood itself influenced conceptions of childhood. Middle-class parents often were preoccupied with the pleasures and challenges of their work lives.[36] They tended to view childhood as a dual opportunity: a chance for play, and for developing talents and skills of value later in life. Mr. Tallinger noted that playing soccer taught Garrett to be "hard nosed" and "competitive," valuable workplace skills. Ms. Williams mentioned the value of Alexander learning to work with others by playing on a sports team. Middle-class parents, aware of the "declining fortunes" of the middle class, worried about their own economic futures and those of their children (Newman 1993). This uncertainty increased their commitment to helping their children develop broad skills to enhance their future possibilities.

Working-class and poor parents' conceptions of adulthood and childhood also appeared to be closely connected to their lived experiences. For the working class, it was the deadening quality of work and the press of economic shortages that defined their experience of adulthood and influenced their vision of childhood. It was dependence on public assistance and severe economic shortages that most shaped poor parents' views. Families in both classes had many worries about basic issues: food shortages, limited access to healthcare, physical safety, unreliable transportation, insufficient clothing. Thinking back over their childhoods, these parents remembered hardship but also recalled times without the anxieties they now faced. Many appeared to want their own youngsters to concentrate on being happy and relaxed, keeping the burdens of life at bay until they were older.

Thus, childrearing strategies are influenced by more than parents' education. It is the interweaving of life experiences and resources, including parents' economic resources, occupational conditions, and educational backgrounds, that appears to be most important in leading middle-class parents to engage in concerted cultivation and working-class and poor parents to engage in the accomplishment of natural growth. Still, the structural location of families did not fully determine their childrearing practices. The agency of actors and the indeterminacy of social life are inevitable.

In addition to economic and social resources, are there other significant factors? If the poor and working-class families' resources were transformed overnight so that they equaled those of the middle-class families, would their cultural logic of childrearing shift as well? Or are there cultural attitudes and beliefs that are substantially independent of economic and social resources that are influencing parents' practices here? The size and scope of this study preclude a definitive answer. Some poor and working-class parents embraced principles of concerted cultivation: They wished (but could not afford) to enroll their children in organized activities (e.g., piano lessons, voice lessons), they believed listening to children was important, and they were committed to being involved in their children's schooling. Still, even when parents across all of the classes seemed committed to similar principles, their motivations differed. For example, many working-class and poor parents who wanted more activities for their children were seeking a safe haven for them. Their goal was to provide protection from harm rather than to cultivate the child's talents per se.

Some parents explicitly criticized children's schedules that involved many activities. During the parent interviews, we described the real-life activities of two children (using data from the 12 families we were observing). One schedule resembled Alexander Williams's: restricted television, required reading, and many organized activities, including piano lessons (for analytical purposes, we said that, unlike Alexander, this child disliked his piano lessons but was not allowed to quit). Summing up the attitude of the working-class and poor parents who rejected this kind of schedule,[37] one white, poor mother complained:

> I think he wants more, I think he doesn't enjoy doing what he's doing half of the time (light laughter). I think his parents are too strict. And he's not a child.

Even parents who believed this more regimented approach would pay off "job-wise" when the child was an adult still expressed serious reservations: "I think he is a sad kid," or, "He must be dead-dog tired."

Thus, working-class and poor parents varied in their beliefs. Some longed for a schedule of organized activities for their children and others did not; some believed in reasoning with children and playing an active role in schooling and others did not. Fully untangling the effects of material and cultural resources on parents and children's choices is a challenge for future research.[38]

Discussion

The evidence shows that class position influences critical aspects of family life: time use, language use, and kin ties. Not all aspects of family life are affected by social class, and there is variability within class. Still, parents do transmit advantages to their children in patterns that are sufficiently consistent and identifiable to be described as a "cultural logic" of childrearing. The white and black middle-class parents engaged in practices I have termed "concerted cultivation"—they made a deliberate and sustained effort to stimulate children's development and to cultivate their cognitive and social skills. The working-class and poor parents viewed children's development as spontaneously unfolding, as long as they were provided with comfort, food, shelter, and other basic support. This commitment, too, required ongoing effort; sustaining children's natural growth despite formidable life challenges is properly viewed as an accomplishment.

In daily life, the patterns associated with each of these approaches were interwoven and mutually reinforcing. Nine-year-old middle-class children already had developed a clear sense of their own talents and skills, and they differentiated themselves from siblings and friends. They were also learning to think of themselves as special and worthy of having adults devote time and energy to promoting them and their leisure activities. In the process, the boundaries between adults and children sometimes blurred; adults' leisure preferences became subordinate to their children's. The strong emphasis on reasoning in middle-class families had similar, diffuse effects. Children used their formidable reasoning skills to persuade adults to acquiesce to their wishes. The idea that children's desires should be taken seriously was routinely realized in the middle-class families we interviewed and observed. In many subtle ways, children were taught that they were entitled. Finally, the commitment to cultivating children resulted in family schedules so crowded with activities there was little time left for visiting relatives. Quantitative studies of time use have shed light on important issues, but they do not capture the interactive nature of routine, everyday activities and the varying ways they affect the texture of family life.[39]

In working-class and poor families, parents established limits; within those limits, children were free to fashion their own pastimes. Children's wishes did not guide adults' actions as frequently or as decisively as they did in middle-class homes. Children were viewed as subordinate to adults. Parents tended to issue directives rather than to negotiate. Frequent interactions with relatives rather than acquaintances or strangers created a thicker divide between families and the outside world. Implicitly and explicitly, parents taught their children to keep their distance from people in positions of authority, to be distrustful of institutions, and, at times, to resist officials' authority. Children seemed to absorb the adults' feelings of powerlessness in their institutional relationships. As with the middle class, there were important variations among working-class and poor families, and some critical aspects of family life, such as the use of humor, were immune to social class.

The role of race in children's daily lives was less powerful than I had expected. The middle-class black children's parents were alert to the potential effects of institutional discrimination on their children. Middle-class black parents also took steps to help their children develop a positive racial identity. Still, in terms of how children spend their time, the way parents use language and discipline in the home, the nature of the families' social connections, and the strategies used for intervening in institutions, white and black middle-class parents engaged in very similar, often identical, practices with their children. A similar pattern was observed in white and black working-class homes as well as in white and black poor families. Thus my data indicate that on the childrearing dynamics studied here, compared with social class, race was less important in children's daily lives.[40] As they enter the racially segregated words of dating, marriage, and housing markets, and as they encounter more racism in their interpersonal contact with whites (Waters 1999), the relative importance of race in the children's daily lives is likely to increase.

Differences in family dynamics and the logic of childrearing across social classes have long-term consequences. As family members moved out of the home and interacted with representatives of formal institutions, middle-class parents and children were able to negotiate more valuable outcomes than their working-class and poor counterparts. In interactions with agents of dominant institutions, working-class and poor children were learning lessons in constraint while middle-class children were developing a sense of entitlement.

It is a mistake to see either concerted cultivation or the accomplishment of natural growth as an intrinsically desirable approach. As has been amply documented, conceptions of childhood have changed dramatically over time (Wrigley 1989). Drawbacks to middle-class childrearing, including the exhaustion associated with intensive mothering and frenetic family schedules and a sapping of children's naivete that leaves them feeling too sophisticated for simple games and toys (Hays 1996), remain insufficiently highlighted.

Another drawback is that middle-class children are less likely to learn how to fill "empty time" with their own creative play, leading to a dependence on their parents to solve experiences of boredom. Sociologists need to more clearly differentiate between standards that are intrinsically desirable and standards that facilitate success in dominant institutions. A more critical, and historically sensitive, vision is needed (Donzelot 1979). Here Bourdieu's work (1976, 1984, 1986, 1989) is valuable.

Finally, there are methodological issues to consider. Quantitative research has delineated population-wide patterns; ethnographies offer rich descriptive detail but typically focus on a single, small group. Neither approach can provide holistic, but empirically grounded, assessments of daily life. Multi-sited, multi-person research using ethnographic methods also pose formidable methodological challenges (Lareau 2002). Still, families have proven themselves open to being studied in an intimate fashion. Creating penetrating portraits of daily life that will enrich our theoretical models is an important challenge for the future.

Notes

1. In a study of mothers' beliefs about child-rearing, Hays (1996) found variations in how working-class and middle-class mothers sorted information, but she concluded that a pattern of "intensive mothering" was present across social classes. My study of behavior found class differences but, as I discuss below, in some instances working-class and poor parents expressed a desire to enroll their children in organized activities.
2. Some significant differences between the study's working-class and poor families (e.g., only the poor children experienced food shortages) are not highlighted here because, on the dimensions discussed in this paper, the biggest differences were between middle-class and non-middle-class families. See Lareau (forthcoming) for a more elaborate discussion as well as Lamont (2000) for distinctions working-class families draw between themselves and the poor; see McLanahan and Sandefur (1994) regarding family structure and children's lives.
3. Case studies of nonrandom samples, such as this one, have the limitation that findings cannot be generalized beyond the cases reported. These examples serve to illustrate conceptual points (Burawoy et al. 1991) rather than to describe representative patterns of behavior. A further limitation of this study is that the data were collected and analyzed over an extended period of time, (see the "Methodology" section).
4. All names of people and places are pseudonyms. The Lawrenceville school was in a white suburban neighborhood in a university community a few hours from a metropolitan area. The student population was about half white and half black; the (disproportionately poor) black children were bused from other neighborhoods.
5. Over three-quarters of the students at Lower Richmond qualified for free lunch; by contrast, Swan did not have a free lunch program.
6. At both sites, we attended school events and observed many parent-teacher conferences. Also, I interviewed the classroom teachers and adults involved in the children's organized activities. These interview data are not presented here.
7. Both schools had computer labs, art programs, and music programs, but Swan had many more resources and much higher average achievement scores. Graffiti and physical confrontations between students were common only at Lower Richmond. At these two sites and in Lawrenceville, white faculty predominated.
8. I located the black middle-class parents through social networks; the white poor families were located through flyers left at welfare offices and social service programs, and posted on telephone poles. Ten white poor families (only) were paid $25 per interview.
9. Of 19 families asked to participate in the intensive study, 7 declined (a response rate of 63 percent). I tried to balance the observational phase sample by gender, race, and class, and to "mix and match" the children on other characteristics, such as their behavior with peers, their relationships with extended family, and their parents' level of involvement in their

education. The aim was to lessen the chance that observed differences in behavior would reflect unknown variables (e.g., church attendance or parents' participation at school). Last, I deliberately included two families (Irwins, Greeleys) who had some "middle-class" traits but who lived in a working-class and poor area, respectively. Including these unusual families seemed conceptually important for disentangling the influences of social class and environment (neighborhood).

10. I analyzed the data for the study as a whole in two ways. I coded themes from the interviews and used Folio Views software to help establish patterns. I also relied on reading the field notes, thinking about similarities and differences across families, searching for disconfirming evidence, and re-reading the field notes.

11. Recruitment to complete the sample was difficult as children needed to be a specific age, race, and class, and to be part of families who were willing to be observed. The white poor boy was recommended by a social service program manager; the black middle-class children were located through extended social networks of mine.

12. We did 12 to 14 observations of the Handlon and Carroll families before settling on the 20-visit pattern. In Alexander Williams's case, the visits occurred over a year. To observe unusual events (e.g., a family reunion), we sometimes went back after formal observations had ended.

13. Families developed preferences, favoring one fieldworker in a team over another. But these preferences were not stable across families, and the field notes did not differ dramatically between fieldworkers. Notes were much more similar than they were different.

14. Wright (1997) uses 12 categories in his neo-Marxist approach. Goldthorpe, a neo-Weberian, operationalizes his class schema at levels of aggregation ranging from 3 to 11 categories (Erikson and Goldthorpe 1993:38–39).

15. Here "poor" refers to the source of income (i.e., government assistance versus labor market) rather than the amount of income. Although lower class is more accurate than poor, it is widely perceived as pejorative. I might have used "underclass," but the literature has defined this term in racialized ways.

16. Dollar figures are from 1994–1995, unless otherwise noted. Income was not used to define class membership, but these data are available from the author.

17. Mr. and Ms. Williams disagreed about the value of their home; the figure here averages what each reported in 1995. Housing prices in their region were lower—and continue to be lower today—than in many other parts of the country. Their property is now worth an estimated $175,000 to $200,000.

18. Alexander's mother goes by Christina Nile at work, but Mrs. Williams at church. Some other mothers' last names also differ from their children's. Here I assign all mothers the same last names as their children.

19. I contacted the Williams family through social networks after I was unable to recruit the black middle-class families who had participated in the classroom observation and interview phase. As a result, I do not have data from classroom observations or parent-teacher conferences for Alexander.

20. The Suzuki method is labor intensive. Students are required to listen to music about one hour per day. Also, both child and parent(s) are expected to practice daily and to attend every lesson together.

21. Hart and Risley (1995) reported a similar difference in speech patterns. In their sample, by about age three, children of professionals had larger vocabularies and spoke more utterances per hour than the *parents* of similarly aged children on welfare.

22. This section focuses primarily on the concerns of black parents. Whites, of course, also benefited from race relations, notably in the scattering of poor white families in working-class neighborhoods rather than being concentrated in dense settings with other poor families (Massey and Denton 1993).

23. Activities coded as "organized" are Scouts/ Brownies, music lessons, any type of sports lesson (e.g., gymnastics, karate), any type of league-organized sports (e.g., Little League), dance lessons, choir, religious classes (excluding religious primary school), arts and crafts classes, and any classes held at a recreation center.

24. As other studies have found, the mothers in my sample were far more knowledgeable than the fathers about their children's daily lives and spent more time caring for children (Crouter et. al. 1999; Thompson 1999). Family observations showed fathers playing a very important role in family dynamics, however, especially by contributing laughter and humor (Lareau 2000b).

25. Some data are missing. The list of activities was so long we sometimes shortened it to conserve time (we always asked respondents, however, whether there were any activities their children had experienced that were not covered in the list). On average, middle-class parents were not queried concerning 2.5 of the approximately 20 items on the list; working-class parents were not asked about 3.0 items; and poor parents were not asked about 2.0 items. Since the sample is non-random, inferential procedures are not applicable. At a reviewer's request, I carried out a Scheffe post hoc test of group differences and found significant differences (at the $p < .001$ level) between the middle-class children and the working-class and poor children. The difference between working-class and poor children is non-significant (at the $p < .05$ level). Statistically significant differences do not occur across racial groups or by gender; nor are there significant interactions between race or gender and class

26. Recent time-diary data suggest that middleclass parents' reports of how much time their children spend watching television are significantly lower than their children's actual viewing time (Hofferth 1999). There is no comparable gap shown in national data for less educated parents.

27. During an interview, Ms. Yanelli estimated that during the previous two weeks, she had used the belt twice, but she noted that her use varied widely. Not all working-class and poor parents in the study used physical punishment, but the great majority did rely heavily on directives.

28. Interviews were open-ended; respondents' varied answers preclude summarizing the data in a single scale that would accurately measure differences in kinship ties by class. For details regarding social class and kin group contact, see Fischer (1982).

29. The overall sample included 36 middle-class, 26 working-class, and 26 poor families. For the question on teachers, there were responses from 31 middle-class parents, 21 working-class parents, and 25 poor parents. For the question on doctors,

the responses by class numbered 26, 21, and 22. Similar results were found for knowing a psychologist, family counselor, or lawyer (data available from the author). Race did not influence the results.

30. How misguided parents' suspicions might be is hard to assess. The counselor at Lower Richmond, who regularly reported children to the Department of Human Services as victims of neglect, maintained that she did so only in the gravest cases and only after repeated interventions had failed. The working-class and poor parents, however, generally saw "the school's actions" as swift, capricious, and arbitrary.

31. Not all professionals accommodated children's participation. Regardless of these adults' overt attitudes, though, we routinely observed that middle-class mothers monitor and intervene in their children's interactions with professionals.

32. Ms. McAllister told me about this visit; we did not observe it. It is striking that she perceived only the black male field-worker as being at risk.

33. Middle-class parents sometimes appeared slightly anxious during parent-teacher conferences, but overall, they spoke more and asked educators more questions than did working-class and poor parents.

34. The higher levels of institutional reports of child neglect, child abuse, and other family difficulties among poor families may reflect this group's greater vulnerability to institutional intervention (e.g., see L. Gordon 1989).

35. In 2002, a single sport could cost as much as $5,000 annually. Yearly league fees for ice hockey run to $2,700; equipment costs are high as well (Halbfinger 2002).

36. Middle-class adults do not live problem-free lives, but compared with the working class and poor, they have more varied occupational experiences and greater access to jobs with higher economic returns.

37. Many middle-class parents remarked that forcing a child to take piano lessons was wrong. Nevertheless, they continued to stress the importance of "exposure."

38. Similarly, whether concerted cultivation and the accomplishment of natural growth are new historical developments rather than modifications of earlier forms of childrearing cannot be determined from the study's findings. The "institutionalization of children's leisure" seems to be increasing (Corsaro 1997). Hays (1996) argues that families increasingly are "invaded" by the "logic of impersonal, competitive, contractual, commodified, efficient, profit-maximizing, self-interested relations" (p. 11). In addition to evidence of a new increase in children's organized activities (Sandberg and Hofferth 2001), none of the middle-class parents in the study reported having childhood schedules comparable to their children's. Change over time in parents' intervention in education and in the amount of reasoning in middle-class families also are difficult to determine accurately. Kohn and Schooler's (1983) study suggests little change with regard to reasoning, but other commentators insist there has been a rise in the amount of negotiating between parents and children (Chidekel 2002; Kropp 2001). Such debates can not be resolved without additional careful historical research.

39. The time-use differences we observed were part of the taken-for-granted aspects of daily life; they were generally unnoticed by family members. For example, the working-class Yanellis considered themselves "really busy" if they had one baseball game on Saturday and an extended family gathering on Sunday. The Tallingers and other middle-class families would have considered this a slow weekend.

40. These findings are compatible with others showing children as aware of race at relatively early ages (Van Ausdale and Feagin 1996). At the two sites, girls often played in racially segregated groups during recess; boys tended to play in racially integrated groups.

References

Aries, Philippe. 1962. *Centuries of Childhood: A Social History of the Family*. Translated by R. Baldick. London, England: Cape.

Bernstein, Basil. 1971. *Class, Codes, and Control: Theoretical Studies towards a Sociology of Language*. New York: Schocken Books.

Bianchi, Suzanne M. 2000. "Maternal Employment and Time with Children: Dramatic Change or Surprising Continuity." *Demography* 37:401–14.

Bianchi, Suzane and John Robinson. 1997. "What Did You Do Today? Children's Use of Time, Family Composition, and Acquisition of Social Capital." *Journal of Marriage and the Family* 59:332–44.

Bourdieu, Pierre. 1976. "Marriage Strategies as Strategies of Social Reproduction." Pp. 117–44 in *Family and Society*, edited by R. Forster and O. Ranum. Baltimore, MD: Johns Hopkins University Press.

———. 1984. *Distinction: A Social Critique of the Judgment of Taste*. Cambridge, MA: Harvard University Press.

———. 1986. "The Forms of Capital." Pp. 241–58 in *Handbook of Theory and Research for the Sociology of Education*, edited by J. C. Richardson. New York: Greenwood.

———. 1989. *The State Nobility: Elite Schools in the Field of Power*. Stanford, CA: Stanford University Press.

Bronfenbrenner, Urie. 1966. "Socialization and Social Class through Time and Space." Pp. 362–77 in *Class, Status and Power*, edited by R. Bendix and S. M. Lipset. New York: Free Press.

Burawoy, Michael, Alice Burton, Ann Arnett Ferguson, and Kathryn J. Fox, eds. 1991. *Ethnography Unbound: Power and Resistance in the Modern Metropolis*. Berkeley, CA: University of California Press.

Chidekel, Dana. 2002. *Parents in Charge*. New York: Simon and Schuster.

Conley, Dalton. 1999. *Being Black, Living in the Red: Race, Wealth, and Social Policy in America*. Berkeley, CA: University of California Press.

Corsaro, William A. 1997. *The Sociology of Childhood*. Thousand Oaks, CA: Pine Forge.

Crouter, Ann C, Heather Helms-Erikson, Kimberly Updegraff, and Susan M. McHale. 1999. "Conditions Underlying Parents' Knowledge about Children's Daily Lives in Middle Childhood: Between—and within—Family Comparisons." *Child Development* 70:246–59.

Daley, Kerry J. 2001. "Deconstructing Family Time: From Ideology to Lived Experience." *Journal of Marriage and the Family* 63:238–94.

Donzelot, Jacques. 1979. *The Policing of Families*. Translated by R. Hurley. New York: Pantheon.

Epstein, Joyce. 2001. *Schools, Family, and Community Partnerships*. Boulder, CO: Westview.

Erikson, Robert, and John H. Goldthorpe. 1993. *The Constant Flux: A Study of Class Mobility in Industrial Societies*. Oxford, England: Clarendon.

Fischer, Claude. 1982. *To Dwell among Friends*. Chicago: University of Chicago Press.

Fordham, Signithia and John U. Ogbu. 1986. "Black Students' School Success: Coping with the 'Burden of Acting White.'" *The Urban Review* 18:176–206.

Gordon, Linda. 1989. *Heroes of Their Own Lives: The Politics and History of Family Violence*. New York: Penguin.

Halbfinger, David M. 2002. "A Hockey Parent's Life: Time, Money, and Yes, Frustration." *New York Times*, January 12, p. 29.

Hart, Betty and Todd Risley. 1995. *Meaningful Differences in the Everyday Experience of Young American Children*. Baltimore, MD: Paul Brooks.

Hays, Sharon. 1996. *The Cultural Contradictions of Motherhood*. New Haven, CT: Yale University Press.

Heath, Shirley Brice. 1983. *Ways with Words*. London, England: Cambridge University Press.

Heimer, Carol A. and Lisa Staffen. 1998. *For the Sake of the Children: The Social Organization of Responsibility in the Hospital and at Home*. Chicago, IL: University of Chicago Press.

Hertz, Rosanna and Nancy L. Marshall, eds. 2001. *Working Families: The Transformation of the American Home*. Berkeley, CA: University of California Press.

Hess, Robert and Gerald Handel. 1974. *Family Worlds: A Psychosocial Approach to Family Life*. Chicago, IL: University of Chicago Press.

Hochschild, Arlie Russell. 1989. *The Second Shift: Working Parents and the Revolution at Home*. New York: Viking.

Hochschild, Jennifer L. 1995. *Facing Up to The American Dream*. Princeton, NJ: Princeton University Press.

Hofferth, Sandra L. 1999. "Family Reading to Young Children: Social Desirability and Cultural Biases in Reporting" (Working paper no. 005-99, May 13, 1999). Institute for Survey Research, Center for Ethnography of Everyday Life, University of Michigan, Ann Arbor, MI. (http://www.ethno.isr.umich.edu/06papers. html).

Hofferth, Sandra and John Sandberg. 2001a. "Changes in American Children's Time, 1981–1997." Pp. 193–232 in *Advances in Life Course Research*, vol. 6, *Children at the Millennium: Where Have We Come From, Where Are We Going?*, edited by S. Hofferth and T. Owens. Oxford, England, Eslevier Science Ltd.

———. 2001b. "How American Children Spend Their Time." *Journal of Marriage and the Family* 63:295–308.

Jacobs, Jerry and Kathleen Gerson. 1998. "Who Are the Overworked Americans?" *Review of Social Economy* 56:442–59.

Juster, F. Thomas and Frank P. Stafford, eds. 1985. *Time, Goods, and Well-Being*. Ann Arbor, MI: Survey Research Center, Institute for Social Research.

Kingston, Paul. 2000. *The Classless Society*. Stanford, CA: Stanford University Press.

Kohn, Melvin and Carmi Schooler, eds. 1983. *Work and Personality: An Inquiry into the Impact of Social Stratification*. Norwood, NJ: Ablex.

Kropp, Paul. 2001. *I'll Be the Parent, You Be the Child*. New York: Fisher Books.

Lamont, Michele. 2000. *The Dignity of Working Men: Morality and the Boundaries of Race, Class, and Immigration*. Cambridge, MA: Harvard University Press.

Lareau, Annette. Forthcoming. *Unequal Childhood: Class, Race, and Family Life*. Berkeley, CA: University of California Press.

———. 2002. "Doing Multi-Person, Multi-Site 'Ethnographic' Work: A Reflective, Critical Essay." Department of Sociology, Temple University, Philadelphia, PA. Unpublished manuscript.

———. 2000a. *Home Advantage: Social Class and Parental Intervention in Elementary Education*. 2d ed. Lanham, MD: Rowman and Littlefield.

———. 2000b. "My Wife Can Tell Me Who I Know: Methodological and Conceptual Issues in Studying Fathers." *Qualitative Sociology* 23:407–33.

Lever, Janet. 1988. "Sex Differences in the Complexity of Children's Play and Games." Pp. 324–44 in *Childhood Socialization*, edited by G. Handel. New York: Aldine de Gruyter.

Marsiglio, William. 1991. "Paternal Engagement Activities with Minor Children." *Journal of Marriage and the Family* 53:973–86.

Massey, Douglas and Nancy Denton. 1993. *American Apartheid*. Cambridge, MA: Harvard University Press.

McLanahan, Sara and Gary Sandefur. 1994. *Growing Up with a Single Parent: What Hurts, What Helps*. Cambridge, MA: Harvard University Press.

Medrich, Elliot, Judith Roizen, Victor Rubin, and Stuart Buckley. 1982. *The Serious Business of Growing Up*. Berkeley, CA: University of California Press.

Menaghan, Elizabeth G. 1991. "Work Experiences and Family Interaction Processes: The Long Reach of the Job?" *Annual Review of Sociology* 17:419–44.

Newman, Kathleen. 1993. *Declining Fortunes: The Withering of the American Dream*. New York: Basic Books.

Pattillo-McCoy, Mary 1999. *Black Picket Fences: Privilege and Peril among the Black Middle-Class*. Chicago, IL: University of Chicago Press.

Presser, Harriet B. 1989. "Can We Make Time for Children? The Economy, Work Schedules, and Child Care." *Demography* 26:523–43.

Robinson, John P. and Geoffry Godbey. 1997. *Time for Life: The Surprising Ways Americans Use Their Time*. University Park, PA: The Pennsylvania State Press.

Rubin, Lillian 1976. *Worlds of Pain: Life in a Working-Class Family*. New York: Basic Books.

Sandberg, John F. and Sandra L. Hofferth. 2001. "Changes in Children's Time with Parents, U.S., 1981–1997." *Demography* 38:423–36.

Shehan, Constance L., ed. 1999. *Through the Eyes of the Child: Re-Visioning Children as Active Agents of Family Life*. New York: JAI Press.

Schemari, James. 2002. "Practice Makes Perfect (and Poorer Parents)." *The New York Times*, January 27, p. 11).

Skolnick, Arlene. 1991. *Embattled Paradise: The American Family in an Age of Uncertainty*. New York: Basic Books.

Tatum, Beverly Daniel. 1997. *Why Are All the Black Kids Sitting Together in the Cafeteria? And Other Conversations about Race*. New York: Basic Books.

Thompson, Shona M. 1999. *Mother's Taxi: Sport and Women's Labor*. Albany, NY: SUNY Press.

Thorne, Barrie. 2001. "Growing Up in Oakland: Orbits of Class, 'Race,' and Culture." Paper presented at the annual meeting of the American Sociological Association, August 19, Anaheim, CA.

Van Ausdale, Debra and Joe R. Feagin. 1996. "Using Racial and Ethnic Concepts: The Critical Case of Very Young Children." *American Sociological Review* 61:779–93.

Waksler, Frances. 1991. *Studying the Social Worlds of Children*. Bristol, England: Falmer.

Waters, Mary. 1999. *Black Identities: West Indian Immigrant Dreams and American Realities*. New York: Russell Sage Foundation.

Wright, Erik Olin. 1997. *Class Counts: Comparative Studies in Class Analysis*. Cambridge, England: Cambridge University Press.

Wrigley, Julia. 1989. "Do Young Children Need Intellectual Stimulation? Experts' Advice to Parents, 1900–1985." *History of Education* 29:41–75.

Zelizer, Vivianna. 1985. *Pricing the Priceless Child: The Changing Social Value of Children*. New York: Basic Books.

Zick, Cathleen D. and W. Keith Bryant. 1996. "A New Look at Parents' Time Spent in Child Care: Primary and Secondary Time Use." *Social Science Research* 25:260–80.

Collective Identity and the Burden of "Acting White" in Black History, Community, and Education

JOHN U. OGBU

Introduction

Having conducted comparative research on minority education for more than 15 years, I came to the conclusion that discrimination in society and school as well as minority responses to the discrimination, though significant, are not enough to explain why there are differences in the school performance among minority groups. My comparative study suggested that two additional factors from the dynamics in minority communities also contributed to the school performance differences. In a joint publication with Dr. Signithia Fordham in 1986, we stated that the two additional factors were *collective identity* or *fictive kinship* and *cultural frame of reference* (Fordham and Ogbu, 1986). We also reported a study of Capital High students in Washington, D. C. where we found that the two factors played a major role in the school performance of Black adolescents.

The joint article has generated responses from the academic community beyond what we anticipated. It is the subject of dissertation studies (Carter, 1999; O'Connor, 1996; Taylor, 2001), several publications (Ainsworth-Darnell and Downey, 1998; Bergin and Cooks, 2002; Cook and Ludwig, 1997) and organized sessions at professional meetings (Epstein, 2003; Horvat and O'Connor, 2001). During the past 2 years, I have reviewed more than a dozen book and journal manuscripts on oppositional culture and schooling for publishers. Although it is gratifying to see the impact of the joint article on the academic community, the potential contributions of these activities to scholarship are limited by misinterpretations of the problem, replacing the thesis, and making a different conclusion.

One of the shortcomings of current scholarship is the failure to distinguish among three different perspectives on collective identity, cultural frame of reference, and the schooling of Black adolescents. This has resulted in the translating of my cultural–ecological framework into a single-factor hypothesis of *oppositional culture*. In effect, critics construct and study a different problem than the one we laid out in the joint article.

An equally serious problem is that there is no evidence that authors are aware that throughout their history Black Americans have experienced the "burden of 'acting White'" because of their oppositional collective identity and cultural frame of reference. Lacking this knowledge, critics ignore the historical and community contexts of Black students' behavior and focus almost exclusively on the transactions between the students and their school. Basing their analysis on data collected at the level of student–school transactions, it is not surprising that some critics accuse Fordham and myself of assigning a race label ("acting White") to a common ridicule, namely, teasing and harassment, endured by academically achieving adolescents or "nerds." They also believe that we have read too much into a "concept that they themselves manufactured."

The purpose of this paper is to correct these misinterpretations. I will start with the meaning of collective identity and how it differs from other identity concepts used in discussing Black students' experiences. This will be followed by a brief account of the evolution of Black American collective identity, a presentation of my study of Black American experience with the "burden of 'acting White'" in contemporary United States, and conclude with an exploration of a possible continuity between Black historical and community experiences with the "burden of 'acting White'" and the experience of Black students that I and my students have studied in Stockton (1968–70), Oakland (1989–93), San Francisco (1991–92), and Shaker Heights (1997).

What Is Collective Identity?

Some Perspectives on Identity

Psychologists have examined the development and school experience of minority children from a number of interesting perspectives as it relates to identity. Among them are (a) *the Ericksonian ego identity* (Hauser, 1972), (b) *ethnic identity* based on Erickson's theory (Phinney and Rosenthal, 1992; Phinney and Rotheram, 1987); (c) *racial identity* as measured by racial attitudes (Branch, 1999); and (d) *underclass oppositional identity* (Cross, Strauss and Fhagen-Smith, 1999, pp. 29–30). Among non-psychologists some have proposed (a) *negotiated identity* (Yon, 2000), and (b) *circumstantial/marketable identity or politics of recognition* (Cornell and Hartman, 1998). These are useful and interesting ways of looking at identity and minority status. But they have to be distinguished from collective identity as used in this paper.

What Is Collective Identity?

Collective identity refers to people's sense of who they are, their "we-feeling" or "belonging." People express their collective identity with emblems or cultural symbols which reflect their attitudes, beliefs, feelings, behaviors, and language or dialect. The persistence of a group's collective identity depends on the continuity of the external (historical and structural) forces that contributed to its formation. It also depends on the continuity of responses of the group (Castile and Kushner, 1981; DeVos, 1995; Spicer, 1966, 1971).

Collective identity usually develops because of people's collective experience or series of collective experiences. Warfare, conquest, colonization, forced labor, mass emigration, imposition of an outcast status, and enslavement are examples of the collective experience that leads to the formation of collective identity (Castile and Kushner, 1981; DeVos, 1995; Spicer, 1967). Usually, the collective identity of an oppressed minority group is created and maintained by two sets of factors: status problems and minority response to status problems.

Status Problems

Status problems are external forces that mark a group of people as a distinct segment from the rest of the population. A group so created is usually bounded and named. For example, the Emperor of Japan, by proclamation, created the Burakumin as an outcast group from the Japanese people when Japan established a four-rigid, caste-like stratification system placing the Burakumin as the outcast group during the Edoera in the 17th century. Before the establishment of the status groups, the people in the outcast category, the Burakumin, had been, like other Japanese, warriors, peasants, and artisans. Designated as an outcast, the Burakumin (people of special hamlet or residential area) were assigned the role of slaughtering animals and executing criminals, functions which the general public perceived as "polluting functions" under Buddhist and Shintoist beliefs. Their social ostracism and discrimination have continued even after they were emancipated in 1871 (DeVos, 1967; Hirasawa and Nabeshima, 1995). Similarly, White Americans created Black Americans as a separate and an enduring segment of the United States society through enslavement. Status problems are collective problems which members of the subordinate group find difficult if not impossible to solve within the existing system of majority–minority relations. They include the following.

1. *Involuntary incorporation into society:* Usually these minorities do not become minorities by choice. Rather they are forced into minority status against their will by conquest, colonization, enslavement (e.g., Black Americans) or arbitrary subjection to the status of a pariah caste (e.g., the Burakumin of Japan).
2. *Instrumental discrimination:* e.g., denial of equal access to good jobs, education, political participation, and housing.
3. *Social subordination:* e.g., residential and social segregation, hostility and violence; prohibition of intermarriage; requirement of the offsprings of intergroup mating to affiliate with one group with no choice. In some cases oppressed minorities are forced against their will to assimilate into the dominant group, although this assimilation usually results in marginalization.
4. *Expressive mistreatment:* e.g., cultural, language, and intellectual denigration.

Dominant group members stigmatize minorities' food, clothing, music, values, behaviors, and language or dialect as bad and inferior to theirs. These four mechanisms are used by the dominant group to create and maintain the collective identity of the minorities; i.e., to "carve them out" and maintain them as a separate segment of society with a distinct identity. The existence of the minorities with distinct collective identity remains as long as these mechanisms or mistreatment of the minorities remain (Ogbu, 2000).

The Response of Minorities to Status Problems

Both minorities as a group and as individuals feel the impact of status problems. The minorities experience their mistreatment regardless of their individual differences in education and ability, in status, physical appearance, or place of residence. They know fully well that they do not have the option of membership in the dominant group; they also know that they cannot easily escape from their more or less ascribed membership in a subordinate and disparaged group. Individuals who "pass" physically or culturally often find that the social and psychological costs are very high. Oppressed minorities are bitter for being forced into minority status and subjected to oppression. They usually hold the dominant group responsible for their "troubles" (e.g., their inferior economic and political status, demeaning social positions, poor health and housing, and stigmatized cultures and languages or dialects). Under this circumstance, involuntary minorities respond collectively as a group and they also respond as individuals in ways that reinforce their separate existence and collective identity. Furthermore, their response often makes their oppositional collective identity vis-a-vis their perceptions of the collective identity of the dominant group. That is, their very attempts to solve their status problem lead them to develop a new sense of who they are, that is in opposition to their understanding of who the dominant group members are.

Cultural and Language Frames of Reference

Closely related to their sense of collective identity is the way minorities interpret the cultural and language or dialect differences between them and the dominant group. We use the term 'cultural frame of reference' to refer to the correct way of behaving and 'language or dialect frame of reference' to refer to the correct way of talking from the point of view of the minorities. Cultural and language frames of reference are closely tied to collective identity, so that we can speak of them as the cultural identity and the language identity of the minorities. Where the latter is oppositional, the former is usually oppositional. Furthermore, where that is the case, we can regard the situation as one of oppositional culture and oppositional language or dialect. The relationship—oppositional or non-oppositional—between the cultural and language frames of reference of the minorities and that of the dominant group, determines to some degree the difficulty individual members of the minority group have in crossing cultural and language boundaries or learning to behave and talk like White people. However, this does not mean that all members of the minority group respond to the culture and language of the dominant group in opposition. As we shall see, minorities usually develop some strategies to deal with the demands that they behave and talk like dominant group members in order to achieve self-betterment in situations controlled by members of the dominant group.

The Case of Black Americans

Black American oppositional collective identity began to form before emancipation and has remained to the present. We have more information on the subject for more recent than earlier periods.

Pre-Emancipation Period

Status Problems

Enslavement and mistreatment under slavery: Black Americans became involuntary minorities when they were enslaved by White Americans. For more than 200 years they were denied basic human rights, exploited economically, politically, socially, and expressively. They were tightly controlled by White slave owners who forced them to behave like slaves. They were forbidden to behave in certain ways considered White prerogatives and were punished if they disobeyed. For example, they were punished for learning to read and write, where slaves were forbidden these activities (Haley, 1976). Punishment was sometimes extended to all slaves on the plantation, not just limited to the slave who committed the offence. This collective punishment was important in the creation of Black collective identity.

The treatment of Blacks following Nat Turner's "insurrection" is a good example of the collective blame and punishment which increased their sense of being a separate people with a collective identity. A slave, Nat Turner, led an "insurrection" in Southampton, Virginia in 1831. Following this incident, the movement of *all* Black people throughout the United States was restricted. Blacks were forbidden to assemble among themselves. The restriction even applied to children. For example, Black children in Washington, DC. were no longer allowed to attend Sunday School with White children as they did previously for no other reason than that they were Black (Fordham, 1984; Styron, 1966).

Instrumental discrimination: During slavery, Blacks were excluded by law and custom from economic, political, and other opportunities open to Whites.

Social discrimination: Non-reciprocal social interaction between Blacks and Whites was instituted during slavery. According to Starker (1971; pp. 6), the ritual of social interaction required Blacks and Whites to behave toward each other in certain prescribed ways. For example, they had to use certain prescribed forms of address that expressed the "ritual." Blacks addressed White slave owners as master (*massa*), mistress (*mistis*), miss (*missy*), boss or *buckra,* with or without given names. Slave owners addressed Blacks as aunt, uncle, mammy, sometimes daddy, boy (Starker, 1971; pp. 6). The etiquette also required slaves to behave in a certain manner when he or she was spoken to by Whites. For example, the slave had to "stand attentively, respond politely, bow servilely to the extent, at times, of extreme evasion and deceit" (Starker, 1971; pp. 7).

Expressive Discrimination: Expressive discrimination refers to White Americans' beliefs that Black slaves were culturally, linguistically and intellectually inferior to them; it also refers to the treatment of Blacks based on such beliefs. Historically, the overarching ideology of White American was that Black Americans belonged to a race that was inferior to the White race biologically, culturally, and socially.

White denigration of Black culture began during slavery, with the myth that the slaves came from the "dark continent" of Africa that had not produced civilizations like other continents (Becknell, 1987). They forced the slaves to give up their African cultures and to adopt superior White culture. White cultural values, behaviors, and speech were presented as correct or proper; in contrast, Black cultural values, behaviors, and speech were presented as incorrect and improper.

In the case of language, slave owners took deliberate steps to rid the slaves of their indigenous African languages. There appeared to be a policy not to have several slaves speaking the same language on a plantation for fear that they would teach others their language, and that speaking the same language would make it easy for slaves to plan an escape or a slave revolt. To avoid such incidents, the slaves were forced to speak English. The language situation during slavery, especially the evolution of Black English dialects, contributed to the creation of Blacks as a separate and enduring people with a distinct collective identity.

Intellectual denigration was (and is) an expressive exploitation because it makes White people feel good to think that they are more intelligent than Blacks.

Black Response to Status Problems During Slavery

Response to forced incorporation: Black Americans began to develop their sense of collective identity and of belonging together during slavery. Collective experience of oppression and exploitation caused them to develop the sense of a Black community which embodied their collective racial identity. It has been suggested that racial identity was more important than class or gender identity for the slaves because they knew only too well that all of them, regardless of class or gender, could be punished for an offence of one slave; and they could also be rewarded because of the good deed of one (Green, 1981; Rawick, 1972). The racial identity formed during slavery has continued to influence Black perceptions of and responses to White treatment to this day. In my ethnographic research in Black communities, I have often found that regardless of social class and gender, Black Americans tend to code their experiences with White Americans and with social institutions in terms of race, and not class or gender.

The expressive response of Blacks was particularly important in their construction and maintenance of oppositional collective identity. As noted earlier, White people forced Blacks to give up their African cultures and languages. Under oppression, Blacks developed a new culture and an English dialect different from and oppositional to the White way of behaving and talking (Green, 1981). Another area of expressing opposition was religion. Black religion evolved to satisfy slave master's expectations that this would make it easier to control Blacks, but it turned out to be the opposite of those expectations. Reverend Calvin Marshall described this paradox as follows:

> (T)he (White)man systematically killed your (i.e., Black) language, killed your culture, tried to kill your soul, tried to blot you out—but somewhere along the way he gave us Christianity and gave it to use to enslave us. But it freed us because we understood things about it and we made it work for us in ways that it never worked for him (Holt 1972).

Black music was yet another aspect of cultural evolution for expressing difference and opposition to White domination and White ways. Blacks used their music not only to entertain, lighten the burden of their labor and other sufferings but also as a means of communication, especially the transmission of messages they did not want White people to understand. For example, when Harriet Tubman sang "Steal Away, Steal Away, Steal Away to Jesus" she was not pleading for Blacks to convert to Christianity. Rather, she was telling them to run away through the Underground Railroad to the North of the United States or to Canada (Baer, 1984; Becknell 1987; pp. 45–49).

The development of the Black English dialect was yet another means of expressing differences, toward collective identity. Blacks developed their dialect because, as noted earlier, slave owners forbaded them to speak indigenous African languages and required them to speak the English dialect. The slaves developed an English dialect that the slave masters did not and could not understand (Becknell, 1987; Holt, 1972).

Black American English dialect differs from White American Standard English in phonology, morphology, and syntax. But these differences are not as important for oppositional collective identity as are differences due to secondary meanings. The secondary meanings arose from dialect inversions. The inversion was that Blacks assigned to words, phrases, or statements reverse meanings or changed their functions from what they mean to White people. Thus, the same words appearing in both White English and Black English may have different and, often, opposite meanings. For example, the word "bad" which always means "bad" in White peoples' English sometimes means "good" in Black English.

According to Holt (1972) Black slaves developed their linguistic opposition because they recognized that to use English like their White masters would mean submitting to an identity defeat. That is, it would mean that they accepted definitions of their slave or caste status built into the White semantic system. Language inversion "emerged during slavery to fight both linguistic and psychological entrapment" (Holt, 1972; pp. 154).

The Burden of Acting White During Slavery

Black Americans became bi-cultural and bi-dialectical during slavery because they lived and worked in two different worlds which expected them to think, act, and react in a particular way, depending on where they found themselves. In the Black community and among themselves, most Blacks felt at ease to talk and do things they would never attempt in a White environment. Conversely, in a White environment, Blacks talked and behaved as White people expected, which would be inappropriate among the Black community (Becknell, 1987; pp. 30).

As noted earlier, the ritual of social interaction between Blacks and Whites established during slavery required the two groups to behave toward each other in certain prescribed ways. Blacks were expected to act and react the way Whites wanted them to, otherwise, they would be punished or even put to death. As survival was the name of the game for Blacks, they talked and behaved the way Whites wanted.

Note, however, that Whites did not require Blacks to talk and behave the same way that White people actually talked and behaved; i.e., White slave owners did not require Blacks to "act White." In fact, Blacks were forbidden to talk like Whites; e.g., they were forbidden to learn to read and write. What the Whites wanted was for Blacks to talk and behave according to White people's construction of Black speech and cultural behavior. When in front of White people, Blacks tried to talk and behave out of compliance to what White people were demanding. But when they were among themselves, they acted according to their cultural ways that White people hardly observed.

The same situation existed with regard to speech. White English dialect was portrayed by Whites and Blacks as proper, correct, good, and standard. Black English dialect, by contrast, was stigmatized as improper, incorrect, flat, country, slangish, and bad. Although White people required Blacks to speak in a particular way, the requirement was not for Blacks to talk like White people actually talked; i.e., White people did not require Black slaves to speak "correct" or "standard English." Rather, they wanted Blacks to talk according to the White construction of Black speech based on Black "improper English." Blacks talked the way Whites wanted them to talk when with Whites out of compliance, but talked "Black" among themselves.

The burden of "acting White" before emancipation was how to comply with the White demand that Blacks should behave and talk like Blacks the way Whites thought that Blacks talked and behaved. It was not that Blacks should choose between behaving and talking the way White people actually behaved and talked and the way they themselves preferred to behave and talk.

There was no uniformity in Black response to this conflicting demand before emancipation. Rather, they evolved several strategies of coping with the "burden of 'acting White." This is evident in the variety of stock characters portrayed in novels, plays, drama, short stories and films of and about that era (Bogle, 1989; Nestby, 1982; Starker, 1971). The characters included accommodatative slaves, rebellious slaves, clowns, tragic mulattoes. Black mammies and coons. These characters represented different responses to the "burden of 'acting White." The accommodative slave (toms, servile Negro), for e.g., accepted his place as defined by Whites; and behaved and talked according to the White definition. The rebellious slave or "bad Negro" defied the law and the ritual of non-reciprocal social interaction. Black mammies were the nurturers of White offspring.

Black Collective Identity After Emancipation

Status Problems

Blacks continued to face status problems after emancipation. Instrumentally, they were subjected to extreme economic exploitation. They were denied free and fair competition with Whites in employment, wages, promotion and entrepreneurship (Moore, 1981; Norgren and Hill, 1964; Novak, 1978). Before 1960, about the only places where Blacks could get jobs based on formal education and ability were segregated educational and health institutions serving the Black community (Frazier, 1957; Marshall, 1967; Ross, 1967).

Although school credentials were a requirement for employment in the wider society, White employers used a job ceiling to deny them access to jobs, promotion, and wages commensurate with their qualifications.

In the social domain, residential, sexual, social, and school segregation continued. Black people were residentially segregated by statute, regulatory authorities, and custom (Ogbu and Margold, 1986). School segregation followed suit. In many states sexual relationship between white women and Black men was forbidden and severely punished when the taboo was violated (Johnson, 1943, p. 220; Myrdal, 1944). Until the year 2000, there was a culturally sanctioned rule backed by statutes in many states, namely, that biracial children should be defined as Black and should affiliate with Blacks (Rockquemore and Brunsma, 2002; Wright, 2001).

Ritual non-reciprocal social interaction continued. White people continued to believe that Blacks were inferior to them. These beliefs were expressed in their treatment of Blacks' jokes, novels, short stories, drama, and movies (Johnson, 1931, p. 100). The beliefs aroused White aversion to Blacks and this, in turn, led to another White belief, namely, that Black Americans were not assimilable. Whites did not mean by this that Blacks were not capable of acquiring the education, economic status, and lifestyle of the White middle class. Rather, what they meant was that it was not desirable or acceptable to assimilate Blacks into White society to share their collective identity because they were colored and inferior (Myrdal, 1944, p. 54, 100).

Whites continued to make Blacks collectively responsible for the offence of a single Black person. For example, in Rosewood, Florida in January, 1923, about 1,500 white men from Rosewood and surrounding communities went to the Black neighborhood in Rosewood and killed 40 black men, women, and children in retaliation for an alleged rape of a White woman by a Black man (CBS Television Magazine, 60 Minutes (August 5, 1984).

The threats of violence, punishment, and the prevalence of lynching led Blacks to petition the United Nations in 1951 to intervene on their behalf (Patterson, 1951). Blacks suffered because Whites used them as scapegoats in times of economic hardships and political crisis (Frazier, 1957, p. 155–156;

Shapiro, 1988). They were denied political power through disenfranchisement in the Southern states and through gerrymandering in the North.

Black Response to Status Problems after Emancipation

Blacks tried both as a group and as individuals to solve their status problems after emancipation. Blacks firmly believed that they were treated differently and badly because of their race and history. This interpretation of their social reality further motivated them to forge collective solutions to their collective status problems that reinforced their oppositional identity. Their collective solutions included the following:

Instrumental solutions: Blacks accepted the criteria of getting good jobs, decent wages, and upward social mobility through education and hard work like Whites. But they soon realized that there was a job ceiling which prevented them from achieving these goals by merely meeting the criteria or rules that worked for White people. For this reason, they developed folk theories of getting ahead in spite of the job ceiling. As a group, they came to believe that they had to meet additional requirements, which included collective struggle at group level and clientship or uncle tomming, as individuals. The various forms of collective struggle up to the 1960s constituted modes of coping with the instrumental aspect of their status problems. They included the following:

Accommodation: Booker T. Washington's idea of accommodation under the caste-like system of the old South was advocated. He believed that Black Americans could achieve economic self-sufficiency through industrial education and vocational training for the Black masses and through independent business enterprise for the higher classes. He emphasized working within mutually separate collective identities for Blacks and Whites (Hall, 1979).

Integration with equality of opportunity: W. E. B. DuBois and the National Association for the Advancement of Colored People (NAACP) disagreed with Washington's view. By contrast, they demanded equality of opportunity with Whites and full acceptance by White people. Actually, some version of this strategy was initiated during slavery by free Blacks like Delany and Douglas. In the 1930s its advocates picketed and boycotted White business in Black communities that discriminated against Blacks (Drake and Cayton, 1970, Hall, 1979; p. 99). This strategy increased the tension and mistrust between Blacks and Whites. More importantly, however, they increased Black Americans' sense of oppositional collective identity (Becknell, 1987).

The third strategy was separatism. The separatists did not believe that it was possible to achieve a satisfactory solution to Black status problems within the American social and economic system. They believed that the solution was for Blacks to leave the United States society both physically and spiritually, while heading for places like Africa, Mexico, Latin America, or a part of the United States set aside for Blacks. The best known separatist movement was led by Marcus Garvey. It appealed to many Blacks, whether or not they formally belonged to it, because the movement promoted Black pride and collective identity (Hall, 1979; Redkey, 1969; Sygnnerstvedt, 1972, p. 133). Another influential separatist movement, especially in its early phase, was the Black Muslim Movement.

Social response: It took about 50 years for the social response to the post-emancipation status problems to crystallize. Locke (1925, p. 631) reports that during the first 50 years, "the minds of Blacks were burrowed in trenches of the Civil War and Reconstruction." But underneath this was a psychological development that eventually enabled Blacks to liberate themselves from "the tyranny of intimidation and implied inferiority" (Locke, 1925, p. 631). The new era arrived in the mid-1920s when Blacks began to demand changes in their representation in the White minds or social image. Until then, the prevailing social image was expressed in the ritualized non-reciprocal interaction and forms of address carried over from slavery, as well as other renditions created by the Civil War (Locke, 1925, p. 631–632). By the 1920s, e.g., "Tom and Sambo" were no longer acceptable. Locke (1925, p. 632) notes that "The Negro today wishes to be known for what he is, even in his faults and shortcomings; (He) scorns a craven and even precarious survival at the price of seeming to be what he is not." Locke quotes an apt passage from a poem by Claude MacKay about the outlook of the *New Negro:*

> Mine is the future, grinding down today
> Like a great landship moving to the sea,
> Where the green hungry waters restlessly
> Heap mammoth pyramids and bark and roar
> Their eerie challenge to the crumbling shore.
> (Locke, 1925; p. 633).

Collective struggle against social discrimination went beyond ending non-reciprocal social interaction. Black Americans demanded social justice and acceptance by White Americans as social equals. Their strategies for achieving these goals included boycotts, protests, riots, civil disobedience, law suits, and lobbying for legislation (Berry, 1971; Weisbrodt, 1991). White Americans, of course, resisted the Black collective struggle for social justice and inclusion. This resistance, in turn, made Blacks more disappointed and mistrustful of White people, a situation that further increased their sense of oppositional collective identity.

Black fear and experience of physical violence also promoted their sense of oppositional collective identity and group loyalty. Group loyalty was also necessary because White violence was often indiscriminate (Fordham, 1985). The Rosewood incident described earlier was an example of White indiscriminate violence after the emancipation period.

Expressive responses: The emergence of the Harlem Renaissance and *The New Negro* also brought changes in the post-emancipation expressive adaptations of Black Americans. New interpretation of the *Negro Spirituals* is a case in point. Before the first quarter of the 20th century, *Negro Spirituals* were not accepted as original creations of folk hymns by Blacks. Instead, they were regarded as imitations of White Wesleyan hymns. Blacks were ashamed of this interpretation, but by the 1920s they were courageous enough to reject the White interpretation that their hymns were not original. Equally important is that Blacks began to express their collective identity at this time in poetry, Jazz Art, and culture (Hayes, nd; p. 666–677).

The Burden of "Acting White" After Emancipation

The burden of "acting White after emancipation, was different from the burden of "acting White" before emancipation. Recall that before emancipation "acting White" was that out of compliance Blacks had to behave and talk in the manner defined for them by the Whites to satisfy White people's expectations. Again, White people did not require that Blacks should behave and talk the way White people themselves actually behaved and talked.

However, after emancipation, Blacks were required to behave and talk the way White people actually behaved and talked: (a) in situations requiring the mastery of certain White knowledge, behaviors, and speech, such as for formal education, upward social mobility, and participation in societal institutions controlled by White people, while (b) Blacks were also now required to behave and to talk like White people to gain social acceptance and to be treated as social equals by White people. Blacks, therefore, now had to master two sets of cultural and dialect frames of reference: (1) Black ways of behaving and talking among themselves; and (2) White ways of behaving and talking in

White-controlled situations. The co-existence of Black and White frames of reference, of course, has had a dynamic relationship and changed over time. What was not required of Blacks was to assume White people's collective identity.

But there was one additional problem: Blacks were often not rewarded or accepted as equal by Whites when they successfully learned to behave and talk like Whites or had obtained stipulated educational qualification.

Coping with the Burden of "Acting White" after Emancipation

After emancipation, Black Americans did not abandon their oppositional cultural and dialect frames of reference to embrace the White cultural frame of reference for education and upward social mobility. However, they accepted the need to behave and talk like White people (to "act White") for education, upward social mobility, equality and acceptance by White people. This was a dilemma for Black people. How they responded to this dilemma, i.e., resolved the tension between the demands that they act according to White frames of reference, rather than the Black frames of reference in situations controlled by White people, constituted their coping with the "burden of acting White." They developed five identifiable coping strategies.

Cultural and linguistic assimilation: Some Black people, after emancipation, chose to assimilate in culture and language. They tried very hard to emulate White people in behavior, speech, and thought because they believed that their chances of success in education, employment in the corporate economy, and in being socially accepted by White people would be better if they abandoned Black frames of reference and emulated White people. Becknell (1987) has described some techniques such Blacks used to assimilate: they straightened their hair with scalp-brushing chemicals because Black people's hair was stigmatized as "bad;" bleached their skin to look more White; some even stopped drinking coffee because coffee made a person "black;" pinched their nose to make it more pointed instead of flat; learned to talk like White people, including going for special coaching to talk more "properly;" distanced themselves socially from other Black people; and joined White churches.

Accommodation without assimilation: Another coping strategy for some was to more or less live in two worlds at different times: Black and White. Within the Black community they behaved and talked according to the Black frames of reference. In the White world, like school, work, and among White people, they behaved and talked like White people required. This category of Blacks could "go home again," according to Becknell (1987).

Ambivalence: The third coping strategy was ambivalence. Ambivalent Blacks knew, for instance, that "proper English" was necessary for school success and for getting good jobs. However, they also knew that no matter how hard a Black person tried to talk like White people, he or she would still sound Black. So, for them, trying to "talk proper" was only "puttin' on" or pretending to be White (Ogbu, 1999), Similarly, some ambivalents believed that the obstacles facing Blacks in employment, wages, promotion, and education were racial; the fact that they were Black, not because they did not behave or talk like White people, was the key (Ogbu, 1999). I will give a concrete example later in the paper.

Resistance or opposition: Some Blacks opposed adopting White cultural and language frames of reference or "acting White" anywhere because they believed or feared that this would mean giving up their Black ways. It would also mean accepting White people's interpretation of the cultural and dialect differences between the two races. From their point of view, White people defined White ways as good and defined Black ways as bad. One informant in Oakland, California, gave a historical explanation of this resistance to "acting White" in the Black community. He said that, since slavery, White Americans have tried to get Black people to replace their inferior culture and dialect with superior White culture and language before White people would accept them. It began with teaching house slaves to imitate their White masters to make them different and superior over field hands. After emancipation, White people established "finishing schools" and "special education" to improve Black speech, manners and behaviors. These programs assumed that Black speech, manners, and behaviors were bad and should be replaced with good White speech, manners, and behaviors. A similar reason was given by some Black parents during ethnographic interviews in San Francisco for not wanting to speak standard English (Luster, 1992).

Encapsulation: Finally, some Blacks were more or less encapsulated in Black cultural and dialect frames of reference. They did not behave or talk like White people because they did not know how to rather than because they were opposed to doing so.

I have limited data on social sanctions or peer pressures against Blacks who chose any of these coping strategies to resolve the conflicting demands. Nor do we have data on how people handled or coped with the social sanctions. But there must have been consequences. More research is needed in this area.

Post-Civil Rights Era Black Responses to "Acting White"
Status Problems

Significant changes have occurred in the status problems of Blacks since the civil rights movement of the 1960s. These changes were most evident in the economic and political sectors. The factors that raised the job ceiling for Blacks included (a) executive orders (e.g., President Kennedy's Committee on Equal Employment Opportunity in 1961); (b) federal legislation (e.g., Title VIII of the Civil Rights Act of 1964); (c) the war on poverty; and (d) pressures from civil-rights organizations (Burkey, 1971; Ferman, Kornbluh and Miller, 1968). Although the changes have benefited mainly college-educated Blacks, not the Black masses, college-educated Blacks in the White establishments have complained of a glass ceiling. They say that they lag behind their White peers in promotion because of their race (Benjamin, 1991; Case, 1995).

Social discrimination: This has decreased but has not been entirely eliminated. Hostility and violence are still directed against Blacks and other minorities in times of economic recession, such as during the 1980s (State of California, 1982). The definition of inter-racial children as Black and their affiliation with Blacks continued until the census of 2000. Children can now choose their affiliation. Residential and school integration is now more or less a matter of economic status, but segregation remains because of "White flight."

Expressive discrimination: Many Whites probably no longer believe that Blacks are inferior to Whites but the residue of this belief remains. A poll conducted by the *Newsweek* magazine in 1978 found that about one quarter of the Whites (25%) still believed that Blacks had less intelligence than Whites, and about 15% thought that Blacks were inferior to White people (Newsweek, February 26, 1979, p. 48). The publication of *The Bell Curve* by Herrnstein and Murray (1994) is a reminder that the Whites' belief in the inferiority of Blacks still exist even in White "scientific" circles. After a recent report in the *San Francisco Chronicle* about my research on Black academic performance, one reader sent me statistics on standardized test performance along with a lengthy letter on the genetic basis of the low score of Blacks. The debate goes on about Black genetic endowment for intelligence (The Gene Media Forum, 2002). As this goes to press, Black culture and language are still stigmatized.

Black Response to Status Problems in Post Civil Rights Era
The civil rights mobilization of the 1960s reinforced Black collective identity, especially with the emergence of the Black Power Movement. For Blacks, the ideology and strategies of the movement removed the stigma attached to being Black, increased race pride and provided a shared slogan that "Black is Beautiful." Thus, their response to the status problems complemented their collective identity as we find it today.

Oppositional Collective Identity in Contemporary Black Community

Black Americans have always aspired to succeed like White Americans, but they have always been aware of the obstacles facing them because of their status or race (Ferman, Kornbluh and Miller, 1968; Myrdal, 1944; Ogbu, 1978; Rowan, 1967; Sochen, 1972). Another obstacle is the "burden of 'acting White.'" Before and after emancipation, as well as after the civil rights movement, they responded to this obstacle with one of the five culturally patterned strategies or copings described earlier: assimilation, accommodation without assimilation, ambivalence, resistance of opposition, and encapsulation. Clearly, resistance or opposition has always been just one of the coping responses. It is probably by no means the most prevalent coping strategy during any of the periods.

Even though it is just one of the strategies for coping with the "burden of acting White," I focus on it in this section to show that oppositional collective identity or oppositional culture exists in the contemporary Black community or post-civil rights movement and provides the context for understanding why Black students label and avoid some attitudes and behaviors as "White."

In the 1980s, I studied the collective identity and frames of reference in the Black community by reviewing ethnographic and other literature (Ogbu and Margold, 1986). The latter included more than 50 Black American autobiographies (Ogbu and Simons, 1998). I discovered in this research six recurring identity themes: (1) oppositional collective identity; (2) oppositional cultural frame of reference;(3) strategies for coping with the burden of "acting White;" (4) interpretations of the coping strategies; (5) social sanctions or peer pressures against some coping strategies; and (6) coping strategies against the social sanctions. I will revisit each of these now.

Oppositional Collective Identity

One indicator of a sense of collective identity among contemporary Black Americans is the frequency that Black authors cite the passage about "double consciousness" from DuBois' (1982/1903) *Souls of Black Folks*. In the second half of the 20th century, a number of events have reinforced this double consciousness. Among them are the civil rights mobilization, the Black Power Movement. and the Black Muslim Movement. As noted earlier, the Black Power Movement was particularly important in reinforcing the oppositional collective identity. Its ideology and tactics removed the stigma attached to being Black and increased race pride and provided an appealing slogan "Black is Beautiful." These practices removed the fear, shame. and stigma as well as the social costs of being Black for those who wanted to express the outward symbols of Black collective identity. They began to display openly what they had always felt covertly, namely, that they were proud to be Black. The new public and psychological acknowledgement and the expression of Black collective identity have not been limited to activists or poor Blacks. They have reached every segment of the Black America. They have permeated the works of Black artists, performers. and scholars (Becknell, 1987). They have been embraced by Black professionals and the Black middle class in general.

This development was taking place during my ethnographic research in Stockton, California, 1968 and 1970, the hey day of the movement. Thus, I had a chance to observe identity transformations among both poor and middle-class Blacks first-hand. The transformation included shifts in identity labels from "Negro" to "Colored" to "Black;" changes in identity symbols, such as from processed to natural hair style; and changes in organizational membership, such as Black teachers in Stockton who refusal to join Black Teachers' Alliance in 1969 (because the term Black was bad and militant) to 100% membership by the same teachers in the Black Teachers' Alliance in 1972. The changes continued. During my research in Oakland in the early 1990s, a conference was organized in New Orleans by Blacks to change their collective identity label to African Americans. We also studied the response to this label change by Blacks in Oakland.

The strongest evidence of oppositional collective identity among contemporary Black Americans is linguistic. For example, Blacks use positive labels among themselves, such as "soul" (implying eternity, spirituality and transcendence); "brother and sister" (implying some of the closest of kin) and "bloods" (referring to the very stuff of life). In contrast, they label White people, particularly White men, "Ofays" (i.e., enemies, foes). According to Johnson (1972, p. 172), Blacks have only one positive label for White men, namely, "blue-eyed soul brother" which was usually reserved for "hippies" in the 1960s.

Oppositional Frames of Reference

The literature review provided evidence that Black and White cultural and dialect frames of reference are different and oppositional. For example, both Smitherman (1977, p. 75) and Boykin (1986, p. 63) describe Black culture as characterized by spirituality, harmony with nature, and being "in time" rather than "on time." Boykin (1986, p. 63) adds other areas in which Black and White cultures are also oppositional. For example, Blacks use more organic metaphors, have more preference for expressive movement, place more emphasis on inter-connectedness, and have a richer oral tradition. The two cultures differ in cognitive modes and non-verbal discourse (Shade, 1984); styles of walking, talking and gesturing (Folb, 1980:45), in attitudes (Davis and Watson 1985, p. 113; Folb, 1980, p. 45; Weis, 1985, p. 35). The strongest evidence of oppositional frame is in language use or communication (Boykin, 1986, p. 58; Daiby, 1972; Folb, 1980; p. 227–260; Holt, 1972; Smitherman, 1977). According to Daiby (1972, p. 175) Black Americans believe that they have to be "one jump ahead" of White people in verbal communication. He goes on to say that the function of Black vernacular English has been to "strengthen the in-group solidarity of Black Americans to the exclusion of Whites, and to deceive, confuse and conceal information from White people in general" (Daiby 1972, p. 172).

Interpretations of Adoption of "White" Culture and Dialect Frames

An important clue as to how Black Americans interpret the adoption of White cultural and language frames of reference or "acting White" for professional success comes from a description in *Black Rage* of the dilemma of successful Black Professionals in White business. As the authors put it:

> The only way out, if indeed it can be so considered, is a poor one at best and the price paid for success is terribly high. *We speak of those Negroes who make it by emulating the White man. They accept as a fact that Negroes are not so smart as White people and decided to reject their blackness and, insofar as possible, embrace whiteness.* They identify with White men in every way and add to that contempt for black people. In the process they gain some of the "White man's magic." They acquire some of the superior qualities they attribute to him. They may as a result feel more competent, but it is a direct function of the feeling that "other Negroes" are incompetent. In this way they develop a contempt for themselves, because, however much they avoid it, they remain black, and there are things about themselves that will yet remind them of their blackness and those reminders will evoke feeling of self hatred and self-depreciation (Grier and Cobbs, 1968; *Emphasis added*).

Many authors state explicitly that they themselves and/or Black Americans in general see successful participation in White institutions (e.g., school, the corporate economy) as an assimilation, a one way acculturation or a subtractive process, that takes away their Black identity (Baker, 1987; Campbell, 1982; Davis and Watson, 1985; Mitchell, 1982; Steele, 1992; Taylor, 1973). Based on her ethnographic findings in a community college, Weis (1985) suggests that the students more or less interpreted mastering academic work as a one-way acculturation. A Black professor told the researcher that "a lot of Black students see (the academic world) as a White world...(If I) tell students, 'you're going to be excellent...' often times excellence means being...White....(and) that kind of excellence is negative here" (Weis 1985, p. 100–101). Labov (1972, p. 135) asserts that it is apparent to some Black youth "that accepting...School values (is) equivalent to giving up self-respect."

Some Black professionals in the corporations, according to Taylor (1973; p. 13), find that it is in their best interest to embrace, overtly the behaviors of Whites. He goes on to say that "the flight into the White role behavior is...at a high cost." This is because for a minority person to be accepted into the top echelons of the corporations, he or she (the minority professional) must "think, manage, be-have like a majority group member and be White except in external appearance." (Taylor, 1973; pp. 16–17). Campbell concluded from her study of Black female executives that they are forced to pull away from their Black cultural identity, and to consciously modify their speech, their laughter, their walk, their mode of dress, and their choice of car to conform to mainstream requirements. Thus, as Black executive women move up, they become isolated from those in their old world (Campbell, 1982; pp. 68–69, 70). Davis and Watson (1985) repeatedly mention the "phenomenal estrangement of corporate Blacks" from Black cultural traditions from their own families and communities, and even from their own pre-corporate life styles, ways of dressing, and sense of humor (see also Baker, 1987; Mitchell, 1982).

Coping Today with the "Burden of Acting White"

In the context of oppositional collective identity and cultural frame of reference as well as negative interpretation of "acting White," contemporary Blacks adopt definite strategies to cope with the demand that they adopt certain "White" attitudes and behaviors in White institutions and establishments. The strategies they use to resolve the tension between meeting the demands of the White controlled situ-ations and the demands to conform to the Black ways are similar to the coping strategies of Blacks after emancipation. They include the following.

Assimilation or Emulation of Whites

Contemporary Black professionals in this category choose to abandon Black cultural and dialect frames of reference to behave and talk primarily according to White frames of reference. Like their predecessors they believe that their choice is more likely to help them succeed in education, upward social mobility in the wider society and acceptance by White people. Some other Blacks think that the assimilating Blacks not only reject Black dialect but also appear have a kind of linguistic self-hatred. Assimilationists try very hard to talk like White people. Some go for special coaching to "talk better" in order to keep their job or get promoted. Some send their children to private school where they will learn to "talk better" or to ensure that they learn to "speak White" when they have to, such as at school, on the job, and in the company of "better class of people."

A strong evidence of the assimilation strategy can be found in studies based on William Cross' theory of negrescence (Cross, 1991) described earlier. Before being influenced by the Black Power Movement (1968–75), these professionals and well-educated Blacks had developed a negative self-image of themselves as Black people. However, when they became involved in the Black Power Movement they underwent a transformation from their pre-involvement identity (a non-Afro-centric identity) to a new identity that is Afro-centric (Cross, 1991; p. 190).

Accommodation Without Assimilation

Another strategy is accommodation without assimilation. Blacks in this category adopt White-cultural and language frames of reference where they have to in order to succeed in school or in other White controlled institutions that are evaluated by White criteria. They do not, however, give up their Black identity or cultural and language frames of reference. They learn and follow the standard practices for success in White Americans in their institutions, without giving up their racial identity and ways of behaving or talking (Haynes, 1985; Sowell, 1974). Marva Collins on (60 Minutes, Hewitt, 1979) will serve as a good example of accommodation without assimilation. She is a Black educator who realizes that Black colloquial language is "not considered good enough" when applying for a job. Her solution was to teach Black children to master and use standard English.

Some Black autobiographers mention two important functions of accommodation: (a) it helps Blacks to maintain their sanity in a racist society, and (b) it helps them get ahead in White establishments. It is in this vein that Wiederman (1985) writes of the "seventh sense" that Blacks need in order to stay sane in America:

> It was a trick I learned early on. A survival mechanism as old as slavery. If you re born Black in America you must quickly teach yourself to recognize the invisible barriers disciplining the space in which you may move. This seventh sense you must activate is imperative for survival and sanity. Nothing is what it seems. You must always take second readings, decode appearances, pick out the abstractions erected to keep you in your place. Then work around them. What begins as a pragmatic reaction to race prejudice gradually acquires the force of an instinctive response (Wiederman, 1985, p. 222).

Edwards (1980, p. 120) sees the need to learn standard English and code-switch for upward mobility:

> My father always had a way of changing his voice when he was talking to White folks. We used to say that he could sound more like them than they could sound like themselves. He was just a regular every day "Blood" right up until a White person came on the scene. And then you never heard so many "gushes" and "golly, gee whizzes" in your life.

Ambivalence

I noted earlier that, after emancipation, some Blacks were ambivalent about adopting White behavior and talk in order to achieve success because they did not believe that the reason Black people are not as successful as White people was because they did not know how to behave or talk like White people. This was brought home to me in 1969 when I was attending a workshop on Black history and culture at the University of California, Los Angeles. One of my teachers narrated a story about a Black applicant enrolled in a program for training minority technicians in the Hollywood movie industry. The applicant was turned down because she did not speak "correct English." My teacher offered a different explanation; she said that until the late 1960s, Blacks could not work, rent, or buy homes in Westwood or Hollywood even when they spoke perfect English. She said that the applicant was turned down because of racism.

Resistance or Opposition

Some are afraid that mastering proper English will cause them to lose their Black dialect identity. They do think that they should not give up their dialect because their collective identity requires them to talk like Black people, not like White people. Several Black women in San Francisco considered "talking proper" an attempt to dissociate oneself from the Black race, to show that one is superior to other Blacks and an act of betrayal (Luster, 1992). The women "consciously resisted learning and using standard English because they believed that it is a White imposition on Blacks."

Encapsulation

Some are encapsulated in Black cultural and dialect frames of reference and do not behave or talk like White people anywhere. The reason may be that they have not learned to behave or speak proper English.

Social Sanctions (Peer Pressures) Against "Act White" Today

The belief that adopting White attitudes, behaviors, and communication style as a one-way assimilation or abandonment of Black identity and frames of reference leads to social sanctions against potential assimilation. Accommodators without assimilation are also potential targets of sanctions. Other Blacks are opposed to individuals in these categories who are perceived as trying to behave or talk like Whites in certain situations because such individuals are seen not merely as "acting White" but also as trying to betray the cause of Black people or trying to "join the enemy." The sanctions are both psychological and social.

Psychologically, some individuals trying to 'act White' may experience psychological stress or what DeVos (1967) calls affective dissonance. That is, because individual Blacks share the group's sense of oppositional racial identity, the would-be assimilationists may feel that by behaving or talking like White people they are, indeed, abandoning or betraying their own people.

There was evidence in the literature of both psychological and social sanctions against "acting White." Some Black professionals not only fear that they are being co-opted by the White world, but also experience social pressures from the Black community. Take the case of Mitchell (1983, p. 22–23). Reflecting on her position as a Black professor at a major research university, she describes the dilemma for Black academics: "the Black community rates service to the community high and research low... also the type of research that the community regards as worthwhile is that which advocates change, helps to get money and speaks in plain language." In contrast, the university regards this type of research as particularistic and subjective.

The sanctions experienced most commonly by Blacks striving for academic and professional success are (a) accusation of Uncle Tomism or disloyalty to the Black cause or Black community (Petroni, 1970, p. 263); (b) threat of personal embarrassment and humiliation (Mitchell, 1983, p. 22–23); and (c) fear of losing friends and/or a sense of community (Abdul-Jabba and Knobles, 1983; Labov, 1972; Weis, 1985). The individual also feels the need to perform a social cost/benefit analysis of his or her chances for making it (Davis and Watson, 1985, p. 51; Mitchell, 1982, p. 35). He or she may experience intense frustration and the perception of a closing down of options (Davis and Watson, 1985, p. 74). In some cases, the latter has led to suicide, while some individuals suffer from self-doubts, guilt, alienation, and paranoia (Luster, 1992).

Reports by Becknell (1987), Kochman (1987), and Luster (1992) as well as my own study in Oakland, California (Ogbu, 1999) provide evidence of contemporary community pressures against "acting White," especially against "talking proper in the community" because it would mean denying and ultimately losing one's Black identity. Becknell (1987, p. 36) talks about the pressure this way:

> When I encounter a group of Blacks on the street in my home community, I can't go up to them and say "Good afternoon, gentlemen. How are you doing today?" (i.e., greet them in Standard English). They would laugh at me and then feel sorry for me. They'd think, "Poor Charles, when he left here for college, he was OK. (That is, he talked appropriately like us and maintained his Black identity). But now, look what they've done (i.e., White people or White educational institutions) to him!" (i.e., he has learned to "talk proper" or "act White").

According to Kochman (1987, p. 228):

Black intonation patterns function as an inside (ethnic) boundary marker; those who do not manifest the distinctive Black intonation in their speech regularly acknowledge the adverse criticism they receive from other Blacks, the substance of which characterizes them as being "assimilation-oriented" or "acting White." I have observed often the nonverbal criticisms directed at these Blacks by other Blacks who do manifest such intonations (a criticisms also often verbalized about them later on, when the person is no longer present). The accused are often called upon to demonstrate the extent of their group affiliation in other ways, and may be further tested for their "Blackness" before the final judgment is rendered. (See also Ogbu, 1999).

Luster tells us that among Black women (and many were parents) who were attending a community school in San Francisco to get their GED, that the biggest opposition was against speaking standard English:

> There is a continual delineation and reinforcement of behaviors, practices, and attitudes that are "Black" (and appropriate) versus those that are "White" (and inappropriate)... "Acting White" is an acknowledged and identifiable practice within the community. The women who were both observed for more than a year and then interviewed consider "speaking proper" or using the Standard English is an attempt to disassociate oneself from the race; an attempt to demonstrate superiority, an act of betrayal. It angered and disgusted the community. The women consciously resisted learning and using the Standard English because it would mean accepting what the White society defines as "right" or "White" to replace what the same White society defines as "wrong" or "Black." (Luster, 1992, p. 202)

I also found that talking proper was a strong signifier of "acting White" in Oakland, California. The parents I studied believed that talking proper in the community was pretentious because, no Black person could really talk like a White person. Talking proper was not natural for Blacks. There was yet another reason for the opposition: Talking proper signified adopting White people's attitude of superiority toward Blacks. Here is how the community would treat a person trying to talk proper, according to my informants:

Parent 1: You know, talkin' all—you know, talkin' like White people.
Interviewer: Oh, talking—so people would not be interested in that...
Parent 1. No.
Interviewer: Ok. Well, how would they treat them?
Parent 1: Probably standoffish...Ignore them... Because they're trying to (show that they are) better than they are...Maybe that type of attitude.
Parent 2. People in the community will say, "He thinks he's smarter than everyone else, or he thinks he's White." We don't want to listen to this. I don't want to listen to this thing or that.
Parent 3: They (other Lafayette Blacks) would probably tend to be somewhat prejudicial of someone speaking very proper English, and they would probably make an assessment on that person's character as being "uppity" or... she is trying to be White, or something like that, you know.

Coping with Social Sanctions Against "Acting White" Today

Contemporary Blacks who must "act White" for whatever reason know full well that their behavior is not endorsed by the community. There are cultural ways of handling or shielding them from the social sanctions. The strategies found in both the literature and my ethnographic studies include the following:

Camouflaging: Involvement in the Black Struggle

This requires activities that give other Blacks the impression that one is for Black people, not for White people. Active participation in the civil rights struggle is a good way to camouflage. Middle class

BISHOP BURTON COLLEGE
LIBRARY

Blacks are expected to be involved in the collective struggle against White oppression. They have to demonstrate their concern for and loyalty to the "race" through "the struggle" to be accepted as good role models for Black youth. Some Black professionals I interviewed reported that they were accused on many occasions of not being for the race because they were "not involved". This is how one Oakland parent describes the attitude of the community toward a professional suspected of abandoning the community. This is followed by a Stockton school administration's description of the dilemma of Black professionals:

Parent 5L: By now they've (i.e., successful Black professionals) gone somewhere else to live in a totally different neighborhood. So, you know, it's really hard to...
Interviewer: That's right. So, they've moved away from the community
Parent 5L: That's right.
School Administrator: Let me tell you something else about this community, about the Black people, that they don't have a lot of trust in each other, either you know.... The Black people who live in north Stockton, professionals) .... if they came to the Black community Council they would be literally attacked by the people from south Stockton (Black ghetto resident). They (from south Stockton Blacks) feel that they (north Stockton Blacks) have abandoned them for having moved up there. So, once you have become a professional, and successful, and others who are not, sort of cast dispersion on you because of it. It's a difficult thing to go back and serve, to help when people are challenging you every step of the way you know (interview, 1970).

Accommodation Without Assimilation
Convincing others that one is able to behave and talk like White people in White-controlled environments and yet behave and talk like Black people in the Black community is another way to handle social sanction. Some Blacks learn to live alternately in the Black world and in the White World (Becknell, 1987). Some Black parents in Oakland recognized the importance of code-switching behavior. One mother said that she mastered proper English to disguise her racial identity, minimize racial discrimination, and increase her chances of getting a good job.

Parent: (Talking proper) is not a problem for me because I can change my tone of voice and speak in a different (way). Well, I appear to speak in a different–with an accent. Certain (White) people don't really know who they're talking to.
Interviewer: Okay.
Parent: Whereas if they were to see me, they would not (have agreed to what I said or wanted)...because of the Afro.

Support Group or Mentorship
Black professional organizations or associations function to provide needed support to Blacks. Getting a mentor helps Black professionals succeed in the mainstream. One function of the mentor is to serve as a stabilizing force against peer pressures and self-doubt. Mentors are very important even in professional sports, as can be seen in the experience of Abdul-Jabbar. Early in his professional sports career, a mentor provided him with tips on how to play. One of two other mentors who gave him emotional support, was a Muslim. His Muslim mentor admonished him to both take his religion seriously and affirm his U.S. citizenship and get all his rights as a citizen (Abdul-Jabbar and Knobles, 1983). However, the literature indicates that mentorship is not frequently available to Black achievers. According to Davis and Watson (1985, p. 89), mentoring is limited by a lack of structural opportunity. They note that, "In the early 60's...Blacks always had a 'godfather' or corporate mentor who would

look out for them. But that did not mean that the mentor would help Black employees rise through the ranks" (Davis and Watson 1985, p. 29–30).

Coping with the Burden of "Acting White" at School

I have discussed at length the collective identity and frames of reference among Blacks in contemporary United States because critics of the Fordham–Ogbu thesis focus almost exclusively and atomistically on Black students attitudes and behaviors in the school context, divorced from Black history and community. But Black students are products of Black history and members of contemporary Black community. They face the same dilemma, due to the same oppositional collective identity and frames of reference characteristics, as members of their community. Therefore, in examining the students' conduct, I will not repeat the above discussions of the dilemma of "acting White" among contemporary Black Americans. Suffice it to say that at school, students responded to required attitudes and behaviors labeled "White" like adult Blacks in White institutions and corporate America. Among the students, as among adults, there are assimilationists, accommodators without assimilation, ambivalents, resisters and the encapsulated. It is important to bear in mind that although Black collective identity and cultural frame of reference are oppositional, only one of the five categories of Blacks among both adults and students is explicitly opposed to adopting White attitudes, behaviors, and speech. In my own study, I have generally found that there are relatively few students who reject good grades because it is "White." On the contrary, they want to make good grades and many report that they are well received by their close friends when they get good grades, such as when they get an A (Ogbu and Simons, 1994a, 95).

What the students reject that hurt their academic performance are "White" attitudes and behaviors conducive to making good grades (Ogbu and Simons, 1998). In Shaker Heights, for example, they include speaking standard English, enrollment in Honors and AP classes, being smart during lessons, and having too many White friends. In Oakland, they include talking proper, studying a lot or doing homework everyday, having mostly White friends, taking hard/advanced placement courses, acting like a nerd, taking mathematics and science classes, spending a lot of time in the library and reading a lot. Black students experience peer pressures from other Black students to discourage them from adopting such White attitudes and behaviors. Black students also experience peer pressures for other reasons than "acting White." In Shaker Heights, these include non-academic priorities like pressure to work too many hours on part-time jobs to pay-off credit card debts, as well as maintaining a certain lifestyle. Oakland students are pressured to sell drugs, smoke weed, cut classes, to hang out with friends and to believe that school does not matter. It is important to note that all peer pressures that hurt students' grades are not for preventing students from "acting White."

Coping with Social Sanctions Against Peer Pressures at School

Like the adults, Black students have strategies for coping with peer pressures. It is difficult to separate strategies for handling pressures against "acting White" from strategies for peer pressures for other reasons. Shaker Heights students reported three major ways they handled peer pressures. One was family upbringing and continued parental supervision, including screening their friends and monitoring their school work. The second was a student's own initiative, whereby he or she carefully chooses Black friends who are serious about school and about making good grades. Finally, some students interpret peer pressures as distractions from their goal of school success and take necessary steps to avoid them.

In Shaker Heights, the school made a significant indent into the peer pressures by establishing an academic identity program for achieving Black students, called The (Minority Achievement Committee

Scholar) MAC Scholars. Academically promising students are invited to join the program. The scholars meet periodically to discuss how they can handle peer pressures and improve their school performance. They also have an annual award ceremony for academic improvement. Equally important is that they wear special symbols identifying them as MAC scholars and greet one another in a special way. Both of these express their pride in academic achievement. The MAC Scholars are generally admired as good role models by other Black students (Ogbu, 2003, p. 125–126).

The most common strategy in Oakland is camouflaging. A good example of this is to be highly involved or to excel in Black activities and avoid "White" activities. Another common strategy is to help friends with their home-work or let them copy one's assignments. Some students act dumb in class or as class clowns. Some study in secret and their good grades, achieved "without studying," are attributed to the fact that they are "naturally smart." A few students get "bullies" to protect them in exchange for helping the latter with assignments. There seem to be more students in Oakland than in Shaker Heights, however, who "give in" to friends or yield to peer pressures and "let their grades suffer."

There are several things to be stressed as a conclusion. First, Black students face the same burden of "acting White" that Black Americans have faced throughout their history and still face in contemporary United States. Under this circumstance, they have developed culturally patterned ways of coping with the dilemma or the burden of "acting White" which one finds both in the contemporary Black community and among the students. Second, in the course of their history, Black Americans have had to cope with peer or community pressures against "acting White" and they have also developed strategies to handle such pressures. The social sanctions or pressures and the coping strategies still exist in contemporary Black community and are shared by Black students. Third, Black students experience peer pressures for other reasons than for "acting White." The peer pressures unrelated to the burden of "acting White" also contribute to their low school performance. Lastly, other and even more important contributors to their low school performance are societal, school and other community forces that discourage academic engagement (Ogbu, 2002, 2003; Ogbu and Simons, 1998).

References

Abdul-Jabbar, K. and Knobles, P. (1983). *Giant Steps; The Autobiography of Kareem Abdul-Jabbar.* New York: Bantam Books.

Ainsworth-Darnell, J. W. and Downey, D. B. (1998). Assessing the oppositional culture explanation for racial/ethnic differences in school performance. *American Sociological Review* 63:536–553.

Alba, R. (1990). *Ethnic Identity: The Transformation of White Americans.* New Haven, CN: Yale University Press.

Baer, H. A. (1984). *The Black Spiritual Movement: A Religious Response to Racism.* Knoxville, TN: The University of Tennessee Press.

Baker, H. A. Jr. (1987). *Modernism and the Harlem Renaissance.* Chicago, IL: University of Chicago Press.

Becknell, C. F. (1987). *Blacks in the Work-force: A Black Manager's Perspective.* Albuquerque, NM: Horizon Communications.

Benjamin, L. (1991). *The Black Elite: Facing the Color Line in the Twilight of the Twentieth Century.* Chicago, IL: Nelson Hail.

Bennett, L. Jr. (1996). 10 Most dramatic events in African-American history. In J. A. Kromkowski (Ed.), *Race and Ethnic Relations: Annual Edition* (pp. 31–32). Sluice Dock, Guilford, CT: Dushkin Publication.

Bergin, D. A. and Cooks, H. C. (2002). High school students of color talk about accusations of "acting white. *The Urban Review* 34(2):113–134.

Berry, M. F. (1971). *Black Resistance!White Law: A History of Constitutional Racism in America.* New York: Appleton-Century-Crofts.

Bethel, E. R. (1997). *The Roots of African American Identity: Memory and History in the Antebellum Free Communities.* New York: St. Martin's.

Bogle, D. (1989). *Toms, Coons, Mulattoes, Mammies, & Bucks: An Interpretive History of Blacks in American Films.* New York: Continuum.

Boykin, A. W. (1986). The Triple Quandary and the Schooling of Afro-American Children. In U. Neisser (Ed.). *The School Achievement of Minority Children: New Perspectives,* (pp. 57–92). Hillsdale, NJ: Lawrence Erlbaum.

Branch, C. W. (1999). Race and human development. In R. H. Sheets and E. R. Hollins (Eds.), *Racial and Ethnic Identity in School Practices: Aspects of Human Development* (pp. 7–28). Mahwah, NJ: Lawrence Erlbaum.

Burkey, R. M. (1971). *Racial Discrimination and Public Policy in the United States.* Cambridge, MA: D. C. Heath.

Campbell, F. (1982). Black executive and corporate stress. *The New York Times Magazine* 12:1–42.

Carter, P. (1999). *Balancing 'Acts': Issues of Identity and Cultural Resistance in the Social and Educational Behaviors of Minority Youth*. Ph.D. Dissertation, Department of Sociology, Columbia University, New York, NY.

Carter, R. I. and Goodwin, A. L. (1994). Racial identity and education. In L. Darling-Hammond (Ed.), *Review of Research in Education* (pp. 291–336). Washington, D.C: American Educational Research Association.

Castile, G. P. and Kushner, G. (1981). *Persistent Peoples: Cultural Enclaves in Perspective*. Tucson, AZ: University of Arizona Press.

CBS Television Network (1984). The Rosewood massacre. *60 Minutes XVI* (47): 16–22.

Cone, J. H. (1972). *The Spirituals and the Blues*. San Francisco, CA: Harper and Row.

Case, E. (1995). *The Rage of the Privileged Class: Why are Middle-class Blacks Angry? Why Should America Care?* New York: Harper Collins.

Cook, P. J. and Ludwig, J. (1997). Weighing the "burden of acting white." Are there differences in attitudes towards education. *Journal of Policy Analysis and Management*, 16(2):256–278.

Cornell, S. E. and Hartman, D. (1998). *Ethnicity and Race: Making Identities in a Changing World*. Thousand Oaks, CA: Pine Forge Press.

Cross, W. E. Jr. (1991). *Shades of Black: Diversity in African American Identity*. Philadelphia, PA: Temple University Press.

Cross, W. E., Strauss, L. and Fhagen-Smith, P. (1999). African American identity development across the life span: educational implications. In R. H. Sheets and E. R. Hollins (Eds.), *Racial and Ethnic Identity in School Practices: Aspects of Human Development* (pp. 29–47). Mahwah, NJ: Lawrence Erlbaum.

Daiby, D. (1972). The African element in American English. In T. Kochman (Ed.), *Rappin' and 'Stylin' Out: Communication in Urban Black America* (pp. 170–188). Urbana, IL: University of Illinois Press.

Davis, G. and Watson, C. (1985). *Black Life in Corporate America: Swimming in the Mainstream*. Garden City, NY: Anchor Books.

DeVos, G. A. (1992). *Ethnic Persistence and Role Degradation: Koreans in Japan*. Boulder, CO: West View Press.

DeVos, C. A. (1967). *Japan's Invisible Race*. Berkeley, CA: University of California Press.

DeVos, G. A. (1995). Ethnic pluralism: conflicts and accommodation. In L. Romanucci-Ross and G. A. DeVos (Eds.), *Ethnic Identity: Creation, Conflict, and Accommodation* (pp. 15–41). Walnut Creek, CA: Altimira Press.

Drake, St. C. and Cayton, H. R. (1970). *Black Metropolis: A Study of Negro Life in a Northern City*, Vol. 1, 2. New York: Harcourt.

DuBois, W. B. (1982, originally 1903). *The Souls of Black Folks*. New York: The New American Library.

Edwards, H. (1980). *The Struggle that must be: An Autobiography*. New York: Macmillan.

Epstein, T. (2003). Adolescent Racial/Ethnic Identity and Academic Achievement Revisited. Paper presented at the AERA Annual Meeting, Chicago, April 21–24, 2003.

Ferman, L. A., Kornbluh, J. L. and Miller, J. A. (Eds.) (1968). *Negroes and Jobs. A Book of Reading*. Ann Arbor, MI: The University of Michigan Press.

Folb, E. A. (1980). *Runnin' Down Some Lines: The Language and Culture of Black Teenagers*. Cambridge, MA: Harvard University Press.

Fordham, S. (1985). Black Students' School Success as Related to Fictive Kinship. Final Report to the National Institute of Education, Washington, D.C.

Fordham, S. (1984). Ethnography in a High School: Learning not to be A Native. A paper presented at the 83rd Annual Meeting of the American Anthropological Association, Denver, CO, November 14–18.

Fordham, S. and Ogbu, J. (1986). Black students' school success: coping with the burden of 'acting white'. *Urban Review* 18(3):176–206.

Frazier, E. F. (1957). *The Negro in the United States* (Rev. Edn.). New York: Macmillan.

Gans, H. (1979). Symbolic ethnicity: The future of ethnic groups and cultures in America." *Ethnic and Racial Studies* 2:1–20.

The Gene Media Forum (2002). *Race, Genes and Intelligence*. New York: The Gene Media Forum.

Green, V. M. (1981). Blacks in the United States: the creation of an enduring people. In G. P. Castile, and G. Kusher (Eds.), *Persistence Peoples: Cultural Enclaves in Perspective* (pp. 69–77). Tucson, AZ: University of Arizona Press.

Grier, W. H. and Cobbs, P. M. (1968). *Black Rage*. New York: Basic Books.

Haley, A. (1976). *Roots: The Saga of an American Family*. New York: Dell.

Hall, R. L. (1979). *Black Separatism in the United States*: Hanover, NH: The New England University Press.

Hauser, S. T. (1972). Black and White identity development: aspects and perspectives. *Journal of Youth and Adolescence* 1(2):113–130.

Hayes, R. (Nd). *Harlem, Mecca of the New Negro, March 1925* (pp. 631–635). Baltimore, MD: Black Classic Press.

Haynes, R. L. (1985). *Minority Strategies for Success*. Unpublished Manuscript, Department of Anthropology, University of California, Berkeley. Special Project.

Herrnstein, R. J. and Murray, C. (1994). *The Bell Curve: Intelligence and Class Structure in American Life*. New York: The Free Press.

Hewitt, D. (Executive Producer). (1979, November 11). *60 Minutes* [Television Broadcast]. New York, NY: CBS Broadcasting Inc.

Hirasawa, Y. and Nabeshima, Y. (1995). *Dowa Education: Educational Challenge Toward a Discrimination-free Japan*. Osaka, Japan: Buraku Liberation Research Institute.

Holt, G. S. (1972). Inversion in Black communication. In T. Kochman (Ed.), *Rappin and Stylin' Out: Communication in Urban Black America* (pp. 152–159). Chicago, IL: University of Illinois Press.

Horvat, E. Mc. and O'Connor, C. (2001). *The Black–White Achievement Gap and Black Cultural Opposition to Acting White: Where do we go from Here?* American Sociological Association, 97th Annual Meeting, Chicago.

Johnson, C. S. (1931). *The Negro in American Civilization*. London, England: Constable and Co.

Johnson, C. S. (1943). *Backgrounds to Patterns of Negro Segregation.* New York: Crowell-Collier.

Johnson, K. (1972). The Vocabulary of Race. In T. Kochman (Ed.). *Rappin' and 'Stylin' out. Communication in Urban Black America,* (p. 140–151). Urbana, IL: University of Illinois Press.

Keyes, C. F. (1981). *Ethnic Change.* Seattle, WA: University of Washington Press.

Kochman, T. (1981). *Black and White Styles in Conflict.* Chicago, IL: University of Chicago Press.

Kochman, T. (1987). The ethnic component in Black language and culture. In J. S. Phinney and M. J. Rotheram (Eds.), *Children's Ethnic Socialization: Pluralism and Development* (pp. 117–133). Beverly Hills, CA: Sage.

Labov, W. (1972). *Language in the Inner City: Studies in the Black English Vernacular.* Philadelphia, PA: University of Pennsylvania Press.

Locke, A. (1925). Enter the New Negro. In Hayes, R. (Nd). *Harlem, Mecca of the New Negro, March 1925* (pp. 631–635). Baltimore, MD: Black Classic Press.

Luster, L. (1992). *Schooling, Survival, and Struggles, Black Women and the GED.* Unpublished Doctoral Dissertation, School of Education, Stanford University.

Marshall, R. (1967). *The Negro Workers.* New York: Random House.

Mitchell, J. (1983). Visible, vulnerable, and viable: emerging perspectives of a minority professor. In J. H. Cones, J. F. Noonan and D. Janha (Eds.), *Teaching Minority Students: New Directions for Teaching and Learning,* No. 16. (pp. 17–28). San Francisco, CA: Jossey-Bass.

Mitchell, J. (1982). Reflections of a Black social scientist: some struggles, some doubts, some hopes. *Harvard Educational Review* 52(1):27–44.

Moore, J. T. Jr. (1981). *A Search for Equality: The National Urban League, 1910–1961.* University Park, PA: The University of Pennsylvania Press.

Myrdal, G. (1944). *An American Dilemma: The Negro Problem and Modern Democracy,* Vol. 1. New York: Harper.

Nestby, J. P. (1982). *Black Images in American Films, 1896–1954: The Interplay Between Civil Rights and Film Culture.* New York: State University of New York Press.

Norgren, P. H. and Hill, S. E. (1964). *Toward Fair Employment.* New York: Columbia University Press.

Novak, D. A. (1978). *The Wheel of Servitude: Black Forced Labor After Slavery.* Lexington, KY: The University of Kentucky Press.

O'Connor, C. (1996). *Optimism Despite Limited Opportunity: Schooling Orientation and Agency Beliefs Amongst Low-income African American Students.* Unpublished Dissertation, University of Chicago, Chicago, IL.

Ogbu, J. (1978). *Minority Education and Caste: The American System in Cross-Cultural Perspective.* New York: Academic Press.

Ogbu, J. (1998). *Community Forces and Minority Educational Strategies: The Second Part of the Problem.* Berkeley, CA: Department of Anthropology, University of California.

Ogbu, J. (1999). Beyond language: ebonics, proper english, and identity in a Black-American speech community. *American Educational Research Journal* (Summer) 36(2).

Ogbu, J. (2000). Collective Identity and Schooling. In H. Fujita and K. Shimizu (Eds.), *Education, Knowledge and Power.* Tokyo: Shinyosha Ltd (English version).

Ogbu, J. (2002). Black-American students and the academic achievement gap: What else you need to know. *Journal of Thought.* 37(4):9–33.

Ogbu, J. (2003). *Black Students in an Affluent Suburb: A Study of Academic Disengagement.* Hillsdale, NJ: Lawrence Erlbaum.

Ogbu, J. and Margold, J. (1986). *A Summary of Literature Review On Black Oppositional Identity And Cultural Frame of Reference.* Unpublished Manuscript, Survey Research Center, University of California, Berkeley, CA.

Ogbu, J. and Simons, F. (1988). *Black Autobiographies: A Search for Cultural Model of Minority Status and American Society.* Unpublished Manuscript, Survey Research Center, University of California, Berkeley, CA.

Ogbu, J. and Simons, H. D. (1994). *Cultural Models of School Achievement: A Quantitative Test of Ogbu's Theory.* Final Report. Graduate School of Education, National Center for the Study of Writing, University of California, Berkeley, CA.

Ogbu, J. and Simons, H. D. (1998). Voluntary and involuntary minorities: A cultural-ecological theory of school performance with some implications for Education. *Anthropology and Education Quarterly* 29(2):155–188.

Patterson, W. L. (1951). *We Charge Genocide.* New York: International Publishers.

Petroni, F. A. (1970). 'Uncle toms': White stereotypes in the Black Movement. *Human Organization* 29(4):260–266.

Phinney, J. S. and Rotheram, M. J. (1987). Children's ethnic socialization: Themes and implications. In J. S. Phinney and M. J. Rotheram (Eds.), *Children's Ethnic Socialization: Pluralism and Development.* Newbury Park, CA: Sage Publications.

Phinney, J. S. and Rosenthal, D. A. (1992). Ethnic identity in adolescent: Process, context and outcome. In G. R. Adams, R. P. Gullotta and R. Montemayor (Eds.), *Adolescent Identity Formation* (pp. 145–172). Newbury Park, CA: Sage Publications.

Rawick, G. P. (1972). *From Sundown to Sunup: The Making of the Black Community.* Westport, CT: Greenwood Publishing Co.

Redkey, E. S. (1969). *Black Exodus: Black Nationalist and Back-to-Africa Movements, 1890–1910.* New Haven, CN: Yale University Press.

Rockquemore, K. A. and Brunsma, D. L. (2002). *Beyond Black: Biracial Identity in America.* Thousand Oaks, CA: Sage.

Ross, A. M. (1967). The Negro in the American economy. In A. M. Ross and H. Hill (Eds.), *Employment, Race and Poverty: A Critical Study of the Advantaged Status of Negro Workers from 1865 to 1965* (pp. 3–48). New York: Harcourt.

Rowan, C. T. (1967). The Negro's Place in the American Dream. In J. D. Harrison and A. B. Shaw (Eds.), *The American Dream: Vision and Reality.* San Francisco, CA: Canfield Press.

Shade, B. (1984). Personal traits of educationally successful black children. *Negro Educational Review* 32(2):6–11.

Shapiro, H. (1988). *White Violence and Black Response: From Reconstruction to Montgomery*. Amherst, MA: The University of Massachusetts Press.

Smitherman, G. (1977). *Talkin' and Testifyin':The Language of Black American*. Detroit, MI: Wayne State University Press.

Sochen, J. (1972). *The Unbridgeable Gap: Blacks and their Quest for the American Dream*. Chicago, IL: Rand McNally.

Sowell, T. (1974). Black excellence: the case of Dunbar High School. *The Public Interest* (Spring):5–7, 10–11, 12.

Spicer, E. H. (1966). The Process of Cultural Enclavement in Middle America." 36th Congress of International de Amerianistas, Seville, vol. 3:267–279.

Spicer, E. H. (1967). *Cycles of Conquest*. Tucson, AZ: University of Arizona Press.

Spicer, E. H. (1971). Persistent cultural systems: a comparative study of identity systems that can adapt to contrasting environments. *Science* 174:795–800.

Starker, C. J. (1971). *Black Portraiture in American Fiction: Stock Characters, Archetypes, and Individuals*. New York: Basic Books.

Steele, C. (1992). Race and the Schooling of Black Americans. *The Atlantic Monthly* (April), 68–73.

Stuckey, S. (1987). *Slave Culture: Nationalist Theory & The Foundations of Black America*. New York: Oxford University Press.

Styron, W. (1966). *The Confessions of Nat Turner*. New York: Random House.

Sygnnerstvedt, S. (1972). *The White Response to Black Emancipation: Second-Class Citizenship in the United States since Reconstruction*. New York: Macmillan.

Taylor, S. A. (1973). Some funny things happened on the way up. Contact 5(1):12–17.

Taylor, B. L. (2001). *Navigating Knowing/Complicating Truth: African American Learners Experiencing Oral History as Real Education*. Unpublished Dissertation, Louisiana State University and Agricultural Mechanical College.

Weis, L. (1985). *Between Two Worlds: Black Students in an Urban Community College*. London: Rutledge.

Weisbrodt, R. (1991). *Freedom Bound: A History of America's Civil Rights Movement*. New York: A Plumer Book.

Wiederman, J. E. (1985). *Brothers and Keepers*. New York: Penguin Books.

Wright, L. (1996). One drop of blood. In J. A. Kromkowski (Ed.), *Race and Ethnic Relations*. Annual Edition, (pp. 10–16). Sluice Dock, Guilford, CT: Dushkin Publication.

Wright, M. A. (2001). *I'm Chocolate, You're Vanilla: Raising Healthy Black and Biracial Children in a Race-Conscious World*. San Francisco, CA: Jossey Bass.

Yon, D. A. (2000). *Elusive Culture: Schooling, Race, and Identity in Global Times*. New York: State University of New York Press.

21

Burden of Acting Neither White Nor Black

Asian American Identities and Achievement in Urban Schools

JAMIE LEW

A growing body of research has challenged Ogbu's theory of the "burden of acting white" and to what extent cultural explanations account for black students' schooling experience and outcome. Emerging studies show that Ogbu's cultural explanations may be limited when examining variability of school achievement among black and white students, and that other social forces, such as class, peer networks, and school context may play a significant role in their schooling aspirations and achievement (Cook & Ludwig, 1998; Downey & Ainsworth-Darnell, 2002; Ferguson, 2001; Tyson, 2002; Tyson, Darity, & Castellino, 2005). In short, variability of school performance among black and white students, for instance, should take into account not only issues of race and culture but also how these processes may be fluid and salient depending on the changing social and school contexts.

These studies are important in light of the widening black and white achievement gap and the prevailing cultural discourse often used to explain school achievement. However, in the midst of this on-going debate, there is a limited understanding of how, if at all, theory of "acting white" plays a role for racial groups other than black and white students. By extending the discussion beyond a black-and-white discourse, researchers may be able to complicate and expand our understanding of the role of culture in school achievement and how it intersects with various structural forces, such as class and schools.

One of the more invisible racial groups discussed in this debate is Asian Americans. Stereotyped as model minorities, Asian American students' negotiation of multiple identities, varied schooling experiences, and racialization process are often ignored (Fong & Shinangawa, 2000; Lee, 1996; Lew, 2006; Nakanishi & Nishida, 1995; Pang & Cheng, 1998; Park, Goodwin, Lee, 2003). However, Asian American status as model minorities—a stereotype that often conflates them with whiteness—plays an important ideological role in perpetuating ideals of individual meritocracy, especially for poor minority students. Such ideals of "American dream" predicated on cultural explanations place both reward and blame on individuals without adequately taking into account important structural factors, such as race, class, and schools. Therefore, stereotype images of Asian "success" or black "failure" cannot be predicated solely on cultural explanations, but has to take into account the changing social contexts.

In order to address such limitations, this study will examine some of these timely issues by asking the following research questions: How do Asian American students in different social and economic contexts negotiate their racial and ethnic identities, and how does this process impact their academic aspirations and achievements? In what ways do peer networks and race relations in schools affect students' negotiation of identities? How do high-achieving Asian Americans who are typically viewed as model minorities negotiate their racial minority status? How is this process similar and different from those Asian American students who are low-achieving or dropping out of high schools? In what ways does this research challenge our understanding of "acting white," and the ways in which students negotiate power relations inherent in the polarized notions of blackness and whiteness?

As a way to answer some of these questions, this study compares experiences of two groups of Korean American students—both high- and low-achieving—in New York City urban schools. I compare experiences of high-achieving middle-class students attending a competitive academic magnet high school with working-class low-achieving high school dropouts attending a community-based GED (General Educational Development) program. The findings indicate that the two groups of Korean American students experienced their racial minority status and adopted different racial strategies depending on their socioeconomic backgrounds, peer networks, and school contexts. For instance, the high-achieving middle-class Korean students, in the school context of academic peer culture attended predominantly by middle-class white and Asian students were more likely to associate and identify with their ethnic backgrounds. Similar to previous studies on Hispanic and children of immigrants, the high-achieving Korean students highlighted their bicultural backgrounds and bilingual ability when noting their experiences as both Korean and American.

On the other hand, the low-achieving Korean American high school dropouts, in the context of urban schools fraught with academic failure and increasing dropout rates that consist predominantly of poor and working-class minorities, were more likely to identify themselves as "minorities." As such, the Korean high school dropouts in this study were careful to disassociate themselves from the "wealthy" and "studious" Koreans and other Asian Americans. It is important to note that neither the high- nor the low-achieving students identified themselves with whiteness; however, the two groups negotiated and interpreted their racial minority status and accompanying marginalization differently depending on their given opportunity structure at home and schools.

This research is particularly timely given the on-going debate of Ogbu's theory of "burden of acting white" and the role of culture on school achievement. It argues that academic achievement among Asian American students involves a complex relationship between culture, class, race, and schools. Asian Americans in schools face conflicting messages regarding their racial minority status: On the one hand, as racial minorities, they are often excluded from whiteness, while on the other hand, they are also stereotyped as model minorities that align them with whiteness. Asian Americans in the context of a black and white racial discourse prevalent in our society learn to negotiate their race and ethnic identities differently from black and white students—a process that is largely shaped by changing social contexts. Although neither the high- nor the low-achieving Korean American students aligned themselves with whiteness, the two groups in different economic and school contexts, learned to interpret their minority status and opportunity structure differently. The findings support earlier studies that note the significance of school structure—peer relations, racial and class composition, and academic culture—and show how these structural factors may play an integral role in fulfilling academic aspirations and achievement among minority students. In so doing, it challenges the prevalent stereotype based on cultural discourse to explain Asian "success" and black "failure." It underscores the significance of examining these processes across and within various ethnic and racial groups, while highlighting the salience of race as well as the relational nature of identities in various school and economic contexts.

"Burden of Acting White" and Oppositional Cultural Frame of Reference

For the past few decades, Ogbu's (1987) seminal research on voluntary and involuntary immigrants has helped educators examine the critical role of race and culture in academic achievement. By making a clear distinction between voluntary and involuntary immigrant experiences, he pointed to the significance of minority students' cultural frame of reference and their interpretation of economic, social, and political barriers. Ogbu and colleagues have argued that involuntary minorities, such as African American students adopt low-school performance as a form of adaptation to their limited social and economic opportunity in adult life. It is argued that involuntary minorities who were forcefully incorporated into the United States tend to attribute academic success with "whiteness" and thus reject school success with their own ethnic and racial identities. Therefore, as a means of developing survival strategies to endure structural barriers such as inferior schooling, job ceiling, and racial discrimination, African Americans form an oppositional cultural frame of reference and oppositional social identity to dominant white society (Fordham, 1988; Fordham & Ogbu, 1986; Labov, 1982; Matute-Bianchi, 1986; Villejas, 1986).

Fordham and Ogbu (1986) argued that this oppositional cultural frame of reference lead African American students who are doing well in school to be associated with and to be labeled as "acting white." For Ogbu, the growing black and white educational gap persists mainly because of this "burden of acting white" and institutionalized racial stratification inherent in our schools and society at large: "school performance gap persists because the forces of racial stratification—white treatment and black responses—that created it continue to some degree" (Ogbu, 1994, p. 264). Ogbu criticizes those scholars who talk about black and white inequality in terms of class stratification, pointing to the "temporality of class membership in contrast to the permanence of racial group membership" (p. 267). He argues that despite class variability among black communities, middle-class blacks continue to perform less academically than middle-class whites, as a result of their oppositional cultural frame of reference and resistance to "acting white."

For Ogbu, black students' attitudes and behaviors in school cannot be separated from the larger historical oppression and systemic racism that African Americans have faced in the United States. In the last article he wrote before his untimely death, Ogbu (2004) defended his position by arguing that many of his critics have misinterpreted his cultural-ecological theory simply as an oppositional culture theory (p. 1). In this last article, he articulated the various types of coping strategies that African Americans have developed in response to the White dominant society: in doing so, he pays particular attention to the processes of oppositional collective identity and cultural frame of reference in the context of African American history. Some of these coping strategies that have developed as a result of historical White oppression include processes such as assimilation, accommodation without assimilation, ambivalence, resistance or opposition, and encapsulation (pp. 21–23). Despite these various coping strategies, however, he illustrates how the strategies aforementioned are largely shaped by history of oppression, giving rise to a collective black experience and the "burden of acting white" that generally frame their attitudes, experiences, and identities (2004).

Despite the significance of Ogbu's theory of "burden of acting white," other studies have criticized Ogbu by pointing to the significance of class, ethnicity, and school context when noting the relationship between race and school achievement (Ainsworth-Darnell & Downey, 1998; Carter, 2003; Cook & Ludwig, 1998; Downey & Ainsworth-Darnell, 2002; Ferguson, 2001; Tyson, 2002; Tyson et al., 2005). For instance, Tyson and colleagues (2005) argued that Ogbu's theory of "burden of acting white" among black students may be more of a problem related to school structure than culture. They found that both black and white students were generally achievement oriented and that racialized peer pressure against high achievement was not prevalent in all schools. Similarly, Ferguson (2001) challenged the black oppositional cultural theory by arguing that depending on the family backgrounds, both blacks and whites shared similar interests and aspiration toward schooling. Carter (2003) also pointed out that low-income black youths exhibit both "dominant" and "nondominant" cultural capital and how they negotiate these cultural expectations in school may be an important factor in analyzing school stratification and achievement.

Flores-Gonzalez (1999), in her research on a group of high-achieving Puerto Rican high school students, found that despite their involuntary immigrant status, these students did not associate school success with "whiteness." These middle-class students were academically successful while maintaining their ethnic identity. In the context of a school culture that embraced academic achievement, these students did not believe that doing well in school was associated with whiteness, but instead, achieving in school was very much in line with their ethnic background. In other words, the students associated achieving in school with their Puerto Rican identity, rather than rejecting their racial minority status as a barrier to their achievement. Therefore, Flores-Gonzalez (1999) highlighted the importance of ethnicity, class, and school context when examining minority student achievement.

Studies of post-1965 immigrants and their second-generation children have also complicated the dichotomous notion of voluntary and involuntary immigrants by pointing out that voluntary black immigrants from countries in the West Indies, for instance, are also likely to adopt oppositional cultural frame of reference from their peers. Portes and Zhou (1993) have argued that certain immigrant groups are more vulnerable to downward mobility depending on the immigrant group's neighborhood incorporation, strength of ethnic networks, and mode of adaptation.

For instance, according to Portes and Rumbaut (1996), the first-generation Haitian American community in Miami, Florida, had strong national identity and solidarity with fellow ethnic Haitian immigrants. However, their national pride and achievement orientation conflicted with the children's everyday experience in school. Little Haiti, located in Miami, is adjacent to Liberty City, which is the main black inner-city area of Miami. Haitian adolescents attended predominantly inner-city schools and were labeled by other native black youths as docile or subservient to whites. They were denigrated for their French, Creole, and Haitian accents. Consequently, second-generation children faced conflicting ideas and values: "To remain Haitian, they would have to face social ostracism and continuing attacks in school; to become American—Black American in this case—they would have to forgo their parents' dreams of making it in America on the basis of ethnic solidarity and preservation of traditional values" (p. 81). Since adversarial stance toward the white mainstream is common among inner-city minority youths, many Haitian second-generation youths were given messages by their peers in their school and community that devalued education as a means for social advancement. This message directly contradicts the first-generation parents' expectations. For many of these students, to be fully assimilated means assimilating into the values and norms of the poor inner-city rather than mainstream middle-class. In the process, the solidarity and support rooted in the Haitian ethnic community dissipates (Portes & Rumbaut, 1996).

Similarly, in Waters' research of black immigrant from the West Indies in Brooklyn, New York, she argues that the high achieving black immigrants were embedded in strong ethnic networks, such as church and community organizations, whereby first-generation parents and other immigrant adults provided important educational and employment information and resources for their second-generation children. By instilling immigrant values of education and ideals of achievement, the high-achieving black immigrant students tend to adopt their ethnic identities and immigrant status, while resisting assimilation into the cultures of their black peers of the inner-city neighborhoods where they resided. On the other hand, the low-achieving black immigrant students, in the context of residing in isolated neighborhoods with limited support from ethnic networks, were more likely to reject their ethnic identities and immigrant status, while adopting oppositional cultural frame of reference from their black peers in schools and neighborhoods.

Gibson (1988) also found that the second-generation Punjabi children in California are able to succeed in schools by sustaining strong ethnic identity and not assimilating to the dominant working-class white culture surrounding them. She noted this process as "accommodation without assimilation" and argued that through selective accommodation, Punjabis learn the skills necessary to succeed in schools but are able to keep from being culturally assimilated.

Similarly, Lew's (2004, 2006) research on Korean American high school students supported earlier findings. She argues that although culture is important, issues of class, race, and school context play an integral role in academic achievement among Asian American students. Although both high-and low-achieving students experienced racism and noted their racial minority status, the two groups adopted different strategies to negotiate such institutional barriers, and hence their racial and ethnic identities. She found that compared to the middle-class high-achievers, the poor and working-class low-achievers, in the context of urban high school that is fraught with increasing school violence and high school dropout rates, are more likely to disassociate from their ethnic identities and adopt oppositional cultural frame of reference from their peers as a way to resist their limited opportunities at home, communities, and school (2006). This finding indicates that resistance to school achievement may not be specific to involuntary immigrant groups, such as African Americans, but may be generalizable beyond specific student groups. Although students' race and sociocultural backgrounds play an important role, factors of class, peer relations, and school structure may also play an integral role when taking into account school achievement among minority students (Lew, 2006).

Research Site and Methods

In order to collect information on social processes, such as intergenerational negotiations, racial and ethnic identity construction, and schooling aspirations, the research is based on in-depth interviews and participant observations. This research took place in the New York City public school and a community-based GED program. A total of 72 Korean American students were interviewed: 42 in the academic magnet high school and 30 high school dropouts in the GED program. Both 1.5-generation (born in Korea but raised in the United States) and second-generation (born and raised in the United States) Korean American students were interviewed.

Although most of the students grew up and lived in Queens, New York—the borough with the largest ethnic enclaves of Korean Americans in the New York metropolitan area—they came from different socioeconomic and family backgrounds. Compared to the Korean high school dropouts, the magnet high school students came from higher socioeconomic backgrounds with a greater number of two-parent households. For instance, 36% of the academic students were eligible for reduced and free lunch, compared to 80% of the dropout students. Furthermore, when we consider their schooling context, we see an important distinction.

As one of the most competitive elite high school in New York City, the magnet high school (MH) prides itself on student academic achievement paralleled by few public high schools. According to the annual school report (NYC Board of Assessment, 2002–2003), approximately 2,700 students were enrolled, and since entrance to the school was based on a competitive standardized exam, students commute to the school from all five of New York City's boroughs. Almost half of the students were Asian (46.5%), while 37% were White, 9.1% Hispanic, and 7.4% black. Only about 1% consists of recent immigrants to the United States (those who immigrated within the last three years).

The Youth Community Center (YCC) is a nonprofit community-based organization in Queens, New York. Its education and outreach programs provide students and adults with counseling, tutoring, classes on the Test of English as a Foreign Language (TOEFL), English-as-a-second language (ESL) classes, and preparatory classes for the GED exam. All of the Korean students in the GED program had officially dropped out of their respective neighborhood public high schools in New York City, most of which had a record of low student academic performance and high school dropout rates, as well as a disproportionate number of poor minority students and recent immigrants, and had been referred to the program by teachers, counselors, parents, community members, and peers.

Findings

Middle-Class and High-Achieving Students: Race, Class, and Schools

At MH the students were steeped in a competitive college-bound curriculum taught by teachers and administrators who are certified in their fields. Students were also surrounded predominantly by middle-class White and Asian American peers who were immersed in the school culture that fostered academic achievement and excellence; thus, the Korean American students at MH were likely to associate with peers of similar socioeconomic status, education background, and academic expectations. Even for those Korean American students at MH whose families were of lower socioeconomic backgrounds, they were more likely to be exposed to and associate with other students of higher socioeconomic backgrounds.

Moreover, by attending a high school where second-generation Asian Americans represented nearly half (46.5%) of the student population, the Korean American students were likely to reinforce old or establish new friendships with other Asian and Korean American peers who also shared similar experiences growing up as children of immigrant parents. In this respect, institutional characteristics of the school played an important role in strengthening peer relations and helping second-generation youths negotiate their ethnic and racial identities.

According to the high-achieving students in the interview, this regular contact with Korean Americans in school and community formed the basis for an important set of shared experiences—growing up with immigrant parents and maintaining close ties to ethnic communities at home and school—which reinforced their ethnic identities. Susan explains:

> The Korean community of my age group, everyone knows everyone in some way. Like, either you're friends with someone that knows this other person…it's like everything is sort of related into one big circle…I started hanging out with Koreans, and then more other Korean friends came along…church especially, tae kwon do, neighborhood, they are all part of this big circle.

By being embedded in such networks at home, community, and school, the high-achieving students also reinforced their Korean language skill. For instance, John spoke about the importance of learning to speak Korean, and how bilingual skill is an important part of identifying with and reinforcing their Korean ethnic background:

> How do you identify yourself?
> Korean American. I have a lot of Korean pride. If I see a Korean kid who can't speak Korean at all, I'd just be like, you gotta learn Korean you know, you are Korean.

Helen also highlighted her ethnicity, identifying herself as a Korean American. However, she was careful to point out that she saw herself as both Korean and American. Her comments illustrate that social constructs such as race and ethnic identity are subject to change, contradiction, and variability within specific determinate contexts. When I asked her how she identified herself, she replied:

> Korean American. I was born here, so I am definitely American in some way, but I am, of course, Korean…Even if I am born here, I look definitely Asian or Korean or whatever and like the way my parents live and the way we are—we are not Americanized…if I compare myself to some of my friends, I am more American. They were born there [Korea] and raised there.

As illustrated, the process of identity construction is relative, filled with contradictions and inconsistencies. However, the students were also keenly aware of their racial minority status and associated becoming American with whiteness. Yet, as Helen noted, in a school context that has such a large number of Asian American students, she takes pride in being identified as "Asian."

I would never consider myself just American. Sometimes, if someone teased me or something, I just wanted and would've been happier if I was American, if I looked American. You know how Asians, they look totally different. So I guess if I looked American, no one would tease me and stuff…Now, since I am going to this school, and a lot of people are Asians, so I think being Asian is good. I would never want to be like someone else.

If the school context reinforced their ethnic and racial identity, their parents also played an important role. For instance, Beth comments that her parents reminded her that regardless of whether she was born and raised in the United States, most people would not accept her as an American because of her minority racial status:

When I think of Americans, I think of white people. My parents always told me that even though you are born here and can speak English as well as them, they won't really think of you as American. I don't completely believe that, but I think there is some basis truth in that. I think that if they look at you, they are going to say, you are Asian—and then attach the American thing after. So, the first impression that people will have of me will not be that she is American, but that she is Asian.

As illustrated, despite the students identification with ethnic backgrounds, the high-achieving Korean American students at MH were also painfully aware of how their racial minority status may be used to label them as foreigners or non-American by outsiders, despite their having been born and raised in the United States. Therefore, as much as the students identified with their ethnicity, this process is also framed by exclusion and marginalization.

According to the students, in order to address such marginalization, their parents emphasized the importance of using education to compensate for their racial barriers. Underlying this advice was a firm belief that to compensate for their racial-minority status, they had to work even harder and excel in school. Therefore, embedded in strong social support at home, communities, and school, the high-achieving Korean students learned to use education as a means to, in part, withstand the stigma accompanying their racial minority status. Yun Shin at MH, reiterated her mother's advice:

My mom would want me to be Americanized and get education, since there is so much racism against Asians and stuff, but she wants me to keep my Korean culture. Being American never entered my mind. It's not that I don't want to be, but it's just that I've never been accepted as one, never been considered one, so I never thought of myself as one. Because I am always surrounded by Asians, being American never entered my mind. You know, if I say, "I am American," they would say, "No, you are not. You are Asian."

The students' responses also echo findings from earlier studies that have shown how children of immigrants who maintain close ties to their ethnic communities are more likely to reinforce their ethnic identity toward excelling in school (Caplan, Choy, & Whitmore, 1991; Gibson, 1988; Lew, 2006, Portes & Rumbaut, 1996; Suarez-Orozco & Suarez-Orozco, 1995, 2001; Zhou & Bankston III, 1996, 1998). Gibson (1988) describes this as a strategy of accommodation or selective assimilation—a process whereby the children in Punjabi community learned skills necessary to be competitive in American society but resisted assimilating with the lower-socioeconomic white community in which they resided. Other studies on Southeast Asian refugee students also indicate that their academic success was primarily attributable to their close ties to their first-generation parental ethnic networks, and their ability to resist downward assimilation into their surrounding poor minority communities (Zhou & Bankston III, 1996, 1998).

Poor and Working-Class High School Dropouts: Race, Class, and Schools

Expanding on Ogbu's (1987) theory of oppositional cultural frame of reference and "acting white," an increasing number of studies have complicated the dichotomy of voluntary and involuntary groups' experiences by illustrating how members of both groups learn to adopt oppositional cultural frames of reference (Portes & Rumbaut 1996, 2001; Waters 1994, 1999). These studies show that children of immigrants who live in poor, isolated neighborhoods without the protection of strong immigrant networks and social capital are likely to assimilate the cultures and norms of their poor minority peers and adopt an oppositional cultural frame of reference that may not be conducive to schooling success.

The working-class Korean American dropouts not only struggled financially at home, but faced limited support in school. These urban schools mostly populated by poor minorities and recent immigrants, were fraught with violence and high dropout rates. In this school context, the low-income Korean American dropouts rarely came into contact with wealthy whites. Rather, most of their peers were working-class and poor Asians, Blacks, and Hispanics. The racial and economic isolation of these youngsters, therefore, perpetuated their distrust of and alienation from wealthy whites. Henry, who was born in Korea but raised in the United States, explained that he and his friends had very little contact with wealthy whites, either in school or in their neighborhoods, and that they saw whites largely through an oppositional lens:

> I feel closer to Blacks and Hispanics than whites. I think most Koreans are closer to black culture. It's not like I hate whites, but I don't like them either. When I see a white person, I don't see them as just a person. I see them as a white person. When I see them, I think, "I don't know you, I don't know what you do, and I don't want to get to know you." My friends don't like whites either, 'cause we sometimes get into fights with whites and the way they talk about white people. When I see a white person, the first thing I think about is that they are rich and educated, and most of Koreans like me are not educated and rich. So when I see them, I think they are from another planet.

It is important to note, however, that my participants also distinguished themselves from the "wealthy" Korean and other Asian Americans who grew up in middle-class homes and privileged neighborhoods. For instance, Emily explained how such "wealthy" Korean Americans from better neighborhoods would not understand her experience and struggles of growing up in housing projects populated by poor Blacks and Hispanics:

> This Korean girl I know at church was brought up in Bayside, which is mostly white and Asian. If she was brought up in Philadelphia, it would be different. For me, where I lived, majority of the people were Hispanics and Blacks. She doesn't know the environment I grew up in. I know their culture and the way they work. She only knows what she knows. It's mixed, but they are wealthier, and they live in houses. We struggled, and she grew up more comfortable. You know, where I grew up, everybody worked to make a living, the houses were dirty, lived in one bedroom with four people in it. You know, that's how I lived. One bedroom with my mother, father, brother, and me.

Emily continued to explain that her low social and economic status represented a kind of collective "minority" experience that distinguished her from the wealthier and privileged whites and Asians:

> We went through a lot living in that environment. She [wealthy Korean American friend] doesn't know a lot about that. She is more to the whites and Asians, and I am more to the Blacks and Hispanics, more toward the minority.

Similarly, Lee (2004) in her study of second-generation Korean American adults in New York City also found that middle-class Koreans touted their ethnicity and model minority status as reasons for their achievement. However, working-class Koreans interpreted their experiences as shaped largely by their class position. In the context of an ethic community that is predominantly middle-class and socially mobile, the working-class Korean Americans, in order to "save face" from being "looked down" upon, tend to distance themselves somewhat from Korean communities at large and downplay their ethnicity (Lee, 2004).

Interestingly enough, as the Korean American high school dropouts distinguished themselves from their co-ethnic peers along class lines, they also distinguished themselves from more educated or "studious" Koreans. Ken explained that he had many Korean American friends whom he had met in Korean churches, clubs, or schools. But he carefully distinguished himself from the "studious" Koreans. He noted that while his Korean American friends "hang out" after church, the "studious" Koreans go home after school with their family:

> I don't hang out with anyone else but Koreans. I used to hang out at the Elmhurst Park a lot. I used to play basketball there, and when you play sports there you meet people, and then you meet their friends. The basketball thing was always after the [church] service. Those kinds of people, you know, the studious people who don't go out much, would leave right after the service. So, you know who they are.

Ken continued to explain how he aligned "studious" and "wealthy" Koreans with whiteness because of the way they spoke, dressed, and succeeded in school:

> They [studious Koreans] live a different world. Totally different. When I look at them, I never had a friend like them, so I don't know. When I see them, it's like I am seeing a white person. They never cut school, they use a different language, they use proper language, and I use slangs. They dress more simple; some try to show off, but they don't care what other people think. Their hairstyles are different. Most of them are like whites because they don't know this kind of life, and they hang out with whites, and most of the time they don't hang out anyway.

The findings show that in addition to distinguishing themselves from wealthy whites, the low-status dropouts also distinguished themselves from socially mobile Koreans and other Asians whom they deemed "wealthy and studious"—attributes of "success" they associated with whiteness. In the process, most of the dropouts aligned their shared experiences of racism and low socioeconomic status with those of their low-income minority peers—Blacks, Hispanics, and Asians (Lew, 2004, 2006).

In a society based on a polarized discourse of success and failure, rich and poor, and Black and white, it is no surprise that students struggled to make sense of their distinctive experience, one marked by low socioeconomic and racial-minority status. Their comments represent their negotiation within a polarized racial discourse that tolerates Asians as either "near-whites" or invisible minorities, and whose experiences are often de-racialized and de-contextualized. Within the Black and white racial paradigm, Asians, American Indians, and Latinos are defined in relation to acting either white or Black. As Okihiro (1994) notes, racial paradigm of being "near-whites" or "just like Blacks" is historically and socially constructed, where Asian Americans have been marginalized throughout U.S. history, as the labels of "near-Blacks" in the past or "near-whites" in the present demonstrate.

Meanwhile, embedded in the students' comments is also the implicit marginalization they experience *within* the Korean community (Lew, 2005, 2006). To be poor and uneducated within a community that is predominantly middle class, college educated, and upwardly mobile also means being looked down on and being excluded. As a means of developing survival strategies to endure and resist such marginalization within their own co-ethnic communities, as well as withstand institutional barriers such as inferior schooling, economic limitation, and racial discrimination within the larger society, the working-class Korean American high school dropouts formed cultural frames of reference and social identities in opposition to the dominant society.

Conclusion

To summarize, both groups of Korean students negotiated their racial and ethnic identities differently according to the changing social and economic context. The high-achieving Korean American students in the context of an academic high school with a significant number of middle-class white and Asian student body, were more likely to identify with their ethnicity. They often described themselves as both Korean and American noting the varied ways in which this process is filled with contradictions. Despite the fluidity of identities, however, the students also saw their racial identities ascribed to them in the form of exclusionary stereotypes and false constructs of homogeneity. As illustrated, the high-achieving Korean American students typically associated being "American" with whiteness and pointed out that because of their racial minority status, they would not be accepted as "American" despite being born and raised in the United States.

In order to resist this racial minority status and marginalization that accompanies it, the middle-class and high-achieving students are more likely to use education as a racial strategy. That is, they firmly uphold the belief that as racial minorities, they would have to work even harder in school to obtain the economic parity with white Americans. This predicament highlights multiple and situational meanings associated with being American, the salience of race, as well as the integral and complex relationship between race and class in the United States.

On the other hand, the Korean high school dropouts in the context of poor urban schools fraught with academic failure and populated by poor minority students, adopted a different mode of adaptation. The Korean dropouts were less likely to identify with their ethnicity. By distinguishing themselves from wealthy and educated Koreans and Asians who symbolically represent whiteness, they identified themselves with other "minorities"—a collective term symbolizing downward mobility and struggles with racism and poverty. In order to negotiate and resist such institutional barriers in their homes, schools, and communities, these low-income Korean American students dropped out of high school and adopted behaviors that were not conducive to school achievement.

The findings poignantly illustrate how social class intersects with identity and school achievement. It shows how middle-class high-achieving students, compared to the poor and working-class high school dropouts, have greater access to educational resources and social capital at their respective schools and ethnic communities—institutional resources that are pivotal for students to achieve academically (Lew, 2004; 2006; in press). The middle-class Korean students in the study, compared to poor and working-class Korean students, are more likely to gain access to teachers, counselors, and peers who can provide important schooling resources toward achieving in school. Therefore, even though both groups of Korean American students bring with them their distinct cultural capital and forge important relationships with fellow peers in schools and communities, the social and cultural resources available to middle-class high-achieving students are more likely to be rewarded by the mainstream school system.

Moreover, the findings point to the importance of noting class variability within ethnic communities and the implications this may have in negotiation of racial and ethnic identities. For instance, as beneficial as ethnic networks can be, depending on the background of the member, it can also serve to exclude: that is, in the context of an ethnic community that is predominantly middle-class and socially mobile, the middle-class and high-achieving Korean Americans are more likely to benefit from their ethnic communities and align themselves with their ethnic backgrounds. However, the poor and working-class high school dropouts, often facing exclusion from their own ethnic communities are less likely to benefit from their ethnic communities and disassociate themselves from their ethnic backgrounds.

The findings also complicate earlier understandings of oppositional cultural frames of reference and "acting white": In the context of a binary Black and white racial discourse, as well as the prevalent model minority stereotype that conflates Asian Americans with whiteness, the findings in this study illustrate how Asian American students in different social and economic contexts negotiate their racial minority status and social class backgrounds. To that end, it is important to distinguish the variability of social class and peer relations, highlight the fluidity of multiple identities, and examine institutional factors and schooling contexts when accounting for students' negotiation of identities and interpretation of opportunity structure.

Moreover, the stereotype of Asian "success" much like Black "failure" cannot be explained solely on their cultural orientation. Although race and cultures play an important role in students' outlook and negotiations of their opportunity structure, this process changes and adapts to given social and school contexts. Through expanding the current debate across and within racial/ethnic lines, this research shows that culture is significant and race remains salient; however, in order to examine academic aspirations and achievement among minority students, researchers may benefit by examining race relations beyond a Black and white discourse, and how students' racial and ethnic identities intersect with culture, class, race, and school context.

References

Ainsworth-Darnell, J. W., & Downey, D. B. (1998). Assessing the oppositional culture explanation for racial/ethnic differences in school performance. *American Sociological Review, 63*(4), 536–553.

Caplan, N., Choy, M. H., & Whitmore, J. K. (1991). *Children of the boat people: A study of educational success.* Ann Arbor: University of Michigan Press.

Carter, Prudence. (2003). "Black" cultural capital, status positioning, and schooling conflicts for low-income African American youth. *Social Problems, 50*(1), 136–155.

Cook, P. J., & Ludwig, J. (1998). The Burden of acting white: Do black adolescents disparage academic achievement. In Jencks, C. & Phillips, M. (Eds.), *The black-white test score gap* (pp. 375–400). Washington D.C.: Brookings Institute Press.

Downey, D. B., & Ainsworth-Darnell, J. W. (2002). The search for oppositional culture among black students. *American Sociological Review, 67*(1), 156–164.

Espiritu, Y. L. (1994). The intersection of race, ethnicity, and class: The multiple identities of second-generation Filipinos. *Identities, 9,* 249–273.

Ferguson, R. (2001). A diagnostic analysis of black-white GPA disparities in Shaker Heights, Ohio. In Ravitch, D. (Ed.), *Brookings Paper on Education Policy 2001* (pp. 347–414). Washington D.C.: Brookings Institute Press.

Flores-Gonzales, N. (1999). Puerto Rican high achievers: An example of ethnic and academic identity compatibility. *Anthropology and Education Quarterly, 30*(3), 343–362.

Fordham, S., & Ogbu, J. U. (1986). Black student's school success: Coping with the "burden of 'acting white.'" *The Urban Review, 18,* 176–204.

Kibria, N. (2002). *Becoming Asian American: Second-generation Chinese and Korean American identities.* Baltimore, MD: Johns Hopkins University Press.

Lew, J. (2004). The "Other" Story of Model Minorities: Korean American High School Dropouts in an Urban Context. *Anthropology and Education Quarterly, 35*(3), 297–311.

Lew, J. (2006). *Asian Americans in Class: Charting the Achievement Gap Among Korean American Youth.* New York: Teachers College Press.

Ogbu, J. U. (1987). Variability in minority school performance: A problem in search of an explanation. *Anthropology & Education Quarterly, 18,* 312–334.

Ogbu, J. U., & Matute-Bianchi, M. E. (1986). Understanding sociocultural factors: Knowledge, identity, and school adjustment. In *Beyond language: Social and cultural factors in schooling language minority students.* Los Angeles: California State University, Evaluation, Dissemination, and Assessment Center.

Ogbu, J. U. (1994). Racial Stratification and Education in the United States: Why Inequality Persists. *Teachers College Record, 96*(2), 264–298.

Okihiro, G. (1994). *Margins and mainstreams: Asians in American history and culture.* Seattle, WA: University of Washington Press.

Omi, M., & Winant, H. (1994). *Racial formation in the United States: From the 1960s to the 1990s.* London: Routledge.

Portes, A. (Ed.) (1996). *The new second generation.* New York: Russell Sage Foundation.

Portes, A., & Rumbaut, R. G. (1996). *Immigrant America: A portrait*. Berkeley: University of California Press.

Portes, A., & Rumbaut, R. G. (2001). *Legacies: The Story of the immigrant second-generation*. Berkeley: University of California Press.

Portes, A., & Zhou, M. (1993). The new second generation: Segmented assimilation and its variants. *Annals of the American Academy, 530*, 74–96.

Suárez-Orozco, C., & Suárez-Orozco, M. (1995). Transformations: Immigration, family, life, and achievement motivation amonz Latino adolescents. Stanford, CA: Stanford University Press.

Suárez-Orozco, C., & Suárez-Orozco, M. (2001). *Children of immigration*. Cambridge, MA: Harvard University Press.

Tyson, K. (2002). Weighing in: Elementary-Age students and the debate on attitudes toward school among black students. *Social Forces, 80*(4), 1157–1189.

Tyson, K, Darity, W. Jr., & Castellino, D. R. (2005). It's not "a black Thing": Understanding the burden of acting white and other dilemmas of high achievement. *American Sociological Review, 70*(4), 582–605.

Waters, M. C. (1999). *Black identities: West Indian immigrant dreams and American realities*. Cambridge, MA: Harvard University Press.

Zhou, M., & Bankston III, C. L. (1996). Social capital and the adaptation of the second generation: The case of Vietnamese youth in New Orleans. In A. Portes (Ed.), *The new second generation* (pp. 197–220). New York: Russell Sage Foundation.

Zhou, M., & Bankston III, C. L. (1998). *Growing up American: How Vietnamese children adapt to life in the United States*. New York: Russell Sage Foundation.

22

The Help-Seeking Orientations of Latino and Non-Latino Urban High School Students

A Critical-Sociological Investigation

RICARDO D. STANTON-SALAZAR, LISA F. CHÁVEZ, AND ROBERT H. TAI

1. Introduction

Scholars across disciplinary domains who study child and adolescent socialization are showing considerable and growing interest in social networks.[1] This scholarly attention includes how the structure, composition, and resourcefulness of young people's interpersonal networks *mediate* the relation between society's social hierarchies and opportunities for developmental gains and educational success.[2] Included here, particularly in the study of minority youth development, are efforts to delineate how the systemic forces of class, race, and gender exercise their power indirectly, by shaping young people's very adaptation to the structural constraints and possibilities characterizing their social networks and environment (Cross, 1990; Ogbu, 1991a, b; Stanton-Salazar, 2000). This is to say that the social engines of class, race, and gender not only determine opportunity structures, but also help shape people's coping responses to these structures in ways that aid social reproduction. In the case of many lower working-class youth, their oppositional or defensive coping strategies are never the root causes of their structural predicament, but in the absence of humanizing ethnic-based or institutional interventions, these coping patterns can often go a long way toward exacerbating already distressful and disempowering circumstances (e.g., Willis, 1977; MacLeod, 1987; Ogbu, 1991a, b; McQuillan, 1998).

This study examines a particular feature of the coping and adaptation process as manifested by adolescents enrolled in working-class urban schools. Specifically, we look at young people's proclivity (or disinclination) to resolve personal, academic, and family problems through the mobilization of relationships and through the seeking of social support (i.e., coping by seeking help). Serious scholarly attention to this aspect of consciousness, conventionally termed *network orientation* and originating in social anthropology (Barnes, 1972; Katz, 1974), is found in the work of community psychologists, epidemiologists, and sociologists who study mental health (Lin, Dean, & Ensel, 1986; Vaux, Burda, & Stewart, 1986; Wallace & Vaux, 1993). Psychologists in particular have alerted us to the important role of network orientation in child development and parenting (Cochran et al., 1990). Apart from a number of recent works which draw attention to a more expanded conception of network orientation (Stanton-Salazar, 1997; Phelan, Davidson, & Yu, 1998), most explicit treatments of this phenomenon in the literature have focused on help-seeking beliefs and practices. In order to provide some conceptual clarity to this and related phenomena, we use the term *help-seeking orientation* to specifically address issues of help seeking and social support, and treat it as one key dimension of a more complex constellation of network-relevant dispositions and skills related to adaptation to environmental demands, stressors, and opportunity structures (whether opened or closed).

In the following pages we attempt to theoretically expand on the role of adolescent help-seeking orientation as an important mediating link between the systemic forces of class, race, and gender and young people's life chances. We also present an empirical study of adolescent help-seeking orientation based on a self-administered questionnaire survey of one urban high school situated in a large west-coast city in the United States. The study examines three measures of help-seeking orientation, and looks at a set of variables known to have predictive value among adult populations. Special attention and discussion are devoted to the influence of social class, gender, English-language proficiency, and academic performance. Our survey of this urban high school, where 67% of the student body was Latino (predominantly Mexican-origin), provided us an opportunity to explore the influence of cultural variations within one particular ethnic group (Mexican-origin/Latino students). In the course of this study, we paid special attention to the well-known distinctive experience of Spanish-dominant immigrant students; we felt this attention was necessary considering their rapidly growing presence in the California school system (Olsen, 1997). We also explored whether the help-seeking orientations of our two Latino student groups might be significantly different from the non-Latino population at the school (EuroAmerican/Whites, African Americans, Asians combined), including whether the predictive value of our antecedent variables differ significantly across our principal ethnolinguistic groupings (Spanish-dominant Latinos, highly English-proficient Latinos, and English-proficient non-Latinos).

Help-Seeking Orientation and 'Social Embeddedness' Within the School

We propose here that students' help-seeking orientation, particularly those exhibited by working-class minority youth, provide one insightful indicator of students' social integration within the school, with 'integration' (of the individual) reconceptualized here in network-analytic terms. Whereas classical depictions of social integration have emphasized the social psychological states of group membership and identity as well as the internalization of norms and values (Durkheim, 1951; Tinto, 1987; Coleman, 1988; Wehlage, Rutter, Lesko, & Fernández, 1989), our interest here is in a group of network processes nicely captured in the term *social embeddedness*, a concept taken from the work of Mark Granovetter (1985).[3] We present our version of embeddedness, and highlight the associated processes, in terms of three principal dimensions.

The first dimension of embeddedness pertains to the network of relations or ties which serve as conduits to vital institutional resources, privileges, and knowledge-forms. Such ties are activated in a number of ways, although our interest here centers on the help-seeking behaviors enacted by the student as part of a coping strategy for dealing with an array of problems associated with life circumstances, schooling, and academic performance (see Frydenberg, 1997). Related aspects of this dimension have to do with the structure and composition of the individual's social network. One aspect, for example, entails the quantity and diversity of relationships Granovetter refers to as weak ties (1982). Such ties, although characterized by trust, are not part of the individual's core network, and usually center on the exchange or provision of a particular or specialized form of social and institutional support. Among low-status youth, positive or empowering embeddedness entails both strong and weak ties to a number of diverse and supportive institutional agents, in contrast to an overdependence on single agents and mentors (i.e., highly multiplex ties). In this scenario, young people actively participate and seek help within a set of diversified social relationships with agents capable and oriented toward providing, or negotiating one's access to, multiple forms of institutional resources.

The second dimension of embeddedness entails aspects that, for low-status groups and their members (e.g., minorities, working-class persons), make relations with institutional agents particularly challenging. For this group, social relations with institutional agents and gate-keepers embody network dynamics tacitly set within multiple social hierarchies and usually oriented towards obstructing the development of trust and authentically supportive relations. Such dynamics, according to Granovetter (1985), are founded upon the greater structural relations and historical tensions existing between different status groups of which interacting parties are a part (e.g., racial, ethnic, religious, class, and gender groupings).

Given this second dimension of embeddedness, key individual and institutional processes play their mediating role. We focus here on those processes at the individual level, and draw particular attention in this article to the social psychological aspects of social embeddedness—the third dimension conceptualized here. Cumulative network experiences across institutional sites shape perceptions, attitudes, beliefs, and dispositions relating generally to the development and maintenance of various relationships and networks, and specifically, to the mobilization of such ties and networks for purposes of resolving personal, academic, and/or family problems. One key aspect of this cognitive orientation, particularly among low-status persons, has to do with coping strategies to either defuse or sustain (or resign to) those latent yet imposing structural dynamics responsible for engendering social distance and distrust between low-status persons and institutional agents (see, Blau, 1964; Erickson & Shultz, 1982; Lareau, 1989).[4] This third dimension, of course, represents the foundation of individual agency in institutional life, and is captured here in this paper in terms of students' help-seeking orientation—that is, their proclivity to seek others for support (or to withdraw from others) in times of need.

In light of these three dimensions, for low-status individuals, positive embeddedness (i.e., large, resourceful networks; network dynamics oriented towards trust, confidence, and dependability; and a proclivity toward help seeking) is never a taken-for-granted feature of 'normal development'. For this population, movement towards positive embeddedness, under 'normal' societal conditions, requires mitigating processes (set into motion by the exceptional individual, by the community, by institutional agents, or by all parties working either collectively or independently), and gradually manifests itself in terms of trusting relations, active help seeking, and authentic institutional support. Negative embeddedness, in contrast, manifests itself as the norm in network dynamics that produces a significant degree of conflict, distrust and/or social distance, in the lack of help seeking, and in the generally experienced scarcity of genuine institutional support.

How do we more closely link these three primary dimensions of embeddedness with the systemic forces of class, race, and gender? We see urban schools organized in ways that work in tandem with society's patterns of stratification and *counterstratification*. On the one hand, schools provide fertile ground for the deleterious effects of class, race, and gender to operate on the subjectivities of lower-status students (Bowles & Gintis, 1976; Fine, 1991; Bourdieu & Wacquant, 1992; McQuillan, 1998). On the other hand, schools provide an institutional arena for some low-status groups and individuals to exercise special psycho-cultural resources which allow them to neutralize the effects of deleterious social forces, to maintain high self-regard and high levels of motivation, and to engage school agents as key sources of social and institutional support (Matute-Bianchi, 1986; Ogbu, 1991a, c; Valenzuela, 1999; Stanton-Salazar, 2001/a).

The important role of help-seeking orientation in the embeddedness experiences of urban high school adolescents can be articulated in both of the scenarios above. In the first scenario, the known detrimental effects of lower social class and racial segregation on adult help-seeking and networking behavior is permitted to recreate itself in school as well, translating into restricted networks and a negative or defensive help-seeking orientation. Such a negative orientation has its effects through a self-regulated social estrangement from school personnel and academically-oriented peers capable of transmitting important forms of social, emotional, and institutional support (e.g., funds of knowledge associated with college admission).

This is not meant to obscure in any way the marginalizing *structural* effects of curricular tracking, overcrowded schools, underfunding, and poorly trained teachers and counselors (e.g., Cicourel & Mehan, 1983; Berliner & Biddle, 1995; Anyon, 1997). Instead, our purpose is to highlight an important way such institutional structures do their 'work'. Lower-status students enter school already psychologically burdened and distressed by the routine effects of race and class on family and community life. Taken this as a given, a school's stratifying structures has its (often hidden) detrimental impact, in great part, by 'embedding' students in conflict-producing or unprotecting social relations which, in turn, restimulate and aggravate students' pre-existing and evolving distress patterns (see Lipsky, 1987; Phelan, Davidson, & Yu, 1998; Valenzuela, 1999; Stanton-Salazar, 2000). Such distress patterns (and associated coping strategies) usually become manifest in terms of students' estrangement and withdrawal from key sources of social and institutional support (Wehlage et al., 1989). Simply put, low-status students embedded in conflict-producing or uncaring social relations in urban schools are the least likely to cope with academic and life distresses by building relationships with, and seeking help from, school personnel and academically-oriented peers (Nelson-Le Gall & Jones, 1991; Stanton-Salazar & Dornbusch, 1995; Stanton-Salazar, Tai, & Bressler, 1999).

Public schools, of course, are the primary institution whereby working-class youth cultivate their orientation toward institutional agents, gate-keepers, and higher status peers. What this means becomes clear in Colleta's (1987) succinct appraisal of this phenomenon:

> It is logical to expect that when an individual has repeatedly had positive experiences finding others willing to help in time of need, and when assistance has proven effective, the individual will develop the general belief that a productive method of dealing with problems is to seek help from others. When, on the other hand, individuals have been rebuffed in their efforts to seek assistance or when that assistance has resulted in negative consequences, they are likely to hold the attitude that it is less threatening to rely on their own resources than to ask for help (p. 150).

Similarly, we argue that defensive help-seeking orientations in high school can potentially translate into similar orientations as young adults (Cochran, 1990b; Wallace & Vaux, 1993), further diminishing opportunities for accessing resources relevant to buffering the adverse effects of class, racial, and gender domination.

Looking at a different scenario, some immigrant communities are able to recreate and sustain communitarian practices which embody the social values of affiliation, attachment and cooperation, mutual trust and social support (Ramirez & Castañeda, 1974; Vélez-Ibáñez, 1980; Zhou & Bankston, 1998). Most importantly, they are able to perceive and interpret the discriminatory forces of class and race through a cultural framework that sustains their optimism and high aspirations (Ogbu, 1991a). Many non-immigrant minority students distance themselves from institutional agents they have learned to distrust. In contrast, many immigrant-oriented students—once they are proficient in English—not only exhibit strong inclinations to seek support from available school personnel, they also find that their distinctive psycho-cultural orientations make them particularly attractive to school agents (i.e., as 'safe', 'nice kids'); this is especially the case when contrasted with the often defiant and distrustful orientations of their non-immigrant and low-achieving peers (Matute-Bianchi, 1991; Stanton-Salazar & Dornbusch, 1995; Valenzuela, 1999).

The Significance of Perceived Support, Help-Seeking Orientations, and Contextual Antecedents: A Review of Selected Empirical Studies

In a recent study, Croninger and Lee (1999) sought to determine whether supportive relations with teachers increases the likelihood that students complete high school, particularly among those students who are at risk of academic failure. Using data from the national educational longitudinal study (NELS:88), these researchers found that evidence of such relations, measured in terms of students' *perceived support*, reduces the probability of dropping out by nearly half. Most importantly, for students from low-income backgrounds and for those who had experienced academic difficulties in the past, supportive relations with teachers were shown to be particularly beneficial. Past studies have shown a close link between high levels of perceived support and a positive help-seeking orientation (discussed below).

In another recent study, Stanton-Salazar, Tai, and Bressler (1999) demonstrate the close associations between students' help-seeking orientation—as an indicator of the social psychological dimension of embeddedness—and access to key forms of academic and institutional support. Students reporting positive help-seeking orientations, as well as those reporting higher levels of *perceived support*, exhibited the greatest likelihood of actively seeking academic assistance from teachers and counselors, net of the other independent variables. These psychologically-connected students also reported a greater likelihood of participation in non-athletic school organizations, relative to those with negative orientations and low levels of perceived support.[5] These findings closely correspond to what researchers have found in their study of help-seeking orientations among adults. Vaux, Burda, and Stewart (1986), using four samples of college students and one sample of adults, found that persons with positive help-seeking orientations, relative to those with negative orientations, reported significantly larger networks—in other words, a greater number of people they could potentially draw upon for social support. Evidence also emerged showing that those respondents with positive orientations showed a significantly greater likelihood of coping with personal problems by seeking assistance from significant others, and in turn, generally enjoyed more advice and guidance, and more material, financial, and emotional support then their counterparts with less than positive orientations. Vaux and Wood (1987), in a similar study utilizing path-analytic modeling, found that relative to persons with a negative help-seeking orientation, those with positive orientations were more likely to feel socially connected and cared for, more likely to actively cultivate supportive ties with significant others, and less likely to experience psychological distress.

The disciplinary domains of community and cross-cultural psychology have also alerted us to how children's help-seeking orientation factor into the developmental experiences of 'resilient' children. Attention has centered on children who develop high levels of competency and sociability, and who demonstrate positive coping patterns, in spite of growing up in stressful and problem-plagued environments (Werner & Smith, 1982; see, Garbarino, Dubrow, Kostelny, & Pardo, 1992, for review). Stable emotional relations with caregivers and a supportive educational environment appear to be the key. Resilient children are able to cope effectively with the social ills and pressures emanating from segregation, economic dislocation, and the distress patterns of community members. "They are able to adapt quickly to new situations, perceived clearly what is occurring, communicate freely, act flexibly, and view themselves in a positive way. Compared to vulnerable children, they are able to…ask for help when they need it" (Garbarino, Dubrow, Kostelny, & Pardo, 1992, p. 103; citing the work of Anthony & Cohler, 1987).

Contextual Effects on Social Networks and Help-seeking Orientation

A substantive body of studies in the areas of mental health, community psychology, and sociology have attempted to delineate the close connection between social structural factors (e.g., low-SES, segregated urban environments) and the conditions for life-long network building—specifically, opportunities for easy entrée into different social and institutional contexts and for cultivating relationships with agents who exert various degrees of influence over social networks, institutional resources and privileges, and opportunities for social mobility and for personal and financial empowerment (Wellman, 1983). In the literature on adult networks, social class is clearly the preeminent force, shaping both the structure and composition of people's networks, as well as the likelihood of forming supportive ties with gate-keepers and those who control the allocation of institutional privileges and resources (Fischer, 1982; Lin, 1982, 1990).

We focus here on the influence of class stratifying forces on the network orientations and coping styles of different status groups. Besides governing the structure of social networks (e.g., size, composition, boundedness), class systemic forces also go a long way toward shaping how different people cope with stressors and crises related to class, racial, and gender oppression. A few studies have demonstrated the effect of social class on help seeking among adults, with social class most often measured in terms of years of schooling and income. Eckenrode (1983) investigated the help-seeking behavior of a group of adult women with children, with coping behavior measured following stressful events. Not only did Eckenrode find positive statistical associations between help-seeking beliefs and SES (income and education measured separately), but also that the usual predictors (number of potential supporters, locus of control, and help-seeking beliefs) had much less impact on help-seeking behavior for those of lower SES and for those of Spanish-speaking background.[6] Referencing Pearlin and Schooler (1978), Eckenrode states that low-status groups "appear doubly at risk for experiencing psychological strain because they are exposed to more stressors as well as having fewer effective coping resources" (p. 524).

Institutional, ethnic, and subcultural influences on people's help-seeking orientation have yet to be fully explored (see Stanton-Salazar, 2000). The multidisciplinary literature on social networks does, however, suggest that help-seeking beliefs are lodged within a particular institution's or community's *network orientation*, understood here as a set of distinctive normative and micro-economic principles which govern social relations, social interactions, and social exchanges. It would seem that such forces would certainly influence the strategies people adopt for coping with environmental stressors and life-crises (e.g., unemployment, sickness, etc.). Yet, the effects of race and ethnicity on a group's network and help-seeking orientations are deeply intertwined with the effects of social class (Cross, 1990). The fundamental cultural manifestations of both *metropolitan* and *rural* working-class groups and ethnic minority groups seem to most easily converge when seen within the context of structural relations with public institutions controlled by agents and authority figures from the middle and upper-middle classes. These relations have been extensively elaborated in the work of Pierre Bourdieu and others.

According to Lamont and Lareau's critique and extension of Bourdieu's work on cultural capital (e.g., Bourdieu & Passeron, 1977), access to valuable institutional resources and opportunities, as well as the rules of engagement with gatekeepers and highly positioned institutional agents, are founded upon the cultural capital of middle- and upper-class institutional agents (Lamont & Lareau, 1988). For low-status persons, effective relations frequently require a hard-to-gain facility with the discourses, cognitive styles, and cultural sensitivities of the dominant group (see also, Gee, 1989; Stanton-Salazar, 1997). Following the framework presented in this paper, we can say that in mainstream institutional arenas (e.g., work, school, government services), low-status individuals are typically embedded in hierarchical social relations marked by distrust and geared toward the inequitable distribution of resources and opportunities. When such individuals are unable to mobilize politically and effectively as a group, they are usually left to their own devices (Blau, 1964). Supportive relations with institutional agents usually require a tolerance as well as particular social competencies for engaging agents from a hierarchically subordinate position, where patronizing behavior, disrespect, coercion, and discriminatory treatment can often become routine.[7] Such dynamics can become part of the institutional culture, solidifying relations of distrust, social distance, cultural resistance and intergroup antagonisms (Blau, 1964; Fischer, 1975; Ogbu, 1991a, b, c). Embeddedness in such contexts, of course, does not provide fertile ground for the development of coping strategies that rely heavily on help-seeking and network-building practices which incorporate institutional agents. In this scenario, individual success in help seeking and network building becomes a curious exception to the rule.

Such problematic embeddedness is perhaps most easily visible in urban public high school settings (Fine, 1991; Anyon, 1997; McQuillan, 1998). Here, the background effects of class, race/ethnicity, and gender (e.g., being a working-class Chicano male) operate to complicate if not undermine the development of trusting relations between low-status students and school agents and to inhibit the help-seeking behavior of the former. The organizational constraints on student help-seeking opportunities further thwart the cultivation of this form of coping behavior (Nelson-Le Gall & Jones, 1991). Schools and classrooms have been shown to impact students' network and help-seeking orientations in other ways as well. Different schools and classrooms are believed to provide different opportunities for cultivating dispositions that foster life-long network-building (Fischer, 1982; Wilcox, 1982; Nelson-Le Gall, 1985; Cochran, 1990a, b; Stanton-Salazar, 1997). Existing research has also shown that high levels of academic performance are associated with greater help-seeking behavior as well as with the incorporation of school agents into students' support networks (Stanton-Salazar & Dornbusch, 1995; Stanton-Salazar, Tai, & Bressler, 1999).

The Role of Gender on Help-seeking Orientation

Considerable attention has been paid to the effect of gender on help-seeking behavior. Throughout this literature, we also see gender manifesting both its stratification and *counterstratification* potentialities. As discussed above, we seek to cast help-seeking orientation—among low-status students—as an important indicator of social psychological embeddedness within the school site. To what degree does gender exert its effect on help seeking, both among adolescents as well as within the adult population? Are low-status adolescent boys particularly at risk of negative embeddedness and social estrangement from key sources of social and institutional support?

Although considerable attention has been paid to the effect of gender on help-seeking beliefs and behavior patterns, there is very little comparative research on gender variation in network and help-seeking orientations across class and racial groups (see, Reiley & Cochran 1987; Cross, 1990, for two exceptions). Overall, many studies have shown that females, compared to males throughout the life-span, are more willing to seek help from both informal (friends, family) and formal (i.e., professionals) sources in times of need or distress. In particular, consistent gender differences have been found among children (Garland & Ziegler, 1994; Salomon & Strobel, 1997), adolescents (see, Offer & Schonert-Reichl, 1992 for a review; Garland & Ziegler, 1994; Rickwood & Braithwaite, 1994; Boldero & Fallon, 1995; Schonert-Reichl & Muller, 1996), and adults (see, McMullen & Gross, 1983 for a review; Good, Dell, & Mintz, 1989). While some researchers have noted some evidence that this relationship varies according to social context and problem type (Boldero & Fallon, 1995), as well as source of support (Blyth & Foster-Clark, 1989), for the most part, there is a consensus that females have stronger pro-help-seeking orientations.

Reasons for this consistent finding vary. One line of research notes the relationship between perceived availability of support and willingness to ask for support (Vaux, Burda, & Stewart, 1986); since, relative to males, females report a larger base of social support, especially with regards to kin, they are much more willing and likely to ask for support (see Feiring & Coates, 1987, for a review; Turner, 1994). Female friendships are also characterized by intimacy and emotional support (Youniss & Smoller, 1985), while male friendships are characterized by mutual activities and 'instrumental support' (see Blyth & Foster-Clark, 1989, for a review of this literature). Another explanation for these gender differences lies in gender-role expectations and socialization. A number of studies have shown that the intensity of negative or ambivalent dispositions toward seeking support vary according to the individual's adherence to traditional male gender roles usually learned during early and adolescent socialization, with the greatest reluctance associated with adherence to rigid gender roles (Good, Dell, & Mintz, 1989). Similarly, another study notes that females' help-seeking orientations become more positive and networks increase in size during adolescence, a time when gender-role specific expectations increase, with girls moving from being nurtured (as children) to their prescribed roles as nurturers (Blyth & Foster-Clark, 1989). As a result, adolescent girls, relative to boys, were more likely to be intimate (defined as having relations characterized by acceptance, shared feelings, understanding and advice receiving) with non-kin adult females (although see Riley & Cochran, 1987 which found that black adolescent boys had more adult non-kin in their social networks).

The implications of these gender differences, combined with those described in our discussion of social class above, do not bode well for low-status males, especially in the arena of schooling. Overall, the research reviewed here tells us that we can expect to find low-status males less positively embedded in their schools when compared with low-status females. Further investigation into the conceptual and theoretical relevance of adult and adolescent help-seeking orientations is sorely needed. Our consideration of this phenomenon, as a proxy for social psychological embeddedness within school and for either developmental resiliency or risk-status, has focused on antecedents such as social class and gender. This focus mirrors our concern that adolescent help-seeking orientation may be operating as an important mediator between stratification forces and life-chances, particularly as this plays out within the segregated urban high school. The purpose of our study is to explore the effect of individual-level characteristics on the help-seeking orientations of high school students—particularly Latinos. The individual-level factors we chose to examine emerged from this focal concern and from our review of the literature.

Data and Method

Our analysis relies on data from a questionnaire survey administered in the spring of 1992 to the student body at a public urban high school in a large southern California city. Two-thirds of the official total school enrollment (1,513) were Latino (67%), while 11% were Black, 20% White, and 8% were Asian and Pacific Islander. Due to a high number of absences on the day of administration, we were only able to survey 78% (1,187) of the entire student body.[8] An English version of the survey was taken by 69% of the participants while 31% took a Spanish version. The high school is stratified into three grade levels; approximately 40% of the students who took the survey were 10th graders or sophomores, 34% were 11th graders or juniors, and 26% were 12th graders or seniors. The survey was conducted at the end of a year-long study by the first author which examined the social networks and help-seeking practices of Mexican-origin students at the school.[9] The solid majority of the student body was composed of Mexican-origin and African American students (about 78%), and resided in about six principal neighborhoods, each of which featured high rates of (official) household poverty (approximately 40–50%).[10] Most of the Euro-American students enrolled at this school were bused in from suburban communities (or outlying metropolitan areas), as part of a voluntary desegregation program at the school; this program featured a considerably exclusive and high-powered academic curriculum as well as specialized teachers. Only about 32% of Latino students surveyed reported participating in this academic program.[11]

Variables

'Help-seeking orientation' is operationalized by the following three measures: *confidence in the support process, interpersonal openness,* and *desire for academic support.* The first two measures were derived from the section of the student survey which contained a 20-item scale developed and tested by Vaux, Burda, and Stewart (1986) and designed to gauge the help-seeking orientations of adults. Our own principal component analysis produced two orthogonal factors, each suggesting a useful indicator of an individual's help-seeking orientation.[12] The first measure, *confidence in the support process,* represents the respondent's confidence in the ability of others to provide support and is based on seven items; two examples are 'Sometimes it is necessary to talk to someone about your problems' and

'Friends often have good advice to give'. The second measure, *interpersonal openness*, represents the respondent's ability and willingness to share problems with others. Items for this factor include 'Other people never understand my problems', and 'If you confide in other people, they'll take advantage of you'. The resulting scales showed reasonably good internal consistency, with Cronbach alphas of 0.76 for *confidence* and 0.61 for *openness*.

Our third measure, *desire for academic support*, originates from a seven-item scale adapted from Hymovich (1983) and used to gauge the areas in which the student would have liked pertinent information and guidance. Students were asked, 'Please indicate if you would or would not like to have help with or to discuss any of the following'. We used one of the seven items: 'Advice and guidance from teachers and counselors in making important educational and academic decisions', as a measure of the desire for academic support. The response format consisted of three choices, 'would not', 'not sure', and 'would like'. The measure was coded 1 if the student answered in the affirmative and 0 if they chose one of the first two responses.

For the purpose of modeling individual-level determinants of help-seeking orientation, we used family, personal, and academic background variables. They are *socioeconomic status, gender, age, English proficiency, grades,* and *self-esteem*. The Duncan socioeconomic index (SEI), an occupational prestige scale constructed by Duncan and associates in 1961, was used as a measure of family socioeconomic status (SES). Our measures relied on student's reports of parents' occupational status; scores represent the average of mother's and fathers' occupational prestige ratings. In the case of single-parent households, the sole parent's score was used. All students, regardless of race-ethnicity or language of questionnaire were asked two questions about the degree to which they understood and spoke English. The response scale ranged from 1 = not at all well, to 5 = extremely well. Students' overall scores were constructed by taking the average of both items.

The *grades* variable was constructed with self-reports of the usual grades the students received in their classes (1 = mostly A's to 8 = mostly below D). We computed a numerical scale with assigned weights based on enrollment in specific academic programs, (e.g., E.S.L., International Baccalaureate, etc.). These weighted grades ranged from 0, the lowest grade, to 5, the highest. Two earlier studies using the same measure (Dornbusch, Ritter, Leiderman, & Roberts, 1987; Valenzuela & Dornbusch, 1994), found correlations of 0.76 and 0.79 (respectively) between self-reported and actual recorded grades.

Finally, a measure of *self-esteem* was included in the analysis. This composite scale is based on a six-item scale originally developed by Harter (1993). The responses were first normalized and then summed to create the values for the variable *self-esteem*. Due to an error in survey construction, the agree–disagree format was not completely consistent between the English and Spanish language versions of the questionnaire. In the English version, the scale ranged from (strongly disagree = 1)–(disagree = 2)–(no opinion = 3)–(agree = 4)–(strongly agree = 5). In the Spanish version, the scale ranged from (strongly disagree = 1)–(disagree = 2)–(agree = 3)–(strongly agree = 4). The 'no opinion' response was not included in the Spanish version. After carefully comparing the responses from students for all the variables relevant to our analysis between the two versions of the survey, we decided to deal with this issue by shifting the values of the Spanish language version for agree = 3 to agree = 4 and for strongly agree = 4 to strongly agree = 5 to match the values for these responses in the English version. This allowed us to maintain a consistent valuation for the responses between the two surveys. Given this correction in the valuation of these responses, we could combine the two surveys and continue with our analysis.[13]

Analytic Approach

Our goal was to model individual-level determinants of our three measures of help-seeking orientation. Two OLS regression models were estimated to measure the effects of our demographic and academic variables on our first two dependent variables *(confidence in the support process, interpersonal openness)* and a logistic regression model was estimated to model *desire for support,* a dichotomous variable. Cases missing data on any independent variable were dropped which resulted in a working file of 1,047 cases. Similar to our original sample, 63.23% of this final sample were Latino, while 36.77% were non-Latino (Whites: 20.06% of overall student sample; African Americans: 10.98%; Asian/Pacific Islanders: 5.25%; five students registered as native Americans).

We were particularly interested in exploring whether the effects of individual-level characteristics differ by Latino subgroup (i.e., recent immigrants versus more acculturated Latinos), and whether either of these two subgroups might experience these characteristics differently than the non-Latino population at the school (e.g., effect of academic grades on help-seeking attitudes). To pursue these analyses, we used English proficiency to distinguish the two principal segments of the Latino student body: Spanish-dominant immigrant students (SPANLAT) and highly English-proficient students (ENGLAT) (virtually all of the Latino students in our sample were either first or second generation, and thus, all those who registered as highly English-proficient can be assumed to have exhibited various degrees of bilingualism).[14] We believe that this sociolinguistic division is a good proxy for one of the most important acculturation differences in the student population, and reflects a well-documented cultural distinction in the Latino community overall. Spanish-dominant immigrant students have been shown to experience practical communicative barriers to accessing the social support of school personnel, particularly in junior and senior high schools where the majority of the school staff often lacks proficiency in Spanish.[15] We proceed below with a brief overview of our descriptive statistics.

Results

Descriptive Analyses

Table 22.1 presents the means and standard deviations for all the continuous variables used in our study, with comparisons across our three principal ethnolinguistic groupings: Spanish-dominant (immigrant) Latinos, English-proficient Latinos, and non-Latinos. Several *T*-tests were conducted to determine significant differences in mean scores. For our dichotomous antecedent variables, the relevant percentages are provided. Each of the three groups registered significantly different SES scores ($p < 0.05$). Non-Latinos showed the highest socioeconomic status (SES) (62.36), due to the influence of higher-status (middle-class) Whites in this group (67.88). The SES score for English-proficient Latinos is considerably lower (43.33), while the score for Spanish-dominant immigrants is even lower (32.88). Spanish-dominant immigrants, as a group, appear to also have a relatively greater representation of slightly older students, and of students reporting relatively high self-esteem. Both Latino subgroups registered significantly lower (self reported) grades than non-Latinos; no discernable differences emerged between Latino groups.

We turn now to our mean differences in the first two measures of help-seeking orientation; the first representing *confidence in the support process* and the second representing *interpersonal openness.* There were no significant group differences in *confidence.* Most noteworthy is that relative to both English-proficient Latinos and non-Latinos, Spanish-dominant immigrant students registered significantly lower degrees of *interpersonal openness.* Auxiliary analyses showed that relative to both of the Latino subgroups, Euro-American/White students registered significantly higher degrees of *openness.* Although Latinos were not significantly differentiated when divided by language status, subsequent regressions did show the significant positive influence of English proficiency on *openness.* We close this section by reporting on our comparative findings for our third key measure, *desire for academic support.* What is most significant is that Spanish-dominants were the only group that did not have a majority reporting a desire for more academic support. Slightly more than two-thirds of this group did not report a desire for such support (68%).

Table 22.1 Means, Standard Deviations and Sample Coverage of Measures Used in the Analysis, Category by Ethnic-Linguistic Group

Variable	Non-Latinos	English-proficient Latinos	Spanish dominant Latinos	F
(N)	385	298	364	
Socioeconomic status	62.36	43.33	32.88	191.01[a]
	(24.63)	(21.71)	(15.24)	
Gender (1 = Male)	0.46	0.46	0.57	
	(0.50)	(0.50)	(0.50)	
English proficiency	4.38	4.25	2.32	836.87[a]
	(0.86)	(0.66)	(0.72)	
Grade level	10.92	10.97	10.73	
	(0.79)	(0.80)	(0.79)	
Age	17.13	17.20	17.40	7.15[b]
	(0.96)	(0.99)	(1.03)	
Grades	3.26	2.68	2.77	32.09[c]
	(1.13)	(1.06)	(0.96)	
	3.87	3.87	4.15	
Self-esteem	(0.87)	(0.90)	(0.70)	13.01[a]
Dependent variables				
Confidence in	21.82	21.63	21.52	0.91
Support process	(3.21)	(3.29)	(2.86)	
Interpersonal openness	16.31	16.10	15.53	7.47[b]
	(2.98)	(2.86)	(2.72)	
Desire for academic support	0.69	0.65	0.32	120.42[d]
	(0.46)	(0.48)	(0.47)	

[a] Mean differences between all three groups at $p < 0.001$.
[b] Mean differences only between Spanish-dominant Latinos and the other two groups at $p < 0.001$.
[c] Mean differences only non-Latinos and the other two groups at $p < 0.001$.
[d] Chi-square statistic, $p < 0.001$.

Multiple-Regression and Logistic Regression Analysis of Operationalized Measures of 'Help-Seeking Orientation'

Tables 22.2, 22.3, and 22.4 display analyses of our three operationalized measures of 'help-seeking orientation': *confidence in support process, interpersonal openness,* and *desire for academic support,* respectively. Given the parsimonious set of predictors studied in this analysis, we would like to remind our readers that our primary objective was not to establish definitive models of these three operationalized outcomes measures, but rather to gain an understanding of the relationship between these three outcomes and our select set of predictors. We present our findings by dependent variable (Tables 22.2, 22.3, & 22.4), then review our overall findings by antecedent variable.

In Table 22.2, the analysis reveals that only three of the main-effects are significant ($p < 0.05$) in our final model, model 1–7, which accounts for 5% of the variance in the outcome variable, *confidence in support process.* Model 1–7 shows that gender (0 for females, 1 for males) is significant at the 0.001 level. The negative relationship between gender and *confidence* reveals that boys had lower confidence in the support process than girls. The negative relationship between self-esteem and *confidence* reveals that students with higher self-esteem reported less confidence in the support process than students with lower self-esteem, a finding that seems at first quite counterintuitive. We return to this finding below. In contrast to the negative effect of self-esteem, the positive relationship between grades and *confidence* reveals that students with higher grades have higher confidence in the support process than students with lower grades (i.e., poorer academic performance). The absence of the SES, English

Table 22.2 A Taxonomy of Fitted Linear Regression Models of Confidence in Support Process on Predictors including SES, Gender, English Proficiency, Age, Grades, Self-Esteem, and the Indicator Variable Pair, ENGLAT and SPANLAT

	Main effects models															
	1-1		1-2		1-3		1-4		1-5		1-6		1-7		1-8	
Predictors	b	(se) t-stat	b	(se) t-stat	b	(se) t-stat	b	(se) t-stat	b	(se) t-stat	b	(se) t-stat	b	(se) t-stat	b	(se) t-stat
SES	0.01*	(0.00) 2.20	0.01	(0.00) 1.79												
Gender			-1.03***	(0.19) -5.43	-1.02***	(0.19) -5.36	-1.03***	(0.19) -5.39	-1.02***	(0.19) -5.36	-1.04***	(0.19) -5.55	-0.98***	(0.19) -5.19	-0.99***	(0.19) -5.20
English prof.					0.16*	(0.08) 2.01	0.17*	(0.08) 2.12	0.13	(0.08) 1.6						
Age							0.07	(0.95) 0.69								
Grades									0.28**	(0.09) 3.13	0.29***	(0.09) 3.38	0.31***	(0.09) 3.57	0.32***	(0.09) 3.49
Self-esteem													-0.35**	(0.11) -3.10	-0.35**	(0.12) -3.11
ENGLAT															-0.00	(0.24) -0.21
SPANLAT															0.06	0.23 0.293
Intercept	21.26***		21.85***		21.58***		20.43***		20.90***		21.32***		22.65***		22.59***	
R^2 statistic	0.01		0.03		0.03		0.03		0.04		0.04		0.05		0.05	

*$p < 0.05$.
**$p < 0.01$.
***$p < 0.001$.
No significant interactions between the indicator variable pair, ENGLAT and SPANLAT, and the predictors, gender, grades, and self-esteem were found ($n = 1047$).

Table 22.3 A Taxonomy of Fitted Linear Regression Models of Interpersonal Openness of Predictors Including SES, Grades, English Proficiency, Age, Grades, Self-Esteem, and the Indicator Variable Pair, ENGLAT and SPANLAT

	Main effects models															
	2–1		2–2		2–3		2–4		2–5		2–6		2–7		2–8	
Predictors	b	(se) t-stat	b	(se) t-stat	b	(se) t-stat	b	(se) t-stat	b	(se) t-stat	b	(se) t-stat	b	(se) t-stat	b	(se) t-stat
SES	0.02***	(0.00) 5.90	0.02***	(0.00) 5.68	0.02***	(0.00) 3.80	0.01***	(0.00) 3.73	0.01**	(0.00) 3.14	0.01***	(0.00) 3.34	0.02***	(0.00) 3.60	0.03***	(0.01) 5.54
Gender			0.47**	(0.17) −2.68	−0.43*	(0.17) −2.47	−0.42*	(0.18) −2.40	−0.43*	(0.17) −2.48	−0.51**	(0.17) −2.93	−0.51**	(0.17) −2.94	−0.53**	(0.17) −3.07
English prof.					0.24**	(0.08) 2.96	0.23**	(0.08) 2.93	0.23**	(0.08) 2.84	0.26***	(0.08) 3.34	0.33**	(0.12) 2.87	0.31**	(0.12) 2.69
Age							−0.07	(0.09) −0.80								
Grades									0.27**	(0.08) 3.26	0.24**	(0.08) 2.89	0.24**	(0.08) 3.03	0.23**	(0.08) 2.85
Self-esteem											0.48***	(0.10) 4.58	0.47**	(0.11) 4.46	0.45***	(0.10) 4.34
ENGLAT													0.27	(0.23) 1.15	1.93***	(0.52) 3.67
SPANLAT													0.39	(0.32) 1.22	2.15***	(0.55) 3.93
Interactions																
ENGLAT*PSEI															−0.03***	(0.01) −3.34
SPANLAT*PSEI															−0.04***	(0.01) −3.57
Intercept	14.99***		15.26***		14.63***		15.85***		14.00***		12.06***		11.54***		10.70***	
R^2 statistic	0.03		0.04		0.05		0.05		0.06		0.08		0.08		0.09	

*$p < 0.05$.
**$p < 0.01$.
***$p < 0.001$.
Interactions between the indicator variable pair, ENGLAT and SPANLAT, and the significant predictors, SES, gender, English proficiency, grades, and self-esteem were modeled, and the interaction between ENGLAT/SPANLAT and SES was found to be significant ($n = 1047$).

proficiency, age, and the indicator pair ENGLAT and SPANLAT in the final model shows that these variables are not significant predictors of *confidence* at the $p < 0.05$ level.

In Table 22.3, the analysis reveals that the interactional model 2–8 accounts for the most variance yielding an $R^2 = 0.09$ with respect to the outcome variable, *interpersonal openness*. Model 2–8 contains gender, English proficiency, grades, and self-esteem as main effects predictors and an interaction between SES and ENGLAT/SPANLAT. Beginning with the predictors included only as main effects, we note that, once again, the negative relationship between gender and *interpersonal openness* suggests that boys report less interpersonal openness than girls. In contrast to the previous model, the positive relationship between English proficiency and *interpersonal openness* suggests that more positive help-seeking orientations are also associated with higher levels of English proficiency. Similar to the previous model, there is a positive relationship between grades and *interpersonal openness*; yet, contrary to our findings for *confidence*, here we see a positive relationship between self-esteem and *interpersonal openness*, suggesting that students with higher self-esteem report greater ability and willingness to share personal problems with others.

Moving on to the interaction between SES and ENGLAT/SPANLAT, we note that we have three groups of students accounted for in our final model 2–8. For non-Latino students (ENGLAT = 0, SPANLAT = 0), we have the parameter estimate of SES equal to 0.03. This result suggests that non-Latino students at higher levels of SES reported higher levels of interpersonal openness than non-Latino students at lower levels of SEI. For English-proficient Latino students (ENGLAT = 1, SPANLAT = 0), we have the parameter estimate for SES equal to 0.00, while a constant for ENGLAT of 1.93 is added to the predicted values of the outcome variable *interpersonal openness*. This result suggests that among English-proficient Latino students, unlike non-Latino students, interpersonal openness is not a function of SES. However, for Spanish-dominant Latino students (ENGLAT = 0, SPANLAT = 1), we have the parameter estimate for SES equal to –0.01, while a constant for SPANLAT of 2.15 is added to the predicted value of the outcome variable, *interpersonal openness*. As a result, the estimated values for *interpersonal openness* appear to be higher for lower levels of SES and lower for higher levels of SES among Spanish-dominant Latinos, a finding that goes counter to the expected effect of SES.

In Table 22.4, the analysis reveals that the interactional model 3–8 accounts for the most variance yielding a pseudo-$R^2 = 0.13$ with respect to the outcome variable, *desire for academic support*. Model 3–8 contains gender, grades, and self-esteem as main effects predictors and an interaction between English proficiency and ENGLAT/SPANLAT. Beginning with the predictors appearing only as main effects, we note that, similar to our previous findings for gender, females are more likely to desire academic support than males across all three ethno-linguistic groups (Spanish-dominant Latinos, English-proficient Latinos, and non-Latinos for students with comparable grades). With respect to grades, comparing across gender groups and then ethno-linguistic groups, students with the highest grades were discovered to be roughly 1.1–1.2 times more likely to desire academic support than students with lowest grades. With respect to self-esteem, comparing across gender groups and then ethno-linguistic groups among students with comparable grades, students who report having low self-esteem are 1.5–2.3 times more likely to desire academic support than students who report having high self-esteem.

Taking a look at the interaction between English proficiency and ENGLAT/SPANLAT, we note that the primary issue appears to be the difference in desire for academic support between the Spanish-dominant Latino students and everyone else (with no statistical difference between the other two ethno-linguistic groups). Comparing among Latino students with moderate English proficiency to those with high English proficiency, we note that highly English-proficient students are no more likely to desire academic support than moderate to low English-proficient students. These odds ratios are much the same for non-Latino students. However, comparing Spanish-dominant Latino students, males with moderate to high English-proficiency are 2.1 times more likely to desire academic support

Table 22.4 A Taxonomy of Fitted Logistic Regression Models of Desire for Academic Support on Predictors Including SES, Gender, English Proficiency, Age, Grades, Self-Esteem, and the Indicator Variable Pair, ENGLAT and SPANLAT

	Base	Main-effects models							
		3–1	3–2	3–3	3–4	3–5	3–6	3–7	3–8
Predictors									
Gender		−0.49***	−0.41**	−0.40**	−0.43**	−0.41**	−0.35**	−0.33**	−0.34*
English prof.			0.51***	0.48***	0.52***	0.49***	0.46***	0.16	−0.09
SES				0.004					
Age					0.12				
Grades						0.23***	0.26***	0.27***	0.26***
Self-esteem							−0.47***	−0.42***	−0.44***
ENGLAT								0.02	−0.58
SPANLAT								−1.01***	−3.18***
Interactions									
ENGLAT*ENGPROF									0.14
SPANLAT*ENGPROF									0.71**
Intercept		0.45***	−1.45***	−1.51***	−3.47***	−2.07***	−0.17***	1.15	2.27**
χ^2 statistic	1441.30	1425.68	1332.95	1331.40	1329.82	1319.14	1287.15	1265.40	1253.66
$\Delta \chi^2$ test		15.62***	92.73***	1.55	3.13	12.26***	31.99***	21.75***	11.74***
(nested modes)		(base, 1)	(1,2)	(2,3)	(2,4)	(2,5)	(5,6)	(6,7)	(7,8)
Δdeg. of freedom		2	1	1	1	1	1	2	2
Pseudo R^2 statistic		0.01	0.08	0.08	0.08	0.08	0.11	0.12	0.13

*$p < 0.05$.
**$p < 0.01$.
***$p < 0.001$.
Interactions between the indicator variable pair, ENGLAT and SPANLAT, and the significant predictors, gender, English proficiency, grades, and self-esteem were modeled and the interaction between ENGLAT/SPANLAT and English proficiency were found to be significant ($n = 1047$).

than males with low English-proficiency. Among Spanish-dominant females, the odds ratio is 1.9 comparing moderately English proficient females to low English-proficient females. If we compare Spanish-dominant Latinos with high English proficiency to those Latinos with low English-proficiency, the odds ratio jumps to 3.2. This result suggests that among Spanish-dominant students, the desire for academic support varies greatly depending on the student's English-proficiency among those students attending the school sampled in this study. Its appears that among Spanish-dominant students, those with some English proficiency are many times more likely to desire academic support than those with little or no English proficiency. As expected, for non-Latinos and English-proficient Latinos, the level of English proficiency appears to play nearly no role in the students' desires to seek academic support—mainly due to the lack of significant variability in this measure.

Review of Findings by Independent Variable

Socioeconomic Status Overall, the independent effect of socioeconomic status did not display a paramount role in our models, although some significant findings did occur. Family socioeconomic status did register significant positive effects on interpersonal openness among non-Latinos at this school. In accordance with published studies, non-Latino students from higher income families tended to report a greater willingness to share problems with others. The findings for interpersonal openness among Latinos is difficult to decipher. Analyses of SES within Latino student populations has been conventionally difficult due to the typically restricted socioeconomic variation (due in part to segregated schools).[16] Particularly perplexing is the reverse relationship among Spanish-dominant immigrant Latinos, with higher SES associated with lower interpersonal openness—opposite to the finding for non-Latinos.

Gender In accordance with published studies, gender displayed its prominent role in the help-seeking orientations of our high school sample, registering significant effects in each of our three principal regression models. Taken together, these findings appear quite unequivocal; boys, relative to girls, consistently reported lower *confidence* in the support process, less willingness to share personal problems with others (i.e., less *openness*), and less *desire* for personalized academic support or assistance from school personnel.

English Proficiency As mentioned above, measures of English proficiency typically act as a particularly key variable differentiating Latino student samples. Although English proficiency shows no effect on *confidence*, it shows itself to be a strong predictor of *interpersonal openness*. The findings connecting English proficiency with *desire* are varied, with this relation apparently only operative among Spanish-dominant Latinos, and in the expected positive direction. Immigrants with the lowest levels of English proficiency are quite unlikely to report a desire for academic support or assistance from school personnel.

Age Although age did not register any significant independent effect, preliminary descriptive analyses by grade level did show that 10th graders (the youngest group) were, overall, less likely to be interested in academic support. Approximately 61% of 11th graders and 60% of 12th graders desired academic support, while only 46.5% of 10th graders desired support. This trend is accentuated when examining Latinos exclusively (only 37% of Latino sophomores desired academic support) (tables available upon request).

Analyses conducted for a different project similarly showed that half of Spanish-dominant sophomore students (50.8%) did not actively seek assistance from a teacher or a counselor regarding academic issues during a six-month period (Stanton-Salazar, Tai, & Bressler, 1999). Also in that study, sophomores, in general (across ethnic groups), appeared the least likely to seek help regarding academic issues, and especially regarding post-high school plans. Regardless of whether age directly affects their help-seeking orientation in high school, it is quite reasonable to expect that, given their relative nearness to high school graduation, seniors as a group would be more interested in receiving academic support than their sophomore counterparts—particularly with regard to post-high school options. On the other hand, considering Latino students' well-known underachievement in school, the fact that between 41% and 63% of the Latino students at this school reported no affirmative desire for advice and guidance in making important academic decisions should be cause for concern.

Academic Performance–Grades Our indicator of academic achievement appears here to consistently substantiate its expected association with the help-seeking orientation of all students, with effects significant across groups. As expected, students with good grades appear to have the most *confidence* in the support process and to exhibit the most *openness*; likewise, relative to low achievers, high achievers show greater *desire* or interest in receiving advice and guidance on academic matters. Low achievers —arguably those most in need of academic help—appear least inclined or prepared to engage the human resources of the school. Low-achieving males would be expected to be particularly disengaged.

Self-Esteem Our findings for self-esteem are mixed and somewhat complex, given that our measure registered negative as well as positive effects on our dependent variables. Although reporting high self-esteem was associated with greater *interpersonal openness*, as would be normally hypothesized, high self-esteem was also associated with low *confidence in the support process* and low *desire for support*. Auxiliary bivariate correlations using the Spanish-dominant student subsample did show, however, a positive relationship between self-esteem and confidence in the support process. These auxiliary findings raise the possibility that the effects of self-esteem may be tied to distinctive perceptions of the help-seeking process, depending upon cultural background and level of acculturation. We elaborate on this possibility in the following section.

In summary, the strongest and most consistent effects across models came from our gender variable, followed by self-reported measures of academic performance. It appears that Latino males, low achievers, and recent immigrants tend to exhibit help-seeking orientations that would normally function to impede supportive interactions across social contexts, and perhaps most importantly, impede the development of supportive relations with school personnel. We further explore the significance of these findings in the following section.

4. Discussion

This study highlighted three indicators of young people's orientation toward cultivating and utilizing relations with significant others and other sources of social and institutional support. Our first two measures were designed to capture adolescents' general orientation to seeking help from all available sources across contexts. Only our last measure focused on seeking support specifically from school personnel. Nonetheless, we argue here that adolescent help-seeking orientation is a key indicator of adolescents' social embeddedness within school, and when manifested as a generalized coping strategy, has important and direct consequences for their access to key forms of support which underlie educational mobility and developmental resiliency.

Technically, low-status students are fully entitled to make use of adult bearers of institutional knowledge and social support within the school. In strictly technical and even mainstream ideological terms, students across social classes have 'equal opportunities' to accumulate school-based 'social capital', that is, to engage in supportive relations with school-based institutional agents. However, structural circumstances and forces in society do permeate the school site and regularly embed students and personnel in relational dynamics rooted in divisive societal forces. The full story, however, is that schools also embody the capacity for *counterstratification*, that is, the potential for mitigating the relation between class, race, and gender forces and the structure, composition, and resourcefulness of young people's social networks. One principal way of doing this would be by creating an environment that would foster cooperative learning and networking skills, and, most importantly, foster positive help-seeking orientations founded on trusting and committed relations between students and school personnel.

Our findings here provide us with a unique type of assessment of whether one particular school has been able to realize this *counterstratification* potential. Evidence of this occurring would show itself in weak or nonexistent statistical associations between our social background and scholastic measures and our indicators of help-seeking orientation—particularly desire for academic assistance and support from school personnel (e.g., low achievers would be as likely to seek help from teachers as high achievers; boys would be as likely as girls to seek help). On the contrary, our findings show that major segments of the student body exhibited orientations that suggest a form of social estrangement from vital sources of support in the school, home, and community. While socioeconomic status did show some evidence as a relevant predictor, gender consistently showed its well-known role in inhibiting the help-seeking initiative of adolescent boys, both non-Latino and Latino. Such findings need to be considered in conjunction with our self-esteem findings. Here we see evidence that high esteem among our English-speaking sample (Latinos and non-Latinos) was associated with dispositions valuing self-reliance over help seeking and cooperative coping strategies. Our findings pertaining to self-esteem run counter to findings in at least one study of adolescents. Colleta's (1987) study of adolescent mothers provides support for the normally-expected association between self-esteem and help-seeking orientation, with younger mothers with high self-esteem registering positive help-seeking orientation scores (relation did not register for older mothers).

In recent years, specific explanations and perspectives have emerged for addressing the relation between self-esteem and help seeking.[17] One perspective focuses on what happens when individuals perceive that others will interpret their request for help as an admission of incompetence or inadequacy; in this scenario, help-seeking initiatives among low-esteem individuals only serve to further damage their sense of competency and self-esteem. In contrast, high self-esteem individuals would not see help seeking as a sign of their inadequacy. A quite distinctive perspective sees high self-esteem individuals having many positive self-cognitions regarding their ability to accomplish difficult tasks. When their self-evaluations of ability become closely associated with their concept of self, the act of seeking help appears inconsistent or threatening to both. Thus, high self-esteem individuals would be less expected to seek assistance in times of need.

Given the cultural variations in our student body, both perspectives may have applicability to our findings. The first perspective above seems, at first, to be applicable to our Spanish-dominant sample; for this group, high self-esteem individuals show their positive inclinations toward seeking help in times of need. High self-esteem individuals in this community exhibit *confidence* in the support process and a relatively high degree of *interpersonal openness*, both known antecedents to active help-seeking behavior.

In contrast, the alternative perspective above seems applicable to our English-speaking students (both Latino and non-Latino). Here high-esteem individuals may interpret help seeking as inconsistent with their highly positive self-perceptions of efficacy and competency. In this scenario, help seeking is only compatible with incompetency. This, of course, raises the issue of whether institutional efforts to bolster students' self-esteem may be working to undermine students' positive embeddedness in resourceful and cooperative networks of support.

Although cautionary, gender studies on help seeking may be suggesting that males may be particularly susceptible to this second scenario. This is to say that the psychological incompatibility between high competency and help seeking may be a conventionally masculine phenomenon in American society, although among our recent immigrants, being male also signaled inhibitions toward seeking help.

Recent Latino immigrants, as it turns out, represent a quite perplexing case study. As revealed in our descriptive analyses, only a third of Spanish-dominants reported a desire for more academic support, and thus, distinguishing themselves from most other student groups. Furthermore, low English proficiency was associated with low *interpersonal openness* as well as low *desire*. In fact, Spanish-dominant immigrants, relative to the two other groups, registered significantly lower group scores on *desire* and *interpersonal openness*. We see then, that Spanish-dominant immigrants are particularly prone to regulating their own marginality from institutional sources of support, despite their well-documented optimism and scholastic motivation.

Their situation may be even more serious than our present findings suggest. In the companion study already mentioned,[18] we found that these same Spanish-dominant students registered the highest scores of *perceived support* (relative to other groups at the school). We also found that while *perceived support* was highly predictive of actual help-seeking behavior at the school, this positive association was not operative for Spanish-dominant students. This suggests that for recent immigrants, their particular (negative) embeddedness in school are founded on different dynamics. Low-status, acculturated Latino students are often considered to be embedded in relations with school personnel plagued by tacit class and racial antagonisms and resultant social distance. For recent immigrants, however, their own disinclination toward help seeking may be rooted in their distinctive and temporary sense of social and psychological marginality within the cultural and linguistic mainstream of the school—a marginality that seems to easily co-exist with positive appraisals of the school environment overall.

This article attempted to bring out the sociological significance underlying variations in students' help-seeking orientation, a construct mainly lodged in mainstream psychological research circles. It is quite possible that help-seeking orientations exhibited by low-status adolescents, particularly in school arenas, may be playing a prominent role in the social reproduction of inequality. This is to suggest that the seeds of negative embeddedness in high school and in other key contexts may very well spell future disaster in adulthood. Low-status adolescents invested in negative orientations and other psychological defenses may find themselves in adulthood inadvertently aiding structural forces in the reconstitution of their earlier bounded and resource-poor networks.

In contrast, the low-status students in our study who exhibited positive help-seeking orientations may very well be the students most prepared to take advantage of the school system's *counterstratification* potentialities. They may also come to represent that sector of their community best prepared to manage the multiple borders and stressors inherent in our class-divided, racialized, and gendered society; more importantly, this sector may likewise be the most prepared to maximize their participation in mainstream arenas, where institutional resources and opportunities for social advancement and political empowerment are abundant, yet lodged within networks that require a considerable deal of negotiation and psychological resiliency.

Notes

1. The research for this paper was supported by grants by the Spencer Foundation, the W.T. Grant Foundation, and the California Policy Research Center. The support from these institutions does not imply their agreement with the arguments and statements expressed herein, and responsibility for any errors of fact or interpretation rests solely with us. Address correspondence to Ricardo D. Stanton-Salazar, Rossier School of Education, WPH 1002, University of Southern California, Los Angeles, California 90089–0031. You may also reach the first author via E-mail: stantons@usc.edu, or via the following numbers: Tel: 213–740–3471; Fax: 213–740–3671.
2. See Cochran (1990c) chapter on Human Development (Chapter 14); also Cochran et al., 1990.
3. The concept of social embeddedness is fully explored in another work (Stanton-Salazar, Tai, & Bressler, 1999) and in Stanton-Salazar, 2001/b.
4. Erickson and Shultz, in their book entitled, The Counselor as Gatekeeper (1982), do a superb job of demonstrating how

class and other status differences can inadvertently sabotage the supportive potential of counselor-student relations. Lareau, in her insightful book, *Home Advantage* (1989), shows how relations between working-class parents and school personnel are regularly characterized by social distance, and mutual suspicion and distrust.

5. These hypothesized relations, however, were not substantiated for Spanish-dominant students. Although this latter group reported the highest levels of perceived support, they exhibited the lowest levels of help-seeking and organizational participation.

6. See Eckenrode (1983) for a review of the literature on the relations between SES and use of psychological services.

7. See the excellent ethnographic study by Patricia Zavella (1987) which illustrates the shop-floor relations between women employees and their supervisors and male co-workers; also see the ethnographic study by Annette Lareau (1989).

8. This high response rate reflects several attempts to reach students who had either been absent on the day of the survey, or who had not completed it. Although the possibility of sampling bias is lowered it remains possible that habitual truants and chronically disengaged students were undersampled.

9. Highlights of this study are provided in Stanton-Salazar (2001b); for the entire study, see Stanton-Salazar (2001a).

10. However, only about 18% of the Latino students surveyed reported receiving some form of government welfare.

11. Of the Latino students who participated in this college-preparatory academic program, about 57% took only one or two courses. One of the most frequently taken courses among participating Latino students was Spanish literature.

12. Vaux, Burda, and Stewart (1986) conducted their validation using a unifactorial measure.

13. One important methodological issue here is that Spanish-version takers (in contrast to the English-version takers) did not have the opportunity to use 'no opinion'. We do not believe our findings would have differed had we used uniform scales. We felt this problem was not severe enough to require dropping the variable from the study. A series of descriptive analyses were conducted to check our data; we present here the results. (1) only 13.7% of students (English-survey takers) took the 'no opinion' option three or more times (out of six items); thus, most students here selected responses relevant to their perceptions of self. (2) We compared those students (English-version takers) who selected 'no opinion' at least once (69.2%) with those who never selected 'no opinion' option; (i) we found no statistically significant differences in SEI, English proficiency, age, self-reported academic grades, and confidence in the support process (a 'help-seeking orientation' variable); (ii) we did find, however, statistically significant differences in interpersonal openness and self-esteem (the 'no opinion' people more 'open', and had slightly higher self-esteem).

14. A combination of measures were used to isolate Spanish-dominant immigrants from their more acculturated counterparts: nativity, length of residence in the U.S., self-reported English proficiency, and language of the questionnaire. 'Spanish-dominant students' were those who immigrated at age 6 or older and who reported English-proficiency scores less than 4 ('very well'); other related variables were used to check for accuracy or for estimating missing data. Spanish-dominants were distinguished from immigrants who were highly bilingual; 'immigrant bilinguals' were grouped with those who were US-born.

15. Initiatory studies show that, although recent immigrants tend to be satisfied with their high schools, their status as newcomers in a foreign land, combined with their lack of English proficiency, serves to inhibit the seeking of support from school staffers as a general rule; exceptions to this non-seeking are, however, common (Stanton-Salazar & Dornbusch, 1995; Stanton-Salazar, Tai, & Bressler, 1999; Stanton-Salazar, 2001a).

16. Approximately 87% of Latino fathers at this school were found to be blue collar workers, and three quarters of Latino mothers had not finished high school (or the equivalent).

17. See Gross and McMullen (1982); Nadler (1983); Nelson-Le Gall (1985) for reviews of relevant theories pertaining to self-esteem and help seeking.

18. See Stanton-Salazar, Tai, & Bressler (1999).

References

Anthony, E. James & Cohler, Bertram J. (Eds.) (1987). *The invulnerable child.* New York: Guildford Press.

Anyon, Jean (1997). *Ghetto schooling: A political economy of urban educational reform.* New York: Teachers College Press.

Barnes, John A. (1972). *Social networks.* Reading, MA: Addison-Wesley.

Berliner, David C. & Biddle, Bruce J. (1995). *The manufactured crisis: Myths, fraud, and the attack on America's public school.* Reading, MA: Addison-Wesley.

Belle, Deborah, Dill, Diana, & Burr, Robin (1991). Children's network orientations. *Journal of Community Psychology, 19*(4), 362–372.

Blau, Peter M. (1964). *Exchange and power in social life.* New York: Wiley.

Blyth, Dale A. & Foster-Clark, Frederick S. (1987). Gender differences in perceived intimacy with different members of adolescents' social networks. *Sex Roles, 17*(11–12), 689–718.

Boldero, Jennifer & Fallon, Barry (1995). Adolescent help-seeking: What do they get help for and from whom? *Journal of Adolescence, 18*(2), 193–209.

Bourdieu, Pierre & Passeron, Jean-Claude (1977). *Reproduction in education, society, and culture.* London: Sage.

Bourdieu, Pierre & Wacquant, Loic J.D. (1992). *An invitation to reflexive sociology.* Chicago: The University of Chicago Press.

Bowlby, John (1969). *Attachment and loss.* New York: Basic Books.

Bowles, Samuel & Gintis, Herbert (1976). *Schooling in capitalist America: Educational reform and the contradictions of economic life.* New York: Basic Books.

Buriel, Raymond (1984). Integration within traditional Mexican American culture and sociocultural adjustment. In J.L. Martinez & R. Mendoza (Eds.), *Chicano psychology.* New York: Academic Press, pp. 95–130.

Coleman, James (1988). Social capital in the creation of human capital. *American Journal of Sociology, 94,* S95–S120.

Colletta, Nancy D. (1987). Correlates of young mothers' network orientations. *Journal of Community Psychology, 15*(2), 149–60.

Cicourel, Aaron V. & Mehan, Hugh (1983). Universal development, stratifying practices and status attainment. *Research in Social Stratification and Mobility, 4*, 3–27.

Cochran, Moncrieff (1990). Environmental factors constraining network development. In M. Cochran, M. Larner, D. Riley, L. Gunnarsson & R.H. Charles (Eds.), *Extending families: The social networks of parents and their children.* New York: Cambridge University Press, pp. 277–296.

Cochran, Moncrieff (1990). Factors influencing personal social initiative. In M. Cochran, M. Larner, D. Riley, L. Gunnarsson & R.H. Charles (Eds.), *Extending families: The social networks of parents and their children.* New York: Cambridge University Press, pp. 297–306.

Cochran, Moncrieff, Larner, Mary, Riley, David, Gunnarsson, Lars, & Henderson, Charles R. Jr. (Eds.) (1990). *Extending families: The social networks of parents and their children.* New York: Cambridge University Press.

Croninger, Robert G. & Lee, Valerie (1999). *Social capital and dropping out of school: Benefits to at-risk students of teachers' support and guidance.* Unpublished manuscript.

Cross, Jr. William E. (1990). Race and ethnicity: Effects on social networks. In M. Cochran, M. Larner, D. Riley, L. Gunnarsson & R.H. Charles (Eds.), *Extending families: The social networks of parents and their children.* New York: Cambridge University Press, pp. 67–85.

Delpit, Lisa D. (1988). The silenced dialogue: Power and pedagogy in educating other people's children. *Harvard Educational Review, 58*(3), 280–298.

Delpit, Lisa D. (1995). *Other people's children: Cultural conflict in the classroom.* New York: The New Press.

DePaulo, Bella M., Leiphart, V., & Dull, W.R. (1983). Help-seeking and social interaction: Person, situation, and process considerations. In E. Staub, D. Bar-Tal, J. Reykowski & J. Karylowski (Eds.), *The development and maintenance of pro-social behavior.* New York: Plenum, pp. 337–357.

Dornbusch, Sanford M., Ritter, Philip L., Leiderman, Herbert, Roberts, Donald F., & Fraleigh, Michael (1987). The relation of parenting style to adolescent school performance. *Child Development, 58*, 1244–1257.

Durkheim, Emile (1951). *Suicide.* Translated by John A. Spaulding and George Simpson. With an introduction by George Simpson (Ed.). Glencoe, IL: Free Press.

East, Patricia L. (1989). Early adolescents' perceived interpersonal risks and benefits: Relations to social support and psychological functioning. *Journal of Early Adolescence, 9* (4), 374–395.

Eckenrode, John (1983). The mobilization of social supports: Some individual constraints. *American Journal of Community Psychology, 11*(5), 509–528.

Eckenrode, John & Wethington, Elaine (1990). The process and outcome of mobilizing social support. In S. Duck (Ed.), *Personal relationships and social support.* Newbury Park, California: Sage Publications, pp. 83–103.

Erickson, Frederick & Shultz, Jeffrey (1982). *The counselor as gatekeeper: social interaction in interviews.* New York: Academic Press.

Feiring, Candice & Coates, Deborah (1987). Social networks and gender differences in the life space of opportunity: Introduction. *Sex Roles, 17*(11/12), 611–620.

Fine, Michelle (1991). *Framing dropouts: Notes on the politics of an urban public high school.* Albany: State University of New York Press.

Fischer, Claude S. (1982). *To dwell among friends.* Chicago: The University of Chicago Press.

Fischer, Claude S. (1975). Toward a subcultural theory of urbanism. *American Journal of Sociology, 80*(6), 1319–1341.

Frydenberg, Erica (1997). *Adolescent coping: Theoretical and research perspectives.* New York: Routledge.

Garbarino, James, Dubrow, Nancy, Kostelny, Kathleen, & Pardo, Carole (1992). *Children in danger: Coping with the consequences of community violence.* San Francisco: Jossey-Bass.

Garland, Ann F. & Zigler, Edward F. (1994). Psychological correlates of help-seeking attitudes among children and adolescents. *American Journal of Orthopsychiatry, 64*(4), 586–593.

Gee, James Paul (1989). Literacy, discourse and linguisitcs: Introduction. *Journal of Education, 171*(1), 5–17.

Gibson, Margaret & Ogbu, John (1991). *Minority status & schooling: A comparative study of immigrant and involuntary minorities.* New York: Garland Press.

Good, Glenn E., Dell, Don M., & Mintz, Laurie B. (1989). Male role and gender role conflict: Relations to help seeking in men. *Journal of Counseling Psychology, 36*(3), 295–300.

Gottlieb, Benjamin H. (1975). The contribution of natural support systems to primary prevention among four subgroups of adolescent males. *Adolescence, 10* (38), 207–220.

Granovetter, Mark (1982). The strength of weak ties: A network theory revisited. *Sociological Theory, 1*, 201–233.

Granovetter, Mark (1985). Economic action and social structure: The problem of embeddedness. *American Journal of Sociology, 91*(3), 481–510.

Gross, Alan E. & McMullen, Patricia A. (1983). Models of the help-seeking process. In J.D. Fisher, A. Nadler & B.M. DePaulo (Eds.), *New directions in helping.* New York: Academic Press, pp. 45–70.

Harter, Susan (1993). Causes and consequences of low self esteem in children and adolescents. In R.F. Baumeister (Ed.), *Self-esteem: The puzzle of low self-regard.* New York: Plenum Press, pp. 87–116.

Hymovich, Debra P. (1983). The chronicity impact and coping instrument: Parent questionnaire. *Nursing Research, 32*(5), 275–281.

Katz, Pearl (1974). *Acculturation and social networks in American immigrants in Israel.* Unpublished Doctoral Dissertation, State University of New York, Buffalo.

Kaplan, Berton H., Cassel, John C., & Gore, Susan (1977). Social support and health. *Medical Care, 15*, (Suppl.), 47–58.

Keefe, Susan E. (1979). Urbanization, acculturation, and extended family ties: Mexican Americans in cities. *American Ethnologist, 6*, 349–362.

Keefe, Susan & Padilla, Amado (1987). *Chicano ethnicity.* New Mexico: University of New Mexico Press.

Keefe, Susan, Padilla, Amado, & Carlos, Manuel (1979). The Mexican American extended family as an emotional support system. *Human Organization, 38*, 144–152.

Lamont, Michele & Lareau, Annette (1988). Cultural capital: Allusions, gaps and glissandos in recent theoretical developments. *Sociological Theory, 6*(2), 153–168.

Lareau, Annette (1989). *Home advantage: Social class and parental intervention in elementary education.* New York: Falmer Press.

Lin, Nan, Dean, Alfred, & Ensel, Walter M. (Eds.) (1986). *Social support, life events, and depression.* Orlando: Academic Press.

Lin, Nan (1982). Social resources and instrumental action. In P. Mardsen & N. Lin (Eds.), *Social structure and network analysis.* Beverly Hills, CA: Sage Publications, pp. 131–145.

Lin, Nan (1990). Social resources and social mobility: A structural theory of status attainment. In R.L. Breiger (Ed.), *Social mobility and social structure.* Cambridge, England: Cambridge University Press, pp. 247–271.

Lomnitz, Larissa Adler de (1977). *Networks and marginality: Life in a Mexican shantytown.* New York: Academic Press.

Matute-Bianchi, María Eugenia (1991). Situational ethnicity and patterns of school performance among immigrant and non-immigarnt Mexican-descent students. In J.U. Ogbu & M.A. Gibson (Eds.), *Minority status and schooling: A comparative study of immigrant and involuntary minorities.* New York: Garland, pp. 205–247.

Matute-Bianchi, María Eugenia (1986). Ethnic identities and patterns of school success and failure among Mexican-descent and Japanese-American students in a California school: An ethnographic analysis. *American Journal of Education, 95*(1), 233–255.

MacLeod, Jay (1987). *Ain't no makin' it: Leveled aspirations in a low-income neighborhood.* Boulder, Colorado: Westview Press.

McMullen, Patricia A. & Gross, Alan E. (1983). Sex differences, sex roles, and health-related help-seeking. In J.D. Fisher, A. Nadler & B.M. DePaulo (Eds.), *New directions in helping: Help-seeking (Vol. 2).* New York: Academic Press.

McQuillan, Patrick J. (1998). *Educational opportunity in an urban American high school: A cultural analysis.* Albany: State University of New York.

Nadler, Arie (1983). Personal characteristics and help-seeking. In J.D. Fisher, A. Nadler & B.M. DePaulo (Eds.), *New directions in helping: Help-seeking (Vol. 2)* New York: Academic Press.

Nelson-Le Gall, Sharon (1985). Help-seeking behavior in learning. In E.W. Gordon (Ed.), *Review of Research in Education, 12*, 55–90.

Nelson-Le Gall, Sharon & Jones, Elaine (1991). Classroom help-seeking behavior of African-American children. *Education & Urban Society, 24*(1), 27–40.

Offer, Daniel & Schonert-Reichl, Kimberly A. (1992). Debunking the myths of adolescence: Findings from recent research. *Journal of the American Academy of Child & Adolescent Psychiatry, 31*(6), 1003–1014.

Ogbu, John U. (1991a). Immigrant and involuntary minorities in comparative perspective. In M.A. Gibson & J.U. Ogbu (Eds.), *Minority status & schooling: A comparative study of immigrant and involuntary minorities.* New York: Garland Press, pp. 3–33.

Ogbu, John U. (1991b). Low school performance as an adaptation: The case of Blacks in Stockton, California. In M.A. Gibson & J.U. Ogbu (Eds.), *Minority status & schooling: A comparative study of immigrant and involuntary minorities.* New York: Garland Press, pp. 249–285.

Ogbu, John U. (1991c). Minority coping responses and school experience. *Journal of Psychohistory, 18*(4), 433–456.

Olsen, Laurie (1997). *Made in America: Immigrant students in our public schools.* New York: New Press.

O'Neil, James M. (1990). Assessing men's gender role conflict. In D. Moore & F. Leafgren (Eds.), *Problem solving strategies and interventions for men in conflict.* Alexandria, VA: American Association for Counseling and Development, pp. 23–38.

Pearlin, Leonard I. & Schooler, Carmi (1978). The structure of coping. *Journal of Health & Social Behavior, 19*(1), 2–21.

Phelan, Patricia, Davidson, Ann Locke, & Yu, Hanh Cao (1998). *Adolescents' worlds: Negotiating family, peers, and school.* New York: Teachers College Press.

Ramírez, Manuel & Castañeda, Alfredo (1974). *Cultural democracy, bicognitive development, and education.* New York: Academic Press.

Riley, Dave & Cochran, Moncrieff (1987). Children's relationships with nonparental adults: Sex-specific connections to early school success. *Sex Roles, 17*(11/12), 637–655.

Rickwood, Debra J. & Braithwaite, Valerie A. (1994). Social-psychological factors affecting help-seeking for emotional problems. *Social Science & Medicine, 39*(4), 563–572.

Salomon, Anne & Strobel, Michael G. (1997). Social network, interpersonal concerns and help-seeking in primary grade school children as a function of sex, performance and economic status. *European Journal of Psychology of Education, 12*(3), 331–347.

Schonert-Reichl, Kimberly A. & Muller, Jennifer R. (1996). Correlates of help-seeking in adolescence. *Journal of Youth & Adolescence, 25*(6), 705–731.

Stack, Carol B. (1974). *All our kin: Struggles for survival in a black community.* New York: Harper and Row.

Stanton-Salazar, Ricardo D. (2001/a). *Manufacturing hope & despair: The school and kin support networks of US-Mexican youth.* New York: Teachers College Press.

Stanton-Salazar, Ricardo D. (2001/b). Defensive network orientations as internalized oppression: How schools mediate the influence of social class on adolescent development. In Bruce J. Biddle (Ed.), *Social class, poverty, and education: Policy and practices.* New York: RoutlegeFalmer, pp. 101–131.

Stanton-Salazar, Ricardo D. (2000). The development of coping strategies among urban Latino youth: A focus on help-seeking orientation and network-related behavior. In M. Montero-Sieburth & F.A. Villaruel (Eds.), *Making invisible Latino adolescents visible: A critical approach to Latino diversity.* New York: Garland Press, pp. 203–238.

Stanton-Salazar, Ricardo D. (1997). A social capital framework for understanding the socialization of racial minority children and youth. *Harvard Educational Review, 67*(1), 1–40.

Stanton-Salazar, Ricardo D. & Dornbusch, Sanford M. (1995). Social capital and the social reproduction of inequality: The formation of informational networks among Mexican-origin high school students. *Sociology of Education, 68*(2), 116–135.

Stanton-Salazar, Ricardo. D., Tai, Robert, & Bressler, Michael (1999). *Social embeddedness: How social networks facilitate academic persistence among high school students.* Unpublished manuscript.

Tinto, Vincent (1987). *Leaving college: Rethinking the causes and cures of student attrition.* Chicago: University of Chicago Press.

Tolsdorf, Christopher C. (1976). Social networks, support, and coping: An exploratory analysis. *Family Process, 15,* 407–417.

Turner, Heather A. (1994). Gender and social support: Taking the bad with the good. *Sex Roles, 30*(7–8), 521–541.

Valenzuela, Angela (1999). *Subtractive schooling: US-Mexican youth and the politics of caring.* Albany: State University of New York Press.

Valenzuela, Angela (1993). Liberal gender role attitudes and academic achievement among Mexican-origin adolescents in two Houston inner-city Catholic schools. *Hispanic Journal of Behavioral Sciences, 15*(3), 310–323.

Valenzuela, Angela & Dornbusch, Sanford M. (1984). Familism and social capital in the academic achievement of Mexican origin and Anglo adolescents. *Social Science Quarterly, 75*(1), 18–36.

Vaux, Alan (1988). *Social support: Theory, research, and intervention.* New York: Praeger.

Vaux, Alan, Burda, Philip C., & Stewart, Doreen (1986). Orientation toward utilization of support resources. *Journal of Community Psychology, 14*(2), 159–170.

Vaux, Alan & Wood, JoAnna (1987). Social support resources, behavior, and appraisals: A path analysis. *Social Behavior and Personality, 15*(1), 107–111.

Vélez-Ibáñez, Carlos G. (1980). Mexicano/Hispano support systems and confianza: Theoretical issues of cultural adaptation. In R. Valle & W. Vega (Eds.), *A natural resource system for health-mental health promotion to Latino/Hispano populations.* Sacramento, California: State of California, Dept. of Mental Health, pp. 45–54.

Wallace, John L. & Vaux, Alan (1993). Social support network orientation: The role of adult attachment style. *Journal of Social and Clinical Psychology, 12*(3), 354–365.

Wellman, Barry (1983). Network analysis: Some basic principles. In R. Collins (Ed.), *Sociological theory.* San Francisco: Jossey-Bass, pp. 155–200.

Werner, Emmy E. & Smith, Ruth S. (1982). *Vulnerable but invincible: A longitudinal study of resilient children and youth.* New York: McGraw-Hill.

Wehlage, Gary G., Rutter, Robert A., Smith, G. A., Lesko, Nancy, & Fernández, Ricardo R. (1989). *Reducing the risk: Schools as communities of support.* Philadelphia: Falmer Press.

Wilcox, Kathleen (1982). Differential socialization in classrooms. In G.D. Spindler (Ed.), *Doing the ethnography of schooling.* New York: Holt, Rinehart & Winston, pp. 268–309.

Willis, Paul E. (1977). *Learning to labor: How working class kids get working class jobs.* New York: Columbia University Press.

Wilson, William Julius (1987). *The truly disadvantaged: The inner city, the underclass, and public policy.* Chicago: The University of Chicago Press.

Wisch, Andrew, Mahalik, James, Hayes, Jeffrey, & Nutt, Elizabeth (1995). The impact of gender role conflict and counseling technique on psychological help seeking in men. *Sex Roles, 33*(1–2), 77–89.

Youniss, James & Smollar, Jacqueline (1985). *Adolescent relations with mothers, fathers, and friends.* Chicago: University of Chicago Press.

Zavella, Patricia (1987). *Women's work and Chicano families: Cannery workers of the Santa Clara valley.* Ithaca: Cornell University Press.

Zhou, Min & Bankston, Carl L. (1998). *Growing up American: How Vietnamese children adapt to life in the United States.* New York: Russell Sage Foundation.

What Do We Know about the Effects of Single-Sex Schools in the Private Sector?

Implications for Public Schools

CORNELIUS RIORDAN

Introduction

Most Americans take coeducation for granted. Typically, their own schooling has been coeducational; often, they have little awareness of single-sex schools. Our political culture reinforces the taken-for-granted character of American coeducation. It implies that schools reflecting the variety of society exemplify what is best about democratic societies. Many people also take for granted that coeducation provides equality of educational opportunity for women. Like racial and ethnic minorities, women have long been excluded from the educational process. Thus, many people regard coeducation as a major milestone in the pursuit of gender equality. Single-sex education, by contrast, appears regressive.

Coeducation began not because of any firm belief in its sound educational effect, but rather because of financial constraints (Riordan, 1990). Historically, mixed-sex schools were economically more efficient. In America, boys and girls have usually attended the same public schools. This practice originated with the "common" school. Of course, at one time in our society only boys received an education. At other times the only education for either boys or girls was single-sex schooling, either public or private. Once mass and state-supported public education had been established, however, it was clearly the exception for boys and girls to attend separate schools. By the end of the nineteenth century, coeducation was all but universal in American elementary and secondary public schools (Bureau of Education, 1883; Butler, 1910; Kolesnick, 1969). Although single-sex schooling remains as an option in private secondary schools, it declines with each decade (Lee and Marks, 1992).

Men's and women's colleges also became coeducational largely as a result of economic forces. This continues to be true today as enrollments dwindle in women's colleges. Thus, coeducation has evolved as a commonplace norm, not because of educational concerns as much as other forces. Women's colleges were established within a context of exclusion in the nineteenth century. And within this context, the underlying assumption, widely held both then and now, was that women's colleges were a temporary, short-term solution on the road to the eventual achievement of coeducation (Tidball et al., 1999).

This historical background has provided a protective halo around coeducation as an institution. Historically, this mode of school organization was never subjected to systematic research. Currently, this protective halo affects the research strategy and logic for comparing single-sex and mixed-sex schools. This "assumptive world" is so deeply ingrained that people often acknowledge the academic superiority of single-sex schools without realizing the aspersion implied for coeducation. A cursory sample of interviews will reveal that most people view single-sex schools as academically tougher, more rigorous, although perhaps less enjoyable than coeducational schools.

The salience of this problem was pointed up with the publication of the report, "How Schools Shortchange Women," commissioned by the American Association of University Women Educational Foundation (1992). (For an update of this study, see AAUW, 1998a.) This study examined more than one thousand publications about girls and education and concluded that bias against females remained widespread in coeducational schools, and was the cause of lasting damage to both educational achievement and self-development. Given these findings, one might think that the burden of proof would shift to coeducational schools, to demonstrate first that they are free of gender bias, and second, that they are at least as effective as single-sex schools in terms of achievement and gender equity. This would replace the current practice, which requires single-sex schools to show greater effectiveness.

A landmark study using expectation states theory was conducted by Elizabeth Cohen and her colleagues at Stanford University (1972). In Cohen's study, and several replications, it was found that simply placing African-American and white students in what appeared to be an equal-status problem-solving situation was *insufficient* to guarantee equal-status outcomes. In fact, the studies have documented and reported relatively extreme manifestations of racism; that is, white dominance in these types of situations. Moreover, in these studies, extensive efforts were made to alter the interaction pattern of white dominance with little success, except under one condition in which the African-American students were literally allocated to a dominant role vis-à-vis the white students, who were allocated a submissive role. These results led Cohen and Roper to the conclusion that:

> The oft made assumption that one has only to join blacks and whites on an officially "equal" footing in the same building for "equal status" relations to develop is not sound.... Belief systems concerning race and other status characteristics are so powerful that they will likely reinforce rather than damage stereotypical beliefs. (1972, pp. 645, 657)

Research has shown that small task groups, such as those characterized by classrooms, exhibit status hierarchies where some group members are more active, influential, and powerful than others (Berger and Zelditch, 1985). These unequal status positions occur in groups in which participants have been carefully matched according to various irrelevant status characteristics such as race, gender, age, height, educational level, and occupational attainment. This process has been termed "status generalization" (Berger, Conner, and Fisek, 1974). Whenever members of a social group are performing lower on average than another group, as is the case regarding boys and girls on many educational outcome measures, sound research suggests that some form of prior "treatment" for the disadvantaged group is helpful before engaging in mixed-group interaction or learning (Cohen and Roper, 1972; Lockheed, 1985). Thus, it is incorrect to conclude that coeducational schooling is best, especially when there are existing inequalities.

If dominance and inequality emerge in groups of people who are otherwise equal in societal status, it is not surprising to learn that this occurs even more predictably when group members differ in status characteristics that are viewed as unequal. Thus, because gender and race have historically been defined as unequal, expectation states theory predicts that higher status actors will assume high status positions in classrooms. In the case of race, whites are more likely to be dominant. In the case of gender, it can go both ways depending on the particular skill being evaluated (Lee, Chen, and Smerdon, 1995; Riordan, 2000; U.S. Department of Education, 2000).

In addition, students typically hold unequal standing in the classroom based on previous academic performance. Students hold relatively clear expectations for each other as to academic competence at various tasks (Cohen, 1994, 2000; Rosenholtz, 1985; Tammivaara, 1982). Furthermore, the research demonstrates that group members who assume and are accorded high status in one area of expertise are expected to be more competent and influential in other nonrelated tasks as well, academic and nonacademic. What this means for classrooms is that some students who are seen as performing specific tasks well, such as reading, are also accorded higher status in performing most other tasks, however unrelated they may be (Rosenholtz, 1985). Specifically, it means that females may be accorded higher status on all academic skills based on their reading ability or that males might be accorded higher status based on their mathematical ability.

Within the context of these introductory remarks, I wish to address four key issues in the remainder of the article:

1. What does research in the private sector tell us about single-sex schooling?
2. Why are single-sex schools more effective than coeducational schools?
3. What are the implications of private school research for single-sex public schools?
4. What does all of this mean in terms of educational policy?

What Is Known Regarding the Effects of Single-Sex Schools in the Private Sector?

Surprisingly, there are very few formal reviews of the relative effects of single-sex and coeducational schools or classrooms. Of course, all researchers have conducted their own literature reviews, but these are often incomplete. However, we can effectively draw upon the two exhaustive reviews of research. The first of these was conducted by Moore, Piper, and Schaefer for a U.S. Department of Education report. This review concluded that "there is sufficient evidence to support the proposition that single-sex schools may produce positive outcomes for young women, and that the countervailing evidence to reject that proposition is not sufficiently convincing" (1992, p. 42). In a more recent and fully exhaustive review, Mael concluded that "the predominance of research certainly shows a role for single-sex schools (as an option if not a norm)" (1998, p. 121). Despite the widespread attention given to the AAUW report, *Separated by Sex* (1998b), it is inappropriate to rely on it or the media stories that followed it as a definitive interpretation in light of the independent reviews of the research that are available.

I argue that the research is "exceedingly persuasive" in demonstrating that single-sex schools are effective in terms of providing both greater equality and greater achievement, especially for low-income and working-class students, most particularly for African-American and Hispanic-American boys *and* girls. I believe that the data are both consistent and persistent when several specifications are made. Note first that I exclude single-sex classes from my contention for exceedingly persuasive positive effects. My argument centers on the notion of an academic culture that is endemic to single-sex schools and cannot be produced in one or two classrooms within an otherwise coeducational school. Note that I draw these conclusions almost entirely from research that has been done on private rather than public schools. I begin with two general findings that rest on sound sociological and educational theory and research.

First, the academic and developmental consequences of attending one type of school versus another are typically insignificant for middle-class or otherwise advantaged students. By contrast, the consequences are significant only for students who are historically or traditionally disadvantaged—minorities and/or lower-class and working-class youth (students at risk). Furthermore, these significant effects for at-risk students are small in comparison with the much larger effects of socioeconomic status and type of curriculum in a given school (for a full review of studies, see Riordan, 1997). This basic social science finding has been shown to be true since first identified in the famous Coleman Report (Coleman et al., 1966, see especially Tables 3.221.1 and 3.221.2 on p. 229). Over the past three decades, the data persistently confirm this educational fact, which is fully consistent with the following points. We need to understand that all the hollering about types of schools (single-sex or otherwise) applies mostly to these students.

Second, single-sex schools work to improve student achievement (Lee, 1997; Lee and Bryk, 1986,

1989; Lee and Marks, 1990; Mael, 1998; Riordan, 1990, 1994a). They work for girls and boys, women and men, whites and nonwhites, *but* this effect is limited to students of lower socioeconomic status and/or students who are disadvantaged historically—females and racial/ethnic/religious minorities (both males and females). The major factor that conditions the strength of single-sex effects is social class, and since class and race are inextricably linked, the effects are also conditioned by race and sometimes by gender.

Specifically, disadvantaged students in single-sex schools, compared to their counterparts in co-educational schools, have been shown to have higher achievement outcomes on standardized tests of mathematics, reading, science, and civics. They show higher levels of leadership behavior in school, do more homework, take a stronger course load, and have higher educational expectations. They also manifest higher levels of environmental control, more favorable attitudes toward school, and less sex-role stereotyping. They acknowledge that their schools have higher levels of discipline and order and, not surprisingly, they have a less satisfactory social life than students in coeducational schools. In the long term, women who attended a girls' school continue to have higher test scores than women who attended coeducational schools (see preceeding citations). In drawing these conclusions, I do not in-clude two studies by Marsh (1989, 1991), which included many variables such as student expectations, which I argue in the following are inappropriate to use as controls. Bryk, Lee, and Holland (1989) also rejected Marsh's analysis on this and other grounds. The preceeding citations are generally confined to American studies only.

It is important to note, however, that single-sex school effects are fairly robust even when social class or race is not partitioned. In their Catholic school study, Lee and Bryk (1989) analyzed the data by statistically controlling for social class, race, and other background characteristics and applied the results to students generally (assuming that there were no differences in social class, race, or back-ground variables). They found sixty-five of seventy-four separate dependent variable effects to be in favor of single-sex schools. Thirty of seventy-four effects obtained an effect size (ES) of .18 or higher, favoring single-sex schools, equally distributed among boys and girls and the mean effect size was .13, favoring single-sex schools. These results are depicted in Figure 23.1.

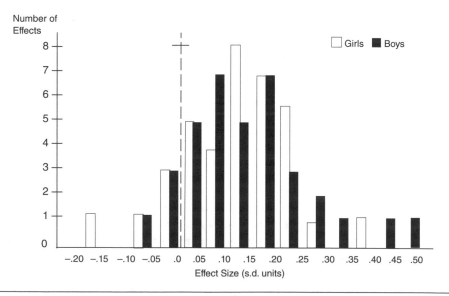

Figure 23.1 Effect sizes of single-sex schooling (Lee and Bryk 1989)

The results for students attending women's colleges parallel and substantiate the secondary school results. They manifest higher levels of environmental control, greater satisfaction with school (although not social life), and higher occupational success despite the fact that there is no difference in educational achievement when compared to women who attended a coeducational college (Miller-Bernal, 2000; Riordan, 1990, 1994b). This latter finding strongly suggests that their schooling has been of a higher quality, because ultimately they have the same level of educational achievement as women attending coeducational schools. Amazingly, women who attend a women's college for even a single year and then transfer obtain a significant gain in occupational success (Riordan, 1994b).

However, these positive effects, are not universal. In a cross national study of four countries (Belgium, New Zealand, Thailand, and Japan), Baker, Riordan, and Schaub (1995) showed that single-sex schools do not have uniform and consistent effects. The effects appear to be limited to those national educational systems in which single-sex schools are relatively rare. We argue that the rarity of a school type may enhance single-sex effects under certain conditions. When single-sex schools are rare in a country, the proacademic choice-making by parents and students results in a more selective student body that brings with it a heightened degree of academic demands. In turn, we believe that rare school types are better able to *supply* the quality of schooling *demanded* by these more selective students. Being less normative, these schools are likely to possess greater autonomy.

I wish to address another related matter that is quite important: How should we control for the distinct possibility of "selection bias" in studies of single-sex and mixed-sex schools? All researchers acknowledge that students attending each type of school vary in a number of ways, including socio-economic status, previous academic achievement, family structure, and the like. And everyone agrees that we need to statistically control (and thereby equate) these preexisting characteristics if we are to sort out the effects of the school from the effect of the home. I part company from those who believe that the appropriate strategy is to control or equate exhaustively. If we do, we end up controlling on some of the very characteristics that I maintain drives the entire success of single-sex schools: making a proacademic choice. Hence, my view is that we need to control for factors that pertain to home background resources (e.g., socioeconomic status) and prior academic achievement (e.g., test scores). But not much else, and certainly not educational expectations or similar variables, which measure and may distinguish students in terms of the value they place on academics. (See Figure 23.4 and the discussion.) In fact, having controlled for social class and academic achievement, students in single-sex schools may still have higher educational expectations than students in coeducational schools (Lee and Bryk, 1986; Lee and Marks, 1990). It is worth a moment to consider the irony of refusing to allow such students to attend a school that will help them to achieve their high educational expectations, especially when the students are desperate, poor, and powerless.

During the 1970s and 1980s, female students benefited from single-sex schools regardless of their social class position because they were historically and traditionally disadvantaged in school. Sometime during the 1980s, and clearly by 1990, this historical disadvantage for females in schools had been remediated (Riordan, 1998, 2000; U.S. Department of Education, 2000; Willingham and Cole, 1997). As a result of this transformation, I now argue that only females of low socioeconomic status are likely to show significant gains (along with boys) in single-sex schools.

Recent research (LePore and Warren, 1997) in the 1990s found that females in Catholic single-sex schools do not outperform their counterparts in coeducational schools. This is contrary to the results obtained by Bryk, Lee, and Holland (1993) and Riordan (1990) for Catholic school students in the 1970s and 1980s. This now seems completely consistent because students in these schools have become increasingly significantly affluent from 1980 to 1992. Figure 23.2 shows that Catholic single-sex schools for girls have undergone a metamorphosis regarding the socioeconomic composition of their student bodies. In 1972, students attending Catholic single-sex schools for girls were approximately

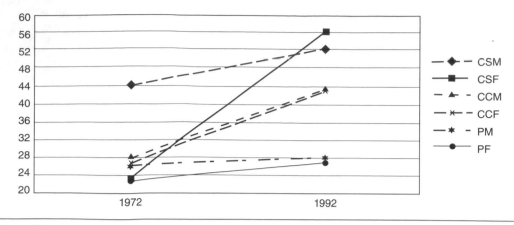

Figure 23.2 Socioeconomic composition (percent highest quartiles) of Catholic and publis schools.

equal to public school students in their socioeconomic background. From 1972 to 1992, their socio-economic status underwent a meteoritic rise. (See Baker and Riordan, 1998, for an elaboration on this phenomenon.) Given the propositions in the preceding, no school effects would be predicted under these demographic conditions.

Lee (1997) also found no differences in educational achievement between students in single-sex and mixed-sex elite independent schools. Thus, it appears that from 1972 to 1982 (and probably earlier) girls in Catholic single-sex schools outperformed girls in Catholic coeducational schools, and their achievements also closed the gender gap in comparison with coeducational males. In the late 1980s and the 1990s, however, the single-sex advantage for girls in "elite" Catholic schools was greatly diminished. Girls in coeducational schools increased their achievement curve surpassing their counterparts in single-sex schools (Riordan, 1998). Thus, we need to note very carefully that the findings from the 1970s to the early 1980s cannot and should not be generalized straightforwardly to the 1990s and beyond. As Catholic single-sex schools received positive media and academic attention in the 1980s, students attending these schools in the 1990s increasingly came from more affluent homes (Baker and Riordan, 1998). And for this reason, the single-sex schooling effects in Catholic schools were attenuated as per the preceding discussion.

However, what is bad for the goose is not always bad for the gander. This troubling news for Catholic schools is not a problem for the potential of single-sex schools in public schools. If single-sex schools are established to serve disadvantaged students, there are always ample numbers of socioeconomically disadvantaged, at-risk youth available in the public sector. Single-sex schools will be effective in the public sector so long as they are earmarked for disadvantaged students. On the other hand, if public schools were to establish single-sex schools and then allow more advantaged students to attend, the single-sex school effect would dissipate. To repeat (perhaps ad nauseam): Single-sex schools do not greatly influence the academic achievement of affluent or advantaged students, but they do for poor disadvantaged students.

It is important to emphasize that white middle-class (or affluent) boys and girls do not suffer any loss by attending a single-sex school. (They are not better off in coeducational schools.) At worse, they realize a neutral outcome, which is the general school effect finding for this subgroup across any two types of schools, as noted. Moreover, there exists the possibility that they do acquire small gains that are undetectable.

Why Are Single-Sex Schools More Effective Than Coeducational Schools?

There are at least a dozen theoretical rationales that provide support for the contention that single-sex schools are more effective academically and developmentally than mixed-sex schools, especially for minorities and at-risk students. Each of these rationales is less applicable when the schools and the students are mostly from high socioeconomic home backgrounds, and/or if single-sex schools are normative in the society or a subculture. Note carefully that all of these conceptual rationales are derived and/or linked to Expectation States Theory, as described in the Introduction to this chapter. These rationales are depicted in Figure 23.3.

The last four items on this list (9 through 12) draw on the work of Valerie Lee and colleagues (1997), who identified several structural and organizational features of schools that generate increased academic achievement as well as increased equity among the students (a decrease in the gap between racial and social class groups).

Single-sex schools provide more successful same-sex teacher and student role models, more leadership opportunities, greater order and discipline, fewer social distractions to academic matters, and the choice of a single-sex school is a proacademic choice. (For an elaboration of rationales 1 through 8, see Riordan, 1990, 1994.) Females also gain advantages because of significant reductions in gender bias in both teaching and peer interaction, and via access to the entire curriculum; the reverse may be true for African-American males. The schools are typically smaller and provide the academic climate features (9 through 12) noted by Lee (1997). Lee also argues (1997, p. 156) that these organizational differences explain the greater effectiveness of single-sex schools. Obviously I agree. But these explanatory variables are set into motion because of an independent variable, which is "school type" (single-sex or coeducational). You cannot just assume that the explanatory variables can be easily operationalized by well-intended educational policymakers and/or administrators.

Single-sex schools are places where students go to learn; not to play, not to hassle teachers and other students, and not primarily to meet their friends and have fun. Aside from affluent middle-class communities and private and alternative schools, coeducational schools are not all about academics. This has been noted often with alarm by respected and distinguished investigators across a variety of disciplines using a variety of methodologies (Devine, 1996; Goodlad, 1984; Powell, Farrar, and Cohen, 1985; Sedlack, Wheeler, Pullin, and Cusick, 1986; Steinberg, Brown, and Dornbusch, 1996; Willis, 1981).

1. The diminished strength of youth culture values
2. A greater degree of order and control
3. The provision of more successful role models
4. A reduction of sex differences in curriculum and opportunities
5. A reduction of sex bias in teacher-student interaction
6. A reduction of sex stereotypes in peer interaction
7. The provision of a greater number of leadership opportunities
8. *Single-gender schools require a proacademic parent/student choice*
9. Smaller school size
10. A core curriculum emphasized academic subjects taken by all students (organization of the curriculum)
11. Positive relationships among teachers, parents, and students that lead to a shared value community with an emphasis on academics and equity (school social organization)
12. Active and constructivist teaching and learning (organization of instruction)

FIGURE 23.3 Theoretical rationales for positive effects of single-sex schools.

What Are the Implications of Private School Research for Single-Sex Public Schools?

Over the course of time, I have come to see the proacademic choice that is made by parents and students as the key explanatory variable. This choice sets into motion a set of relationships among teachers, parents, and students that emphasize academics and deemphasize youth culture values, which as I have suggested, dominate coeducational schools. I want to be absolutely clear about this point. The choice is not at all about sex and romance nor is it about exclusion. It is about the rejection of antiacademic values that predominates in our culture and schools. Moreover, this rejection comes from the bottom up rather than the top down. In my view, it drives all that follows.

Single-sex schools, of course, provide a set of structural norms conducive to academic learning, as shown in Figure 23.3. This proacademic single-sex school environment operates in concert and harmony with the choice-making process made by students who attend single-sex schools. In this regard, it is entirely different from a set of structures or programs that are put into place by educators. In single-sex schools, the academic environment is normative in a true sociological sense. It is a set of rules established by the subjective reality (definitions) of participants that takes on an objective reality as a set of social structural norms (Berger and Luckman, 1967). This idea is similar to that proposed by Bryk, Lee, and Holland (1993) of a "voluntary community" for public school policy, which would resemble Catholic schools in every respect except for religion.

Figure 23.4 depicts this reciprocal relationship between organizational structures and student affirmations of those structures. Moreover, as I have indicated, these academic definitions of school contradict the nonacademic definitions that students otherwise bring to school and that come to constitute a youth culture. In effect, single-sex schools mitigate the single largest obstacle that stands in the way of effective and equitable schooling by using a fundamental sociological principle about how real social structures are created. Structures that are imposed and that contradict deeply cherished beliefs (regardless of how wrong-headed and problematic) will be rejected out of hand by any group with substantial power in numbers, such as students in schools.

By contrast, we can consider some alternatives that have been suggested for creating a proacademic environment in coeducational schools or schools generally. Specifically, we should consider the previously mentioned organizational features of effective schools from Lee (1997). In this 1995

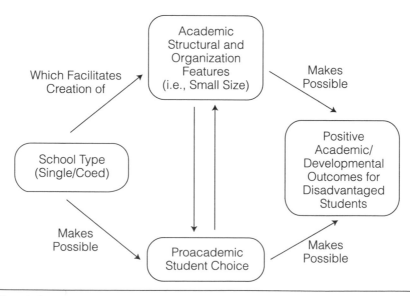

Figure 23.4 A Theoretical model of single-sex school type effects.

study for AAUW, she reported several cautionary findings regarding the effect of this set of school climate variables on the gender gap. For example, the same set of school level variables emphasizing academics (as in numbers 9 through 12 in Figure 23.3) increased mathematics, science, social studies, and reading achievement, but these same variables often did not reduce the gender gap favoring either males or females in these subject area tests.

In some cases, these positive school level variables actually made matters worse—greater parental involvement increased the gender gap, favoring males in mathematics achievement, and a whole set of positive academic school variables (e.g., positive student-teacher relations and an academic learning environment) increased the gender gap in social studies. In fact, aside from decreasing the gender gap in school engagement (which favors females), the school variables either had no effect or negative effects on the gender gap. Lee, Chen, and Smerdon (1995) demonstrate convincingly that a whole range of positive school climate variables will increase student achievement and engagement with school, but these same variables have either null or negative effects on increasing gender equity for these same measures.

The challenge of effective and equitable schooling in the next century is to overcome the resistance and recalcitrance of youth cultures in and out of school (Devine, 1996; Goodlad, 1984; Steinberg, Brown, and Dornbusch, 1996; Willis, 1981). This is not a new problem and undoubtedly predates the modern school. However, the intensity and complexity of the problem are new and represent the most important obstacles in schools today. It is not just about youthful anti-intellectualism, antisocial behavior, athletics and rock concerts, sexual harassment, heterosexual attraction and subsequent distraction, and the contentiousness that comes from increased diversity in the schools; it is about all these things and more.

How do schools get to be small or how do they develop communal relationships, authentic instruction, and/or a core academic curriculum? How can schools provide more successful academic role models and reduce the strength of antiacademic youth culture values? In essence, this requires reconstruction of schools. It requires a proacademic choice on the part of administrators, teachers, parents, and students (see Figure 23.4). Of these, I argue that students are the key stakeholders. In contrast to private schools, public schools often serve poor, disadvantaged, lower-class and working-class youth who are often racially stigmatized as well. These are the children and young adults who can benefit most from single-sex schools.

Single-Sex Public Schools

One of the interesting by-products of the questionable legal status of single-sex schools and classes has been that it has provided a backdrop for *Profiles in Courage* among public school principals (borrowing the term from John Kennedy's book by that name). During the 1990s, in various public schools across the country, principals were asked (or in some cases they did the asking) to allow teachers to establish single-sex classes. In view of the questionable legal status of single-sex schools and/or classes (see chapter 4 of this volume and Salomone, 1999), most principals were reluctant to venture away from anything but business as usual (carrying out the bureaucratic ethos). Not many were sufficiently courageous as to take on single-sex schooling. Yet, as a result of the problems in coeducational schools for both boys and girls, and the potential offered by single-sex schools (as per the preceding discussion), a variety of efforts were made throughout the 1990s to establish single-sex public schools for disadvantaged students. Some of these experiments were successful, whereas others were stymied by opponents of single-sex schools or other factors described in the following. In the examples that follow, the reader should note that only the California single-sex school experiment and the Young Women's Leadership School in New York City have been subjected to systematic and independent evaluations.

Several Unsuccessful Examples In 1989, the principal of Martin Luther King Jr. Elementary School in Rochester, New York, heeding the advice of several of her teachers, established a set of single-sex classrooms for both males and females. Students (and their parents) could choose between a single-sex or coeducational classroom in each grade. From the outset, her administrative decision was viewed with criticism from the central office, even though she had full and enthusiastic teacher, parental, student, and community support.

At the time (1989), the school had been identified as the thirteenth worst school in the state of New York as judged by performance standards. It is an inner city school attended predominantly by very poor Hispanic-American and African-American students. During the years 1989 to 1993, school records indicate that the students in the single-sex classrooms showed greater NCE gains on the reading and mathematics tests, higher attendance rates, lower suspension rates, and higher parental participation rates than students in the coeducational classes. Perhaps most remarkably, in one all-male class of African-American and Hispanic-American students, twenty-one of twenty-four *fathers* attended monthly parent-teacher meetings on a regular basis during the time that the program was intact (Riordan, 1993).

During the course of the 1989 to 1993 time period, Anita Boggs received no praise nor support for her work. Rather, she and her staff were pressured by the American Civil Liberties Union (ACLU) and National Organization for Women (NOW) to justify this organizational form of schooling. In 1993, she was abruptly transferred to another school. Single-sex schooling was shut down at Martin Luther King Jr. Elementary School. However, during 1989 to 1993, Boggs increased achievement and equality, she energized a group of teachers by simply supporting and organizing and making possible their pedagogical desires, and she brought forth social capital from the home by the involvement of African-American and Hispanic-American fathers and mothers in the schooling of their children. She utilized educational research to organize her school and for this she was banished to the suburbs where her efforts were not even needed.

Similar examples occurred throughout the 1990s. In 1991, Detroit school officials proposed three all-male academies for African-American boys that were ruled in violation of Tide IX; in 1993, school officials in Ventura, California, attempted for several years to experiment with single-sex classes but they too were destroyed by a set of legal challenges, and in 1994 again a courageous principal attempted to establish single-sex classes (see Richardson, 1995; Walsh, 1996). Anthony Palone, Principal of Myrtle Avenue School in Irvington, New Jersey, established single-sex classes for several years. Students flourished and parents were satisfied until the same antisingle-sex school forces that had appeared in other cities moved into action in Irvington. like Anita Boggs, Anthony Palone was shortly forced to abandon his efforts (Walsh, 1996).

Hubbard and Datnow (2002) describe a large experimental effort in the state of California to open single-sex schools for both boys and girls. Here I will only note that Governor Pete Wilson established these schools in 1997 by offering grants as incentives to districts to open schools for both boys and girls. In 1997, money was available for twenty schools (ten for boys and ten for girls) to be opened across the state. As of fall 2000, only one set of these schools (one boys' and one girls' school) remains in operation and each has a different story to tell.

Many of the schools in the California single-gender experiment violated a basic assumption of key theoretical rationales that have been identified in the preceding: namely, that principals and teachers in a single-sex school must believe in the basic philosophy of this kind of school organization, and not simply be in it for the grant money provided to the school. The downfall of the California single-sex school experiment was not pressure by political forces against single-sex schooling, but rather the result of a failure of the experiment itself to assure that principals and teachers minimally embraced the proacademic single-sex school concept. Hubbard and Datnow suggest that these schools could have been sustainable and successful if some of the fundamental components were in place.

Several Successful Examples Some schools have been successful in warding off the opponents of single-sex schools. They have obtained the services of principals and teachers who fully embrace the potential value of single-sex schooling (the major flaw in the California single-sex school experiment). In 1995, philanthropist and former journalist Ann Rubenstein-Tish, together with her husband Andrew Tish, initiated plans to open what has come to be called the Young Women's Leadership School in New York City. Tish secured the help of a legal team as well as the consulting services of this author and opened the school in fall 1996 as a regular public (not a charter) school in Community School District 4 of New York City. The school was designed to provide both a middle school (grades seven and eight) and upper school (grades nine through twelve) with a demanding college preparatory course of study. Funding for the school is the same as any of the other schools in District 4. Priority for admission to the school is given to students residing in District 4, which is a predominantly poor African-American and Hispanic-American East Harlem community in New York City.

Currently, the school serves about 310 students in grades seven to twelve. The school curriculum focuses on mathematics, science, technology, humanities, and leadership. The student population is diverse: 59 percent are Hispanic-American, 40 percent are African-American, and 67 percent fall below the poverty line, therefore qualifying for a free or reduced-price school lunch. Test scores for reading and mathematics are 30 percent higher than average for New York City coeducational schools. Although initially "only 40 percent [of the students] could read and do math at grade level, by the end of the year, 70 percent could read at or above grade level and 65 percent could meet the standard in math" (*New York Post,* 1997). Remarkably, 100 percent of this year's first graduating class are bound for college.

Following the New York City model, a group of prominent professional women in business, law, the arts, and philanthropy formed an advisory council and developed plans to open a school for girls in Chicago. In fall 2000, the Young Women's Leadership Charter School of Chicago opened its doors to 150 sixth-grade and ninth-grade students for girls only. The school focuses on math, science, technology, and leadership for girls and is located on the campus of the Illinois Institute of Technology. Students are selected by a lottery, and in the first draw 80 percent of the girls qualified for free or reduced-price lunch and 73 percent were African American. At full enrollment, the school will house 525 girls in grades six to twelve. Students are required to be residents of Chicago and in good academic standing.

Finally, brief mention should be made of several other public single-sex schools currently in operation. The Philadelphia School for Girls has existed since 1848, and although it was ordered to admit boys in a 1983 court decision, it remains today as a public all-girl magnet school by default. The school serves fifteen hundred students who come from predominantly poor families. Admission standards are rigorous, and the school was cited for excellence by the U.S. Department of Education in 1987. The school has a 98 percent college acceptance rate.

Western High School in Baltimore, Maryland, was founded in 1844 and remains today as a thriving all-girls' school. The school enrolls 1,250 students, and over 75 percent of these girls attend four-year colleges. The school is 80 percent African-American, and 38 percent of the students qualify for a free or reduced-price lunch. In the 1998 to 1999 academic year, 96 percent of the eleventh-grade students passed the Maryland state exams in reading, mathematics, writing, and citizenship.

In Hartford, Connecticut, the Lewis Fox Middle School houses the Benjamin E. Mays Institute for Boys and its sister program, the Mary M. Bethune Institute for Girls. Approximately eight hundred students attend this school, which is physically divided into separate clusters for boys and girls as well as for mixed-sex classes (schools within the school). About two hundred boys and girls attend classes separated by sex. The institutes share classes for physical education, but all other classes are conducted in separate areas as well as the lunch period. This school was established in 1996 and serves predominantly poor students (89 percent qualify for a free or reduced-price lunch). According to

Judith Glover (2001), a school guidance counselor, students in the single-sex classes always excel in the Hartford citywide testing program in comparison with students in mixed-sex classes.

And finally, the New York State Board of Regents has approved a proposal to open two single-sex charter schools. The Brighter Choice Charter School for Boys and the Brighter Choice Charter School for Girls will open in fall 2002 in Albany, New York. Both schools target economically disadvantaged at-risk youth (largely African-American and Hispanic-American), which are precisely the groups most likely to benefit from single-sex schools. In fact, the school will admit only students who qualify for a federal free lunch. It even comes with a guarantee. Any student who is there for three years is guaranteed to pass the state exams in math, reading, and science. Those who do not will be given a private scholarship to any other public or private school (*Wall Street Journal*, 2000).

It is interesting to note that three strategies have been used by these schools to defend against legal attacks from opponents. In New York, Chicago, and Albany, the schools utilized the services of legal consultants and social scientists to develop the school charters. In the California schools, the entire initiative was made available to both boys and girls with exactly equal resources for each school, down to the number of pencils and desks provided. In the case of the Philadelphia and Baltimore schools, the ACLU and other opponent organizations have been unable to find a boy willing to attend the school; moreover, the mayor of Baltimore has literally challenged the ACLU to take the schools to court. Because the school has enjoyed great success and is extremely popular with the citizenry of the city, local officials simply rely on community support to legitimatize the school.

Educational Research, Politics, and Policy

Data alone will not save single-sex schools; nor will data alone be sufficient to change the persistent problems that exist for both boys and girls in coeducational schools. This is not to say that research is not important, but only that ultimately the politics of education dictates the future of single-sex schools. It is useful to contrast educational research and educational policy about single-sex schools and the use of uniforms in schools. There exists a substantial degree of empirical research, which contrasts the relative effects of single-sex and mixed-sex schooling. Moreover, that base is both theoretical and empirical. And, although it is not entirely consistent, there is a preponderance of evidence supporting the positive value of single-sex education (under the conditions I have noted). Now, regarding the relative effects of wearing or not wearing uniforms in schools, we know next to nothing. There are all sorts of anecdotal reports and small sample studies, but there are very little hard data, although there is some good theory.

It is instructive to observe how easy it can be for an educational practice such as requiring uniforms to become educational policy without any educational research. Just a short time ago (February 24, 1995), President Clinton instructed the U.S. Department of Education to distribute manuals to all the school districts in the nation advising them how they can legally enforce a policy of uniforms in public schools. With this and several other speeches, the movement toward a national policy of school uniforms is racing ahead full speed, despite the fact that no one knows whether this educational policy will produce any positive educational results by and of itself, including the reduction of violence in the schools, which is the major claim of its proponents.

If you think about this for a moment, you can actually experience what it must have been like when the movement toward coeducation began to take hold about a century ago. In fact, coeducation (as a form of school organization) was institutionalized with little regard for educational research or educational or sociological theory. Just as coeducation was (and continues to be) politically correct, so too are school uniforms. Thus, political correctness can and often does override educational research and sociological theory in the formation of educational policy. Rosemary Salomone (1996) identified this as the perils of ideology.

Single-sex schools are politically incorrect; they are downright politically threatening to many people, and many of these people are in fact educational researchers, policymakers, and special interest stakeholder groups such as the AAUW Educational Foundation. This is not a very inspiring thought, but it is important to realize that this is the nature of what we are working with. It is not just about which type of school works best. It is about what most people think is politically expedient. In the long haul, however, I submit that educational politics may offer a deceiving foundation for educational policy in the absence of educational research and theory.

We desperately need more research on single-sex schools and less attention to educational politics and the formation of educational policy. One of the central problems is that single-sex schools cannot remain in place sufficiently long to develop a systematic long-term plan of action and a viable set of single-sex organizational norms, as I have outlined in this article. In all of the public school examples described herein, the period of existence for the schools has been too short to merit a valid evaluation. However, beyond the central question of which type of school works best in terms of achievement and gender equity, there are other questions that researchers have not even attempted to address.

For example, no one in the world has a clue as to the relative effects of single-sex and coeducational schools on identity formation (which is not at all the same as self-esteem). However, we do know from the work of Maccoby and Jacklin (1987; see also, Jacklin and Maccoby, 1978) that young children (two years of age and older) manifest a strong proclivity and greater compatibility in same-sex pairs, that girls exhibit more assertive behavior in same-sex groups, and that these facts remain true despite the efforts of adults to structure mixed-sex groups in such a way as to obtain equal status interaction (Lockheed, 1985; Lockheed and Harris, 1984).

Some people still think the gender gap is a one-way street, with males enjoying all the advantages. Beyond the schoolhouse door, this may still be true; but in elementary and secondary schools, it is not true and perhaps never was. Thus, issues of equity in coeducational schools can no longer be jump started by the phrase "when we shortchange girls, we shortchange America." Recent reports have now confirmed that both boys *and* girls are on the unfavorable side of the gender gap in education and developmental matters (Hedges and Nowell, 1995; Lee, Chen, and Smerdon, 1995; Linn and Hyde, 1989; Nowell, 1997; Riordan, 1998, 2000; U.S. Department of Education, 2000; Willingham and Cole, 1997). Lee, Chen, and Smerdon (1995) suggest that a more balanced approach to the study of gender equity is in order. What is becoming increasingly clear is that coeducational schools will have to provide special attention to boys in reading and writing and engagement, and this is going to complicate the entire equation for creating equity in coeducational schools.

Conclusions

Single-sex schools remain an effective form of school organization for disadvantaged students. The schools provide a structure that is conducive to learning, as I have detailed in this article. In selecting a single-sex school with its structure in place, students reject the antiacademic norms that permeate most public coeducational schools attended by at-risk youth. They make a proacademic choice. I have no illusions that students do this gleefully and go off to school dancing in the streets. Of course, for most students the choice is made by parents for their children. The point is this: An effective school requires a minimal level of compliance (even if it is begrudging) on the part of the students to the academic norms of the school.

Specifically, in order for a school to provide high levels of achievement and equity for students, it should provide a challenging academic program to all students; the teaching style should be active and constructive; the relationships among teachers, administrators, parents, and students should be communal; and the school should be small. Youth culture and antiacademic values should be minimized, order and control should prevail, successful student role models should be abundant, sex (and race) bias in peer and student-teacher interaction should be nonexistent, and leadership and educational opportunities should be free of sex (and race) bias.

One can try to set this up by instituting rules and regulations and structures and norms from the desks of either superintendents and/or principals. In lieu of any other alternative, this is how it will be done. But institutions simply do not work very well that way, especially when the clients are youth who understandably and justifiably want a stake in the creation of social organizations that ultimately control their behavior. Single-sex schools provide an avenue for students to make a pro-academic choice, thereby affirming their intrinsic agreement to work in the kind of environment we identify as effective and equitable. Single-sex schools should not be expected to correct the gender equity problems that exist in society and in coeducational schools. Nor should anyone fear that their existence would detract in any way from efforts that should be made to provide greater gender equity in public coeducational schools.

References

American Association of University Women (AAUW). (1998a). *Gender Gaps*. Commissioned and researched by the American Institute for Research, Washington, D.C.: The American Association of University Women Educational Foundation.
———. (1992). *How Schools Shortchange Girls*. Commissioned and researched by S. Bailey. Wellesley, MA: Wellesley College Center for Research on Women.
———. (1998b). *Separated by Sex*. Washington, D.C.: The American Association of University Women Educational Foundation.
Baker, D. P. and Riordan, C. (1998). "The 'Eliting' of the Common American Catholic School and the National Educational Crisis." *Phi Delta Kappan*. September: 16–23.
Baker, D. P., Riordan, C., and Schaub, M. (1995). "The Effects of Sex-Grouped Schooling on Achievement: The Role of National Context." *Comparative Education Review* 39: 468–481.
Berger, J., Conner, T. L., and Fisek, M. H. (Eds.). (1974). *Expectation States Theory*. Cambridge, MA: Winthrop Publishers.
Berger, J. and Zelditch, Jr., M. (eds.). (1985). *Status, Rewards, and Influence*. San Francisco: Jossey-Bass.
Berger, P. L., and Luckman, T. (1967). *The Social Construction of Reality*. Garden City, NY: Doubleday-Anchor.
Bryk, A. S., Lee, V. E., and Holland, P. B. (1993). *Catholic Schools and the Common Good*. Cambridge, MA: Harvard University Press.
Bureau of Education. (1883). *Co-education of the Sexes in the Public Schools of the U.S.A.* Washington, D.C.: United States Government Printing Office.
Butler, N. M. (Ed.). (1910). *Education in the United States*. New York: American Book Company.
Cohen, E. G. (1994). *Designing Groupwork: Strategies for the Heterogeneous Classroom* (2nd ed.). New York: Teachers College Press.
Cohen, E. G. (2000). "Equitable classrooms in a changing society." In M. Hallinan (Ed.), *Handbook of the Sociology of Education*. New York: Kluwer Academic Publishers.
Cohen, E. G., and Roper, S. S. (1972). "Modification of Interaction Disability: An Application of Status Characteristics Theory." *American Sociological Review* 37: 643–657.
Coleman, J. S., Campbell, E. Q., Hobson, C. J., McPartland, J., Mood, A. M., Weinfeld, F. D., et. al. (1966). *Equality of Educational Opportunity*. Washington, D.C.: U.S. Government Printing Office.
Devine, J. (1996). *Maximum Security: The Culture of Violence in Inner-City Schools*. Chicago: University of Chicago Press.
Glover, J. (2001). Personal telephone conversation on August 2, 2001.
Goodlad, J. (1984). *A Place Called School*. New York: McGraw-Hill.
Hedges, L. V., and Nowell, A. (1995, July). "Sex Differences in Mental Test Scores, Variability, and Numbers of High-Scoring Individuals." *Science* 269: 41–45.
Hubbard, L., and Datnow, A. (2002). Are single-sex schools sustainable in the public sector. In A. Datnow and L. Hubbard (Eds.), *Gender in policy and practice* (pp. 109–132). New York: Routledge/Falmer.
Jacklin, C. N., and Maccoby, E. E. (1978). "Social Behavior at Thirty-Three Months in Same-Sex and Mixed-Sex Dyads." *Child Development* 49: 557–569.
Kolesnik, W. B. (1969). *Co-education: Sex Differences and the Schools*. New York: Vantage Press.
Lee, V. E. (1997). "Gender Equity and the Organization of Schools." In B. J. Bank and P. M. Hall (Eds.), *Gender, Equity, and Schooling*. New York: Garland Publishing.
Lee, V. E., and Bryk, A. S. (1986). "Effects of Single-Sex Secondary Schools on Students Achievement and Attitudes." *Journal of Educational Psychology* 78: 381–395.
———. (1989). "Effects of Single-Sex Schools: Response to March." *Journal of Educational Psychology* 81(4): 647–650.
Lee, V. E., Chen, X., and Smerdon, B.A. (1995). *The Influence of School Climate on Gender Differences in Achievement and Engagement of Young Adolescents*. Washington, D.C.: Paper commissioned by the American Association of University Women, 1995.
Lee, V. E., and Marks, H. M. (1990). "Sustained Effects of the Single-Sex Secondary School Experience on Student Achievement and Attitudes." *Journal of Educational Psychology* 82(3): 378–392.

———. (1992). "Who Goes Where? Choice of Single-Sex and Coeducational Independent Secondary Schools." *Sociology of Education* 65: 226–253.

LePore, P. C., and Warren, J. R. (1997). "A Comparison of Single-Sex and Coeducational Catholic Secondary Schooling: Evidence from the National Educational Longitudinal Study of 1988." *American Educational Research Journal* 34: 485–511.

Linn, M. C., and Hyde, J. S. (1989). "Gender, Mathematics, and Science." *Educational Researcher* 18: 17–27.

Lockheed, M. E. (1985). "Sex and Social Influence: A Meta-Analysis Guided by Theory." In J. Berger, and M. Zelditch Jr. (Eds.), *Status, Rewards, and Influence.* San Francisco: Jossey-Bass, 406–427.

Lockheed, M. E., and Harris, A. M. (1984). "Cross-Sex Collaborative Learning in Elementary Classrooms." *American Educational Research Journal* 21: 275–294.

Maccoby, E. E., and Jacklin, C. N. (1987). "Gender Segregation in Childhood." *Advances in Child Development and Behavior* 20: 239–287.

Mael, F. A. (1998). "Single-Sex and Coeducational Schooling: Relationships to Socioemotional and Academic Development." *Review of Educational Research* 68: 101–129.

———. (1989). "Effects of Attending Single-Sex and Coeducational High Schools on Achievement, Attitudes, Behavior, and Sex Differences." *Journal of Educational Psychology* 81(1): 70–85.

Marsh, H. W. (1991). "Public, Catholic Single-Sex, and Catholic Coeducational High Schools: Effects on Achievement, Affect, and Behaviors." *American Journal of Education* 11: 320–356.

Miller-Bernal, L. (2000). *Separate by Degree: Women Students' Experiences in Single and Coeducational Colleges.* New York: Peter Lang.

Moore, M., Piper, V., and Schaefer, E. (Mathematica Policy Research, Inc.). (1992). "Single-Sex Schooling and Educational Effectiveness: A Research Overview." In *Single-Sex Schooling: Perspectives from Practice and Research. A Special Report from the Office of Educational Research and Improvement.* Washington, D.C.: U.S. Department of Education.

New York Post. (September 19, 1997).

Nowell, A. (1997). "Trends in Gender Differences in Academic Achievement from 1960 to 1994." Paper read at the annual meeting of the American Educational Research Association.

Powell, A. G., Farrar, E., &. Cohen, D. K. (1985). *The Shopping Mall High School: Winners and Losers in the Educational Marketplace.* Boston: Houghton Mifflin Company.

Richardson, J. (1995). "Troubled N.J. School Turns to Single-Sex Classes." *Education Week,* 14(24): 1, 10.

Riordan, C. (1997). *Equality and Achievement: An Introduction to the Sociology of Education.* New York: Addison-Wesley Longman.

———. (1990). *Girls and Boys in School: Together or Separate?* New York: Teachers College Press.

———. (1993). Personal observations, interviews, correspondence, and research regarding the Martin Luther King, Jr. Elementary School, Rochester, New York.

———. (1994a). "Single-Gender Schools: Outcomes for African and Hispanic Americans." *Research in Sociology of Education and Socialization* 10: 177–205.

———. (2000). "Student Experiences in Home and School: Gender Gap Comparisons among 1990 Sophomores in the National Educational Longitudinal Study." Paper read at the annual meeting of the American Sociological Association.

———. (1998). "Student Outcomes in Public and Catholic Secondary Schools: Gender Gap Comparisons from 1972 to 1992." Paper read at the annual meeting of the American Sociological Association.

———. (1994). "The Value of Attending a Women's College." *Journal of Higher Education,* 65(4): 486–510.

Rosenholtz, S. J. (1985). "Modifying Status Expectations in the Traditional Classroom." In J. Berger, and M. Zelditch, Jr. (Eds.), *Status, Rewards, and Influence.* San Francisco: Jossey-Bass, 445–470.

Salomone, R. (1996). "Rich Girls, Poor Girls, and the Perils of Ideology." Keynote Address given at the Annual Leadership Conference of the Connecticut Chapter of the American Association of University Women, Wesleyan University.

———. (1999). "Single-Sex Schooling: Law, Policy, and Research." In D. Ravitch, (Ed.), *Brookings Papers on Education Policy.* Washington, D.C.: Brookings Institution Press.

Sedlak, M. W., Wheeler, C. W., Pullin, D. C., and Cusick, P. A. (1986). *Selling Students Short: Classroom Bargains and Academic Reform in the American High School.* New York: Teachers College Press.

Steinberg, L. B., Brown, B., and Dornbusch, S. M. (1996). *Beyond the Classroom.* New York: Simon & Schuster.

Tammivaara, J. (1982). "The Effects of Task Structure on Beliefs about Competence and Participation in Small Groups." *Sociology of Education* 55: 212–222.

Tidball, M. E., Smith, D. G., Tidball, C. S., and Wolf-Wendel, L. E. (1999). *Taking Women Seriously: Lessons and Legacies for Educating the Majority.* Phoenix, AZ: The American Council on Education and The Oryx Press.

U.S. Department of Education. (1992). *Single-Sex Schooling: Perspectives from Practice and Research* (vol. I). Washington, D.C.: Office of Educational Research and Improvement.

U.S. Department of Education. (2000). *Trends in Educational Equity of Girls and Women.* Written and researched by Y. Bae, S. Choy, C. Geddes, J. Sable, and T. Snyder. Washington, D.C.: Office of Educational Research and Improvement, NCES, 2000–03.

Wall Street Journal. (December 26, 2000). "A Brighter Idea." A-10.

Walsh, M. (1996). "Educators Debate Impact of Ruling on Single-Sex Classes." *Education Week* 15(40): 1, 31.

Willingham, W. W., and Cole, N. S. (1997). *Gender and Fair Assessment.* Mahwah, NJ: Lawrence Erlbaum Associates.

Willis, P. (1981). *Learning to Labor: How Working-Class Kinds Get Working Class Jobs.* New York: Columbia University Press.

Arnot, M. (2002). *Reproducing gender: Selected critical essays on educational theory and feminist politics.* London: Falmer.

Arnot, M., David, M., & Weiner, G. (1999). *Closing the gender gap: Postwar education and social change.* Cambridge: Polity.

Attewell, P. (2001) The winner-take-all high school: Organizational adaptations to educational stratification. *Sociology of Education, 74*, 267–296.

Baker, D. P., & Stevenson, D. L. (1986). Mothers' strategies for children's school achievement: Managing the transition to high school. *Sociology of Education, 59*, 156–166.

Becker, H. S. (1952). Social-class variations in the teacher-pupil relationship. *Journal of Educational Sociology, 25*(8), 451–466.

Braddock, J. H., II. (1990). Tracking the middle grades: National patterns of grouping for instruction. *Phi Delta Kappan, 71*, 445–449.

Braddock, J. H., II, & McPartland, J. M. (1990). Alternatives to tracking. *Educational Leadership, 47*(7), 76–79.

Braddock, J. H., & Dawkins, M. P. (1993). Ability grouping, aspirations, and attainments: Evidence from the National Educational Longitudinal Study of 1988. *Journal of Negro Education, 62*, 324–336.

Catsambis, S. (1994). The path to math: Gender and racial-ethnic differences in mathematics participation from middle school to high school. *Sociology of Education, 67*, 199–215.

Cicourel, A. V., & Kitsuse, J. I. (1963). *The educational decision makers.* New York: Bobbs-Merrill

Coleman, J. S., et al. (1966). *Equality of educational opportunity.* Washington D.C.: U.S. Government Printing Office.

Coleman, J. S., & Hoffer, T. (1987). *Public and private schools: The impact of communities.* New York: Basic Books.

Coleman, J .S., Hoffer, T., & Kilgore, S. (1982). *High school achievement: Public, Catholic and private schools compared.* New York: Basic Books.

Cookson, P.W., & Persell, C. H. (1985). *Preparing for power: America's elite boarding schools.* New York: Basic Books.

Darling-Hammond. L. (2004). Inequality and the right to learn: Access to qualified teachers in California's public schools. *Teachers College Record, 106*(10), 1936–1966.

Datnow, A., & Hubbard, L. (2002). *Gender in policy and practice.* New York: Routledge/Falmer.

DiMaggio, P. (1982). Cultural capital and school success. *American Sociological Review 47*, 189–201.

DiMaggio, P., & Mohr, J. (1985). Cultural capital, educational attainment, and marital selection. *American Journal of Sociology, 90*, 1231–1261.

Dougherty, K. J. (1996). Opportunity-to-learn standards: A sociological critique. *Sociology of Education*, Extra Issue (Special Issue on Sociology and Educational Policy: Bringing Scholarship and Practice Together), 40–65.

Dumais, S. A. (2002). Cultural capital, gender, and school success: The role of habitus. *Sociology of Education, 77*, 44–68.

Eder, D. (1995). *School talk.* New Brunswick, NJ: Rutgers University Press.

Eder, D., & S. Parker. (1987). The cultural reproduction of gender: The effect of extracurricular activities on peer-group culture. *Sociology of Education 60*, 200–213.

Entwisle, D., Alexander, K., & Olson, L. S. (1997). *Children, schools and inequality.* Boulder, CO: Westview.

Entwisle, D., & Alexander, K. (1992). Summer setback: race, poverty, school composition, a mathematics achievement in the first 2 years of school. *American Sociological Review, 57*, 72–84.

Epstein, J. L. (1991). Effects on student achievement of teacher practices of parent involvement. In S. Silvern (Ed.), *Advances in reading/language research, Vol. 5. literacy through family, community and school interaction.* Greenwich, CT: JAI Press.

Farkas, G. (1996). *Human capital or cultural capital: Ethnicity and poverty groups in an urban school district.* New York: Aldine DeGruyter.

Ferguson, A. (2001). *Bad boys.* Ann Arbor: University of Michigan Press.

Fordham, S. (1997). *Blacked out: Dilemmas of race and identity and success at Capital High.* Chicago: University of Chicago Press.

Fordham, S., & Ogbu, J. U. (1986). Black students' school success: Coping with the "burden" of acting white. *The Urban Review, 18*(3), 176–206.

Gamoran, A. (1987). The stratification of high school learning opportunities. *Sociology of Education, 60*, 135–155.

Gamoran, A. (1993). Alternative uses of ability grouping in secondary schools: Can we bring high-quality instruction to low-ability classes? *American Journal of Education, 101*, 1–22.

Gamoran, A. (1996). Curriculum standardization and equality of opportunity in Scottish secondary education, 1984–1990. *Sociology of Education, 29*, 1–21.

Gamoran, A., & Berends, M. (1987). The effects of stratification in secondary schools: synthesis of survey and ethnographic research. *Review of Educational Research, 57*, 415–435.

Gamoran, A. Nystand, M,, Berends, M., & LePore, P. (1995). An organizational analysis of the effects of ability grouping. *American Educational Research Journal, 32*, 59–87.

Gamoran, A., & Mare, R. D. Secondary school tracking and educational inequality: enforcement, compensation, or neutrality? *American Journal of Sociology, 94*, 1146–1183.

Gartner, A., & Lipsky, D. K. (1987). Beyond special education: Toward a quality system for all students. *Harvard Educational Review 57*, 367–395.

Hallinan, M. T. (1987). Ability grouping and student learning. In M. T. Hallinan (Ed.), *The social organization of schools: New conceptualizations of the learning process* (pp. 41–69). New York: Plenum.

Hallinan, M. T. (1994). School differences in tracking effects on achievement. *Social Forces 72*, 799–820.

Hallinan, M. T. (1994). Tracking: From theory to practice. *Sociology of Education, 67*, 79–84.

Hallinan, M. T. (2001). Sociological perspectives on Black-White inequalities in American schooling. *Sociology of Education, 74* (Extra Issue), 50–70.

Hoffer, T. B. (1992). Middle school ability grouping and student achievement in science and mathematics. *Educational Evaluation and Policy Analysis, 14*, 205–227.

Horvat, E. M. (2003). Reassessing the burden of 'acting White': The importance of peer groups in managing academic success. *Sociology of Education, 76*, 265–280.

Jencks, C., & Phillips, M. (Eds.) (1998). *The Black-White achievement gap*. Washington, D.C.: Brookings.

Kerckhoff, A. (1986) The effects of ability grouping. *American Sociological Review, 51*, 842–858.

Kilgore, S. (1991). The organizational context of tracking in schools. *American Sociological Review, 56*, 189–203.

Lareau, A. (1987). Social class differences in family-school relationships: The importance of cultural capital. *Sociology of Education, 60*, 73–85.

Lareau, A. (1989). *Home advantage: Social class and parental intervention in elementary education*. New York: Falmer Press.

Lareau, A. (2002). Invisible inequality: Social class and childrearing in Black families and white families. *American Sociological Review, 67*(5), 747–776.

Lareau, A. (2003). *Unequal childhood: Class, race and family life*, University of California Press.

Lareau, A., & Horvat, E. M. (1999). Moments of social inclusion and exclusion: Race, class, and cultural capital in family-school relationships. *Sociology of Education, 72*, 37–53.

Lee, V. E., & Burkham, D. (2002). *Inequality at the starting gate: Social background differences in achievement as children begin school*. Washington D.C.: Economic Policy Institute.

Lee, V. E., Marks, H. M., & Byrd, T. (1994). Sexism in single-sex and coeducational independent secondary school classrooms. *Sociology of Education, 67*, 92–120.

Lew, J. (2006). *Asian Americans in class: Charting the achievement gap among Korean American youth*. New York: Teachers College Press.

Lewis, A. (2003). *Race in the schoolyard: Negotiating the color line in classrooms and communities*. New Brunswick, NJ: Rutgers University Press.

Losen, D., & Orfield, G. (Eds.) (2002). *Racial inequity in special education*. Cambridge, MA: Harvard Education Publishing Group.

Lucas, S. R. (1999). *Tracking inequality: Stratification and mobility in American high schools*. New York: Teachers College Press.

Lucas, S. R. (2001). Race, class, and tournament track mobility. *Sociology of Education, 74*, 139–156.

Lucas, S. R. (2002). Socio-demographic diversity, correlated achievement, and de facto tracking. *Sociology of Education, 75*, 328–348.

MacLoud, J. (1995). *Ain't no makin' it: Aspirations and attainment in a low income neighborhood*. Boulder, CO: Westview.

McDermott, R. P. (1977). Social relations as contexts for learning. *Harvard Educational Review, 47*, :198–213.

McDermott, R. P. (1994). More than misapplied technology: A normative and political response to Hallinan on tracking. *Sociology of Education 67*, 84–89.

McDermott, R. P., & Varenne, H. (1995). Culture as disability. *Anthropology and Education Quarterly, 26*(3), 324–348.

McDonaugh, P. (1994). Buying and selling higher education: The social construction of the college applicant. *Journal of Higher Education, 65*, 4.

Mickelson, R. A. (1990). The attitude-achievement paradox among Black adolescents. *Sociology of Education, 63*, 44–61.

Mickelson, R. A., & Ray, C.A. (1994). Fear of falling from grace: The middle class, downward mobility, and school desegregation. *Research in Sociology of Education and Socialization, 10*, 207–238.

Mickelson, R. A. (2003a). Gender Bourdieu, and the anomaly of women's achievement redux. *Sociology of Education, 75*, 373–375.

Mickelson, R. A. (2003b). When are racial disparities in education the result of racial discrimination? A social science perspective. *Teachers College Record, 105*(6), 1080–1114.

Noguera, P. A. (2004) Social capital and the education of immigrant students: Categories and generalizations. *Sociology of Education, 77*, 180–184.

Oakes, J. (2006). *Keeping track: How schools structure inequality* (2nd ed.). New Haven, CT: Yale.

Oakes, J. (1994). More than misapplied technology: A normative and political response to Hallinan. *Sociology of Education, 67*, 84–88.

Ogbu, J. U. (1987). Variability in minority school performance: A problem in search of an explanation. *Anthropology and Education Quarterly, 10*(1).

Ogbu, J. U. (1992). *Minority status and schooling: A comparative study of immigrants and involuntary minorities.* New York: Garland Publishing (with M. A. Gibson).

Ogbu, J. U. (1999). Beyond language: Ebonics, proper English, and identity in a Black-American speech community. *American Education Research Journal, 36*(2), 147–184.

Ogbu, J. (2003). *Black Americans students in an affluent suburb: A study of academic disengagement.* Mahwah, NJ: Erlbaum.

Ogbu, J. U. (2004). Collective identity and the burden of acting white in black history, community and education. *The Urban Review, 36*(1): 1–35.

Orfield, G. (2004) *Dropouts in America: Confronting the graduate rate crisis.* Cambridge, MA: Harvard.

Orfield, G., & Lee, C. (2002) *Why segregation matters: Poverty and educational inequality.* Cambridge, MA: The Civil Rights Project, Harvard University.

Power, S., Warren, S., Gillborn, D., Clark, A., Thomas, S., & Coate, K. (2001). *Education in deprived areas.* London: Institute of Education University of London.

Page, R. N. (1991). *Lower-track classrooms: A curricular and cultural perspective.* New York: Teachers College Press.

Pallas, A. M., Entwisle, D. R., Alexander, K. L., & Stluka, M. F. (1994). Ability group effects: Instructional, social, or institutional. *Sociology of Education, 67,* 27–46.

Persell, C. H. (1997). *Education and inequality.* New York: The Free Press.

Persell, C. H., & Cookson, P. W. (1985). Chartering and bartering: Elite education and social reproduction. *Social Problems, 33*(2), 114–129.

Reardon, S. F. (2001). Suburban racial change and suburban school segregation: 1987–96. *Sociology of Education, 74,* 79–101.

Riordan, C. (1985). Public and Catholic schooling: The effects of gender context policy. *American Journal of Education, 93,* 518–540.

Riordan, C. (1990). *Girls and boys in school: Together or separate?* New York: Teachers College Press.

Rosenbaum, J. (1976). *Making inequality: The hidden curriculum of tracking.* New York: Wiley.

Rumberger, R. W., & Gandara, P. (2004). Seeking equity in the education of California's English learners. *Teachers College Record, 106*(10), 2032–2056.

Salomone, R. (2003). *Same, different, equal: Rethinking single-sex schooling.* New Haven, Yale University Press.

Salomone, R. C. (2006). Single-sex programs: Resolving the research Conundrum. *Teachers College Record, 108*(4), 778–802.

Shavit, Y., & Blossfeld, H. P. (Eds.). (1993). *Persistent inequalilty: Changing educational attainment in thirteen countries.* Boulder, CO: Westview Press.

Spade, J., Columba, L., & Vanfossen, B. E. (1997). Tracking in mathematics and science: Courses and course-selection procedures. *Sociology of Education, 70*(2), 108–127.

Stanton-Salazar, R. D., & Dornbusch, S. M. (1995). Social capital and the reproduction of inequality: Information networks among Mexican-origin high school students. *Sociology of Education, 68*(2), 116–135.

Stanton-Salazar, R. D. (2001). *Manufacturing hope and despair: The school and kin support networks of U.S.-Mexican youth.* New York: Teachers College Press.

Stanton-Salazar, R., Chavez, L., & Tai, L. (2001). The help-seeking orientation of Latino and non-Latino urban high school students: A critical-sociological investigation. *Social Psychology of Education, 5,* 49–82.

Stevenson, D. L., Schiller, K. S., & Schneider, B. (1994). Sequences of opportunities for learning. *Sociology of Education, 67,* 184–198.

Thorne, B. (1993). *Gender play: Girls and boys in school.* New Brunswick, NJ: Rutgers University Press.

Tyson, K. (2003). Notes from the back of the room: Problems and paradoxes in the schooling of young Black students. *Sociology of Education, 76,* 326–343.

Useem, E. L. (1991). Student selection into course selection sequences in mathematics: The impact of parent involvement and school policies. *Journal of Research on Adolescence, 1,* 231–250.

Useem, E. L. (1992). Getting on the fast track in mathematics: School organizational influences on math track assignment. *American Journal of Education, 100*(3), 325–353.

Useem, E. L. (1992). Middle schools and math groups: Parents' involvement in children's placement. *Sociology of Education 65*: 263–279.

Vanfossen, B. E., Jones, J.D., & Spade, J. Z. (1987). Curriculum tracking and status maintenance. *Sociology of Education, 60,* 104–122.

Van Hook, J. (2002). Immigration and African American educational opportunity: The transformation of minority schools. *Sociology of Education, 75,* 169–189.

Valenzuela, A. (1999). *Subtractive schooling: U.S. Mexican youth and the politics of caring.* Albany: SUNY Press.

Velez, W. (1989). Why Hispanic students fail: Factors affecting attrition in high schools. In Jeanne H. Ballantine (Ed.), *Schools and Society: A Unified Reader,* (2nd ed.). Palo Alto: Mayfield Publishing Company.

Walters, P. B. (2001). Educational access and the state: Historical continuities and discontinuities in racial inequality in American education. *Sociology of Education, 74* (Extra Issue), 35–45.

Weis, L. (1985). *Between two worlds: Black students in an urban community college.* Boston: Routledge & Kegan Paul.

Weis, L. (1992). *Working class without work.* Albany: SUNY Press.

Weis, L. (1993). White male working-class youth: An exploration of relative privilege and loss. In Lois Weis and Michelle Fine (Eds.), *Beyond silenced voices,* pp. 237–258. Albany: SUNY Press,.

Weis, L. ,& Fine, M. (2000). *Construction sites: Escavating race, class and gender among Urban youth.* New York: Teachers College Press.

Weis, L. (2004). *Class reunion: The remaking of the American white working class.* New York: Routledge.

Wells, A. S. (1995). Reexamining social science research on school desegregation: Long-versus short-term effects. *Teachers College Record, 96,* 691–706.

Wells, A. S., & Serna, I. (1996). The politics of culture: Understanding local political resistance to de-tracking in racially mixed schools. *Harvard Educational Review 66,* 93–118.

Wells, A. S., & Crain, R. L. (1997). *Stepping over the color line: African-American students in white suburban schools.* New Haven, CT: Yale University.

Wenglinsky, H. (1997). How money matters: The effect of school district spending on academic achievement. *Sociology of Education, 70,* 221–237.

Wexler, P. (1992). *Becoming Somebody.* London: Falmer Press.

Willis, P. (1981). *Learning to labor: How working class students get working class jobs.* New York: Columbia University Press.

Wrigley, J. (Ed.). (1992). *Education and gender equality.* London: Falmer.

Young, Michael. (1958). *The rise of the meritocracy, 1870–2033: An Essay on Education and Equality.* London: Thames and Hudson.

PART **VI**

Educational Reform and Policy

From the 1980s, standards-based reform has dominated educational policy. In 1983, the National Commission on Educational Excellence's report *A Nation at Risk* argued that U.S. schools were mediocre at best and that as a nation we faced falling behind the Japanese and Germans, whose students performed better on international examinations of reading, science, and mathematics. Following this report, state and national educational policies stressed higher standards for all students. By the beginning of the twenty-first century, the 1960s and 1970s concern for equity began to reemerge, with President George W. Bush's 2001 No Child Left Behind Act (NCLB) requiring the elimination of the achievement gap among different groups by 2014. Today, educational policy makers are concentrating on setting high academic standards for all children and ensuring that all children can meet them. Although most policy makers support the goal of eliminating the achievement gaps, there is disagreement as to whether this can be done and, if so, how. A critical question is whether nonschool factors such as poverty, family dysfunction, or health and environmental problems make the elimination of the gap, especially for poor children, unrealistic, or whether these factors are simply excuses for ineffective schools. The following readings examine different types of educational reforms and provide empirical evidence for considering this difficult question.

Chapter 24, "Complexity, Accountability, and School Improvement" by American Institutes for Research sociologist Jennifer A. O'Day, analyzes the effects of standards-based reforms on school districts and how complexity theory provides a tool for understanding the limits and possibilities of district and school based reforms.

Chapter 25, "False Promises: The School Choice Provisions in No Child Left Behind" by University of North Carolina, Chapel Hill, sociologist Douglas Lauen, examines the limits and possibilities of the public school choice provision in NCLB to improve educational opportunities for children in low-performing schools. Through an overview of the school choice debates and the implementation of the choice provision under NCLB, Lauen provides a sociological analysis of the effects of educational reform policies.

Chapter 26, "Our Impoverished View of Educational Reform" by educational psychologist David Berliner, provides a critical sociological analysis of the limits of school reform. Berliner examines the pernicious effects of poverty on the lives of low-income families and the failure of educational reform to address these effects.

Questions for Reflection and Discussion

1. According to O'Day, how does complexity theory help us to understand and improve schools and districts? What are the factors that should be considered when implementing standards-based reforms? Based on this article, if you became a school superintendent in a large, urban district, what types of policies would you implement to increase academic achievement?

BISHOP BURTON COLLEGE
LIBRARY
435

2. According to Lauen, what are the arguments in favor and against public and private school choice? Do you think that all parents should have the right to send their children to a school of their choice? Do you think that low-income families should receive publicly funded vouchers to send their children to private and religious schools? Based upon Lauen's findings, do you think that the reauthorization of NCLB should include a private school choice option for children in failing public schools, funded with public dollars?

3. According to Berliner, can school reform succeed in eliminating the achievement gaps in the United States? Why or why not? Do you think schools have the potential of reducing these gaps, without the types of economic policies discussed by Berliner? How do you think teachers and principals in schools with low-income children would respond to Berliner's argument?

References

National Commission on Excellence in Education (1983). *A Nation at Risk*. Washington, D.C.: U.S. Department of Education.

24

Complexity, Accountability, and School Improvement[1]

JENNIFER A. O'DAY

School-Based Accountability: Tensions and Problems

This discussion starts from the premise that school accountability mechanisms by their very nature seek to increase student performance by improving the functioning of the school organization. Mechanisms of school accountability vary from jurisdiction to jurisdiction, but generally include the establishment of some target level of performance (aggregated across the school, though targets may include disaggregated benchmarks as well), with consequences (and sometimes assistance) meted out to the school unit for achieving or not achieving the target performance. Whatever their differences in terms of the targets or the consequences, policies that take the school as the basic unit of accountability must contend with a number of inherent problems if they are to effect organizational change. I raise three such problems here and return to them at the conclusion of this article.

Problem 1: The school is the unit of intervention, yet the individual is the unit of action. The first of these problems concerns the relationship between collective accountability and individual action. School accountability by definition targets the school unit for monitoring, intervention, and change. But schools are collections of individuals, and to the extent that the needed change involves the behavior of the members of the organization, it must occur ultimately at the individual level. That is, individual teachers, administrators, and parents must in some way change what they are doing in the hope that this will change what students do (individually and in interaction with teachers) in such a way as to increase or deepen student learning. School-level accountability approaches bank on school members' identification and interaction with their organizational environment to motivate and direct individual action. In other words, such policies assume that targeting the school unit will generate the necessary and desired changes in the behavior of individuals within that unit. This assumption leads to two questions: How will school accountability mechanisms reach beyond the collective level to mobilize such changes among individuals? What conditions need to be in place for this connection to occur?

Problem 2: External control seeks to influence internal operations. Just as individuals operate within schools, schools are nested within larger systems and environments. New accountability approaches, by their very nature, seek to influence from the outside what goes on inside schools. Moreover, such policies assume that external forces can play a determining role in changing the internal workings of schools. The limitations of such assumptions, however, have provided grist for the vast literature on policy implementation in education.[6]

The heart of the issue is the problematic relationship between external and internal sources of control and the implications of this relationship for organizational learning and improvement. Organizational systems have several mechanisms at their disposal to control the behavior of individuals and subunits. Two such mechanisms are formal rules and normative structures. Large systems—like public education—tend toward bureaucracy and reliance on rules. Teachers work a certain number of hours a day, teach their classes in a prescribed order, and follow a variety of district, state, and federal mandates. But rules decreed from on high often have little impact, especially when it comes to the core technology of teaching and learning (Elmore, 1996; Marion, 1999). One reason is that externally generated rules may come up against the power of an organization's internal norms of behavior. Normative structures inside schools, such as the privacy of classroom practice, are often the determining factor not only in the implementation of policy, but, more importantly, in the school's overall effectiveness in fostering student learning.[7] The resulting questions for school accountability policies are profound. What is the appropriate and most effective balance between external and internal control? What are the mechanisms for achieving this balance? Can external accountability measures influence the development of internal norms that are more conducive to improving student learning?

Problem 3: Information is both problematic in schools and essential to school improvement. The third problem in school accountability concerns the nature and role of information in school improvement. Indeed, information is the lifeblood of all accountability mechanisms: one accounts to someone for something, and this accounting gets done by conveying information. Current school accountability policies, such as public reporting of student test scores, assume that, armed with accurate information about the achievement of students in the school, stakeholders and participants in the instructional process will take whatever action is necessary to improve learning outcomes. But again, this simple assumption raises a host of questions, the answers to which are anything but straightforward. What are the most effective forms and uses of information in the school improvement process? What is the potential for the external accountability system to generate and disseminate the information needed to accomplish the accountability goals? What are the motivational and learning links between information on the one hand and individual and collective action?

These three problems—collective accountability versus individual action, internal versus external sources of control, and the nature and uses of information for school improvement—undergird this paper on school accountability. To illuminate their interrelationships, I turn to theories of organizational complexity and adaptation, focusing on the central role of information in both accountability and school improvement processes.

Complex Adaptive Systems and Change: A Framework for Understanding School Accountability

Complexity Theory and Organizations

Complex systems theory draws on parallel developments in the physical, biological, and social sciences that challenge traditional notions of linear causality and externally imposed or predetermined order.[8] Complexity theorists use the term *complex adaptive systems* (CAS) to describe "a world in which many players are all adapting to each other and where the emerging future is very hard to predict" (Axelrod & Cohen, 1999, p. xi). A few central concepts from complexity theory as applied to organizations are particularly instructive in understanding both the potential and the limitations of current approaches to school accountability.

- Interaction and Interdependence in Complex Adaptive Systems

A central characteristic of complex adaptive systems is the interdependence of individual and collective behavior. CAS are defined as populations of interacting "agents" (be they cells, animals, people, organizations, or other systems), each of which pursues a limited set of strategies in response to its surroundings and in pursuit of its goals. The systemic nature of a complex adaptive system derives from the patterns of interaction and to some extent from a commonality of strategies among like agents (Axelrod & Cohen, 1999; Marion, 1999).

In a school, for example, teachers interact with students, with other teachers, with administrators, with parents, and so forth. In each of these interactions, the individual actor follows his or her own goals and strategies, which differ from those of other actors to varying degrees. One teacher may seek to develop her students' mathematical reasoning while another is more focused on keeping students safe and off the streets. These teachers' differing goals may be manifested in somewhat different strategies in the classroom. Similarly, while one student may show up because he wants to hang out with friends and avoid the truancy officer, another has his eyes on an elite university. Again, students' particular activities will vary according to their goals. This variation among individual actors and their strategies is central to the notion of complexity and adaptation.

Equally central, however, are the constraints placed on that variation by the interaction of actors within the organization and between them and the larger environment. Thus, what a teacher does in her classroom depends greatly on what her students do, and vice versa; and what individuals in one classroom do is shaped in part by their interaction with individuals in other classrooms, in the hallways, and on the grounds of the school. The more frequent and powerful those interactions are, the more influence they are likely to have on the behavior of individual actors. Conversely, the more weakly connected—or loosely coupled (Weick, 1976)—the organization, the more independent and self-determined the actions of individuals and subunits within it. The nature and strength of the patterns of interaction are thus key to understanding the relationship between individual and organizational behavior and change.

- Stability and Change

In complex systems, the strategies that individual agents and organizations pursue reflect both stability and change over time—with both these characteristics being manifestations of learning. As new members come into the organization, they become socialized into (i.e., learn) its "code"—the languages, beliefs, and routines that make up the dominant behaviors of the organization and define it as an interactive system (March, 1991); hence, the stability of the system. But organizational codes and practices also change. Such change occurs through the selection, recombination, and adaptation of strategies, based on information derived from the interactions of system members with one another and with their environment. Thus, second-grade teacher Mrs. Cardenas moves Anton to a different seat because she notices that he is distracted by activity outside the window near his current seat. Meanwhile, Mr. Arthur and his third-grade colleagues introduce cross-class reading groups, based on feedback and modeling from a literacy coordinator working with the school. And Washington Elementary selects a new mathematics curriculum after receiving notice from the school board about a new testing policy. As Huber (1991) explains: "An entity learns if, through its processing of information, the range of its potential behaviors is changed. This definition holds whether the entity is a human or other animal, a group, an organization, an industry, or a society" (p. 89).

- Information and Learning

At the heart of the learning process in any complex system is the role of information and the movement of information among agents and subunits through patterns of interaction. Several characteristics of this information are important to note.

First, information and adaptation derive from variation. Without variation among the agents of a system or in the surrounding environment, there is little information on which to act. For example, students—individually and as a group—vary from teachers in knowledge and maturity, vary from each other, and vary from their prior behavior over time as they grow and learn. Much of teachers' activity is bound up with responding to these variations in and among students. At the system level, monitoring and responding to variation is also at the heart of current accountability efforts, as differences in reported test scores become the basis on which progress, success, and failure are judged.

Second, information in this model is not a static entity that is disseminated unchanged. Rather, information is dynamic, constantly changing as it is interpreted based on prior experience, recombined with other information and knowledge, and passed on through interaction with others. Interpretation is "the process though which information is given meaning" (Daft & Weick, 1984, p. 294). As such, it depends on "a person's prior cognitive map (or belief structure or mental representation or frame of reference)" (Huber, 1991, pp. 102–103), which is socially constructed and varies across organizational units having different responsibilities. One implication is that the process of spreading information will itself become a source of variation—as in the classic children's game "telephone" (Marion, 1999). In essence, the message changes each time it is passed on. Spillane (2000, 2002) has found, for example, that variation in the implementation of state standards derives in part from variation in the way that district leaders interpret and then convey those standards to school personnel, who then reinterpret them based on their own context and frames of reference.[9] A second implication is that the meaningfulness of the information generated by the system will vary in relation to the knowledge and skills of the users. To the extent that such knowledge and skills are weak or are unequally distributed, so too will be the meaning and usefulness of the accountability information.

Finally, not all information leads to learning and change. As implied above, for information to be useful, members of the system must first have access to it, through interaction with other members of the environment.[10] Moreover, if they are to incorporate the information into their cognitive maps or repertoire of strategies, they must attend to it and must have sufficient knowledge and stability to interpret it. Action does not necessarily follow, even once learning occurs, as this step often requires motivation and resources beyond those necessary for the learning itself. As I will discuss later, these elements—access, attention, knowledge, motivation, and resources—are all essential. A breakdown in any one of them may disrupt the connection between information and change.

- Learning and Improvement

Even when learning and change occur, they do not necessarily lead to improvement. This may seem counterintuitive, given popular notions about learning and "learning organizations" (Senge, 1993), but this conclusion flows from the conception of learning and of complex systems just described. Complexity theorists Robert Axelrod and Michael Cohen (1999) use the term *adaptation* to indicate when learning and change lead to "improvement along some measure of success" (p. 7). This concept of adaptation is highly consistent with the goals of school accountability systems, which seek improvement in terms of specific assessments of student performance. In complex systems, however, the relationship between learning (an "increase in the range of potential behaviors)" (Huber, 1991, p. 89) and adaptation is obscured. For one thing, individual agents vary in their goals and thus in measures of success; adaptation for one might not be adaptation for others (Axelrod & Cohen, 1999).

In addition, interaction and interpretation of information make learning unreliable. Agents and organizations may misinterpret feedback from their environment, causing "superstitious learning" (Levitt & March, 1988).[11] If individuals and organizations act on that superstitious learning—for example, using it to select a strategy—the results may be maladaptive rather than adaptive; that is, they may lead to a decline rather than an improvement in relevant measures of success. Finally, learning at one point in an individual's or system's experience may inhibit learning and change at another point. As individuals and organizations gain competence in certain activities through learning, they may actually decrease their range of potential strategies (Levinthal, 1991). By repeatedly selecting strategies that have led to success in the past and interacting with other entities based on those strategies, an organization reduces variation, thus potentially reducing future learning and adaptation. The end result is that individuals and mature organizations over time may get caught in "competency traps," becoming prisoners of their own past success (Levitt & March, 1988).[12] One might argue that the general inertia of the educational system is a reflection of such competency traps.

Barriers to Improvement in Schools

This discussion of complex adaptive systems has implications for how we think about the potential relationship between accountability policies and school improvement and, more specifically, about the organizational barriers that accountability policies must overcome in order to foster successful adaptation. These barriers center on the generation, interpretation, and use of information for school and system improvement.

- Too Much or Too Little Information

  Teachers and schools are constantly bombarded by information and by demands to do something about that information—requests from parents, notices from the central office or federal and state departments, publishing companies, external advocates and programs, community groups, counselors, etc. In many schools, teachers' and students' work is subject to continual interruption as others try to thrust new information upon them. What's worse, much of the information is irrelevant to the improvement of instruction and learning. It merely distracts attention and resources from what is supposed to be the main work of school personnel and students. Sifting through the morass to find that which is likely to lead to improvement requires time, resources, and knowledge that school personnel may not possess. Unable to make productive choices, some teachers and schools move chaotically from one demand or source of information to another, with insufficient focus and time to learn. The classic "Christmas tree school" is an example of this pattern.[13]

  Alternatively, teachers and schools may metaphorically and literally close the door on new information, shutting out the noise. This is a coping strategy that potentially allows them to focus, but it also leads to isolation. Such isolation prevents their having sufficient opportunity to encounter variation and the information it engenders, and thus little opportunity for learning. Norms of private practice in education and loose coupling (Weick, 1976) throughout the system reinforce this isolation.[14] On the one hand, loose coupling prevents failure in one unit (school or classroom) from cascading throughout the system (Marion, 1999; Weick, 1976), but at the same time, it may inhibit learning that can lead to improvement.

  Consider a veteran teacher typical of those in many U.S. urban schools. Extended survival in the system implies that he or she has learned and selected strategies that have been successful by at least some measure of success—perhaps student learning, perhaps social competence, perhaps simply control. As described earlier, one such strategy has been to shut out the cacophony of information and distracting interactions by literally closing the classroom door on them. Other teachers in the school, many of them also veterans in the system, have adopted a similar approach, so that the school has become a collection of virtually private domains demarcated by the walls surrounding each classroom. Moreover, protecting the sanctity of those domains has become an integral part of the school code. New teachers quickly learn this code if they intend to continue in the organization; they develop their own strategies for what they do in the classroom, leaving their colleagues to do the same. The structure of the school day and the school building reinforce this pattern. The teachers survive, and over time survival increasingly becomes the measure of success, not only for individuals but for the school as a whole. That this means of survival has been enhanced through isolation has implications for future change. In a sense, one could say the "egg-crate" structure of U.S. schooling, with its separate and isolated classroom structures designed to buffer each component from change, is a kind of competency trap. That is, separating teachers and students in independent and isolated classrooms is a strategy that has worked in the past for survival, control, and sorting, but that may not work well if the measure of success changes (e.g., to high levels of student learning for all students). The "trap" of the egg crate is that such isolation prevents teachers from taking advantage of the variation in their individual classroom strategies in order to learn from one another and select more successful ways of doing things.

On the one hand, external sources thrust an overload of information on schools and school personnel, while on the other hand, isolation creates a lack of information sharing among teachers. What seems to be needed is some middle ground—as in the story of Goldilocks and the just-right porridge. For Goldilocks, only the porridge of just the right temperature could ensure taste, consumption, and eventual satisfaction. Likewise, teachers, given the right amount of information, will be able to attend to it, interpret it, and use it for learning and adaptation. The question is, how will the accountability system ensure that school personnel receive an adequate amount of information, can interpret the information, and have the ability to focus on what is most appropriate for improving teaching and learning?

- Complexity and the Problem of Attribution in Schools

The amount of information encountered is only one part of the problem. Also of concern are the kinds of information available, how that information is interpreted, and whether the interpretations will lead to learning and to selecting strategies that lead to adaptation.

Theorists (e.g., Levitt & March, 1988) tell us that organizations are oriented toward targets and adapt based on feedback (information) about those targets. Discrepancies between observed outcomes and aspirations for those outcomes can provide motivation for change (Simon, 1986). Such is certainly the assumption of outcomes-based accountability. First of all, agents within schools vary in their definition of a target (sometimes it is just getting through the day!), and schools also have multiple and changing targets. Moving a school community from an emphasis on discipline and order to a focus on student learning, for example, is difficult and represents this sort of change. Second, even taking a single generally agreed-upon goal, such as independent reading by the third grade, does not remove the ambiguity. Other targets remain, agents have differing views about what independent reading entails, and measurement is difficult.

But perhaps most important, even in an ideal situation where the goals and measures are clear, the complexity of interaction patterns inside and outside the organization and of the learning process itself makes attribution of cause and effect difficult and unreliable. Consider the following hypothetical example: Only 15 percent of third graders in Bryant Elementary are reading independently by time of the spring assessment. Do we conclude that the third-grade teachers are not teaching appropriately? And if so, in what particular ways is the instruction inadequate? Are the textbooks too difficult? Too easy? Too boring? Perhaps the low performance is due to constant interruptions during reading time or lack of order in the school. Maybe the problem is that the students do not see any reason for reading, or perhaps they speak a language other than English and do not have the requisite English vocabulary. Perhaps the real problem lies in first- or second-grade instruction, in the fear induced by violence in the neighborhood, or in the low expectations of the adults. Perhaps it is all or some combination of the above. Alternatively, if the majority of students at Bryant are doing well, we are not necessarily any closer to understanding the cause of their performance. Is it class background? School selection processes? Motivated teachers? Effective instruction? All of the above? Indeed, it is often more difficult to pinpoint the cause of success than it is of failure.

The difficulty of attribution, and thus of selection and prediction, is endemic to complex systems. Complexity theorists use terms like *circular causality* and *multiple interactions* to discuss the problem of attribution where individual actors are responding to (and providing) feedback from (and to) multiple sources (Marion, 1999; Weick, 1976). Mutual adaptation inevitably leads to mistakes in attribution.[15]

The tendency toward faulty attribution in education is commonplace. It is exacerbated by the lack of accurate, valid, and appropriately detailed information on outcomes. For example, a test given in the spring with the results reported to teachers (about their now former students) in the fall does not solve the attribution problem for teachers. That problem is also exacerbated when those involved in interpreting the results know little about the type and distribution of strategies and resources used to produce those results, or when they lack the opportunity and knowledge to reflect on and explore alternative interpretations of the information they have. As we will see, school accountability systems generally seek to address the first of these conditions—the lack of information on outcomes—but often ignore the other information needed for appropriate attribution.

- Faulty Incentive and Resource Allocation Structures

Adaptation in schools is also inhibited by incentive and resource structures that undermine motivation and the opportunity for organizational learning or that preclude the adoption of more productive strategies. These inhibitors include such things as incentives that pull attention and effort to goals other than student learning,[16] insufficient time or other resources for collaboration and sharing information about instruction, and human resource systems that reward mediocrity and concentrate the most knowledgeable teachers where they are least needed. One might think about such allocation as a "strategy" of the larger system in which the unit or individual is embedded. Thus, we would ask whether the school has an effective strategy for allocating resources to foster student learning. Does the district? As with other aspects of the system, resource allocation is dependent on accurate and reliable information. Again, the goal of the accountability system should be to supply that information.

School Accountability Framework

This discussion suggests a framework for analyzing the potential impact of accountability-based interventions on school improvement. School accountability mechanisms will be successful in improving the functioning of school organizations to the extent that those interventions are able to:

- *Generate and focus attention on information relevant to teaching and learning and to changes in that information as it is continually fed back into and through the system.* Note that in order to alter what happens in classrooms, this focus must occur not only at the school level, but at the level of individual teachers as well. Interaction patterns are likely to be very important in the generation and spread of such information.
- *Motivate educators and others to attend to relevant information and to expend the effort necessary to augment or change strategies in response to this information.* Central here is the problematic relationship of collective accountability and individual action. Motivation must ultimately occur at the individual level, but it is likely to be dependent in part on the normative structures of the school as well as on individual characteristics of educators and students.
- *Develop the knowledge and skills to promote valid interpretation of information and appropriate attribution of causality at both the individual and system levels.* As discussed above, learning takes place through the interpretation of information, whether that information is data from a student assessment, research on reading instruction, or observation of a colleague's lesson. Interpretation is dependent on prior learning and is constrained and informed by such. Data often remain unused because educators lack the knowledge base for interpretation and incorporation of the new information. If accountability systems are to be successful, they will need not only to build knowledge and skills for interpretation in the short run, but also to establish mechanisms for continued learning through use of information generated by the system.
- *Allocate resources where they are most needed.* Information at all levels can promote the allocation of resources—human and material—to where they are most needed. A classroom teacher might reallocate resources by spending more of her time and attention on a student she sees is having

trouble understanding a new concept. Similarly, district administrators might move additional resources to a low-performing school or one taking on a new challenge. To what extent does the accountability system encourage allocation (or reallocation) of resources to foster student learning based on information generated?

Bureaucratic Accountability and School Improvement

How do current school accountability policies fare with respect to the framework outlined above? That is, to what extent do accountability policies generate and focus attention on relevant information, motivate the use of that information for individual and collective change, contribute to the knowledge base needed for appropriate interpretation of that information, and use information to provide adequate resources where needed? To answer this question requires that we first define what is meant by "current school accountability policies." Here I turn to analyses of the new accountability in education (Elmore et al., 1996), as well as the more expansive typologies of educational accountability (Adams & Kirst, 1999; Darling-Hammond & Ascher, 1991; O'Reilly, 1996).

Accountability systems, according to these and other observers, differ in large part by the way they respond to four central questions: *Who* is accountable? *To whom* are they accountable? *For what* are they accountable? And *with what consequences*? Fuhrman notes that one of the distinguishing characteristics of the new accountability in standards-based reform is that the "who" in this formulation is generally the school unit and, as previously indicated, this article focuses exclusively on school-level accountability.[17] In addition, while school accountability policies differ in their particulars from jurisdiction to jurisdiction, the "to whom" designation almost universally refers to the district and/or state agencies.[18] That is, schools as collective entities are accountable to the higher levels of the educational system. In this respect, such policies represent a form of administrative (O'Day & Smith, 1993) or bureaucratic accountability (Adams & Kirst, 1999; Darling-Hammond & Ascher, 1991). However, they differ from traditional forms of bureaucratic accountability in one very important respect: they hold schools and school personnel accountable not for delivering designated educational inputs and processes but for producing specific levels or improvements in student learning outcomes. Thus, they are examples of what might best be termed "outcome-based bureaucratic accountability."[19] In this section, I will use Chicago as an exemplar of this form of school accountability.[20]

Addressing the Framework: Outcomes-Based Accountability, Chicago Style

The Chicago Public Schools (CPS) provide a particularly useful model to illustrate this framework, since the Illinois legislature amended the Chicago School Reform Act in 1995 to include specific provisions for school accountability. Following those provisions, the Chicago School Board designated school-level targets for student performance and instituted sanctions (probation and reconstitution) for schools falling below those targets. The district has now accumulated six years of experience with school accountability. Several colleagues and I have had the opportunity to follow the design, practice, and results of this system over the past several years. Our investigation has included in-depth interviews with business, political, education, and community stakeholders; analyses of school improvement plans and the planning process; interviews and shadowing of support providers; school case studies; and multilevel analyses of survey and achievement data on all CPS elementary schools since 1994 (two years prior to the implementation of sanctions). Our data are thus both rich and varied. They provide an inroad into understanding the links between outcomes-based school accountability and school improvement.

At first glance, CPS and similar school accountability systems seem to address well the criteria laid out in the framework above. Below I discuss how the four components of the school accountability framework are reflected in the CPS accountability system.

Attention: On the most basic level, these accountability systems call attention to information on student outcomes by designating a particular indicator (or indicators) of those outcomes and by defining specific performance targets. In Chicago's case, the focus is sharpened by the district's use of a single indicator—the Iowa Test of Basic Skills (ITBS)[21]—in only two subject areas, reading and mathematics. Moreover, the targeted performance benchmark is simple, measurable, and clear: schools must have at least 20 percent of their students in grades 3–8 or 9–11 reading at or above national grade-level norms in the spring administration of the ITBS, or be declared "on probation." Attention to the outcomes is further enhanced through school planning and reporting mechanisms that single out reading and math scores and require all schools to provide information on how they will increase student performance in these areas. Such mechanisms establish priorities in the organization and thus should help school personnel sift through the usual information overload to focus on that most directly related to student achievement and improvement strategies.

Motivation: Chicago's policy, like outcomes-based policies in other jurisdictions, provides motivation for this sifting process and related improvement efforts by attaching consequences to the outcome targets. For all schools, these consequences come in the form of public and administrative scrutiny of reported school outcome data. For schools falling below the target, sanctions include the stigma of the "probation" label, decreased autonomy as local school councils lose authority to select their principals, additional requirements for planning, monitoring, and assistance, and potentially even reconstitution or reengineering, both of which entail involuntary changes in personnel.[22] Policy designers believe that even the threat of such sanctions will increase educator motivation and efforts to improve student learning.

Knowledge Development: Attending to outcome information is of little value if school personnel do not know how to interpret it, and motivation to act will produce nothing if educators do not know what actions they should take. Recognizing the need for site-based knowledge and skill development, CPS administrators instituted an elaborate program of assistance for schools, including mentoring for principals, help with business and school improvement plans, and professional and organizational development provided by external partners. A particularly interesting feature of the CPS design of external assistance is the district's response to the tension between internal and external sources of control discussed earlier. In an effort to balance these sources of control and enhance normative buy-in among school personnel, CPS allows probation schools to select their own partners from an approved list. The policy designers hoped that this selection process would both enhance motivation and ensure that support providers pay attention to the particular conditions in each school.

Resource Allocation: Finally, funding for this assistance demonstrates a major way in which the district has used information generated by the accountability system to allocate resources. Low test scores trigger the targeting of discretionary monies—initially from the district surplus and then from federal programs, including the Comprehensive School Reform Demonstration (CSRD) program and class-size reduction—to probation schools.[23] The district covers 100 percent of the cost of the first year of assistance, 50 percent of the second year, and the school bears the full cost in subsequent years. In the first two years of the probation policy, CPS spent $29 million for external support alone.[24]

Other jurisdictions, both states and other districts, have set in place similar systems—in part in response to the accountability requirements incorporated into Title I of the Elementary and Secondary Education Act (ESEA) in 1994.[25] Of course, jurisdictions vary considerably in the specifics of their policies. One important dimension of this variation is in the definition of targets. Some jurisdictions have set improvement targets for all schools and rewards for those meeting or exceeding targets. The intent is to focus and motivate improvement in both higher performing schools and lower performing ones.[26] Jurisdictions also vary in the forms of assistance provided and in the consequences attached to either high or low performance relative to the targets. Yet, despite these variations, the general school accountability model is the same in that it defines certain expected levels of performance, designates schools as high or low performing based on student assessments, requires planning to focus attention and coordinate action in the school, provides assistance in some form, and administers sanctions for continued failure to improve.

• Impact of Outcomes-Based Accountability

Although experience with and research on school accountability are still in the early stages, some evidence of its impact is beginning to accumulate. Our data from Chicago (Finnigan & Gross, 2001) and CPRE research in Kentucky and Charlotte-Mecklenburg, North Carolina (Kelley, Odden, Milanowski, & Heneman, 2000), indicate that teachers are working harder in response to the accountability measures and are more focused on externally set student-learning goals. In addition, many systems (e.g., Boston, San Diego, Tennessee, and California) are using school-level data on student outcomes to allocate additional discretionary resources where they appear to be most needed. Some jurisdictions, such as New York City and Baltimore, have even put in place special monetary incentives to attract and retain highly skilled teachers and principals for the lowest performing schools (Westat, 2001).

There is also evidence of an impact on achievement, as measured by standardized tests. In each of the first four years after instituting its school accountability policy, the Chicago schools posted increased scores in both reading and mathematics, though reading scores have begun to level off since 2000 (Chicago Public Schools, 2002). Similarly, Kentucky, California, Texas, Tennessee, and other jurisdictions have claimed that their accountability policies have resulted in higher student achievement. However, some observers question whether increases in test scores really indicate higher levels of student learning or whether later scores have been artificially inflated by concentrated "teaching to the test" and increased familiarity with test questions and format.[27] In Texas and Tennessee, rising scores on the National Assessment of Educational Progress (NAEP) seem to validate similar increases on the state assessments, but in these and in all other cases it is difficult to attribute such increases to school accountability mechanisms.

Schools respond unevenly to outcomes-based accountability policies and this unevenness may be directly tied to internal conditions in schools that make them more or less able to use the information generated by the accountability systems. The CPRE research team led by Richard Elmore and Leslie Siskin, for example, has found that schools that are better positioned in terms of their socioeconomic composition (i.e., higher SES students) and their prior academic performance respond more readily and coherently to the demands of external performance-based accountability systems than those schools less well situated (DeBray, Parson, & Woodworth, 2001; Elmore, 2001). This research suggests that lower performing schools actually lose ground relative to the well-positioned schools once an external accountability system is instituted.

Our research on the lowest performing schools in Chicago extends the CPRE analysis, identifying variations in responses among schools that might all be considered less well positioned—that is, among those at similarly low socioeconomic and achievement levels.[28] The first indication of this variation is a rapid bifurcation in the achievement trends for all elementary schools placed on probation in 1996, despite comparable initial achievement. More specifically, one group of schools—those that came off the probation list by spring of 1998—posts a significantly sharper increase in scores than those schools that remained on probation after 1998. Multilevel analysis of survey data for this rapidly improving group suggests that they differed significantly from other probation schools along several dimensions of initial school capacity: peer collaboration, teacher-teacher trust, and collective responsibility for student learning (Gwynne & Easton, 2001). Referring to the earlier discussion of organizational complexity, we might surmise that the first two of these dimensions—peer collaboration and teacher-to-teacher trust—reflect stronger patterns of interaction among the organizational agents (teachers in this case). The third dimension—collective responsibility for student learning—suggests that attention and effort in these schools were already directed to a higher degree to student learning and were bolstered by the normative structure of the school—what Elmore and his colleagues call "internal accountability" (DeBray et al., 2001; Elmore, 2001).

That schools with such patterns of interaction and attention would be more successful at adaptation makes sense in light of the earlier discussion of complexity, information, and learning, as these patterns would facilitate the dissemination, selection, and interpretation of information relevant to student learning. Meanwhile, the failure of other schools to show similar improvement and their propensity to stay on probation for as long as five years or more suggests something about the limitations of bureaucratic accountability for catalyzing school improvement in low-capacity schools—that is, in schools lacking the internal accountability structures or knowledge base to generate or use information well. Indeed, our qualitative data on the policy, assistance, and individual school response point to significant limitations of bureaucratic outcomes-based accountability for fostering school improvement.

Limitations of Bureaucratic, Outcomes-Based School Accountability

The earlier discussion of complex adaptive systems suggests that adaptation (improvement) is based on the feedback (information) agents receive from one another and from the environment, on the interpretations and dispersal of this information through patterns of interaction in the organization, and then on the invention, selection, and recombination of strategies to produce improvement along some measure of performance. Our data from Chicago indicate several ways in which bureaucratic outcomes-based accountability may inhibit—or at least fail to promote—widespread organizational adaptation.

- Inadequate Information

   A central limitation of school accountability in Chicago and elsewhere is that the nature and quality of the information produced and dispensed by the system are simply inadequate for effective organizational adaptation and learning. Three aspects of this inadequacy stand out.

   The first limitation of the information dispensed in an outcomes-based school accountability system concerns the validity of the outcome measure on which improvement is to be based. Much of the criticism of Chicago's model of school accountability has centered on the use of a norm-referenced basic skills test that is not fully aligned with either the district or the state standards, that emphasizes fragmented and discrete skill acquisition, and that lacks validation for the types of decisions (e.g., probation and grade retention) made on the basis of its results. Validity with respect to measurement of the goals (e.g., standards) is a critical aspect of an assessment's quality: if the assessment does not measure what it purports to measure, it could actually draw attention away from the goals of the system rather than toward them. This potential problem is compounded in a situation like that in Chicago, where the use of a single measure and the attachment of consequences to that measure (see below) intensifies attention to the measure rather than to the larger goal of increased student learning. In this regard, it is important to note that the Iowa Test of Basic Skills has not been validated for the purpose of either school or student accountability.

   A second limitation of Chicago's and most other school accountability systems concerns the periodicity and specificity (grain size) of the information provided by the outcome measure.[29] On the one hand, a test given once a year that reports a general indication of the content and skills that students have and have not mastered can be extremely valuable for identifying schools and subject areas that may need additional attention, resources, or, possibly, changes in strategies. An important contribution of school accountability systems in places like Chicago and Maryland, for example, is that they have directed the spotlight at failing parts of the system that can then be given additional assistance.[30] However, while such information is useful at these higher levels of aggregation, its potential for directly improving strategies in the classroom is limited. Such assessments are usually administered in the spring to measure student learning during the academic year, but the results are not available in time for the relevant teacher to alter instruction in response to the test. Even if the scores were available earlier in the year, the infrequency and lack of specificity of results is still a problem.

In short, the measure of outcomes through such a test is simply too distant from the complexities of instructional inputs for the teacher to make reasonable attributions of causality. Superstitious learning is common under such circumstances (Levitt & March, 1988). For this reason, some schools supplement the annual testing with more regular and focused assessments aligned with the ITBS. These periodic tests can give teachers more information on outcomes, though they may also underscore concerns about teaching to the test.

A third limitation of the quality of the information is an extension of the second, and concerns the appropriate balance of information about outcomes and information about processes. The implication is that the actor—whether that actor is an individual or an organization—must have valid and reliable information on both outcomes and processes. Yet, school accountability systems focus almost exclusively on outcomes, producing little in the way of reliable information on instruction or organizational practices. Some authors have argued that the production of such process-based information at aggregated levels would introduce further measurement problems and unduly constrain practice.[31] That the external accountability system does not generate information on practice might not be a problem if such information were available at the school level. Substantial research suggests that when teachers share information about instruction as well as student learning, they are better able to adapt their practice to the needs and progress of their students.[32] However, the egg-crate structure of U.S. schools impedes such adaptation; information on instructional strategies and processes is held privately by teachers and only rarely shared across the school as the basis for future learning (Lortie, 1975; McLaughlin & Talbert, 2001). Our research in Chicago suggests that bureaucratic school accountability policies are insufficient to establish the patterns of interaction that might foster more effective information sharing in low-capacity schools.

- Patterns of Interaction

Indeed, if CPS is any indication, bureaucratic school accountability mechanisms serve to maintain interaction patterns that foster compliance and hierarchy over system learning. Our data reveal a fairly unidirectional (top-down) flow of information throughout the system. For example, rather than being opportunities for collective sharing of information and knowledge, meetings between assistance providers and central office staff and between principals and district liaison personnel were reportedly occasions in which schools and those working with them were simply the recipients of information and mandates rather than sources of valuable information in their own right. When information did flow the other way (from schools and those working with them up into the system), it focused on whether people were carrying out prescribed tasks—that is, whether external partners were providing agreed-upon services, whether schools were implementing specifics of school plans, and whether teachers were understanding and using the tools and techniques disseminated by the external partners (Finnigan, O'Day, & Wakelyn, 2001).

Even those instances in which one might expect more collective problem-solving—such as in the school improvement planning process—more often than not became symbolic exercises in responding to formulaic requirements of the district office rather than thoughtful and inclusive learning experiences for the staff.[33] The planning template was handed down from the Office of Accountability and schools complied, with emphasis on compliance over self-reflection being noticeably stronger in the least improving, lowest capacity schools.[34] What was perhaps most distressing was that this transmission model of information flow also characterized the professional development provided by the external partners, the bulk of which consisted of traditional short workshops rather than intensive inquiry-based explorations of either content or instructional practice (Finnigan et al., 2001).

The end result is that much of the response we saw in schools involved their reacting to directions imposed from above and outside the school rather than reflecting on internal practices. This response is perhaps unsurprising. Hierarchical control and information dissemination are characteristic of large bureaucracies like CPS, and well-established, internalized organizational codes are difficult to change (March, 1991). Moreover, the "get tough" theory of action and the urban politics underlying the school probation policy could be expected to exacerbate these tendencies. By defining the problem as low expectations and a lack of effort on the part of school staff, the forces that come from higher in the system and outside the schools seek to push those inside to work harder. The accompanying incentives only reinforce control and enforcement over system learning.

- Maladaptive Incentive Structures

While much of the benefit of current school accountability schemes is supposed to be that they provide incentives to motivate improvement, we found that the incentive structures in Chicago actually exacerbated the problem of motivation in some low-performing, low-capacity schools.

The emphasis on negative incentives (stigma of probation, threat of reconstitution) tied to a single measure (ITBS) appears to have resulted in two tendencies that work against long-term improvement. First, attention in these schools became focused not so much on student learning per se, but on getting off or staying off probation. This goal essentially places adult desires (to remove the professional stigma and avoid administrative scrutiny) over the needs of students (Wei & Evans, 2001). Second, to achieve this goal, probation schools exhibited an emphasis on strategies to produce immediate increases in test scores, often to the neglect of longer-term success. The combination of these tendencies produced a number of dysfunctional practices.

Most common was the emphasis on test preparation in the form of intensive drill and practice to raise student scores. Some schools even redesigned their curriculum not only to reflect the general skills on the ITBS but to align the proportion of time allotted in the curriculum to a given discrete skill with the proportion of test items measuring that skill. In such cases, the test specifications became the curriculum specifications as well. Another common practice was to triage assistance (mostly test preparation) to students scoring near grade-level cutoffs in the hope that, by raising these students' scores slightly, the school could escape probation. These and similar practices suggest the allocation of resources to achieve adult ends (e.g., getting off probation), rather than to meet the greatest student needs.

Such patterns, which have been noted in prior research on high-stakes testing in education, are not uncommon in organizations in crisis.[35] A focused search for short-term strategies to satisfy a specific target is typical when an organization's performance falls below its aspirations or goals (March, 1994; Simon, 1986). When low performance is combined with negative incentives, including a threat to the organization's position or survival (as is the case of school probation), the potential for maladaptive response increases.

A comprehensive review of research on organizational response to threat (Staw, Sanderlands, & Dutton, 1981) uncovered two dominant and often maladaptive patterns, both of which are relevant to the earlier discussion of organizational learning. First, rather than expanding their use of information to find solutions to the problem, threatened organizations and individuals actually restrict their information processing, relying instead on previously held internal hypotheses and expectations. Exacerbated by stress, this reliance produces a rigidity of action rather than an expansion of strategies and adaptation. A second pattern associated with the presence of a threat is centralization of authority, which in the case of schools serves to further enhance the bureaucratic, control-oriented patterns of interaction mentioned earlier (Staw et al., 1981). Both patterns were observed in low-performing schools in Chicago. We can expect individual and system learning to be constrained under these conditions, as well as innovation and examination of existing practice and assumptions.[36]

A second limitation of the incentive structures is the unbalanced reliance on collective incentives. This problem was raised at the beginning of this article regarding the relationship between individual action and collective accountability. With a focus on schoolwide consequences, the policy offers few incentives for individuals to improve their practice. Individual teacher evaluation is not well aligned with either outcome measures or standards of practice likely to produce those outcomes. In many schools there is little accountability for individual teachers at all, and in others, teachers receive little recognition for improving their practice. One revealing example occurred at one of our case study schools in which a teacher who was working hard to improve practice was repeatedly told by her principal that she could not get an "excellent" rating because "if we had excellent teachers, this school would not be on probation." In other words, until the school as a whole was removed from probation, this teacher could not expect any reward for her individual efforts, no matter what the actual quality of her work. The effect of this proclamation was a sharp decrease in this teacher's motivation and commitment to the school. While we could attribute this result to the actions of a single principal, what becomes clear is that the policy relies on the ability of the principal (or others in the school community) to motivate the individuals on the school's staff. Where the principal is unable to provide such motivation (often the case in low-performing schools), the effect of the policy on individual teachers is likely to be weak, or even negative. Alternatively, where the principal is an effective motivator or where the connections among individuals are mutually reinforcing, the lack of individual incentives may be mitigated by the strong identification of individuals with the group. This may help to explain why probation schools with higher levels of teacher-to-teacher trust, peer collaboration, and collective responsibility improved more rapidly than others in our Chicago study (Gwynne & Easton, 2001). Perhaps other incentives are at work in these schools to motivate individual behavior.[37]

- Weak Resource Allocation and Knowledge Development Strategies

As stated earlier, one of the most promising aspects of outcomes-based school accountability is the use of information to direct attention and resources where they are most needed. In Chicago, this reallocation mainly took the form of external assistance to low-performing schools. Our data indicate, however, how the potential effect of this substantial reallocation of resources was mitigated by the low intensity and lack of focus of most of the support actually provided to schools. For example, external partners[38] on average spent only one or two person-days per week in the schools and, with few exceptions, their work provided neither a consistent and coherent focus on literacy instruction (the target of the policy) nor a clear strategy for organizational change (Finnigan et al., 2001). The limitations of the assistance may be attributed in part to problems of implementation, such as the weak quality control in the selection of the external partner candidates. In addition, however, the weak specification of the policy with regard to the content or goals of the assistance gave little guidance to either the schools or the support providers themselves about where to concentrate their energies. Such weak specification is common in school accountability policies in other jurisdictions as well. It derives on the one hand from a desire to respond to internal school context and on the other from the policy's emphasis on student outcomes to the neglect of information—or a theory of action—about instruction. The resulting diffuseness of the assistance, however, does little to highlight or solve problems of attribution discussed earlier. Moreover, the policy neglect of other inputs—such as reallocation of human or other resources—also weakens the potential impact.

Summary

What does this discussion of the CPS experience add up to in light of the framework and central problems of school accountability outlined earlier? On the one hand, school accountability policies, like those in Chicago have clearly helped focus attention throughout the system on student outcomes and have provided data that can be used for targeting resources and assistance where they are most needed—particularly in low-performing schools. On the other hand, this outcomes-based school accountability approach suffers from a number of inherent weaknesses that make it, as it is currently construed, unlikely to effect the deep changes necessary for long-term improvement, particularly in low-performing, low-capacity schools. Four weaknesses stand out:

1. The problems of validity, periodicity, and specificity in the outcome measures, coupled with inattention to information on instructional practice, make attribution and thus learning at the school or individual teacher level difficult.

2. Most school accountability systems still operate from a bureaucratic control model and thus fail to create the interaction patterns and normative structures within schools that encourage sustained learning and adaptation. Most low-performing schools lack such patterns and structures.

3. Reliance on negative incentives undermines innovation and risk-taking in threatened schools and diverts attention to organizational survival rather than student learning. Moreover, most current incentive structures fail to foster individual motivation or to reward learning and changes in practice that might lead to sustained improvement.

4. Finally, the reallocation of assistance and resources for increasing the capacity of low-performing schools is generally inadequate and weakly specified. Unfocused assistance based on transmission models of learning does little to build the knowledge base needed for valid interpretation of information produced by the system.

While some of these shortcomings are exacerbated by poor implementation, they derive from fundamental assumptions inherent in the design of current school accountability systems. Current approaches have not solved any of the three problems outlined at the beginning of this article: the relationship between collective accountability and individual action; the tension between external and internal sources of control; and the production, spread, and use of information that can help solve problems of attribution caused by the complexity of school organizations. Thus, reliance on bureaucratic forms of accountability, even with better implementation, is unlikely to lead to the kind of improvement desired.

Is there an alternative?

Professional Accountability: Alternative or Addition?

Perhaps the most commonly posed alternative to bureaucratic or administrative accountability in education is that of professional accountability (Adams & Kirst, 1999; Darling-Hammond & Ascher, 1991; O'Reilly, 1996). Professional accountability is rooted in the assumption that teaching is too complex an activity to be governed by bureaucratically defined rules and routines. Rather, like other professions, effective teaching rests on professionals acquiring specialized knowledge and skills and being able to apply such knowledge and skills to the specific contexts in which they work. In mature professions, the requisite knowledge is articulated in professionally determined standards of practice, and professional accountability involves members of those professions assuming responsibility for the definition and enforcement of those standards.

In education, the focus of professional accountability might be described as three-fold. First, it is centered on the process of instruction—that is, on the work of teachers as they interact with students around instructional content (Cohen & Ball, 1999; McLaughlin & Talbert, 2001). Professional accountability thus concerns the performance of adults in the system at least as much as the performance of students.[39] Second, much of the focus of professional accountability concerns ensuring that educators acquire and apply the knowledge and skills needed for effective practice. Knowledge development is front and center. Third, professional accountability involves the norms of professional interchange. These norms include placing the needs of the client (students) at the center of professional work, collaborating with other professionals to address those needs and ensure the maintenance of standards of practice, and committing to the improvement of practice as part and parcel of professional responsibility.

At the system level, mechanisms of professional accountability center on teacher preparation, teacher licensure, and peer review. At the school level, professional accountability rests both on individual educators assuming responsibility for following standards of practice and on their professional interaction with colleagues and clients. Mentoring, collaboration, and collective problem-solving in response to student needs and some form of peer review to ensure quality of practice are all aspects of school-site professional accountability. Advocates for professionally based forms of accountability argue that this approach holds the most promise for the improvement of teaching and, by extension, for the improvement of student learning.

The Promise and Limitations of Professional Accountability

The earlier discussion of complexity and organizational adaptation lends some theoretical support for the claims of advocates of professionalism. In particular, professional accountability at the school site would seem to address problems of attribution and motivation more productively than what we have seen from bureaucratically based models.

With respect to the use of information for effective attribution, three aspects of professional accountability seem most pertinent. First, professionalism draws attention both to instructional practice (agents' strategies) and to teachers' collective responsibility for student learning (outcomes). Second, norms of collaboration around instruction enhance patterns of interaction at the school site that allow for the generation and spread of information about both practice and outcomes and the dissemination of effective strategies based on analysis of that information (i.e., data-driven change). This information is naturally more fine-grained and immediate than that accumulated at higher levels of aggregation, and thus the links between specific strategies and their effects are more easily discerned. This is in part because the articulation of both outcome targets and of standards of practice allows for the testing of hypotheses about those links, particularly where experience or results run contrary to expectations (Axelrod & Cohen, 2000; Sitkin, 1992). Finally, more successful attribution is also likely because of the emphasis on professional knowledge and skills, which lay the groundwork for meaningful interpretations of the information available and more meaningful sharing of information with others. Standards of practice, constructed generally across the profession and more particularly within the professional community of the school, provide the cognitive maps for this process of meaning creation (Huber, 1991).

In addition to addressing problems of attribution, professional accountability expands the incentives for improvement, with particular emphasis on the intrinsic motivators that bring teachers into teaching in the first place, a commitment to students (clients) and an identity as an educator (O'Day, 1996). Scott (1998) has delineated three types of incentives in organizations: material incentives such as monetary rewards and job promotion or loss; community/solidarity incentives based on an identity as a member of a community or profession and a desire to maintain or gain position in that community; and purposive incentives, for example, satisfaction from achieving a valued goal such as a learning objective for students. Our work in schools on probation in Chicago suggests that school accountability policies often fail to tap into solidarity and intrinsic purposive incentives, focusing instead on the threat of material sanctions such as reassignment or job loss or on rewards (Finnigan & Gross, 2001). In contrast, research on professional communities of practice note the motivational aspects of membership in those communities and of normative structures that focus on student learning (goal attainment) and professional identity (Darling-Hammond, 1996; McLaughlin & Talbert, 2001).

Beyond the theoretical appeal of professional accountability, a growing body of empirical evidence points to aspects of professionalism as important components of school improvement. Lee and Smith (1996), for example, find a significant positive relationship between student achievement gains and teachers' collective responsibility for students' academic success in high school.[40] Meanwhile, various researchers have pointed to the positive impact on instruction and student achievement of teacher interaction and collaboration in school-based professional communities (Little, 1990; McLaughlin & Talbert, 1993, 2001; Newmann & Wehlage, 1995). Community School District 2 in New York City provides proof of the deep impact professional culture and professional development can have as a strategy for improvement and system management (Elmore, 1997). Finally, as mentioned previously, there is some recent evidence that professionally based aspects of internal school accountability and capacity are essential for a school's ability to respond effectively to outcomes-based accountability (DeBray et al., 2001; Elmore, 2001) and can help explain the differential gains among schools that are targets of accountability policies (Gwynne & Easton, 2001).

Limitations of Professional Accountability

Despite its promise, however, reliance on professional accountability alone cannot ensure that all students' needs are addressed. The most obvious limitation of such a strategy is the overall weakness of professionalism and professional accountability throughout U.S. education. Most U.S. schools are atomized structures in which responsibility rests with the individual educator rather than with the collective body or the profession as a whole (Abelmann & Elmore, 1999; Lortie, 1975). Mentoring and collaboration are simply too rare to ensure the information sharing necessary for ongoing organizational learning. In addition, teachers' knowledge and skills are not what they need to be, especially in light of more challenging goals for *all* students, and professional standards of practice are only beginning to be defined and enforced.[41] Given this situation, U.S. public school systems may well need external incentives and administrative assistance to stimulate the development of professional accountability and attention to learning objectives for all students.

A second limitation of professionalism concerns the problem of equity. Failure of professionalism is most notable in schools serving disenfranchised groups, especially schools in inner cities with large proportions of low-income students and students of color. Many of these schools have been allowed to languish for years, during which time the profession has not stepped forth to fight for the needs of these students. External administrative accountability is needed to address this failure of professionalism and help ensure equal opportunity.

Tied to the equity limitations of professionalism is the fact that outcomes-based school accountability is able to address some systemic purposes and needs more readily than professional accountability alone. For example, at more aggregated levels of the system, performance reporting and other outcomes-based accountability tools provide a useful mechanism for managing the resources necessary for instruction and school improvement. Low performance can be a marker indicating areas of greatest need. In addition, monitoring and reporting of outcomes are important avenues for informing the public about the status of the system and the degree to which it is addressing the needs of and providing opportunities to all students. This is particularly true in the United States, where neither the public nor its representatives are ready to fully trust professional educators (Cohen & Spillane, 1993).

A Better Way: Combining the Bureaucratic and the Professional

A combination of professional and administrative/bureaucratic school accountability may be most useful to create an environment that would foster long-term school improvement. Such combinations are common in other professions. In medicine, for example, physicians establish and enforce standards of medical practice but hospitals, insurance companies, and sometimes governments pay attention to outcome (as well as process [42]) data to identify and respond to breakdowns and problems in the distribution and management of medical resources.

Similarly, some educational jurisdictions are experimenting with combinations of outcomes-based administrative accountability to identify areas of low performance and professionally based interventions and accountability to foster school adaptation to address these problems. One such example is the recently formed CEO District in Baltimore, Maryland. Maryland established outcome targets based on the Maryland Student Performance Assessment Program, and identifies schools that are the farthest from and declining in relation to those targets. Such schools are deemed "reconstitution eligible." The preponderance of reconstitution-eligible schools in Baltimore City was one factor contributing to a change in governance for the district, to a district-state partnership, and to additional funding being directed to the district (reallocation of resources based on outcomes).[43] Once in place, the new leadership of the district collected a group of the lowest performing schools into a special configuration, the CEO District, and turned to the local education fund (LEF) to assist these schools in becoming effective learning organizations.[44]

The resulting intervention incorporates many of the aspects of teacher professionalism discussed above, as well as the characteristics of adaptive organizations. These include a focus on literacy for teacher and student work and for generating and sharing information about that work; ongoing assessments through Running Records and regular evaluation of student work to provide frequent, fine-grained information about learning outcomes; team structures like regular grade-level meetings to foster teacher interaction, sharing of strategies, and collective responsibility; and ongoing professional development designed to build a "culture of shared learning" (Fund for Educational Excellence, 2001). Professional development, which is central to the intervention in the CEO District, is site based, focuses on literacy standards, and incorporates teachers' professional interchange through collective study, interclass visitations, and common planning. A client-centered focus, which is also central to notions of professionalism, is manifested throughout these endeavors, but especially in the identification of, targeted assistance to, and monitoring of all students reading below grade level. Finally, the CEO District intervention fosters a full range of incentives, from material rewards for principals and teachers for taking on the challenge of and showing progress in these schools to solidarity incentives derived from membership in a profession, and, finally, to the intrinsic purposive rewards of success with students.[45]

An interesting characteristic of this and several similar approaches is the apparent division of labor between the generation and use of information at the state level, which is following a more administrative/bureaucratic model, and that at the local level, which has a strong infusion of professionalism.[46] This division of labor suggests a necessary distinction in the balance of accountability approaches depending on the level of aggregation, and thus on the distance from or closeness to the point of instruction and school change. What seems critical here is that the bureaucratic accountability mechanisms from the more aggregated levels of the system not get in the way of the development of professional norms, structures, and standards at the school site.

The Baltimore CEO District and similar models represent only one approach to combining professional and bureaucratic accountability. What is important to note is the synergistic interplay of professional and bureaucratic accountability. On the one hand, outcomes-based targets for schools and performance reporting are critical for identifying problem areas, for allocating of resources to address those problems, and for monitoring progress. But the real action at the school site and across school sites is on developing professional knowledge through focused assistance on instruction, professional norms, and the professional patterns of interaction necessary for establishing the basis for ongoing organizational adaptation. This combination allows for a more thorough and balanced incorporation of all aspects of the accountability framework discussed earlier. It generates and draws attention to information relevant to teaching and learning (i.e., to both adult and student performance);

it motivates individuals and units through intrinsic as well as extrinsic incentives to attend and to use that information; it builds the knowledge base for valid interpretations of information; and it allocates resources where they are most needed.

The combination also addresses the three underlying problems and tension in school accountability described at the beginning of this article. Recall that the first of these problems concerned the interplay between collective accountability for the school unit and the requisite change in behavior of the individuals within that unit. The addition of professional accountability at the school site strengthens the links between individual teachers and their schools by fostering interaction around common work, a sense of shared purpose, and identity as members of the school community. These ties increase individual motivation to act in accordance with the community's collectively defined endeavor. Moreover, the deprivatization of practice through sharing of student work and teacher strategies, as well as interclass visitations, provides a mechanism for developing and enforcing common standards of practice.

This latter point also has implications for the second problem identified earlier, the relationship between external and internal mechanisms of control. Attempts to control individual and group behavior by means of external rules and policies are notorious for their inevitable failure, especially in situations where tasks and environments are complex and ambiguous.[47] Resistance and superficial compliance are the common responses. In the case of education, compliance with externally produced rules can even be counterproductive, as it does not allow for the flexible application of professional knowledge to specific contexts and students. In contrast, the strong professional norms generated by the infusion of professional accountability, especially collective responsibility for student learning, become potential resources and mechanisms for orienting the entire school community toward the higher levels of student performance sought by reformers and the general public.

Finally, with respect to the third problem—the generation, flow, and use of information for organizational learning and adaptation—the combination of professional and outcomes-based school accountability holds considerable promise. Drawing on the discussion of complexity theory and the examples described above, we might posit several principles of information generation and use for accountability purposes. The first of these, which is the subject of considerable scholarship and debate, is that information on performance must be valid and accurate and must reflect the goals of teaching and learning.[48] This principle applies to all forms of accountability, regardless of target or mechanism.

With respect to school accountability and improvement, four additional principles derive from our discussion here. First, for individuals and systems to evaluate performance, make appropriate attributions, and adapt their strategies, information must be available both on student performance (achievement) and on adult performance (instructional and other relevant strategies). Second, the grain size and periodicity of the information feedback should match the level and purposes of its use. For the improvement of instructional practice at the school and classroom level, fine-grained and frequent information, including instructionally integrated diagnostic assessments of student learning and feedback on instructional practice tied to that learning, provides the basis for professional reflection. Meanwhile, at higher levels of the system, more aggregate and less frequent information feedback provides a sufficient basis for allocating resources and evaluating and refining policies. Third, because information in complex systems derives from interaction, accountability systems should foster connections within and across units to allow access to and reflection on information relevant to teaching and learning. And, finally, accountability systems must pay particular attention to developing the knowledge base necessary for valid interpretation of the information so generated.

A thoughtful combination of outcomes-based school accountability and professional accountability provides the means of addressing all these information needs and thus for fostering the data driven improvement sought by many system reformers and policymakers. Whether such a thoughtful combination is likely to come about, however, particularly in light of the highly prescriptive and stringent testing and accountability provisions of the No Child Left Behind Act, is another matter.

Notes

1. Work for this paper was supported in part by Office of Educational Research and Improvement (Grant No. R308A60003) to the Consortium for Policy Research in Education and by two grants from the Spencer Foundation (one to the Wisconsin Center for Educational Research for the study of school probation in Chicago elementary schools and the other to Marshall S. Smith to explore implementation issues in standards-based reform). All findings, opinions, and conclusions expressed in this paper are those of the author and do not necessarily reflect the views of any of the funders.

2. The Consortium for Policy Research in Education unites five leading research institutions—the University of Pennsylvania, Harvard University, Stanford University, the University of Michigan, and the University of Wisconsin–Madison—in collaborative efforts to improve educational systems and student learning through research on educational reform, policy, and finance.

3. The No Child Left Behind Act (NCLB), the most recent reauthorization of the Elementary and Secondary Education Act (ESEA), requires annual testing of all students in grades three through eight, a twelve-year timeline to achieve universal proficiency in reading and mathematics, identification of low-performing schools based on aggregated and disaggregated test scores, and administration of severe consequences (including public school choice) for low-performing schools that fail to improve.

4. Chicago's school accountability policy is explained in greater detail in the section on bureaucratic accountability and in Note 22. In brief, the Chicago system identifies low-performing schools for "probation" based on student test results and metes out both assistance and sanctions to spur improvement in those schools. This article draws on data from a three-year study of school probation policies and practices in Chicago elementary schools.

5. While this article focuses on the explicit organizational improvement goals of school accountability, these policies have symbolic and political purposes as well. For a fuller discussion of some of the politics underlying Chicago's school probation policies, see Bennett (2001).

6. For a range of implementation discussions over the past three decades, see, for example, Berman and McLaughlin (1974), Goertz, Floden, and O'Day (1995), McLaughlin (1987), Spillane (2000), and Weatherly and Lipsky (1977).

7. See, for example, DeBray, Parson, and Woodworm (2001), Elmore (2001), McLaughlin and Talbert (1993), or Newmann and Wehlage (1995) for a discussion of the power of internal norms.

8. For popular accounts of complexity theory in the natural and social sciences, see Kauffman (1995), Lewin (1992), and Waldrop (1992).

9. See also McLaughlin and Talbert (1993) and Cohen (1990).

10. Interaction patterns among agents within the system are thus critical in understanding how information from the outside becomes available (or not) and used (or not) by its members for learning.

11. "Superstitious learning occurs when the subjective experience of learning is compelling but the connections between actions and outcomes are misspecified" (Levitt & March, 1988, p. 325).

12. It is important to note that organizational inertia is enhanced as the web of supporting relationships grows, creating codependencies among units of the organization and between it and external systems. For a discussion of how initial advantage and increasing returns serves to lock in certain solutions and strategies, see Arthur (1989) or Marion (1999).

13. The term *Christmas tree school* is often used to indicate a school that adds on multiple uncoordinated and inconsistent programs, much as a Christmas tree displays a mélange of multicolored and decorative ornaments.

14. Coupling, in organizations literature, refers to the connections and interdependence of elements of a system. According to Weick (1976), loosely "coupled events are responsive [to one another], *but* each event also preserves its own identity and some evidence of its physical or logical separateness … and their attachment may be circumscribed, infrequent, weak in its mutual effects, unimportant, and/or slow to respond…. Loose coupling also carries connotations of impermanence, dissolvability, and tacitness, all of which are potentially crucial properties of the 'glue' that holds organizations together" (p. 3).

15. Axelrod and Cohen (1999) identify three types of attribution mistakes: crediting or blaming a part when a larger ensemble of forces is responsible for a given outcome; crediting or blaming a particular ensemble of factors when a different ensemble is actually responsible; and failing to appreciate the role of context—that is, believing that what was successful in one context may be equally successful in another. Each type of mistake is common in education at every level of the system.

16. An example of such incentives would be salary increases given to teachers for taking additional course credits whether or not such coursework has any bearing on school improvement plans and strategies, any effect on teachers' actual instructional knowledge, or any impact on student performance.

17. In addition to school accountability, student accountability—in which consequences for individual students such as graduation or grade promotion are based on standardized measures of academic performance—has become an increasingly prevalent aspect of standards-based reform in the past several years. School accountability remains the lynchpin in most jurisdictions, however, as well as in the No Child Left Behind Act.

18. In the case of federal policies (e.g., Title I), *to whom* may also refer indirectly to the federal government, but still by way of the state and local education agencies (SEAs and LEAs). Similarly, where authority for a given policy derives from state law (legal accountability) and the courts are the ultimate arbiter, administration remains the responsibility of the superordinate levels of the educational bureaucracy to whom the schools are most directly accountable. From the perspective of the schools, then, these cases are almost indistinguishable from other examples of bureaucratic accountability.

19. *Note:* In this article, the terms *bureaucratic accountability, outcomes-based accountability,* and *outcomes-based bureaucratic accountability* will be used interchangeably with school accountability. This discussion excludes choice systems in which schools are held accountable directly to parents through the market.

20. It may be important here to note that the designation "outcomes-based bureaucratic accountability" differs somewhat from the terms used in prior typologies—in large part because it incorporates two somewhat different approaches to categorizing accountability systems. Adams and Kirst (1999) focus their typology on the differences in *who* is accountable *to whom.* According to these authors, "Bureaucratic accountability ensures that the preferences and decisions of organizational leaders govern the work of employees throughout the organization. It is based on the relationship between superiors and subordinates and operates through a system of supervisory control characterized by hierarchical structure, standard operating procedures, and rewards and punishments" (p. 467). Darling-Hammond (1990) agrees, underscoring the importance of standardized rules and procedures for practice, established at the top of the system and followed by teachers and others in schools. "New accountability" models do not entirely fit this description, however, as they loosen the standardization of *practice,* replacing it with standardization of *outcomes* (or progress toward the outcomes). O'Reilly (1996) tries to incorporate this distinction by developing a typology based on the operational assumptions that various approaches to accountability make in order to effect systemic change. She thus identifies four operational "theories" of accountability: performance reporting, changes in governance, market-based approaches, and professional accountability. Performance reporting comes closest to the Chicago Public Schools and similar models in that "performance reporting assumes that the collection and reporting of information on student academic performance can be used to stimulate strategies for improving teaching and learning" (p. 5). However, O'Reilly's category falls short in two respects. First, it overlaps with and is integral to other categories in the typology, confounding its interpretation. Second, it does not distinguish between performance and outcomes. While test scores may be a direct indicator of *student* performance, they are only an indirect indicator of *adult* performance. Campbell and his colleagues underscore the importance of distinguishing between performance (behavior) and the results (outcomes) of that performance if there is to be any hope of making valid attributions between the two (Campbell, McCloy, Oppler, & Sager, 1993). This distinction becomes important in understanding the limitations of current models of school accountability to foster improved instruction. It is for this reason that I have chosen the term *outcomes-based* bureaucratic accountability.

21. The ITBS is an example of the type of commercially produced, norm-referenced, multiple-choice, timed assessment used in many jurisdictions for accountability, monitoring, and placement purposes.

22. All probation schools are required to develop a corrective action/school improvement plan and literacy plan to organize their improvement efforts. These plans are reviewed at the central office, and their implementation is monitored by the probation manager assigned to the school. Assistance comes in the form of additional resources for external support providers called external partners. If the necessary improvement in test scores is not manifest at the end of a vaguely specified number of years, school personnel may be replaced en masse (reconstitution) or individually through a more extended peer review process (reengineering). Such consequences, however, have rarely been administered.

23. The Comprehensive School Reform Demonstration (CSRD) Program, is a federal effort encouraging the adoption of research-based, whole school reform models, especially in Title I schools identified as being in need of improvement.

24. This does not include the resources allocated for remedial summer or after school classes or for practice and testing materials. See Finnigan, O'Day, and Wakelyn (2001) for a fuller discussion of the assistance program.

25. The most recent reauthorization of ESEA, the No Child Left Behind Act of 2001, tightens and extends these requirements and the consequences for continued low performance (see Note 3).

26. An example is California's Public School Accountability Act of 1999, which metes out monetary awards to all schools in the state (both high and low performers) that reach their annual improvement targets on the state's Academic Performance Index (API).

27. For varying perspectives of the impact of these accountability systems, see Grissmer, Flanagan, Kawata, and Williamson (2000), Haney (2000), Klein, Hamilton, McCaffrey, and Stecher (2000), and Koretz and Barron (1998).

28. This research was conducted by a team of researchers from the University of Wisconsin–Madison and the Consortium on Chicago School Research and was sponsored by the Spencer Foundation and the Office of Educational Research and Improvement.

29. By periodicity I mean the frequency and regularity of information on student learning generated by the system. Specificity refers to the degree of detail of the information. For example, information on student knowledge regarding particular decoding skills (like facility with beginning or ending consonants) is more specific than would be a single test score covering all aspects of decoding, let alone a single score for reading.

30. The No Child Left Behind Act of 2001 promises to substantially alter the specifics of many existing school accountability systems—for example, the nature of the assessments or the timeframe for improvement—but the general intent (to implement a system that identifies lower performing units for intervention) remains.

31. See, for example, *The Debate on Opportunity to Learn Standards: Supporting Works* (National Governors' Association, 1993) or the "Report of the National Academy of Education Panel on Standards-Based Education" (McLaughlin & Shepard, 1995).

32. See, for example, the literature on the role of professional community (e.g., McLaughlin & Talbert, 1993, 2001; Newmann & Wehlage, 1995) and on information sharing in high-performing schools (Darling-Hammond, 1996; Mohrman & Lawler, 1996).

33. This conclusion derives primarily from our observations and interviews regarding the planning process in our ten case study schools but is augmented by additional analysis of the planning documents and processes in a slightly larger and more diverse group of schools. See Gross, Wei, and O'Day (2002) for further discussion of this pattern.

34. Some exceptions exist, of course, with the more self-reflective school communities generally showing the greater gains in performance (Gross, et al., 2002).

458 • Jennifer A. O'Day

35. See, for example, Firestone and Mayrowetz (2000), Nolen, Haladaya, and Haas (1992), and Smith and Rottenberg(1991).
36. These tendencies might be mitigated if a policy included positive incentives (rewards) for learning and for improvements in instructional practice. While some systems do include rewards, these are tied to improvements in outcomes, not practice or learning. Observers often note the need for interim indicators of organizational practice and a capacity to be included in the accountability structures, but they rarely are.
37. For a discussion of these other incentives, see, for example, Mohrman and Lawler (1996) and Darling-Hammond (1996).
38. External partners are the official external support providers approved and funded through the school probation policy (see Note 22).
39. See Campbell et al. (1993) for the importance of the distinction between performance and outcomes.
40. See also Porter and Brophy (1988).
41. The work of the National Board for Professional Teaching Standards (NBPTS), the Interstate New Teacher Assessment and Support Consortium (INTASC), and the National Council for Accreditation of Teacher Education (NCATE) are promising but still beginning efforts in this regard.
42. An example of process data in the medical field might be the number of patients seen in a day or the average length of hospital stay, indicators with which health maintenance organizations and insurance companies have become noticeably concerned in recent years.
43. The partnership between the Baltimore City Public School System (BCPSS) and the Maryland State Department of Education (MSDE) was established by Maryland State Senate Bill 795 in 1997 and is a unique arrangement in educational governance. The partnership decoupled BCPSS from control of Baltimore's city government and established a new Board of School Commissioners that was jointly appointed by the mayor and the governor. It also set in place certain steps for the new board to take in its reform efforts and provided additional monies to support implementation of those steps. For a description and evaluation of the partnership, see Westat (2001).
44. Local education funds (LEFs) are community-based organizations and coalitions centered on improving public schools and student achievement through community involvement in specific locales. The Baltimore LEF, the Fund for Educational Excellence, is partnering with BCPSS in the implementation of Achievement First, a whole-school standards-based reform effort focused on improving literacy instruction through professional development of teachers and principals. See Fund for Educational Excellence (2001) and Westat (2001).
45. Teachers, for example, receive an 11 percent supplement to their base salary and seven days of paid professional development at the beginning of the school year. See Kim (2001).
46. Other jurisdictions are also experimenting with combinations of professional and bureaucratic accountability, each of which focuses substantially on intense site-based professional development and efforts to develop professional patterns of interaction and collegiality. These include the Boston Public Schools, Community School District 2 and the Chancellor's District in New York City, and the San Diego City Schools, among others.
47. To paraphrase McLaughlin (1988), you can't mandate what matters.
48. See, for example, Linn (2001, 1997).

References

Abelman, C., & Elmore, R. (1999). *When accountability knocks, will anyone answer?* (CPRE Research Report Series RR-42). Philadelphia: Consortium for Policy Research in Education.
Adams, J. E., & Kirst, M. (1999). New demands for educational accountability: Striving for results in an era of excellence. In J. Murphey & K. S. Louis (Eds.), *Handbook of research in educational administration* (2nd ed., pp. 463–489). San Francisco: Jossey-Bass.
Arthur, W. B. (1989). The economy and complexity. In D. L. Stein (Ed.), *Lectures in the sciences of complexity* (pp. 713–740). Redwood City, CA: Addison-Wesley.
Axelrod, R., & Cohen, M. D. (1999). *Harnessing complexity: Organizational implications of a scientific frontier.* New York: Free Press.
Bennett, A. (2001, April). *The history, politics and theory of action of the Chicago probation policy.* Paper presented at the annual meeting of the American Educational Research Association, Seattle.
Berman, P., & McLaughlin, M. (1978). *Federal programs supporting educational change: Vol. VII. Factors affecting implementation and continuation.* Santa Monica, CA: RAND.
Campbell, J. P., McCloy, R. A., Oppler, S. H., & Sager, C. E. (1993). A theory of performance. In N. Schmitt, W. C. Borman, & Associates (Eds.), *Personnel selection in organizations* (pp. 35–70). San Francisco: Jossey-Bass.
Chicago Public Schools. (2002). *Iowa test of basic skills: Citywide results over time, 1997–2002* (Report ITOT-CW-white). Chicago: Author. Available at http://research.cps.k12.il.us/resweb/pdf/itbs_over_read_a.p
Cohen, D. K. (1990). A revolution in one classroom. *Educational Evaluation and Policy Analysis, 12,* 327–345.
Cohen, D. K., & Ball, D. L. (1999). *Instruction, capacity, and improvement.* Philadelphia: Consortium for Policy Research in Education.
Cohen, D. K., & Spillane, J. P. (1993). Policy and practice: The relationship between governance and instruction. In S. H. Fuhrman (Ed.), *Designing coherent education policy: Improving the system* (pp. 35–95). San Francisco: Jossey-Bass.
Daft, R. L., & Weick, K. E. (1984). Toward a model of organizations as interpretation systems. *Academy of Management Review, 9,* 284–295.
Darling-Hammond, L. (1990). Teacher professionalism: Why and how? In A. Lieberman (Ed.), *Schools as collaborative cultures: Creating the future now* (pp. 25–50). Bristol, PA: Falmer Press.

Darling-Hammond, L. (1996). Restructuring schools for high performance. In S. Fuhrman & J. A. O'Day (Eds.), *Rewards and reform: Creating educational incentives that work* (pp. 144–192). San Francisco: Jossey-Bass.

Darling-Hammond, L., & Ascher, C. (1991). *Creating accountability in big city school systems* (Urban Diversity Series No. 102). New York: ERIC Clearinghouse on Urban Education.

DeBray, E., Parson, G., & Woodworth, K. (2001). Patterns of response in four high schools under state accountability policies in Vermont and New York. In S. Fuhrman (Ed.), *From the capitol to the classroom: Standards-based reform in the states* (pp. 170–192). Chicago: University of Chicago Press.

Elmore, R. F. (1996). Getting to scale with successful educational practices. In S. Fuhrman & J. A. O'Day (Eds.), *Rewards and reform: Creating educational incentives that work* (pp. 294–329). San Francisco: Jossey-Bass.

Elmore, R. F. (1997). *Investing in teacher learning: Staff development and instructional improvement in Community District 2.* Philadelphia: Consortium for Policy Research in Education and the National Commission on Teaching and America's Future.

Elmore, R. F. (2001, April). *Psychiatrists and light bulbs: Educational accountability and the problem of capacity.* Paper presented at the annual meeting of the American Educational Research Association, Seattle.

Elmore R. F., Abelmann, C. H., & Fuhrman, S. H. (1996). The new accountability in state education reform: From process to performance. In H. F. Ladd (Ed.), *Holding schools accountable: Performance-based reform in education* (pp. 65–98). Washington, DC: Brookings Institution.

Evans, L. E., & Wei, H. H. (2001, April). *Focusing the work of teachers and schools: The Chicago public schools probation policy.* Paper prepared for the annual meeting of the American Educational Research Association, Seattle.

Finnigan, K., O'Day, J., & Wakelyn, D. (2001). *Buddy, can you lend us a hand? The provision of external assistance to Chicago elementary schools on probation.* Chicago: Consortium on Chicago School Research.

Finnigan, K. S., & Gross, B. M. (2001, April). *Teacher motivation and the Chicago probation policy.* Paper presented at the annual meeting of the American Educational Research Association, Seattle.

Firestone, W. A., & Mayrowetz, D. (2000). Rethinking "high stakes": Lessons from the United States and England and Wales. *Teachers College Record, 102,* 724–749.

Fuhrman, S. H. (1999). *The new accountability* (CPRE Policy Brief No. RB 27). Philadelphia: Consortium on Policy Research in Education.

Goertz, M., Floden, R., & O'Day, J. (1995). *Studies of education reform: Systemic reform, volume 1. Findings and conclusions.* New Brunswick, NJ: Consortium for Policy Research in Education.

Grissmer, D., Flanagan, A., Kawata, J., & Williamson, S. (2000). *Improving student achievement: What state NAEP test scores tell us* (Report MR-924-EDU). Santa Monica, CA: RAND.

Gross, B., Wei, H., & O'Day, J. A. (2002). *Planning for improvement in Chicago schools on probation.* Unpublished report, University of Wisconsin–Madison.

Gwynne, J., & Easton, J. Q. (2001, April). *Probation, organizational capacity, and student achievement in Chicago elementary schools.* Paper presented at the annual meeting of the American Educational Research Association, Seattle.

Haney, W. (2000). The myth of the Texas miracle in education [Electronic version]. *Education Policy Analysis Archives, 8*(41). Available at http://epaa.asa.edu/epaa/v8n41/

Huber, G. P. (1991). Organizational learning: The contributing processes and the literatures. *Organizational Science, 2,* 1, 88–115.

Kaufmann, S. (1995). *At home in the universe: The search for the laws of self-organization and complexity.* New York: Oxford University Press.

Kelley, C., Odden, A, Milanowski, A., & Heneman, H. (2000). *The motivational effects of school-based performance awards* (CPRE Policy Brief No. RB-29). Philadelphia: Consortium for Policy Research in Education.

Kim, T. (2001, November 14). News in brief: Some Baltimore teachers set to receive extra pay [electronic version]. *Education Week.* Available at http://www.edweek.org/ew/newstory.cfm?slug=11 briefs.h21

Klein, S. P., Hamilton, L. S., McCaffrey, D. F., & Stecher, B. M. (2000). *What do test scores in Texas tell us?* Washington, DC: RAND.

Koretz, D., & Barron, S. (1998). *The validity of gains on the Kentucky instructional results information system* (Report MR 1014-EDU). Santa Monica, CA: RAND.

Lee, V., & Smith, J. (1996). Collective responsibility for learning and its effects on gains in achievement for early secondary school students. *American Journal of Education, 104,* 103–147.

Levinthal, D. A. (1991). Organizational adaptation and environmental selection: Interrelated processes of change. *Organizational Science, 2,* 140–145.

Levitt, B., & March, J. G. (1988). Organizational learning. *Annual Review of Sociology, 14,* 319–340.

Lewin, R. (1992). *Complexity: Life at the edge of chaos.* New York: Macmillan.

Linn, R. L. (1997). Evaluating the validity of assessments: The consequences of use. *Educational Measurement: Issues and Practice, 16,* 2, 14–16.

Linn, R. L. (2001). *The design and evaluation of educational assessment and accountability systems* (CSE Technical Report). Los Angeles: University of California, Los Angeles, Center for Research on Evaluation, Standards, and Student Testing.

Little, J. W. (1990). The persistence of privacy: Autonomy and initiative in teachers' professional relations. *Teachers College Record, 91,* 509–536.

Lortie, D. C. (1975). *Schoolteacher: A sociological study.* Chicago: University of Chicago Press.

March, J. G. (1991). Exploration and exploitation in organizational learning. *Organizational Science, 2*(1), 71–87.

March, J. G. (1994). *A primer on decision making: How decisions happen.* New York: Free Press.

Marion, R. (1999). *The edge of organization: Chaos and complexity theories of formal social systems.* Thousand Oaks, CA: Sage.

McLaughlin, M. (1988) Learning from experience: Lessons from policy implementation. *Educational Evaluation and Policy Analysis, 9,* 171–178.

McLaughlin, M. W., & Shepard, L. A. (1995). *Improving education through standards-based reform: A report by the National Academy of Education Panel on Standards-Based Reform.* Stanford, CA: National Academy of Education.

McLaughlin, M. W., & Talbert, J. E. (1993). *Contexts that matter for teaching and learning.* Stanford, CA: Stanford University, School of Education, Center for Research on the Context of Teaching.

McLaughlin, M. W., & Talbert, J. E. (2001). *Professional communities and the work of high school teaching.* Chicago: University of Chicago Press.

Mohrman, S. A., & Lawler, E. E. (1996). Motivation for school reform. In S. H. Fuhrman & J. A. O'Day (Eds.), *Rewards and reform: Creating educational incentives that work* (pp. 115–143). San Francisco: Jossey-Bass.

National Governors' Association. (1993). *The debate on opportunity-to-learn standards: Supporting works.* Washington, DC: Author.

Newmann, F. M., & Wehlage, G. G. (1995) *Successful school restructuring: A report to the public and educators by the Center on Organization and Restructuring of Schools.* Madison, WI: Center on Organization and Restructuring of Schools.

Nolen, S. B., Haladyna, T. M., & Haas, N. (1992). Uses and abuses of achievement test scores. *Educational Measurement: Issues and Practice, 11*(2), 9–15.

O'Day, J. A. (1996). Incentives and school improvement. In S. Fuhrman & J. A. O'Day (Eds.), *Rewards and reform: Creating educational incentives that work* (pp. 1–16). San Francisco: Jossey-Bass.

O'Day, J., & Smith, M. S. (1993). Systemic school reform and educational opportunity. In S. H. Fuhrman (Ed.), *Designing coherent education policy: Improving the system* (pp. 250–312). San Francisco: Jossey Bass.

O'Reilly, F. E. (1996). *Educational accountability: Current practices and theories in use.* Cambridge, MA: Harvard University, Consortium for Policy Research in Education.

Porter, A., & Brophy, J. (1988). Good teaching: Insights from the work of the Institute for Research on Teaching. *Educational Leadership, 45,* 75–84.

Scott, W. R. (1998). *Organizations: Rational, natural, and open systems* (4th ed.). Upper Saddle River, NJ: Prentice Hall.

Senge, P. M. (1993). *The fifth discipline: The art and practice of the learning organization.* London: Century Business.

Simon, H. A. (1986). Theories of bounded rationality. In C. B. McGuire & R. Radner (Eds.), *Decision and organization: Volume 2* (pp. 161–176). Minneapolis: University of Minnesota Press.

Siskin, L. S. (in press). The challenge of the high schools. In S. H. Fuhrman & R. F. Elmore (Eds.), *Redesigning accountability systems.* New York: Teachers College Press.

Sitkin, S. B. (1992). Learning through failure: The strategy of small losses. *Research in Organizational Behavior, 14,* 231–266.

Smith, M. L., & Rottenberg, C. (1991). Unintended consequences of external testing in elementary schools. *Educational Measurement: Issues and Practice, 10*(4), 7–11.

Spillane, J. (2000). Cognition and policy implementation: District policy-makers and the reform of mathematics education. *Cognition and Instruction, 18,* 141–179.

Spillane, J. (2002). Local theories of teacher change: The pedagogy of district policies and programs. *Teachers College Record, 104,* 377–420.

Staw, B. M., Sanderlands, L. E., & Dutton, J. E. (1981). Threat-rigidity effects in organizational behavior: A multilevel analysis. *Administration Science Quarterly, 26,* 501–524.

Waldrop, M. M. (1992). *Complexity: The emerging science at the edge of order and chaos.* New York: Simon & Schuster.

Weatherly, R., & Lipsky, M. (1977) Street-level bureaucrats and institutional innovation: Implementing special-education reform. *Harvard Educational Review, 47,* 171–197.

Weick, K. (1976). Educational organizations as loosely coupled systems. *Administrative Science Quarterly, 21,* 1–19.

25

False Promises

The School Choice Provisions in No Child Left Behind

DOUGLAS LAUEN

Stratification and Equality of Educational Opportunity

Scholars have long debated the extent to which education enhances mobility chances or simply maintains existing patterns of inequality. On the one hand, social scientists have argued that mobility based on achievement, rather status maintenance, is a hallmark of the U.S. social system (Blau & Duncan, 1967). The U.S. educational system has been characterized as one with "contest," rather than "sponsored" mobility. Unlike the British system, in which elites induct a select group of youth at an early age to groom them for high-status positions, youth in the U.S. compete in multiple contests, with every effort taken to keep students in the game (Turner, 1960). Alternative views argue that through hidden curriculum and tracking, the U.S. system "cools out" the mobility aspirations of disadvantaged students, thereby reinforcing, rather than overturning, existing patterns of stratification (Rosenbaum, 1976; MacLeod, 1995; Oakes, 1985).

If the United States is indeed characterized by mobility through achievement, one must consider the rules of the game. To establish the legitimacy of contest mobility regimes and maintain social control, participants must believe that differential outcomes, and the rewards that flow from these outcomes, are due not to differential access to the resources necessary to compete in the contest, but rather to effort and merit. Stated in terms of education in particular, in order for success in school to be viewed as an effective mechanism to attain the rights and privileges of high status, all students must have access to high quality teachers, curricula, and schools.

Throughout the 19th and 20th centuries, promoting equality of educational opportunity has been a persistent goal of U.S. education policy. Expanding access has taken various forms over time, from extending schooling in rural areas, to ensuring that immigrants attended common schools in urban areas, to school desegregation, and, as some have argued, expanding school choice. Though expansion of educational opportunity has been a hallmark of the U.S. system, structural inequality and entrenched power dynamics have made providing students the same starting point a highly contentious area of public policy. Due to the relatively high level of inequality in American society and the decentralized nature of the educational system, efforts to use education policy to reduce inequality have faced political opposition and myriad policy implementation difficulties. While there is often widespread agreement among the public and policymakers that students *should* receive equal access to education, implementing reform has often foundered on entrenched interests seeking to maintain their advantages (Hochschild & Scovronick, 2003).

The expansion of school choice through vouchers, charter schools, and NCLB has been framed by advocates as a way to enhance equality of educational opportunity; critics claim that school choice would reduce, rather than increase, educational opportunities for disadvantaged students. The stakes of this debate have been raised now that school choice is being funded and encouraged through federal policy. The D.C. Opportunity Scholarship program, begun in the 2004-2005 school year, currently serves about 1,700 students who each receive up to $7,500 of federal funds to attend one of 68 private schools (about two-thirds of which are religiously affiliated) (Wolf et al., 2006). A policy that affects many more students and schools is the school choice provision in NCLB, which requires that students in schools that have failed to make adequate yearly progress (AYP) in consecutive years be given the option of transferring to a school that has done so. The implication of this provision is that because states and local school districts have failed to provide adequate access to educational resources to low-income children, the federal government must use its authority to regulate student enrollment policy.

In order to justify what has become a significant incursion of federal government power into educational policy since the original ESEA law was passed in 1965, the president and Congressional leaders sought to instill in the public and other members of Congress a sense that urgent reform was required to fix a dysfunctional educational system. The image of "freeing" students from "failing" schools was central in this effort. For example, upon introducing his educational agenda on January 23, 2001, President George W. Bush said: "American children must not be left in persistently dangerous or failing schools. When schools do not teach and will not change, parents and students must have other meaningful options."[1]

Not surprisingly, the exertion of federal authority over student enrollment policy has proved controversial and implementation of these provisions has been uneven across local school districts. In fact, one could argue that the school choice provisions have been remarkably ineffective. Despite the fact that 3.3 million students were eligible for NCLB transfers in the 2003-04 school year, only 31,500, or 1%, of eligible students actually transferred to a school that was making AYP (United States Government Accountability Office, 2004).

The purpose of this chapter is to assess the extent to which public school choice either through local or federal policy is likely to expand equality of educational opportunity. I begin by outlining some important design principles for school choice programs. I then discuss some different modes of school choice policy, with careful consideration of NCLB choice and its relationship to other forms of school choice. Though very little research exists on NCLB choice in particular, I review what social scientific research says about the potential risks and benefits of various choice policies. With the broader context of school choice research understood, I discuss the challenges local districts have faced when attempting to comply with the NCLB transfer mandates. I conclude by drawing implications for NCLB's 2007 reauthorization and for future research on NCLB choice.

The Promises and Perils of School Choice

The most common and least controversial policy of assigning students to schools is by geographic catchment area, with all students in a given set of neighborhoods going to the same neighborhood school. This policy is the norm in American education, in which local school district officials determine which students attend which schools through drawing attendance area boundaries. Neither parents nor school principals have much choice over enrollment decisions.[2] School choice advocates criticize this type of school enrollment policy for creating monopolistic conditions in which students are essentially a captive clientele. This view holds that these monopolistic conditions stifle both diversity of educational approach and educational excellence. In 2003, about 74% of students in grades 1–12 attend an assigned public school (Wirt et al., 2004). Ten years previously, in 1993, about 80% of students attended an assigned neighborhood school, one indication of the erosion of support for assigned public schools through the 1990s and early 2000s.

School choice advocates seek to replace the neighborhood-based school with a wide variety of schools tailored to fit the needs and interests of various student groups. Advocates argue that school choice can help parents both find a school that better fits their child's educational needs and potentially leverage school reform by promoting competition among schools for students. For example, a cultural divide between teachers and poor parents has been identified as a barrier to school improvement (Lareau, 1989; Comer, 1988). A goal of school choice policy, therefore, is to bridge this divide by allowing schools to recruit parents aligned with their educational approaches. This should promote parent satisfaction and trust if teachers and administrators adhere to these approaches and serve the needs of the students (Bryk & Schneider, 2002). Moreover, some have argued that schools in which educational values are aligned among staff, parents, and students may produce more functional learning communities (Coleman & Hoffer, 1987; Bryk et al., 1993). Therefore, choice has the potential to raise parent satisfaction, student engagement, and improve the incentives that influence school leaders.

Choice, if paired with deregulation of curricular foci, could promote a better match between family values and school mission. Promoting innovation of educational approach increases the likelihood of a match between student and family interests and a school's educational approach. If one assumes that the needs of students and families vary too much to be served by one type of school, a goal of school choice policy is to subvert the common school ideal, which promotes a unitary conception of educational values. In its place, choice policy promotes a wide variety of schools, each tailored to a particular conception of educational values, with the ability to attract students and families based on shared values: the "interests of children are best served in a decentralized polity giving maximum scope to free, chosen, communal relationships that are generally organized on a small scale" (Coons & Sugarman, 1978, 2). School choice advocates have argued that it is not the state's place to enforce conformity to one set of values: "Our problem today is not to enforce conformity; it is rather that we are threatened with an excess of conformity. Our problem is to foster diversity, and the alternative [vouchers] would do this far more effectively than a nationalized system" (Friedman, 1962, 97).

Education organized around a plurality of value commitments raises the possibility that school choice might harm social cohesion. While some voucher proponents have advocated reforms to create a system of pluralistic value competition—education as a "marketplace of ideas" (Coons & Sugarman, 1978, 102)—the fact that education is a public good paid for by tax dollars makes political contestation over curricular content inevitable. As controversies over the teaching of evolution suggest, matters of curriculum involve deeply held value commitments. Because schools are one of society's most important institutions of socialization and national identity, school curricula are fiercely contested.

From an egalitarian standpoint, therefore, school choice is problematic because it threatens the common school ideal of educating children of many different social, racial, and achievement backgrounds in the same institution. It has been argued that the common school has benefits for social cohesion and perhaps even peer effects on test scores if low ability and high ability students share classrooms. Therefore, allowing students to exercise school choice to attend schools that better suit their values, racial/ethnic preferences, or abilities, would harm social cohesion and may have negative spill-over effects on the students who remain in neighborhood schools. Expanding school choice could promote "creaming" (i.e., more advantaged students would be more likely to take advantage of school choice and leave less advantaged students in failing schools). Given that the social isolation of disadvantaged groups has been shown to harm student outcomes (Hanushek et al., 2002), one could predict that school choice could increase inequality in test scores, college enrollment rates, and incomes over time.

From a meritocratic standpoint, on the other hand, school choice could promote equity. The fact that highly motivated parents and children are able to gain access to alternatives to their neighborhood schools can be viewed as unproblematic assuming the admission rules are fair. In other words, in its ideal form school choice replaces the current system of school stratification based on race and class with one governed by merit, measured by test scores, effort, grades, or some other criterion. This could improve the incentives for families to seek out schools that serve their interests and for schools to attract and hold students who place a high value on learning (Coleman, 1992). Therefore, access to high ability peers becomes a result of a fair process rather than some combination of ascriptive characteristics.

While my characterizations of these two divergent viewpoints may be roughly hewn, these perspectives are critical to understanding whether expanding school choice will increase or decrease social inequality through changes in access to educational opportunities. I now turn to the particular policies that have attempted to expand educational opportunity through school choice, with particular attention to NCLB's public school choice provision.

Varieties of School Choice

As we might expect from decentralized educational system in the U.S., choice policy varies somewhat across the country. Most areas of the country allow some degree of choice within school districts, most states allow charter schools, and vouchers are quite rare. NCLB choice, which has largely been implemented within (rather than across) school districts can be viewed as a form of intradistrict choice that has been mandated by the federal government onto local school districts. Before summarizing the features of the NCLB choice provisions, I outline the other varieties of choice to provide a context for understanding the policy environment into which NCLB choice is being implemented.

Intradistrict Choice

A major change to the traditional mode of catchment area student assignment came with busing, or mandatory student assignment in the 1960s. Busing, imposed by federal judges as a remedy for school segregation, proved to be very unpopular with politicians and many community groups (Orfield & Eaton, 1996). While busing has been largely abandoned as a remedy for segregation, voluntary student assignment programs, such as magnet schools, have proven to be longer lived. These programs encourage racial integration by creating enriched learning environments in minority schools to attract white (and now Asian-American) students to enroll. Concurrently with efforts to promote racial integration, school districts also responded to the desire of parents for separate learning environments for students with unique needs. The addition of these types of programs increased the options available for most students, but within certain limits. Students generally had to meet certain criteria to be admitted to such schools, and the schools were subject to many of the same regulations and collective bargaining agreements as other schools. There are currently 1,736 magnet schools in 28 states (Kafer, 2005).

More recently, other forms of public school choice have greatly expanded the options available to American students. Intradistrict choice allows students to attend traditional neighborhood schools or specialized programs within larger schools. Selection criteria vary across districts, schools, and programs, but these options often involve interest in specialized curriculum or educational approaches, such as occupationally-focused curriculum, military academies, international baccalaureate academics, foreign language academics, and the like. Intradistrict choice can provide a relatively high degree of both density and diversity of schooling choices, but student selection criteria can be highly regulated, requiring a certain level of test score achievement, grades, and lack of disciplinary problems.

Interdistrict Choice

Interdistrict choice, student transfers across school district boundaries, was held up as a remedy for school desegregation in the 1970s (Orfield & Eaton, 1996). While some urban districts (e.g., Boston and St. Louis) have been able to negotiate agreements with surrounding suburban districts to accept minority student transfers, suburban districts are under no obligation to enter into such agreements due to a 1974 Supreme Court decision (Milliken v. Bradley). Consequently, this type of school choice is relatively rare. Furthermore, because most school district funds come from local property taxes, not state income taxes, wealthy suburban school districts are unlikely to accept students from poorer urban school districts without compensation from state funds.

Charter School Choice

Since 1991, charter schools have emerged as one of the fastest growing forms of alternative governance in American education. Run by independent groups, charter schools are granted a fixed term performance contract by public authorities, usually local school districts. Currently, 40 states have laws authorizing charter schools (Kafer, 2005), though the extent to which charter schools are allowed to penetrate the educational marketplace varies widely. Most states allow only a limited number of charters in a small set of locales and allow local school districts to reject charter school proposals as they see fit. These laws tend to produce what might be considered "pilot" schools that do little to expand options for most students in the state. These schools are usually subject to desegregation laws and student testing programs, but have a great deal more autonomy over hiring, procurement, and curriculum decisions. In return, school charters may be revoked for failing to perform adequately. Unlike traditional schools, charter schools face a stronger form of accountability from above (in the sense that schools that fail to perform can be more easily shut down than traditional public schools) and from below (in the sense that all parents are clients who can vote with their feet). There are currently 3,400 charter schools in the United States (ibid).

States with more liberal charter school laws allow either multiple authorizing entities or charter districts. While most state laws allow only local school districts to approve charter applications, at least 11 states and the District of Columbia allow multiple public entities to authorize charter school applications (Allen & Marcucio, 2005). This tends to expand the density and diversity of choice options because local school district officials often view charter schools as a threat to the public schools under their authority. Student selection regulations are typically consistent across authorizing entities, with enrollment by lottery typically the method to handle over-subscription. The locus of accountability is more complicated in mixed authority charter states, with some charter schools accountable to local school boards, some to universities, and others to the state board of education or a state-level charter school authorizing entity. In rare cases, state laws provide for charter-only districts, most often in cases in districts subject to state take-over due to chronic under-performance or fiscal mismanagement.

Choice through Vouchers

Finally, parents in some parts of the country have the ability to receive a school voucher. Unlike charter school laws, states or local school districts do not directly contract for educational services, but instead provide parents with funds for use in a public or private school. In general, this form of educational governance provides for more autonomy and less accountability to public entities, though like charter schools, vouchers provide for more accountability to parents. Most publicly funded voucher programs are targeted to low-income students. The NCLB Act's choice provisions were, in fact, modeled after Florida's A++ Plan (Levin, 2004), which unlike programs in Cleveland, Milwaukee, and the District of Columbia does not means-test by income level. This plan provides "Opportunity Scholarships" to students in schools that fail to meet state benchmarks twice in a four-year period. In the 2003–04 school year, 650 students received such scholarships. In January 2006, Florida's Supreme Court ruled that this plan violated the state's constitutional provision to provide a "uniform" system of public schools. Florida Governor Jeb Bush's attempt to pass an amendment to the Florida constitution through the Republican-controlled legislature failed in May of 2006.

NCLB Choice

NCLB choice is a form of intradistrict choice mandated by federal law and implemented by local school districts. The NCLB school transfer provisions, which only apply to schools receiving Title I funds, are designed as a negative incentive for under-performing schools. They are triggered when a high poverty school fails to make "adequate yearly progress" (AYP) for two years in a row. AYP applies to standards set by states (and subject to the approval of the U.S. Department of Education) in reading and math. AYP describes an improvement trajectory leading to 100% proficiency in both subjects for all students by the 2013–2014 school year, measured by testing results from students in grades 3–8. A school can be judged as not making adequate yearly progress for failing to meet performance targets or for failing to test 95% of their students. In addition, schools can miss AYP for not testing at least 95% of students in a number of subgroups—major ethnic/racial groups, the economically disadvantaged, limited English proficient students, and students with disabilities—or if the average subgroup score fails meet a certain threshold.[3] If a school fails to make AYP in two consecutive years, it must offer students the opportunity to attend another public school in the same district or one nearby that is making AYP.[4] A school forced to provide NCLB transfers must do so until it succeeds in meeting AYP in two consecutive years. Students who transfer to a receiving school must be allowed to stay through the highest grade offered in the school. In implementing school transfer policies, the act requires that local school districts (LEAs) give low-income and low-achieving students priority to school transfers in the event that not enough spaces in eligible schools are available.

Based in part on comments to regulation and additional questions to the U.S. Department of Education, in February of 2004 the department provided additional guidance to states attempting to implement the laws requirements (U.S. Department of Education, 2004). While additional funding would provide a positive incentive for schools receiving NCLB transfer students, the law does not require Title I funds to "follow the child."[5] LEAs must spend an amount equal to 20% of its Title I allocation on choice-related transportation and/or tutoring, with no less than 5% of this allocation going to either transportation or tutoring. LEAs may delimit student transfer options to designated transportation zones to reduce costs. However, LEAs are not required to provide transportation to students whose original school is no longer in improvement status.

LEAs are not required to change admission requirements in schools with specialized missions (like arts magnets, science and math academies, and selective enrollment schools) even if these schools are the only ones identified by the district as eligible to receive transfers. They may, however, give NCLB transfer students priority in charter school lotteries. LEAs must not use lack of capacity to deny students the transfer option, but may take capacity under consideration in deciding which choices to make available. LEAs with a lack of capacity must create new capacity for NCLB transfers by building new classroom space, erecting portables, building new schools, starting charter schools, developing distance learning programs, sending students to another school district, or contracting with private schools. Finally, LEAs subject to desegregation orders are not exempt from the NCLB transfer provisions. They must attempt to comply with both the dictates of the order and the transfer provisions.

In summary, the NCLB choice provision is explicitly linked to school accountability, requires LEAs to use Title I funds for transportation, and forbids overcrowding from preventing student transfers. I now turn to what research says about the potential benefits and costs of policy reforms aimed expanding educational choice for families.

What Does Research Say About School Choice?

Because school choice advocates have proposed radical transformations of the educational system, the amount of research on school choice, competition in the educational sector, and similar topics is vast. Instead of summarizing the entire corpus of existing research, I will focus this review on the aspects of school choice research that seem the most relevant to understanding both the policy context of NCLB and the implementation difficulties school policymakers have faced since its passage. Unfortunately, either because NCLB choice is a recent phenomenon, or because participation rates have been so low, the extant research base on the implementation and outcomes of NCLB choice is quite thin. Therefore, I focus this review on research about other types of choice programs. I will review the few studies that exist on NCLB choice in the next section.

School choice research can be organized by at least three hypotheses: the liberation hypothesis, the competition hypothesis, and the stratification hypothesis. I begin with research that addresses the extent to which choice in education will "free" students from "failing" schools.

The Liberation Hypothesis

To understand the policy context in which NCLB was proposed and debated, it is critical to examine how school choice advocates have framed their claims. The school choice provisions in NCLB were proposed by a Republican president, George W. Bush, who like his father before him, had championed school choice as a policy issue in the presidential campaign. President Bush and many other school choice advocates align their cause with what Gunnar Myrdal called the American Creed (Myrdal et al., 1944), which espouses liberty, equality of opportunity, and civil rights. Such advocates argue that expanding school choice promotes equity by allowing students in bad schools to escape to either private schools, or public schools in better neighborhoods. This perspective, dubbed the "liberation" hypothesis by Archbald (2004), argues that wealthy families are able to reproduce their values by shopping for the appropriate school for their children, whereas poor families are captives of professional elites in school systems that are increasingly unable to serve their needs (Coons & Sugarman, 1978; Tyack, 1974). National data confirm that parents with higher levels of education, for example, are more likely to report moving to their current neighborhood for the school system (Wirt et al., 2004). School choice programs provide more educational options to parents blocked from exercising "choice through mortgage" by resource constraints or practices of racial exclusion.

School choice advocates point to the Milwaukee public voucher experiment and four private school voucher experiments in New York City, Washington, D.C., Charlotte, and Dayton (all of which employed random assignment research designs) as the best evidence on the promise of choice to reform education policy in the United States. Evidence from these studies is highly contested due to the threat vouchers present to the cherished American notion of the public and community based, common school. An initial study of the Milwaukee experiment by the state's own evaluator claimed that there was no consistent positive effect of using a voucher on educational outcomes (Witte, 2000). A group of scholars analyzed the voucher study data with a different comparison group and claimed to find consistently positive results for voucher children (Green et al., 1997). Another scholar analyzed the same data a third time and found effects for math achievement, but not in reading (Rouse, 1998). Studies of private voucher programs in five other cities are similarly contested, with scholars reporting modest effects for low income black males in a few grade levels (Gill, 2001). In a reanalysis of a private voucher experiment in New York City, Krueger & Zhu (2004) found that claims of test score gains to black students were not statistically significant when students with missing baseline scores were included in the analysis and when both mother's and father's race were taken into account when coding student's race.

In summary, school- and program-level studies offer no resounding endorsement of school choice. Treatment effects across studies are mixed, with some students in some grades and on some outcomes showing positive results, while students in other grades and on other outcomes showing null results. Studies on particular schools or programs provide what economists call "partial equilibrium" results. In other words, they tell us about the intention-to-treat effect or the average effect on the treated, but not about the effect on an entire district from school choice. To examine the general equilibrium effect of choice on student outcomes, one must expand the level of analysis from the school/program level to the district level.

The Competition Hypothesis

School choice advocates argue that school choice, by promoting competition, could transform low-performing school districts, thereby reducing inequality between poor and non-poor districts. In other words, by expanding school choice in areas, such as central cities, where access to high quality schools is severely constrained and residential mobility options are also constrained, average achievement in such areas would increase to levels approaching areas, such as affluent suburbs, where affluent middle class residents have chosen to live in part because of the quality of the schools.

If school choice produces benefits from competition, the concern that students left behind in low performing schools would be harmed by the exodus of highly motivated students abandoning their assigned schools becomes less salient. In what might be called the "competition hypothesis," advocates argue that choice might be the "tide that lifts all boats" (Hoxby, 2003). Competition can emerge from three sources: choice between private and public schools (sectoral choice), choice between public school districts (Tiebout, or interdistrict choice), or choice among public schools in the same district (intradistrict choice) (Belfield & Levin, 2002). Educational productivity has been defined as "achievement per dollar spent, controlling for incoming achievement differences of its students" (Hoxby, 2003, 287). Therefore, this hypothesis predicts that in areas with larger private school sectors, public schools would be forced to improve for fear of losing enrollment to private schools. Similarly, in areas with more extensive public school choice programs, or in areas where it is easier to move between school districts, school productivity would be higher because the consequence of under-performance would be lost enrollment.

There is some empirical support for the competition hypothesis. A meta-analysis of peer-reviewed studies testing the competition hypothesis found that a majority of studies report that increased competition positively predicts test scores and graduation rates, while at the same time increasing teacher salaries and decreasing student-teacher ratios (Belfield & Levin, 2002). This review also notes that the effect of competition on school spending is mixed. For example, a study of the effect of private school competition on public school performance and spending finds that public school students in states with larger private school sectors tended to have higher test scores than those with smaller private school sectors (Arum, 1996). This author uses resource dependency theory (Pfeffer & Salancik, 1978) to argue that the improved performance of students in states with more private school competition is due not to increased efficiency, but to higher public funding spurred by the threat of competition from the private sector.

A contrasting view is offered by a study of the competition engendered by interdistrict public school choice. Hoxby (2000) uses an instrumental variables approach to estimate the effect of public school competition on student outcomes and productivity net of the selection effects of parents of high achieving children selecting into more productive school districts. This study finds that metropolitan areas with more public school competition (which in this case is operationalized as the number of school districts in the area), tend to beget higher test scores and *lower* spending, thus producing higher productivity.[6] Positive results from competition have also been shown by Hoxby (2003) schools in Milwaukee facing voucher threats and in Arizona and Michigan among schools facing charter school threats.

Perhaps the ideal research design for studying the impact of school choice on student outcomes is to conduct an experiment. This would involve randomly assigning districts (in the simplest case) to two treatment conditions: 1) school choice, and 2) no school choice and tracking student outcome differences between treated and control districts. Assuming adequate samples of treatment and control districts, compliance with treatment condition, and fidelity of implementation, it is at least theoretically possible to estimate a district-level causal effect of school choice based on average student outcomes. Due to the political and logistical complexities of conducting an experiment on such a broad scale, a more feasible design would be to exploit the natural experiment of policy variation across districts. One would take one or more districts, each of which implemented a comparable form of school choice at roughly the same time. Student outcomes would be measured before and after the imposition of the school choice policy of interest. A subsample of control districts would provide a comparative baseline to interpret any changes in student outcomes. Because school choice policies and comparable before and after measures vary a great deal across districts, however, such studies have been difficult to design.

In sum, the policy context in which the NCLB choice provisions were proposed and debated was informed by an ideological commitment to two ideas, both backed up with some evidence, that promoting school choice would both enhance educational opportunities for low-income students and promote competition in a sector that was perceived to be under-performing.

While school choice advocates place faith in the market to generate overall benefits, school choice critics argue that relying on market incentives to deliver educational services will worsen inequities in an already stratified school system. The family's role in school selection is central due to the decentralized nature of the U.S. educational system. Middle-class parents jockey for positions in early childhood programs, schedule every spare minute of the child's day with extracurricular activities, and advocate on behalf of their children for favorable course and school placements (Lareau, 2002). Educational transition points—such as those between kindergarten and primary school and between primary and secondary school—are times when the family's role in reproducing class become particularly salient (Baker & Stevenson, 1986). Research has found, for example, that parents who exert a high degree of control over the management of their children's educational careers are more likely to successfully place them in nonneighborhood schools and keep them there once enrolled (Wells & Crain, 1997). Therefore, school choice critics focus on the role race and class play in the causes of school selections and potential consequences of school choice programs.

The Stratification Hypothesis

Though school choice programs are targeted at low-income students, research shows that this is precisely the population that is hardest to serve by school choice. In what might be called the "stratification critique," this perspective holds that marketization will compound racial and class inequality by failing to compensate for the inability of disadvantaged families to negotiate the school choice process. A relatively consistent finding in school choice research is that the most disadvantaged families seem to be less likely to exercise school choice. For example, one study found that lower income and minority parents are less aware of magnet programs (Henig, 1995). Another found that among low-income parents, those with higher education levels are more likely to exercise school choice for their children (Lee et al., 1996). A third study found that higher SES and white parents are more likely to exercise school choice (Teske & Schneider, 2001).

One reason disadvantaged families may be less likely to exercise school choice is that minority and low income parents may have less access to useful information about schools through their social networks (ibid.). More advantaged parents, on the other hand, are embedded in social networks which provide knowledge more relevant to choosing schools (Archbald, 2000) and about objective measures of school quality (Schneider et al. 1998). Another reason the disadvantaged may be less likely to attend nonneighborhood schools may be that middle class white parents, by virtue of their cultural capital, face an advantage when negotiating educational bureaucracies and in relating to teachers (Lareau, 1989).

Researchers have also questioned whether parents choose schools based on school quality or on racial/ethnic composition (Wells & Crain, 1997; Saporito, 2003; Saporito & Lareau, 1999; Glazerman, 1998).

Most studies rely on inferences drawn from the end result of a choice process, such as those provided by an intra- or interdistrict choice program. Studies of "revealed preferences" do not necessarily prove that racial preferences are driving ethnic separation since they do not directly measure preferences, but rather are the end result of a complex social process. Ideally we want to study the same-race and different-race preferences of families, something hard to measure due to the (now) widespread unacceptability of racist views. One study has attempted to directly measure preferences. By examining the online search patterns of parents interested in schools of choice in the District of Columbia, this study found that characteristics of the student body were among the most frequently searched attributes of schools (Schneider & Buckley, 2002), a finding that supports the results in revealed preference studies. Such studies call into question a central claim of school choice advocates. If parents define school quality purely in terms of poverty rates and racial composition, then schools face no incentive to improve since they are not being held accountable by parents for academic performance.

The possibility that school choice reforms would worsen segregation is a concern because since the civil rights era, federal policy has sought to mitigate between-school racial segregation. The implication of this line of research is that school choice programs must be carefully designed and regulated to avoid worsening segregation. This is particularly critical because studies have found that unrestricted choice programs worsen between-school segregation by racial/ethnic and class background (Fiske & Ladd, 2000). In the United States, there is some evidence suggesting that charter schools, which face much lower levels of government oversight, may contribute, rather than mitigate between-school segregation. A study found that Arizona's charter schools are more racially homogeneous than nearby schools (Cobb & Glass, 1999).[7] A nationwide study finds that in more integrated districts, charter schools tend to enroll higher proportions of white students, thereby worsening between-school segregation in otherwise relatively integrated districts (Renzulli & Evans, 2005). On the other hand, scholars have found that the U.K.'s country-wide choice program, in which students may attend any public school in the country, has contributed to social class integration (Gorard & Fitz, 2000; Gorard, 2000).

In sum, while research shows that school choice presents some promise as an educational reform effort, policymakers must contend with class disparities in uptake, and the potential that the effort to improve schools through choice and competition may worsen segregation. Keeping in mind the literature about how choice policy should be designed, I now turn to how it has been actually implemented by states and local school districts.

NCLB Choice Implementation

I begin my discussion of NCLB choice implementation by first providing a nation-wide overview of the difficulties school districts have had with implementing the transfer provisions of the Act. Following this, I describe in some detail what is known about Chicago's implementation of the transfer provisions. To place Chicago's compliance with federal mandates into perspective, I draw on research I conducted on the history and current operation of school choice programs in Chicago (Lauen, 2006).

Nationwide Overview

The NCLB transfer provisions have been called among the hardest provisions in the Act for local school districts to implement (Casserly, 2004). They require districts to identify schools that have failed to make AYP for two consecutive years, identify schools that are both eligible to accept transfers under the Act and have the space available for student transfers, notify parents of their eligibility for a school choice transfer, set up a selection process to assign students to schools in the event that more students apply for transfers than can be accommodated, and provide transportation for transferring students. In some districts, this process is relatively straightforward and involves very few students. Three cities in Texas, for example, Houston, Dallas, and Austin, had no schools that were in "school improvement" status in 2003–04,[8] so these districts did not have to create a transfer process. Philadelphia, on the other hand, had 74% of the schools in improvement status, and was forced by NCLB to set up an elaborate transfer program (ibid).

Nationwide, about 1% of eligible students in both the 2003–04 and 2004–05 school years actually switched schools through NCLB choice (Center for Education Policy, 2005; United States Government Accountability Office, 2004). About 15% of school districts had schools designated to offer NCLB transfers in 2004–05, and large urban districts tended to have more schools facing this sanction (Center for Education Policy, 2005). In large urban districts, NCLB transfers have been a small, but rising, percentage of the overall student population. Based on a survey of the 50 largest urban districts in 2003–04, 44,373, or 3.8%, of eligible students requested a NCLB transfer (Casserly, 2004). Of these requests, 17,879, or 40.3%, were granted. For comparison purposes, the number of NCLB transfer requests granted by these large urban districts in 2002-03 was 5,661 (ibid).

According to a survey of state and school district officials, finding enough space in schools meeting AYP to satisfy requests, identifying eligible families in a timely manner, and communicating with parents were the most challenging barriers to implementing the choice provisions (Center for Education Policy, 2005). Capacity constraints were particularly severe in some rural districts with only one school and in overcrowded urban districts and large proportions of schools in improvement status. Interdistrict choice is a potential solution to this problem, but virtually no districts have been willing or able to create cross-district agreements to allow interdistrict NCLB transfers (Brown, 2004).

Notifying families of their options in a timely manner has been a particular challenge due to testing, data cleaning, and reporting schedules. Given the high stakes attached to testing results, the complex NCLB achievement and testing participation criteria for each subgroup, and recent scandals involving mistakes in test scoring (see, for example, Duchesne (2000)), states must carefully scrutinize student, subgroup, and school test scores to ensure accuracy. While NCLB has increased the demand for accuracy, there has been a concurrent demand for results to be processed more rapidly. To ensure that testing results reflect what students have learned in a school year, students are typically tested as late in the spring as possible. Providing adequate notification to families eligible for NCLB transfers, however, requires results to be processed in a matter of months, before the next school year. This presents problems for most school districts. According to a survey of large urban districts, no district had testing results processed by the end of the 2002-03 school year, and more than half did not have results by the beginning of the next school year (Casserly, 2004).

Lack of adequate notification is one barrier that contributes to the broader challenge of parent participation in the NCLB transfer program. While NCLB is designed to serve disadvantaged families, it is precisely these families that are the least likely to know whether they are eligible for a transfer. A survey in Massachusetts found that most parents whose children qualify for an NCLB transfer do not know whether their child's school is in improvement status and is thus required to offer their child a transfer. Specifically, only one in four parents of eligible children correctly identified the improvement status of their school (Howell, 2004).

Evidence suggests that uptake for NCLB transfers has been low because parents have strong commitments to local schools and may be getting conflicting signals from the overlapping federal, state, and district accountability regimes. Opinion surveys consistently indicate that public school parents think highly of the schools their children attend, but not highly of schools in general. For example, in 2004 more than two-thirds of public school parents gave the school their oldest child attends a grade of "A" or a "B." Less than one-quarter of public school parents, however, gave public schools in the nation as a whole a grade of "A" or "B" (Rose & Gallup, 2004). This suggests that parents might be willing to support efforts like those called for in NCLB to reform schools in general, but may resist efforts to punish or reform their own child's school. Despite high levels of parent satisfaction among those whose children attend schools of choice (Gill, 2001, 128–37), most parents prefer reforming the existing school system to creating expanding school choice. Poll figures suggest that even if their child's school was in NCLB improvement status, only a small minority of parents would opt to exercise school choice. The vast majority (85%) of parents preferred that instead of choice, additional efforts should be made to improve their neighborhood school (ibid).[9]

Some evidence also suggests that parents do not believe the alternatives to their home school are markedly better. In some cases, this is understandable because state and federal quality designations sometimes vary. In some cases, states may recognize a school as being a school of excellence, but because of the under-performance of one subgroup, or because of the test participation rate of a particular subgroup, the school may miss AYP standards. In other cases, it may be that districts identify schools as NCLB transfer options that are only marginally better than the sending schools themselves.

Scholars have questioned the effectiveness of relying on an accountability program that can lead to an overly broad definition of school failure. In other words, if large majorities of schools are deemed to be "failures" by NCLB rules, then the stigmatizing effect of the label may be limited. If, however, only a small proportion of schools are deemed as failing to meet a more relaxed set of standards, then arguably the stigmatizing effect would be more likely to lead to productivity improvements. For example, in 2003 75% of Florida's elementary schools were deemed as failing to meet AYP, whereas only 10% of schools in 2002 received failing marks under the state's A++ accountability plan (which, as noted above, offered vouchers to students in failing schools) (West & Peterson, 2006). A study of Florida's A++ program found that schools facing, or at risk of facing, the voucher threat produced positive impacts on school performance; schools at risk of facing sanctions through NCLB, however, did not produce similar effects (ibid). This provides some evidence supporting the hypothesis that targeted sanctions work better than overly broad ones. Further study is needed to determine the extent to which 1) the proportion of schools facing a sanction, 2) the type of choice offered (public versus private), or 3) the extent of state and local commitment to providing teeth to negative sanctions through policy implementation are the most effective at bringing about school improvement through stigmatization and negative sanctions.

In summary, the low NCLB transfer rates stem from several sources: 1) capacity constraints, 2) the logistical hurdles inherent in meeting both annual testing and notification requirements, 3) strong commitment to local schools, 4) race and class disparities in access to information about school quality and 5) the fact that federal and state accountability regimes send conflicting signals about the quality of local schools. To provide more institutional detail and a sense of how policy implementation can evolve over time, I now turn to a more in-depth examination of one case.

Chicago Case Study

Chicago is a highly segregated city with a predominantly low income and minority student population. Its schools were once decried by William Bennett (former Secretary of Education under President Reagan) as the "worst in the nation" (Johnson, 1987). While some strides have been made to reform schools and improve student achievement, large numbers of the city's schools remain on academic probation and are deemed under-performing by local and federal standards. The District is currently identified by NCLB as being in "improvement" status for failing to meet goals in math.

Chicago has a large intra-district high school choice program in which public or private school choice is the norm. About half of secondary students exercise public school choice and almost one-fifth attend private high school (see Figure 25.1). Public alternatives include career academies, selective enrollment college preparatory high schools, magnet schools and programs, charter schools, and military academies; private alternatives are predominantly Catholic schools. Only about one-third of secondary students in Chicago attend an assigned public school. The district also runs a liberal open enrollment transfer program which allows high school students to attend any high school in the district on a space-available basis.

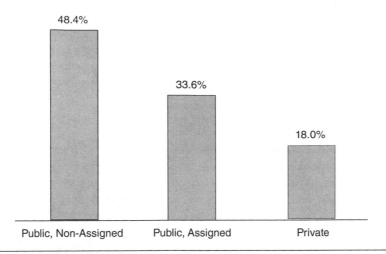

Figure 25.1 Chicago Secondary School Enrollment, by School Type, 2000. *Note*: Data on private school enrollment is from author calculations of 2000 IPUMS data. Data on nonneighborhood public school enrollment is from author calculations of CPS administrative data.

The Emergence of School Choice from Desegregation Chicago's history with school choice began as a response to the problem of school segregation. Though Chicago formally desegregated its school system in 1874, due to real estate practices, public housing policy that situated projects in black neighborhoods, and a neighborhood schools policy, Chicago's schools were segregated de facto (Hess, 1984). Despite calls for action from community groups, policy recommendations in reports by academic experts, student boycotts, and the constant threats of federal civil rights enforcement, the Chicago school board refused to implement any substantial school desegregation policy between 1960 and 1980 (Peterson, 1976). Unlike in the South, where national guard troops escorted black students through the hallways of Little Rock high school, the federal role in enforcing civil rights in Chicago was minimal. After passage of the Civil Rights Act in 1964, Chicago became an early test case in enforcement of the act's provisions. When the Office of Education withheld federal education funds from Chicago due to the board's inaction on school integration, Mayor Daley complained to President Johnson, who quickly intervened on Chicago's behalf. The funds were quickly released (Peterson, 1976; Hess, 1984). Johnson's intervention set a precedent. At least in key Democratic strongholds like Chicago and other northern cities, the federal role in enforcement would be an empty threat until 1980, the turning point for both the history of desegregation and school choice in Chicago.

To avoid a federal lawsuit, in 1980 the District negotiated a consent decree with the U.S. Department of Justice to create a voluntary transfer program called "Options for Knowledge" to entice students away from segregated schools. Creating and maintaining integrated schools was a central goal of this program, so transfer requests were evaluated to determine the impact of a student transfer on the racial composition of the sending and receiving schools. Applications to schools under this program were sorted by grade, race, and gender. Students were chosen by lottery if schools or programs were oversubscribed. The plan established a standard to guide student reassignment and transfers: if a school was more than 70% of one race or ethnicity, then it was considered segregated and was subject to student reassignment policies including boundary changes and racial/ethnic quotas on incoming student transfers. Therefore, what emerged in Chicago was a program that sought to expand school choice, while also regulating schools' racial mix.

Mayoral Takeover and a Turn Towards Selectivity During the mid to late 1990s, Mayor Richard M. Daley, Jr. used authority granted to him by a school reform law in 1995 to close chronically under-performing schools and open new schools.[10] In Chicago and other cities during the 1990s, professional discretion and union control gave way to a business-led movement to give authority to big city mayors who then hired technocrats, businessmen, and military leaders to run schools. The reform act was passed by a Republican legislature and informed by extensive input from the Chicago United and the Civic Committee of the Commercial Club, both influential Chicago-based business organizations (Klonsky, 1995). The mayor, and Paul Vallas, the mayor's former budget director (who was himself not a professional educator) tightened accountability for both students and schools. They put an end to social promotion, the practice of promoting students from one grade to the next whether or not students performed at grade level on standardized tests. In 1997, for example, 11,000 students were retained in the 3rd, 6th, and 8th grades due to poor performance on standardized tests in reading and math (Roderick et al., 1999). Vallas also used his expanded authority to use standardized test scores as a basis for evaluating schools and closing them for chronic under-performance.

Neighborhood schools, which had not fared well under the "Options for Knowledge" program, were further stigmatized by rising academic standards. One study found that schools on probation for low test score performance lost the highest proportion of their attendance area student enrollment to schools of choice (Duffrin, 2001). As neighborhood high schools gained poor reputations, families with the information and ability to negotiate the school choice process (or pay for private schooling) sent their children elsewhere. Those students who had fewer options or special needs became disproportionately represented in neighborhood high schools. In South Shore High School, once a school with a good reputation in an integrated middle class neighborhood, for example, a reporter found that a typical classroom of 28 students had 10-12 students with learning disabilities or behavior disorders (ibid).

Given the poor reputation of many neighborhood schools in Chicago, the Daley regime sought to close dysfunctional schools, open new schools in their place, and build new school buildings. Between 1995 and 2004, 22 schools were closed and 53 schools opened. Of those that opened, only 16 had attendance areas, and 37 were schools of choice such as charters, magnets, and selective enrollment high schools. One objective in creating these new schools was to change the image of the Chicago Public Schools from one of fraud, mismanagement, and failure to one of performance and innovation. Daley and Vallas sought to keep more middle class families in the city and attract students from the private sector to the district's selective enrollment schools and programs. The administration built eight new selective enrollment high schools, expanded International Baccalaureate programs (a selective high school program leading to a high school diploma set to worldwide standard), and created Math/Science/Technology academies in schools with large outflows of attendance area students. In addition, the school district created fee-based preschool programs and neighborhood set-asides in gentrifying neighborhoods in an effort to entice young professionals to consider sending their children to the public schools.[11]

Features of the Existing System Several features of Chicago's existing school choice regime are worth noting before exploring the District's implementation of the NCLB transfer provisions. At least in part because most high schools have an application process to admit some or all of their students, students with social and academic advantages are more likely to participate in public school choice programs in Chicago. Students with higher prior achievement, and students with parents who had successfully negotiated the elementary school choice process, are more likely to attend a private or public alternative to their assigned public high school (Figure 25.2). Poor students (measured by whether the student was eligible for a free or reduced priced lunch), on the other hand, are less likely to exercise private or public high school choice.[12]

There is also evidence that, consistent with prior research (Schneider & Buckley, 2002; Saporito & Lareau, 1999; Glazerman, 1998), parents in Chicago choose schools based on race. Net of assigned

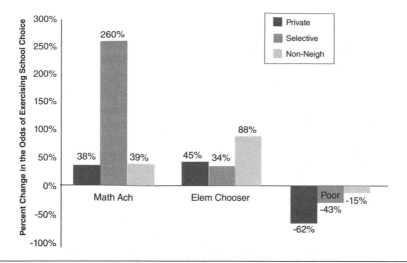

Figure 25.2 Effect of Measures of Student Social and Academic Status on High School Choice, 2000. Source: Lauen (2006). 2000–2001 Chicago Public Schools Administrative Data. 9th grade destinations of 8th Grade Public School Students Only. Effects shown control for gender, race/ethnicity, special education status, age, number of previous school moves, and measures of elementary school context.

high school average achievement, non-black families tend to avoid neighborhood high schools with high percentages of black students (Figure 25.3). This suggests that high minority schools, no matter how productive, may be at a disadvantage in Chicago's system of school choice.

Ideally, we would like to be able to separate parent racial and class preferences from their preferences for high performing schools. It could be that parents assume that schools serving disadvantaged student populations are of low quality. The evidence from Chicago is that parents prefer high schools with high compositional quality, defined as a composite of aggregate achievement, safety, mobility,

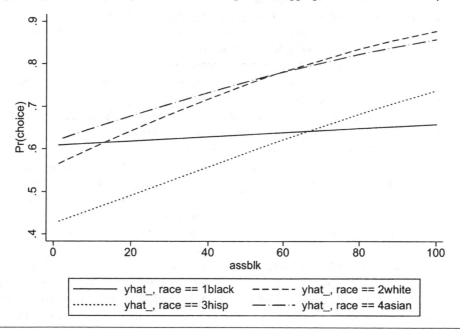

Figure 25.3 Effect of Percentage Black Students on Propensity to Exercise School Choice, by Race/Ethnicity, 2000. Source: Lauen (2006). 2000–2001 Chicago Public Schools Administrative Data. Eighth Grade Public School Students Only. Effects shown control for student-level covariates such as prior achievement, poverty, and race-ethnicity, and neighborhood high school average achievement.

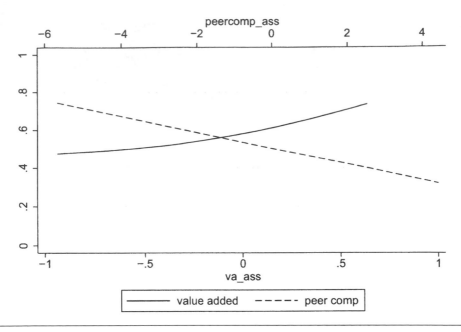

Figure 25.4 Effect of Assigned School Peer Composition and Productivity on Propensity to Exercise School Choice, by Poverty Level, 2000. Source: Lauen (2006). 2000–2001 Chicago Public Schools Administrative Data. Eighth Grade Public School Students Only. Effects shown control for student-level covariates such as prior achievement, poverty, and race-ethnicity. Peer composition is a principal components measure of assigned high school characteristics such as percent poor, mobility rate, and average achievement. Productivity is defined as the average residual 8th to 9th grade test score gain, controlling for student background and elementary school quality.

poverty, motivation, and attainment measures. (These school-level measures are all highly correlated.) The evidence also suggests, however, that parents are also likely to avoid enrolling their children in highly productive assigned high schools. This could be because parents are unaware that, controlling for student background, prior educational experiences, and elementary school quality, disadvantaged high schools in Chicago tend to produce higher 8th to 9th grade test score gains.[13] Figure 25.4 displays the opposite effects of compositional quality and productivity.

In summary, Chicago's existing system of school choice emerged from school desegregation. At first, policymakers focused on expanding educational opportunities for black students in segregated schools. After a mayoral takeover of the school system in the mid-1990s, however, the focus of school choice policy shifted somewhat to expand educational opportunities for high achieving students. By the year 2000, choice of high school in Chicago was designed as a "winner-take-all" system, with high achieving students receiving a disproportionate share of the benefits of school choice (Lauen, 2006). There is evidence to support the hypothesis that parents are sensitive to school quality differences; unfortunately, whether due to lack of access to school quality information or due to assumptions that schools serving disadvantaged students are of low quality, families seem to be avoiding schools with relatively high productivity levels.

Chicago and NCLB Choice Elected and appointed officials have been openly critical of NCLB and the transfer provisions. Mayor Daley has been quoted as arguing that NCLB should have given schools more time to improve before they were subject to the transfer threat: "it's 'ridiculous' to think schools can improve 'overnight.' ... 'Many of the schools are not performing. Everybody knows that,' Daley said. 'We know it. Where are you going to go? To another nonperforming school? You can't.'" (Rossi & Spielman, 2002). Arne Duncan, the CEO of the Chicago Public School system (CPS), has expressed doubt that NCLB would improve student learning and was "burdensome ...complex and impractical" (Rossi, 2003b).

The U.S. Department of Education official responsible for overseeing the transfer provisions of NCLB, Nina Reece, said, "Based on every single news report and discussion we've had with the city of Chicago, we feel, when it comes to choice, they are not looking at creative ways to extend capacity and meet the needs of students in low-performing schools" (Rossi, 2003a). Two options for complying with federal mandates include providing trailers for students on the grounds of schools making AYP and creating inter-district agreements for transfers across district lines. Duncan has been quoted as saying that CPS has no funds to purchase trailers and that he hasn't asked neighboring districts to accept CPS transfers because, "I don't think yellow school buses from Chicago would be well-received" (ibid.).

From these exchanges in the newspapers, it seems fair to characterize the attitude of important elected and appointed officials as being hostile to the transfer provisions of NCLB. This is perhaps understandable given that the federal share of funding is low, federal requirements under NCLB are extensive, and that NCLB labels large portions of Chicago's schools as in need of improvement, a problem that policymakers had been attempting to address in various ways for at least the past 10–15 years.

According to data provided by the Illinois State School Board, in the 2003–04 school year, three-quarters of elementary schools and 90% of high schools failed to make AYP. In subsequent years, the proportion of elementary schools failing to make AYP fell to two-thirds; the high school proportion fell and then increased to 94% (Table 25.1). By the 2005–06 school year, 64% of elementary school students and 94% of high school students attended schools that failed to make AYP according to federal guidelines. Approximately 256,000 students were eligible by federal regulation to transfer to a school making AYP in 2005–06.[14] In a district with approximately 436,000 students enrolled in the fall of 2005 eligible for a transfer under NCLB, it is clear that CPS faces implementation problems; short of shutting down all schools that missed AYP, it is impossible for the district to find spaces for all students eligible for an NCLB transfer under federal guidelines.

For 2003–04, the first year of NCLB choice implementation, CPS determined that 1,100 spaces would be made available by lottery to eligible students, which for this year was determined to be 270,000 students. Approximately 19,000 students entered the lottery. Lottery winners were given

Table 25.1 Selected NCLB Statistics, Chicago, 2003-2006.

	School Year		
	03-04	**04-05**	**05-06**
Panel A, Federal Definitions			
Elementary			
% of Schools that Failed AYP	75%	65%	64%
% of Students in Schools that Failed AYP	80%	70%	64%
High School			
% of Schools that Failed AYP	90%	84%	92%
% of Students in Schools that Failed AYP	90%	84%	94%
Panel B, Chicago Implementation of NCLB Transfers			
Eligible students (As Defined by CPS)	270,757	2,500	1,100
Applications	19,246	5,933	267
Spaces Made Available	1,100	440	550

Source: Percent of schools failing AYP from author calculations of data provided by the Illinois State Board of Education. Chicago implementation of choice transfer policy from newspaper reports, e-mail communication with CPS officials, and Center on Education policy reports (Center for Education Policy, 2005, 2006).

one day to decide whether to accept a choice seat (Rossi, 2003b). For the 2004–05 school year, CPS changed eligibility rules and determined that about 2,500 students were eligible for 440 slots. About 5,933 students applied for these slots (Center for Education Policy, 2006). It is clear that the decline in the number of students eligible for a choice transfer was due not to a large decline in the number of schools subject to the choice sanction, to a redefinition of eligibility by local officials. In 2005-06, the definition of eligibility was further restricted to students in three schools that both missed AYP and had been identified for closure under CPS' accountability regime. 550 slots were made available to students in these three schools, but only 267 students applied for an NCLB transfer to one of 20 schools that were making AYP.[15] This left more than 800 students who chose to attend schools in neighborhood adjacent to their old schools, none of which were making AYP (Grossman, 2005). The number of students applying for NCLB transfers has been falling (Table 25.1). No high school students were given opportunity to exercise NCLB choice during the 2004–05 and 2005–06 school years.

In addition to capacity constraints, CPS has had difficulty identifying schools that were significantly better than those subject to the choice sanction. Students in Chicago could only choose from schools that had, on average, very high poverty levels. The average proficiency level of the receiving schools in Chicago, while generally higher than the sending schools, was significantly below the average proficiency level of the pool of potential receiving schools (Kim & Sunderman, 2004). Of the 11 schools slated to be receiving schools of students affected by school closures in the spring of 2002, however, six were identified as needing improvement and eligible for choice in the fall of 2002 (Rossi & Spielman, 2002). In some cases, receiving schools had worse test scores than some of the sending schools (Rossi, 2003b). In at least one case, this was the case because the receiving school had not been in existence long enough to be subject to the choice sanction.

Illinois state law prevents local school districts from complying with some federal mandates. Though federal regulations state that local school districts must allow NCLB transfers even to overcrowded schools, Illinois state law forbids such an action. State law also prevents NCLB transfer students from taking precedence in admissions to academically selective schools (Center for Education Policy, 2006).

In summary, Chicago is a large and diverse urban school system that has been struggling for many years to improve student learning. NCLB choice is but a small portion of the choice transfers that exist in a district in which 30% of elementary school students and 60% of public school students attend a public school of choice. Despite the fact that NCLB was perhaps designed with school districts like Chicago in mind, the ability of federal officials to force compliance with the laws dictates has been limited. For four years local officials have been largely free to craft policies that severely constrain the number of NCLB transfer slots and limit the pool of eligible students that has little, if any, resemblance to federal regulations.

Implications for Reauthorization

Rather than encouraging the rise of new school forms that could expand educational opportunity, the NCLB transfer provisions are a blunt system of negative sanctions. Without careful attention to mid-course modifications informed by additional research in exactly how school choice leads to benefits to students, NCLB choice is likely to hold an empty promise to American school children.

To be most effective, school choice policy must encourage innovation, reform, and productivity while also promoting (or at least not harming) social cohesion, accountability, and equity (National Working Commission on Choice in K-12 Education, 2003; Levin, 2004). Policy aimed at promoting a diverse array of educational options must, therefore, regulate enough to maintain social cohesion and ensure that public dollars are being put to productive use, but not so much that schools cannot innovate, take risks, and reach populations aligned with their mission. If enough new (or reconstituted) schools enter the market, policy must also create a level playing field to foster competition between new entrants and existing schools (National Working Commission on Choice in K-12 Education, 2003). This involves providing both new and old schools adequate and equitable funding, budgetary control, and the flexibility to hire and fire teachers aligned with reform objectives. The goal of policy would be to allow teachers and families to focus on a shared mission and the technical core of education—teaching and learning—while also fostering competition among educational providers and ensuring quality standards.

In short, the state must use its powers at the federal, state, and local levels to ensure innovation and competition in education while also holding schools accountable, promoting social cohesion, and protecting the rights of students to gain access to equal access to educational opportunity. Some of these powers include maintaining an adequate and equitable flow of funding to schools, providing or paying for transportation to schools outside of a student's neighborhood, providing extra funds to schools with harder to serve student populations, funding parent information centers and social marketing campaigns to facilitate an efficient and equitable school-to-parent matching process, promoting a mix of schools with a variety of selectivity criteria and lotteries for student admission, holding schools accountable for their "value added" (the achievement gain for the students who remain in the school long enough to produce a treatment effect), widely disseminating the performance measurement results, and closing schools with persistent failure records or records of financial malfeasance.

It would be hard to conclude from the early phase of NCLB choice that the policy as currently implemented is living up to the rhetoric of "liberation" used by the framers of the act. The choice provisions are difficult for many, if not most, districts to implement, give struggling schools only one year to improve before facing sanctions, and penalize too many schools for the sanction to be effective. The vast majority of students who desire a school transfer are not being allowed one. Testing schedules, capacity constraints, the large variation in state standards, and the high between-district variation in access to high quality alternatives represent substantial barriers to the prospect of NCLB transfers actually improving the plight of students in low-performing, high-poverty schools.

Absent significant changes in the implementation of the transfer provisions, and perhaps regulatory and legislative action, NCLB choice will probably have very little effect on educational reform. Because local school districts have a great deal of latitude in designing transfer programs, those districts that want to use the negative sanction will have legislative cover to do so and those that do not will be able to design programs that render the negative sanction impotent. Until state and local officials see evidence that negative sanctions work and that school choice is directly related to educational achievement, state and local resistance is also likely to remain strong.

The implementation difficulties of the NCLB school choice provisions likely stem from several sources. First, school choice is a flash-point issue in American educational policy. It threatens the interests of powerful actors in the educational system, such as teacher unions and school boards. There is ample evidence that the NCLB transfer provisions have been resisted by powerful local actors. Second, school choice threatens the cherished notion of the common school ideal. NCLB school choice may have had such a limited impact because of strong parental loyalty to neighborhood schools. Third, the potential costs and benefits of school choice are poorly understood. As a consequence, it is not clear what system of regulation and incentives should be employed to achieve the appropriate balance of educational equity and efficiency. This suggests that the NCLB transfer policy has been ineffective simply because it was poorly conceived and implemented. Finally, it could be that the federal role in education policy is too limited to present a credible threat to local entities that ignore legal mandates. Further research is needed to test the tenability of these propositions.

NCLB dramatically alters the balance of governmental authority in education, away from local control and toward state and federal control. While it fails to set national standards and test these standards with a national test, it provides a common set of negative sanctions. Based on local and state resistance to NCLB, the limits of this expanded federal role are being severely tested. The fact that the federal share of education spending was 8% in 2003 indicates that the federal role is limited. Furthermore, because this federal share varies across states (from 4% to 18%), the leverage federal power can exert over education at the local level may also vary.[16]

A good indication of the limits of federal power in education, and a substantial limitation of the NCLB Act, is the inability of the federal government to set national standards and hold states accountable to these standards with a national test. The wide fluctuation of standards across the states results in the problem that cities with high proportions of schools in need of improvement are not necessarily those cities with the lowest NAEP scores (Casserly, 2004).[17] Therefore, while NCLB is informed by the "liberation" hypothesis, in which students are to be freed from failed schools, the federal government cannot ensure the quality of standards across states, much less the quality of particular schools slated by local districts to accept NCLB transfers. To ensure comparability of educational opportunity across states, federal policymakers should carefully scrutinize state standards. As it stands now, the easiest way to ensure that maximum number of schools in a state meets AYP is to water down state academic standards and tests.

This suggests that the ability of federal authority to enforce compliance is sharply limited. Compliance with NCLB offers a good case study of the difficulty of enforcing federal accountability provisions in a loosely coupled educational system (Meyer & Rowan, 1977). It is clear in Chicago at least that local officials are seeking to maintain the charade of minimal compliance with federal mandates to continue receiving federal funds.

There is some evidence that the Bush administration is using low transfer rates under NCLB as justification for a nationwide voucher program. Margaret Spellings, Secretary of the U.S. Department of Education, recently touted the Bush administrations $100 million "Opportunity Scholarship" program at a Christian school in New York:[18]

> In some districts, public school choice is non-existent because no public schools are meeting state standards and waiting lists for charter schools are out the door. I've heard stories about parents cramming into rooms like this one to draw numbers to see which students will make it off the waiting list. You shouldn't need to win the lottery to send your child to a high-performing school …More than 1,700 schools around the country have failed to meet state standards for five or six years in a row. And many of these schools are in districts where public school choice isn't a real option. We're proposing a new $100 million Opportunity Scholarship Fund to help thousands of low-income students in these schools attend the private school of their choice or receive intensive one-on-one tutoring after school or during the summer.

If passed by the Congress, the scholarship program would be offered to students in the restructuring phase of NCLB. The fact that private schools would become options could increase participation rates (Howell, 2004), but given the mixed results from voucher experiments and studies of private schools (Neal, 1997; Lubienski & Lubienski, 2006), substantially improved student outcomes are not likely. In addition, providing vouchers to private schools would raise the question of whether private schools funded in part by public funds should be subject to the same accountability framework as public schools. This is not likely to be something private schools would accept; without this, however, public and private schools would not be on an even playing field, and vouchers could lose support if funds were spent without appropriate evaluation and accountability.

Implications for Research

The research base about the NCLB transfer provision is surprisingly thin. For example, I am aware of no peer-reviewed studies that address the causal effect of receiving an NCLB transfer on educational outcomes. With reauthorization of NCLB slated for 2007, there is an urgent need for policy-relevant research addressing the effects of the NCLB transfer policy on students and schools. Researchers will no doubt be hampered by low participation rates in NCLB choice programs, though it may be possible to conduct studies in urban districts with relatively large transfer programs.

The liberation hypothesis predicts that those who exercise choice through an NCLB transfer would outperform students who remain in schools failing to meet AYP. Fortunately, the provisions of the Act itself provides an opportunity to exploit a research design to estimate causal effects. Specifically, because the act gives priority to low-achieving students, we may be able to employ a regression discontinuity design to examine treatment effects. This design examines the change in the slope of a treatment effect just below and just above a cutoff point. In this case, the cutoff point would be a point in a test score distribution. The logic of this approach is similar to a randomized design. While a student's test score is not as random as a flip of a coin, once we compare students just above and just below a cutoff, we can narrow our attention to a range of students whose score on a test may approximate a random difference that assigns students to two different treatment conditions. Of course, this research design may not be feasible in particular districts, It may be that the number of students transferring between two schools is too small to produce statistically significant results. If sample sizes are adequate and transfer slots are, in fact, distributed on the basis of student prior achievement, this research design provides a promising approach to estimating the causal effect of receiving an NCLB transfer opportunity.

A skeptical view of the NCLB choice sanction is that shuffling students among a number of dysfunctional urban schools will do more harm than good. The nightmare scenario goes like this: Once schools become stigmatized as nonimproving, families flee with or without an NCLB transfer and the school eventually closes. The mostly low-income students attend different schools in the same area. These new schools struggle to compensate for inadequate early childhood experiences and elementary school teaching and are soon themselves subject to sanctions, thereby encouraging yet more student mobility.

The competition hypothesis suggests that the threat of exit will force schools to do a better job serving students. If this hypothesis is correct, therefore, we could predict that rather than simply shuffling students from one school to the other, NCLB transfers could have a positive general equilibrium effect on student achievement. Thus, research could address whether, and under what conditions, the NCLB transfer provision forces school improvement through the negative sanction of being labeled as a school "in need of improvement" and by losing students under a transfer program. As shown by West and Peterson (2006), schools subject to an overly broad stigmatizing sanction may not force school improvement. It is possible, however, to test an alternative hypothesis. Specifically, that schools facing larger transfer outflows would improve more than those facing smaller transfer outflows. In other words, one might be able to design a "dose response" study to examine the effects of the NCLB transfer program where the treatment is a continuous variable—the proportion of the student body that exits the school with an NCLB transfer.

The stratification hypothesis predicts that school choice only worsens educational stratification and inequality in student outcomes. This perspective focuses attention on inequality in who benefits from choice and the social process through which education produces a stratified social order. With respect to NCLB choice in particular, research might address race and class disparities in who transfers under the act and what types of schools are made available to students wishing to transfer. While the act specifies that low achieving and poor students should get priority for transfers, it could be that few low achieving and poor students apply for transfers. The act specifies that overcrowding should not be used as an excuse to exclude students from higher quality schools; in practice it appears that in Chicago most students eligible for a transfer under NCLB are not able to attend schools with substantially lower poverty rates and substantially higher quality. Finally, the stratification hypothesis would predict that students who transfer under the act would not become integrated into the academic and social life of their receiving schools. Specifically that NCLB transfer students would be stigmatized outsiders, tracked into low ability classrooms, and, like refugees from New Orleans, part of a separate subculture.

In closing, a major methodological barrier to assessing school choice is identifying the mechanisms linking school choice with student outcomes. Any effects of school choice on student outcomes, like the effects of schools themselves, are necessarily indirect. "Choice is not a teacher, a classroom, or an instructional resource. If choice affects what students learn, it works indirectly, by leading to changes in what students experience, read, and hear" (National Working Commission on Choice in K-12 Education, 2003, 10). The effects of schooling work largely through teacher-student interaction and peer effects. To the extent that school choice can alter these processes to promote better academic achievement and attainment, it will only do so by altering what goes on in the classroom and the relationships between and among teachers and students. So the question then becomes, how does NCLB choice affect patterns of interaction among students and teachers? For example, we might expect that in schools with large outflows of students and strong professional communities, the choice sanction may spark critical dialogue about teaching practices, which could then, in turn, result in changes in teaching practices and improved student achievement. By contrast, in schools with weak professional communities, we might expect large outflows to prompt a worsening of ties between teachers.

Conclusion

NCLB represents a dramatic shift in federal education policy aimed at expanding equal access to educational opportunity for poor students. While the initial ESEA legislation focused on infusing federal funds into poor schools to address resource inequalities, NCLB focuses on the issue of school quality and whether poor children and those from traditionally under-served populations are learning what they need to know to succeed. The Act assumes that schools can spur complete proficiency in all students, including the disadvantaged and those with special educational needs. This, while it may be impossible without dramatic improvements in early childhood education system, parent participation, and anti-poverty programs, is a laudable goal.

Unfortunately, NCLB relies on blunt negative sanctions on low performing schools and must rely on local school districts to implement what is in many districts across the country an unworkable set of transfer policies. Schools are given only one year after being labeled as at-risk of facing the choice sanction to make changes in practice and improve student achievement in all the necessary subgroups. The elaborate formula used to define whether or not a school is meeting AYP labels so many schools as "in need of improvement" that the sanction becomes meaningless.

This chapter has summarized three primary hypotheses that inform a great deal of school choice research. For decades, scholars have debated the promises and perils to educational opportunity of expanding school choice policies. Scholars informed by the *liberation* hypothesis (Archbald, 2004), argue that school choice has the potential to free students from "failing" schools. Studies informed by the *competition* hypothesis claim that when parents are given greater latitude to choose alternatives to their neighborhood schools, school systems tend to become more competitive. On the other hand, sociologists of education have offered a *stratification* critique. Scholars from this tradition argue that schools choice tends to worsen inequality in an already stratified social system.

With the 2007 reauthorization of NCLB fast approaching, more research is urgently needed to test the tenability of these hypotheses with particular attention to whether and how NCLB choice promotes educational opportunity for those who transfer and encourages competition among schools. Research is also needed to determine the extent to which families offered a transfer receive the information and time to make an informed choice, receive opportunities to transfer to qualitatively better schools, and become integrated into the academic and social life of their receiving schools.

Notes

1. Quote is from a White House press conference transcript: http://www.whitehouse.gov/news/releases/2001/01/20010123-2.html, last accessed on May 26, 2006.
2. Many parents do, however, take school quality into consideration when determining where to live. National estimates suggest that about one-quarter of parents report moving to their current neighborhood for the schools (Wirt *et al.*, 2004).
3. Exceptions to this rule are made if there are too few students in a subgroup to provide statistically reliable results. The minimum subgroup size is determined by each state.
4. Schools that fail to meet AYP for three years in a row must allow students free after-school tutoring. Schools failing to make AYP for five years face school restructuring. School restructuring may include conversion to a charter school or contracting out to private management organizations.
5. Of course, if enough poor students enter a new school, it is possible that the receiving school could become eligible for Title I funds. This would then make the school subject to school choice transfer provisions, however.
6. It should be noted that the robustness of Hoxby's results have been called into question by Rothstein (2005). The instrumental variable in Hoxby's study is the number of streams of various lengths running through an area (areas with streams running through them tend to be broken into more jurisdictions, which creates an exogenous source of variation school district size). Rothstein finds that effect of choice on productivity is highly sensitive to how the lengths of streams is coded. See also Hoxby's response (2005).
7. Arizona has the highest concentration of charter schools in the country and is considered by charter school advocates to be a model for other states to follow.
8. "School improvement" status is the designation for schools that fail to make AYP in two consecutive years.
9. This 2001 Phi Delta Kappa poll found that 54% of parents oppose vouchers to choose private schools at public expense, while 42% favor them. There is some evidence, however, that those who favor vouchers care more about this issue than those who oppose it. When asked whether knowing that a candidate for a national office supports vouchers, 43%. said that this position would make supporting that candidate more likely, while only 37% said that this position would make supporting that candidate less likely (Rose & Gallup, 2004).
10. The mayoral takeover occurred just seven years after a radical decentralization reform plan passed the legislature in 1988.
11. Some analysis indicates that this policy has yet to bear fruit. In neighborhoods with the highest levels of gentrification, white enrollment in the school system has decreased rather than increased. As one observer noted, "Yuppies don't have kids, they have dogs" (Weissman, 2002).
12. Figures are from multilevel models that control for a number of student- and school-level models. See Lauen (2006, Chapter 5) for tables and more details.
13. School productivity is defined as the average student-level residual from the following OLS test score gain model: $9thGr\ Read_{ij} = \beta 0 + \beta 1\ (8thGr\ Road)_{ij} + \beta 2X_{ij} + \Sigma_{j=1}^{J-1} Ej\alpha j + e_{ij}$, where $9thGr\ Read_{ij}$ is the 9th grade reading test score (in grade-equivalent units) for student i who attended elementary school j in 8th grade; $8thGr\ Read_{ij}$ is the ith student's 8th grade reading test score (in grade-equivalent units); X_{ij} is a vector of student background characteristics such as poverty, gender, and race/ethnicity; $\Sigma_{j=1}^{J-1} Ej\alpha j$ is a vector of elementary school fixed effects to control for prior school quality differences; and e_{ij} is the student-specific error component of test score gain. High school k's value added measure. $\hat{V}_k$, is defined as the within-high-school average of the student-level residual: $\hat{V}_k = \frac{\Sigma e_{ik}}{N_k}$. This specification of the value added model was proposed by Cullen *et al.* (2005). Defining and measuring school productivity is a contentious area of educational policy; further research is needed to determine the validity of this particular specification of the productivity of Chicago's neighborhood high schools.
14. This figure is the result of author calculations based on data provided by the state. It is not shown in the table because comparable figures are not available for previous years.
15. CPS later offered the unaccounted for slots to students in 15 other of the lowest performing schools. Data on the number of students who applied for transfers from this group are unavailable.
16. Figures are from author calculations of state-level federal funding shares and are based on 2003 Census Bureau statistics. (U.S. Census Bureau, 2005)
17. NAEP, or the National Assessment of Educational Progress, is a national test that is "low stakes." In other words, states are not currently held accountable for sub-par performance on NAEP.
18. Remarks published online at www.ed.gov/news/pressreleases/2006/04/04052006.html. Last accessed on May 26, 2006.

References

Allen, J., & Marcucio, A. V. 2005. *The simple guide to charter school laws.* Tech. rept. Center for Education Reform.

Archbald, D. A. 2000. School choice and school stratification: Shortcomings of the stratification critique and recommendations for theory and research. *Educational Policy*, 14(2), 214–240.

Archbald, D. A. 2004. School choice, magnet schools, and the liberation model: An empirical study. *Sociology of Education*, 77, 283–310.

Arum, R. 1996. Do private schools force public schools to compete? *American Sociological Review*, 61(1), 29–46.

Baker, D. P., & Stevenson, D. L. 1986. Mothers' strategies for children's school achievement: Managing the transition to high school. *Sociology of Education*, 59(3), 156–166.

Belfield, C. R., & Levin, H. M. 2002. The effects of competiton between schools on educational outcomes: A review for the United States. *Review of Educational Research*, 72(2), 279–341.

Blau, P. M., & Duncan, O. D. 1967. *The American occupational structure*. New York: Wiley.

Brown, C. G. 2004. *Choosing better schools: A report on student transfers under the No Child Left Behind Act*. Tech. rept. Citizen's Commission on Civil Rights.

Bryk, A., Lee, V. E., & Holland, P. B. 1993. *Catholic Schools and the Common Good*. Cambridge, MA: Harvard University Press.

Bryk, A. S., & Schneider, B. L. 2002. *Trust in schools: a core resource for improvement*. New York: Russell Sage Foundation.

Casserly, M. 2004. Choice and supplemental services in America's greatcity schools. In F. M. Hess & C. E. Finn (Eds.), *Leaving no child behind? Options for kids in failing schools* (pp. 191–211). New York: Palgrave Macmillan.

Center for Education Policy. 2005. *From the capital to the classroom: Year 3 of the No Child Left Behind Act*. Tech. rept. Center for Education Policy.

Center for Education Policy. 2006. *From the capital to the classroom: Year 4 of the No Child Left Behind Act*. Tech. rept. Center for Education Policy.

Cobb, C. D., & Glass, G. V. 1999. Ethnic segregation in Arizona charter schools. *Education Policy Analysis Archives*, 7(1), Retrieved June 23, 2005 (http://epaa.asu.edu/epaa/v7nl/).

Coleman, J. S. 1992. Some points on choice in education. *Sociology of Education*, 65(4), 260–262.

Coleman, J. S., & Holler, T. 1987. *Public and private high schools: the impact of communities*. New York: Basic Books.

Comer, J. P. 1988. Educating poor minority children. *Scientific American*, 259(5), 42–48.

Coons, J. E., & Sugarman, S. D. 1978. *Education by choice: The case for family control*. Berkeley: University of California Press.

Cullen, J. B, Jacob, B. A., & Levitt, S.. 2005. *The effect of school choice on student outcomes: Evidence from randomized lotteries*. NBER Working Paper.

Duchesne, P. D. 2000. 8,000 Passed test after all: Scoring firm blamed for basic-skills test error that kept hundreds from graduating. *Star Tribune* (Minneapolis, MN), July 29, 1A.

Duffrin, E. 2001. Why Kids Flee. *Catalyst Chicago*, December Edition.

Fiske, E. B., & Ladd, H. F. 2000. *When schools compete: A cautionary tale*. Washington, D.C.: Brookings Institution Press.

Friedman, M. 1962. *Capitalism and freedom*. Chicago: University of Chicago Press.

Gill, B. P. 2001. *Rhetoric versus reality: What we know and what we need to know about vouchers and charter schools*. Santa Monica, CA: Rand Education.

Glazeman, S. 1998. *Determinants and consequences of parental school choice*. Doctoral, University of Chicago.

Gorard, S. 2000. Questioning the crisis account: a review of evidence for increasing polarization in schools. *Education Research*, 42(3), 309–21.

Gorard, S., & Fitz, J. 2000. Markets and stratification: A view from England and Wales. *Educational Policy*, 14(3), 405–428.

Green, J. P., Peterson, P. E., & Du, J. 1997. *Effectiveness of school choice: The Milwaukee Experiment*. Tech. rept. Harvard University Program in Education Policy and Governance, Cambridge, MA.

Grossman, K. 2005. Parents declining to send children to top schools: Only a quarter of kids from closing schools apply for open schools. *Chicago Sun-Times*, April 27, News, 34.

Hanushek, E. A., Kain, J. F., & Rivkin, S. G. 2002. *New Evidence about Brown v. Board of Education: The Complex Effects of School Racial Composition on Achievement*. NBER Working Paper No. 8741, January 2002.

Henig, J. R. 1995. Race and choice in Montgomery County, Maryland, Magnet Schools. *Teachers College Record*, 96(4), 729–734.

Hess, G. A. 1984. Renegotiating a multicultural society: Participation in desegregation planning in Chicago. *Journal Of Negro Education*, 53(2), 132–146.

Hochschild, J. L., & Scovronick, N. B. 2003. *The American dream and the public schools*. New York: Oxford University Press.

Howell, W. 2004. Fumbling for an exit key: Parents, choice, and the future of NCLB. In F. M. Hess & C. E. Finn (Eds.), *Leaving no child behind? Options for kids in failing schools* (pp. 161–190). New York: Palgrave Macmillan.

Hoxby, C. M. 2000. Does competition among public schools benefit students and taxpayers? *American Economic Review*, 90(5), 1209–1238.

Hoxby, C. M. 2005 (Mar.). *Competition among public schools: A reply to Rothstein (2004)*. Tech. rept. 11216. National Bureau of Economic Research, Inc. available at http://ideas.repec.org/p/nbr/nberwo/11216.html.

Hoxby, C. M. 2003. School choice and School productivity: Could school choice be a tide that lifts all boats? In C. M. Hoxby (Ed.), *The economics of school choice* (pp. 287–341). Chicago: University of Chicago Press.

Johnson, D. 1987. Chicago leads aay in city school woe. *The New York Times*, December 9, Late City Final Edition, 7.

Kafer, K. 2005. *Choices in Education: 2005 Progress Report*. Tech. rept. 1848. The Heritage Foundation.

Kim, J., & Sunderman, G. 2004. *Does NCLB provide good choices for students in low-performing schools*. Tech. rept. The Civil Rights Project at Harvard University.

Klonsky, M. 1995. GOP clears field, Daley runs with the ball. *Catalyst Chicago*, September Edition.

Krueger, A. B., & Zhu, P. 2004. Another look at the New York City school voucher experiment. *American Behavioral Scientist*, 47(5), 658–698.

Lareau, A. 1989. *Home advantage: social class and parental intervention in elementary education*. Education policy perspectives. Social analysis series. London; New York: Falmer Press.

Lareau, A. 2002. Invisible inequality: Social class and childrearing in black families and white families. *American Sociological Review*, 67(5), 747–776.

Lauen, D. L. 2006. *Opportunity for all? The hidden causes and consequences of school choice in Chicago*. Doctoral, University of Chicago.

Lee, V. E., Croninger, R. G., & Smith, J. B. 1996. Equity and choice in Detroit. In B. Fuller & R. F. Elmore (Eds.), *Who chooses? Who loses?* (pp. 70–94). New York: Teachers College Press.

Levin, H. 2004. Multiple choice questions: The road ahead. In N. Epstein (Ed.), *Who's in charge here? the tangled web of school governance and policy* (pp. 228–255). Denver Washington, D.C.: Education Commission of the States; Brookings Institution Press.

Lubienski, C., & Lubienski, S. T.. 2006. *Charter, private, public schools and academic achievement: New evidence from NAEP Mathematics Data*. Tech. rept. National Center for the Study of Privatization in Education.

MacLeod, J. 1995. *Ain't no makin' it: aspirations and attainment in a low-income neighborhood*. Boulder: Westview Press.

Meyer, J. W., & Rowan, B. 1977. Institutionalized organizations: Formal structure as myth and ceremony. *American Journal of Sociology*, 83(2), 340–363.

Myrdal, G., Sterner, R. M. E., & Rose, A. M. 1944. *An American dilemma; the Negro problem and modern democracy*. New York and London: Harper.

National Working Commission on Choice in K-12 Education. 2003. *School choice doing it the right way makes a difference*. Tech. rept. Brookings Institution.

Neal, D. 1997. The effects of catholic schooling on educational achievement. *Journal of Labor Economics*, 15, 98–123.

Oakes, Je. 1985. *Keeping track: how schools structure inequality*. New Haven: Yale University Press.

Orfield, G., & Eaton, S. E. 1996. *Dismantling desegregation: the quiet reversal of Brown v. Board of Education*. New York: New Press: Distributed by W.W. Norton and Company.

Peterson, P. E. 1976. *School politics, Chicago style*. Chicago: University of Chicago Press.

Pfeffer, J., & Salancik, G. R. 1978. *The external control of organizations: a resource dependence perspective*. New York: Harper and Row.

Renzulli, L. A., & Evans, L. 2005. School choice, charter schools, and white flight. *Social Problems*, 52(3), 398–418.

Roderick, M., Bryk, A. S., Jacob, B. A., Easton, J. Q., & Allensworth, E. 1999. *Ending social promotion*. Tech. rept. Consortium on Chicago Schools Research, Chicago.

Rose, L. C., & Gallup, A. M. 2004. The 36th annual Phi Delta Kappa/Gallup Poll of the public's attitudes toward the public schools. *Phi Delta Kappa*, 86(1), 41–52.

Rosenbaum, J. E. 1976. *Making inequality: The hidden curriculum of high school tracking*. New York: Wiley.

Rossi, R. 2003a. Feds: City falling short of school transfer goals. *Chicago Sun-Times*, October 27, News Special Edition, 10.

Rossi, R. 2003b. To Duncan, No Child Left Behind Law is 'burdensome' and 'tmpractical'. *Chicago Sun-Times*, August 29, News Special Edition, 12.

Rossi, R., & Spielman, F. 2002. Daley protests student transfers. *Chicago Sun-Times*, July 17, News Special Edition, 5.

Rothstein, J. 2005 (Mar.). *Does competition among public schools benefit students and taxpayers? A Comment on Hoxby (2000)*. Tech. rept. 11215. National Bureau of Economic Research, Inc. available at http://ideas.repec.org/p/nbr/nberwo/11215.html.

Rouse, C. E. 1998. Private school vouchers and student achievement: An evaluation of the Milwaukee Parental Choice Program. *Quarterly Journal of Economics*, 113(2), 553–602.

Saporito, S. 2003. Private choices, public consequences: Magnet school choice and segregation by race and poverty. *Social Problems*, 50(2), 181–203.

Saporito, S., & Lareau, A. 1999. School selection as a process: The multiple dimensions of race in framing educational choice. *Social Problems*, 46(3), 418–439.

Schneider, M., Teske, P., Marschall, M., & Roch, C. 1998. Shopping for schools: In the land of the blind, the one-eyed parent may be enough. *American Journal of Political Science*, 42(3), 769–793.

Schneider, M., & Buckley, J. 2002. What parents want from schools? Evidence from the Internet. *Educational Evaluation and Policy Analysis*, 24(2), 133–44.

Teske, P., & Schneider, M. 2001. What research can tell policymakers about school choice. *Journal of Policy Analysis and Management*, 20(4), 609–631.

Turner, R. H. 1960. Sponsored and contest mobility and the school-system. *American Sociological Review*, 25(6), 855–867.

Tyack, D. B. 1974. *The one best system: a history of American urban education*. Cambridge, MA: Harvard University Press.

United States Government Accountability Office. 2004. *No Child Left Behind Act: Education needs to provide additional technical assistance and conduct implementation studies for school choice provision: report to Secretary of Education*. Washington, D.C.: United States Government Accountability Office.

U.S. Census Bureau. 2005. *Public education finances, 2003*. Tech. rept. U.S. Census Bureau.

U.S. Department of Education. 2004. *Public school choice: Non-regulatory Guidance*.

Weissman, D. 2002. Gentrifiers slow to buy CPS. *Catalyst Chicago*, Febrauary Edition.

Wells, A. S., & Crain, R. L. 1997. *Stepping over the color line: African-American students in white suburban schools*. New Haven: Yale University Press.

West, M. R., & Peterson, P. E. 2006. The efficacy of choice threats within School accountability systems: Results from legislatively induced eExperiments. *The Economic Journal*, 116(March), C46–C62.

Wirt, J., Choy, S., Rooney, P, Provasnik, S., Sen, A., & Tobin, R. 2004. *The condition of education 2004*. Tech. rept. U.S. Department of Education.

Witte, J. F. 2000. *The market approach to education*. Princeton University Press.

Wolf, P., Butmann, B., Puma, M., & Silverberg, M.. 2006. *Evaluation of the D.C. Opportunity Scholarship Program: Second year report on participation*. Washington, D.C.: U.S. Government Printing Office. U.S. Department of Education, Institute of Education Sciences.

26

Our Impoverished View of Educational Research

DAVID C. BERLINER

Over the last three years, I have co-authored three reports about the effects of high-stakes testing on curriculum, instruction, school personnel, and student achievement (Amrein & Berliner, 2002; Nichols & Berliner, 2005; Nichols, Glass & Berliner, 2006). They were all depressing. My co-authors and I found high-stakes testing programs in most states ineffective in achieving their intended purposes, and causing severe unintended negative effects, as well. We believe that the federal No Child Left Behind (NCLB) law is a near perfect case of political spectacle (Smith, 2004), much more theater than substance. Our collectively gloomy conclusions led me to wonder what would really improve the schools that are not now succeeding, for despite the claims of many school critics, only some of America's schools are not now succeeding (Berliner, 2004).

I do not believe that NCLB is needed to tell us precisely where those failing schools are located, and who inhabits them. We have had that information for over a half century. For me, NCLB is merely delaying the day when our country acknowledges that a common characteristic is associated with the great majority of schools that are most in need of improvement; it is this common characteristic of our failing schools that I write about, for by ignoring it, we severely limit our thinking about school reform.

This is an essay about poverty and its powerful effects on schooling. So these musings could have been written also by Jean Anyon, Bruce Biddle, Greg Duncan, Jeanne Brooks-Gunn, Gary Orfield, Richard Rothstein, and many others whose work I admire and from whom I borrow. Many scholars and teachers understand, though many politicians choose not to, that school reform is heavily constrained by factors that are outside of America's classrooms and schools. Although the power of schools and educators to influence individual students is never to be underestimated, the out-of-school factors associated with poverty play both a powerful and a limiting role in what can actually be achieved.

In writing about these issues, I ask for the tolerance of sociologists, economists, child development researchers, and others who read this essay because I discuss variables that are the subject of intense debate within the disciplines. Although scholars dispute the ways we measure the constructs of social class, poverty, and neighborhood, we all still manage to have common enough understandings of these concepts to communicate sensibly. That will suffice for my purposes. In this essay it is not important to argue about the fine points at which poverty is miserable or barely tolerable, or whether a person is stuck in the lowest of the social classes or merely belongs to the working poor, or whether families are poor at the federal poverty level or at 200% of the federal poverty level (which is still poor by almost everyone's standards). We know well enough what we mean when we talk of poverty, communities of poverty, the very poor, and the like. We also know that the lower social classes and the communities in which they live are not at all homogenous. It is a simplification, and therefore a mistake, to treat a group as if the individuals who comprise that group were the same. I also ask for my readers' tolerance for ignoring these distinctions in what follows.

The Basic Problem of Poverty and Educational Reform

It seems to me that in the rush to improve student achievement through accountability systems relying on high-stakes tests, our policy makers and citizens forgot, or cannot understand, or deliberately avoid the fact, that our children live nested lives. Our youth are in classrooms, so when those classrooms do not function as we want them to, we go to work on improving them. Those classrooms are in schools, so when we decide that those schools are not performing appropriately, we go to work on improving them, as well. But both students and schools are situated in neighborhoods filled with families. And in our country the individuals living in those school neighborhoods are not a random cross section of Americans. Our neighborhoods are highly segregated by social class, and thus, also segregated by race and ethnicity. So all educational efforts that focus on classrooms and schools, as does NCLB, could be reversed by family, could be negated by neighborhoods, and might well be subverted or minimized by what happens to children outside of school. Improving classrooms and schools, working on curricula and standards, improving teacher quality and fostering better use of technology are certainly helpful. But sadly, such activities may also be similar to those of the drunk found on his hands and knees under a street lamp. When asked by a passerby what he was doing, the drunk replied that he was looking for his keys. When asked where he lost them, the drunk replied "over there," and pointed back up the dark street. When the passerby then asked the drunk why he wasn't looking for the keys where they were located, the drunk answered "the light is better here!"

I believe we need to worry whether the more important keys to school reform are up the block, in the shadows, where the light is not as bright. If we do choose to peer into the dark we might see what the recently deceased sociologist Elizabeth Cohen saw quite clearly: That poverty constitutes the unexamined 600-pound gorilla that most affects American education today (cited in Biddle, p. 3, 2001).

When I think about that gorilla it immediately seems ludicrous to me that most of what we try to do to help poor youth is classroom and school based. Education doesn't just take place in our schools, a point that Pulitzer prize-winning historian Lawrence Cremin tried to make as the reform movement gained momentum in the late 1980s (Cremin, 1990). It is a fact of contemporary American life that many of the poorest of the children who come to our schools have spent no time at all in school-like settings during the first five years of their life. And then, when of school-age, children only spend about 30 of their waking hours a week in our schools, and then only for about two-thirds of the weeks in a year. You can do the arithmetic yourselves. In the course of a full year students might spend just over 1,000 hours in school, and almost 5 times that amount of time in their neighborhood and with their families.

For all youth those 5,000 hours require learning to be a member of one or more cultural groups in that community, learning to behave appropriately in diverse settings, learning ways to get along with others, to fix things, to think, and to explain things to others. These are natural and influential experiences in growing up. But for poor kids, ghetto kids, what is learned in those settings can often be unhelpful. It was Jean Anyon, among others, who some time ago alerted us to the fact that many of the families in those impoverished neighborhoods are so poorly equipped to raise healthy children, that the schools those children attend would have a hard time educating them, even if they weren't also so poorly organized and run. Anyon (1995) said

> It is has become increasingly clear that several decades of educational reform have failed to bring substantial improvements to schools in America's inner cities. Most recent analyses of unsuccessful school reform (and prescriptions for change) have isolated educational, regulatory, or financial aspects of reform from the social context of poverty and race in which inner city schools are located. (p. 69)

...the structural basis for failure in inner-city schools is political, economic, and cultural, and must be changed before meaningful school improvement projects can be successfully implemented. Educational reforms cannot compensate for the ravages of society. (p. 88)

More recently Anyon (2005, p. 69) bluntly evaluated the pervasive failure of school reform. She says:

Currently, relatively few urban poor students go past ninth grade: The graduation rates in large comprehensive inner-city high schools are abysmally low. In fourteen such New York City schools, for example, only 10 percent to 20 percent of ninth graders in 1996 graduated four years later. Despite the fact that low-income individuals desperately need a college degree to find decent employment, only 7 percent obtain a bachelors degree by age twenty-six. So, in relation to the needs of low-income students, urban districts fail their students with more egregious consequences now than in the early twentieth century.

Oakland, California, where my grandson goes to school, announced recently that its high-school graduation rate is 48% (Asimov, 2005). Oakland has been reforming its schools at least since 1973 when I first started working there. Oakland's educators are not ignorant or uncaring, and neither are Oakland's parents. But no one has been able to fix Oakland's public schools. In Oakland and elsewhere, is that because we are looking for the keys in the wrong place?

As educators and scholars we continually talk about school reform as if it must take place inside the schools. We advocate, for the most part, for adequacy in funding, high-quality teachers, professional development, greater subject matter preparation, cooperative learning, technologically enhanced instruction, community involvement, and lots of other ideas and methods I also promote. Some of the most lauded of our school reform programs in our most distressed schools do show some success, but success often means bringing the students who are at the 20th percentile in reading and mathematics skills up to the 30th percentile in those skills. Statistical significance and a respectable effect size for a school reform effort is certainly worthy of our admiration, but it just doesn't get as much accomplished as needs to be done.

Perhaps we are not doing well enough because our vision of school reform is impoverished. It is impoverished because of our collective views about the proper and improper roles of government in ameliorating the problems that confront us in our schools; our beliefs about the ways in which a market economy is supposed to work; our concerns about what constitutes appropriate tax rates for the nation; our religious views about the elect and the damned; our peculiar American ethos of individualism; and our almost absurd belief that schooling is the cure for whatever ails society. These well-entrenched views that we have as a people makes helping the poor seem like some kind of communist or atheistic plot, and it makes one an apostate in reference to the myth about the power of the public schools to affect change.

James Traub (2000) writing in the New York Times said this all quite well a few years ago. He noted that it was hard to think of a more satisfying solution to poverty than education. School reform, as opposed to other things we might do to improve achievement, really involves relatively little money and, perhaps more importantly, asks practically nothing of the nonpoor, who often control a society's resources. Traub also noted that school reform is accompanied by the good feelings that come from our collective expression of faith in the capacity of the poor to overcome disadvantage on their own. Our myth of individualism fuels the school reform locomotive.

On the other hand, the idea that schools *cannot* cure poverty by themselves sounds something like a vote of no confidence in our great American capacity for self-transformation, a major element in the stories we tell of our American nation. Traub notes that when we question the schools' ability to foster transformation we seem to flirt with the racial theories expressed by Charles Murray and

Richard Herrnstein, who argued in *The Bell Curve* (1994) that educational inequality has its roots in biological inequality. But an alternative explanation to Herrnstein and Murray, "is that educational inequality is rooted in economic problems and social pathologies too deep to be overcome by school alone. And if that's true, then there really is every reason to think about the limits of school" (Traub, 2000, p. 54). Schooling alone may be too weak an intervention for improving the lives of most children now living in poverty.

Those who blame poor children and their families, like Herrnstein and Murray, or those who blame the teachers and administrators who serve those kids and families in our public schools, like Rod Paige, Jeanne Allen, Checker Finn, William Bennett, and dozens of other well-known school critics, are all refusing to acknowledge the root problem contended with by too many American schools, namely, that there is a 600-pound gorilla in the school house.

The economist Richard Rothstein understands this. In his recent book *Class and Schools* (2004), he states:

> Policy makers almost universally conclude that existing and persistent achievement gaps must be the result of wrongly designed school policies—either expectations that are too low, teachers who are insufficiently qualified, curricula that are badly designed, classes that are too large, school climates that are too undisciplined, leadership that is too unfocussed, or a combination of these.
>
> Americans have come to the conclusion that the achievement gap is the fault of "failing schools" because it makes no common sense that it could be otherwise.... This common sense perspective, however, is misleading and dangerous. It ignores how social class characteristics in a stratified society like ours may actually influence learning in schools. (pp. 9–10)

Like Anyon, Rothstein goes on to note:

> For nearly half a century, the association of social and economic disadvantage with a student achievement gap has been well known to economists, sociologists and educators. Most, however, have avoided the obvious implication of this understanding—raising the achievement of lower-class children requires the amelioration of the social and economic conditions of their lives, not just school reform. (Rothstein, p. 11)

Anyon, Rothstein, and others provide the framework for the issues I raise in this essay. But first, having raised the spectre of the gorilla, let me provide information on the magnitude of the American problem. I can do that by benchmarking American rates of childhood poverty against the rates in other industrialized nations.

America's Poverty Problem

The UNICEF report from the Innocenti Foundation (UNICEF, 2005), which regularly issues reports on childhood poverty, is among the most recent to reliably document this problem. The entire report is summarized quite simply in one graph, presented as Figure 26.1.

In this set of rich nations, the United States is among the leaders in childhood poverty over the decade of the 1990s. The only nation with a record worse than ours is Mexico, and, contrary to UNICEF, I would not consider Mexico a rich nation. Using 2003 data to compute Gross National Income per capita (using Purchasing Power Parity [PPP] as the method of comparison), the United States ranked fourth at $37,750 per capita, while Mexico ranked 80th with $8,900 per capita (World Bank, 2005). We should not be in the same league as Mexico, but, alas, we are closer to them in poverty rate than to others whom we might, more commonly, think of as our peers.

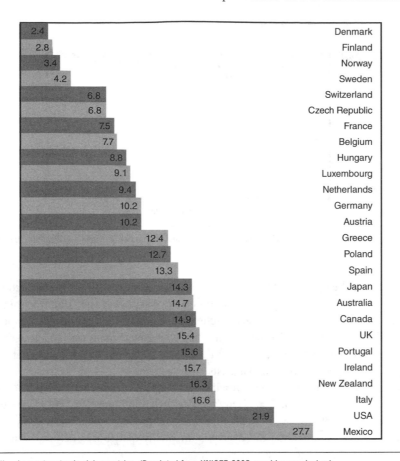

Figure 26.1 Childhood poverty rates in rich countries. (Reprinted from UNICEF, 2005, used by permission.)

Figure 26.1 informs us that we have the highest rate of childhood poverty among the rich nations, which is what other studies have shown for over a decade (Berliner and Biddle, 1995). Our rank has been remarkably steady. The United States likes to be #1 in everything, and when it comes to the percent of children in poverty among the richest nations in the world, we continue to hold our remarkable status.

One bit of good news about poverty in the United States is that over the decade of the 1990s we lowered our embarrassing rate of poverty a great deal, almost 2.5%. So in the graph presented in Figure 26.1 you are seeing a measure of childhood poverty in the United States after years of improvement! But there is also some bad news. First, the expansion of jobs and income growth in our nation stopped at the end of the 1990s, and the gains that had been made have been lost. With the sharp increase in housing prices that has occurred since then, no noticeable increases in the real wages for the poor, an economic expansion that has failed to create jobs, and a reduction in tax revenues (resulting in a reduction of aid to the poor), it is quite likely that our rate of childhood poverty is back to where it was. That would be about 2 or more percentage points higher than the figure given in this UNICEF report. Apparently this is about where we as a nation want the rate to be, since the graph makes it abundantly clear that if we cared to do something about it, we could emulate the economic policies of other industrialized nations and not have the high rate of poverty that we do.

In Figure 26.2 we note the percentage of people in the United States who are living at half the rate of those classified as merely poor (Mishel, Bernstein & Allegretto, 2005, p. 323, from data supplied

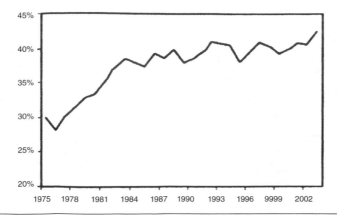

Figure 26.2 Percent of the poor living at half the official poverty rate. (Reprinted from Mishel, Bernstein and Allegretto, 2005. Used by permission of the publisher, Cornell University Press.)

by the US Bureau of the Census). These are the poorest of the poor in our nation, constituting over 40% of the tens of millions of people that are officially classified as the "poor" by our government. But I need to also note that the classification scheme used by our government is suspect. Almost all economists believe that the level of income at which the government declares a person to be poor misleads us into thinking there are fewer poor than there really are. So it is likely that there are many more very poor people than this graph suggests.

I call attention in Figure 26.2 to the overall upward trend of the desperately poor in this graph, particularly the upturn after 2000. That is why the rates given in Figure 26.1 may be an underestimate of the conditions that pertain now, in 2006. Something else needs to be noted about the poverty we see among children. It is not random. Poverty is unequally distributed across the many racial and ethnic groups that make up the American nation.

Figure 26.3 makes clear that poverty is strongly correlated with race and ethnicity (Mishel, Bernstein & Allegretto, p. 316, from data supplied by the U.S. Bureau of the Census). Note once again the

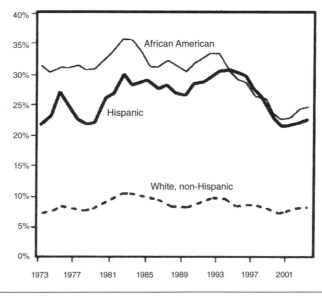

Figure 26.3 U.S. poverty rates by ethnicity. (Reprinted from Mishel, Bernstein and Allegretto, 2005, by permission of the publisher, Cornell University Press.)

upward trend for poverty among minorities after the roaring 90s ended. New immigrants, African-Americans, and Hispanics, particularly those among these groups who live in urban areas, are heavily overrepresented in the groups that suffer severe poverty. Thus, while this is a paper about poverty, it is inextricably tied to issues of race in America. I have found no way to separate the two, though here I focus on poverty, perhaps the more tractable issue.

The UNICEF report (2005, p. 8) also reminds us that there is a charter about the rights of children to which 192 United Nations members have agreed. It is sad, I know, that many member nations sign such a charter and then do little to live up to it. But still, at the very least, signing is an acknowledgment of the underlying concept and only two nations have refused to sign this treaty. One of these nations is Somalia.

Can you guess which is the other nation? You guessed correctly if you chose the United States of America. We will not sign a charter guaranteeing the rights of already born children, though we somehow managed to get a bill through our congress that guarantees the rights of unborn children. As Congressman Barney Frank was said to mutter one day, there are many people who "believe that life begins at conception, and ends at birth!" (Erbe & Shiner, 1997).

Apparently we, the American people, do not agree with such radical ideas as those expressed in article 27 of the UN charter. There it is stated that governments should "recognize the right of every child to a standard of living adequate for the child's physical, mental, spiritual, moral and social development" (UNICEF, 2005, p. 8).

Article 27 also makes clear that parents or others responsible for the child "have the primary responsibility to secure…the conditions of living necessary for the child's development," but that governments should assist parents "to implement this right and shall in case of need provide material assistance and support programs, particularly with regard to nutrition, clothing and housing" (UNICEF, 2005, p. 8).

We actually have many programs to help parents and children, but because they are fragmented, do not cover everyone eligible, are subject to variability in funding, they end up not nearly as good nor as serious in intent as those in many other countries. While school critics delight in talking about our inadequate achievement vis-à-vis other nations, it seems just as important to talk about other nations' attention to the poor and the mechanisms each has for helping people out of poverty as soon as possible. This should also be an important indicator for judging one nation's performance against another. If we do that, our country does not look good.

Table 26.1 shows that we are a leader among the rich nations of the world in terms of failing to help people exit from poverty once they have fallen into poverty (Mishel, Berstein & Allegretto, p. 409, from data supplied by the OECD). One column in this table shows the percent of individuals who became impoverished once in a three-year time period, say through illness, divorce, childbirth, or job loss—the big four poverty producers among those who had been non-poor. There we see that the U.S. rate is quite high, but not much different than that of many other nations. Poverty befalls many people, in many countries, once in a while.

Our national problem shows in the next column, displaying the percent of people who stayed poor for the entire three years after they had fallen into poverty. At a rate roughly twice that of other wealthy nations, we lead the industrialized world! Unlike other wealthy countries, we have few mechanisms to get people out of poverty once they fall into poverty.

In the last column of Table 26.1 we can see how awful it can be to stumble into poverty in the United States compared to other nations. In that column we see the percent of people who stayed below the poverty level on a relatively permanent basis. The United States likes to lead the world, and here we are, champs once again! We can claim the highest rate of the permanently poor of all the other industrialized nations! If you compare the data from Denmark, Ireland, or the Netherlands to

Table 26.1 Poverty in OECD Countries over a Three-Year Period, and Permanent Poverty, During the 1990s.

Country	Percent poor once in three years	Percent poor for all three years	Percent in nation permanently poor
United States	23.5	9.5	14.5
Denmark	9.1	0.8	1.8
Ireland	15.3	1.3	5.3
Netherlands	12.9	1.6	4.5
France	16.6	3.0	6.6
Italy	21.5	5.6	10.4
United Kingdom	19.5	2.4	6.5
Canada	18.1	5.1	8.9
Belgium	16.0	2.8	5.2
Germany	19.2	4.3	8.1
Finland	25.1	6.5	12.2
Portugal	24.2	7.8	13.4
Spain	21.3	3.7	8.7

Source: Reprinted from Mishel, Bernstein and Allegretto, 2005. Used by permission of the publisher, Cornell University Press.

that of the United States, it is easy to see the difference between societies that abhor poverty, and one such as ours, that accepts poverty as a given.

Poverty and Student Achievement

I have now pointed out that in the United States the rates of childhood poverty are high, poverty is racialized, and that those who once get trapped in poverty have a hard time getting out of poverty. But what does this mean for us in terms of student achievement? There are, of course, thousands of studies showing correlations between poverty and academic achievement. Nothing there will surprise us, though I do wonder why, after hundreds of studies showing that cigarettes were related to a great number of serious illnesses we eventually came to believe that the relationship between smoking and cancer, or smoking and emphysema, was causal. And yet when we now have research establishing analogous connections between poverty and educational attainment we ignore them. Instead we look for other causal mechanisms, like low expectations of teachers, or the quality of teachers' subject matter knowledge, to explain the relationship. Of course the low expectations of teachers and their subject matter competency are important. But I keep thinking about that 600-pound gorilla out there asking for more attention than it is getting. That big ape may be causal in the relationships we consistently find between poverty and achievement.

Since the relationship is well known, let us look briefly at how U.S. poverty is related to student achievement in just the international studies, since it is our international competitiveness that worries so many in industry and government, and it is those worries that kindled the reform movement in education. We can start with the recent Trends in International Mathematics and Science Study, known as TIMSS 2003, released at the end of 2004 (Gonzales, Guzmán, Partelow, Pahlke, Jocelyn, Kastenberg, & Williams, 2004). Table 26.2 presents data on mathematics and science scores for American 4th and 8th grade youth disaggregated by the degree of poverty in the schools they attend.

In this table three aspects of our performance with regard to other nations are instructive. First, our scores in both subject areas and at both grade levels were correlated perfectly with the percent of poor students who attend a school. In the five categories presented, schools with the wealthier students had the highest average score, the next wealthier set of schools had students who had the next highest average score, and so forth, until we see that the schools with the poorest students had the students who scored the lowest. This pattern is common.

Table 26.2 Fourth and Eighth Grade Mathematics and Science Scores from TIMMS 2003

Poverty level of school (percent free or reduced lunch)	Fourth grade math scores	Fourth grade science scores	Eighth grade math scores	Eighth grade science scores
Less than 10% in poverty (schools with wealthy students)	567	579	547	571
10%–24.9% in poverty	543	567	531	554
25%–49.9% in poverty	533	551	505	529
50%–74.9% in poverty	500	519	480	504
75% or more in poverty (schools with poor students)	471	480	444	461
U.S. Average Score	518	536	504	527
International Average Score	495	489	466	473

Source: Gonzales et al., 2004.

The second thing to note is that the average scores for the schools with less than 50% of their students in poverty exceeded the US average score, while the average scores for the schools with greater than 50% of their students in poverty fell below the US average score. This tells us who is and who is not succeeding in the United States.

The third thing to notice pertains to the schools that serve the most impoverished students, where 75% or more of the students are eligible for free or reduced lunch. That is, almost all the students in these schools live in extreme poverty and those are the students that fall well below the international average obtained in this study. In general, Table 26.2 informs us that our poor students are not competitive internationally while our middle classes and wealthy public school children are doing extremely well in comparison to the pool of countries that made up TIMSS 2003.

As we go through these data and learn that poor students are not doing well in international competitions, the question we seem unable to raise and debate intelligently is this: Why do we put so much of our attention and resources into trying to fix what goes on inside low-performing schools when the causes of low performance may reside outside the school? Is it possible that we might be better off devoting more of our attention and resources than we now do toward helping the families in the communities that are served by those schools? That would certainly be a competitive strategy for solving the problem of low academic performance if it is simply poverty (along with its associated multitude of difficulties) that prevents most poor children from doing well.

There are more international data to examine. The OECD has instituted a three-year cycle for looking at reading, mathematics, and science for 15-year-olds, called the PISA studies—the Program for International Student Assessment (Lemke, Calsyn, Lippman, Jocelyn, Kastberg, Liu, Roey, Williams, Kruger, & Bairu, 2001). Unfortunately PISA doesn't do a very good job of breaking down the data by social class. So I report on ethnicity and race to discuss the effects of poverty on achievement. Given the high inter-correlations between poverty, ethnicity, and school achievement in our country, it is (sadly) not inappropriate to use ethnicity as a proxy for poverty.

Tables 26.3, 26.4, and 26.5 display the performance in 2000 of US 15-year-olds in mathematics, literacy, and science, in relation to other nations. What stands out first is a commonly found pattern in international studies of achievement, namely, that US average scores are very close to the international average. But in a country as heterogeneous and as socially and ethnically segregated as ours, mean scores of achievement are not useful for understanding how we are really doing in international comparisons. Such data must be disaggregated. I have done that in each of the three tables presenting

Table 26.3 Mathematics Scores (mean 500) from PISA 2000

Country	Score
Japan	557
Korea, Republic of	547
New Zealand	537
Finland	536
Australia	533
Canada	533
United States Average Score for White Students	**530**
Switzerland	529
United Kingdom	529
Belgium	520
France	517
Austria	515
Denmark	514
Iceland	514
Sweden	510
Ireland	503
Norway	499
Czech Republic	498
United States Average Score	**493**
Germany	490
Hungary	488
Spain	476
Poland	470
Italy	457
Portugal	454
Greece	447
Luxembourg	446
United States Average Score for Hispanic Students	**437**
United States Average Score for African American Students	**423**
Mexico	387

Source: Lemke et al., 2001.

PISA data. From those tables we see clearly that our white students (without regard for social class) were among the highest performing students in the world. But our African American and Hispanic students, also undifferentiated by social class, were among the poorest performing students in this international sample.

Looking at all three tables reveals something very important about inequality in the United States. If the educational opportunities available to white students in our public schools were made available to all our students, the United States would have been the 7th highest scoring nation in mathematics, 2nd highest scoring nation in reading, and the 4th highest scoring nation in science. Schooling for millions of US white children is clearly working quite well. On the other hand, were our minority students "nations," they would score almost last among the industrialized countries of the world.

Given these findings, and a scientific attitude, we should be asking what plausible hypotheses might differentiate the education of white, African American, and Hispanic students from one another? Segregated schooling seems to be one obvious answer. Orfield and Lee (2005) in their recent report on school segregation make clear how race and schooling are bound together, as is shown in Table 26.6.

Orfield and Lee's data suggests that segregation is an overriding contributor to the obvious scoring disparities that exist between races. Only 12% of white children go to schools where the majority of the students are not white. And only 1% of white students go to schools that are over 90% minority. Eighty-eight percent of white children are attending schools that are majority white. In contrast,

Table 26.4 Literacy Scores (mean 500) from PISA

Country	Score
Korea, Republic of	552
Japan	550
United States Average Score for White Students	**538**
Finland	538
United Kingdom	532
Canada	529
New Zealand	528
Australia	528
Austria	519
Ireland	513
Sweden	512
Czech Republic	511
France	500
Norway	500
United States Average Score	**499**
Hungary	496
Iceland	496
Belgium	496
Switzerland	496
Spain	491
Germany	487
Poland	483
Denmark	481
Italy	478
Greece	461
Portugal	459
United States Average Score for Hispanic Students	**449**
United States Average Score for African American Students	**445**
Luxembourg	443
Mexico	422

Source: Lemke et al., 2001.

almost all African American and Latino students, usually poorer than their white age-mates, are in schools where there are students very much like them racially and socioeconomically. Latinos and African Americans are as segregated by poverty as they are by race and ethnicity, which may be the more important issue with which our schools have to deal.

In the 2003 PISA studies that came out at the end of 2004, the US position relative to other OECD nations slipped. No one is sure why this happened, and we will have to see if this holds up when the 2006 PISA results are analyzed. But relative positions of white, African American, and Hispanic students remained the same and quite discrepant. For example, Table 26.7 presents the PISA 2003 scores in mathematics literacy, the latest international scores we have. These data are disaggregated by both race and social class (Lemke, Sen, Pahlke, Partelow, Miller, Williams, Kastberg, & Jocelyn, 2004).

The pattern of results in Table 27.7 looks familiar, regardless of whether we examine race or social class. White students (disregarding social classes) and upper-income students (of all races) score well. Their test scores in mathematics literacy are significantly above the international average. But lower social class children of any race and black or Hispanic children of all social classes are not performing well. They score significantly below the international average. Clearly those who are poor do not have the mathematical skills to compete internationally, and those particular children are often African American and Hispanic. Poverty, race, and ethnicity are inextricably entwined in the United States.

One more study is informative in this brief look at poverty and the performance of US students in international comparisons. This is the PIRLS study (Ogle, Sen, Pahlke, Jocelyn, Kastberg, Roey, &

Table 26.5 Science Scores (mean 500) from PISA 2000

Country	Score
Korea, Republic of	552
Japan	550
Finland	538
United States Average Score for White Students	**535**
United Kingdom	532
Canada	529
New Zealand	528
Australia	528
Austria	519
Ireland	513
Sweden	512
Czech Republic	511
France	500
Norway	500
United States Average Score	**499**
Hungary	496
Iceland	496
Belgium	496
Switzerland	496
Spain	491
Germany	487
Poland	483
Denmark	481
Italy	478
Greece	461
Portugal	459
Luxembourg	443
United States Average Score for Hispanic Students	**438**
United States Average Score for African American Students	**435**
Mexico	422

Source: Lemke et al., 2001.

Williams, 2003). PIRLS stands for Progress in International Reading Literacy, a reading assessment administered to 9- and 10-year-olds in 35 nations. The data from this comparison are presented in Table 26.8. The United States did quite well. Our nation ranked ninth, though statistically, we tied with others at third place. This is quite heartening since these data prove our President and former Secretary of Education wrong in their belief that teachers in the United States cannot teach reading.

But PIRLS revealed more than the fact that for the second time in about a decade US 9-year-olds showed remarkably high literacy skills. For instance, the mean score of US white children, without any concern about their social class status, was quite a bit higher than that of the Swedish children who, it should be noted, are also a very white group, and in this study the leading nation in the world.

Table 26.6 Minority Makeup of Schools Attended by Different Racial/Ethnic Groups

	Minority make-up of school		
	50–100%	90–100%	99–100%
White Students	12	1	0
Latino Students	77	38	11
Black Students	73	38	18

Source: Orfield & Lee, 2005.

Table 26.7 Mathematical Literacy Scores in PISA 2003, by both Race and Social

	White	512
Race	African American	417
	Hispanic	443
	Q1 (Lowest SES)	448
Social class	Q2	477
By quartile	Q3	497
	Q4	530

Source: Lemke et al., 2001.

Once again we see that millions of US white children are doing well against international benchmarks. Further, when we take social class into consideration by looking at the scores of students who attend schools where there are few or no children of poverty, we learn that this group of public school children performed quite well. In fact, these higher social class children from the United States walloped the Swedes, scoring 585, an average of 24 points higher than the average score obtained by Swedish students. Public school students by the millions, from US schools that do not serve many poor children, are doing fine in international competition.

But the scores obtained by students attending schools where poverty is prevalent are shockingly low. The mean score in literacy in schools where more than 75% of the children are on free and reduced lunch was 485, 100 points below the scores of our wealthy students, and well below those of many nations that are our economic competitors. The PIRLS study also informed us that, compared to other nations, the United States had the largest urban/suburban score difference among the competing nations. In that finding, as in the segregation data, we see a contributor to many of our nations' educational problems. The urban/suburban social class differences in the United States result in de facto segregation by race and ethnicity. Middle- and upper-class white families in the suburbs live quite separately from the poor and ethnically diverse families of the urban areas. School and community resources differ by social class, and therefore differ also by race and ethnicity.

From these recent international studies, and from literally thousands of other studies both domestic and international, we learn that the relationship between social class and test scores is positive, high, and well embedded in theories that can explain the relationship. This suggests a hypothesis that is frightening to hear uttered in a capitalist society, namely, that if the incomes of our poorest citizens were to go up a bit, so might achievement scores and other indicators that characterize a well-functioning school. Sometimes a correlation exists precisely because causation exists.

Table 26.8 Highest Scoring Nations in Reading Literacy for Nine- and Ten-years-olds in 35 Countries

Rank	Country	Scorer
1	Sweden	561
2	Netherlands	554
3	England	553
4	Bulgaria	550
5	Latvia	545
6	Canada	544
7	Lithuania	543
8	Hungary	543
9	United States	542
10	Italy	541

Source: PIRLS 2001; Ogle et al., 2003.

How Poverty Affects Achievement

Can a reduction of poverty improve the achievement of the poor and the schools they are in? I will only mention a few of the many studies that have caught my attention while thinking about this issue. One that impressed me greatly demonstrated that poverty, pure and simple, prevents the genes involved in academic intelligence to express themselves (Turkheimer, Haley, Waldron, D'Onofrio, & Gottesman, 2003).

We all have heard of the occasional feral child, or about the child kept locked in a closet for some years. We learned from those cases that under extreme environmental conditions whatever genetic potential for language, height, or intellectual functioning a child had, that potential was unable to be expressed. The powerful and awful environment in which such children lived suppressed the expression of whatever genes that child had for complete mastery of language, for full height, for complete intellectual functioning, for competency in social relationships, and so forth.

This is the same point made by evolutionary biologist Richard Lewontin (1982), who discussed how two genetically identical seeds of corn planted in very different plots of earth would grow to very different heights. In the plot with good soil, sufficient water, and sunshine, genetics accounts for almost all of the noticeable variation in the plants, while environment is much less of a factor in the variation that we see. On the other hand, when the soil, water, and sun are not appropriate, genetics do not account for much of the noticeable variation among the lower-growing and often sickly plants that are our harvest. Genes do not have a chance to express themselves under poor environmental conditions.

Lewontin's example now has a human face. There is strong evidence that the influence of genes on intelligence is quite dependent on social class. For example, Turkheimer and his colleagues determined the hereditability of IQ for those who were and were not economically advantaged. The total sample studied began with almost 50,000 women, followed from pregnancy on, in the National Collaborative Perinatal Project. These women gave birth to hundreds of twins, both mono- and di-zygotic. At the lowest end of the socioeconomic spectrum were families with a median income of $17,000 a year in 1997 dollars. One in five of these mothers was younger than 21, one-third of them were on public assistance, and more than one-third did not have a husband. These were the most impoverished of the family groupings studied, the kind of people that we ordinarily refer to as very poor. Unlike most other studies of hereditability in twins, there were enough of these families in the sample to do a separate estimate of the hereditability of IQ in their children. Wechsler IQ was measured for the twins when they were 7 years old, old enough to get a good fix on what their adult IQ was likely to be. The findings are clear and presented in Figure 26.4.

Figure 26.4 presents the smoothed curve of the relationship between genotype and phenotype, between hereditability and its expression. It shows that at the low end of the 100 point scale that was used to measure socioeconomic status, the heritability of IQ was found to be about 0.10 on a scale of zero (no hereditability) to one (100% hereditable, as is eye-color); at the other end of the SES scale, we see that for families of the highest socioeconomic status, the heritability was estimated to be 0.72.

That is, among the lowest social classes, where the mean IQ is quite a bit lower than that of those in the higher social classes, only 10% of the variation we see in measured IQ is due to genetic influences. Thus, the environment accounts for almost all the variation in intelligence that we see. Just as in Lewontin's corn growing example, genetic variation in intelligence in these impoverished environments is not being expressed in the measures we use to assess intelligence. And also as in Lewontin's example, at the top end of the SES scale, almost three quarters of the variation we see in measures of intelligence is due to genetic influences. These findings suggest a number of things.

First, put bluntly, poverty sucks. Among the poor the normal variation we see in academic talent has been sucked away, like corn growing in bad soil.

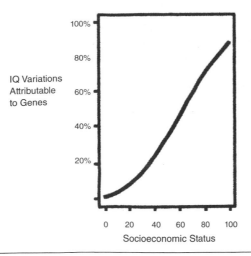

Figure 26.4 Percentage of variation in IQ attributable to genes, for various levels of socioeconomic status (Turkheimer et al., 2003, used by permission of the authors).

Second, all charges of genetic inferiority in intelligence among poor people, minorities or not, have little basis. Genes are not accounting for much of their phenotypic IQ. Environment is the overwhelming influence on measured IQ among the poor. This suggests that unless environments for the most impoverished improve we will not see the expression of the normal human genetic variation in intelligence that is expected. The problem we have, however, is that we don't yet know with much certainty how to improve those environments, because we don't yet know what it is about those environments that is so debilitating. However, Occam's razor suggests that the simplest explanation should be given precedence when attempting to explain any phenomenon. The simplest explanation available is that poverty, and all it entails, causes a restriction of genetic variation in intelligence. We do not need to wait until we understand the micro environments of the poor to know that the macro environment of the poor needs to be changed if we desire to let all the genetic talent that exists among the poor flower.

A third thought arises from this study, and others like it. That is, if genes are not accounting for a great deal of variation in IQ among the poor, and environment is, then environmental interventions for poor people are very likely to change things. In fact, environmental changes for poor children might be predicted to have much bigger effects than similar changes made in the environments for wealthier children. This often appears to be the case, a conclusion reached by Duncan and Brooks-Gunn (2001) using different data. When I look at the studies of the effects of small class size for the poor, or the effects of early childhood education for the poor, or the effects of summer school programs for the poor, the largest effects are found among the poorest children. Thus it seems to me that Turkheim et al. bring us remarkably good news from their study of genetic influences on IQ. The racism and pessimism expressed in *The Bell Curve* by Herrnstein and Murray (1994) can now be seen as completely unjustified because among the very poor genes are not very powerful influences on intelligence, while environments are.

Point four arising from this study is derived from Figure 26.5, also taken from the Turkheimer et al. study. This graph informs us that most of the variation in IQ at the bottom of the SES ladder is due to the environments shared by family members, and that the family's role in the expression of intelligence is less and less important as you go up in social class standing.

Figure 26.5 is the inverse of what was presented in Figure 26.4. Here we see that the variance in intelligence that is due to shared family factors is four times larger among the poor than it is among

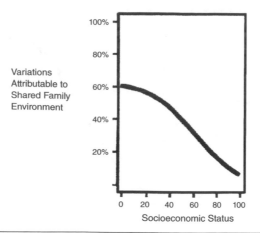

Figure 26.5 Percentage of variation in IQ attributable to shared family environment, across various levels of socioeconomic status (Turkheimer et al., 2003, used by permission of the authors).

the rich. This is another way of saying that environments matter a lot more in the determination of IQ for poor children than they do for wealthier children. After a certain point of environmental adequacy is achieved by means of economic sufficiency, it apparently doesn't much matter what gets added to the environment. A healthy childhood environment supported by adequate family economics is an amalgam of many factors, but probably includes a regular supply of nutritious food, stability in feelings of security, quick medical attention when needed, high-quality child-care, access to books and exposure to rich language usage in the home, and so forth.

Children with these kinds of environments were planted in good soil, and under those conditions the variation we see is mostly genetic and not environmental, however counterintuitive that seems. But the flip side of this is that positive changes in environments for the poor, say high-quality child-care, are expected to have much bigger effects on outcomes we value than they would have when provided to middle-class and wealthier students. That is why high-quality child-care, good nutrition, and medical attention don't just matter for the poor: They matter a lot!

School reformers are doing their best. But they are often planting in poor soil. While you can eke out a living doing that, and occasionally you even see award-winning crops come from unlikely places, we all know that the crops are consistently better where the soil is richer. Healthy trees do not often grow in forests that are ailing, though there are always some resilient ones that thrive, making us forget that most do not. Resilient children and the occasionally exemplary school that exists amidst poverty should be lauded and supported. But the focus of our attention must be on the fact that most children in poverty and most schools that serve those children are not doing well.

The simplest way to get a healthier environment in which to raise children is to provide more resources for parents to make those changes for themselves. Despite the shortcomings of many parents at every level of social class, I still believe the proper place to begin solving the problem of low achievement among poor families is by making those families less poor. I am not talking about a government giveaway. I seek only employment that can supply families with the income that gives them the dignity and hope needed to function admirably, allowing them to raise their children well.

How Money Affects School Achievement

How would a bit more income per family influence educational attainment? The two answers that immediately spring to mind are about health and neighborhood, which I address next.

Health Issues Affecting the Poor

The many medical problems that are related to social class provide obvious and powerful examples of problems affecting school achievement that are remediable with a little extra money. For example, at the simplest level are medical problems such as otitis media and those associated with vision.

Otitis media is a simple and common childhood ear infection, frequently contracted by rich and poor children alike between birth and 3 years of age. In a number of studies, recurring otitis media in the first 3 years of life has been related to hearing impairments, and thus to language development, and thus to reading problems in school, and therefore to deficits on tests such as the Stanford-Binet intelligence test. Otitis media is also implicated in the development of ADHD (see, for example, Agency for Healthcare Research and Quality, 2005; Hagerman & Falkenstein, 1987; Knishkowy, Palti, Adler 8c Tepper, 1991; Luotonen, Uhari, Aitola, Lukkaroinen, Luotonin, Uhari, & Korkeamaki, 1996). This literature makes clear that poor children have more untreated cases of otitis media than do those that are financially better off, especially those with medical insurance. The cause of otitis media may not be directly linked to poverty, but its prevalence and lack of treatment in children is quite clearly affected by poverty.

For example, recurrent otitis media as well as other childhood diseases before age 3 are found to be strongly and negatively related to breastfeeding—the less breast-feeding, the greater the rate of a number of childhood diseases. But breast-feeding of infants in America is done significantly less frequently by women who are poor (Centers for Disease Control, 2005). Breast-feeding is also done significantly less often by those who only have high school degrees or have not finished high school and by those mothers who are under 19 and who are not married (Centers for Disease Control, 2005).

In other words, poverty affects otitis media and other childhood diseases indirectly through home practices that are more common among the poor and less common in the middle class. Another example makes this point as well. The relationship to recurring odds media is also strongly positive for pacifier use (Niemela, Pihakari, Pokka, Uhari, & Uhari, 2000). Pacifiers are used more commonly, and for longer periods of time, among the lower social classes.

In the final analysis, while otitis media isn't a disease of the poor, the characteristics of child rearing and of home environment among the poor of all races and ethnicities leads to more medical problems for the children of the poor. And then, since the poor often lack proper medical insurance, they have a much greater chance of having hearing handicaps at the stage of their lives where language is being developed. In just a few years those handicaps will emerge as reading problems in the classroom.

Otitis media is precisely the kind of problem that is likely not to be much of a factor if the poor were a little richer and in possession of adequate health insurance. Note also that the norms regarding breast-feeding and pacifier use influence all who live in middle-class neighborhoods in a positive way, while the neighborhood norms for these same factors result in negative effects on children in the communities of the poor. A little more money in the lives of the poor would buy them neighborhoods with healthier norms for behavior, as well as medical insurance.

Vision is another simple case of poverty's effects on student behavior outside the teachers' control. For example, two different vision screening tests, one among the urban poor in Boston and one among the urban poor in New York, each found that over 50% of the children tested had some easily correctable vision deficiency, but most such cases were not followed up and corrected (Gillespie, 2001).

An optometrist working with poor children notes that the mass screening vision tests that schools typically use rarely assess the ability of children to do close-up work—the work needed to do reading, writing, arithmetic, and engage in computer mediated learning (Gould & Gould, 2003). What optometrists point out is that a better set of mathematics standards seems less likely to help these students improve in school than does direct intervention in their health and welfare, perhaps most easily accomplished by ensuring that the families of these children earn adequate incomes and are provided medical insurance.

The complexity of the medical problems increases when we discuss asthma. Asthma has now has reached epidemic proportions among poor children. One survey in the South Bronx found a fourth grade teacher where 12 of his 30 students have asthma and 8 of those have to bring their breathing pumps to school every day (Books, 2000). Seven years ago, according to the National Institutes of Health, asthma alone resulted in 10 million missed school days a year, with many individual children missing 20 to 40 school days a year (National Institutes for Health, 1998, cited in Books, 2000). This year, however, a survey puts missed school days due to asthma at 21 million (Children & Asthma in America, 2005). Asthma is simply preventing millions of children of all social classes from attending school and studying diligently. But asthma's effects on children from middle-income families are not nearly as severe as they are on the children of low-income families. Time-on-task, as we all know, is one of the strongest predictors of learning in schools. So it is no great leap of logic to point out that poor children, compared to their middle-class counterparts, will be missing a lot more school because of asthma, and thus will be learning a lot less.

Another level up in the seriousness of the medical problems that afflict the poor has to do with the effects of lead on mental functioning. Michael Martin (2004) of the Arizona School Boards Association has convinced me that this is much more of a problem than I had thought. No one I could find in the medical profession disputes the fact that very small amounts of lead can reduce intellectual functioning and diminish the capacity of a child to learn. The damage that lead does is almost always permanent. The good news is that lead poisoning is in decline. The bad news is that the Centers for Disease Control still estimates that some 450,000 children in the United States between 1 and 5 years of age show levels of lead in their blood that are high enough to cause cognitive damage (Centers for Disease Control, 2004). A simple extrapolation gives us a K–6 schooling population of another half million students with levels of lead in the blood high enough to cause neurological damage. The epidemiological data suggests that another half million brain-damaged students are enrolled in our middle and high schools. The effects of lead poisoning may be small or large, but whatever damage is done by the lead in the system, it is usually permanent.

Do the millions of children affected in small and big ways by lead poisoning have anything in common? They sure do. They are mostly poor and mostly children of color. The poor live in older inner-city buildings where lead contamination from paint, and lead dust from many other sources, is prevalent. But the poor cannot move and cannot afford the paint removal costs since they do not have the income to do so.

Figure 26.6 presents data from California showing the age of the school and the lead that children are exposed to. It is likely to be the case that the relationship shown in Figure 26.6 holds for all states. Essentially what is demonstrated there is that children attending schools built since 1980 are not being exposed to lead in the schools or in the soil around the schools, while the children in older schools are exposed to toxic levels of this dangerous metal. The children who attend new and old schools are not a random selection of children from the population. The poor are exposed to lead's toxicity many times more than the rich.

The literature on the symptoms of lead poisoning remind me of the problems new teachers tell me about when they teach in schools that serve the poor. A lead-damaged nervous system is associated with a variety of problems including learning disabilities, ADHD, increased aggression, and lower intelligence, and those symptoms among older children are also linked with drug use and a greater likelihood of criminal behavior (see reviews by Books, 2000; and Rothstein, 2004).

Though a reduction of, say, 4 or 5 IQ points is not disastrous in a single poisoned child, that IQ reduction in a population will increase by 50% the number of children who qualify for special education, just about what we see in the schools serving the poor. Bailus Walker, a member of both the National Academy of Sciences and the Institute of Medicine says:

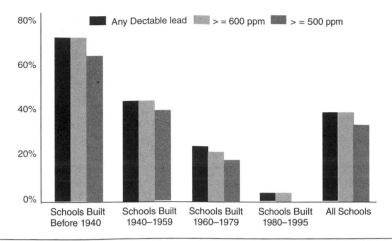

Figure 26.6 Percent of California public elementary schools with various levels of lead paint and lead deterioration, by age of school. (U.S. Environmental Protection Agency, 2003, based on data from the late 1990s.)

The education community has not really understood the demensions of this because we don't see kids falling over and dying of lead poisoning in the classroom. But there's a very large number of kids who find it difficult to do analytical work or [even] line up in the cafeteria because their brains are laden with lead. (cited in Martin, 2004)

Space limitations do not allow me to discuss mercury poisoning—a terribly powerful neurotoxin that gets into the air around medical waste disposal plants and coal fired power plants. But just ask yourselves who lives in the vicinity of the big urban medical waste fascilities or are downwind of a coal-fired power plant? The answer, of course, is that poor families, mostly Hispanics and African Americans, are those who live closest to these toxic facilities. That is the basis for charges about environmental racism.

Perhaps it is even more accurate to call it environmental classism, because the poor feel the brunt of these problems regardless of ethnicity. What is clear is that poor children and their parents are getting more lead and more mercury in their systems than their wealthier kin.

What is also important to note is that the symptoms presented by lead and mercury exposure, like ADHD, irritability, problems of concentration, and the like, are problems that display degrees of impairment. It is not like being pregnant, where a woman either is or is not. So if the lower classes suffer from exposure to lead and mercury more than those in the higher social classes, then there will be more impairments that are slight, as well as those that are more obviously noticeable. In fact at least one recent study of lead effects claims that there is absolutely no safe level for lead. It *always* causes negative cognitive and behavioral effects (Lanphear, Dietrich, Auinger, & Cox, 2000). These invisible medical problems often translate into misbehavior in school, probably resulting in more poor children receiving punishment and having negative school experiences than might their healthier middle-class peers.

The set of environmentally caused problems, both small and large, become teacher and school problems that cannot be fixed by administrators and teachers. Yet we have many politicians who worry little about environmental pollution but are quick to blame educators for the poor achievement of some schools, although that poor achievement may be, in part, a result of problems they could help to solve. I believe that more politicians need to turn their attention to the outside-of-school problems that affect inside-of-school academic performance.

There is another medical problem that is directly related to poverty. Premature births and low birth weight children are much more common problems among the poor. Neural imaging studies show that premature and low birth weight children are several times more likely to have an atomic brain abnormalities than do full-term, full birth weight controls (Peterson, Anderson, Ehrenkranz, Staib, Tageldin, Colson, Gore, Duncan, Makuch & Mendt 2003). Quantitative comparisons of brain volumes in 8-year-old children born prematurely and age-matched full-term control children also found that brain volume was less in the prematurely born. The degree of these morphologic abnormalities was strongly and inversely associated with measures of intelligence (Peterson, Vohr, Staib, Cannistraci, Dolberg, Schneider, Katz, Westerveld, Sparrow, Andersobn, Duncan, Makuch, Gore, & Mendt, 2000). Unfortunately social class and birth defects have been found to be significantly correlated in hundreds of studies. Some of the relationships seem associated with lifestyle problems (drug and alcohol use, vitamin deficiencies), while some seem neighborhood related (waste sites, lead, pesticides). But in either case, the children will still go to public schools five years later.

How Neighborhoods Affect the Poor

Neighborhoods communicate norms for behavior, such as in the case of drugs and alcohol, breast-feeding or pacifier use, and achievement. For example, Garner and Raudenbush (1991) looked at student achievement in literacy in 16 secondary schools and in 437 neighborhoods in a set of school districts. The neighborhoods were scaled to reflect sociodemographic characteristics, precisely the kinds of things that make one choose to live in (or not live in) a neighborhood. These included overall unemployment rate, youth unemployment rate, number of single-parent families, percent of low-earning wage earners, overcrowding, and permanently sick individuals. When Hierarchical Linear Modeling was used to analyze these data, significant school-to-school variance was found even when controlling for family background and neighborhood. Happily, this tells us that we should continue working on making schools better. This study and many others demonstrate that school effects are real and powerful: Schools do exert positive influences on the lives of the poor.

But the analysis did not stop there. The neighborhood deprivation variable showed a negative effect on educational attainment even after variation in the individual students and the schools they attend were stringently controlled. This was not a trivial statistical finding. For two students with identical prior background in achievement, with identical family backgrounds, and even with identical school membership, the differences in their educational attainment as a function of their neighborhood deprivation was estimated to be a difference of between the 10th and the 90th percentile on an achievement test.

More recently sociologists Catsambis and Beveridge, verified these finding using NELS 88 data with mathematics achievement as the outcome (2001). They found that neighborhood had significant direct and indirect effects on achievement, often by depressing parental practices that were usually associated with better student achievement.

The combination of home circumstances, neighborhood, and school are powerful influences on a secondary students' life circumstances. But independent of the other factors, neighborhood deprivation showed powerful effects on its own. Tragically, good parents too frequently lose their children to the streets: neighborhood effects are strong. Families who have enough money to move out of a dysfunctional neighborhood do so. On the other hand, poverty traps people in bad neighborhoods that affect their children separately from the effects of home and school.

Jeanne Brooks-Gunn and her colleagues (Brooks-Gunn, Duncan, Klebanov, & Sealand, 1993) also found that neighborhood effects rival family effects in influencing child development. In addition they found that the absence of more affluent neighbors is more important than the presence of low-income neighbors (Brooks-Gunn, Duncan, Klebanov, & Sealand, 1993). This means that well-functioning adult role models are needed in low-income neighborhoods, and that such positive role models count for a lot in the lives of poor children.

In sum, zip codes matter. Zip codes can determine school achievement as much or more than does the influence of a persons' family, and they often have more power then the quality of the school a child attends. While family involvement and school improvement programs are each to be supported, and some have garnered success (Comer, 2004), they cannot be expected to do all that needs to be done. Most low-performing schools serve poor children who live in neglected neighborhoods and we pay a price for our communal neglect.

We all know that urban segregation of the poor, along with segregation of language minorities and ethnic groups, is the reason that zip codes matter. Since the end of World War II there has been a gradual decline of white middle- and upper-class families in large metropolitan centers. As those families moved to suburbs or small cities, the white middle-class students in the schools of the central cities were replaced by large concentrations of black and Latino students. As Orfield and Lee point out (2005), these minority and poor communities had to cope with inadequate and decaying housing, weak and failing urban infrastructures, shortages of jobs, and perhaps among the most important of these problems, a critical lack of mentors for urban youth. As Rumberger (1987) noted some time ago, without strong positive peer influences, children attending high poverty schools are not likely to achieve well. Zip codes do matter. They determine who is around to exert an influence during a child's formative years.

The zip codes of the middle class have influence too. Several empirical studies have found that attending a middle-class school exposes minority students to higher expectations and more educational and career options. One team of researchers studied voluntary transfer policies in metropolitan St. Louis (Wells & Crain, 1997). They observed that minority students who attend middle- and upper-class schools had higher educational achievement and college attendance rates than their peers in schools where poverty was concentrated. Studies of Boston students who attended suburban public schools revealed that they had access to knowledge and networks of knowledge that their peers in inner-city Boston lacked (Eaton, 2001). These experiences increased their educational and professional opportunities. The famous Gautreaux study of Chicago made this plain years ago (Rubinowitz & Rosenbaum, 2000). In that natural experiment a random set of families received vouchers to move from the 'hood to the 'burbs. Their children succeeded much better than did an equivalent control group. The Gautreaux study provides convincing evidence of the power of neighborhood, and the schools available to those neighborhoods, to influence our nation's youth.

Although we have no idea what the micro elements of a middle-class culture are, when such a culture is well entrenched in a neighborhood, it is the best insurance that the schools in that neighborhood will have the quality and the student norms of behavior that lead to better academic achievement. Perhaps it is because middle-class and residentially stable neighborhoods often manifest a collective sense of efficacy and that, in turn, determines the ways that youth in those neighborhoods are monitored as they grow up (Sampson, Raudenbush & Earls, 1997).

On the other hand, neighborhoods that perpetuate the culture of poverty cannot help but have that culture spill over into the schools their children attend. Obviously, one way to help the American schools achieve more is to weave low-income housing throughout more middle-class zip codes. This would provide more low-income people with access to communities where stability exists, efficacy is promoted, and children have access to a variety of role models. But we are an economically segregated country, a condition perpetuated in various ways by the more affluent and powerful in the nation. So this is not likely to happen.

Yet another way to harness neighborhood effects on achievement is ensuring that low-income people have access to better-paying jobs so they can make and spend more on decent housing. Poverty is what drives families into zip codes that are not healthy for children and other living things. And all those unhealthy things they experience end up, eventually, being dealt with inside the school house.

I could go on. The rates of hunger among the poor continue to be high for an industrialized nation (Nord, Andrews & Carlson, 2004). In 2003 about 12.5 million households, around 36 million people, suffered food insecurity. About 4 million of those households, or around 9.5 million people, actually went hungry some time in that year. And sadly, one-third of this group experienced *chronic* hunger. Seventeen percent of the households with food insecurity have children, and these children do not ordinarily learn well. Perhaps equally unfortunate is the fact that the neighborhood norms for people who are poor promote non-nutritional foods and diets that lead to medical problems. Anemia, vitamin deficiencies, obesity, diabetes, and many other conditions that affect school learning help to keep the academic achievement of poor children lower than it might otherwise be.

The lack of high-quality affordable day care and quality early childhood learning environments is a problem of poverty that has enormous effects on later schooling. The early childhood educational gap between middle-class and poor children is well documented by Valerie Lee and David Burkham in their book *Inequality at the Starting Gate* (2002). More recent studies of the economic returns to society of providing better early childhood education for the poor have looked at the most famous of the early childhood programs with longitudinal data. From projects such as the Perry Preschool, the Abecedarian Project, the Chicago Child-Parent Centers, and the Elmira Prenatal/Early Infancy Project, scholars find that the returns to society range from $3 to almost $9 for every dollar invested. Grunewald and Rolnick (2004, p. 6) of the Minneapolis Federal Reserve noted that when expressed as a rate of return "the real (adjusted for inflation) internal rates of return on these programs range from about seven percent to above 16 percent annually" (see also Lynch, 2004, for a similar argument). Thus, since the return on investment to society for making high-quality early childhood programs available to all of our nation's children is remarkably large, why are we *not* making those investments? A plausible answer is that we won't invest in poor children's futures, nor our own, due to simple mean-spiritedness. It is clearly not due to economics!

Income also plays a role in determining the learning opportunities that are available to children during the summer months. Children of the poor consistently show greater learning losses over summer than do children of the middle class (Cooper, Nye, Charlton, Lindsay & Greathouse, 1996). Middle-class children apparently get a more nutritious cultural and academic diet during the summer than the poor. This results in middle-class children gaining in reading achievement over the summer, while lower-class children lose ground. Every summer the gap between the affluent and the poor that shows up on the first day of kindergarten gets larger and larger.

The effects of smoking, alcohol and other drugs, lack of adequate dental and medical care, increased residential mobility, fewer positive after-school groups in which to participate, and many other factors all take their toll on the families and children of the poor. While these factors all interact with the quality of the teachers and the schools that poor children attend, these social, educational, medical, and neighborhood problems are also independent of the schools, and thus beyond their control. Poverty severely limits what our schools can be expected to accomplish.

Let me take stock here so my argument is clear. I have provided reliable information that a) we have the largest percentage of poor children in the industrialized world, b) people stay poor longer in the United States than elsewhere in the industrialized world, c) poverty is negatively related to school achievement and poverty's effects on our international competitiveness appear to be serious, d) poverty has powerful effects on individuals that limit the expression of genetic diversity as well as strongly influencing the health and place of residence in which children are raised, and e) improvement in the school achievement of students from low-income families will have to come as much from improvements in their outside-of-school lives as from their inside-of school lives.

Because the out-of-school environment is so important an influence on the academic attainment of poor people, there is every reason to suspect that changes in the income of poor families will lead to changes in the school-related behavior and achievement of their children. So let us now examine my thesis, namely, that the simplest way to deal with poverty's effects on achievement is to increase the income of poor people so that they are less poor.

How Increased Family Income Affects Student Behavior and School Achievement

Two studies from a growing number about the effects of income growth on families and children have impressed me. First is the study by Dearing, McCartney, and Taylor (2001), who used as a measure of poverty the ratio of income available to the needs faced by a family. A ratio of 1.00 means that the family is just making it, that their family income and their needs such as housing, food, transportation, and so forth, are matched. A ratio of 3.00 would be more like that of a middle-class family, and a ratio of .8 would indicate poverty of some magnitude. A large and reasonably representative sample of poor and non-poor families were followed for three years and their income-to-needs ratios computed regularly, as were their children's scores on various social and academic measures. What was found was that as poor families went from poor to a lot less poor, for whatever reasons, their children's performance began to resemble that of the never poor children with whom they were matched.

Figure 26.7 presents data illustrating the performance of poor children on a measure of school readiness, as the income of poor and non-poor children changed over these three years. The mean change in income-to-needs ratios over the time period of the study is where the lines cross. That is, the mean change in income-to-needs was a positive 73, though some families went up more and some families lost ground over this time period. Plotted against a measure of school readiness, the slope of the non-poor children is seen to hardly have changed at all. Whether family income-to-need ratios went up or went down seemed unrelated to the school readiness scores of the non-poor. But the slope of the poor children showed quite a large change. Poor children in families experiencing loss of income over the three years lost ground to the non-poor on this measure of academic readiness. But children in families whose income improved showed growth in school readiness over the three years. Most interesting of all, the poor children in families whose income went up ended up scoring as well as the students who had never been poor. This was true even though the set of families who were not poor earned considerably more money than those who had been poor. Although there are many possible explanations for this, a reasonable one is that rising incomes provide families with dignity and hope, and these in turn promote greater family stability and better childcare.

An almost identical relationship was found when plotting change in income-to-needs ratios against other academic-like outcome measures such as measures of a child's expressive language, or of their receptive language. And in Figure 26.8 we see the same relationship shown for a measure of social behavior, a non-academic measure that identifies children whose presence in classes will promote or impede the work of their teachers.

Figure 26.8 illustrates that as income-to-need ratios changed for the poor and the non-poor, the poor again showed significant slope changes and the non-poor once again did not. Furthermore, poor children in families experiencing growth in income over the three years once again ended up scoring as well in social behavior as the children who had never been poor.

Figure 27.7 The relationship between school readiness and income change among poor and non-poor families (reprinted from Dearing, McCartney, & Taylor, 2001, used by permission of the authors).

Figure 26.8 The relationship between positive social behavior and income change among poor and non-poor families (reprinted from Dearing, McCartney, & Taylor, 2001, used by permission of the authors).

As noted earlier, bigger changes are expected to occur for the poor than the non-poor as positive changes in their environments occur. We see that here. Also worth noting is that Duncan and Brooks-Gunn (2001) found that the greatest impact of family income on children's academic outcomes is when they are the youngest, and this was a study of children from birth to three years of age.

In an interesting follow-up to the original study, these researchers went on to estimate the effect size of making permanent the income changes that had occurred in the sample of poor families, and comparing that effect size to those that the Department of Health and Human Services estimates for the early head start program (Taylor, Dearing & McCartney, 2004). Both in the Head Start study and this one, the same Mental Development Index was used to look at intellectual functioning and both studies measured students' negative behavior, as well. Those interesting findings are presented as Table 26.9.

In the first row of Table 26.9 we see that Head Start researchers estimate that children enrolled in that program increased between 12% and 15% of a standard deviation on the Mental Development Index. These children also showed a decline of 10% to 11% percent of a standard deviation in their negative behavior. Those outcomes are socially significant and large enough to claim effectiveness for the gigantic head start apparatus. The second row of this table are Taylor, Dearing & McCartney's (2004) estimates of what would happen were the income of the poor families in their study increased one standard deviation, or about $13,000 per year. This estimate shows that the children for low-income families would have had gains in IQ of about 15% of a standard deviation, and that the children would decline in negative behavior about 20% of a standard deviation.

The success brought about by an increase in the incomes of poor families apparently matches or exceeds the success our nation obtains from running a giant program like Head Start, that enrolls only about 60% of those who are eligible. Equally intriguing in this study was that raising the income of families to improve the lives of poor children was actually a bit less expensive than the annual cost per-child of attending Head Start. It is impossible not to speculate about what the results might be for our society if we combined both approaches to school improvement, providing both high-quality early childhood programs and better incomes for the poor!

Table 26.9 Comparison of the Effects of Traditional Head Start and Simple Growth in Family Income on Children's Cognitive and Affective Behavior

	Mental Development Index (percent of a standard deviation)	**Negative Behavior Index** (percent of a standard deviation)
Head Start Program	Up 12–15 percent	Down 10–11 percent
Income Growth Study	Up 15 percent	Down 20 percent

Source: Reprinted from Taylor, Dearing, & McCartney, 2004, by permission of the authors.

The second study of income change and school success is from North Carolina and is almost a natural experiment in income redistribution (Costello, Compton, Keeler, & Angold, 2003). A Duke University team noticed that their study of psychiatric disorders and drug abuse within a rural community included a group of people who had risen out of poverty because of the income derived from a recently opened gaming casino. During these changes the researchers had been giving annual psychiatric assessments to about 1,400 children, 350 of them American Indians, and they did so over an eight-year period. The children ranged in age from 9 to 13 and were in three distinct groups: those who had never been poor, those who had been persistently poor, and a group that had been poor until the casino came to the reservation.

The researchers discovered that moving out of poverty was associated with a decrease in frequency of psychiatric symptoms over the ensuing four years. In fact, by the fourth year, the psychiatric symptom level was the same among children whose families moved out of poverty as it was among children whose families were never in poverty. A small replication of the findings was available for a group of non-Indians who also moved out of poverty over this same time period. Once again, as in the Dearing, McCartney and Taylor (2001) study, and in the main part of this study, negative psychiatric symptoms disappeared as income rose. The researchers offered an explanation for these findings, namely, that relieving poverty appeared to increase the level of parental supervision of children. One last finding of interest from this study is that additional income for the families of the never-poor had no effect on frequency of behavioral or emotional symptoms. As is common in this area of research, and noted earlier, improving the income of the very poor has large effects, while improving the income of the less poor has negligible effects.

Although the literature is not voluminous, these are not the only studies to show that a lessening of poverty helps young children succeed better at school and in life. The negative income tax was studied 20 years ago and it revealed that increases in family income resulted in increased school attendance and better school achievement for the families that gained in income (Salkind & Haskins, 1982). The work assistance programs of the 1990s have also been examined and again there is some evidence that as family income went up, the achievement and behavior of children in those families improved (Huston, Duncan, Granger, Bos, McLoyd, Mistry, Crosby, Gibson, Magnuson, Romich, & Ventura, 2001). The evidence of the positive influence on student achievement when families are able to leave poverty is consistent and replicable, suggesting that inside-of-school reform needs to begin with outside-of-school reform. Otherwise, like the drunk in the allegory I began with, we will be looking for our keys in the wrong place.

What We Need To Do

Poverty, through its many connections to other parts of people's lives, is an obstacle that is not easy for most educators to overcome. Poverty in a community almost ensures that many of the children who enter their neighborhood schools cannot maximally profit from the instruction provided there. Helping to eliminate some of that poverty is not just morally appropriate, though it is that, first of all. But to a convincing degree finding ways to reduce poverty to improve schooling is evidence based: It takes no great wisdom to realize that families with increasing fortunes have more dignity and hope, and are thus able to take better care of their children, than do families in more dire straights, where anxiety and despair are the more common emotional reactions.

So when we push for higher qualifications for the teachers of the poor, as we should, we also may need to push ourselves and others to stop shopping at companies like Wal-Mart. The logic of this is simple: if we want to primarily hold our teachers responsible for increasing their students' educational attainment, then we need at a minimum to provide those teachers with children who enter their classrooms healthy and ready to learn. Twenty years ago this was one of our national goals, to be reached by the year 2000. But one of the impediments to reaching that goal was Wal-Mart, now the largest employer in the United States. Wal-Mart and companies like them do not provide the great majority of their employees the income, medical insurance, or retirement plans needed to promote healthy families or raise healthy children. Wal-Mart and companies like it have a terrible record in its treatment of woman with children, a group who make up a big share of the poor households in this country (Shulman, 2003). Thus Wal-Mart is an impediment to school reform and although it is not usually noted, Wal-Mart is one reason we did not reach our national goal.

There are so many other problems we need to address, as well. When we push for more rigorous standards in our schools, we should also push for a raise in the minimum wage, or better yet, for livable wages. If we do not do this then we will ensure that the vast majority of those meeting the increasingly rigorous requirements for high school graduation will be those students fortunate enough to be born into the right families. If we really want a more egalitarian set of educational outcomes, our nation needs a more equalitarian wage structure.

For these same reasons when we push for more professional development for teachers and mentoring programs for new teachers, we need also to demand that women's wages be set equal to those of men doing comparable work, since it is working women and their children who make up a large percentage of America's poor.

When we push for advanced placement courses, or college preparatory curricula for all our nation's students, we must simultaneously demand universal medical coverage for all our children. Only then will all our children have the health that allows them to attend school regularly and learn effectively, instead of missing opportunities to learn due to a lack of medical treatment.

When we push for all-day kindergarten, or quality early childhood care, or de-tracked schools we need also to argue for affordable housing throughout our communities, so neighborhoods have the possibility of exerting more positive influences on children and people can move from lead and mercury polluted areas to those that are less toxic, and thus less likely to cause birth defects. This goal requires educators, parents, and other concerned citizens to be in the forefront of the environmental fight. To fight for clean air and water, and for less untested chemicals in all our food products, is a fight to have more healthy children for our schools to educate. The psychological and financial costs on families and the broader society because of students needing special education can be markedly reduced by our demands for a healthier environment.

In my estimation we will get better public schools by requiring of each other participation in building a more economically equitable society. This is of equal or greater value to our nation's future well-being than a fight over whether phonics is scientifically based, whether standards are rigorous enough, or whether teachers have enough content knowledge.

Conclusion

All I am saying in this essay is that I am tired of acting like the schools, all alone, can do what is needed to help more people achieve higher levels of academic performance in our society. As Jean Anyon (1997, p. 168) put it, "Attempting to fix inner city schools without fixing the city in which they are embedded is like trying to clean the air on one side of a screen door."

To clean the air on both sides of the screen door we need to begin thinking about building a two-way system of accountability for contemporary America. The obligation that we educators have accepted to be accountable to our communities must become reciprocal. Our communities must also be accountable to those of us who work in the schools, and they can do this by creating social conditions for our nation that allow us to do our jobs well. Accountability is a two-way process; it requires a principal and an agent. For too long schools have thought of themselves only as agents who must meet the demands of the principal, often the local community, state, or federal government. It is time for principals (and other school leaders) to become principals. That is, school people need to see communities as agents as well as principals and hold communities to standards that ensure all our children are accorded the opportunities necessary for growing well.

It does take a whole village to raise a child, and we actually know a little bit about how to do that. What we seem not to know how to do in modern America is to raise the village to promote communal values that ensure that all our children will prosper. We need to face the fact that our whole society needs to be held as accountable for providing healthy children ready to learn, as our schools are for delivering quality instruction. One-way accountability, where we are always blaming the schools for the faults that we find, is neither just nor likely to solve the problems we want to address.

I am tired, also, of those among us who say the poor are not really bad off, as claimed recently in a lengthy research report from the Heritage Foundation (Rector & Johnson, 2004). Our poor today, they say, are really much better oil than the poor in other countries, or compared to the immigrant poor at the turn of the 20th century. Because of refrigerators, televisions, and automobiles, the poor in America today actually might live as well or better than royalty did in the 13th century. But that completely fails to capture what poverty is like for poor children. As a reminder about the reality of poverty, and to shame the Heritage Foundation and all who vote to keep income inequality as it is, I want to close this essay with the introduction to *Amazing Grace,* by Jonathan Kozol (1995). In doing this 1 move away from the analytic and quantitative ways to think about poverty and its effects, and move to the only way we might actually comprehend the reality of poverty for our young, through the use of narrative.

> The number 6 train from Manhattan to the South Bronx makes nine stops in the 18-minute ride between East 59th Street and Brook Avenue. When you enter the train, you are in the seventh richest congressional district in the nation. When you leave, you are in the poorest.
>
> The 600,000 people who live here and the 450,000 people who live in Washington Heights and Harlem, which are separated from the South Bronx by a narrow river, make up one of the largest racially segregated concentrations of poor people in our nation.
>
> Brook Avenue, which is the tenth stop on the local, lies in the center of Mott Haven, whose 48,000 people are the poorest in the South Bronx. Two thirds are Hispanic, one third black. Thirty-five percent are children. In 1991, the median household income of the area, according to *The New York Times,* was $7,600.
>
> St. Ann's Church, on St. Ann's Avenue, is three blocks from the subway station. The children who come to this small Episcopal Church for food and comfort, and to play, and the mothers and fathers who come here for prayer, are said to be the poorest people in New York. "More than 95 percent are poor," the pastor says—"the poorest of the poor, poor by any standard I can think of."
>
> At the elementary school that serves the neighborhood across the avenue, only seven of 800 children do not qualify for free school lunches. "Five of those seven," says the principal, "get reduced-price lunches, because they are classified as only 'poor,' not 'destitute.'"
>
> In some cities, the public reputation of a ghetto neighborhood bears little connection to the world that you discover when you walk the streets with children and listen to their words. In Mott Haven, this is not the case. By and large, the words of the children in the streets and schools and houses that surround St. Ann's more than justify the grimness in the words of journalists who have described the area.
>
> Crack-cocaine addiction and the intravenous use of heroin, which children I have met here call "the needle drug," are woven into the texture of existence in Mott Haven. Nearly 4,000 heroin injectors, many of whom are HIV-infected, live here. Virtually every child at St. Ann's knows someone, a relative or neighbor, who has died of AIDS, and most children here know many others who are dying now of the disease. One quarter of the women of Mott Haven who are tested in obstetric wards are positive for HIV. Rates of pediatric AIDS, therefore, are high.

514 • David C. Berliner

Depression is common among children in Mott Haven. Many cry a great deal but cannot explain exactly why.

Fear and anxiety are common. Many cannot sleep.

Asthma is the most common illness among children here. Many have to struggle to take in a good deep breath. Some mothers keep oxygen tanks, which children describe as "breathing machines," next to their children's beds.

The houses in which these children live, two thirds of which are owned by the City of New York, are often as squalid as the houses of the poorest children I have visited in rural Mississippi, but there is none of the greenness and the healing sweetness of the Mississippi countryside outside their windows, which are often barred and bolted as protection against thieves.

Some of these houses are freezing in the winter. In dangerously cold weather, the city sometimes distributes electric blankets and space heaters to its tenants. In emergency conditions, if space heaters can't be used, because substandard wiring is overloaded, the city's practice is to pass out sleeping bags.

"You just cover up ... and hope you wake up the next morning," says a father of four children, one of them an infant one month old, as they prepare to climb into their sleeping bags in hats and coats on a December night.

In humid summer weather, roaches crawl on virtually every surface of the houses in which many of the children live. Rats emerge from holes in bedroom walls, terrorizing infants in their cribs. In the streets outside, the restlessness and anger that are present in all seasons frequently intensify under the stress of heat.

In speaking of rates of homicide in New York City neighborhoods, the *Times* refers to the streets around St. Ann's as "the deadliest blocks" in "the deadliest precinct" of the city. If there is a deadlier place in the United States, I don't know where it is.

In 1991, 84 people, more than half of whom were 21 or younger, were murdered in the precinct. A year later, ten people were shot dead on a street called Beekman Avenue, where many of the children I have come to know reside. On Valentine's Day of 1993, three more children and three adults were shot dead on the living room floor of an apartment six blocks from the run-down park that serves the area.

In early July of 1993, shortly before the first time that I visited the neighborhood, three more people were shot in 30 minutes in three unrelated murders in the South Bronx, one of them only a block from St. Ann's Avenue. A week later, a mother was murdered and her baby wounded by a bullet in the stomach while they were standing on a South Bronx corner. Three weeks after that, a minister and elderly parishioner were shot outside the front door of their church, while another South Bronx resident was discovered in his bathtub with his head cut off. In subsequent days, a man was shot in both his eyes and a ten-year-old was critically wounded in the brain.

What is it like for children to grow up here? What do they think the world has done to them? Do they believe that they are being shunned or hidden by society? If so, do they think that they deserve this? What is it that enables some of them to pray? And when they pray, what do they say to God?[1]

Notes

1. My thanks to Jonathan Kozol for permission to use this lengthy quote. His insightful and poignant writing has educated and moved so many of us, but as is clear, not yet enough of us.

References

Agency for Healthcare Research and Quality (2005). Archived Clinical Practices Guidelines, National Library of Methcine. No. 12. *Otitis metha with effusion in young children*, Retrieved May 17, 2005 from http://www.ncbi.nlm.nih.gov

Arnrein, A. L., & Berliner, D. C. (2002, March 28). High-stakes testing, uncertainty, and student learning. *Education Policy Analysis Archives, 10*(18), Retrieved May 15, 2005 from http:// epaa.asu.edu/epaa/v10n18/

Anyon, J. (1995). Race, social class, and educational reform in an inner city school. *Teachers College Record, 97,* 69-94.

Anyon, J. (1997). Ghetto schooling. *A political economy of urban school reform.* New York: Teachers College Press.

Anyon, J. (2005). What "Counts" as Educational Policy? Notes toward a New Paradigm. *Harvard Educational Review, 75*(1), 65–88.

Asimov, N. (2005, April 5). Study puts Oakland dropout rate at 52%, Mayor decries crisis—district questions research accuracy. *San Francisco Chronicle,* Retrieved May 15, 2005 from http://sfgate.com/

Berliner, D. C (2004). If the underlying premise for No Child Left Behind is false, how can that act solve our problems? In K. Goodman, P. Shannon, Y. Goodman, & R. Rapoport (Eds.), *Saving our schools.* Berkeley, CA: RDR Books.

Berliner, D. C, & Biddle, B. J. (1995). *The manufactured crisis. Myth, fraud, and the Attack on America's Public Schools.* Reathng, MA: Adthson-Wesley.

Biddle, B. J. (Ed.) (2001). *Social class, poverty, and education.* New York: RoutlegeFarmer.

Books, S. (2002). Poverty and environmentally induced damage to children, in V. Polakow (Ed.), *The public assault on America's children: Poverty, violence, and juvenile injustice.* New York:Teachers College Press.

Brooks-Gunn, J., Duncan, G. J., Klebanov, P. K., & Sealand, N. (1993). Do neighborhoods influence child and adolescent development? *American Journal of Sociology, 99,* 353–395.

Catsambis, S., & Beveridge, A. W. (2001). Does neighborhood matter? Family, neighborhood, and school influences on eighth grade mathematics achievement. *Sociological Focus, 34(4),* 435–457.

Centers for Disease Control (2004). *Children's blood lead levels in the United States.* Retrieved May15, 2005 from http://www.cdc.gov/

Centers for Disease Control (2005). *Breastfeeding Practices: Results from the 2003 National Immunization Survey.* Retrieved May 17, 2005 from http://www.cdc.gov

Children & Asthma in America (2005). Retrieved May 15, 2005 from http://www.asthmainamerica.com/

Comer, J. P. (2004). *Leave no child behind: Preparing today's youth for tomorrow's world.* New Haven, CT: Yale University Press.

Cooper, H., Nye, B., Charlton, K., Lindsay,J., & Greathouse, S. (1996). The effects of summer vacation on achievement test scores: a narrative and meta-analytic review. *Review of Ed-ucatumal Research, 66*(3), 227–268.

Costello, E. J., Compton, S. N., Keeler, G., & Angold, A. (2003). Relationships between poverty and psychopathology: A natural experiment. *Journal of the American Medical Association, 290,* 2023–2029.

Cremin, L. A. (1990). *Popular education and its discontents.* New York: Harper & Row.

Dearing, E., McCartney, K., & Taylor, B. A. (2001). Change in family income-to-needs matters more for children with less. *Child Development, 72*(6), 1779–1793.

Duncan, G. J., & Brooks-Gunn, J. (1997). *Consequences of growing up poor.* New York: Russell Sage Foundation.

Duncan, G. J., & Brooks-Gunn, J. (2001). Poverty, welfare reform, and children's achievement (49–75). In B. J. Biddle (Ed.), *Social class, poverty, and achievement.* New York: Routlage-Farmer.

Eaton, S. (2001). *The other Boston busing story: What's won and lost across the boundary line.* New Haven, CT: Yale University Press.

Erbe, B, & Shiner, J. (1997, March 29). What Kate for the 'Partial-Birth' Bill. *Washington Times* p. 1.

Garner, C. L., & Raudenbush, S. W. (1991). Neighborhood effects on educational attainment: A multilevel analysis. *Sociology of Education, 64,* 251–262.

Gillespie, K. (2001). *How vision impacts literacy: An educational problem that can be solved.* Harvard Graduate School of Education News, 17 April 2001. Retrieved May 15, 2005 from http:// www.gse.harvard.edu/

Gonzales, P., Guzmán, J. C, Partelow, L., Pahlke, E, Jocelyn, L., Kastberg, D., & Williams, T. (2004). *Highlights from the Trends in International Mathematics and Science Study (T1MSS) 2003. (NCES 2005–005).* U.S. Department of Education, National Center for Education Statistics. Washington, D.C.: U.S. Government Printing Office. Retrieved May 15, 2005 from http:// nces.ed.gov/pubs2005/2005005.pdf

Gould, M., & Gould, H. (2003). A clear vision for equity and opportunity. *Phi Delta Kappan, 85(4),* 324–328.

Grunewald, R, & Rolnick, A. (2004). *A proposal for achieving high returns on early childhood Development.* Minneapolis, MN: Federal Reserve Bank of Minneapolis. Retrieved May 16, 2005 from http://minneapolisfed.org/research/studies/early-child/draft_ecd_proposal.pdf

Hagerman, R. J., & Falkenstein, A. R. (1987). An association between recurrent otitis media in infancy and later hyperactivity. *Clinical Pethatrics, 26(5),* 253–257.

Herrnstein, R. J., & Murray, C. (1994). *The bell curve: intelligence and class structure in American life.* New York: The Free Press.

Huston, A. C, Duncan, G. J., Granger, R., Bos, J., McLoyd, V., Mistry, R., Crosby, D., Gibson, C, Magnuson, K., Romich, J., & Ventura, A. (2001). Work-based antipoverty programs for parents can enhance the school performance and social behavior of children. *Child Development, 72,* 318–336.

Knishkowy, B., Palti, H., Adler, B., & Tepper D,. (1991). Effect of otitis media on development: a community-based study. *Early Human Development, 26(2),* 101–111.

Kozol, J. (1995). *Amazing grace: The lives of children and the conscience of a nation.* New York: Crown.

Lanphear, B. P., Dietrich, K., Auinger, P., & Cox, C. (2000). Subclinical lead toxicity in U.S. children and adolescents. *Public Health Reports, 115,* 521–529 Retrieved May 15, 2005 from http://www.nmic.org/

Lee, V. E., & Burkam, D. T. (2002). *Inequality at the starting gate.* Washington, D.C.: Economic Policy Institute.

Lemke, M., Calsyn, C, Lippman, L., Jocelyn, L., Kastberg, D., Liu, Y. Y., Roey, S., Williams, T., Kruger, X, & Bairu, G. (2001). *Outcomes of Learning: Results from the 2000 Program for International Student Assessment of 15-year-olds in reading, mathematics, and science literacy, NCES 2002-115.* Washington, D.C.: U.S. Department of Education, National Center for Education Statistics.

Lemke, M., Sen, A., Pahlke, E., Partelow, L., Miller, D., Williams, T., Kastberg, D., & Jocelyn, L. (2004). *International outcomes of learning in mathematics literacy and problem solving: PISA 2003, results from the U.S. perspective* (NCES 2005–003). Washington, D.C.: U.S. Department of Education, National Center for Education Statistics.

Lewontin, R. (1982). *Human diversity.* New York: Freeman.

Luotonen, M., Uhari, M., Aitola, L., Lukkaroinen, A., Luotonen, J., Uhari, M., & Korkeamaki, R-L. (1996). Recurrent otitis media during infancy and linguistic skills at the age of nine years. *Pethatric Infectious Disease Journal, 15(10),* 854–858.

Lynch, R. G. (2004). *Exceptional Returns: Economic, Fiscal, and Social Benefits of Investment in Early Childhood Development.* Washington, D.C.: Economic Policy Institute.

Martin, M. (2004). *A strange ignorance: The role of lead poisoning in "failing schools."* Retrieved May 15, 2005 from http://www.azsba.org/lead.htm

Mishel, L., Bernstein, J., & Allegretto, S. (2005). *The state of working America 2004/2005.* A publication of the Economic Policy Institute, Washington, D.C.. Ithaca, NY: Cornell University Press.

Nichols, S. N., & Berliner, D. C. (2006). *The inevitable corruption of indicators and educators through high-stakes testing.* Tempe, AZ: College of Education, Education Policy Studies Laboratory Report EPSL-0503–101-EPRU. Retrieved May 15, 2005 from http://www.asu.edu

Nichols, S. N., Glass, G.V, & Berliner, D. C. (2005). High-Stakes Testing and Student Achievement: Does accountability pressure increase student learning? *Education Policy Analysis Archives,* (14)1. Retrieved April 3, 2006, from http://epaa.asu.edu/epaa/vi4nl/.

Niemela, M., Pihakari, O., Pokka, T., Uhari, M., & Uhari, M. (2000). Pacifier as a risk factor for acute otitis media: A randomized, controlled trial of parental counseling. *Pediatrics,106*(3), 483–488.

Nord, M., Andrews, M., & Carlson, S. (2004). *Household food security in the United States, 2003.* Food Assistance and Nutrition Research Report No. (FANRR42). Washington, D.C.: Economic Research Service, United States Department of Agriculture. Retrieved May 16, 2005 from: http://www.ers.usda.gov/publications/fanrr42/

Ogle, L., Sen, A., Pahlke, E., Jocelyn, L., Kastberg, D., Roey, S., & Williams, T. (2003). *International comparisons in fourth-grade reading literacy: findings from the Progress in International Reading Literacy Study (PIRLS) of 2001* (NCES 2003–073). U.S. Department of Education, National Center for Educational Statistics. Washington, D.C.: U.S. Government Printing Office.

Orfield, G., & Lee, C. (2005). *Why segregation matters: Poverty and educational inequality.* Cambridge, MA: Harvard University The Civil Rights Project. Retrieved May 15, 2005 from http://www.civilrightsproject.harvard.edu

Peterson, B. S., Anderson, A. W., Ehrenkranz, R., Staib, L. H., Tageldin, M., Colson, E., Gore, J. C, Duncan, C. C, Makuch, R., & Mendt, L. (2003). Regional brain volumes and their later neurodevelopmental correlates in term and preterm infants. *Pediatrics, 111(5),* 939–948.

Peterson B, S., Vohr, B., Staib, L. H., Cannistraci, C. J., Dolberg, A., Schneider, K. C, Katz, K. H., Westerveld, M., Sparrow, S., Anderson, A. W., Duncan, C. C, Makuch, R. W., Gore, J. C, & Ment, L. R. (2000). Regional brain volume abnormalities and long-term cognitive outcome in preterm infants. *Journal of the American Medical Association, 284,* 1939–1947.

Rector, R. E., & Johnson, K. A. (2004). *Understanding poverty in America.* Washington, D.C.: Heritage Foundation Backgrounder #1713. Retrieved May 15, 2005 from http://www.her-itage.org/

Rothstein, R. (2004). *Class and schools: Using social, economic, and educational reform to close the black-white achievement gap.* Washington, DC: Economic Policy Institute.

Rubinowitz, L. S., & Rosenbaum, J. E. (2000). *Crossing the class and color lines: from public housing to white suburbia.* Chicago: University of Chicago Press.

Rumberger, R. (1987). High school dropouts: A review of issues and evidence. *Review of Eduncational Research, 57(2),* 101–121.

Salkind, N. J., & Haskins, R. (1982). Negative income tax: The impact on children from low-income families. *Journal of family Issues, 3,* 165–180.

Sampson, R. J., Raudenbush, S. W., & Earls, F. (1997). Neighborhoods and violent crime: A multilevel study of collective efficacy. *Science, 277,* 918–924.

Shulman, B. (2003). *The Betrayal of Work: How Low-Wage Jobs Fail 30 Million Americans.* New York: New Press.

Smith, M. L. (2004). *Political spectacle and the fate of American schools.* New York: Routledge-Farmer.

Taylor, B. A., Dearing, E., & McCartney, K. (2004). Incomes and Outcomes in Early Childhood. *Journal of Human Resources, 39(4),* 980–1007.

Traub, J. (2000, January 16). What no school can do. *New York Times Magazine.* Retrieved May 19, 2005, from http://www.augsburg.edu/

Turkheimer, E., Haley, A., Waldron, M., D'Onofrio, B., & Gottesman, 1. (2003). Socioeconomic status modifies hereditability of IQ in young children. *Psychological Science, 14(6),* 623–628.

UNICEF (2005). *Child poverty in rich countries, 2005.* Innocenti Report Card No. 6. Florence, Italy: UNICEF Innocenti Research Centre. Retrieved May 16, 2005 from www.unicef.org/ ire and www.unicef-irc.org

U.S. Environmental Protection Agency 2003. America's children and the environmental measures contaminants, body burdens, and illnesses. Washington, D.C.: Author. Retrieved July 23, 2005 from http://www.epa.gov

Wells, A., & Crain, R. (1997). *Stepping over the color line: African-American students in white, suburban schools.* New Haven, CT: Yale University Press.

World Bank (2005). World Development Indicators database. Retrieved May 15, 2005 from http ://www. worldbank.org

PART **VI**

Suggested Readings

Anyon, J. (1997). *Ghetto schooling: A political economy of urban educational reform.* New York: Teachers College Press.

Anyon, J. (2005a). *Radical possibilities: Public policy, urban education and a new social movement.* New York: Routledge.

Anyon, J. (2005b). What "counts" as educational policy? Notes toward a new paradigm."*Harvard Educational Review, 75*(1), 65–88.

Apple, M. W. (2006). *Educating the "Right" Way.* New York: Routledge.

Belfield, C. R. & Levin H. M. (2002b). The effects of competition between schools on educational outcomes: A review for the United States. 72. *Review of Education Research, 279.*

Berends, M., Bodilly, S., & Kirby, S. (2002). Looking back over a decade of whole-school reform: The experience of new American schools. *Phi Delta Kappan, 84*(2), 168–175.

Berliner, D. (2006). Our impoverished view of educational reform Teachers College Record, 108(6), 949–995.

Berliner, D. and Biddle, B. (1996). *The manufactured crisis.* New York: Longman.

Binder, A. J. (2000). Why do some curricular challenges work while others do not? The case of three Afrocentric challenges. *Sociology of Education, 73,* 69–91.

Borman, K.M., Cookson, Jr., P.W., Sadovnik, A. R., & Spade, J. Z. (1996). *Implementing educational reform: Sociological perspectives on educational policy.* Wesport, CT: Ablex.

Borman, G., Hewes, G., Overman, L., & Brown, S. (2003). Comprehensive school reform and student achievement: A meta-analysis. *Review of Educational Research, 73*(2), 125–230.

Borman, K. M., Kersaint, G., Boydston, T., Lee, R. Cotner, B., Uekawa, K., Baber, G., Kromrey, J., & Katzenmeyer, W. (2004). *Meaningful urban education reform: confronting the learning crisis in mathematics and science.* Albany: SUNY Press.

Bulkley, K., & Wohlstetter (Eds.) (2004). *Taking account of charter schools: What's happened and what's next.* New York: Teachers College Press.

Darling-Hammond, L. (1996). The right to learn and the advancement of teaching: Research, policy, and practice for democratic education. *Peabody Journal of Education, 67*(3), 123–154.

Darling-Hammond, L. (1997). *The right to learn: A blueprint for creating schools that work.* San Francisco, CA: Jossey-Bass.

Datnow, A., Borman, G., Stringfield, S., Overman, L., & Castellano, M. (2003). Comprehensive school reform in culturally and linguistically diverse contexts: Implementation and outcomes from a four-year study. *Educational Evaluation and Policy Analysis, 25*(2), 25–54.

Datnow, A., & Stringfield, S. (2000). Working together for reliable school reform. *Journal of Education for Students Placed at Risk, 5*(1 & 2), 183–204.

Edmonds, R. (1979). Effective schools for the urban poor. *Educational Leadership, 37,* 15–27.

Edmonds, R. (1982). Programs of school improvement: An overview. *Educational Leadership, 40,* 4–11.

Elmore, R. (2004). *School reform from the inside out: Policy, practices and performance.* Cambridge, MA: Harvard.

Epstein, J. (2001). *School, family and community partnerships: Preparing educators and improving schools.* Boulder, CO: Westview Press.

Fine, M. (Ed.). (1994). *Chartering urban school reform.* New York: Teachers College Press.

Fullan, M. G., & Stiegelbauer, S. (1991). *The new meaning of educational change.* New York: Teachers College Press.

Fuller, B. (2000). *Inside charter schools.* Cambridge, MA: Harvard.

Gamoran, A. (1996). Student achievement in public magnet, public comprehensive, and private city high schools. *Educational Evaluation and Policy Analysis.*

Henig, J. (1994). *Rethinking school choice. Limits of the market metaphor.* Princeton, NJ: Princeton University Press.

Hess, G. Alfred, Jr. (1995). *Restructuring Urban schools: A Chicago perspective.* New York: Teachers College Press.

Hubbard, L., Stein, M. K., & Mehan, H. (2006). *Reform as learning: When school reform collides with school culture and community politics.* New York: Routledge

Lauen, D. L. (2007). The false promises of school choice in NCLB. In A. R. Sadovnik, J. A. O' Day, G. Bohrnstedt, & K. Borman (Eds.), *No child left behind and the reduction of the achievement gap: Sociological perspectives on federal educational policy.* New York: Routledge.

Lee, V. E., & Smith, J. B. (1995, October). Effects of high school restructuring and size on gains in achievement for early secondary school students. *Sociology of Education, 68*(4), 241–270.

Lee, V. E., & Smith, J. B. (2001). *Restructuring high schools for equity and excellence: What works.* New York: Teachers College Press.

Lipman, P. (1998). *Race, class and power in school restructuring.* New York: SUNY Press.

Lipman, P. (2003). *High stakes education: Inequality, globalization, and urban school reform.* New York: Routledge.

McNeil, L. M. 2000. *Contradictions of school reform: Educational costs of standardized testing.* New York: Routledge.

Mickelson, R. A. (2001). Subverting swan: first- and second-generation segregation in the Charlotte-Mecklenburg school. *American Educational Research Journal, 38*(2), 215–252.

Mickelson, R. A. (1999). International business machinations: A case study of corporate involvement in local educational reform. *Teachers College Record, 100*(3), 476–512.

Noguera, P. A. (2003). *City schools and the American dream: Reclaiming the promise of public education.* New York: Teachers College Press.

Oakes, J. (2004). Investigating the claims in Williams v. the State of California: An unconstitutional denial of education's basic tools. *Teachers College Record, 106*(10), 1889–1906.

O'Day, J. A. (2002). Complexity, accountability, and school improvement. *Harvard Educational Review, 72*(3), 293–329.

O'Day, J. A., & Smith, M. S. (1992). Systemic reform and equal educational opportunity. In S. H. Fuhrman (Ed.), *Designing coherent education policy* (pp. 250–312). San Francisco: Jossey-Bass.

Odden, A. (1993). School finance reform in Kentucky, New Jersey and Texas. *Journal of Education Finance, 18*, 293–317.

Orfield, G., & Ashkinaze, C. (1991). *The closing door: Conservative policy and Black opportunity.* Chicago: University of Chicago Press.

Orfield G., & Easton, S. (1996). *Dismantling segregation: The quiet reversal of Brown v. Board of Education.* New York: New Press.

Orfield, G., & Lee, J. (2004). *Brown at 50: King's dream or Plessy's nightmare?* http://www.civilrightsproject.harvard.edu/research/deseg/reseg_schools99.php.

Orfield, G., & John Yun, J. T. (1999). Resegregation in American schools. Cambridge, MA: The Civil Rights Project, Harvard University. http://www.civilrightsproject.harvard.edu/research/deseg/reseg_schools99.php.

Powers, J. M. (2004) High-Stakes accountability and equity: Using evidence from California's Public Schools Accountability Act to address the issues in *Williams v. State of California. American Educational Research Journal, 41*(4), 763–795

Powers, J. M., & Cookson, Jr., P. W. (1999). School choice as a political movement. *Educational Policy, 13*(1,2), 104–122.

Ray, C. A., & Mickelson, R. A. (1993). Restructured students for restructured work: The economy, school reform, and noncollege-Bound Youth. *Sociology of Education, 66*, 1–23.

Ready, D. G., Lee, Valerie E., & Welner, K. (2004). Educational equity and social structure: School size, overcrowding, and school-within-schools. *Teachers College Record,106*(10), 1989–2014.

Rosenbaum, J. E. (2001). *Beyond college for all: Career paths for the forgotten half.* New York: Russell Sage Foundation.

Rothstein, R. (2004). *Class and schools: Using social, economic, and educational reform to close the Black-White achievement gap.* New York: Teachers College Press.

Sadovnik, A. R., O' Day, J. A., Bohrnstedt , G., & Borman, K. M. (Eds.) (2007). *No child left behind and the reduction of the achievement gap: Sociological perspectives on federal educational policy.* New York: Routledge.

Van Dunk, E., & Dickman, E. (2003). *School choice and the question of accountability.* New Haven, CT: Yale University Press.

Wells, A. S. (1993). *Time to choose: America at the crossroads of school choice policy.* New York: Hill and Wang.

Wells, Amy, Artiles, L., Carnochan, S., Cooper, C. Grutzik, C. Holme, J. Lopez, A., Scott, J., Slayton J., & Vasuveda, A. (1998). *Beyond the rhetoric of charter school reform: A study of ten California districts.* Los Angeles: UCLA.

Wells, A .S., Holme, J. J., Tijerina Revilla, A., & Korantemaa Atanda, A. (2004). How desegregation changed us: The effects of racially mixed schools on students and society: A study of desegregated high schools and their class of 1980 Graduates. http://www.tc.columbia.edu/faculty/documents.htm?facid=asw86. Forthcoming in *In search of Brown*, Harvard University Press.

Whitty, G. (1996). Creating quasi-markets in education: A review of recent research on parental choice and school autonomy in three countries. *Review of Research in Education, 22.*

Witte, J. F. (2000). *The market approach to education.* Princeton, NJ: Princeton University Press.

Wohlstetter, P., Malloy, C., Chau, D., & Polhemus, J. (2003). Improving schools through networks: A new approach to urban school reform. *Educational Policy, 17*(4), 399–430.

Permissions

Durkheim, Emile, "On Education and Society" from pp. 92–105. Reprinted with permission from Routledge, a member of Taylor & Francis Books.

Collins, Randall, "Functional and Conflict Theories of Educational Stratification" from *American Sociological Review,* Vol. 36, No. 6 (Dec. 1971), pp. 1002–1019, ©1971. Reprinted with permission of the American Sociological Association.

Bowles, Samuel and Gintis, Herbert, "Broken Promises: School Reform in Retrospect from *Schooling in Capitalist America,* pp. 18–41, ©1976 by Basic Books. Used by permission of Perseus Books Group.

Rist, Ray, "On Understanding the Processes of Schooling: The Contributions of Labeling Theory" from *Power and Ideology* (1997) pp. 292–305, ©1997. By permission of Oxford University Press, Inc.

Bourdieu, Pierre, "The Forms of Capital Pierre Bourdieu" from John Richardson *Handbook of Theory and Research for the Sociology of Education,* John Richardson, © 1986. Reprinted with permission of Greenwood Publishing Group, Inc., Westport, CT.

Bernstein, Basil, "Social Class and Pedagogic Practice" from *The Structuring of Pedagogic Discourse: Class, Code and Control, Volume 4,* pp. 63–93, ©1990 by Routledge. Reprinted with permission from Routledge, a member of Taylor & Francis Books.

Meyer, John, "The Effects of Education as an Institution" from *American Journal of Sociology,* 85:1 (1977) pp. 55–77, ©1977 by permission of The University of Chicago Press.

Gamoran, Adam, Secada, Walter, and Marrett, Cora, "The Organizational Contexts of Teaching and Learning: Changing Theoretical Perspectives" from Maureen Hallinan, *Handbook of the Sociology of Education,* pp. 37–64 (Gamoran et al.), ©2000. Reprinted with kind permission from Springer Science and Business Media.

Richard, Ingersoll, "Is there Really a Teacher Shortage?" from *Center for the Study of Teaching and Policy,* pp. 1–32, © 003. By permission of The University of Washington.

Apple, Michael W., "Whose Markets, Whose Knowledge" from Michael Apple, *Educating the "Right" Way,* 2nd ed., ©2006. Reprinted with permission from Routledge, a member of Taylor & Francis Books.

Ramirez, Francisco and Boli, John, "The Political Construction of Mass Schooling: European Origins and Worldwide Institutionalization" from *Sociology of Education,* Vol. 60, No. 1. (Jan. 1987), pp. 2–17, ©1987. Reprinted with permission of the American Sociological Association.

Whitty, Geoff and Power, Sally, "Mercerization and Privatization in Mass Education Systems" from *International Journal of Educational Development,* Vol. 20, No. 2 (2000), pp. 93–107, ©2000. Reprinted with permission of Elsevier.

Baker, David P. and LeTendre, Gerald K., "Nation Versus Nation: The Race to Be the First in the World" *from National Differences, Global Similarities: World Culture and the Future of Schooling*. ©2005 by the Board of Trustees of the Leland Stanford Jr. University. All rights reserved.

Karen, David, "Changes in Access to Higher Education in the United States: 1980–1982".from *Sociology of Education,* Vol. 75, No. 3 (Jul, 2002), pp 191–210, ©2002. Reprinted by the American Sociological Association.

Dougherty, Kevin J. and Kienzl, Gregory S., "It's Not Enough to get Through the Open Door: Inequalities by Social Background in Transfer from Community Colleges to Four-Year Colleges" from *Teachers College Record,* Vol. 108.i, pp. 452–487. Reprinted with permission from Blackwell Publishing, Oxford, UK.

Rosenbaum, James E., "Colleges-for-All: Do Students Understand What College Demands? From *Social Psychology of Education,* Vol. 2 (1998), pp. 50–85, ©1998. Reprinted with kind permission from Springer Science and Business Media.

Hallinan, Maureen, "Tracking: From Theory to Practice" and Oakes, Jeannie, "More than Misplaced Technology: A Normative and Political Response to Hallinan on Tracking" from *Sociology of Education,* Vol. 67, No. 2. (Apr, 1994), pp. 79–91, ©1994. Reprinted by the American Sociological Association.

Lareau, Annette, "Invisible Inequality: Social Class and Childrearing in Black Families and White Families" from *American Sociological Review,* Vol. 67, No. 5. (Oct., 2002), pp. 747–776, ©2002. Reprinted with permission from the American Sociological Association.

Ogbu, John, "Collective Identity and the Burden of Acting White in Black History, Community and Education" from *Urban Review,* Vol. 36, No.1 (2004), pp. 1–35, ©2004. Reprinted with kind permission from Springer Science and Business Media.

Lew, Jamie, "Burden of Acting Neither White Nor Black: Asian American Identities and Achievement in Urban Schools" from *Urban Review,* Vol. 38, No. 5 (2006), pp. 335–352, ©2006. Reprinted with kind permission of Springer Science and Business Media.

Salazar-Stanton, Ricardo, Chavez, Lisa and Tai, Robert, "The Help-Seeking Orientation of Latino and non-Latino Urban High School Students: A Critical-Sociological Investigation" from *Social Psychology of Education,* Vol. 5 (2001), pp. 49–82, ©2001. Reprinted with kind permission from Springer Sciences and Business Media.

Riordan, Cornelius, "What do we Know About the Effects of Single-Sex Schools in the Private Sector?: Implications for Public Schools" from *Gender in Policy and Practice,* pp. 10–30, ©2002. Reprinted with permission from Routledge, a member of Taylor & Francis Books.

O'Day, Jennifer A., "Complexity, Accountability, and School Improvement" from *Harvard Educational Review,* Vol. 72, No. 3(Fall 2002), pp. 293–329. ©2002 by the President and Fellows of Harvard College. All rights reserved.

Berliner, David C., "Our Impoverished View of Educational Reform" from *Teachers College Record,* Vol. 108.16, pp. 949–995. Reprinted with permission from Blackwell Publishing, Oxford, UK.

Index

Page numbers in italic refer to figures or tables.